ECONOMICS

ECONOMICS

an introduction to traditional and radical views

SECOND EDITION

E. K. HUNT AND HOWARD J. SHERMAN
University of California, Riverside

Harper & Row, Publishers
New York   Evanston   San Francisco   London

To Linda and Barbara

Sponsoring Editor: John Greenman
Project Editor: William B. Monroe
Designer: Michel Craig
Production Supervisor: Will C. Jomarrón

Economics: An Introduction to Traditional and Radical Views, Second Edition.

Library of Congress Cataloging in Publication Data
Hunt, E   K
    Economics: an introduction to traditional and rad-
    ical views.
    Bibliography: p.
    Includes index.
    1. Economics.   I. Sherman, Howard J., joint author.
II. Title.
HB171.5.H83   1975   330   74-11769
ISBN 0-06-043016-8

CONTENTS

FOREWORD

At last! Beginning economics students have for too long been denied a thoroughly critical analysis of the society in which they live. Hunt and Sherman have now provided them with such a critique, and at the same time they have supplied professional expositions of traditional economic theory. Other authors of elementary textbooks have presented this aspect or that of traditional theory as well as or even better or more fully than Hunt and Sherman have, good as their treatment generally is, but no authors, to my knowledge, have given elementary economics students a truer picture of modern capitalism in its national and world dimensions. There are many ways to present traditional economic theory, and each instructor undoubtedly has his favorites, but the theory presented in this book is by social critics rather than by apologists for the system, and that should make all the difference to students who truly wish to gain a deeper understanding of what is going on in the world today.

Radical economists are dissatisfied, to put the point gently, with the conventional approach to economics, which takes the capitalist system for granted, considering it more or less eternal, and so skimps on the history of both the system and its ideology. Accordingly, conventional textbooks serve capitalism to the students on a platter, as though there was nothing else in the kitchen or ever would be. Hunt and Sherman break with that approach, right off the bat, by devoting Part One of their book to the evolution of economic institutions and ideologies. Joseph Schumpeter once wrote that "nobody can hope to understand the economic phenomena of any, including the present, epoch who has not an adequate command of historical facts and an adequate amount of historical sense. . . ." The authors of this book have taken those words seriously.

There is another reason for discontent with the conventional approach. It distorts reality by assuming harmonies of interest throughout society, ignoring the deep class conflicts that prevail in our society. Such sweetness and light enable conventional economists to refer to "the general interest," "the public welfare," "the common good," and other equally soothing expressions and to assume that the State represents everyone's interests. Hunt and Sherman, I am pleased to say, look upon their discipline as "political economics" rather than economics in the narrow sense, and so throughout the book they study economic problems within the context of ruler-subject relations—always sensitive to the fact that there are pervasive relationships of domination and servitude throughout our society. That this makes a difference can easily be seen by comparing their analyses of income distribution, discrimination, economic waste, international finance, and development of poor countries with corresponding treatments in other textbooks. Hunt and Sherman come out on top because their conception of the world—which includes power, conflict, and disruptive change within a historical setting—is more accurate than the paradigms used by bourgeois economists.

Do we have to put up with the misinformation in the thin and slanted chapters in one elementary textbook after another, which are supposed to pass for serious analyses of socialism, communism, and Marxism? Not any longer. I do not mean that Hunt and Sherman have given us glowing accounts of the supreme joy of living in the Soviet Union and China, for they have not. What I mean is that we now have a serious discussion of alternative economic systems by experts who have more than their share of critical faculties. The five chapters that make up the last part of the book will inform and stimulate a large number of beginning economics students.

Radical economics still has a long way to go, as Hunt and Sherman well know, before it can sweep away most of the rubbish in present-day bourgeois economics. This book is an excellent contribution toward that end.

John G. Gurley

PREFACE

This book is very different from the traditional elementary economics text.

We do present the traditional economic theory. In addition, we present radical critiques and radical theories. In the traditional economics category we include economists who are generally classified as liberal as well as those generally considered conservative. The traditional view rests on Adam Smith's notion that in a market economy the forces of supply and demand act as an "invisible hand" to guide resources into their most efficient uses and to distribute the proceeds of the productive process in a reasonably fair manner.

Most economists realize that the forces of supply and demand do not always maximize social welfare. In some circumstances they might even be pernicious. In these instances it is necessary for the government to intervene in the market to ensure a socially acceptable outcome. Varying assessments of the extent and significance of these "special cases" differentiate liberals and conservatives. Liberals believe that promoting the society's welfare requires relatively frequent government intervention into market processes. Conservatives believe that these interventions should be relatively less frequent. Neither liberals nor conservatives seriously question the basic institutional framework of the private property, market capitalist economy within which the forces of supply and demand operate.

Radicals, however, subject these institutions to critical scrutiny. In this book we shall use the term *radical* in its traditional meaning. Traditionally, the adjective *radical* has referred to "leftist" or "socialist" criticisms or actions, and the noun *radical* has referred to these leftists and socialists. In recent times, particularly since the 1964 American presidential election, references have been made to the *radical right*. Included in the radical right have been various political conservatives, reactionaries, and assorted cranks. We do not refer to these right-wing radicals when we use the term. We mean only radicals of the left.

Thus, in this book we shall be concerned with radical criticism of the fundamental institutions of capitalism as well as the orthodox views on how the market capitalist system functions.

A HISTORICAL APPROACH

In Part One we introduce economics by way of a history of the great economists (some of them wild and wonderful). We present their ideas as set within the context of the institutions of their times, and therefore we sketch an economic history.

There is no easier and more pleasant way of learning economics than to follow the evolution of the main ideas of the great thinkers in the field. This will also impress upon the reader, as nothing else could, that there are at least two (and usually more) views on every subject in economics.

It is interesting to see how our modern economic institutions slowly evolved from feudal times. The usual textbooks start off cold from the present situation. We believe it is much more meaningful to witness all of the curious zigzags and the fighting that occurred in the development of our present institutions. How things developed in the past gives us a key to understanding the present and, hopefully, the future.

The history of economic ideas and the history of economic institutions are not totally independent of each other. In reality, they are very closely related, each affecting the other at all times. Thus, we shall see that the specific problems and interests of various groups gave rise to very specific economic ideologies and that these ideologies served as an excuse for the status quo or as a call for drastic change. For example, we shall see in the first few chapters that the dominant ideology in the medieval period fully supported the feudal economic system as just and correct and eternal. Eventually, however, the contrary ideas of the new groups of merchants and industrialists were reflected in new economic ideologies, which then helped overturn the old restrictive feudal order.

TEACHING ECONOMIC THEORY

The traditional approach concentrates on explaining how the consumer may maximize his satisfaction from spending, how the businessman may maximize his profits, and how the government may aid private business to maximize growth. This approach is often dull and mechanical. We include these usual and somewhat mechanical subjects, but to a lesser degree, focusing on the more exciting present-day social and political issues. In fact, ours is more of a political economics textbook than a purely economics textbook.

Thus, in Part Two we discuss the traditional microeconomic problems of the individual consumer and the individual business firm. We also investigate often neglected problems—for example, poverty, racism, sexual discrimination, monopoly power, unequal education opportunities, and tax loopholes.

Similarly, in Part Three we discussed the usual macroeconomic problems of the economy as a whole, including the standard questions of economic growth and unemployment. In addition, we examine such problems as inflation, pollution and waste, population, war spending, the less developed countries, and imperialism.

OBJECTIVITY

Some traditional economists will complain that we do not present the conservative or traditional views completely enough. We do try, especially in the historical presentations of Part One, to state both the traditional and radical views as impartially as possible. Of course no one is impartial, so we undoubtedly state the radical view somewhat more effectively. In Parts Two and Three we again state the traditional views first, before giving the radical view, but our sympathy with the radical view will be quite apparent.

Some radical economists who have read this book before publication have complained of the opposite. They said that we sound too impartial between the conservative and radical views, especially in their historical presentation.

Other radicals have complained that it is not necessary to state the orthodox views at all because they are wrong. We believe, first, that students should be acquainted with all views; second, that present radical views can be understood only in their historical context, which definitely includes the traditional theories, criticism of which led to the radical theories; and third, we do not like a know-nothing radicalism of the type that says: Poverty and racism are bad, so we should just go out and demonstrate against them and toss tomatoes at their defenders. On the contrary, we believe one must put some hard study into political economics in order to understand the causes of poverty and racism and other evils and their possible cures.

A COMPARATIVE APPROACH

In Part Four we take the reader on an excursion through some of the countries that call themselves socialist, particularly Russia, China, and Yugoslavia. Various chapters examine their historical development, current institutions, and current problems. Their development and institutions are compared with those of the Western capitalist countries. This does not merely give us an idea of what the rest of the world looks like. It is also important because the comparisons bring out more clearly many of the features of the Western capitalist countries. For example, in studying the market process of the United States, it is very interesting and helpful to compare it with the planned nonmarket economies of eastern Europe.

SOME OTHER SPECIAL FEATURES

The usual elementary economics text is filled with nothing but graphs and mathematics. We have used graphs only where necessary to illustrate a point, but we have always explained it first in ordinary English and have kept the graphs as simple as possible.

For the convenience of students, summaries are provided at the end of each chapter. *Warning:* No summary can explain a chapter; it may merely remind you of the most important points. *Another warning:* No summary can be very accurate because it is too short to include all the necessary qualifications.

For instructors accustomed to standard textbooks, we have presented most theory in its usual order and covered the usual topics. In a few places that is not so. For example, international trade is sometimes placed in the microeconomics part, even though it always contains many macroeconomic observations. Because we found that the macroecenomic issues in international trade are the most interesting, we have emphasized them and put the discussion in that part. (It is independent enough of the surrounding chapters so that it can be used at a different point.) Also, we have omitted production functions, a traditional topic, because we approach the subject differently and believe recent theory has shown this approach to be based on indefensible assumptions.

HOW TO USE THIS BOOK

This book has been designed so that it may be used as the main text for a one-year course, but with plentiful use of supplements. Many good collections of readings are available. It may also be used for a one-semester or one-quarter course if one wishes to cover the material somewhat lightly or emphasize particular areas.

Most instructors prefer to teach macroeconomics before microeconomics. That is understandable because microeconomic theory is usually especially dull and lifeless in most texts. This book is so arranged that the instructor may, if he wishes, teach the macroeconomics first, even though it comes second. In other words, the two parts are sufficiently independent, even though they refer to each other at the appropriate points.

After some heated discussion between the authors, we decided to put the microeconomics part first. For one, we believe our microeconomics section is much more interesting than the average. We go through the usual supply and demand graphs, although as simply as possible. But the section also emphasizes the radical views on poverty, government behavior, and racial and sexual discrimination—all of which, we believe, the reader will find exciting. We also present the usual graphs on monopoly theory but give a great deal more attention than most books to the history and facts of monopoly in the United States. We believe the material on income distribution and monopoly is particularly important in understanding the later macro material on waste and cyclical unemployment in the United States. (But again, we emphasize that the instructor could conceivably teach Part Three ahead of Part Two if he so desired.)

Finally, the book may be used in special ways in one-quarter or one-semester courses emphasizing only one aspect of economics. First, in a macroeconomics course we would suggest that Part One on history be assigned so as to be read lightly in the first few weeks. (Chapter 11 on Keynes could be emphasized.) Then jump to Part Three on macroeconomics; this is a lengthy part and will give plenty of meat, although a supplement could certainly be used as well (several paperbacks go more fully into the traditional subjects of income accounting and determination).

Second, in a course on microeconomics we would again suggest beginning with Part One so that the student sees how microeconomics developed through the history of thought (particularly emphasizing the chapters on the neoclassical economists and on Marx). Part Two will then follow naturally. Since Part Two is fairly short, you may have time for the comparative material of Part Four, which examines several microproblems in the context of economic planning. You should also have time to include a supplement.

Third, some courses emphasize history and institutions and de-emphasize theory. We believe our book is better suited for such a course than any other available complete textbook. All of Part One could be emphasized. In Part Two, most of Chapters 14, 15, 18, and 19 could be omitted. On the other hand, Chapters 16, 17, 20, and 21 are mainly institutional. In Part Three, Chapters 24 and 25 could be omitted. The other chapters are mainly institutional, although certain sections might be omitted. In Part Four, Chapter 43 is somewhat theoretical and could be omitted. The rest of this part is heavily historical and institutional. In the second edition, we have also moved more of the difficult theoretical material to Appendixes, where it may easily be omitted in some courses.

ACKNOWLEDGMENTS

We are profoundly grateful to those whose teaching or direct help made this book possible: Professors Sidney Coontz, William Davisson, Douglas Dowd, Robert Edminster, David Felix, John Gurley, J. W. Hanks, Kiyotoshi Iwamoto, Robert Lekachman, Lawrence Nabors, Andreas Papandreou, Lynn Turgeon, Benjamin Ward, Thomas Weisskopf, and Stephen Worland. Extensive research help, for which we express our thanks, was furnished by Professor Maryanna Boynton.

We also wish to thank various publishers for giving us permission to use certain materials from our previous books: Hunt, *Property and Prophets* (Harper & Row, 1972); Sherman, *Elementary Aggregate Economics* (Appleton, 1966); Sherman, *The Soviet Economy* (Little, Brown, 1969); Sherman, *Profit Rates in the United States* (Cornell University Press, 1968); and Sherman, *Radical Political Economy* (Basic Books, 1972).

In the second edition, we gratefully acknowledge the extensive but constructive criticism of several reviewers: Professors James Cypher, Clint Jencks, John Pool, Ross La Roe, and Jim Starkey. Useful research work was done by William Harnett and Michael Sheehan, and we appreciate the typing and clerical help of Poinka Wong and Susan Bradley.

For the future, we invite any useful ideas for improvements in the book. Please write to us and we will take your suggestions very seriously.

E. K. Hunt
Howard J. Sherman

INTRODUCTION

This book is about traditional and radical economics. It may surprise you to learn that there is no single *truth* in economics but, rather, two or more conflicting approaches to it. That is, however, the sad fact in economics and in all the other social sciences. In studying society there is no important point that is noncontroversial; on every important issue there are a range of opinions from the most conservative to the most radical. Certainly there are some facts that most economists agree on, and there are some tools that most economists use—but we differ over what the important problems are, how to approach them, and how to interpret the findings.

One basic area of disagreement concerns the possibility of changing things. Radicals contend that society can and should be drastically changed. Conservatives contend that nothing can ever change because our behavior is rooted in an unchanging human nature. This basic difference is shown in an amusing imaginary dialogue between an old, conservative cannibal named Wowsy and his young, idealistic, and radical friend, another cannibal, named Bongo:

BONGO: Human beings should not eat each other.

WOWSY: Good Gooey Gow! You can't dictate to people what they're going to eat and what they're not going to eat. Men have always eaten each other and always will. It's natural. You can't change human nature.

BONGO: I love my fellow men.
WOWSY: So do I—with gravy on them.[1]

The conservative economists, like Wowsy, argue that people are born with certain ideas—such as eating people, or holding slaves, or being a competitive capitalist—and that there is no way to change those ideas. Since these ideas are held by everyone, our behavior is determined by these ideas and cannot be changed. Where do they come from? Some conservatives say God gives us our ideas. Others claim that certain ways of living are just "natural" and obvious, so everyone naturally knows they are best. Others, like Freud, simply say we are born with innate, inherited drives—for example, all men are aggressive and domineering; all women are passive and like to be dominated.

Similarly, conservatives in the South before the Civil War said that slavery was natural, that the blacks were happy only as slaves, and that the whites were natural slave owners. The clergy added that slavery was divinely ordained by God, that keeping slaves so that they would be happy—and whipping them occasionally for their own good—was the Christian white man's burden.

In the Middle Ages, conservative religous leaders and social thinkers held that serfdom was natural and reflected human nature. The serfs were happy working for landlords because that was a serf's nature. The landlords were happy directing serfs, judging them, and even executing them (but only when necessary) because that was a landlord's nature. Thomas Aquinas contended that some prices are normal and natural and that it is a sin to buy or sell at more or less than these prices. Chapter 1 will explore medieval economic views more fully.

During the Industrial Revolution, a school of economists known as the classical school preached that capitalism is natural and eternal, earlier economic systems being "unnatural." They claimed that it is the natural proclivity of every person to be greedy, to compete relentlessly, to calculate rationally every purchase and every other economic activity. These views are further explored in Chapter 4 of this book.

Finally, most traditional economists of today (called neoclassical economists) take as given at birth all the preferences of individual consumers. They seem to think that we are born with a certain order of preferences for Cadillacs or TV sets. In Chapter 7 we shall see that these natural consumer preferences constitute the heart of their economics.

[1]From a newspaper column by the radical satirist, Mike Quinn, in the *Daily Peoples World*, 1938.

THE RADICAL VIEW

By contrast with conservatives, radical economists believe that all ideas and preferences—such as our desire for Cadillacs—are shaped by the society in which we live. Consumers are influenced not only by obvious means like advertising but also by more subtle and pervasive means like family upbringing, religion, education, and the mass media. Similarly, it is no coincidence that the dominant view or ideology under slavery supports slavery, that under serfdom supports serfdom, and that under capitalism supports capitalism. Social scientists are human beings like everyone else and thus have their own ideas and preconceptions shaped by society.

Since our ideology is determined by our social environment, radical economists contend that a change in our socioeconomic structure will eventually change the dominant ideology. For example, before the Civil War most Southerners (including their social scientists) declared that slavery was natural and good; but after 100 years of capitalist socioeconomic institutions, most Southerners (including their social scientists) declare that capitalism is natural and good. So the dominant ideas are not given by human nature but are shaped by socioeconomic relations and can be changed by changes in the underlying relationships. There is thus hope for a completely new and better society with new and better views by most people.

This does not mean that ideas are unimportant in the process of social change. The ideas of at least a large number of people must change before a revolutionary social change is possible. The point is only that our ideological views are not God-given and do not change at random. New views—such as the revolutionary ideology of liberty, equality, and fraternity—appeared and caused the French and U.S. revolutions only because they reflected underlying social conflicts. The needs of most people (farmers and workers and industrialists) came into conflict with the old socioeconmic relationships (the French feudal monarchy, British colonialism). These conflicts caused social thinkers, such as Voltaire and Tom Paine, to present new ideologies. The new ideologies caught on because they reflected most people's needs and desires. This led to political revolutions, which changed socioeconomic structures. The new structures reinforced the new ideas and made their ideological conquest complete. This circular process is charted in Figure I.1.

Economic forces are defined here to include all the labor that workers do, the tools and machinery with which they work, use of known natural resources, and use of the available level of technology. *Economic relations* are the relations among people doing economic activity—for example, the relations between slaves and slaveowners, workers and capitalists, debtors and creditors. In Chapter 6 we shall

IDEAS AND ECONOMICS

Figure I.1

find that Karl Marx said that economic activity and relations, defined in this broad manner, form the *base* or foundation of society; on this base is built a *superstructure* consisting of institutions and ideologies. The social and political *institutions* include the family, government, organized religions, all the laws, the educational system, and the media of communication. *Ideologies* include philosophy, much of the social sciences, religion, and all folk customs and biases (such as white or male supremacy).

In any nonrevolutionary period, all the elements of this system reinforce each other. Suppose the economic forces consist of a fairly low level of technology in isolated agricultural estates, while the economic relations are those of feudalism, of landlords ruling over serfs. The political institutions reflect feudal relations in a hierarchy of power up to the largest landlord, the king. The ideology reflects this hierarchy, claiming that the whole system—especially the king—is divinely ordained. So the ideology reinforces the existing institutions, which reinforce the existing economic relations.

In the rare revolutionary situations, conflicts (which are always there to some extent) suddenly become very evident among the elements of the system. For example, over a long period in feudal Europe commerce and industry slowly replaced agricultural economic activity. As a result, a new economic class of capitalists and merchants appeared. There was conflict because the old feudal lords had control of the political institutions and did not want to surrender any power to the upstart capitalists. Eventually, these conflicts led to revolutionary new ideologies, new institutions, and new relations.

PRIMITIVE ECONOMIES

As an example of the various economies that have existed, let us examine the so-called *primitive* type. One British archaeologist lists the characteristics of most areas of human settlement in our first half-million years or so as follows: (1) very small communities; (2) communities quite isolated, self-sufficient, with little or no trade; (3) no writing; (4) a homogeneous group of people; (5) no full-time specialists; (6) the economic unit is the family or extended family of kinsmen; (7) relationships personal and status hereditary rather than economic; and (8) little or no political institutions.[2] There is one still-existing primitive community where even today "there is no private property in productive goods, and whatever the hunting band manages to kill is shared out among the members of the group."[3] In general, the most primitive societies have no market exchange, no money, and no economic competition in the modern sense. It is true that even the most primitive peoples known to anthropologists usually own their weapons, tools, and ornaments as individual private property; but the basic means of production at this stage are the hunting grounds, and these are owned collectively.

The point cannot be overstressed that in primitive societies men are not hired for jobs; they are not paid money; and purely economic relations do not prevail in any area (nor is force used in most cases). Rather, "men work together because they are related to each other, or have social obligations to one another."[4] Furthermore, work is done collectively and the results shared collectively. Or, as another anthropologist writes, "with qualifications such as the special shares locally awarded for special contributions to the group endeavor—the principle remains . . . 'goods collectively produced are distributed through the collectivity.' "[5]

The striking thing about such primitive societies from our present view is that everyone is on about the same plane of economic and political power. There is no ruling class, such as the ancient Roman or Greek or Egyptian slave owners, and no ruled class, such as the slaves in those societies. How did some collectivist, primitive societies evolve into class-divided societies—as in Greece, Rome, and Egypt?

[2]V. Gordon Childe, *Social Evolution* (London: Watts, 1951), passim.

[3]Manning Nash, in George Dalton, ed., *Tribal and Peasant Economies* (Garden City, N.Y.: Natural History Press, 1967), p. 3.

[4]Daryll Forde and Mary Douglas, in ibid., p. 17.

[5]Marshall Sahlins, "On the Sociology of Primitive Exchange," in Michael Barton, ed., *The Relevance of Models for Social Anthropology* (New York: Praeger, 1965), p. 142.

THE TRANSITION TO CLASS SOCIETY

When "civilizaton" became established in the Middle East in the Bronze and Iron Ages, it was marked by large communities, taxes, public works, writing, use of mathematics and astronomy, internal and foreign trade, full-time specialists like farmers and metallurgists, political organization beyond family or kinship, a privileged ruling class, and an exploited class of workers, whether slaves or feudal serfs or peasants paying tribute. The key revolution, however, is the earlier transformation from hunting and gathering food to animal herding and agriculture.

How did the agricultural revolution occur, and how did it end the primitive classless societies of these areas and bring about class rule? We know there was a slow expansion of technical knowledge and improvement of tools over hundreds of thousands of years. Then, in a few particularly fertile areas—perhaps more or less independently in China, Mesopotamia, Egypt, Mexico, and Peru—people discovered how to tame and breed animals and how to grow the most edible plants. This "revolution" did not occur in a momentary flash of insight to some individual. Rather, it seems to have been a very gradual process over thousands of years.

Recent work presents a detailed picture of this process in Mesopotamia and the Aztec areas of Mexico.[6] First, communities became more permanently settled, intensively collected food, and hunted in a smaller given area than previously. Second, the New Stone Age saw better tools being produced, including improved bows, drills, digging tools, and even boats and nets. Third, some crop—wheat, for example—that was already growing in the area might be moved to different areas as desired, protected by such means as removing any weeds, and eventually selected so as to obtain the desired food characteristics. Similarly, hunters of goats or cows might begin to follow one particular herd, protect it against its other enemies, and finally feed and shelter it at times. All these changes could take thousands of years.

Once the pastoral-agricultural revolution is well under way, several important changes occur as a direct result. Obviously the level of productivity per worker increases. The first consequence of this fact is a much higher population density; herding and agriculture can support many people per square mile, whereas hunting and gathering require several square miles per person. At the same time, agriculture means that the population must settle in one place rather than moving here and there around the country. Such large, settled

[6]See Robert Adams, *The Evolution of Urban Society* (Chicago: Aldine, 1965), pp. 39–43.

agglomerations mean the founding of permanent villages and, eventually, towns and cities in the most favored places.

There is enough economic surplus over immediate needs so that the economy may support various specialists, such as carpenters, shoemakers, and the like. Specialization, in turn, calls for exchange of products between individuals and between groups. Moreover, the higher productivity makes available wealth in the form of cattle and gold as well as consumer durables. Then the specialization and exchange slowly destroy the collective use and possession of property, so some individuals come to own more wealth than others.

With this increase of private property and larger, more permanently located groups of people, there is a need for a broader and stronger political structure to replace the family unit. At first, in both possession of private property and control of political power, the families or clans retain the semblance of unity and direction. Individuals slowly accumulate private property as there is more of it; so, too, do individuals slowly accumulate more political power as politics grows more complex.

A war chief may be elected from time to time as a result of small tribal conflicts; the post is likely to become a lifetime one or even hereditary as larger armies come into being. The area and intensity of wars increase at this time because wars for economic motives are used by advanced agricultural societies for the acquisition of cattle or slaves. Most large-scale introductions of slavery seem to follow as the effect of a war of conquest. Yet such wars seem to occur only as the effect of a new technology high enough so that it is profitable to keep a slave (because he can produce a surplus). Slavery and wars of conquest are thus intertwined as cause and effect at a certain level of economic evolution.

To oversimplify a bit: Better technology following the agricultural revolution led to higher productivity per worker. The higher productivity, in turn, meant that a society could for the first time "afford" to have some nonworking individuals (such as slave owners, landlords, priests, full-time warriors). Conversely, until product per worker passed the point at which one worker could just keep himself alive, there could have been no surplus left for the ruling classes. Before that point, slavery or serfdom could not pay—hence prisoners were simply killed or eaten.

A similar increase of power may accrue to those in charge of public works. A director of irrigation for a small tribe may be appointed for a short time in one season; a director of irrigation for a large agricultural area along the Nile must be given more power for a lengthy period. Thus, in Egypt the government separates from and rises above family or clan for two different kinds of reasons: (1)

to carry through public projects, including irrigation and warfare, and (2) to guard private property, including slaves (and to prevent slave revolt).

TYPES OF ECONOMIES

There have been many different types of economy in the world. We have examined in detail the *primitive* type, in which people worked in collective groups and shared the fruits of their labors. Another type is the *slave* economy, in which one class, the slaves, does all the work. The class of slave owners legally owns both the slaves and their whole product. They give the slaves barely enough to live on, keeping the surplus for themselves.

Still another economic system is *feudalism*, varieties of which appeared at different times in Europe, Asia, and Africa. Under feudalism the serf is bound to the land of some estate. The serf owes to the landlord—by tradition, but by force if necessary—150 to 200 days a year of service on the landlord's land. Yet the serf is better off than a slave, since he is not owned in body by the landlord and may work his own tiny plot of land when he finishes his chores on the landlord's land. In Chapters 1 and 2 we discuss the transition from feudalism to capitalism in Western Europe.

Most of this book discusses *capitalism*, the system existing at present in the United States. In this system capitalists are the class of people who own all factories and equipment. Capitalists employ workers, paying them a wage. Workers are not forced to work by physical coercion, as are slaves and serfs, but are "free" to work for a capitalist or not to work and hence to starve. Capitalists own the entire product beyond wages and material costs; they produce only if they expect to make a profit.

Part Four of this book discusses *socialist* economies. *Socialism* means ownership and control of the economy by the entire working population. Production is carried on for the benefit of society. Many countries, such as Cuba, the Soviet Union, and China, claim to have socialist economies.

PART ONE

**property
and
prophets:
the
evolution
of
economic
institutions
and
ideologies**

the
ideology
of
pre-capitalist
europe

Human beings must exist in societies in order to survive. Unlike some species of animals, whose individual members can exist fairly adequately in relative isolation, human beings are not equipped by nature with the physical prowess to provide the material requisites of life by themselves. Humans survive and indeed prosper because by living in groups they have learned to subdivide tasks and use tools. It was this division of labor and the accumulation of more and better tools (or capital) that made possible the impressive increases in man's control over nature, or increases in man's potential to produce the material necessities of life.

This division of labor also resulted, of necessity, in a differentiation of the roles that the different members of a society occupy. This differentiation was probably purely functional in earliest times; that is, when productivity was low, all members of a society lived near the subsistence level and social class, or hierarchical differentiation, was absent. Increasingly elaborate divisions of tasks, combined with more sophisticated tools, however, led to higher productivity, which made possible an escape from the drudgery of everyday toil for at least a small part of society.

A small leisure class could be supported because with higher per capita productivity the labor of a smaller number of people could support the entire society at its customary standard of living or at an even higher standard. When this occurred, societies began to differentiate among their members according to social class. This hierarchical class differentiation was generally economic in nature. Those who worked were usually assigned to the lowest classes; those who escaped the burdens of ordinary labor were of higher class standing. Although these higher-class people were no longer directly connected with the production of everyday necessities, they often performed rites, rituals, or extensive duties, some of which were undoubtedly beneficial to the society.

Such a system could not continue to exist for long if the majority of its members did not share common feelings about the proper way of conducting economic and social affairs. These common feelings and values, which generally stemmed from a common world view, or system of metaphysics, justified both the division of productive tasks and the class differentiation that existed. These common feelings and values were expressed in ideologies.

An *ideology*, as the term is used in this book, refers to ideas and beliefs that tend to justify morally a society's social and economic relationships. Most members of a society internalize the ideology and thus believe their functional role as well as those of others are morally correct and that the method by which society divides its produce is fair. This common belief gives society its cohesiveness and viability. Lack of it creates turmoil and strife—and ultimately revolution, if the differences are deep enough.

This book is concerned primarily with our present economic system, capitalism. We sketch the broad outlines of the evolution of this system. In doing so, we focus on conflicts and social antagonisms and examine the ideologies with which the capitalist system attempted to mitigate these conflicts and to promote social cohesiveness. By way of background, we begin with the economic systems and ideologies of precapitalist Europe.

ANCIENT GREEK AND ROMAN SLAVERY

In ancient Greece and Rome as many as 80 percent of the people were slaves. The slaves did all the manual work and even much of the clerical, bureaucratic, and artistic work of these societies. They were given just enough food and clothing for bare subsistence. The slave owners owned and utilized the entire surplus produced by the slaves above their own subsistence. Most of the economy was agricultural, aside from a few cities where the central government was located. On each agricultural plantation the slave owner was king and lived in splendid luxury—though he might also have a villa in Athens or Rome. In addition to his wife, who was treated as a valuable piece of property, he sexually exploited his slave women.

What sort of economic ideology existed? There were a few

treatises, especially in the Roman period, on the best ways to plant crops, the best agriculural implements to use, and the best ways to supervise, control, and punish slaves. In addition, there were a large number of justifications of slavery. Even such brilliant philosophers as Plato and Aristotle argued that slavery was "natural," was the only possible system, and would exist forever; they argued that some men and women were born to be slaves and were inherently inferior, while others were born superior and were meant to be slave owners. Plato and Aristotle were not verbal apologists; this was the dominant ideology and they simply took it for granted.

Slavery had many limitations, though it did result in many great public works and the advance of science and culture. One limitation was the fact that slaves could not be given complex or delicate machinery of any sort; they would break it up and would often use it for weapons to revolt. Moreover, agricultural organization had to be very simple, usually limited to one crop tilled with crude implements. As a result, much land was totally ruined and the agricultural product limited. Another effect of slavery was the view that all work was demeaning. This attitude spread even to invention, so the Roman period saw little technological advance and the economy stagnated.

Its economic weaknesses—and accompanying political and social weaknesses—made the Roman Empire vulnerable to attack by the primitive Germanic and Slav tribes. The Empire collapsed in the West, and out of the chaos eventually arose the system of feudalism. The kings of the feudal states were mostly former chiefs of the primitive tribes that invaded the area.

FEUDALISM

The decline of the western part of the old Roman Empire left Europe without the laws and protection the empire had provided. The vacuum was filled by the creation of a feudal hierarchy. In this hierarchy, the serf, or peasant, was protected by the lord of the manor, who, in turn, owed allegiance to and was protected by a higher overlord. And so the system went, ending eventually with the king. The strong protected the weak, but they did so at a high price. In return for payments of money, food, labor, or military allegiance, overlords granted the fief, or feudum—a hereditary right to use land—to their vassals. At the bottom was the serf, a peasant who tilled the land. The vast majority of the population raised crops for food or clothing or tended sheep for wool and clothing.[1]

[1]For a more complete discussion of the medieval economic and social system, see J. H. Claphan and Eileen E. Power, eds., *The Agrarian Life of the Middle Ages*, 2d ed, The Cambridge Economic History of Europe, vol. I (London: Cambridge University Press, 1966).

Custom and tradition are the key to understanding medieval relationships. In place of laws as we know them today, the *custom* of
the manor governed. There was no strong central authority in the
Middle Ages that could have enforced a system of laws. The entire
medieval organization was based on a system of mutual obligations
and services up and down the hierarchy. Possession or use of the
land obligated one to certain customary services or payments in
return for protection. The lord was as obligated to protect the serf
as the serf was to turn over a portion of his crop to or perform
extensive labor for the lord.

Customs were broken, of course; no system always operates in
fact as it is designed to operate in theory. One should not, however,
underestimate the strength of custom and tradition in determining
the lives and ideas of medieval people. Disputes between serfs were
decided in the lord's court according to both the special circumstances of each case and the general customs of the manor for such
cases. Of course, a dispute between a serf and a lord would usually
be decided in his own favor by the lord. Even in this circumstance,
however, especially in England, an overlord would impose sanctions
or punishments on a lord who, as his vassal, had persistently violated
the customs in his treatment of serfs. This rule by the custom of the
manor stands in sharp contrast to the legal and judicial system of
capitalism. The capitalist system is based on the enforcement of
contracts and universally binding laws, which are softened only
rarely by the possible mitigating circumstances and customs that
often swayed the lord's judgment in medieval times.

The extent to which the lords could enforce their "rights" varied
greatly from time to time and from place to place. It was the
strengthening of these obligations and the nobleman's ability to
enforce them through a long hierarchy of vassals and over a wide
area that eventually led to the emergence of the modern nation-
states. This process occurred during the period of transition from
feudalism to capitalism. Throughout most of the Middle Ages, however, many of these claims were very weak because political control
was fragmented.

The basic economic institution of medieval rural life was the
manor, which contained within it two separate and distinct classes:
noblemen, or lords of the manors, and serfs (from the Latin word
servus, "slave"). Serfs were not really slaves. Unlike a slave, who
was simply property to be bought and sold at will, the serf could
not be parted from either his family or his land. If his lord transferred possession of the manor to another nobleman, the serf simply
had another lord. In varying degrees, however, obligations were
placed upon the serfs that were sometimes very onerous and from

which there was often no escape. Usually, they were far from being "free."

The lord lived off the labor of the serfs who farmed his fields and paid taxes in kind and money according to the custom of the manor. Similarly, the lord gave protection, supervision, and administration of justice according to the custom of the manor. It must be added that although the system did rest on reciprocal obligations, the concentration of economic and political power in the hands of the lord led to a system in which, by any standard, the serf was exploited in the extreme.

The Catholic church was by far the largest owner of land during the Middle Ages. While bishops and abbots occupied much the same place as counts and dukes in the feudal hierarchy, there was one important difference between the religious and secular lords. Dukes and counts might shift their loyalty from one overlord to another, depending on the circumstances and the balance of power involved, but the bishops and abbots always had (in principle at least) a primary loyalty to the church in Rome. This was also an age during which the religous teaching of the church had a very strong and pervasive influence throughout western Europe. These factors combined to make the church the closest thing to a strong central government throughout this period.

Thus the manor might be secular or religious (many times secular lords had religious overlords and vice versa), but the essential relationships between lord and serfs were not significantly affected by this distinction. There is little evidence that serfs were treated any less harshly by religious lords than by secular ones. The religious lords and the secular nobility were the joint ruling classes; they controlled the land and the power that went with it. In return for very onerous appropriations of the serf's labor, produce, and money, the nobility provided military protection and the church provided spiritual aid.

In addition to manors, medieval Europe had many towns, which were important centers of manufacturing. Manufactured goods were sold to manors and, sometimes, traded in long-distance commerce. The dominant economic institutions in the towns were the guilds—craft, professional, and trade associations that had existed as far back as the Roman Empire. If anyone wanted to produce or sell any good or service, he had to join a guild.

The guilds were as involved with social and religious questions as with economic ones. They regulated their members' conduct in all their activities: personal, social, religious, and economic. Although the guilds did regulate very carefully the production and sale of commodities, they were less concerned with making profits than with saving their members' souls. Salvation demanded that the individual lead an orderly life based on church teachings and custom. Thus the guilds exerted a powerful influence as conservators of the status quo in the medieval towns.

THE CHRISTIAN PATERNALIST ETHIC

The feudal lords, secular as well as religious, needed an ideology that would reflect and justify the feudal status quo. This ideology, which provided the moral cement holding feudal Europe together and protecting its rulers, was the medieval version of the Judeo-Christian tradition. This tradition evolved a moral code sometimes called the Christian corporate ethic, reflecting the fact that all of society was considered a single entity or corporation. To emphasize another feature of it, the Judeo-Christian moral code, as interpreted in the medieval period, will be called the *Christian paternalist ethic* in this book. It can be understood most easily by comparing society with a family. Those with positions of power and wealth can be likened to the father or keeper of the family. They have strong paternalistic obligations toward the common people—the poor or, in our analogy, the children. The common man, however, is expected to accept his place in the society and to subordinate himself willingly to the leadership of the wealthy and the powerful in much the same way that a child accepts the authority of his father.

The Old Testament Jews[2] quite literally regarded themselves as the children of one God. This relationship meant that all Jews were brothers; the Mosaic law was intended to maintain this feeling of membership in one big family. This brotherhood was one of grown children who acknowledged their mutual obligations, even though they no longer shared possessions.

From the confused mass of duties and regulations governing the early Jews, the most salient feature is the large number of provisions made for the prevention and relief of poverty. Their humane treatment of debtors was also notable. Each Jew was to be his brother's keeper; indeed, his obligations extended to caring for his neighbor's animals should they wander his way.[3] The first duty of all, however, and particularly of the wealthy, was to care for the poor: "Thou shalt open thine hand wide unto thy brother, to the poor, and to the needy, in the land."[4] An important element in this paternalistic code was the sanction against taking a worker's tools as a means of satisfying a debt: "No man shall take the nether or the upper millstone

2This account relies on Alexander Gray, *The Socialist Tradition* (London: Longmans, 1963), chap. 2.
3Deut., 22:1-4.
4Deut., 15:7-11.

to pledge: for he taketh a man's life to pledge."[5] The same point was made elsewhere in the Old Testament: "He that taketh away his neighbor's living slayeth him."[6]

All Jews did not, of course, live up to these lofty professions. Great extremes of wealth and poverty existed that would have been impossible had the Moisaic law been strictly observed. Many of the prophets, who were often radical champions of the poor, eloquently denounced the rich for their abuse of their wealth, for their wicked, slothful luxury and general unrighteousness. The important point is not that they failed to live up to the code but that the moral code of this small tribe left so important an imprint on much of subsequent history.

The teachings of Christ in the New Testament carry on part of the Mosaic tradition relevant to economic ideology. He taught the necessity of being concerned with the welfare of one's brother, the importance of charity and almsgiving, and the evil of selfish acquisitiveness and covetousness. His emphasis on the special responsibilities and obligations of the rich is even more pronounced than that of the earlier Jewish writers. In fact, on the basis of a reading of the Gospel of Luke, one might conclude that Christ condemned the rich simply because they were rich and praised the poor simply because they were poor: "Woe unto you that are rich! . . . Woe unto you that are full! for ye shall hunger. Woe unto you that laugh now! for ye shall mourn and weep."[7] However, on examining the other gospels, it must be concluded that this is probably Luke speaking, not Christ. Luke must be seen as the radical "leveller among the apostles."[8]

In the other gospels, there are warnings that wealth may be a stumbling block in getting to heaven, but there is no condemnation of wealth as such. The most important passages in this regard deal with the wealthy young man who wants to know what he must do to attain eternal life.[9] Christ's first answer amounts to nothing more than a brief statement of the Ten Commandments. It is only after being pressed further that Christ goes beyond the binding, universal moral requirements to a counsel of perfection. "If thou wilt be perfect"[10] begins the statement in which he tells the young man to sell whatever he has and give to the poor.

The Christian paternalist ethic, with its parental obligations of the wealthy toward the poor, was developed more specifically and

[5]Deut., 24:6.
[6]Eccles., 34:22.
[7]Quoted in Gray, op. cit., p. 41.
[8]Ibid., p. 42.
[9]Matt., 19:16–26; Mark, 10:17–27; Luke, 18.
[10]Matt., 19.

elaborately by most of the later Christian fathers. The writings of
Clement of Alexandria are a reasonably good reflection of the
traditional attitudes of the early church. He emphasized the dangers
of greed, love of material things, and acquisition of wealth. Those
who had wealth were under a special obligation to treat it as a gift
of God and to use it wisely in the promotion of the general well-
being of others.

Clement's *The Rich Man's Salvation* was written in order to free
the rich of the "unfounded despair" they might have acquired from
reading passages in the gospels like those found in Luke. Clement
began by asserting that, contrary to anything one might find in
Luke, "it is no great or enviable thing to be simply without riches."
Those who were poor would not for that reason alone find God's
blessedness. In order to seek salvation, the rich man need not re-
nounce his wealth but need merely "banish from the soul its opinions about riches, its attachment to them, its excessive desire, its
morbid excitement over them, its anxious cares, the thorns of our
earthly existence which choke the seed of the true life."[11]

Not the possession of wealth but the way in which it was used
was important to Clement. The wealthy were given the responsibility of administering their wealth, on God's behalf, to alleviate the
suffering and promote the general welfare of their brothers. In de-
creeing that the hungry should be fed and the naked clothed, God
certainly had not willed a situation in which no one could carry out
these commandments for lack of sufficient material prerequisites.
It followed, thus, that God had willed that some men should have
wealth but had given them the important functions of paternalisti-
cally caring for the well-being of the rest of society.

In a similar vein, Ambrose wrote that "riches themselves are not
blamable" as long as they are used righteously. In order to use
wealth righteously, "we ought to be of mutual help one to the other,
and to vie with each other in doing duties, to lay all our advantages
. . . before all, and . . . to bring help one to the other."[12]

The list of Christian fathers who wrote lengthy passages to the
same effect could be expanded greatly. Suffice it to say that by the
early feudal period the Christian paternalist ethic was thoroughly
entrenched in western European culture. Greed, avarice, materialistic self-seeking, the desire to accumulate wealth—all such individualistic and materialistic motives—were sharply condemned. The
acquisitive, individualistic person was considered the very antithesis
of the good man, who concerned himself with the well-being of all
his brothers. The wealthy man had the potential to do either great

[11]Quoted in Gray, op. cit., p. 48.
[12]Ibid., p. 49.

good or great evil with his wealth and power, and the worst evil resulted when wealth was used either exclusively for self-gratification or as a means of continually acquiring more wealth for its own sake. The righteously wealthy were those who realized that their wealth and power were God's gift, that they were morally obligated to act as paternalistic stewards, and that they were to administrate their worldly affairs in order to promote the welfare of all.

THE ANTICAPITALIST
NATURE OF FEUDAL IDEOLOGY

The philosophical and religious assumptions on which medieval people acted were extensions of the Christian paternalist ethic. The many particular additions to the ethic were profoundly conservative in purpose and content. Both the continuity in and conservative modifications of the ethic can be seen in the writings of Thomas Aquinas, the preeminent spokesman of the Middle Ages.

Tradition was upheld in his insistence that private property could be justified morally only because it was a necessary condition for almsgiving. The rich, he asserted, must always be "ready to distribute, . . . [and] willing to communicate."[13] Aquinas believed, with the earlier fathers, that "the rich man, if he does not give alms, is a thief."[14] The rich man held wealth and power for God and for all society. He administered his wealth for God and for the common good of mankind. Without proper use and administration of this wealth, it could no longer be religiously and morally justified, in which case the wealthy man was to be considered a common thief.

Aquinas' and, indeed, most of the medieval church fathers' profoundly conservative addition to the Christian paternalistic ethic was their insistence that the economic and social relationships of the medieval manorial system reflected a natural and eternal ordering of these relationships—indeed, that these relationships were ordained by God. They stressed the importance of a division of labor and effort, with different tasks assigned to the different classes, and insisted that the social and economic distinctions between the classes were necessary to accommodate this specialization.

If one was in the position of a lord, secular or religious, it was necessary to have an abundance of material wealth in order to do well the tasks providence had assigned. Of course, it took little wealth to perform the tasks expected of a serf. It was every person's duty to labor unquestioningly at the task to which providence had assigned him, to accept the station into which he was born, and

13Ibid., p. 57.
14Ibid.

to accept the rights of others to have and do the things appropriate to their stations in life. Thus the Christian paternalist ethic could be, and was, used to defend as natural and just the great inequities and intense exploitation that flowed from the concentration of wealth and power in the hands of the Church and nobility.

Any account of medieval social and economic thought must also stress the great disdain with which people viewed trade and commerce and the commercial spirit. The medieval way of life was based on custom and tradition; its viability depended on the acceptance by the members of society of that tradition and their place within it. Where the capitalist commercial ethic prevails, greed, selfishness, covetousness, and the desire to better oneself materially or socially are accepted by most people as innate qualities. Yet they were uniformly denounced and reviled in the Middle Ages. The serfs (and sometimes the lower nobility) tended to be dissatisfied with the traditions and customs of medieval society and thus threatened the stability of the feudal system. It is not surprising, therefore, to find pervasive moral sanctions designed to repress or to mitigate the effects of these motives.

One of the most important of such sanctions, repeated over and over throughout this period, was the insistence that it was the moral duty of merchants and traders to transact all trade or exchanges at the just price. This notion illustrates the role played by paternalistic social control in the feudal era. A *just price* was one that would compensate the seller for his efforts in transporting the good and in finding the buyer at a rate that was just sufficient to maintain the seller at his *customary* or *traditional* station in life. Prices above the just price would, of course, lead to profits, which would be accumulated as material wealth.

It was the lust for wealth that the Christian paternalist ethic consistently condemned. Thus the doctrine of the just price was intended as a curb on such acquisitive and socially disruptive behavior. Then as now, accumulation of material wealth was a passport to greater power and upward social mobility. This social mobility was eventually to prove totally destructive of the medieval system because it put an end to the status relationships that were the backbone of medieval society.

Another example of this condemnation of acquisitive behavior was the prohibition of usury, or the lending of money at interest. A "bill against usury" passed in England reflected the attitudes of most of the people of those times. It read in part:

> But forasmuch as usury is by the word of God utterly prohibited, as a vice most odious and detestable . . . which thing, by no godly teachings and persuasions can sink in to the hearts of divers

greedy, uncharitable and covetous persons of this Realm . . . be it enacted . . . that . . . no person or persons of what Estate, degree, quality or condition so ever he or they be, by any corrupt, colorable or deceitful conveyance, sleight or engine, or by any way or mean, shall lend, give, set out, deliver or forbear any sum or sums of money . . . to or for any manner of usury, increase, lucre, gain or interest to be had, received or hoped for, over and above the sum or sums so lent . . . as also of the usury . . . upon pain of imprisonment.[15]

The church believed usury was the worst sort of acquisitive behavior because most loans on which interest was charged were granted to poor farmers or peasants after a bad crop or some other tragedy had befallen them. Thus, interest was a gain made at the expense of one's brother at a time when he was most in need of help and charity. Of course, the Christian ethic strongly condemned such rapacious exploitation of a needy brother.

Many historians have pointed out that bishops and abbots as well as dukes, counts, and kings often flagrantly violated these sanctions. They themselves granted loans at interest, even while they were punishing others for doing so. We are more interested, however, in the values and motives of the period than in the sins and infractions of the rules. The values of the feudal system stand in stark, antithetical contrast to those that were shortly to prevail under a capitalist system. The desire to maximize monetary gain, accumulate material wealth, and advance oneself socially and economically through acquisitive behavior was to become the dominant motive force in the capitalist system.

The sins that were most strongly denounced within the context of the Christian paternalist ethic were to become the behavioral assumptions on which the entire capitalist market economy was to be based. It is obvious that such a radical change would render the Christian ethic, at least in its medieval version, inadequate as the basis of a moral justification of the new capitalist system. The ethic would have to be modified drastically or rejected completely in order to elaborate a defense for the new system. Attempts to do both are explored in later chapters.

SUMMARY

Economic systems organize human effort to transform the resources given in nature into usable articles, or economic goods. Ideologies

---

[15]Quoted in Leo Huberman, *Man's Worldly Goods* (New York: Monthly Review Press, 1961), p. 39.

are systems of ideas and beliefs that are used to justify morally the economic and social relationships within an economic system.

The Christian paternalist ethic was used to justify the feudal economy and its attendant social and economic relationships. This ideology contained elements that were antithetical to the functioning of a capitalist market system. In later chapters we shall examine the ways in which men attempted to substitute new ideologies for the older Christian paternalist ethic or to modify this ethic in such a way that it could be used to provide a moral justification of a capitalist market economic system.

the transition to early capitalism and the beginnings of the mercantilist view

The medieval society was an agrarian society. The social hierarchy was based on individuals' ties to the land, and the entire social system rested on an agricultural base. Yet, ironically, increases in agricultural productivity were the original impetus to a series of profound changes. These changes, occurring over several centuries, resulted in the dissolution of medieval feudalism and the beginnings of capitalism.

CHANGES IN TECHNOLOGY

The most important technological advance in the Middle Ages was the replacement of the two-field system of crop rotation with the three-field system. Although there is evidence that the three-field system was introduced into Europe as early as the eighth century, its use was probably not widespread until around the eleventh century.

Yearly sowing of the same land would deplete the land and eventually make it unusable. Consequently, in the two-field system half of the land was always allowed to lie fallow in order to recover from the previous year's planting.

With the three-field system, arable land was divided into three equal fields. Rye or winter wheat would be planted in the fall in the first field. Oats, beans, or peas would be planted in the spring in the second, and the third would lie fallow. In each subsequent year there was a rotation of these positions. Any given piece of land would have a fall planting one year, a spring planting the next year, and none the third year.

A dramatic increase in agricultural output resulted from this seemingly simple change in agricultural technology. With the same amount of arable land, the three-field system could increase the amount under cultivation at any particular time by as much as 50 percent.[1]

The three-field system led to other important changes. Spring sowing of oats and other fodder crops enabled the people to support more horses, which began to replace oxen as the principal source of power in agriculture. Horses were much faster than oxen, and consequently the region under cultivation could be extended. Larger cultivated areas enabled the countryside to support more concentrated population centers. Transportation of men, commodities, and equipment was much more efficient with horses. Greater efficiency was also attained in plowing: A team of oxen required three men to do the plowing; a horse-drawn plow could be operated by one man. The costs of transporting agricultural products were substantially reduced in the thirteenth century, when the four-wheeled wagon with a pivoted front axle replaced the two-wheeled cart.

These improvements in agriculture and transportation contributed to two important and far-reaching changes. First, they made possible a rapid increase in population growth. The best historical estimates show that the population of Europe doubled between 1000 and 1300.[2] Second, closely related to the expansion of population was a rapid increase in urban concentration. Before the year 1000, most of Europe, except for a few Mediterranean trade centers, consisted of only manors, villages, and a few small towns. By 1300, there were many thriving cities and larger towns.

The growth of towns and cities led to a growth of rural-urban specialization. With urban workers severing all ties to the soil, the output of manufactured goods increased impressively. Along with increased manufacturing and increased economic specialization came many additional gains in human productivity. Interregional, long-distance trade and commerce was another very important result of this increased specialization.

THE INCREASE IN LONG-DISTANCE TRADE

Many historians have argued that the spread of trade and commerce was the single most important force leading to the disintegration of

[1]Lynn White, Jr., *Medieval Technology and Social Change* (Oxford: Clarendon, 1962), pp. 71–72.

[2]Harry A. Miskimin, *The Economy of Early Renaissance Europe, 1300–1460* (Englewood Cliffs, N.J.: Prentice-Hall, 1969), p. 20.

medieval trade and customs. The importance of trade cannot be doubted, but it must be emphasized that this trade did not arise by accident or by factors completely external to the European economy, such as increased contact with the Arabs. On the contrary, it was shown in the previous section that this upsurge in trade was prepared for by the internal economic evolution of Europe itself. The growth of agricultural productivity meant that a surplus of food and handicrafts was available for local and international markets. The improvements in power and transportation meant that it was possible and profitable to concentrate industry in towns, to produce on a mass scale, and to sell the goods in a widespread, long-distance market. Thus the basic agricultural and industrial developments were necessary prerequisites for the spread of trade and commerce —which then further encouraged industry and town expansion.

The expansion of trade, particularly long-distance trade in the early period, led to the establishment of commercial and industrial towns that serviced this trade. And the growth of these cities and towns, as well as their increased domination by merchant capitalists, led to important changes in both industry and agriculture. Each of these areas of change, particularly the latter, brought about a weakening and ultimately a complete dissolving of the traditional ties that held together the feudal economic and social structure.

From the earliest part of the medieval period, some long-distance trade had been carried on throughout many parts of Europe. This trade was very important in southern Europe, on the Mediterranean and Adriatic seas, and in northern Europe, on the North and Baltic seas. Between these two centers of commercialism, however, the feudal manorial system in most of the rest of Europe was relatively unaffected by commerce and trade until the later Middle Ages.

From about the eleventh century onward, the Christian Crusades gave the impetus to a marked expansion of commerce. Yet the Crusades themselves cannot be viewed as an accidental or external factor to European development. The Crusades were not undertaken for religious reasons, nor were they the result of Turkish molestation of pilgrims, for the Turks continued the Moslem policy of tolerance. Developments on the Moslem side did lead to increased attacks on Byzantium, but the West would normally have sent only token aid, since it had no great love for Byzantium. The basic reasons for the Crusades may be seen in the internal developments of France, where they had their most powerful backing. France had been growing stronger; it had more trade relations with and interest in the East; and it needed an outlet for social unrest at home. Additional propaganda for the Crusades came from the oligarchy of Venice, which wanted to expand its own Eastern trade and influence.

The development of trade with the Arabs—and with the Vikings in the North—led to increased production for export and to the great trade fairs that flourished from the twelfth through the late fourteenth centuries. Held annually in the principal European trading cities, these fairs usually lasted for one to several weeks. Northern European merchants exchanged their grain, fish, wool, cloth, timber, pitch, tar, salt, and iron for the spices, silks, brocades, wines, fruits, and gold and silver that were the dominant items in southern European commerce.[3]

By the fifteenth century the fairs were being replaced by commercial cities where year-round markets thrived. The trade and commerce of these cities was incompatible with restrictive feudal customs and traditions. Generally the cities were successful in gaining independence from church and feudal lords. Within these commercial centers there arose complex systems of currency exchange, debt-clearing, and credit facilities, and modern business instruments like bills of exchange came into widespread use. New systems of commercial law developed. Unlike the system of paternalistic adjudication based on custom and tradition that prevailed in the manor, the commercial law was fixed by precise code. Hence it became the basis of the modern capitalistic law of contracts, negotiable instruments, agency sales, and auctions.

In the manorial handicraft industry, the producer (the master craftsman) was also the seller. The industries that burgeoned in the new cities, however, were primarily export industries in which the producer was distant from the final buyer. Craftsmen sold their goods wholesale to merchants, who, in turn, transported and resold them. Another important difference was that the manorial craftsman was also generally a farmer. The new city craftsman gave up farming to devote himself to his craft, with which he obtained a money income that could be used to satisfy his other needs.

THE PUTTING-OUT SYSTEM
AND THE BIRTH OF CAPITALIST INDUSTRY

As trade and commerce thrived and expanded, the need for more manufactured goods and greater reliability of supply led to increasing control of the productive process by the merchant-capitalist. By the sixteenth century the handicraft type of industry, in which the craftsman owned his workshop, tools, and raw materials and functioned as an independent, small-scale entrepreneur, had been

---

[3]For a more complete discussion of the rise of trade and commerce, see Dudley Dillard, *Economic Development of the North Atlantic Community* (Englewood Cliffs, N.J.: Prentice-Hall, 1967), pp. 3–178.

largely replaced in the exporting industries by the *putting-out system*. In the earliest period of the putting-out system, the merchant-capitalist would furnish an independent craftsman with raw materials and pay him a fee to work the materials into finished products. In this way the capitalist owned the product throughout all stages of production, although the work was done in independent workshops. In the later period of the putting-out system, the merchant-capitalist owned the tools and machinery and often the building in which the production took place. He hired workers to use these tools, furnished them with the raw materials, and took the finished products.

The worker no longer sold a finished product to the merchant. Rather, he sold only his labor power. The textile industries were among the first in which the putting-out system developed. Weavers, spinners, fullers, and dyers found themselves in a situation where their employment, and hence their ability to support themselves and their families, depended on the merchant-capitalists, who had to sell what the workers produced at a price that was high enough to pay wages and other costs and still make a profit.

Capitalist control was, then, extended into the process of production. At the same time, a labor force was created that owned little or no capital and had nothing to sell but its labor power. These two features mark the appearance of the economic system of capitalism. Some writers and historians have defined capitalism as existing when trade, commerce, and the commercial spirit expanded and became more important in Europe. Trade and commerce, however, had existed throughout the feudal era. Yet as long as feudal tradition remained the organizing principle in production, trade and commerce were really outside the social and economic system. The market and the search for money profits replaced custom and tradition in determining who would perform what task, how the task would be performed, and whether a given worker could find work to support himself. When this occurred, the capitalist system was created.[4]

Capitalism became dominant with the extension to most lines of production of the relationship that existed between capitalists and workers in the sixteenth-century export industries. For such a system to evolve, the economic self-sufficiency of the feudal manor had to be broken down and manorial customs and traditions undermined or destroyed. Agriculture had to become a capitalistic venture in which workers would sell their labor power to capitalists, and capitalists would buy labor only if they expected to make a profit in the process.

[4]See Maurice H. Dobb, *Studies in the Development of Capitalism* (London: Routledge & Kegan Paul, 1946), particularly chap. 4.

A capitalist textile industry existed in Flanders in the thirteenth century. When for various reasons its prosperity began to decline, the wealth and poverty it had created led to a long series of violent class wars, starting around 1280, that almost completely destroyed the industry. In the fourteenth century a capitalist textile industry flourished in Florence. There, as in Flanders, adverse business conditions led to tensions between a poverty-stricken working class and their affluent capitalist employers. The results of these tensions were violent rebellions in 1379 and 1382. Failure to resolve these class antagonisms significantly worsened the precipitous decline in the Florentine textile industry, as it had earlier in Flanders.

In the fifteenth century England dominated the world textile market. Its capitalist textile industry solved the problem of class conflict by ruralizing the industry. Whereas the earlier capitalist textile industries of Flanders and Florence had been centered in the densely populated cities, where the workers were thrown together and organized resistance was easy to initiate, the English fulling mills were scattered about the countryside. This meant that the workers were isolated from all but a small handful of other workers, and effective organized resistance did not develop.

The later system, however, in which wealthy owners of capital employed propertyless craftsmen, was usually a phenomenon of the city rather than of the countryside. From the beginning, these capitalistic enterprises sought monopolistic positions from which to exploit the demand for their products. The rise of livery guilds, or associations of merchant-capitalist employers, created a host of barriers to protect their position. Different types of apprenticeships, with special privileges and exemptions for the sons of the wealthy, excessively high membership fees, and other barriers, prevented ambitious poorer craftsmen from competing with or entering the new capitalist class. Indeed, these barriers generally resulted in the transformation of poorer craftsmen and their sons into a new urban working class that lived exclusively by selling its labor power.

THE DECLINE OF THE MANORIAL SYSTEM

Before a complete system of capitalism could emerge, however, the force of capitalist market relations had to invade the rural manor, the bastion of feudalism. This was accomplished as a result of the vast increase of population in the new trading cities. Large urban populations depended on the rural countryside for food and much of the raw materials for export industries. These needs fostered a rural-urban specialization and a large flow of trade between the rural manor and the city. The lords of the manors began to depend on the cities for manufactured goods and increasingly came to desire luxury goods that merchants could sell to them.

The peasants on the manor also found that they could exchange surpluses for money at the local grain markets; the money could be used by the peasants to purchase commutation of their labor services.[5] Commutation often resulted in a situation in which the peasant became very nearly an independent small businessman. He might rent the land from the lord, sell the produce to cover the rents, and retain the remaining revenues himself. This system gave peasants a higher incentive to produce and thereby increased their surplus marketings, which led to more commutations, more subsequent marketings, and so forth. The cumulative effect was a very gradual breaking down of the traditional ties of the manor and a substitution of the market and the search for profits as the organizing principle of production. By the middle of the fourteenth century, money rents exceeded the value of labor services in many parts of Europe.

Another force that brought the market into the countryside and was closely related to commutation was the alienation of the lords' demesnes. The lords who needed cash to exchange for manufactured goods and luxuries began to rent their own lands to peasant farmers rather than having them farmed directly with labor service obligations. This process led increasingly to a situation in which the lord of the manor was simply a landlord in the modern sense of that term. In fact, he very often became an absentee landlord, as many lords chose to move to the cities or were away fighting battles.

The breakup of the manorial system, however, stemmed more directly from a series of catastrophies in the late fourteenth and fifteenth centuries. The Hundred Years' War between France and England (1337–1453) created general disorder and unrest in those countries. The Black Death was even more devasting. On the eve of the plague of 1348–1349, England's population stood at 4 million. By the early fifteenth century, after the effects of the wars and the plague, England had a scant 2.5-million population. This was fairly typical of trends in other European countries. The depopulation led to a desperate labor shortage, and wages for all types of labor rose abruptly. Land, now relatively more plentiful, began to rent for less.

These facts led the feudal nobility to attempt to revoke the commutations they had granted and to reestablish the labor service obligations of the serfs and peasants (peasants were former serfs who had attained some degree of independence and freedom from

---

[5]Commutation involved the substitution of money rents for the labor services required of the serf.

feudal restrictions). They found, however, that the clock could not be turned back. The market had been extended into the country-side, and with it had come greater freedom, independence, and prosperity for the peasants. They bitterly resisted efforts to rein-state the old obligations, and their resistance did not go unchallenged.

The result was the famous peasant revolts that broke out all over Europe from the late fourteenth through the early sixteenth cen-turies. These rebellions were extreme in their cruelty and ferocity. A contemporary French writer described a band of peasants who killed a "knight and putting him on a broach, roasted him over a fire in the sight of his wife and children. Ten or twelve of them ravished the wife and then forced her to eat of her husband's flesh. Then they killed her and her children. Wherever these ungracious people went they destroyed good houses and strong castles."[6] Rebellious peasants were ultimately slaughtered with equal or greater cruelty and ferocity by the nobility.

England experienced a series of such revolts in the late fourteenth and fifteenth centuries. But the revolts that occurred in Germany in the early sixteenth century were probably the bloodiest of all. The peasant rebellion in 1524–1525 was crushed by the Imperial troops of the Holy Roman emperor, who slaughtered peasants by the tens of thousands. Over 100,000 persons probably were killed in Germany alone.

These revolts are mentioned here to illustrate the fact that funda-mental changes in the economic and political structure of a social system are often achieved only after traumatic and violent social conflict. Any economic system generates a class or classes whose privileges are dependent on the continuation of that system. Quite naturally, these classes go to great lengths to resist change and to protect their positions. The feudal nob. ity fought a savage rearguard action against the emerging capitalist market system, but the forces of change ultimately swept them aside. Although the important changes were brought about by aspiring merchants and minor noble-men, the peasants were the pathetic victims of the consequent social upheavals. Ironically, they were usually struggling to protect the status quo.

OTHER FORCES IN THE TRANSITION TO CAPITALISM

The early sixteenth century is a watershed in European history. It vaguely marks the dividing line between the old, decaying feudal order and the rising capitalist system. After 1500, important social

[6]N. S. B. Gras, *A History of Agriculture in Europe and America* (New York: Appleton, 1940), p. 108.

and economic changes began to occur with increasing frequency, each reinforcing the other and together having the cumulative effect of ushering in the system of capitalism. The population of western Europe, which had been relatively stagnant for a century and a half, increased by nearly one-third in the sixteenth century and stood at about 70 million in 1600.

The increase in population was accompanied by the *enclosure movement*, which had begun in England as early as the thirteenth century. The feudal nobility, in ever-increasing need of cash, fenced off, or enclosed, lands that had formerly been used for communal grazing. Enclosed lands were used to graze sheep to satisfy the booming English wool and textile industries' demand for wool. The sheep brought good prices, and a minimal amount of labor was needed to herd them.

The enclosure movement reached its peak in the late fifteenth and sixteenth centuries, when in some areas as many as three-fourths to nine-tenths of the tenants were forced out of the countryside and into the cities to try to support themselves. The enclosures and the increasing population further destroyed the remaining feudal ties, creating a large new labor force—a labor force without land, without any tools or instruments of production, and with only labor power to sell. This migration to the cities meant more labor for the captalist industries, more men for the armies and navies, more men to colonize new lands, and more potential consumers, or buyers of products.

Another important source of change was the intellectual awakening of the sixteenth century, which fostered scientific progress that was promptly put to practical use in navigation. The telescope and the compass enabled men to navigate much more accurately for much greater distances. Hence the "age of exploration." Within a short period, Europeans had charted sea routes to India, Africa, and the Americas. These discoveries had a twofold importance. First, they resulted in a rapid and large flow of precious metals into Europe, and second, they ushered in a period of colonization.

Between 1300 and 1500, European gold and silver production had stagnated. The rapidly expanding capitalist trade and the extension of the market system into city and countryside had led to an acute shortage of money. Because money consisted primarily of gold and silver coin, the need for these metals was critical. Beginning around 1450, this situation was alleviated somewhat when the Portuguese began extracting metals from the African Gold Coast, but the general shortage continued until the middle of the sixteenth century. After that date there occurred such a large inflow of gold and silver from the Americas that Europe experienced the most rapid and long-lasting inflation in history.

During the sixteenth century prices rose in Europe between 150 and 400 percent, depending on the country or region chosen. Prices of manufactured goods rose much more rapidly than either rents or wages. In fact, the disparity between prices and wages continued until late in the seventeenth century. This meant that the landlord class (or feudal nobility) and the working class both suffered, because their income rose less rapidly than their expenses. The capitalist class was the great beneficiary of the price revolution. They recived larger and larger profits as they paid lower real wages and bought materials that appreciated greatly as they held them as inventories.

These larger profits were accumulated as capital. *Capital* refers to the materials that are necessary for production, trade, and commerce. It consists of all tools, equipment, factories, raw materials and goods in process, means of transporting goods, and money. The essence of the capitalist system is the existence of a class of capitalists who own the capital stock. It is by virtue of their ownership of this capital that they derive their profits. These profits are then plowed back, or used to augment the capital stock. The further accumulation of capital leads to more profits, which leads to more accumulation, and the system continues in an upward spiral.

The term *capitalism* describes this system of profit-seeking and accumulation very well. Capital is the source of profits and hence the source of further accumulation of capital. But this chicken-egg process had to have a beginning. The substantial initial accumulation, or *primitive accumulaton*, of capital took place in the period under consideration. The four most important sources of the initial accumulation of capital were (1) the rapidly growing volume of trade and commerce, (2) the putting-out system of industry, (3) the enclosure movement, and (4) the great price inflation. There were several other sources of initial accumulations, some of which were somewhat less respectable and often forgotten—for example, colonial plunder, piracy, and the slave trade.

During the sixteenth and seventeenth centuries the putting-out system was extended until it was common in most types of manufacturing. Although this was not yet the modern type of factory production, the system's increased degree of specialization led to significant increases in productivity. Technical improvements in shipbuilding and navigation also lowered transportation costs. Thus during this period capitalist production and trade and commerce thrived and grew very rapidly. The new capitalist class (or middle class or bourgeoisie) slowly but inexorably replaced the nobility as the class that dominated the economic and social system.

The emergence of the new nation-states signaled the beginning of the transition to a new dominant class. The new monarchs usually drew on the bourgeois capitalist class for support in their efforts to defeat feudal rivals and unify the state under one central power. This unification freed the merchants from the feudal maze of different rules, regulations, laws, weights and measures, and moneys; consolidated many markets; and provided military protection for commercial ventures. In return, the monarch relied on the capitalists for much-needed sources of revenues.

Although England was nominally unified much earlier, it was not until Henry VII (1485–1509) founded the line of Tudor monarchs that England was unified in fact. Henry VIII (1509–1547) and Elizabeth I (1558–1603) were able to complete the work of nation building only because they had the support of Parliament, which represented the middle classes of the shires and boroughs. In the revolutions of 1648 and 1688, the supremacy of Parliament, or of the bourgeois middle classes, was finally established.

The other important early capitalist nation-states also came into existence during this period. In France, Louis XI (1461–1483) was the first king to unify France effectively since the time of Charlemagne. The marriage in 1469 of Ferdinand of Aragon and Isabella of Castile, and their subsequent defeat of the Moors, led to the unification of Spain. The Dutch republic, the fourth of the important early nation-states, did not win its independence until 1690, when it finally expelled its Spanish oppressors.

By the late sixteenth and early seventeenth centuries, most of the large cities in England, France, Spain, and the Low Countries (Belgium and Holland) had been transformed into thriving capitalist economies dominated by the merchant-capitalists, who controlled not only commerce but also much of the manufacturing. In the modern nation-states, coalitions of monarchs and capitalists had wrested effective power from the feudal nobility in many important areas, especially those related to production and commerce. This period of early capitalism is generally referred to as *mercantilism*.

MERCANTILISM: FEUDAL PATERNALISM IN EARLY CAPITALISM

The earliest phase of mercantilism, usually called *bullionism*, originated in the period (discussed earlier) during which Europe was experiencing an acute shortage of gold and silver bullion and hence did not have enough money to service the rapidly expanding volume of trade. Bullionist policies were designed to attract a flow of gold and silver into a country and to keep them there by prohibiting their export. These restrictions lasted from the late Middle Ages into the sixteenth and seventeenth centuries.

Spain, the country into which most of the gold from the Americas flowed, applied bullionist restrictions over the longest period and imposed the most severe penalty for the export of gold and silver:

death. Yet the needs of trade were so pressing and such large profits could be made by importing foreign commodities that even in Spain merchant-capitalists succeeded in bribing corrupt officials or in smuggling large quantities of bullion out of the country. Spanish bullion rapidly found its way all over Europe and was, to a large extent, responsible for the long period of inflation described above. Spain did not legalize the export of gold and silver until long after the bullionist restrictions had been removed in England and Holland in the middle of the sixteenth century.

After the bullionist period, the mercantilists' desire to maximize the gold and silver within a country took the form of attempts by the government to create a favorable balance of trade. To them a *favorable balance of trade* meant that money payments into the country would be greater than money flowing out of the country. Thus exports of goods as well as such things as shipping and insuring, when they were performed by countrymen and paid for by foreigners, were encouraged, and imports of goods and shipping and insurance charges paid to foreigners were discouraged. A favorable balance of trade would ensure the augmentation of the country's treasure. Even though some gold and silver would be paid out in the process, more would come in than would leave.

One of the most important types of policies designed to increase the value of exports and decrease that of imports was the creation of trade monopolies. A country like England could buy most cheaply (from a backward area, for example) if only one English merchant bargained with the foreigners involved rather than having several competing English merchants bidding the price up in an effort to capture the business. Similarly, English merchants could sell their goods to foreigners for much higher prices if there was only one seller rather than several sellers bidding the price down to attract each other's customers.

The English government could prohibit English merchants from competing in an area where such a monopoly had been established. It was much more difficult, however, to keep out French, Dutch, or Spanish merchants. Various governments attempted to exclude such rival foreign merchants by establishing colonial empires that could be controlled by the mother country to ensure a monopoly of trade. Colonial possessions could thereby furnish cheap raw materials to the mother country and purchase expensive manufactured goods in return.

In addition to the creation of monopolies, all the western European countries (with the exception of Holland) applied extensive regulations to the businesses of exporting and importing. These regulations were probably most comprehensive in England, where exporters who found it difficult to compete with foreigners were given tax refunds or, if that was not enough, subsidized. Export duties were placed on a long list of raw materials to keep them within England. Thus the price English merchant-manufacturers would have to pay for these raw materials would be minimized. Sometimes, when these items were in short supply for British manufacturers, the state would completely prohibit their export. The English textile industry received this type of protection. In the early eighteenth century it accounted for about half of England's exports. The English prohibited the export of most raw materials and semifinished products, such as sheep, wool, yarn, and worsted, which were used by the textile industry.

Measures aimed at discouraging imports were also widespread. The importation of some commodities was prohibited, and other commodities had such high duties that they were nearly eliminated from trade. Special emphasis was placed on protecting England's principal export industries from foreign competitors attempting to cut into the export industries' domestic markets.

Of course these restrictions profited some capitalists and harmed others. As would be expected, coalitions of special interest groups were always working to maintain the restrictions or to extend them into different areas in different ways. Attempts such as the English Navigation Acts of 1651 and 1660 were made to promote the use of British ships (both British-made and British-manned) in both import and export trade. All these regulations of foreign trade and shipping were designed to augment the flow of money into the country while decreasing the outflow. Needless to say, many of the measures also stemmed from appeals and pressures by special interest groups.

In addition to these restrictions on foreign trade, there was a maze of restrictions and regulations aimed at controlling domestic production. Besides the tax exemptions, subsidies, and other privileges used to encourage larger output by industries that were important exporters, the state also engaged in extensive regulation of production methods and of the quality of produced goods. In France, the regime of Louis XIV codified, centralized, and extended the older decentralized guild controls. Specific techniques of production were made mandatory, and extensive quality control measures were enacted, with inspectors appointed in Paris charged with enforcing these laws at the local level. Jean Baptiste Colbert, Louis XIV's famous minister and economic advisor, was responsible for the establishment of extensive and minute regulations. In the textile industry, for example, the width of a piece of cloth and the precise number of threads contained within it were rigidly specified by the government.

In England, the Statute of Artificers (1563) effectively transferred to the state the functions of the old craft guilds. It led to central control over the training of industrial workers, over conditions of employment, and over allocation of the labor force among different types of occupations. Regulation of wages, of the quality of many goods, and of other details of domestic production was also tried in England during this period.

What was the source of this extensive state control of trade, commerce, and domestic production? It might seem at first glance that the state was merely using its powers to promote the special interests of capitalists. This view is reinforced by the fact that most of the important writers of this period who dealt with economic issues were either merchants or employees of merchants. Undoubtedly many of the particular statutes and regulatory measures were backed by special interest groups that benefited handsomely from these measures.

However, the rising new middle class of merchant and industrial capitalists were often constrained in their pursuit of profits by the maze of state regulations. Therefore, throughout the period one finds extensive arguments advanced by these capitalists and their spokesmen for greater freedom from state controls. Economic regulation increasingly became anathema to the capitalists and their spokesmen. In fact, the mercantilist period represents an era in which an outdated economic ideology, the medieval version of the Christian corporate ethic, came into increasingly sharp conflict with a new social and economic order with which it was incompatible. Chapter 3 will be concerned with this conflict.

SUMMARY

A series of profound changes resulted in the decline of feudalism and the rise of a new, market-oriented economy. Perhaps the most important of these changes were the improvements in agricultural technology that occurred between the eleventh century and the end of the thirteenth century. These improvements in farming techniques were the original force that set into motion a centuries-long chain of events that ushered in capitalism.

Population grew rapidly and urban concentration increased, which led to a resurgence of long-distance trade. In the cities, the putting-out system was created to produce items that were sold in this trade. This, in turn, led to an urban-rural specialization that could be accomplished only by the monetization of economic tasks and productive activities. The transformation of feudal social relationships into market cash relations destroyed the social base of feudalism. Attempts to preserve the fuedal system resulted in bloody suppressions of peasant revolts.

The new capitalist market system was ushered in by the enclosure movement, the intellectual awakening, world exploration, the discovery of large quantities of precious metals, the price inflation of the sixteenth and seventeenth centuries, and the creation of the new nation-states.

In the early stages of capitalism mercantilist policies resulted in extensive government intervention into market processes, particularly those related to international commerce. These policies were generally aimed at securing high profits for the great merchant trading companies, raising revenues for national governments, and, more generally, bringing a maximum of precious metals into the country concerned.

the conflict in mercantilist thought

The Christian paternalist ethic, with its condemnation of acquisitive behavior, conflicted with the interests of merchants throughout the feudal period. As the importance of trade and commerce grew, the intensity of the conflict grew. There were two principal themes underlying the development of English mercantilism.[1] "One was the biblical injunction to promote the general welfare and common good of God's corporate world and its creatures. The second was the growing propensity to define God's estate as the civil society in which the Christian resided."[2] During this period the state began to take over the role of the church in interpreting and enforcing the Christian paternalist ethic. The basic issue for the earliest formulators of mercantilist policies was whether the growing merchant class was to be allowed to pursue its profits recklessly, regardless of the social and economic consequences of that pursuit. The Christian ethic demanded that the activities of the merchants be checked and controlled in the interest of the welfare of the entire community.

---

[1]We will concentrate primarily on English mercantilism in this chapter because industrial capitalism developed first in England and because most of the ideas in the capitalist ideology that we will discuss in Chapter 4 were developed in England.

[2]William Appleman Williams, *The Contours of American History* (New York: Quadrangle, 1966), p. 33.

THE MEDIEVAL ORIGINS
OF MERCANTILIST POLICIES

The first indications of a mercantilistic type of economic policy can be traced to Edward I (1272–1307), who evicted several foreign economic enterprises from England, established the English wool trade in Antwerp, and made various attempts to control commerce within England. A short time later, Edward III significantly extended these policies of economic control. The long war with France (1333–1360) led him to attempt to mitigate the harsh effects of wartime inflation on the laborers. He did this by fixing wages and prices in a ratio that was more favorable to the laborers. In return for this aid, Edward required all men to work at whatever jobs were available. "As this *quid pro quo* indicates, mercantilism was grounded in the idea of a mutual, corporate responsibility. God's way was based on such reciprocal respect and obligation, and Jerusalem provided the example to be followed."[3]

Richard II (1377–1399) extended and systematized his predecessors' policies. The principal problems facing England during his reign were the social and economic conflict that led to the Peasants' Rebellion of 1381 (see Chapter 2) and the necessity of countering foreign competition more effectively. The latter led to the Navigation Act of 1381, which was designed to favor English shippers and traders and to bring gold and silver into England. This money was needed for his program of building England into a "well and rightly governed kingdom" in which greater economic security for all would mitigate the social tensions that existed.

Henry II (1485–1509) renewed these policies. He commissioned numerous voyages of explorers and adventurers and attempted in various ways to secure legislation and negotiate treaties advantageous to English merchants. At the same time he subjected merchants to many controls and regulations imposed by the crown, for he believed that the unlimited pursuit of self-interest in the quest for profits was often harmful to general social interests and harmony.

Henry was still balancing feudal and capitalist interests; neither was dominant enough to persuade him to favor one over the other. The rapid growth of mining and wool raising during his reign led to an unfortunate neglect of food production. Moreover, the general excesses of the merchants had alienated both the peasants and the agrarian aristocracy. The merchants seemed to understand these problems and accepted a relationship in which, in return for Crown policies that would benefit them in foreign dealings, they submitted to domestic regulation of manufacturing and commerce.

[3]Williams, op. cit., p. 34. The following several pages draw heavily on Williams' excellent book.

THE SECULARIZATION
OF CHURCH FUNCTIONS

During the reign of Henry VIII England broke with Roman Catholicism. This event was significant because it marked the final secularization (in England at least) of the functions of the medieval church. Under Henry, "the state in the form of God's monarchy assumed the role and the functions of the old universal church. What Henry had done in his own blunt way was to sanctify the processes of this world."[4] During his reign as well as those of Elizabeth I, James I, and Charles I (1558–1649), there was widespread social unrest. The cause of this unrest was poverty, and the cause of much of the poverty was unemployment.

The enclosure movements (discussed in Chapter 2) were responsible for much of the unemployment. Another factor, however, was the decline in the export of woolens in the second half of the sixteenth century, which created a great deal of unemployment in England's most important manufacturing industry. There were also frequent commercial crises similar to, but without the regularity of, the depression phase of later business cycles. In addition to these factors, seasonal unemployment put many workers out of work for as many as four months of the year.

The people could no longer look to the Catholic church for relief from widespread unemployment and poverty. Destruction of the power of the church had eliminated the organized system of charity. The state attempted to assume responsibility for the general welfare of society. In order to do this, "England's leaders undertook a general, coordinated program to reorganize and rationalize . . . industry by establishing specifications of standards of production and marketing."[5] All these measures were designed to stimulate English trade and alleviate the unemployment problem.

In fact, it appears that the desire to achieve full employment is the unifying theme of most policy measures advocated by mercantilist writers. The mercantilists preferred measures designed to stimulate foreign rather than domestic trade "because they believed it contributed more to employment, to the nation's wealth and to national power. The writers after 1600 stressed the inflationary effect of an excess of exports over imports and the consequent increase in employment which inflation produced."[6]

Among the other measures taken to encourage industry during this period was the issuance of patents of monopoly. The first

[4]Ibid., p. 36.
[5]Ibid., p. 40.
[6]William D. Grampp, *Economic Liberalism*, vol. 1 (New York: Random House, 1965), p. 59.

important patent was granted in 1561, during the reign of Elizabeth I. Monopoly rights were given in order to encourage inventions and to establish new industries. These rights were severely abused, as might be expected. Moreover, they led to a complex system of special privileges and patronage and a host of other evils, which outraged most mercantilist writers every bit as much as similar abuses outraged late nineteenth-century American reformers. The evils of monopoly led to the Statute of Monopolies of 1624, which outlawed all monopolies except those that involved genuine inventions or would be instrumental in promoting a favorable balance of payments. Of course these loopholes were large, and abuses continued almost unchecked.

The Statute of Artificers (1563) specified conditions of employment and length of apprenticeships, provided for periodic wage assessments and established maximum rates that could be paid to laborers. The statute is important because it illustrates the fact that the Crown's paternalistic ethic never led to any attempt to elevate the status of the laboring classes. Monarchs of this period felt obliged to protect the working classes but, like their predecessors in the Middle Ages, believed those classes should be kept in their proper place. Maximum wage rates were designed to protect the capitalists, and furthermore, the justices who set these maximums and enforced the statute generally belonged to the employing class themselves. It is probable that these maximums reduced the real wages of laborers because prices generally rose faster than wages during the succeeding years.

Poor laws passed in 1531 and 1536 attempted to deal with the problems of unemployment, poverty, and misery then widespread in England. The first sought to distinguish between "deserving" and "undeserving" poor. Only the deserving poor were allowed to beg. The second decreed that each individual parish throughout England was responsible for its poor and that the parish should, through voluntary contributions, maintain a poor fund. This proved completely inadequate, and the "pauper problem" grew increasingly severe.

Finally, in 1572 the state accepted the principle that the poor would have to be supported by tax funds and enacted a compulsory "poor rate." And in 1576 "houses of correction" for "incorrigible vagrants" were authorized and provisions made for the parish to purchase raw materials to be worked up by the more tractable paupers and vagrants. Between that time and the close of the sixteenth century, several other poor law statutes were passed.

The Poor Law of 1601 was the Tudor attempt to integrate these laws into one consistent framework. Its main provisions included formal recognition of the right of the poor to receive relief, imposition of compulsory poor rates at the parish level, and provision for differential treatment for various classes of the poor. The aged and the sick could receive help in their homes; pauper children who were too young to be apprenticed in a trade were to be boarded out; the deserving poor and unemployed were to be given work as provided for in the act of 1576; and incorrigible vagrants were to be sent to houses of correction and prisons.[7]

From the preceding discussion it is possible to conclude that the period of English mercantilism was characterized by acceptance, in the spirit of the Christian paternalist ethic, of the idea that "the state had an obligation to serve society by accepting and discharging the responsibility for the general welfare."[8] The various statutes passed during this period "were predicated upon the idea that poverty, instead of being a personal sin, was a function of the economic system."[9] They acknowledged that those who were the victims of the deficiencies of the economic system should be cared for by those who benefited from the system.

THE RISE OF INDIVIDUALISM

After civil war of 1648 to 1660 and the Glorious Revolution of 1688, the English government was dominated by the gentry and the middle-class capitalists. The medieval world view that underlay the Christian paternalist ethic was eclipsed. A fundamental shift in the philosophy of the role of the State in society took place over the next 100 years. In 1776, with the publication of Adam Smith's *The Wealth of Nations*, a new individualistic philosophy—classical liberalism[10]—had definitely gained the ascendancy in England. This individualistic philosophy had existed throughout the mercantilist period, struggling to break the hold of the older paternalist world view. In the end the new classical liberalism prevailed because it— and not the older, essentially medieval world view—reflected the needs of the new capitalist order.

In condemning greed, acquisitive behavior, and the desire to accumulate wealth, the medieval Christian paternalist ethic condemned what had become the capitalist order's dominant motive force. The capitalist market economy, which had been extended by the late eighteenth century to almost every phase of production,

---

[7]For an extension of this discussion of the poor laws, see Arthur Birnie, *An Econmic History of the British Isles* (London: Methuen, 1936), chaps. 12 and 18.

[8]Williams, op. cit., p. 41.

[9]Ibid., p. 44.

[10]We use the adjective *classical* to differentiate the traditional liberal world view from what is called liberalism in the twentieth century. This distinction is clarified further in Chapter 4.

demanded self-seeking, acquisitive behavior to function successfully. In this context new theories about human behavior began to emerge. Writers began to assert that selfish, egoistic motives were the primary if not the only ones that moved men to action.

This interpretation of man's behavior is expressed in the writings of many important thinkers of the period. Many philosophers and social theorists began to assert that every human act was related to self-preservation and hence was egoistic in the most fundamental sense. The English nobleman Sir Robert Filmer was greatly alarmed by the large number of people who spoke of "the natural freedom of mankind, a new, plausible and dangerous opinion" with anarchistic implications.[11] Thomas Hobbes' *Leviathan*, published in 1651, trenchantly articulated a widely held opinion—that all human motives stem from a desire for whatever promotes the "vital motion" of the organism (man). Hobbes believed that all man's motives, even compassion, were merely so many disguised species of self-interest: "Grief for the calamity of another is *pity*, and ariseth from the imagination that the like calamity may befall himself; and therefore is called . . . *compassion*, and . . . fellow-feeling. . . ."[12]

Except for the few special interest groups that benefited from the extensive restrictions and regulations of commerce and manufacturing during this period, most capitalists felt constrained and inhibited by state regulations in their quest for profits. The individualistic and egoistic doctrines were eagerly embraced by such men. This view began to dominate economic thinking, even among the mercantilists. One careful history asserts that "most of the mercantilist . . . policy assumed that self-interest governs individual conduct. . . ."[13]

The majority of mercantilist writers were either capitalists or employees of the great capitalist trading companies. It was quite natural for them to perceive the motives of the capitalists as universal. From the capitalists' views of the nature of man, and their needs to be free from the extensive economic restrictions that inhibited them in the conduct of their everyday business, grew the philosophy of individualism that provided the basis of classical liberalism. Against the well-ordered, paternalistic view Europe had inherited from the feudal society, they asserted "the view that the human person ought to be independent, self-directing, autonomous, free—ought to be, that is, an individual, a unit distinguished from the social mass rather than submerged in it."[14]

[11]Lee Cameron McDonald, *Western Political Theory: The Modern Age* (New York: Harcourt Brace Jovanovich, 1962), p. 29.
[12]Quoted in Harry K. Girvetz, *The Evolution of Liberalism* (New York: Colliers, 1963), pp. 28–29.
[13]Grampp, op. cit., p. 69.
[14]McDonald, op. cit., p. 16.

PROTESTANTISM AND
THE INDIVIDUALIST ETHIC

One of the most important examples of this individualistic and middle-class philosophy was the Protestant theology that emerged from the Reformation. The new middle-class capitalists wanted to be free not only from economic restrictions that encumbered manufacturing and commerce but also from the moral opprobrium the Catholic church had heaped upon their motives and activities. Protestantism not only freed them from religious condemnation but eventually made virtues of the selfish, egoistic, and acquisitive motives the medieval church had so despised.[15]

The principal originators of the Protestant movement were quite close to the Catholic position on such questions as usury and the just price. On most social issues they were deeply conservative. During the German peasant revolt of 1524, Luther wrote a virulent pamphlet, *Against the Murdering Hordes of Peasants*, in which he said princes should "knock down, strangle and stab. . . . Such wonderful times are these that a prince can merit heaven better with bloodshed than another with prayer." His advice contributed to the general atmosphere in which the slaughter of over 100,000 peasants was carried out with an air of religious righteousness.

Yet despite the conservatism of the founders of Protestantism, this religious outlook contributed to the growing influence of the new individualistic philosophy. The basic tenet of Protestantism, which laid the groundwork for religious attitudes that were to sanction middle-class business practices, was the doctrine that men were justified by faith rather than by works. The Catholic church had taught that men were justified by *works*, which generally meant ceremonies and rituals. In the Catholic view no man could be justified on his own merit alone. "Justification by works . . . did not mean that an individual could save himself: it meant that he could be saved through the Church. Hence the power of the clergy. Compulsory confession, the imposition of penance on the whole population . . . together with the possibility of withholding absolution, gave the priests a terrifying power."[16] These powers also created a situation in which the medieval doctrines of the Catholic church were not easily abandoned and in which the individual was still subordinated to society (as represented by the church).

The Protestant doctrine of justification by faith asserted that

[15]The classic studies of the relationship between Protestantism and capitalism are Max Weber, *The Protestant Ethic and the Spirit of Capitalism* (New York: Scribner, 1958), and Richard H. Tawney, *Religion and the Rise of Capitalism* (New York: Mentor Books, 1954).

[16]Christopher Hill, "Protestantism and the Rise of Capitalism," in D. S. Landes, ed., *The Rise of Capitalism* (New York: Macmillan, 1966), p. 43.

motives were more important than specific acts or rituals. Faith was "nothing else but the truth of the heart."[17] Each man had to search his own heart to discover if his acts stemmed from a pure heart and faith in God. Each man had to judge for himself. This individualistic reliance on each person's private conscience appealed strongly to the new middle-class artisans and small merchants. "When the business-man of sixteenth and seventeenth century Geneva, Amsterdam or London looked into his inmost heart, he found that God had planted there a deep respect for the principle of private property. . . . Such men felt quite genuinely and strongly that their economic practices, though they might conflict with the traditional law of the old church, were not offensive to God. On the contrary: they glorified God."[18]

It was through this insistence on the individual's own interpreta-tion of God's will that the "Puritans tried to spiritualize [the new] economic processes" and eventually came to believe that "God insti-tuted the market and exchange."[19] However, it was only a matter of time before the Protestants expounded dogma that they expected everyone to accept. But the new dogma was radically different from medieval doctrines. The new doctrines stressed the necessity of doing well at one's earthly calling as the best way to please God, and emphasized diligence and hard work.

The older Christian distrust of riches was "translated" into a condemnation of extravagance and needless dissipation of wealth. Thus the Protestant ethic stressed the importance of asceticism and abstemious frugality. A theologian who has studied the connection between religion and capitalism sums up the relationship in this way: "The religious value set upon constant, systematic, efficient work in one's calling as the readiest means of securing the certainty of salvation and of glorifying God became a most powerful agency in economic expansion. The rigid limitations of consumption on the one hand and the methodical intensification of production on the other could have but one result—the accumulation of capital."[20] Thus, although neither Calvin nor Luther was a spokesman for the new middle-class capitalist, within the context of the new religious individualism the capitalists found a religion in which, over time, "profits . . . [came to be] looked upon as willed by God, as a mark of his favor and a proof of success in one's calling."[21]

[17]Ibid.
[18]Ibid., pp. 46–47.
[19]Ibid., p. 49.
[20]Kemper Fullerton, "Calvinism and Capitalism; an Explanation of the Weber Thesis," in Robert W. Green, ed., *Protestantism and Capitalism: The Weber Thesis and Its Critics* (Lexington, Mass.: Heath, 1959), p. 19.
[21]Ibid., p. 18.

THE ECONOMIC
POLICIES OF INDIVIDUALISM

Throughout the mercantilist period this new individualism led to innumerable protests against the subordination of economic affairs to the will of the state. From the middle of the seventeenth century, almost all mercantilist writers condemned state-granted monopolies and other forms of protection and favoritism in the internal economy (as opposed to international commerce). Many believed that in a competitive market that pitted buyer against buyer, seller against seller, and buyer against seller, society would benefit most greatly if the price were left free to fluctuate and find its proper (market equilibrating) level. One of the earliest mercantilist writers of importance, John Hales, argued that agricultural productivity could best be improved if husbandmen were allowed to

> have more profit by it than they have, and liberty to sell it at all times, and to all places, as freely as men may do their other things. But then no doubt, the price of corn would rise, specially at the first more than at length; yet that price would evoke every man to set plough in the ground, to husband waste grounds, yes to turn the lands which be enclosed from pasture to arable land; for every man will gladder follow that wherein they see the more profit and gains, and thereby must need ensue both plenty of corn, and also much treasure should be brought into this realm by occasion thereof; and besides that plenty of other victuals increased among us.[22]

This belief—that restrictions on production and trade within a nation were harmful to the interests of everyone concerned—became increasingly widespread in the late seventeenth and early eighteenth centuries. Numerous statements of this view can be found in the works of such writers as Malynes, Petty, North, Law, and Child.[23] Of these men, perhaps Sir Dudley North (1641–1691) was the earliest clear spokesman for the individualistic ethic that was to become the basis for classical liberalism. North believed that all men were motivated primarily by self-interest and should be left alone to compete in a free market if the public welfare were to be maximized. He argued that whenever merchants or capitalists advocated special laws to regulate production or commerce, "they usually esteem the immediate interest of their own to be the common Measure of Good and Evil. And there are many, who to gain a little in their own Trades, care not how much others suffer; and each man

---

[22]Quoted in Grampp, op. cit., p. 78.
[23]Ibid., pp. 77–81.

strives that all others may be forced in their dealings to act sub-
serviently for his Profit, but under the cover of the Publick."[24] The
public welfare would best be served, North believed, if most of the
restrictive laws that bestowed special privileges were entirely removed.

In 1714 Bernard Mandelville published *The Fable of the Bees:
or Private Vices, Publick Benefits*, in which he put forth the seemingly strange paradox that the vices most despised in the older moral
code, if practiced by all, would result in the greatest public good.
Selfishness, greed, and acquisitive behavior, he maintained, all tended
to contribute to industriousness and a thriving economy. The answer
to the paradox was, of course, that what had been vices in the eyes
of the medieval moralists were the very motive forces that propelled
the new capitalist system. And in the view of the new religious,
moral, and economic philosophies of the capitalist period these
motives were no longer vices.

The capitalists had struggled throughout the mercantilist period
to free themselves from all restrictions in their quest for profits.
These restrictions had resulted from the paternalistic laws that were
the remnants of the feudal version of the Christian paternalist ethic.
Such an ethic simply was not compatible with the new economic
system that functioned on the basis of strict contractual obligations
between people rather than on traditional personal ties. Merchants
and capitalists who invested large sums in market ventures could not
depend on the forces of custom to protect their investments.

Profit seeking could be effective only in a society based on the
protection of property rights and the enforcement of impersonal
contractual commitments between individuals. The new ideology
that was firmly taking root in the late seventeenth and eighteenth
centuries justified these motives and relationships between individuals. It is to a consideration of this new individualistic philosophy
of classical liberalism that we turn in Chapter 4.

SUMMARY

There is a basic continuity between medieval and mercantilist social
thought. State intervention in economic processes was originally justified in terms of the medieval Christian notion that those to whom
God had given power were obligated to use this power to promote
the general welfare and common good of all society. In early capitalism the state began to assume many of the roles formerly held by
the church.

[24]Quoted in Robert Lekachman, ed., *The Varieties of Economics*, vol. I
(New York: Meridian, 1962), p. 185.

The Christian paternalist ethic, however, had thoroughly con-demned the acquisitive behavior that was to become the dominant motive force of the new capitalist system. It was therefore necessary to create a new philosophical and ideological point of view that morally justified individualization, greed, and profit seeking.

Protestantism and the new philosophies of individualism furnished the bases for the new ideology. The economic writings of the mer-cantilists reflected the new individualism. The new point of view emphasized the need for greater freedom for capitalists to seek profits and hence the need for less government intervention in the market. Thus the presence of two fundamentally different general points of view in mercantilist writings created an intellectual conflict that was not resolved until the classical liberal philosophy, including classical economics, effectively ferreted out all remnants of the me-dieval Christian paternalist ethic.

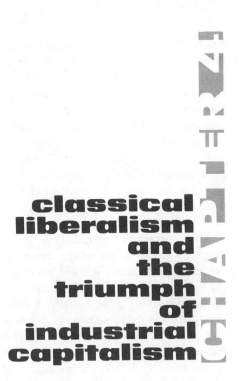

classical liberalism and the triumph of industrial capitalism

A single theme runs through the works of the mercantilist writers (considered in the latter part of Chapter 3) that distinguishes them from the later classical liberal writers. They argued for a minimum of internal restriction and regulation, but they favored an active governmental policy designed to further England's commerce in the international trading markets. The classical liberals, however, advocated free trade internationally as well as domestically. In this chapter we examine the changes in England's commercial position that encouraged its economists to favor free trade.

THE INDUSTRIAL REVOLUTION

Between 1700 and 1770 the foreign markets for English goods grew much faster than did England's domestic markets. During the period 1700–1750, output of domestic industries increased by 7 percent, while that of export industries increased by 76 percent. For the period 1750–1770, the figures are 7 percent and 80 percent. This rapidly increasing foreign demand for English manufactures was the single most important cause of the most fundamental transformation of human life in history: the Industrial Revolution.

Eighteenth-century England was an economy with a well-developed market and one in which the traditional anticapitalist market bias in attitudes and ideology had been greatly weakened. In this

England, larger ouputs of manufactured goods produced at lower prices meant ever-increasing profits. Thus profit seeking was the motive that, stimulated by increasing foreign demand, accounted for the virtual explosion of technological innovations that occurred in the late eighteenth and early nineteenth centuries—and radically transformed all England and eventually most of the world.

The textile industry was the most important in the early Industrial Revolution. In 1700 the woolen industry had persuaded the government to ban the import of Indian-made "calicoes" (cotton) and thus had secured a protected home market for domestic producers. As outlined earlier, rising foreign demand spurred mechanization of the industry.

More specifically, an imbalance between the spinning and weaving processes led to many of the innovations. The spinning wheel was not as productive as the hand loom, especially after the 1730s, when the flying shuttle was invented and the weaving process was speeded up considerably. This imbalance led to three inventions that reversed it: the spinning jenny, developed in the 1760s, with which one person could spin several threads simultaneously; the water frame, invented in 1768, which improved spinning by using both rollers and spindles in the process; and the mule, developed in the 1780s, which combined features of the other two and permitted the application of steam power. These new inventions could be used most economically in factories located near sources of water power (and later steam power). Richard Arkwright, who claimed to be the inventor of the water frame, raised sufficient capital to put a great many factories into operation, each employing anywhere from 150 to 600 people. Others followed his example, and textile manufacturing in England was rapidly transformed from a cottage to a factory industry.

The iron industry was also very important in the early drive to mechanized factory production. In the early eighteenth century England's iron industry was quite inconsequential. Charcoal was still used for smelting and had been since prehistoric times. By this time, however, the forests surrounding the iron mines were almost completely depleted. England was forced to import pig iron from its colonies, as well as from Sweden, Germany, and Spain. In 1709 Abraham Darby developed a process for making coke from coal for use in the smelting process.

Despite the relative abundance of coal near the iron mines, it was not until the latter part of the eighteenth century (when the military demands on the arms and munitions industries were very great) that the iron industry began using coke extensively. This increased demand led to the development of the puddling process, which eliminated the excess carbon left by the coke. A whole series of innovations followed, including the rolling mill, the blast furnace, the steam hammer, and metal-turning lathes. All these inventions led to a very rapid expansion of the iron and coal-mining industries, which permitted the increasingly widespread use of machines made of iron in a great variety of industries.

Entrepreneurs in many other industries saw the possibilities for larger profits if they could increase output and lower costs. In this period there was a "veritable outburst of inventive activity":

> During the second half of the eighteenth century, interest in technical innovations became unusually intensive. For a hundred years prior to 1760, the number of patents issued during each decade had reached 102 only once, and had otherwise fluctuated between a low of 22 (1700–1709) and a high of 92 (1750–1759). During the following thirty-year period (1760–1789), the average number of patents issued increased from 205 in the 1760's to 294 in the 1770's and 477 in the 1780's.[1]

Undoubtedly the most important of these innovations was the development of the steam engine. Industrial steam engines had been introduced in the early 1700s, but mechanical difficulties had limited their use to the pumping of water in mines. In 1769 James Watt designed an engine with such accurate specifications that the straight thrust of a piston could be translated into rotary motion. A Birmingham manufacturer named Boulton formed a partnership with Watt, and with Boulton's financial resources they were able to go into large-scale production of steam engines. By the turn of the century steam was rapidly replacing water as the chief source of power in manufacturing. The development of steam power led to profound economic and social changes.

> With this new great event, the invention of the steam engine, the final and most decisive stage of the industrial revolution opened. By liberating it from its last shackles, steam enabled the immense and rapid development of large-scale industry to take place. For the use of steam was not, like that of water, dependent on geographical position and local resources. Whenever coal could be bought at a reasonable price a steam engine could be erected. England had plenty of coal, and by the end of the eighteenth century it was already applied to many different uses, while a network of waterways, made on purpose, enabled it to be carried everywhere very cheaply: the whole country became a privileged land, suitable above all others for the growth of industry. Factories were now no longer bound to the valleys, where they had

[1]Reinhard Bendix, *Work and Authority in Industry* (New York: Harper & Row, Torchbooks, 1963), p. 27.

grown up in solitude by the side of rapid-flowing streams. It became possible to bring them nearer the markets where their raw materials were bought and their finished products sold, and nearer the centers of population where their labor was recruited. They sprang up near one another and thus, huddled together, gave rise to those huge black industrial cities which the steam engine surrounded with a perpetual cloud of smoke.[2]

The growth in the major manufacturing cities was truly spectacular. For example, the population of Manchester rose from 17,000 in 1760 to 237,000 in 1831 and 400,000 in 1851. Output of manufactured goods approximately doubled in the second half of the eighteenth century and grew even more rapidly in the early nineteenth century. By 1801, nearly 30 percent of the English work force was employed in manufacturing and mining; by 1831, this figure had risen to over 40 percent. Thus the Industrial Revolution transformed England into a country of large urban manufacturing centers, where the factory system was dominant. The result was a very rapid growth of productivity that vaulted England into the position of the greatest economic and political power of the nineteenth century. The effects of the Industrial Revolution on the lives of the English people will be discussed in Chapter 5.

THE RISE OF CLASSICAL LIBERALISM

It was during this period of industrialization that the individualistic world view of classical liberalism became the dominant ideology of capitalism.[3] Many of the ideas of classical liberalism had taken root and even gained wide acceptance in the mercantilist period, but it was in the late eighteenth and nineteenth centuries that classical liberalism most completely dominated social, political, and economic thought in England. The Christian paternalist ethic was still advanced in the writings of many of the nobility and their allies as well as many socialists, but in this era these expressions were, by and large, dissident minority views.

THE PSYCHOLOGICAL CREED

Classical liberalism's psychological creed was based on four assumptions about human nature. People were believed to be egoistic, coldly calculating, essentially inert, and atomistic. (See Chapter 3

[2]Paul Mantoux, *The Industrial Revolution in the Eighteenth Century* (New York: Harcourt Brace Jovanovich, 1927), pp. 344–345.
[3]This account of classical liberalism relies heavily on Harry K. Girvetz, *The Evolution of Liberalism* (New York: Collier, 1963), pp. 1–149.

for a discussion of the egoistic theory of human nature.) The ego-ism argued by Hobbes furnished the basis for this view, and in the works of later liberals, especially Jeremy Bentham, it was blended with psychological hedonism: the view that all actions are motivated by the desire to achieve pleasure and avoid pain.

"Nature," Bentham wrote, "has placed mankind under the gov-ernance of two sovereign masters, *pain*, and *pleasure*. . . . They govern us in all we do, in all we say, in all we think."[4] Pleasures differed in intensity, Bentham believed, but there were no qualitative differences. He argued that "quantity of pleasure being equal, push-pin is as good as poetry." This theory of human motivation as purely selfish is found in the writings of many of the most eminent thinkers of the period, including John Locke, Bernard Mandeville, David Hartley, Abraham Tucker, and Adam Smith. Smith's ideas will be examined in some detail later in this chapter.

Man's intellect played a significant role in the classical liberal's scheme of things. Although all motives stemmed from pleasure and pain, the decisions people made about what pleasures or pains to seek or avoid were based on a cool, dispassionate, and rational as-sessment of the situation. Reason would dictate that all alternatives in a situation be weighed in order to choose that which would maxi-mize pleasure or minimize pain. It is this emphasis on the importance of rational measurement of pleasures and pains (with a correspond-ing deemphasis of caprice, instinct, habit, custom, or convention) that forms the calculating, intellectual side of the classical liberal's theory of psychology.

The view that individuals were essentially inert stemmed from the notion that pleasure or the avoidance of pain were men's only motives. If men could see no activities leading to pleasurable conclu-sions or feared no pain, then they would be inert, motionless, or in simpler terms just plain lazy. Any kind of exertion or work was viewed as painful and therefore would not be undertaken without the promise of greater pleasure or the avoidance of greater pain. "Aversion," wrote Bentham, "is the emotion—the only emotion—which labor, taken by itself, is qualified to produce: of any such emotion as *love* or *desire*, *ease*, which is the *negative* or *absence* of *labor*—ease, not labor—is the object."[5]

The practical outcome of this doctrine (or perhaps the reason for it) was the widespread belief of the time that laborers were incurably lazy. Thus only a large reward or the fear of starvation and depriva-tion could force them to work. The Reverend Joseph Townsend

---

[4]Jeremy Bentham, "An Introduction to the Principles of Morals and Legisla-tion," in A. I. Melden, ed., *Ethical Theories* (Englewood Cliffs, N.J.: Prentice-Hall, 1955), p. 341.
[5]Quoted in Girvetz, op. cit., p. 38.

put this view very succinctly: "Hunger is not only peaceable, silent and unremitted pressure, but, as the most natural motive to industry and labor, it calls forth the most powerful exertions." Townsend believed that "only the experience of hunger would goad them [laborers] to labor."[6]

This view differed radically from the older, paternalistic ethic that had led to the passage of the Elizabethan Poor Relief Act of 1601. The paternalistic concern for the poor had lasted for two centuries and had culminated in 1795 in the *Speenhamland system*, which guaranteed everyone, able-bodied or not, working or not, a minimal subsistence to be paid by public taxes. It was against this system that the classical liberals railed. They eventually succeeded in passing the Poor Law of 1834, the object of which, according to Dicey, "was in reality to save the property of hard-working men from destruction by puting an end to the monstrous system under which laggards who would not toil for their support lived at the expense of their industrious neighbors. . . ."[7]

Classical liberals were persuaded, however, that the "higher ranks" of men were motivated by ambition. This differentiation of men into different ranks betrayed an implicit elitism in their individualistic doctrines. In order to ensure ample effort on the part of the "elite," the classical liberals believed the state should put the highest priority on the protection of private property. Although the argument began "as an argument for guaranteeing to the worker the fruits of his toil, it has become one of the chief apologies for the institution of private property in general."[8]

The last of the four tenets was atomism, which held that the individual was a more fundamental reality than the group or society. "Priority . . . [was] . . . assigned to the ultimate components out of which an aggregate or whole . . . [was] composed; they constituted the fundamental reality."[9] With this notion the classical liberals rejected the concept, implicit in the Christian paternalist ethic, that society was like a family and that the whole and the relationships that made up the whole were more important than any individual. The liberal's individualistic beliefs were inconsistent with the personal and human ties envisioned in the Christian paternalist ethic. The group was no more than the additive total of the individuals that constituted it. They believed that restrictions placed on the individual by society were generally evil and should be tolerated only when an even worse evil would result without them.

[6]Bendix, op. cit., p. 74.
[7]Albert V. Dicey, *Law and Public Opinion in England*, 2d. ed. (London: Macmillan, 1926), p. 203.
[8]Girvetz, op. cit., p. 50.
[9]Ibid., p. 41.

This atomistic psychology can be contrasted with a more socially oriented psychology that would lead to the conclusion that most of the characteristics, habits, ways of perceiving and thinking about life processes, and general personality patterns of the individual are significantly influenced, if not determined, by the social institutions and relationships of which he is a part. Atomistic psychology, however, sees the makeup of the individual as somehow independently given. It therefore regards social institutions as both tools for and the handiwork of these individuals. In this view society exists only because it is useful, and if it were not for this usefulness each individual could go his own way, discarding society much as he would discard a tool that no longer served its purpose.

THE ECONOMIC CREED

Several explanations are necessary for an understanding of why the classical liberals thought society so useful. For example, they talked about the "natural gregariousness of men," the need for collective security, and the economic benefits of the division of labor, which society makes possible. The latter was the foundation of the economic creed of classical liberalism, and the creed was crucial to classical liberalism because this philosophy contained what appear to be two contradictory or conflicting assumptions.

On the one hand, the assumption of man's innate egoism had led Hobbes to assert that, in the absence of restraints, men's selfish motives would lead to a "natural state" of war, with each man pitted against all others. In this state of nature, Hobbes believed, the life of man was "solitary, poor, nasty, brutish, and short." The only escape from brutal combat was the establishment of some source of absolute power—a central government—to which each man submitted in return for protection from all other men.[10]

On the other hand, one of the cardinal tenets of classical liberalism was that men (or, more particularly, businessmen) should be free to give vent to their egoistic drives with a minimum of control or restraint imposed by society. This apparent contradiction was bridged by the liberal economic creed, which asserted that if the competitiveness and rivalry of unrestrained egoism existed in a capitalist market setting, then this competition would benefit the individuals involved and all society as well. This view was put forth in the most profound single intellectual achievement of classical liberalism: Adam Smith's *The Wealth of Nations*, published in 1776.

Smith believed that "every individual . . . [was] continually exerting himself to find out the most advantageous employment for

[10]Hobbes, *Leviathan*, reprinted in Melden, op. cit., pp. 192–205.

whatever capital he can command."[11] Those without capital were always searching for the employment at which the monetary return for their labor would be maximized. If both capitalists and laborers were left alone, self-interest would guide them to use their capital and labor where they were most productive. The search for profits would ensure that what was produced would be what people wanted most and were willing to pay for. Thus Smith and classical liberals in general were opposed to having some authority or law determine what should be produced. "It is not from the benevolence of the butcher, the brewer, or the baker, that we expect our dinner, but from their regard to their own interest,"[12] wrote Smith. Producers of various goods must compete in the market for the dollars of consumers. The producer who offered a better-quality product would attract more consumers. He would therefore be led by his self-interest to constant improvement of the quality of his product. The producer could also increase profits by cutting his costs of production to a minimum.

Thus a *free market*, in which producers competed for consumers' money in an egoistic quest for more profits, would guarantee the direction of capital and labor to their most productive uses and ensure production of the goods consumers wanted and needed most (as measured by their ability and willingness to pay for them). Moreover, the market would lead to a constant striving to improve the quality of products and to organize production in the most efficient and least costly manner possible. All these beneficial actions would stem directly from the competition of egoistical men, each pursuing his self-interest.

What a far cry from the "solitary, poor, nasty, brutish" world Hobbes thought would result from man's competitiveness. The wonderful social institution that could make all this possible was the free and unrestrained market, the forces of supply and demand. The market, Smith believed, would act as an "invisible hand" channeling selfish, egoistic motives into mutually consistent and complementary activities that would best promote the welfare of all society. And the greatest beauty of it was the complete lack of any need for paternalistic guidance, direction, or restrictions. Freedom from coercion in a capitalist market economy was compatible with a natural orderliness in which the welfare of each, as well as the welfare of all society (which was, after all, only the aggregate of the individuals that constitute it), would be maximized. In Smith's words, each producer

[11]Adam Smith, *The Wealth of Nations* (New York: Modern Library, 1937), p. 421.
[12]Ibid., p. 14.

intends only his own security; and by directing that industry in such a manner as its produce may be of the greatest value, he intends only his own gain, and he is in this, as in many other cases, led by an invisible hand to promote an end which was no part of his intention. Nor is it always the worse for the society that it was not part of it. By pursuing his own interest he frequently promotes that of society more effectually than when he really intends to promote it. I have never known much good done by those who affected to trade for the public good. It is an affectation, indeed, not very common among merchants, and very few words need be employed in dissuading them from it.[13]

With this statement it is evident that Smith had a philosophy totally antithetical to the paternalism of the Christian paternalist ethic. The Christian notion of the rich promoting the security and well-being of the poor through paternalistic control and almsgiving contrasts sharply with Smith's picture of a capitalist who is concerned only with "his own advantage, indeed, and not that of the society. . . . But the study of his own advantage naturally, or rather necessarily leads him to prefer that employment which is most advantageous to the society."[14]

Not only would the free and unfettered market channel productive energies and resources into their most valuable uses, but it would also lead to continual economic progress. Economic well-being depended on the capacity of an economy to produce. Productive capacity depended, in turn, on accumulation of capital and division of labor. When one man produced everything he needed for himself and his family, production was very inefficient. But if men subdivided tasks, each producing only the commodity for which his own abilities best suited him, productivity increased. For such a subdivision of tasks a market was necessary in order to exchange goods. In the market each person could get all the items he needed but did not produce.

This increase in productivity could be extended further if the production of each commodity were broken down into many steps or stages. Each person would then work on only one stage of the production of one commodity. In order to achieve a division of labor of this degree, it was necessary to have many specialized tools and other equipment. It was also necessary that all the stages of production for a particular commodity be brought together and coordinated, as, for example, in a factory. Thus an increasingly fine division of labor required accumulation of capital in the form of tools,

[13] Ibid., p. 423.
[14] Ibid., p. 421.

equipment, factories, and money. This capital would also provide wages to maintain workers during the period of production before their coordinated efforts were brought to fruition and sold on the market.

The source of this capital accumulation was, of course, the profits of production. As long as demand was brisk and more could be sold than was being produced, capitalists would invest their profits in order to expand their capital, which would lead to an increasingly intricate division of labor. The increased division of labor would lead to greater productivity, higher wages, higher profits, more capital accumulation, and so forth in a never-ending, upward-moving escalator of social progress. The process would be brought to a halt only when there was no longer sufficient demand for the products to warrant further accumulation and more extensive division of labor. Government regulation of economic affairs, or any restriction on the freedom of market behavior, could only decrease the extent of demand and bring the beneficial process of capital accumulation to a halt before it would have ended otherwise. So here again there was no room for paternalistic government meddling in economic affairs.

THE THEORY OF POPULATION

Thomas Robert Malthus' population theory was an important and integral part of classical liberal economic and social doctrines. He believed most men were driven by an insatiable desire for sexual pleasure and that consequently natural rates of human reproduction, *when unchecked*, would lead to geometric increases in population—that is, population would increase each generation at the ratio of 1, 2, 4, 8, 16, and so forth. But food production, at the very best, increases at an arithmetic rate—that is, each generation it can increase only at a rate such as 1, 2, 3, 4, 5, and so on.

Obviously, something would have to hold the population in check. The food supply could not support a population that was growing at a geometric rate. Malthus believed there were two general kinds of checks that limited population growth: preventive checks and positive checks. Preventive checks reduced the birth rate, whereas positive checks increased the death rate.

Moral restraint, vice, and birth control were the primary preventive checks. Moral restraint was the means by which the higher ranks of men limited their family size in order not to dissipate their wealth among larger and larger numbers of heirs. For the lower ranks of men, vice and birth control were the preventive checks; but they were grossly insufficient to curb the vast numbers of the poor.

Famine, misery, plague, and war were the positive checks. The fact that preventive checks did not succeed in limiting the numbers of lower-class people made these positive checks inevitable. Finally, if the positive checks were somehow overcome, the growing population would press upon the food supply until starvation—the ultimate and unavoidable check—succeeded in holding the population down.

Before starvation set in, Malthus advised that steps be taken to help the positive checks do their work:

> It is an evident truth that, whatever may be the rate of increase in the means of subsistence, the increase in population must be limited by it, at least after the food has once been divided into the smallest shares that will support life. All the children born, beyond what would be required to keep up the population to this level, must necessarily perish, unless room be made for them by the deaths of grown persons. . . . To act consistently therefore, we should facilitate, instead of foolishly and vainly endeavouring to impede, the operation of nature in producing this mortality; and if we dread the too frequent visitation of the horrid form of famine, we should sedulously encourage the other forms of destruction, which we compel nature to use. Instead of recommending cleanliness to the poor, we should encourage contrary habits. In our towns we should make the streets narrower, crowd more people into the houses, and court the return of the plague. In the country, we should build our villages near stagnant pools, and particularly encourage settlements in all marshy and unwholesome situations. But above all, we should reprobate specific remedies for ravaging diseases; and those benevolent, but much mistaken men, who have thought they were doing a service to mankind by projecting schemes for the total extirpation of particular disorders. If by these and similar means the annual mortality were increased . . . we might probably every one of us marry at the age of puberty, and yet few be absolutely starved.[15]

The masses of men, in Malthus' opinion, were incapable of exercising moral restraint, which was the only real remedy for the population problem. They were therefore doomed to live perpetually at a bare subsistence level. If all income and wealth were distributed among them, it would be totally dissipated within one generation because of profligate behavior and population growth, and they would be as poor and destitute as ever.

Paternalistic attempts to aid the poor were thus doomed to failure. Furthermore, they were a positive evil because they drained

[15]Thomas Robert Malthus, *Essay on the Principle of Population*, vol. 2 (New York: Dutton, 1961), pp. 179–180.

wealth and income from the higher (more moral) ranks of men. These higher-class individuals were responsible, either in person or by supporting others, for all the great achievements of society. Art, music, philosophy, literature, and the other splendid cultural attainments of Western civilization owed their existence to the good taste and generosity of the higher classes of men. Taking money from them would dry up the source of such achievement; using the money to alleviate the conditions of the poor was a futile, foredoomed exercise.

It is obvious that the Malthusian population theory and the liberal economic theories led to the same conclusion: Paternalistic government should avoid any attempt to intervene in the economy on behalf of the poor. Malthusian views—that poverty is the fault of the poor, who have too many babies, and that nothing can be done to end poverty—are still held by many people today.

THE POLITICAL CREED

The economic and population doctrines of classical liberalism gave rise quite naturally to a political creed that rejected the State, or government, as an evil to be tolerated only when it was the sole means of avoiding a worse evil. Much of this antipathy stemmed directly from the many corrupt, despotic, capricious, and tyrannical actions of several European kings, as well as from the actions of the English Parliament, which was notoriously unrepresentative and often despotic. The liberal creed was not put forward as an objection against particular governments, however, but against governments in general. Thomas Paine reflected the sentiment of classical liberals when he wrote: "Society in every state is a blessing, but government, even in its best state, is but a necessary evil; in its worst state an intolerable one. . . ."[16]

What were the functions that classical liberals thought should be given to governments? In *The Wealth of Nations* Adam Smith listed three: protection of the country against foreign invaders, protection of citizens against "injustices" suffered at the hands of other citizens, and the "duty . . . of erecting and maintaining those public institutions and those public works, which, though they may be in the highest degree advantageous to a great society, are, however, of such a nature, that the profit could never repay the expense to any individual or small number of individuals, and which it therefore cannot be expected that any individual or small number of individuals should erect and maintain."[17]

[16]Quoted in Girvetz, op. cit., p. 66.
[17]Smith, op. cit., p. 681.

This list is very general, and almost any kind of government action could be justified under one of these three functions. In order to understand the specific functions the liberals believed government should have, it is necessary to deal first with an objection that is frequently raised when the writings of Adam Smith are said to comprise part of an ideology justifying capitalism. It is often pointed out not only that Smith was *not* a spokesman for the capitalists of his day but also that many of his passages show that he was in general suspicious and distrustful of capitalists.[18] This contention is certainly true. Nevertheless capitalists used the arguments put forward by Smith to justify their attempts to eliminate the last vestiges of paternalistic government when these stood in the way of their quest for profits. It was Smith's rationale that enabled them to quiet their consciences when their actions created widespread hardship and suffering. After all, they were only following his advice and pursuing their own profits; and this was the way they should act if they wished to be of the greatest service to society.

Finally, most classical liberals interpreted Smith's theory of the three general governmental functions in a way that showed they were not hesitant about endorsing a paternalistic government when they, the capitalists, were the beneficiaries of paternalism. Thus "the original doctrine of laissez faire . . . passed, for the most part, from the care of intellectuals like Adam Smith . . . into the custodianship of businessmen and industrialists and their hired spokesmen."[19]

First, the requirement that the government protect the country from external threats was often extended in the late nineteenth century to a protection or even enlargement of foreign markets through armed coercion. Second, protection of citizens against "injustices" committed by other citizens was usually defined to mean protection of private property, enforcement of contracts, and preservation of internal order. Protection of private property, especially ownership of factories and capital equipment, is of course tantamount to protection of the sine qua non of capitalism. It was their ownership of the means of production that gave the capitalists their economic and political power. Giving the government the function of protecting property relations meant giving the government the job of protecting the source of power of the economically and politically dominant class: the capitalists.

Contract enforcement was also essential for the successful functioning of capitalism. The complex division of labor and the neces-

[18]For a statement of this view, as well as a scholarly inquiry into classical economics from a viewpoint that differs from the one presented in this book, see Lionel Robbins, *The Theory of Economic Policy in English Classical Political Economy* (London: Macmillan, 1953).

[19]Girvetz, op. cit., p. 81.

sity of complex organization and coordination in production, as well as the colossal capital investments necessary in many commercial ventures, meant that capitalists had to be able to depend on people to meet contractual commitments. The medieval notion that custom and the special circumstances of a case defined an individual's obligations was just not compatible with capitalism. Therefore the duty to enforce contracts amounted to governmental coercion of a type necessary for capitalism to function.

The preservation of internal order was (and is) always necessary. In the late eighteenth and early nineteenth centuries, however, it often meant brutally crushing labor union movements or the English Chartist movement, which capitalists considered threats to their profit-making activities.

Finally, the function of "erecting and maintaining those public institutions and those of public works" that were in the public interest generally was interpreted to mean the creation and maintenance of institutions that fostered profitable production and exchange. These included the provision of a stable and uniform currency, standard weights and measures, and the physical means necessary for conducting business. Roads, canals, harbors, railroads, the postal services, and other forms of communication were among the prerequisites of business. Although these were often privately owned, most capitalist governments were extensively involved in their erection and maintenance either through financial subsidies to private businesses or through the government's direct undertaking of these projects.

Thus it may be concluded that the classical liberals' philosophy of laissez faire was opposed to government interference in economic affairs only if such interference was harmful to the interests of capitalists. They welcomed and even fought for any paternalistic interferences in economic affairs that stabilized business or made larger profits possible.[20]

CLASSICAL LIBERALISM
AND INDUSTRIALIZATION

The Industrial Revolution and the triumph of the classical liberal capitalist ideology occurred together during the late eighteenth and early nineteenth centuries. Liberalism was the philosophy of the new industrial capitalism, and the new liberal ideas created a political and intellectual atmosphere in eighteenth-century England that fostered the growth of the factory system.

[20]Considerable evidence for this assertion can be found in Warren J. Samuels, *The Classical Theory of Economic Policy* (New York: World Publishing, 1966).

In its medieval version, the Christian paternalist ethic had led to a pervasive system of restrictions on the behavior of capitalists during the mercantilist period. Capitalists and their spokesmen opposed most of these restrictions with a new individualistic philosophy that advocated greater freedom for the capitalist to seek profits in a market free of encumbrances and restrictions. It is not surprising that the triumph of this philosophy should coincide with the greatest achievement of the capitalist class: the Industrial Revolution. The Industrial Revolution vaulted the capitalist class into a position of economic and political dominance, and this fact goes far in explaining the triumph of classical liberalism as the ideology of the new age of industrial capitalism.

SUMMARY

The pressure of rapidly increasing demand and the prospect of larger profits led to a "veritable outburst of inventive activity" in the late eighteenth and early nineteenth centuries. This period of widespread innovation—the Industrial Revolution—transformed England (and later western Europe and North America) into urban societies dominated by great manufacturing cities in which large numbers of workers were subjected to the dehumanizing discipline of factory production.

During this period the classical liberal ideology of capitalism came to dominate social and economic thinking. The new ideology pictured individuals as egoistic, coldly calculating, lazy, and generally independent of the society of which they were a part. Adam Smith's analysis of the market as an "invisible hand" that channeled egoistic drives into the most socially useful activities supported a doctrine of laissez faire. The only functions this philosophy assigned to the government were those that would support and encourage profit-making activities.

Finally, the Malthusian theory of population taught that social action designed to mitigate the suffering of the poor was not only useless but even had socially deleterious effects. Acceptance of this view necessitated complete abandonment of the Christian paternalist ethic.

socialist protest amid the industrial revolution

The Industrial Revolution brought about increases in human productivity without precedent in history. The widespread construction of factories and extensive use of machinery represented the mechanical basis of this increase. In order to channel the economy's productive capacity into the creation of capital goods, however, it was necessary to devote a relatively much smaller part of this capacity to the manufacture of consumer goods. Capital goods had to be purchased at a social cost of mass deprivation.

THE SOCIAL COSTS
OF THE INDUSTRIAL REVOLUTION

Historically, in all cases in which society has had to force a bare subsistence existence on some of its members it has always been those with the least economic and political power who have made the sacrifices. And so it was in the Industrial Revolution in England. The working class lived near the subsistence level in 1750, and their standard of living (measured in terms of the purchasing power of wages) deteriorated during the second half of the eighteenth century. The trend of working class living standards in the first several decades of the nineteenth century is a subject of dispute among historians. The fact that many eminent scholars find sufficient evidence to argue that the living standard failed to increase, or even decreased, leads to the conclusion that any increase during this period was slight at best.

Throughout the period of the Industrial Revolution, there is no doubt that the standard of living of the poor fell precipitously in relative terms. A detailed analysis shows that "relatively the poor grew poorer, simply because the country, and its rich and middle class, so obviously grew wealthier. The very moment when the poor were at the end of their tether . . . was the moment when the middle class dripped with excess capital, to be wildly invested in railways and spent on the bulging opulent household furnishings displayed at the Great Exhibition of 1851, and on palatial municipal constructions . . . in the smoky northern cities."[1] There can be no doubt about which class paid the social costs in terms of the sacrificed consumption that was necessary for industrialization.

Yet the costs in terms of decreased consumption were by no means the only, and perhaps not even the worst, hardships forced upon the laboring class by the Industrial Revolution. The new factory system completely destroyed the laborers' traditional way of life, throwing them into a nightmare world with which they were completely unprepared to cope. They lost the pride of workmanship and close personal relationships that had existed in handicraft industries. Under the new system their only relationship with their employer was through the impersonal market, or *cash nexus*. They lost direct access to the means of production and were reduced to mere sellers of labor power totally dependent on market conditions for their livelihood.

Perhaps worse than any of these was the monotonous, mechanical regularity imposed on the worker by the factory system. In pre-industrial Europe the worker's tasks were not so specialized. He went from one task to another, and his work was interrupted by variations in the seasons or the weather. When he felt like resting or playing or changing the pace of his work routine, he had a certain amount of freedom to do so. Factory employment brought the tyranny of the clock. Production was mechanized. Absolute regularity was necessary to coordinate the complex interaction of processes and to maximize the use of new, expensive machinery. The pace of work was no longer decided by the man but by the machine.

The machine, which had formerly been an appendage to the man, was now the focal point of the productive process. Man became a mere appendange to the cold, implacable, pace-setting machine. During the late eighteenth and early nineteenth centuries, a spontaneous revolt against the new factory system saw bands of workers smash-

---

[1] E. J. Hobsbawm, *Industry and Empire: An Economic History of Britain Since 1750* (London: Weidenfeld & Nicolson, 1968), p. 72. Several of Hobsbawm's ideas appear in this chapter.

ing and destroying machines and factories, which they believed were responsible for their plight. These revolts, called the Luddite revolts, ended in 1813 when large numbers of workers were hanged or deported for their activities.

The extensive division of labor in the factory made much of the work so routine and simple that untrained women and children could do it as well as men. Because women and children could be hired for much lower wages than men, and because in many cases entire families had to work in order to earn enough to eat, women and children were employed widely. Many factory owners preferred women and children because they could be reduced to a state of passive obedience more easily than men. The widespread ideology in this period that the only good woman is a submissive woman was a great help to their employers.

Children were bound to factories by indentures of apprenticeship for 7 years, or until they were 21. In these cases almost nothing was given the children in return for long hours of work under the most horrendous conditions. Poor-law authorities could indenture the children of paupers. This led to "regular bargains . . . [where] children . . . were dealt with as mere merchandise . . . between the spinners on the one hand and the Poor Law authorities on the other. Lots of fifty, eighty or a hundred children were supplied and sent like cattle to the factory, where they remained imprisoned for many years."[2]

These children endured the cruelest servitude. They were totally isolated from anyone who might take pity on them and were thus at the mercy of the capitalists or their hired managers, whose main concern was the challenge of competitive factories. The children's workday was from 14 to 18 hours, or until they dropped from complete exhaustion. The foremen were paid according to how much the children produced and therefore pushed them mercilessly. In most factories the children had hardly more than 20 minutes a day for their main (and often only) meal. "Accidents were very common, especially towards the end of the overlong day, when the exhausted children almost fell asleep at their work. The tale never ended of fingers cut off and limbs crushed in the wheels."[3] The children were disciplined in such savage and brutal ways that a recitation of the methods used would appear completely incredible to the reader of today.

Women were mistreated almost as badly. Work in a factory was long, arduous, and monotonous. Discipline was harsh. Many times

[2]Paul Mantoux, *The Industrial Revolution in the Eighteenth Century* (New York: Harcourt Brace Jovanovich, 1927), pp. 410–411.
[3]Ibid., p. 413.

the price of factory employment was submission to the sexual advances of employers and foremen.[4] Women in the mines toiled 14 to 16 hours a day, stripped naked to the waist, working with men and doing the work of men. There were reports of women who came out of the mines to bear children and were back in the mines within days after the birth. Many accounts have been written of the fantastically cruel and dehumanizing working conditions for women during this period. And of course the workingmen were not much better off than the women or the children. Industrialization was stern, harsh, and cruel in the extreme for men as well as for women and children.

Another important consideration in assessing the living standard of the working class during the period of capitalist industrialization was the rapid urbanization that took place at that time. In 1750, only 2 cities in Britain had populations over 50,000. In 1850, there were 29. By the latter date nearly one person in three lived in a city with over 50,000 inhabitants.

Conditions in the cities of this period were terrible:

And what cities! It was not merely that smoke hung over them and filth impregnated them, that the elementary public services— water-supply, sanitation, street-cleaning, open spaces, etc.—could not keep pace with the mass migration of men into the cities, thus producing, especially after 1830, epidemics of cholera, typhoid and an appalling constant toll of the two great groups of nineteenth-century urban killers—air pollution and water pollution, or respiratory and intestinal disease. . . . The new city populations . . . [were] pressed into overcrowded and bleak slums, whose very sight froze the heart of the observer. "Civilization works its miracles" wrote the great French liberal de Tocqueville of Manchester, "and civilized man is turned back almost into a savage."[5]

Included in these slums was a district of Glasgow that, according to a report of a government commissioner, housed

a fluctuating population of between 15,000 and 30,000 persons. This district is composed of many narrow streets and square courts and in the middle of each court there is a dunghill. Although the outward appearance of these places was revolting, I was nevertheless quite unprepared for the filth and misery that were to be found inside. In some bedrooms we visited at night, we found a whole mass of humanity stretched on the floor. There

[4]Ibid., p. 416.
[5]Hobsbawm, op. cit., pp. 67–68.

were often 15 to 20 men and women huddled together, some
being clothed and others naked. There was hardly any furniture
there and the only thing which gave these holes the appearance of
a dwelling was fire burning on the hearth. Thieving and prostitu-
tion are the main sources of income of these people.[6]

The total destruction of the laborers' traditional way of life and
the harsh discipline of the new factory system, combined with deplorable living conditions in the cities, generated social, economic,
and political unrest. Chain reactions of social upheaval, riots, and
rebellion occurred in the years 1811–1813, 1815–1817, 1819, 1826,
1829–1835, 1838–1842, 1843–1844, and 1846–1848. In many areas
these were purely spontaneous and primarily economic in character.
In 1816, one rioter from the Fens exclaimed: "Here I am between
Earth and Sky, so help me God. I would sooner lose my life than go
home as I am. Bread I want and bread I will have."[7] In 1845, an
American named Colman reported that the working people of Manchester were "wretched, defrauded, oppressed, crushed human nature lying in bleeding fragments all over the face of society."[8]

There can be no doubt that industrial capitalism was erected on
the base of the wretched suffering of a laboring class denied access
to the fruits of the rapidly expanding economy and subjected to the
most degrading of excesses to increase the capitalists' profits. The
basic cause of the great evils of this period was "the absolute and
uncontrolled power of the capitalist. In this, the heroic age of great
undertakings, it was acknowledged, admitted and even proclaimed
with brutal candor. It was the employer's own business, he did as he
chose and did not consider that any other justification of his conduct
was necessary. He owed his employees wages and once those were
paid the men had no further claim on him."[9]

LIBERAL SOCIAL LEGISLATION

From the earliest introduction of factory production in the textile
industries, workmen tried to band together to protect their interests
collectively. In 1787, during a period of high unemployment, the
Glasgow muslin manufacturers attempted to lower the piece rates
they were paying. The workers resisted collectively, refused to work
below a certain minimum rate, and organized a boycott of the manufacturers who would not pay the minimum rate. The struggle led

---

[6]Quoted in F. Engels, *The Condition of the Working Class in England in
1844* (New York: Macmillan, 1958), p. 46.
[7]Quoted in Hobsbawm, op. cit., p. 74.
[8]Ibid., p. 75.
[9]Mantoux, op. cit., p. 417.

to open rioting and shooting, but the workingmen proved to have a strong and well-disciplined group, and they built a strong union. In 1792, a union of weavers forced a collective agreement upon Bolton and Bury Manufacturers.

Labor organizations spread rapidly in the 1790s. As a result of this and the concurrent growth of social and economic discontent, the upper classes became very uneasy. The memory of the French Revolution was fresh in their minds, and they feared the power of united workingmen. The result was the Combination Act of 1799, which outlawed any combination of workers whose purpose was to obtain higher wages, shorter hours, or the introduction of any regulation constraining the free action of their employers. Proponents couched their arguments in terms of the necessity of free competition and the evils of monopoly—cardinal tenets of classical liberalism—but did not mention combinations of employers or monopolistic practices of capitalists. The effects of this legislation have been summarized as follows:

The Combination Laws were considered as absolutely necessary to prevent ruinous extortions of workmen, which, if not thus restrained, would destroy the whole of the trade, manufactures, commerce and agriculture of the nation. . . . So thoroughly was this false notion entertained, that whenever men were prosecuted to conviction for having combined to regulate their wages or the hours of working, however heavy the sentence passed upon them was, and however rigorously it was inflicted, not the slightest feeling of compassion was manifested by anybody for the unfortunate sufferers. Justice was entirely out of the question: They could seldom obtain a hearing before a magistrate, never without impatience or insult . . . could an accurate account be given of proceedings, of hearings before magistrates, trials at sessions and in the Court of King's Bench, the gross injustice, the foul invective, and terrible punishments inflicted would not, after a few years have passed away, be credited to any but the best evidence.[10]

Another cause for which the classical liberals campaigned vigorously was the abolition of the Speenhamland system of poor relief that had come into existence in 1795. This system was (continuing in the tradition of the Elizabethan Statute of Artificers) the result of the Christian paternalist ethic. It held that unfortunates would be entitled to a certain minimum living standard whether employed or not. To be sure, the system had serious drawbacks: It actually depressed wages below the relief level in many cases (with the parish

[10]Quoted in ibid., p. 449.

taxes making up the difference) and severely limited labor mobility at a time when greater mobility was needed.

The important issue, however, is not the deficiencies of the Speenhamland system but rather the type of legislation the liberals enacted in its place when they succeeded in abolishing it in 1834. The view of the classical liberals was that workers should accept any job the market offered, regardless of the conditions or pay involved. Any person who would not or could not do so should be given just enough to prevent physical starvation. His dole should be substantially lower than the lowest wage offered in the market, and his general situation should stigmatize him sufficiently to motivate him to seek gainful employment. Thus the new law

> was an engine of degradation and oppression more than a means of material relief. There have been few more inhuman statutes than the Poor Law Act of 1834, which made all relief "less eligible" than the lowest wage outside, confined it to the jail-like workhouse, forcibly separated husbands, wives and children in order to punish the poor for their destitution, and discourage them from the dangerous temptation of procreating further paupers.[11]

THE PATERNALISM OF THE TORY RADICALS

It might seem from this discussion that the Christian paternalist ethic was completely eclipsed during the Industrial Revolution. This was not so. Among the landed or aristocratic wealthy, there were many Tory radicals, men who often had a "gentleman's disdain" for the "vulgar, money-grubbing" middle-class merchants and manufacturers. They asserted that it was the obligation of the "higher classes" to think for and protect the poor. Some of the most vivid descriptions and outspoken denunciations of the excesses of the factory managers came from the pens of Tory radicals.

The ideas of the traditionalist Tories were summarized by John Stuart Mill (who was critical of the point of view he was summarizing). According to Mill, the traditionalists believed that

> the lot of the poor, in all things which affect them collectively, should be regulated *for* them, not *by* them. They should not be required or encouraged to think for themselves, or give to their own reflection or forecast an influential voice in the determination of their destiny. It is supposed to be the duty of the higher classes to think for them, and to take the responsibility of their lot, as

[11]Hobsbawm, op. cit., pp. 69–70.

the commander and officers of an army take that of the soldiers composing it. This function, it is contended, the higher classes should prepare themselves to perform conscientiously, and their whole demeanour should impress the poor with a reliance on it, in order that, while yielding passive and active obedience to the rules prescribed for them, they may resign themselves in all other respects to a trustful *insouciance*, and repose under the shadow of their protectors. The relationship between the rich and poor, according to this theory, should be only partly authoritative; it should be amiable, moral and sentimental: affectionate tutelage on the one side, respectful and grateful deference on the other.[12]

Most of these traditionalists believed that the greedy profit seeking of the vulgar, unrefined, acquisitive middle classes was responsible for the social ills of the Industrial Revolution. Capitalism would function properly, in their opinion, only when capitalists functioned as gentlemen rather than moneygrubbers. These ideas were put into practice in several industrial enterprises owned either by the aristocracy or by humane middle-class capitalists with traditionalist views. Perhaps the most famous of the latter was Robert Owen.

Born in 1771, Owen served as a draper's apprentice from the age of 10. At 20 he was the manager of a large mill. Wise business decisions and good luck soon resulted in the acquisition of a considerable fortune. Owen was a perfect example of a benevolent autocrat. His factory at New Lanark became known throughout all England because he insisted on decent working conditions, livable wages, and education for working-class children. His workers received "affectionate tutelage" from him, and he thought of himself as their trustee and steward.

This paternalistic attitude did not interfere with Owen's very strict organizational discipline in his factory. Owen has described one of his methods of maintaining discipline:

that which I found to be the most efficient check upon inferior conduct was the contrivance of a silent monitor for each one employed in the establishment. This consisted of a four-sided piece of wood, about two inches long and one broad, each side colored—one side black, another blue, the third yellow, and the fourth white, tapered at the top, and finished with wire eyes, to hang upon a hook with either side to the front. One of these was suspended in a conspicuous place near to each of the persons employed, and the color at the front told the conduct of the indi-

[12]John Stuart Mill, *Principles of Political Economy* (Clifton, N.J.: Augustus M. Kelley, 1965 [first published in 1848]), p. 753.

vidual during the preceding day, to four degrees of comparison. Bad, denoted by black and No. 4; indifferent by blue, and No. 3; good by yellow, and No. 2; and excellent by white, and No. 1. Then books of character were provided, for each department, in which the name of each one employed in it was inserted in the front of succeeding columns, which sufficed to mark by the number the daily conduct, day by day, for two months; and these books were changed six times a year, and were preserved; by which arrangement I had the conduct of each registered to four degrees of comparison during every day of the week, Sundays excepted, for every year they remained in my employment.[13]

So in his life and deeds, Owen, like other capitalists of his era, strove to maximize his profits. He believed his competitors' harsh treatment of their workers was stupid and shortsighted, and he based his life on the assumption that the Christian paternalist ethic was compatible with the capitalist system, at least at the factory level. In his own words, "My time, from early to late, and my mind, were continually occupied in devising measures and directing their execution, to improve the condition of the people, and to advance at the same time the works and the machinery as a manufacturing establishment."[14]

THE SOCIALIST VERSION
OF THE CHRISTIAN PATERNALIST ETHIC

Although Owen's life and actions did not differentiate him from many of the conservative Tory radicals of his time, some of his ideas did. He did not believe that any society in which one class was elevated to a position of power and used this power to exploit the lower classes could ultimately become a truly good society. Private ownership of the means of production (factories, machinery, tools) was the social institution by which one small class in the existing economic system gained immense power over the mass of farmers and workers. The profit motive was the force that drove this small class to use its power to exploit the workers and farmers in order to gain profits.

Owen believed that in an ideal society the people could most effectively control nature because they would reap the greatest collective benefit if they cooperated. This cooperation should take the form of self-governing industrial and agricultural communities. In such communities private ownership of the means of production would be abolished and the selfish quest for profits eliminated. He

---

[13]M. Beer, ed., *Life of Robert Owen* (New York: Knopf, 1920), p. 111.
[14]Ibid., p. 112.

maintained that only when such a society was established would it be true that

> One portion of mankind will not, as now, be trained and placed to oppress, by force or fraud, another portion, to the great disadvantage of both; neither will one portion be trained in idleness, to live in luxury on the industry of those whom they oppress, while the latter are made to labor daily and to live in poverty. Nor yet will some be trained to force falsehood into the human mind and be paid extravagantly for so doing while other parties are prevented from teaching the truth, or severely punished if they make the attempt.[15]

There was something in these writings that differed very radically from his description of the way in which he ran his own factory at New Lanark. The ideal society, for Owen, would be one in which the paternalism of the traditional Christian ethic would be expressed as a brotherhood of equals, a considerable shift from the parent–child type of subordination expressed in the medieval and Tory radical versions of the Christian paternalist ethic.

The feudal version of that ethic had accepted a hierarchical society. In this version, those at the top lived lavishly (by the standards of the day, at least), and they did so by exploiting those at the bottom. Chaucer's parson's description of the medieval view is apt: "God has ordained that some folk should be more high in estate and degree and some folk more low, and that everyone should be served in his estate and his degree."[16] This traditional feudal ethic seemed to most capitalists to be incompatible with the capitalist order, and it was gradually replaced by the new individualist philosophy of classical liberalism.

Classical liberalism, however, was a two-edged sword. It became an ideology justifying the new capitalist order (see Chapter 4). But the individualistic assumptions of classical liberalism were very radical. If the old feudal aristocracy had no inherent superiority over the middle class and if any member of the middle class was to be freed of the old restraints, and if each individual should be the best judge in deciding his own affairs, then how could one stop short of asserting the same rights and advantages for the lowest classes? The ideal that each individual ought, in some abstract way, to be considered as important as any other individual was radical indeed.

[15]Robert Owen, "The Book of the New Moral World," reprinted in part in Carl Cohen, ed., *Communism, Fascism and Democracy* (New York: Random House, 1962), pp. 47–48.

[16]Quoted in J. L. and Barbara Hammond, *The Rise of Modern Industry* (New York: Harper & Row, Torchbooks, 1969), p. 215.

If individualism seemed to imply equality in theory, however, it certainly did not lead to it in practice. The rugged battles for more profits led not only to the social misery described earlier but also to a new class division of society that was as sharply defined and as exploitative in nature as the medieval class structure. Membership in the higher class of the new system depended not on genealogy but on ownership. Capitalists derived their income and their power from ownership of the means of production.

Socialism, then, was a protest against the inequalities of capitalism and the social evils resulting from these inequalities. The inequalities themselves, in the opinion of socialists from the earliest times to the present, resulted inevitably from the institution of private property in the means of production. Hence socialism asserted as its most cardinal tenet that social justice demanded the abolition of private ownership of capital.

Intellectually, socialism was a wedding of the liberal notion of the equality of all men to the notion inherent in the traditional Christian paternalist ethic that every man should be his brother's keeper. Incorporating the egalitarian elements of classical liberalism into the traditional Christian ethic made this a utopian ethic, and in comparison with it existing society was criticized. Without this egalitarian element the Christian ethic served well as an ideological justification of the hierarchical class system of the Middle Ages and was sometimes used to defend the capitalist system, particularly in the late nineteenth and twentieth centuries (of which more will be said later).

IMPORTANT PRE-MARXIST SOCIALISTS

When Owen asserted that in the ideal society private property and acquisitive profit seeking would be eliminated, he became part of a socialist tradition that was already firmly established by his time. One of the first voices of socialist protest against capitalist property relations was that of Gerrard Winstanley (1609–1652), a cloth merchant who had been bankrupted in the depression of 1643. He blamed his own misfortune as well as that of others on the "cheating art of buying and selling."[17] In 1649 he led a strange band of followers from London to Saint George's Hill, Surrey. There they occupied unused crown lands, which they cultivated in common and, in general, shared in a communal existence.

In the same year Winstanley published *The True Levellers Standard Advanced*, in which he rebuked "the powers of England" and "the powers of the world" for their failure to realize that "the great

[17]Quoted in Lee Cameron McDonald, *Western Political Theory: The Modern Age* (New York: Harcourt Brace Jovanovich, 1962), p. 63.

creator . . . made the Earth a common treasury for beasts and man."[18] He asserted that all who derived their incomes in part or in full from property ownership were violating God's commandment "Thou shalt not steal." "You pharaohs, you have rich clothing and full bellies, you have your honors and your ease; but know the day of judgment is begun and that it will reach you ere long. The poor people you oppress shall be the saviours of the land."[19]

Throughout the eighteenth and nineteenth centuries, a large number of writers argued that private property was the source of the inequities and exploitation that existed in the capitalist economy. In this chapter we can mention only a few of the better known among them. One of the most interesting was the Frenchman Gracchus Babeuf (1760–1797). Babeuf argued that nature had made all men equal in rights and needs. Therefore the inequalities of wealth and power that had developed should be redressed by society. Unfortunately, most societies did the opposite: They set up a coercive mechanism to protect the interests of the property holders and the wealthy. For Babeuf the presence of inequality meant, of necessity, the presence of injustice. Capitalist commerce existed, he said, "for the purpose of pumping the sweat and blood of more or less everybody, in order to form lakes of gold for the benefit of the few."[20] The workers who created the wealth of society got the least; and until private property was eliminated, the inequalities in society could never be redressed.

Babeuf led the extreme left wing of the French revolutionary movement. After the fall of Robespierre he masterminded a conspiracy to destroy the French government and replace it with one dedicated to equality and brotherhood. The plot was betrayed by Georges Grisel, and its leaders were arrested. Babeuf and his lieutenant, Darthe, were executed on February 24, 1797.

Babeuf is important in the socialist tradition because he was the first to advance the notion that if an egalitarian socialist state is to be achieved, the existing government must be toppled by force. The issue of whether socialism can be achieved peacefully has divided socialists since Babeuf's time. Babeuf also believed that if his revolt were successful a period of dictatorship during the transition from capitalism to the communist democracy he envisioned would be necessary to extirpate the surviving remnants of the capitalist system. Thus in several important ways Babeuf was a precursor of the twentieth-century Russian Bolsheviks.

[18]Ibid.
[19]Ibid.
[20]Alexander Gray, *The Socialist Tradition* (London: Longmans, 1963), p. 105.

Other important ideas in the socialist critique of capitalism can be seen in the writings of the Englishman William Godwin (1756–1836). While the classical liberals were bemoaning the natural laziness and depravity of the lower classes, Godwin argued that the defects of the working class were attributable to corrupt and unjust social institutions. The capitalist society, in Godwin's opinion, made fraud and robbery inevitable: "If every man could with perfect facility obtain the necessaries of life . . . temptation would lose its power."[21] Men could not always obtain the necessities because the laws of private property created such great inequalities in society. Justice demanded that capitalist property relations be abolished and that property belong to that person whom it would benefit most:

> To whom does any article of property, suppose a loaf of bread, justly belong? To him who most wants it, or to whom the possession of it will be most beneficial. Here are six men famished with hunger, and the loaf is, absolutely considered, capable of satisfying the cravings of them all. Who is it that has a reasonable claim to benefit by the qualities with which the loaf is endowed? They are all brothers perhaps, and the law of primogeniture bestows it exclusively to the eldest. But does justice confirm this award? The laws of different countries dispose of property in a thousand different ways; but there can be but one way which is most conformable to reason.[22]

That one way, of course, must be based on the equality of all men. To whom could the poor turn to correct the injustices of the system? In Godwin's opinion it most certainly would not be the government. With economic power went political power. The rich are "directly or indirectly the legislators of the state; and of consequence are perpetually reducing oppression into a system."[23] The law, then, is the means by which the rich oppress the poor, for "legislation is in almost every country grossly the favorer of the rich against the poor."[24]

These two ideas of Godwin's were to be voiced again and again by nineteenth-century socialists: (1) that capitalist social and economic institutions, particularly private property relations, were the causes of the evils and suffering within the system and (2) that the government in a capitalist system would never redress these evils because it was controlled by the capitalist class. But Godwin had an

---

[21]William Godwin, *An Inquiry Concerning Political Justice*, pp. 33, 34. Quoted in Gray, op. cit., p. 119.
[22]Ibid., p. 131.
[23]Ibid., p. 119.
[24]Ibid.

answer to this seemingly impossible situation. He believed human reason would save society. Once men became educated about the evils of the situation, they would reason together and arrive at the only rational solution. As Godwin saw it, this solution entailed the abolition of government, the abolition of laws, and the abolition of private property. For this radical social transformation Godwin believed socialists could rely primarily on education and reason. Most subsequent socialists argued that education and reason alone were insufficient. Education, they believed, should be only a part of the larger objective of creating a mass socialist movement. The importance of education and intellectual persuasion in attaining socialist ends has remained a much-debated issue to this day.

Other important socialist ideas were advanced by Henri de Saint-Simon (1760–1825), who was actually closer to the Tory radicals than the socialists in many ways. He came from an impoverished family of nobility, and his writings show an aristocrat's disdain for the antisocial egoism of the rich capitalists.

He also condemned the idle rich who lived off the labor of the poor but contributed nothing to society's well-being:

> Suppose that France preserves all the men of genius that she possesses in the sciences, fine arts and professions, but has the misfortune to lose in the same day Monsieur the King's brother [and all of the other members of the royal household]. . . . Suppose that France loses at the same time all the great officers of the royal household, all the ministers . . . all the councillors of state, all the chief magistrates, marshals, cardinals, archbishops, bishops, vicars-general and canons, all the prefects and subprefects, all the civil servants, and judges, and, in addition, ten thousand of the richest proprietors who live in the style of nobles. This mischance would certainly distress the French, because they are kind-hearted, and could not see with indifference the sudden disappearance of such a large number of their compatriots. But this loss of thirty thousand individuals . . . would result in no political evil for the state.[25]

Saint-Simon was the first to emphasize the efficiency of huge industrial undertakings and argued that the government should actively intervene in production, distribution, and commerce in the interest of promoting the welfare of the masses. He sanctioned both private property and its privileges as long as they were used to promote the welfare of the masses.

Many of his followers were more radical. They wrote endless

[25]F. M. H. Markham, ed., *Henri Comte de Saint-Simon, Selected Writings* (Oxford: Blackwell, 1952), pp. 72–73.

pamphlets and books exposing abuses of capitalism, attacking private property and inheritance, denouncing exploitation, and advocating government ownership and control of economic production in the interest of the general welfare. It was from Saint-Simon and his followers that socialism inherited the idea of the necessity of government administration of production and distribution in a socialist economy.

There were many other famous socialists in the first half of the nineteenth century. The Frenchman Charles Fourier popularized the idea of cooperatives (or *phalanxes*, as he called them). He attempted to change society by encouraging the formation of phalanxes. His failure proved to many socialists that capitalism could not be reformed by the mere setting of examples. He was also one of the first socialists to predict that competition among capitalists would lead inevitably to monopoly:

> Among the influences tending to restrict man's industrial rights, I will mention the formation of privileged corporations which, monopolizing a given branch of industry, arbitrarily close the doors of labour against whomsoever they please. . . . Extremes meet, and the greater the extent to which anarchical competition is carried, the nearer the approach to *universal monopoly*, which is the opposite excess. . . . Monopolies, . . . operating in conjunction with the great landed interest, will reduce the middle and labouring classes to a state of commercial vassalage. . . . The small operators will be reduced to the position of mere agents, working for the mercantile coalition. We shall then see the reappearing of feudalism in an inverse order, founded on mercantile leagues, and answering to the Baronial Leagues of the Middle Ages.[26]

Fourier believed that in a capitalist economy only one-third of the people really did socially useful work. The other two-thirds were directed, by the corruption and distortion caused by the market system, into useless occupations or were useless, wealthy parasites. He divided these wastes into four categories:

First Waste: Useless or destructive labour. (1) the army (2) the idle rich (3) ne'er-do-wells (4) sharpers (5) prostitutes (6) magistrates (7) police (8) lawyers (9) philosophical cranks (10) bureaucrats (11) spies (12) priests and clergymen.

---

[26]Quoted in Sydney H. Coontz, *Productive Labor and Effective Demand* (Clifton, N.J.: Augustus M. Kelley, 1966), p. 54.

Second Waste: Misdirected work, since society makes it repellent, and not a vehicle of man's personality, attractive to him.

      (a) Deflection of the passions into greed and morbidity, instead of being utilized as society's motors.

      (b) Scale of production too small to utilize labour properly.

      (c) No co-operation.

      (d) No control of production.

      (e) No adjustment of supply to demand, except by the mechanism of the "blind" market.

      (f) The family: this economic and educational unit is absurdly small.

Third Waste: Commerce dominated by middlemen. It takes a hundred men to do what society, with warehouses, distributed according to need, could do with one. A hundred men sit at counters, wasting hours waiting for someone to enter, a hundred people write inventories, etc., competitively. These hundred wasted merchants eat without producing.

Fourth Waste: Wage labour in indirect servitude; cost of class antagonisms. Since class interests are opposed, the costs of keeping men divided are greater than the gains in making them co-operate.[27]

Most socialists agreed that capitalism was irrational and wasteful and led to extreme inequalities, and hence was unjust and immoral. They disagreed, however, on the tactics they should use to achieve socialism. Many famous socialists, such as Louis Blanc (1811–1882), believed that the government could be used as an instrument of reform and that socialism could be achieved through gradual, peaceful, piecemeal reform. Others, such as Auguste Blanqui (1805–1881), the pupil of Babeuf, based his ideas on the assumption that capitalism involved a constant class war between capitalists and workers. He believed that as long as capitalists occupied the position of power that ownership of capital gave them, they would exploit the workers, and the government and laws would be weapons used in this exploitation. He therefore saw no hope through gradual political reform. Revolution was, for him, the only answer.

Pierre Joseph Proudhon (1809–1865), in his well-known book

[27]Ibid., p. 55.

What Is Property?, answered the question posed in the title with a
slogan that made him famous: "Property is theft." He believed property was "the mother of tyranny." The primary purpose of the state
was the enforcement of property rights. Because property rights
were simply sets of special privileges for the few and general restrictions and prohibitions for the masses, they involved coercion,
of necessity, in their establishment and continued enforcement.
Hence the primary function of the state was to coerce.

"Every state is a tyranny," declared Proudhon. The state was the
coercive arm of the ruling class, and Proudhon advocated resistance
rather than servitude: "Whoever lays a hand on me to govern me is
a usurper and a tyrant. I declare him to be my enemy." There could
be no justice until property relations were abolished and the state
was made unnecessary:

> To be governed is to be watched over, inspected, spied on, di-
> rected, legislated, regimented, closed in, indoctrinated, preached
> at, controlled, assessed, evaluated, censored, commanded; all by
> creatures that have neither the right, nor wisdom, nor virtue. . . .
> To be governed means that at every move, operation, or transac-
> tion one is noted, registered, entered in a census, taxed, stamped,
> priced, assessed, patented, licensed, authorized, recommended, ad-
> monished, prevented, reformed, set right, corrected. Government
> means to be subjected to tribute, trained, ransomed, exploited,
> monopolized, extorted, pressured, mystified, robbed; all in the
> name of public utility and the general good. Then, at the first
> sign of resistance or word of complaint, one is repressed, fined,
> despised, vexed, pursued, hustled, beaten up, garroted, imprisoned,
> shot, machine-gunned, judged, sentenced, deported, sacrificed,
> sold, betrayed, and to cap it all ridiculed, mocked, outraged, and
> dishonored. That is government, that is its justice and its morality!
> . . . O human personality! How can it be that you have cowered
> in such subjection for sixty centuries?"[28]

Property rights were not only the source of tyranny and coercion,
they were also the source of economic inequality. Whereas the
amount of labor expended determined how much was produced in
a capitalist society, ownership of property determined how that produce was divided. It was divided in such a way that those who
produced got almost nothing of what they produced, whereas those
who owned property used the laws of private ownership to "legally

[28]Quoted in Daniel Guerin, *Anarchism* (New York: Monthly Review
Press, 1970), pp. 15–16; the quotations in the preceding paragraph are from the
same source.

steal" from the workers. Proudhon's ideal state rejected not only capitalist property relations but industrialization as well. Like Thomas Jefferson, Proudhon envisioned a golden age of small-scale agriculture and handicraft production, in which each farmer and worker owned his own capital and no one lived through property ownership alone.

The list could be continued, but we have included most of the important pre-Marxist socialist ideas and have introduced some of the most famous socialist thinkers. Unquestionably the most influential socialist thinker was Karl Marx, and it is to a summary of his ideas that we turn in Chapter 6.

SUMMARY

The workers bore the social costs of industrialization. The new factory system reduced most of them to poor, unhealthy, dehumanized wretches. Classical liberalism was not only impervious to their plight, it even taught that the desire to improve the conditions of the poor was quixotic and doomed to failure. Two groups of thinkers, the Tory radicals and the socialists, took strong exception to this view.

The Tory radicals had a gentleman's disdain for the "vulgar, money-grubbing" middle-class merchants and manufacturers. They clung to an essentially reactionary version of the Christian paternalist ethic—reactionary because it seemed to assume that they could ignore industrialism and go back to an earlier agrarian way of life.

The socialists protested the inequalities of capitalism. They believed that by eliminating private ownership of capital they could create an industrial society in which every man and woman was treated with dignity and in which the fruits of production were equitably divided.

socialist protest: the economics of marx

Karl Marx (1818–1883) has been the most influential of all socialists. His writings have had, and continue to have, a profound impact not only on socialist thought but also on policy decisions that affect a large percentage of the world's population. Although he worked in close collaboration with Friedrich Engels (1820–1895) and was unquestionably deeply influenced by Engels, Marx was the intellectual leader in most matters of political economy, so no attempt is made in this chapter to distinguish Engels' separate contributions.

HISTORICAL MATERIALISM

Marx believed that most of the late eighteenth- and early nineteenth-century socialists were humanitarians who were rightly indignant about the harsh exploitation that accompanied early capitalism. Despite his admiration for many of them, he gave to them the derisive label "utopian socialists." He believed most of them to be quixotic utopians who hoped to transform society by appealing to the rationality and moral sensibilities of the educated class. In Marx's view, educated men were usually members of the upper classes, and thus they owed their position, prosperity, and superior knowledge and education to the privileges inherent in the capitalist system. Therefore they would generally do everything within their power to preserve that system. The few heretics and humanitarians among them would certainly never constitute the power base from which a transition from capitalism to socialism could be effected. Yet Marx had an undying faith that such a social and economic transition would occur. This faith was not the result of his belief in the rationality and humanity of men but rather was based on an analysis of capitalism. He concluded that internal contradictions and antagonisms within the capitalist system would eventually destroy it.

Marx based his study of capitalist society on a historical approach that has been called *historical materialism*. When he looked at the mass of ideas, laws, religious beliefs, mores, moral codes, and economic and social institutions that were present in all social systems, he tried to simplify the complex cause-and-effect relationships among these many facets of social systems. Such a simplification, he believed, would enable him to focus his attention on the relationships that were most fundamental in determining a social system's overall direction of movement and change.

Although all social institutions and intellectual traditions were reciprocally related in a complex web of cause-and-effect relationships (each affecting and, in turn, affected by the other), he believed that a society's economic base, or mode of production, exerted the most powerful influence in determining the other social institutions as well as social and religious thought. The *mode of production* consisted of two elements: (1) the forces of production and (2) the relations of production. The *forces of production* included tools, factories, equipment, production skills and knowledge of the labor force, natural resources, and the general level of technology. The *relations of production* were the social relationships between men, particularly the relationship of each class of men to the means of production, which included the ownership of productive facilities and the division of the fruits of productive activity. The whole economic system, or mode of production, Marx called the *base*, or *substructure*. The religions, ethics, laws, mores, and institutions of society he called the *superstructure*.

Although the mode of production and the superstructure interacted reciprocally as both cause and effect, the mode of production was the base on which the superstructure was built. Therefore the line of causation running from this economic base to the superstructure was much more powerful and important than the reverse line of causation. To argue that Marx believed the economic base determined, completely and rigidly, every aspect of the superstructure is grossly inaccurate (although it is often done). He did assert, however, that the mode of production was the most important single aspect in determining not only the present social superstructure but also the direction of social change.

When he referred to the relations of production, Marx meant the class structure of society, the most important single aspect of the mode of production. The antagonisms between social classes were, for Marx, the propelling force in history. "The history of all hitherto existing society is the history of class struggles,"[1] he proclaimed. The importance of the mode of production and the class antagonisms it engendered have been summarized by Marx in a famous passage:

> In the social production which men carry on they enter into defi-nite relations that are indispensable and independent of their will; these relations of production correspond to a definite stage of de-velopment of their material powers of production. The sum total of these relations of production constitutes the economic structure of society—the real foundation, on which rise legal and political superstructures and to which correspond definite forms of social consciousness. The mode of production in material life determines the general character of the social, political, and spiritual pro-cesses of life. It is not the consciousness of men that determines their existence, but, on the contrary, their social existence deter-mines their consciousness. At a certain stage of their development, the material forces of production in society come into conflict with the existing relations of production, or—what is but a legal expression for the same thing—with the property relations within which they had been at work before. From forms of development of the forces of production these relations turn into their fetters. Then comes the period of social revolution. With the change of economic foundation the entire immense superstructure is more or less rapidly transformed. In considering such transformations the distinction should always be made between the material trans-formation of the economic conditions of production which can be determined with the precision of natural science, and the legal, political, religious, aesthetic, or philosophic—in short ideological forms in which men become conscious of this conflict and fight it out.[2]

Marx identified four separate economic systems, or modes of pro-duction, through which the European civilization had evolved: (1) primitive communal, (2) slave, (3) feudal, and (4) capitalist. In any one of these economic systems, there was a unique mode of produc-tion that included forces of production as well as a particular class structure, or relations of production. Increasing demands for more

[1]Karl Marx and Friedrich Engels, "The Communist Manifesto," in Arthur P. Mendel, ed., *Essential Works of Marxism* (New York: Bantam, 1965), p. 13.
[2]Karl Marx, *Critique of Political Economy*, reprinted in part in Howard Selsam and Harry Martel, eds., *Reader in Marxist Philosophy* (New York: International Publishers, 1963), pp. 186–187.

production inevitably led to changes in the forces of production, yet the relationships of production, or class positions, remained fixed and were fiercely defended. Therefore there were conflicts, tensions, and contradictions between the changing forces of production and the fixed social relations (and vested interests) of production. These conflicts and contradictions grew in intensity and importance until a series of violent social eruptions destroyed the old system and created a new system that would have new class relationships compatible (for a time at least) with the changed forces of production.

In each mode of production the contradictions that developed between the forces of production and the relations of production showed themselves in the form of a class struggle. The struggle raged between the class that controlled the means of production and received most of the benefits and privileges of the system (e.g., the Roman slaveholders) and the much larger class they controlled and exploited (e.g., the Roman slaves). In all economic systems prior to capitalism, this class struggle had destroyed one system only to create a new system based on exploitation of the masses by a new ruling class, and hence the beginning of a new class struggle. Capitalism, however, was, in Marx's opinion, the last mode of production that would be based on the existence of antagonistic classes. The capitalist class, which ruled by virtue of ownership of the means of production, would be overthrown by the proletariat, or working class, which would establish a classless society in which the means of production were owned in common by all. The transition from capitalism to socialism will be discussed in greater detail later. Before proceeding further, however, it is necessary to examine the basis of Marx's moral condemnation of capitalism.

MARX'S MORAL CRITIQUE OF CAPITALISM

According to Marx, two most important features define capitalism and distinguish it from other economic systems: (1) The separation of the worker from the means of production created a class of owners and a class of workers; (2) the market, or cash nexus, was extended into all human relationships involved in production and distribution. Like most socialists before him, Marx deplored the extremes of wealth and poverty this class relationship created.

His moral condemnation of capitalism, however, went beyond an ethical rejection of these great inequalities. His most important criticism of capitalism involved the idea that in a capitalist system people could not develop their potentialities. They could not become emotionally or intellectually fully developed human beings.

Man differed from animals because in order to satisfy his needs he created tools and worked with them to shape and control his environment. Man's senses and intellect were developed and refined through working. Through his relations with what he produced, man achieved both pleasure and self-realization. In precapitalist social systems like feudalism, man could achieve this self-realization through work despite an exploitative class structure. Because the exploitative social relations were also personal and paternalistic, work was not merely a means of making money.

This changed with capitalism, when, in Marx's opinion:

> the bourgeoisie, wherever it has got the upper hand, has put an end to all feudal patriarchal, idyllic relations. It has pitilessly torn asunder the motley feudal ties that bound man to his "natural superiors," and has left remaining no other nexus between man and man than naked self-interest, than callous "cash payment." It has drowned the most heavenly ecstasies of religious fervor, of chivalrous enthusiasm, of philistine sentimentalism, in the icy water of egotistical calculation. It has resolved personal worth into exchange value. . . .[3]

In a capitalist society the market separated and isolated "exchange value," or money price, from the qualities that shaped man's relations with things as well as with other human beings. This was especially true in the work process. To the capitalist, wages were merely another expense of production to be added to the costs of raw materials and machinery in the profit calculation. Labor became a mere commodity to be bought if a profit could be made on the purchase. Whether the laborer could sell his labor power was completely beyond his control. It depended on the cold and totally impersonal conditions of the market. The product of this labor was likewise totally outside of the laborer's life, being the property of the capitalist.

Marx used the term *alienation* to describe the condition of men in this situation. They felt alienated or divorced from their work, from their institutional and cultural environment, and from their fellow men. The conditions of work, the object produced, and indeed the very possibility of working were determined by the numerically small class of capitalists and their profit calculations, not by human need or aspirations. The effects of this alienation can best be summarized in Marx's own words:

> What, then, constitutes the alienation of labour? First, the fact that labour is external to the worker, i.e., it does not belong to his essential being; that in his work, therefore, he does not affirm

[3]Marx and Engels, "The Communist Manifesto," op. cit., p. 15.

himself but denies himself, does not feel content but unhappy, does not develop freely his physical and mental energy but mortifies his body and ruins his mind. The worker therefore only feels himself outside his work, and in his work feels outside himself. He is at home when he is not working, and when he is working he is not at home. His labour is therefore not voluntary but coerced; it is *forced labour*. It is therefore not the satisfaction of a need; it is merely a *means* to satisfy needs external to it. Its alien character emerges clearly in the fact that as soon as no physical or other compulsion exists, labour is shunned like the plague. External labour, labour in which man alienates himself, is a labour of self-sacrifice, or mortification. Lastly, the external character of labour for the worker appears in the fact that it is not his own, but someone else's, that it does not belong to him, that in it he belongs, not to himself, but to another. . . . As a result, therefore, man (the worker) no longer feels himself to be freely active in any but his animal functions—eating, drinking, procreating, or at most in his dwelling and in dressing up, etc.; and in his human functions he no longer feels himself to be anything but an animal. What is animal becomes human and what is human becomes animal.[4]

It was this degradation and total dehumanization of the working class, thwarting man's personal development and making an alien market commodity of man's life-sustaining activities, that Marx most thoroughly condemned in the capitalist system. Thus his moral critique went far beyond those of most of his socialist precursors. His faith in the possibility of a better future for the working class, however, was not based on the hope that ever-increasing numbers of people would share his moral indignation and therefore attempt to reform the system. Rather, he believed the capitalist mode of production and the class conflict inherent in it would lead to the destruction of capitalism. Capitalism, like all previous modes of production in which class conflicts were present, would destroy itself. In order to understand the basis for this faith, it is necessary to examine his economic theory, in which he attempted to analyze the "laws of motion" of capitalism.

THE LABOR THEORY OF VALUE AND SURPLUS VALUE

Because for Marx the capitalist mode of production was based on the opposition of labor and capital, he began by analyzing the capital-

---

[4]Karl Marx, *Economic and Philosophic Manuscripts of 1844* (Moscow: Progress Publishers, 1959), p. 69.

labor relationship. This relationship was essentially one of exchange. The worker sold his labor power to the capitalist for money, with which the worker bought the necessities of life. Thus this exchange relation was obviously merely a special case of the general problem of exchange values within a capitalist market economy. Marx therefore began volume 1 of *Capital* with a section entitled "Commodities," in which he defined *commodities* as objects that are usually intended for exchange rather than for the direct personal use of the producer. He then attempted to analyze the basic determinant of the exchange value of commodities. In other words, he analyzed the ratio in which commodities could be exchanged for other commodities, as opposed to use value, which was a measure of the usefulness of commodities to their possessor.

Like Adam Smith, David Ricardo, and most of the pre-Marxist classical economists, Marx believed the exchange value of a commodity was determined by the amount of labor time necessary for its production. His theory is therefore usually called the *labor theory of value*. He recognized that laborers differed in abilities, training, and motivation, but he believed skilled labor could be calculated as a multiple of unskilled labor. Thus all labor time could be reduced to a common denominator.

He also realized that labor time expended in the production of a useless commodity (one for which there was no demand) would not create a commodity with an exchange value equal to the labor time embodied in it. The desire of capitalists to maximize their profits would, however, prevent the production of objects for which there was no demand. Capitalists would produce only commodities for which market demand would permit the realization of at least their costs of production. Market demand would determine not only what commodities were produced but also the relative quantities in which they were produced.

Marx began by describing how the capitalist buys the means of production and the labor power. Then, when the laborers complete the production process, he sells the commodities for more money. Thus the amount with which he ends up is greater than that with which he started. This difference is what Marx called *surplus value*. He considered it the source of capitalist profits.

Surplus value originated in the fact that capitalists bought one commodity—labor power—and sold a different commodity—that which labor produced in the production process. Profits were made because the value of labor power was less than the value of the commodities produced with the labor power. The value of labor power was "determined, as in the case of every other commodity, by the labor time necessary" for its maintenance and reproduction, which meant that "the value of labor power . . . [was] the value of the means of subsistence necessary for the maintenance of the laborer at a socially defined minimal standard of living."[5] The fact was that the average length of the working day exceeded the time necessary for a laborer to produce the value equivalent of his subsistence wage, which enabled the capitalist to appropriate the surplus produced over and above this subsistence. Marx called this process the *exploitation* of workers by capitalists. If the worker works for 8 hours but uses only 6 hours to produce the value of his wage goods, then he is exploited because he works 2 surplus hours for the capitalist.

THE ACCUMULATION OF CAPITAL

The capitalist gained his profits because of his ownership of capital. Most of these profits were plowed back to increase his capital and hence increase future profits, which could then be plowed back into more capital, and so forth. This was the process of capital accumulation: Capital led to profits, which led to more capital. When and how did the process originate? Many classical economists and liberals, particularly the English economist Nassau Senior (1790–1864), had answered this question in a way favorable to the capitalist, arguing that through hard, diligent work and abstemious behavior the capitalist had begun a modest saving program, which enabled him to accumulate slowly the fortunes many nineteenth-century capitalists owned. Laborers, on the contrary, rather than devoting themselves to working and living abstemiously, had profligately squandered their earnings.

Marx accused these defenders of the capitalist system of being totally ignorant of history. In a famous passage, which gives the flavor of some of his most colorful writing, Marx described the process of "primitive accumulaton" by which the fortunes were originally made:

> This primitive accumulation plays in Political Economy about the same part as original sin in theology. Adam bit the apple, and thereupon sin fell on the human race. Its origin is supposed to be explained when it is told as an anecdote of the past. In times long gone by there were two sorts of people; one, the diligent, intelligent, and above all, frugal elite; the other, lazy rascals, spending their substance, and more, in riotous living. . . . Thus it came to pass that the former sort accumulated wealth, and the latter sort had nothing to sell except their own skins. And from this original

[5]Karl Marx, *Capital*, vol. 1 (Moscow: Foreign Language Publishing House, 1961), pp. 170–171.

sin dates the poverty of the great majority that, despite all its labour, has up to now nothing to sell but itself, and the wealth of the few that increases constantly although they have long ceased to work. Such insipid childishness is every day preached to us in the defence of property. . . . As soon as the question of property crops up, it becomes a sacred duty to proclaim the intellectual food of the infant as the one thing fit for all ages and for all stages of development. In actual history it is notorious that conquest, enslavement, robbery, murder, briefly force, play the great part. . . . The methods of primitive accumulation are anything but idyllic.[6]

Marx listed the important forms of primitive accumulaton as the enclosure movement and the dislocation of the feudal agrarian population, the great price inflation, monopolies of trade, colonies, "the extirpation, enslavement and entombment in mines of the aboriginal population, the beginning of the conquest and looting of the East Indies, [and] the turning of Africa into a warren for the commercial hunting of black skins."[7]

Once this initial accumulation of capital had taken place, the drive to acquire more capital became the moving force of the capitalist system. The capitalist's social standing and prestige as well as his economic and political power depended on the size of the capital he controlled. He could not stand still; he was beset on every side by fierce competition. The system demanded that he accumulate and grow more powerful in order to outdo his competitors, or else his competitors would force him to the wall and take over his capital. Competitors were constantly developing new and better methods of production. Only by accumulating new and better capital equipment could this challenge be met. Thus Marx believed the capitalist

shares with the miser the passion for wealth as wealth. But that which in the miser is a mere idiosyncrasy, is in the capitalist the effect of the social mechanism of which he is but one of the wheels. Moreover, the development of capitalist production makes it constantly necessary to keep increasing the amount of capital laid out in a given industrial undertaking, and competition makes the immanent laws of capitalist production to be felt by each individual capitalist as external coercive laws. It compels him to keep constantly extending his capital, in order to preserve it, but extend it he cannot except by means of progressive accumulation.[8]

[6]Ibid., pp. 713–714.
[7]Ibid., p. 751.
[8]Ibid., p. 592.

SECTORAL IMBALANCES
AND ECONOMIC CRISES

It was this ceaseless drive to accumulate more capital that created many of the contradictions of capitalist development. The capitalist would begin with the acquisition of more machines and tools of the types that were currently being used. This would require a proportional increase in the number of workers employed in order to operate the new equipment. But the capitalists had been able to keep the wage rate at the subsistence level only because there existed what Marx called an "industrial reserve army" of unemployed labor, which was living below the subsistence level and striving to take jobs that would pay a mere subsistence wage. Therefore capitalists usually had no problem in keeping wage rates down. As the industrial expansion took place, however, the increasing demand for labor soon depleted the ranks of the reserve. When this happened, the capitalist began to find that he had to pay higher wages to get enough labor.

The individual capitalist took the wage level as given and beyond his power to change, so he attempted to make the best of the situation. The most profitable course of action seemed to be changing the techniques of production by introducing new labor-saving machinery so that each laborer would then be working with more capital, and output per laborer could be increased. This labor-saving investment would enable the capitalist to expand output with the same or an even smaller work force. When all or most of the capitalists, acting individually, did this, the problem of high wages was temporarily alleviated as the reserve army was replenished by workers displaced by the new productive techniques. The creation of technological unemployment saved the day. But not without introducing new problems and contradictions.

Labor-saving expansion permitted increases in total production without increasing the wages paid to workers. Therefore, while new goods were flooding the market, workers' wages were being restricted, with the result that consumer demand was limited. As Marx put it, the workers were still producing more profits in the form of goods, but the capitalists could not "realize" the profits by selling these goods in the market because of lack of consumer demand.

In order to clarify this process further, Marx divided the capitalist economy into two sectors, one producing consumer goods and the other producing capital goods. Lack of consumer demand meant that capitalists in the consumption goods sector would find that they could not sell their entire output and thus would lower their expectations of profits and would certainly *not* want to add to their productive facilities. They would therefore cancel any plans to add to their already excessively large capital stock. These decisions would, of course, significantly reduce the demand for capital goods, which would result in a decrease in production in the capital goods sector. Unlike the naïve underconsumptionist theories of the earlier socialists, Marx's view held that the first obvious sign of a depression might thus appear in the capital goods sector.

The actual decrease in capital goods production would mean that some workers in that sector would be fired, which would lower total wages, decrease national income, and reduce consumer demand. Thus there would be a cutback in consumer goods production, and layoffs of workers would spread to those industries. Wages and incomes would then be further reduced, causing a glut, or surfeit, of consumer goods. The entire process of successive repercussions in both sectors would then be one of economic collapse.

The resulting depression would more than restore the reserve army of unemployed and push labor's standard of living back to or below the subsistence level. Marx, however, was not a "stagnationist"—that is, he did not believe capitalism would suffer one long depression or that mass unemployment at high levels would last forever. In the depression workers' wages would fall, but not as rapidly as the output of goods. Thus eventually supply would be lower than consumer demand, and therefore recovery would occur. Marx believed that capitalism does grow, but jerkily, in cycles of boom and bust, with periodic high levels of unemployment for the workers.

ECONOMIC CONCENTRATION

Concentration of wealth and economic power in the hands of fewer and fewer capitalists was another important consequence of capital accumulation. This concentration was the result of two forces. First, competition between capitalists tended to create a situation in which the strong either crushed or absorbed the weak. "Here competition rages in direct proportion to the number, and in inverse proportion to the magnitudes, of the antagonistic capitals. It always ends in the ruin of many small capitalists, whose capitals partly pass into the hands of their conquerors, partly vanish."[9]

Second, as technology improved there was "an increase in the minimum amount of . . . capital necessary to carry on a business under its normal conditions." In order to remain competitive, a firm would constantly have to increase the productivity of its laborers. The "productiveness of labor . . . [depended] on the scale of production."[10] Thus changing technology as well as competition among

[9]Ibid., p. 626.
[10]Ibid.

capitalists created an inexorable movement of the capitalist system toward larger and larger firms owned by fewer and fewer capitalists. In this way the gulf between the small class of wealthy capitalists and the great majority of society, the proletariat, continually widened.

THE IMMISERIZATION OF THE PROLETARIAT

At the same time that this increasing concentration of capital was taking place, the misery of the proletariat grew constantly worse. In his famous "doctrine of increasing misery" (immiserization), Marx argued that the conditions of labor would worsen relative to the affluence of the capitalists until the laborers could stand no more. And then revolution was inevitable. Because Marx's doctrine of immiserization is very often misrepresented, we will quote his own writings on this point:

> Within the capitalist system all methods for raising the social productiveness of labour are brought about at the cost of the individual labourer; all means for the development of production transform themselves into means of domination over, and exploitation of, the producers; they mutilate the labourer into a fragment of a man, degrade him to the level of an appendage of a machine, destroy every remnant of charm in his work and turn it into hated toil; they estrange from him the intellectual potentialities of the labour-process in the same proportion as science is incorporated in it as an independent power; they distort the conditions under which he works, subject him during the labour-process to a despotism the more hateful for its meanness; they transform his life time into working time, and drag his wife and child beneath the wheels of the Juggernaut of capital. But all methods for the production of surplus-value are at the same time methods of accumulation; and every extension of accumulation becomes again a means for the development of those methods. It follows therefore that in proportion as capital accumulates, the lot of the labourer, be his payment high or low, must grow worse. The law . . . establishes an accumulation of misery, corresponding with accumulation of capital. Accumulation of wealth at one pole is, therefore, at the same time accumulation of misery, agony of toil, slavery, ignorance, brutality [and] mental degradation at the opposite pole. . . .[11]

It should be noted that Marx asserted that the laborer would become worse off even if his wages increased. There were two

[11]Ibid., p. 645.

reasons for this. First, Marx believed that even if workers' wages increased they would not increase by as much as capitalists' profits increased. The worker would therefore become continuously worse off relative to the capitalist. Second, Marx correctly foresaw that as the capitalist system progressed there was to be an increasingly minute division of labor.

A finer division of labor makes the worker's activities less varied, and his job becomes more repetitious and tedious. Marx agreed with Adam Smith, who had stated that "the man whose whole life is spent in performing a few simple operations . . . generally becomes as stupid and ignorant as it is possible for a human creature to become."[12] Forced into a condition of stupor and increasingly severely alienated, "the lot of the labourer, *be his payment high or low*, must grow worse."[13]

THE CAPITALIST STATE

Marx rejected the notion that socialism could be created through gradual, piecemeal reforms undertaken by the state. By *the state* Marx meant something more than simply any government: ". . . we may speak of a state only where a special public power of coercion exists which, in the form of an armed organization, stands over and above the population."[14]

Many socialists believed the state was (or could be) an impartial arbiter in the affairs of society, and they had faith in moral and intellectual appeals to the state. Marx rejected this idea. "Political power," he declared in the *Communist Manifesto*, "is merely the organized power of one class for oppressing another." During each period of history, or for each mode of production, the state is the coercive instrument of the ruling class.

Friedrich Engels has summarized the Marxist argument:

Former society, moving in class antagonisms, had need of the state, that is, an organization of the exploiting class at each period for the maintenance of external conditions of production; that is, therefore, for the forcible holding down of the exploited class in the conditions of oppression (slavery, villeinage or serfdom, wage labor) determined by the existing mode of production. The state was the official representative of society as a whole, its embodiment in a visible corporation; but it was this only in so far as it

[12]Adam Smith, *The Wealth of Nations*, ed. Andrew Skinner (London: Penguin Books, 1970), p. 80.
[13]Marx, *Capital*, op. cit., p. 645.
[14]Sidney Hook, *Towards the Understanding of Karl Marx* (New York: Day, 1933), p. 256.

was the state of that class which itself, in its epoch, represented society as a whole; in ancient times, the state of the slave-owning citizens; in the Middle Ages, of the feudal nobility; in our epoch, of the bourgeosie.[15]

Thus the state is simply a dictatorship of the ruling class over the remainder of society.

In the capitalist system the state has two functions. First, it has the traditional function of enforcing the dictatorship of the capitalists over the rest of society. The state achieves this primarily by enforcing property rights, the source of the capitalists' economic power. It also serves in innumerable other ways—for example, jailing or harassing critics of capitalism, fighting wars to extend capitalists' markets, and providing roads, railroads, canals, postal service, and hundreds of other prerequisites for profitable commerce. Second, the government acts as the arbiter of rivalries between capitalists. Each capitalist is interested only in his own profits, and therefore it is inevitable that the interests of capitalists will clash. If not resolved, many of these clashes would threaten the very existence of the system. Thus the government intervenes, and in doing so it protects the viability of the capitalist system. This is why it is sometimes possible to observe the government acting in a way that is contrary to the interests of some of the capitalists. But the government never acts in a way that is contrary to the interests of *all* capitalists taken as a class.

For these reasons, Marx rejected the notion that socialists could rely on the government for help in bringing about the transition from capitalism to socialism. The establishment of socialism, in Marx's opinion, would require a revolution.

THE SOCIALIST REVOLUTION

In his overall view of capitalism Marx saw the process of capital accumulation as inevitably involving several steps. Business cycles or crises would occur regularly and with increasing severity as the capitalist economy developed. There would be a long-run tendency for the rate of profit to fall, and this would exacerbate the other problems of capitalism. Industrial power would become increasingly concentrated in fewer and fewer giant monopolistic and oligopolistic firms, and wealth would become concentrated in the hands of fewer and fewer capitalists. The plight of the laborer would steadily deteriorate.

[15]Friedrich Engels, "Anti-Duhring," in *Handbook of Marxism* (New York: Random House, 1935), p. 295.

Given these increasingly bad conditions, the system could not be perpetuated. Eventually life under capitalism would become so intolerable that workers would revolt, overthrow the whole system, and create a more rational socialist economy.

Along with the constantly diminishing number of magnates of capital, who usurp and monopolize all advantages of this process of transformation, grows the mass of misery, oppression, slavery, degradation, exploitation; but with this too grows the revolt of the working-class, a class always increasing in numbers, and disciplined, united, organized by the very mechanism of the process of capitalist production itself. The monopoly of capital becomes a fetter upon the mode of production, which has sprung up and flourished along with, and under it. Centralization of the means of production and socialization of labour at last reach a point where they become incompatible with their capitalist integument. This integument is burst asunder. The knell of capitalist private property sounds. The expropriators are expropriated.[16]

In subsequent chapters we shall examine the defenses of capitalism offered in opposition to Marx, as well as the further development of socialist thought after Marx.

SUMMARY

Karl Marx, the most influential of all socialists, based his economic analysis on a theory of history called historical materialism. Most social and political institutions, he believed, were significantly shaped by the economic base of society: the mode of production. Over time, conflicts developed between the forces of production and the relations of production. The working out of these conflicts was the most important element in the historical evolution of society.

Marx's economic writings were aimed at understanding the conflicts between the class system (or private property system) of capitalism and the methods of production and commodity exchange under capitalism. These conflicts, he believed, would ultimately lead to the overthrow of capitalism and its replacement by a classless, socialist society.

[16]Marx, *Capital*, op. cit., p. 763.

the
rise
of
corporate
capitalism
and
the
defense
of
laissez
faire

The period from the mid-1840s to 1873 (the year that marked the beginning of the Long Depression in Europe) has been called the golden age of competitive capitalism.[1] These were years of rapid economic expansion throughout most of Europe. Industrialization was getting under way in the United States and continental Europe. The new capital goods necessary for industrialization were, to a large extent, imported from England. Between 1840 and 1860, England experienced an expansion of exports that was more rapid than ever before or since. Capital goods increased from 11 percent of English exports to 22 percent, and exports of coal, iron, and steel also rose sharply.

Between 1830 and 1850, England experienced a railroad-building boom in which some 6,000 miles of railroads were constructed. This railroad building created a strong demand for iron, and iron production doubled between the mid-1830s and the mid-1840s. During the next 30 years the increases in industrial production were also very impressive. Between 1850 and 1880, the production of pig iron increased from 2,250,000 to 7,750,000 tons per year; steel production went from 49,000 to 1,440,000 tons; and coal increased by 300 percent, to 147,000,000 tons. The Bessemer converter (in the 1850s),

[1]Dudley Dillard, *Economic Development of the North Atlantic Community* (Englewood Cliffs, N.J.: Prentice-Hall, 1967), p. 363.

the open-hearth furnace (in the 1860s), and the basic process (in the 1870s) completely revolutionized the steel industry, making large-scale mass production of high-quality steel possible at much lower costs. The capital goods industries also prospered in the second half of the nineteenth century. Production of machines, ships, chemicals, and other important capital goods employed twice as many men in 1881 as in 1851.

THE CONCENTRATION
OF CORPORATE POWER

Just as competitive capitalism seemed to be achieving its greatest successes, the forces Marx had predicted would lead to the concentration of capital began to show themselves. Improvements in technology were such that larger-sized plants were necessary to take advantage of more efficient methods of production. Competition became so aggressive and destructive that small competitors were eliminated. Large competitors, facing mutual destruction, often combined in cartels, trusts, or mergers in order to ensure their mutual survival. In the United States this competition was particularly intense. (It is described in greater detail in Chapter 8.)

A factor that Marx had nearly overlooked, the revolutionary changes in transportation and communication, led to ever-widening markets that could be efficiently supplied by single companies or corporations. The joint stock company, or corporation, became an effective means by which a single business organization could gain control over vast amounts of capital. And a large, well-organized money market evolved in Europe and North America that successfully channeled the smaller capital holdings of many thousands of individuals and small businesses into the hands of large corporations.

In the late nineteenth-century world of giant corporations, in which articles were mass produced for nationwide or worldwide markets, price competition (and indeed sometimes any kind of competition) proved so destructive that it was abandoned almost completely in the large and important industries. There was an inexorable trend toward monopoly power by a few corporations. Many business giants entered into voluntary combinations in which each firm remained somewhat autonomous (e.g., cartels and pools). Other combinations used a financial enterprise such as a trust or holding company to control the voting stock of the corporations involved. Still others used direct mergers and amalgamations from which a single unified corporation emerged.

The English Case

England, where the classical liberal laissez faire philosophy had taken root most firmly, was perhaps least affected by this movement to corporate monopolies. Advances in technology led to a steel industry made up of very large producers. Nevertheless, the fact that England had very few restrictions on imports prevented the industry from combining into an effectively coordinated group until after the trade restrictions of 1932. However, producers of some heavy steel products, such as ship and boiler plate, were able to create effective monopolies much earlier.

In other industries amalgamations led to heavy concentrations. English railroads were combined very early into four main companies. Banking was consolidated until five large commercial banks dominated the industry by the time of World War I. In 1896 the five rivals in the cotton sewing-thread industry had merged into a single monopoly (J. & P. Coats), which came to dominate the world market for that commodity and regularly made profits of 20 percent or more. The firm of Lever Brothers, through amalgamations, gained dominance over the soap business in England as well as in several other countries. Monopolies or closely coordinated oligopolies came to control the wallpaper, salt, petroleum, and rubber industries. Many other industries were either dominated or strongly influenced by a few large firms.

The German Case

In Germany, the classical liberal ideology had never really taken root. During Germany's rapid rise to industrial power during the second half of the nineteenth century, there were neither philosophical nor ideological nor legal barriers to large-scale monopolistic industries. It is therefore not surprising that monopolies and combinations were more widespread in Germany than in any other country in Europe. The cartel was the main type of monopolistic business combination in Germany. There were approximately 16 cartels in 1879; the figure rose to 35 by 1885, 300 by 1900, 600 by 1911, 1000 by 1922, and 2100 by 1930.

Thus by the early twentieth century monopolistic cartels completely dominated almost all the important sectors of the German capitalist economy. (The legal and philosophical justifications of these monopolistic German cartels will be discussed in Chapter 8.)

The American Case

In the United States, the Civil War gave a great stimulus to industrialization. The war not only increased the demand for industrially produced commodities but also led to the passage of laws that were beneficial to the newly emerging corporations that were soon to dominate American industry.

In an effort to provide civil and political rights for all Americans, Congress had passed the first Civil Rights Act in 1866. By 1868, the

Fourteenth Amendment to the U.S. Constitution had been ratified by the states. The ostensible aim of these laws was to confer citizenship and equal rights on American blacks. The Civil Rights Act declared that citizens "of every race and color" were to have equal rights to make contracts, to sue, and enjoy "full and equal benefit of all laws and proceedings for the security of person and property."[2]

Most of the Civil Rights Act was incorporated into the Fourteenth Amendment. The Amendment also included the famous due process clause, which prohibited any state government from depriving "any person of life, liberty, or *property*, without due process of law."[3]

For decades after its ratification the Fourteenth Amendment had no effect at all on the civil rights of American blacks; many of them were thrust into situations worse than slavery. Rather, most court decisions based on the Fourteenth Amendment involved corporations. The courts ruled that corporations were persons and, as such, were protected under the due process clause.

Each time a state government attempted to curb the extravagant excesses of corporations by passing regulatory legislation, the federal courts would invalidate the legislation because it violated the due process clause of the amendment. State governments became powerless before the growing strength of large corporations.

Representative John A. Bingham, who had written the due process clause, later admitted that he had phrased it "word for word and syllable for syllable" to protect the rights of private property and corporations. Representative Roscoe Conkling, who had also helped frame the Amendment, later declared: "At the time the Fourteenth Amendment was ratified, individuals and *joint stock companies* were appealing for congressional and administrative protection against invidious and discriminating state and local taxes. . . . [the Fourteenth amendment embodies] the Golden Rule, so entrenched as to curb the many who would do to the few as they would not have the few do to them."[4]

With the knowledge that they could go to almost any length in their pursuit of profits without fear of state government controls, the corporations thrived. They grew through internal expansion and, more important, by absorbing their competitors. As the giant corporations flourished, the entire American economy thrived and grew.

By the turn of the century, the United States had become the

---

[2]Quoted in Kenneth M. Stampp, *The Era of Reconstruction, 1865–1877* (New York: Random House, Vintage Books, 1967), p. 136.
[3]Ibid.; italics added.
[4]Ibid., p. 137.

leading industrial power in the world. By 1913, when the American economy produced over one-third of the world's industrial output—more than double that of its closest competitor, Germany—most of the strategic industries (railroads, meatpacking, banking in the large cities, steel, copper, and aluminum) and important areas of manufacturing were dominated by a relatively small number of immensely powerful corporations.

With the exception of the railroads, most industries in the immediate post-Civil War years had been relatively atomistic by present-day standards. Although accurate statistics are not available for this early period, it has been estimated that the largest 200 nonfinancial enterprises would have controlled a very minor and inconsequential percentage of all business assets. By the end of the 1920s, this had grown to 33 percent of all assets.[5]

The primary cause of this concentration was the wave of combinations and mergers that took place at an unprecedented rate during the last quarter of the nineteenth century. This merger movement was the outgrowth of the particularly severe competition that had ravaged and destroyed scores of businesses. During this period many people began to question seriously the liberal notion of the invisible hand. It seemed to them that unrestrained individualism had led to unrestrained warfare.

As growing giant businesses locked horns, railroad against railroad, steel mill against steel mill, each sought to assure the coverage of its fixed expenses by gaining for itself .as much of the market as it could. The outcome was the steady growth of cutthroat competition among massive producers. . . . On the railroads for example, constant rate-wars were fought in the 1870's. In the oil fields, the coal fields, among the steel and copper producers, similar price-wars repeatedly broke out as producers sought to capture the markets.[6]

The outcome of such competition was the destruction or absorption of small competitors. Eventually only giants remained, and at this point further competition was immensely destructive to all competitors. The merger movement represented the means whereby the surviving firms could escape this competition.

The scope of the merger movement was so great that by 1904 it had basically altered the structure of American industry. By

[5]Joe S. Bain, *Industrial Organization* (New York: Wiley, 1959), pp. 191–192.
    [6]Robert L. Heilbroner, *The Making of Economic Society* (Englewood Cliffs, N.J.: Prentice-Hall, 1962), p. 120.

the beginning of that year there were over three hundred large industrial combinations with a combined capitalization in excess of $7,000,000,000. They controlled more than two-fifths of the manufacturing capital of the country and had affected about four-fifths of important American industries.[7]

THE CONCENTRATION OF INCOME

Accompanying this concentration of industry was an equally striking concentration of income in the hands of a small percentage of the population. Despite the fact that no accurate statistics for the early part of the period exist, it seems reasonably certain that the degree of concentration increased substantially between 1870 and 1929. By 1929, just 5 percent of the population received 34 percent of personal disposable income in the United States.[8] The degree of concentration had probably reached this extreme as early as 1913. By the end of the 1920s, the highest one-fifth of "families and unattached individuals" were receiving over 50 percent of all personal income.[9]

REEMERGENCE OF THE CLASSICAL LIBERAL IDEOLOGY

With this immense concentration of economic power in the hands of a small number of giant firms and a small percentage of the population, it would seem that the classical liberal ideology of capitalism would have been abandoned. The economic creed of classical liberalism, as developed by Adam Smith and refined by such well-known classical economists as David Ricardo, Nassau Senior, and J. B. Say, was based on an analysis of an economy composed of many small enterprises. In such an economy no individual enterprise could exercise a significant influence on the market price or on the total amount sold in the market. The actions of any firm were dictated to it by consumer tastes, as registered in the marketplace, and by the competition of innumerable other small firms, each vying for the consumer's dollars.

As wide as the gulf between classical economic theory and late nineteenth-century economic reality seems to have been, the eco-

[7]Joe S. Bain, "Industrial Concentration and Anti-Trust Policy," in Harold F. Williamson, ed., *Growth of the American Economy*, 2d ed. (Englewood Cliffs, N.J.: Prentice-Hall, 1951), p. 619.

[8]U.S. Department of Commerce, *Historical Statistics of the United States* (Washington, D.C.: GPO, 1961), p. 167.

[9]Ibid.; the data for 1913 do not give a figure for the income going to the top 5 percent. The amount going to the top 1 percent, however, was 14.98 percent in 1913 and 14.94 percent in 1928.

nomic creed of classical liberalism did not fall by the wayside in this later period. Rather, it was combined with Benthamite utilitarianism (which was already implicit in Adam Smith's normative model of the invisible hand) and refurbished within an elaborate and esoteric framework of algebra and calculus. This resurgence of the classical liberal economic creed was accomplished by a new school of economic thinkers known as *neoclassical* economists.

THE NEOCLASSICAL THEORY OF UTILITY AND CONSUMPTION

During the early 1870s, at precisely the time when the drive toward the economic concentration of corporate capitalism was taking place, three very famous economics texts were published. William Stanley Jevons' *The Theory of Political Economy*[10] and Karl Menger's *Grundsätze der Volkswirtschaftslehre*[11] both appeared in 1871, and three years later Léon Walras's *Eléments d'économie politique pure* was published.[12] Although there were many differences between the analyses of these men, the similarities in both approach and content of these books were striking.

Their theories pictured an economy made up of large numbers of small producers and consumers, each having insufficient power to influence the market significantly. The business firms hired or bought factors of production; they utilized the factors in the production process in such a way that their profits were maximized. Prices of the final products and factors of production were taken as given and beyond their control. The firms could control only the productive process chosen and the amount produced.

Households likewise sold their land and capital, as well as their labor, at prices determined in the market and used the receipts (their incomes) to buy goods and services. Consumers apportioned their income among the various commodities they wished to purchase in a way that maximized the utility they received from these commodities.

Commodities were the ultimate source of pleasure or utility, and the utility they yielded was assumed to be quantifiable. Jevons wrote: "A unit of pleasure or pain is difficult even to conceive; but it is the amount of these feelings which is continually prompting us

[10]William Stanley Jevons, *The Theory of Political Economy*, 1st ed. (London:: Macmillan, 1871).

[11]Karl Menger, *Grundsätze der Volkswirtschaftslehre* (Vienna: Braumuller, 1871), translated as *Principles of Economics* (New York: Free Press, 1950).

[12]Léon Walras, *Eléments d'économie politique pure* (Lausanne: Corbaz et Cie, 1874); translated as *Elements of Pure Economics* (Homewood, Ill.: Irwin, 1954).

to buying and selling, borrowing and lending, laboring and resting, producing and consuming; *and it is from the quantitative effects of the feelings that we must estimate their comparative amounts.*"[13]

Walras was less ambiguous in arguing that utility was quantifiable: "I shall, therefore, assume the existence of a standard measure of intensity of wants or intensive utility, which is applicable not only to similar units of the same kind of wealth but also to different units of various kinds of wealth."[14]

These economists, having presumably quantifiable magnitudes with which to work, next set up general mathematical formulas purporting to show a functional relationship between the utility a consumer received and the amounts of the various commodities he consumed. The problem then was to show how the consumer could get the maximum utility, given his income and the commodity prices prevailing in the market.

Consumers maximized utility when the increase in utility derived from the last unit consumed, expressed as a ratio over the price of that commodity, was an equal proportion for all other commodities. In other words, the last dollar spent on a commodity should yield the same increase in the utility derived by the consumer as the last dollar spent on any other commodity. Jevons explained the same thing in a different way, stating that the consumer maximized utility because he "procures such quantities of commodities that the final degrees of utility of any pair of commodities are inversely as the ratios of exchange [prices] of the commodities."[15]

Suppose there was a free market in which consumers could freely exchange their incomes for commodities. They would be led by their self-interest to maximize utility. Therefore it was concluded that consumers distributed their income among purchases of commodities in such a way that the welfare of all would be maximized, given the existing distribution of wealth and income.

THE NEOCLASSICAL THEORY OF PRODUCTION

In neoclassical production theory the analysis of the business firm was perfectly symmetrical with the analysis of consumer behavior. In order to maximize profits, the firm would operate at its highest efficiency and hence produce at the lowest possible cost. It purchased factors of production (such as labor) up to the point at which the amount added to production by the last unit of each fac-

---

[13]Jevons, op. cit., p. 11.
[14]Walras, op. cit., p. 117.
[15]Jevons, op. cit., p. 139.

tor of production, expressed as a ratio over the price of the factor, was an equal proportion for all factors. The last dollar spent on each factor should yield the same increase in production from all factors. In a free market firms would always attempt to maximize efficiency in order to maximize profits. Therefore this condition would always hold. Thus the factors of production would all be used in such a way that no possible reorganization of production (given the existing technology) could result in a more efficient use of the factors of production.

Neoclassical economists also believed that if an economy were characterized by a free market with many small competitive firms, then each commodity would be produced in such quantities and with such methods that it would be impossible to shift resources from the production of one commodity to the production of a different one without diminishing the total value of what was produced in the market economy.

LAISSEZ FAIRE

Thus the neoclassical economists gave a very elaborate and esoteric analytical defense of Adam Smith's notion of the invisible hand of market competition and the economic policy of laissez faire. They showed that, in a competitive market economy made up of innumerable small producers and consumers, the market would guide consumers in such a way that they would end up with an optimal mix of commodities, *given their original income and wealth*. Factors of production would be used in the most efficient way possible. Moreover, commodities would be produced in amounts that would maximize the value of society's production. This optimal result depended, however, on a minimum of interference by government in the processes of the free market.

They recognized that this result was optimal only if one accepted the existing distribution of income. Some (particularly the American economist John Bates Clark) tried to defend the distribution of income that obtained in a free-market economy. They argued that the principles of profit maximization would lead to a situation in which each category of productive factors would be paid an amount equal to the value of its marginal contribution to the productive process. This seemed to them a model of distributive justice, with each unit of the productive factors being paid an amount equal to what it produced. Critics were quick to point out, however, that units of productive factors were not people (at least as far as land, natural resources, and capital were concerned). In order for such a system to be fair, these critics insisted, an equitable distribution of ownership of the factors of production would be necessary.

Nevertheless, the neoclassical economists did succeed in erecting an impressive intellectual defense of the classical liberal policy of laissez faire. But they did it by creating a giant chasm between economic theory and economic reality. From the 1870s until today, many economists in the neoclassical tradition have abandoned any real concern with existing economic institutions and problems. Instead, many of them have retired to the rarefied stratosphere of mathematical model building, constructing endless variations on esoteric trivia.

SUBSEQUENT MODIFICATIONS
OF NEOCLASSICAL THEORY

Some economists in the second and third generations of neoclassical analysis recognized the need to make the theory more realistic. The economic system was *not* characterized by "perfect competition"; it had flaws. The principal admitted weaknesses were as follows: (1) Some buyers and sellers *were* large enough to affect prices; moreover, the economies of large-scale production seemed to render this inevitable. (2) Some commodities should be "consumed socially," and their production and sale might never be profitable in a laissez faire capitalist economy, even though they might be deemed highly desirable by most citizens (e.g., roads, schools, armies). (3) The costs to the producer of a commodity (such as automobiles) might differ significantly from the social costs (such as smog) of producing that commodity. In such a case it was possible that for society as a whole the costs of production might exceed the benefits of production for the commodity, even though the producer still profited from making and selling it. For example, consider the poisoning of the water and air by producers making profits but doing little or nothing about this evil, even though its side effects could endanger human life itself. (4) An unrestrained free-market capitalist system appeared to be quite unstable, being subject to recurring depressions that incurred enormous social waste.

It was generally agreed that such flaws did exist and did disrupt the otherwise beneficial workings of the capitalist system, but they could be corrected only by some amount of government intervention in the market system. Government antitrust actions, it was argued, could force giant firms to act as if they were competitive, and something called "workable competition" could be achieved. Roads, schools, armies, and other socially consumed commodities could be provided by the government. Extensive systems of special taxes and subsidies could be used to equate private and social costs in cases where they differed. Finally (especially after the 1930s), it was believed that through wise use of fiscal and monetary policy the government could eliminate the instability of the system. (This last point will be discussed in more detail in Chapter 11.)

The flaws in the system were thus seen as minor and ephemeral. An enlightened government could correct them and free the invisible hand once again to create the best of all possible worlds. There did develop, however, an inability to agree on the extent and significance of the flaws. Those who believe them to be fairly widespread and quite significant have, during the course of the twentieth century, become known as *liberals*. They have sometimes advocated fairly extensive government intervention in the economic system, but most have continued to use neoclassical economic theory as an ideology to defend the private ownership, capitalist market economic system.

Economists who see the flaws as minor and unimportant continue to advocate a minimum of government intervention in the market economy. Despite the fact that the laissez faire policies advocated by these economists have been much closer to those advocated by the nineteenth-century classical liberals, they have become known in the twentieth century as *conservatives*. Both liberals and conservatives, as we have described them here, have used neoclassical economic theory to justify the capitalist system.

LAISSEZ FAIRE
AND THE SOCIAL DARWINISTS

Before leaving the topic of late nineteenth- and early twentieth-century advocates of laissez faire capitalism, a brief discussion of *social Darwinism* is necessary. Social Darwinists believed the government should allow capitalists to compete freely in the marketplace with a minimum of government restrictions and, in general, favored as little government intervention as possible in all spheres of life. Therefore many people have imagined their defense of laissez faire capitalism to be similar to that of the neoclassical economists. This is not so. Their policy recommendations were based on a substantially different theoretical framework.

The social Darwinists took Darwin's theory of evolution and extended it to a theory of social evolution (in a manner that Darwin himself strongly disapproved, it may be added). Competition, they believed, was a teleological process in which each succeeding generation was superior to the preceding one. This upward progress was made possible because those least fit to survive did not succeed in maintaining themselves and procreating. Greater ability to survive was equated with a biological as well as a moral superiority.

Herbert Spencer (1820–1903), the father of social Darwinism, based his evolutionary as well as his moral theory on what he called the *law of conduct and consequence*. He believed survival of the human species could be ensured only if society distributed its benefits in proportion to a person's merit, measured by his power to sustain himself. Each person ought to reap the benefits or suffer the evil results of his own actions. Thus the people most adapted to their environment would prosper, and those least adapted would be weeded out—provided that the laws of conduct and consequence were observed. If the government, wishing to mitigate the inequalities of wealth and income in society, took "from him who . . . [had] prospered to give to him who . . . [had] not, it [violated] its duty towards the one to do more than its duty towards the other."[16] This type of action slowed social progress and could, if carried to excess, destroy the human species. Survival and progress could be ensured only if the weak were weeded out and destroyed by the impersonal forces of social evolution.

In Spencer's opinion, "the poverty of the incapable, the distresses that come upon the imprudent, the starvation of the idle, and those shoulderings aside of the weak by the strong . . . are the decrees of a large, far-seeing benevolence."[17] Spencer categorically opposed any action by the government that interfered with trade, commerce, production, or the distribution of wealth or income. He rejected welfare payments of any kind, attempts to decrease the economic insecurity of workers, and government provision of schools, parks, or libraries as detrimental to human progress. His laissez faire was thus much more extreme than that of the classical economists or most of the conservative neoclassical economists.

Social Darwinists accepted the large monopolistic and oligopolistic industries as the beneficient result of evolution. Neoclassical economists, if they did not simply define away or ignore the concentrations of economic power, believed government should attempt to create a more competitive and atomistic market situation. Thus in this very important respect the two theories were quite antagonistic.

LAISSEZ FAIRE AND THE IDEOLOGY OF BUSINESSMEN

Most businessmen, however, were not very concerned with intellectual consistency. They feared radical and socialist reformers who wanted to use the government as a means of achieving greater equality and they welcomed any theory that concluded that the government should not intervene in the economic process. Even

---

[16]Quoted in Sidney Fine, *Laissez Faire and the General Welfare State* (Ann Arbor: University of Michigan Press, 1964), p. 38.
[17]Ibid.

though they themselves used the government extensively to promote their own interests (through special tariffs, tax concessions, land grants, and a host of other special privileges), they relied on laissez faire arguments when threatened with any social reform that might erode their status, influence, wealth, or income. Thus in the ordinary businessman's ideology of the late nineteenth and early twentieth centuries there was a general attempt to combine neoclassical economics and social Darwinism.

In this ideology the accumulation of wealth was considered de facto proof of evolutionary superiority, whereas poverty was believed to be evidence of evolutionary inferiority. Success, asserted writer Benjamin Woods, was "nothing more or less than doing thoroughly what others did indifferently." Andrew Carnegie equated success with "honest work, ability and concentration"; another businessman argued that "wealth has always been the natural sequence to industry, temperance, and perseverance, and it will always so continue." At the same time, S. C. T. Dodd, solicitor for Standard Oil, maintained that poverty existed "because nature or the devil has made some men weak and imbecile and others lazy and worthless, and neither man nor God can do much for one who will do nothing for himself."[18]

The beneficial results of competition in neoclassical economic theory seemed to reinforce reliance on the "survival of the fittest" in the "struggle for survival." "Competition in economics," asserted Richard R. Bowker, "is the same as the law of . . . 'natural selection' in nature."[19]

Although some businessmen and their spokesmen were trying to perpetuate the laissez faire conclusions of the classical liberal ideology of capitalism, many defenders of the capitalist system believed that in the new age of mass production (with gigantic concentrations of wealth and power in the hands of so few corporations and capitalists) the older, individualistic, laissez faire ideology was no longer appropriate. The late nineteenth century witnessed a rebirth of the older paternalistic ethic. In Chapter 8 we will examine a new ideology of capitalism that was based, in many essential respects, on a new version of the Christian paternalist ethic.

SUMMARY

In the late nineteenth century capitalism was characterized by the growth of giant corporations. Control of most of the important industries became more and more concentrated. Accompanying this

18All quotations in this paragraph are cited in Fine, op. cit., p. 98.
19Ibid., p. 100.

concentration of industry was an equally striking concentration of income in the hands of a small percentage of the population.

In view of these facts it would seem that the classical liberal ideology (which depended on an analysis of an economy based on many small, relatively powerless enterprises) would have to be abandoned. The gulf that separated the theory from reality had widened into a giant chasm. But the idea that the market economy channeled acquisitive profit seeking into socially benevolent practices was simply too elegant an apologia for unrestrained profit-making activity. So the classical liberal ideology of capitalism was even more assiduously disseminated in a new school of neoclassical economics.

An elaborate deductive theory permitted the neoclassical economists to defend the classical policy prescription of laissez faire. Conservative neoclassical economists assigned to the government only the tasks that would directly or indirectly promote business profits. Liberal neoclassical economists also believed the government should enter a limited number of other areas in which the operation of the free market did not maximize the social welfare. Whether in the hands of the conservative or the liberal faction, neoclassical economics remained essentially an ideological defense for the status quo.

Finally, social Darwinist ideology and the ideology of most businessmen defended many of the neoclassical economists' conclusions. They did so, however, on entirely different grounds. They accepted the fact that corporate power, personal wealth, and personal income were highly concentrated. This, they believed, was evidence of the evolutionary superiority of the wealthy and, as such, was socially beneficial.

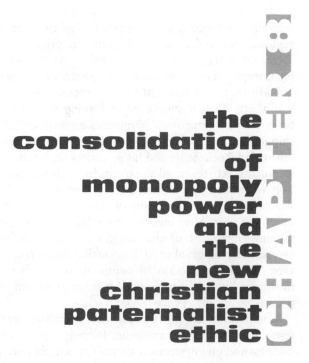

the consolidation of monopoly power and the new christian paternalist ethic

The process of industrialization in the United States after the Civil War involved, in its initial stages, a competition among industrial and financial capitalists that was unique in its ferocity. From 1860 until the early 1880s, the strongest and shrewdest businessmen built great empires with the fruits of economic conquest. The great improvements in transportation that occurred during this period, the rise of standardization in parts and finished products, and the increased efficiency in large-scale mass production created the possibility of nationwide markets. The stakes in the economic struggle were very large, and the participants neither asked for quarter nor received any.

COMPETITION AS INDUSTRIAL WARFARE

Examples of the industrial warfare of the time have filled many books.[1] In the oil industry, for example, John D. Rockefeller and Henry M. Flagler shipped so much oil that they were able to demand large concessions from the railroads. With this cost advantage they could undersell competitors. Their company, which was incorporated in 1870 under the name of Standard Oil Company of Ohio,

[1]See, for example, Matthew Josephson, *The Robber Barons* (New York: Harcourt Brace Jovanovich, Harvest Books, 1962), for a fascinating account of the exploits of the capitalists of this era.

was able to force many competitors to the wall and thus achieve regional monopolies, at which point the price could be substantially increased without fear of competition. After securing large rebates on transport costs, Standard Oil's share in the petroleum industry quickly increased from 10 to 20 percent. But the company did not stop there. Next it succeeded in forcing the railroads to give it rebates on its *competitors'* shipments as well as "all data relating to shipper, buyer, product, price and terms of payment," a scheme that "provided Rockefeller and his associates with rebates on all their own shipments, rebates on all shipments by their competitors, and in addition a complete spy system on their competitors."[2] With this power Rockefeller was able to smash most of his competitors. By 1879, only nine years after incorporation, Standard Oil controlled between 90 and 95 percent of the nation's output of refined petroleum. A sympathetic biographer of Rockefeller has written: "Of all the devices for the extinction of competition, this was the cruelest and most deadly yet conceived by any group of American industrialists."[3]

Competition among the railroad magnates was particularly intense. Rate wars were common, forcing weaker competitors out of business and giving stronger competitors monopoly power over large regions. The battles sometimes got so brutal that locomotives were crashed into each other and track was destroyed. The railroads also extorted money from towns along proposed railroad lines. A member of the California Constitutional Convention of 1878 described the technique.

> They start out their railroad track and survey their line near a thriving village. They go to the most prominent citizens of that village and say, "If you will give us so many thousand dollars we will run through here; if you do not we will run by." And in every instance where the subsidy was not granted this course was taken and the effect was just as they said, to kill off the little town.[4]

According to the same report, the railroad "blackmailed Los Angeles County for $230,000 as a condition of doing that which the law compelled them to do." The railroads also manipulated connections with politicians to get government handouts of public lands. It is estimated that these giveaways amounted to 158,293,000 acres—a

[2]Dudley Dillard, *Economic Development of the North Atlantic Community* (Englewood Cliffs, N.J.: Prentice-Hall, 1967), p. 410.
[3]Allan Nevins, *John D. Rockefeller, The Heroic Age of American Enterprise*, vol. 1 (New York: Scribner, 1940), p. 325.
[4]Quoted in Josephson, op. cit., pp. 84–85.

greater land area than that of some whole countries.[5] The railroads were certainly not in favor of a laissez faire policy in practice.

The great entrepreneurs of that age were definitely not men of estimable social conscience. Many founded their fortunes on the Civil War. When shortages of supplies became desperate, they received high prices for selling to the army "shoddy blankets, so many doctored horses and useless rifles, [and] . . . stores of sickening beef."[6] In order to eliminate their competitors, they did not hesitate to use hired thugs, kidnaping, and dynamite. Likewise, they stopped at nothing as they mulcted the public of millions of dollars through stock frauds, schemes, and swindles. Some of these actions were legal and some were not, but the dominant mood of these capitalist entrepreneurs was expressed by Cornelius Vanderbilt, who, when cautioned about the questionable legality of a desired course of action, exclaimed, "What do I care about the law? Hain't I got the power?"[7] Much the same idea was expressed by William Vanderbilt during a public outcry against one of his policy decisions: "The public be damned. I am working for my stockholders."[8]

BUSINESS COLLUSION
AND GOVERNMENT REGULATION

After a few years of this type of competition, however, most of the remaining business firms were battle-tested giants. Continuing such competition would have been ruinous for all. So, whereas competition was the road to large profits before 1880, after that date it became obvious that cooperative collusion would be more beneficial for the remaining firms. In that way they could exercise monopolistic power for their mutual benefit. Thus pools, trusts, and mergers (described in Chapter 7) were the consequence of the earlier competition. Increasingly as the turn of the century neared, the neoclassical vision of many small competing firms diverged from the reality of massive corporations acting cooperatively to maximize their joint profits.

With the rise of big corporations there was a parallel growth of grass-roots popular opposition to these companies and their blatant disregard for the public welfare. This popular antagonism became so widespread and intense that in the presidential campaign of 1888 both the Democrats and the Republicans advocated federal laws to curb the abuses of big corporations.

[5]Ibid., p. 79.
[6]Ibid., p. 67.
[7]Ibid., p. 72.
[8]Ibid.

After the 1888 election both parties became extremely reluctant to take any such action. Many of the most important Republicans controlled the very corporations they had promised to curb, and the Democrats were only slightly less involved with big business. Only when public pressure reached incredible heights did Congress respond, in December 1889, by passing the Sherman Antitrust Act. The act, an obvious concession to aroused public opinion, passed both houses of Congress with only a single dissenting vote. But the wording of the law was so weak and vague that it appeared to be designed to ensure that it would be ineffective. Another proposal that recommended meaningful punishment of firms that violated the law was overwhelmingly defeated.

The law proscribed "every contract, combination in the form of a trust or otherwise, or conspiracy, in restraint of trade or commerce among the several states or with foreign nations. . . ." It also declared a person guilty of a misdemeanor if he attempted "to monopolize, or combine or conspire with any other person . . . to monopolize any part of the trade or commerce among the several states, or with foreign nations. . . ."

The primary effect of the Sherman Act over the next few decades was to weaken labor unions. What had begun as a concession to the public's hatred of abuses by big business became an antilabor law. This effect followed because the courts ruled that many union strikes constituted constraints of trade. On this basis the government arrested numerous union leaders and broke up many unions.

While President McKinley was in office there were only five cases initiated under the Sherman Act, despite the fact that 146 major industrial combinations were formed between 1899 and 1901 alone. One of these was the massive United States Steel Corporation, which in 1901 controlled or acquired 785 plants worth a whopping $1,370,000,000.

Staggeringly high profits, graft, corruption, and discriminatory practices on the part of the nation's railroads led to the establishment of the first federal government regulatory agency. The Interstate Commerce Act of 1887 established the Interstate Commerce Commission (ICC), which was designed to regulate the railroads in order to protect the public interest.

Competition among the railroads had been so destructive that the railroads themselves were the leading advocates of extended federal regulation. A few years after the passage of the Interstate Commerce Act, U.S. Attorney General Olney wrote a letter to a railroad president that read, in part: "The Commission [ICC] . . . is, or can be made, of great use to the railroads. It satisfies the popular clamor for a government supervision of railroads, at the same time that supervision is almost entirely nominal. Further, the older such a commission gets to be, the more inclined it will be found to take the business and railroad view of things. . . ."[9]

The attorney general's prediction has certainly been borne out by the facts. In the years since the establishment of the ICC, many other federal regulatory agencies have been established. The Federal Communications Commission (FCC), the Civil Aeronautics Board (CAB), and the Securities and Exchange Commission (SEC) were among the federal agencies that joined the ICC as "protectors" of the public interest. Most serious students of government regulation would agree that "the outstanding political fact about the . . . regulatory commissions is that they have in general become promoters and protectors of the industries they have been established to regulate."[10] The agencies help the industries make extraordinary profits at the expense of the public.

Many oligopolistic industries seemed unable to cooperate and act collectively as a monopoly. For these industries there is a considerable body of evidence indicating that they turned to the government and to federal regulatory agencies as a means of achieving this monopolistic coordination.[11] Regulatory agencies have generally performed this function very effectively.

The collusive behavior of the oligopolistic businesses seemed to go unnoticed by neoclassical economists. They continued to frame their analyses in terms of innumerable small, competing business firms. In their advocacy of laissez faire policies, they failed to see that it was primarily big business that supported active government intervention.

Neoclassical economists also continued to accept the classical economists' view that as long as free competition prevails the economy will tend toward full utilization of its productive capacity and full employment will be more or less continuous. During the second half of the nineteenth century, however, economic depressions became more frequent and more severe. During the first half of the nineteenth century, the United States had had two economic crises (in 1819 and 1837), and England had had four (in 1815, 1825, 1836, and 1847). During the second half of the century, the number increased to five in the United States (in 1854, 1857, 1873, 1884, and 1893), and six in England (in 1857, 1866, 1873, 1882, 1890, and 1900).

[9]Quoted in Grant McConnell, "Self-Regulation, the Politics of Business," in D. Mermelstein, ed., *Economics: Mainstream Readings and Radical Critiques* (New York: Random House, 1970), p. 197.

[10]Ibid., p. 199.

[11]The most thoroughly documented defense of this assertion can be found in Gabriel Kolko, *The Triumph of Conservatism* (New York: Free Press, 1963).

Thus the neoclassical economic ideology was as poor a reflection of economic performances as it was of industrial concentration.

**A NEW
CHRISTIAN PATERNALIST ETHIC**

The distance separating the neoclassical liberal ideology of capitalism and economic reality impressed itself on the minds of many academicians and businessmen. The result was a new ideology for the new age of corporate capitalism. Just as the new industrial and financial entrepreneurs came to resemble the feudal robber barons, so the new ideology resembled the feudal version of the Christian paternalist ethic. It emphasized the natural superiority of a small elite, the new industrial and financial magnates, and the paternalistic functions of that elite in caring for the masses.

The new ideology reflected the fact that many of the wealthy capitalists of the era were becoming something of folk heroes among the general public. The last two decades of the nineteenth century and the first three of the twentieth were an age during which the businessman became the most admired social type. The success of businessmen was viewed as de facto proof that they possessed virtues superior to those of the ordinary man. This version of success was the theme of the biographies of William Makepeace Thackeray and the novels of Horatio Alger. These men and other writers created a cult of success that viewed the increase of industrial concentration as proof of Darwinian superiority on the part of the industrialists, glorified the self-made man, and kept the Horatio Alger rags-to-riches myth constantly in the public mind.

The veneration of businessmen, added to the strong rejection of destructive competition by both businessmen and the general public, led to a new conservative version of the Christian paternalist ethic, which resembled the philosophy of the Tory radicals of the late eighteenth and early nineteenth centuries. The unfortunate plight of the poor received prominent mention in the new writings. This problem, as well as that of economic instability, could best be solved, according to the new ideology, by encouraging cooperation among the leaders of the giant corporations. Competition was viewed as antisocial. Through cooperation business cycles could be eliminated and the plight of the poor improved.

This new version of the Christian paternalist ethic received the support of Pope Leo XIII (1810–1903). Between 1878 and 1901 the pope sought to analyze the problems of corporate capitalism and to suggest remedies in a series of encyclicals. In *Rerum novarum* (1891) he argued that "a remedy must be found . . . for the misery and wretchedness which press so heavily at this moment on the large majority of the very poor." He continued with a condemnation of unrestrained laissez faire competition:

> Working men have been given over, isolated and defenseless, to the callousness of employers and the greed of unrestrained competition. The evil has been increased by rapacious usury . . . still practiced by avaricious and grasping men. And to this must be added the custom of working by contract, and the concentration of so many branches of trade in the hands of a few individuals, so that a small number of very rich men have been able to lay upon the masses of the poor a yoke little better than slavery itself.[12]

This passage, which sounds so socialist in tone and content, was followed by a strong condemnation of socialism and a defense of private property. The pope hoped the problems could be corrected by rejection of competition and a return to the Christian virtues of love and brotherhood, with the leaders of business and industry leading the way to a new Christian paternalism within the context of a private property capitalist system.

The German Version

The new paternalistic ideology was probably strongest in Germany, where classical liberalism had never gained a good hold and industrial concentration was most pronounced. A famous German economist expressed the very widely held view that

> the proper kind of cartelization creates more or less a system of justice and equity. . . . The directors of the cartels are educators who wish to bring about the triumph of wide interests of a branch of industry over the egoistic interests of the individual. . . . The cartel system is, like a co-operative or merchants' association, an important element in the education of commercial and technical officials who want to make money but who have also learned to put themselves in the service of general interests and to administer the property of others in a loyal and honorable fashion.[13]

Cartels were also widely justified as means of eliminating economic crises. A German court decision, one of several that formed the legal justification of the cartel system in that country, stated that "Indeed the formation of syndicates and cartels . . . has repeatedly

---

[12]Quoted in Daniel R. Fusfeld, *The Age of the Economist* (Glenview, Ill.: Scott, Foresman, 1966), p. 86.

[13]Gustave Schmoller, quoted in Koppel S. Pinson, *Modern Germany: Its History and Civilization* (New York: Macmillan, 1954), p. 236.

been considered a device especially useful for the economy as a whole, since they can prevent uneconomic overproduction and ensuing catastrophe."[14]

The American Version

In the United States, as mentioned earlier, the new ideology thrived in an atmosphere that venerated the successful businessman and was extremely weary of destructive competition. The view of many American industrial and financial magnates was expressed by Andrew Carnegie, one of the most successful of the magnates:

> Not evil, but good, has come to the race from the accumulation of wealth by those who have the ability and energy that produce it. . . . We have the true antidote for the temporary unequal distribution of wealth, the reconciliation of the rich and the poor—a reign of harmony—another ideal, differing, indeed, from that of the Communist in requiring only further evolution of existing conditions, not the total overthrow of our civilization. . . . Under its sway we shall have an ideal state, in which the surplus wealth of the few will become in the best sense, the property of the many, because administered for the common good, this wealth passing through the hands of the few can be made a more potent force for the elevation of our race than if it were distributed in sums to the people themselves.[15]

Carnegie argued, and many businessmen and their spokesmen agreed, that the millionaire would be "a trustee for the poor, entrusted for a season with a great part of the increased wealth of the community, but administering it for the community far better than it could or would have done for itself."[16]

The Right Reverend William Lawrence gave the new elitist view the sanction of religion. "In the long run, it is only to the man of morality that wealth comes. . . . Godliness is in league with riches."[17] And railroad president George F. Baer had the same idea in mind when he tried to assure railroad workers that "the rights and the interests of the laboring man will be protected and cared for, not by the labor agitators, but by the Christian men to whom God in his infinite wisdom, has given control of the property interests of the country."[18]

[14]Quoted in Dillard, op. cit., p. 396.
[15]Andrew Carnegie, "Wealth," in Gail Kennedy, ed., *Democracy and the Gospel of Wealth* (Lexington, Mass.: Raytheon/Heath, 1949), pp. 3, 5, 6.
[16]Cited in Kennedy, op. cit., p. xii.
[17]Ibid.
[18]Ibid.

SIMON PATTEN'S ECONOMIC
BASIS FOR THE NEW ETHIC

Perhaps the most influential academic spokesman for the new corporate ideology was Dr. Simon N. Patten, professor of economics at the University of Pennsylvania from 1888 to 1917 and one of the founders of the American Economic Association.[19] In keeping with the paternalistic element of the new ideology, Patten denounced the poverty and economic exploitation of his era. The following passage could almost have been written by a Marxist of that era:

> There have flowed then, side by side, two streams of life, one bearing the working poor, who perpetuate themselves through qualities generated by the stress and mutual dependence of the primitive world, and the other bearing aristocracies, who dominate by means of the laws and traditions giving them control of the social surplus.[20]

In the same vein, 15 years late, he wrote that

> The glow of Fifth Avenue is but the reflection of a distant hell into which unwilling victims are cast. Some resource is misused, some town degraded, to create the flow of funds on which our magnates thrive. From Pennsylvania, rich in resources, trains go loaded and come back empty. For the better half no return is made except in literary tomes designed to convince the recipients that exploitation is not robbery. . . . But Nature revolts! Never does the rising sun see children yanked from bed to increase the great Strauss dividends, nor the veteran cripples of the steel mill tramping in their beggar garb, but that it shrivels, reddens, and would strike but for the sight of happier regions beyond.[21]

This poverty and exploitation were, in Patten's opinion, the last vestiges of an earlier age characterized by scarcity. In the economy of scarcity capitalists competed aggressively with each other, with the result that laborers as well as the general public suffered. The fierce competition of the robber barons, however, had marked a watershed in history. The merger movement that followed this competition was the beginning of a new era, an era of plenty rather than scarcity. Capitalists were becoming socialized. They were put-

[19]For a more complete account of Patten's idea, see E. K. Hunt, "Simon N. Patten's Contribution to Economics," *Journal of Economic Issues*, December 1970, pp. 38–55.
[20]Simon Nelson Patten, *The New Basis of Civilization* (New York: Macmillan, 1907), p. 39.
[21]Simon Nelson Patten, *Mud Hollow* (Philadelphia: Dorrance, 1922), p. 226.

ting the public welfare ahead of their pursuit of profits, and in doing this they eschewed competition, recognizing that the public welfare could best be promoted by cooperation. (Of course we have seen that capitalists cooperated with each other mostly to squeeze more profit from the public.)

Evidence that the conditions of economic prosperity at the turn of the century were socializing capitalists could be seen in the fact that "hospitals . . . [were] established, schools . . . [were] made free, colleges . . . [were] endowed, museums, libraries, and art galleries . . . [received] liberal support, church funds . . . [grew] and missions . . . [were] formed at home and abroad."[22] On almost every policy issue of his day, Patten took a strongly proindustrial capitalist position. He viewed the late nineteenth-century captains of industry as a paternally beneficient elite:

> The growth of large-scale capitalism has resulted in the elimination of the unsocial capitalist and the increasing control of each industry by the socialized groups. . . . At bottom altruistic sentiment is the feeling of a capitalist expressing itself in sympathy for the laborer. This desire of upper class men to improve the conditions of lower classes is a radically different phenomenon from the pressure exerted by the lower classes for their own betterment. The lower class movement stands for the control of the state by themselves in their own interests. The upper class movement directs itself against the bad environmental conditions preventing the expression of character.[23]

He believed competition should be discouraged by taxing competitive firms and exempting trusts and monopolies from these taxes. This would benefit all society by eliminating the extensive waste created by competition. In *The Stability of Prices* he argued that competition was largely responsible for the economic instability of the late nineteenth century. When the movement toward trusts and monopolies had been completed, production would be controlled and planned in such a way that this instability would be eliminated.

Patten's paternalistic ideology was, like the liberal ideology of capitalism, ultimately a plea for a minimum of government interference with the actions of businessmen. The government was to interfere in the economy only by encouraging trusts and monopolies and discouraging competition. In Patten's scheme all important social

[22]Simon Nelson Patten, *The Theory of Prosperity* (New York: Macmillan, 1902), p. 170.

[23]Simon Nelson Patten, "The Reconstruction of Economic Theory," reprinted in Simon Nelson Patten, *Essays in Economic Theory*, ed. Rexford Guy Tugwell (New York: Knopf, 1924), p. 292.

and economic reforms were to be carried out voluntarily by the socialized capitalists in a system of cooperative corporate collectivism.

THE NEW
PATERNALISM AND THE NEW DEAL[24]

Patten's version of the new ideology of corporate capitalism was to
be very important. historically. When the Great Depression of the
1930s struck, two of Patten's students and devotees, Rexford Guy
Tugwell and Frances Perkins, had influential positions as members
of Roosevelt's original cabinet. Tugwell had asserted that Patten's
views "were the greatest single influence on my thought. Neither
Veblen nor Dewey found their orientation to the future as completely
and instinctively as did Patten. The magnificence of his conceptions
and the basic rightness of his vision become clearer as time passes.
I am eternally grateful to him."[25] Perkins believed her former teacher
to be "one of the greatest men America has ever produced."[26]

Through these two former students Patten exerted a considerable
influence on the economic policies of the early phase of the New
Deal. His ideas helped create the intellectual basis of the National
Industrial Recovery Act of 1933 (NIRA).[27] Patten was not, of
course, the only source of these ideas. During World War I, the
War Industries Board had generated enthusiasm for corporate collectivism. Throughout the 1920s, trade associations prospered, and
the doctrine of business self-government gained many adherents in
the business world. In 1922, Franklin Roosevelt was president of one
such association: the American Construction Council. However,
Patten's teachings were unquestionably influential. His protégés,
Tugwell and Perkins, were both instrumental in the actual framing
of the NIRA.

The National Industrial Recovery Act proclaimed the intent of
Congress "to promote the organization of industry for the purpose
of cooperative action among trade groups."[28] The bill contained
sections providing for codes of fair competition that permitted and
even encouraged cooperative price fixing and market sharing and for
virtually complete exemption from antitrust laws. Section 7A was
designed to promote labor organization but was so diluted that very

[24]For a more complete discussion of the material covered in this section, see
E. K. Hunt, "A Neglected Aspect of the Economic Ideology of the Early New
Deal," *Review of Social Economy*, September 1971, pp. 180–192.
[25]Quoted in Allan G. Gruchy, *Modern Economic Thought: The American
Contribution* (Clifton, N.J.: Augustus M. Kelley, 1967), p. 408.
[26]Quoted in Arthur M. Schlesinger, Jr., *The Coming of the New Deal*
(Boston: Houghton Mifflin, 1965), p. 229.
[27]Schlesinger, op. cit., p. 98.
[28]Quoted in ibid., pp. 98–99.

often it promoted the formation of company unions. "If it [the NIRA] worked, Tugwell thought, each industry would end with a government of its own under which it could promote its fundamental purpose ('production rather than competition'). NIRA could have been administered, Tugwell later wrote, so that a 'great collectivism' would have channeled American energy into a disciplined national effort to establish a secure basis for well-being."[29]

In explaining the bill to the National Association of Manufacturers, General Hugh S. Johnson, the first head of the National Recovery Administration (NRA), declared that "NRA is exactly what industry organized in trade associations makes it." He further asserted that before the NRA the trade associations had about as much effectiveness as an "Old Ladies' Knitting Society; now I am talking to a cluster of formerly emasculated trade associations about a law which proposes for the first time to give them power."[30]

Most of the economics literature that appeared in 1934 recognized that the early New Deal reforms had not significantly extended government control over business. On the contrary, it had given voluntary trade associations the support of the government in forcing the controls of trade associations on all industry.[31]

This experiment in business self-government proved disastrous. The distinguished historian Arthur M. Schlesinger, Jr., has assessed the success of this phase of the early New Deal. With Schlesinger we concur:

> And the result of business self-government? Restriction on production, chiseling of labor and of 7A, squeezing out of small business, savage personal criticism of the President, and the general tendency to trample down everyone in the rush for profits. Experience was teaching Roosevelt what instinct and doctrine had taught Jefferson and Jackson; that, to reform capitalism you must fight the capitalists tooth and nail.[32]

The early New Deal philosophy underlying the NIRA was very quickly abandoned, and the NIRA was declared unconstitutional. The new paternalistic ideology of capitalism, however, was to receive more elaborate statements after World War II. (These state-

[29]Ibid., p. 108.

[30]Quoted in ibid., p. 110.

[31]See Leo Rogin, "The New Deal: A Survey of Literature," *Quarterly Journal of Economics*, May 1935, pp. 338, 346, 349-355. Typical of the comments of supporters of the early New Deal is this quotation from Tilly: "Here *industry* is setting up a legal and enforceable Golden Rule." Ibid., p. 351.

[32]Arthur M. Schlesinger, Jr., "The Broad Accomplishments of the New Deal," in Edwin C. Rozwenc, ed., *The New Deal: Revolution* (Lexington, Mass.: Raytheon/Heath, 1959), pp. 30-31.

ments and the later New Deal policies will be discussed in subsequent chapters.)

SUMMARY

The industrial warfare of the late nineteenth century led to an era of mergers and collusion among the giant corporations. Through collusion the few corporations that controlled an industry could act effectively as monopolists and maximize their joint profits. Where collusion was difficult, the corporations relied heavily on government regulatory agencies to help enforce mutual cooperation.

Within this economic and political context many ideologists of capitalism rejected classical liberalism because of its unrealistic assumptions. These thinkers created a new version of the Christian paternalist ethic that pictured the new industrial and financial magnates as beneficent, fatherly protectors of the public welfare.

This new ethic was to become particularly influential in the social and economic legislation of the early New Deal of the 1930s.

economic prosperity and evolutionary socialism

In the late nineteenth and early twentieth centuries, the socialist analysis of capitalism was profoundly affected by two developments: (1) the economic and political gains made by the working class and (2) the imperialistic carving up of the economically less developed areas of the world by the major capitalist powers. These developments split the socialist movement into two camps. Some became convinced that governmental power could be peacefully acquired by socialists and used to promote economic and social reforms that would result in a gradual evolution to socialism. The more militant socialists, however, continued to accept the Marxist view of the class nature of capitalist governments and to insist on the necessity of revolution. This chapter considers the economic and political gains of the working class and the resultant conservative reformist tendency in the socialist movement. Imperialism and revolutionary socialism will be discussed in the next chapter.

THE ECONOMIC AND POLITICAL GAINS OF THE WORKING CLASS

During the second half of the nineteenth century, the real income of workers rose throughout the capitalist world. In England the average real wage increased rapidly throughout the 1860s and early 1870s. By 1875, it was 40 percent higher than it had been in 1862.

After ten years in which wages sagged, they again rose sharply between 1885 and 1900. By 1900, the average real wage was 33 percent higher than in 1875 and 84 percent higher than in 1850. Most of the gains in real wages are attributable to the advent of mass production techniques that permitted the prices of many commodities consumed by laborers to be lowered. As a result of new methods of producing and labor's greater purchasing power, there was a fundamental change in patterns of consumption. Workingmen began to eat more meats, fruits, and sweets. Mass-produced shoes and clothing, furniture, newspapers, bicycles, and other new products came within the reach of many. Unquestionably, the average workingman's lot improved substantially during the period.

It should be mentioned, however, that averages can be misleading. Two late nineteenth-century social surveys revealed that about 40 percent of the working class in London and York still lived in abject poverty. The fact that this could be so after a half-century of rapid increases in average real wages gives an indication of the truly pitiful conditions that must have existed in the early nineteenth century.

Similar gains were being made in western Europe and the United States during this period, and in most of these countries economic gains were accompanied by political gains. Most of the industrialized capitalist countries had nearly complete male suffrage by the early twentieth century. Political parties were created that were devoted to furthering the cause of workingmen. The most successful of these was the German Social Democratic Party, formed at a meeting in Gotha in 1875 between the followers of Marx, led by Wilhelm Liebknecht and August Bebel, and the followers of Ferdinand Lassalle. The program adopted in this first party congress was known as the *Gotha Programme*. It represented a compromise that was bitterly attacked by Marx.

Marx believed his followers had made too many concessions to the Lassallian outlook, which conceived of the government as a neutral instrument to be used by workers to achieve socialism through peaceful reform. Excessive concern with reformism could, he believed, divert workers from their task of overthrowing capitalism. The conflict between the revolutionary socialists and the reformers was to remain important in the Social Democratic Party for the next 40 years. Ultimately Marx's misgivings proved prophetic, however, and the reformists became dominant in the party.

In 1874 the two socialist groups had polled 340,000 votes. In the election of 1877 the newly formed party received more than 500,000 votes and had 12 representatives elected to the Reichstag. This show of strength frightened Bismarck, and in 1878 a series of infamous anti-socialist laws was passed. Many of the more militant socialist leaders were exiled, and the Social Democratic Party was prohibited from holding meetings or publishing newspapers.

In spite of this repression the party continued to grow. It received 549,000 votes in 1884 and 763,000 in 1887. By 1890 the Social Democratic Party polled 1,427,000 votes and had become the largest single party in the Reich. The repression had not worked; the anti-socialist laws were abandoned.

In both England and Germany, as well as several other western European countries, it appeared to many socialists that the capitalist system had provided the workers with an escalator on which they could steadily and peacefully advance in both economic well-being and political power.

THE FABIAN SOCIALISTS

In England, despite the brilliant achievements of individual Marxists like William Morris, the socialist movement was largely non-Marxist. The Fabian Society was the primary influence on English socialism, and it rejected Marx's analysis completely. In their economic analysis the Fabians used orthodox neoclassical utility theory. They believed labor received an amount equal to what it produced, and capitalists and landlords received the value of what was produced with their capital and land. The chief cause of injustice was not that labor's surplus value was appropriated by capitalists but rather that all the income from ownership accrued to a tiny percentage of the population. The only way to achieve an equitable society would be to divide the income from ownership equally, and this could be done only through government ownership of the means of production.

On the issue of the nature and role of the government, the Fabians differed radically from Marx. For Marx, the government was an instrument of coercion controlled and used by the ruling class to perpetuate the privileges inherent in the capitalist system. The Fabians believed that, in a parliamentary democracy based on universal suffrage, the State was a neutral agency that could be freely used by the majority to reform the social and economic system. Because the working class was the majority in a capitalist economy, they were confident that, step by step, piecemeal reforms would strip away the privileges of the owning class and result in socialism achieved by peaceful evolution rather than violent revolution.

The most influential of the Fabians were George Bernard Shaw, Sidney and Beatrice Webb, and Graham Wallas. For many years Shaw was the principal draftsman of Fabian publications and was widely known as the society's most lucid and forceful spokesman. The worst evil of capitalism was, in Shaw's opinion, the enormous inequality of wealth and income that prevailed in every capitalist country. The cause of the most egregious inequity was the income that accrued from ownership of land and capital. Such unearned incomes, which Shaw combined under the label of "rents," created extremes of incredible wealth and power for a tiny minority while the majority of those who created the wealth lived in poverty. He also believed the capitalist system suffered from periods of chronic underproduction and incurred enormous wastes by devoting productive capacity to the creation of mountains of useless consumption goods for the rich. By expropriating these rents and eliminating the wastes and inefficiencies of capitalism, a socialist government could easily provide economic security and an ample livelihood for everyone.

The only ultimately just distribution of income was absolute equality. To achieve this, it would be necessary to sever any connection between productive services rendered and monetary remuneration. This, in turn, would require a reliance on noneconomic, or social, incentives to accomplish the necessary productive tasks. Shaw envisioned this equality not as an immediate possibility but only as a long-run goal.

Perhaps the least attractive aspect of Shaw's socialism was his extreme elitist bias. He had little faith in democracy. Rather, he believed an efficient and just organization of society required that policy making and administrative tasks be handled by experts. According to one eminent historian of socialism, Shaw "was apt to admire dictators, if only they would give the experts a free hand."[1]

Shaw's elitism was shown most clearly in his defense of British imperialism. He believed that

> no group or nation had any right to stand in the way of the full development in the interest of the whole world of any productive resource of which it stood possessed, and that accordingly higher civilizations had a complete right to work their will upon backward peoples and to override national or sectional claims, provided only that by doing so they increased the total wealth of the human race.[2]

In view of these opinions, Shaw's leadership of the pro-imperialist faction of the Fabian Society is easily understandable.[3]

Among the general public Shaw was probably the most influential of the Fabians. Within the Fabian Society itself, however, the most

---

[1]G. D. H. Cole, *A History of Socialist Thought*, vol. III, pt. 1 (London: Macmillan, 1956) p. 211.

[2]Ibid., p. 219.

[3]See Chapter 10, p. 132.

influential theoreticians were Sidney and Beatrice Webb. The Webbs were probably the most serious scholars in the Fabian Society and undoubtedly among the most prolific writers in the history of socialism.

One of their first and most influential books, *Industrial Democracy*, rejected the notion that workers might democratically manage their own industries under socialism. They believed workers had neither the desire nor the capability to run their enterprises. Rather, industrial democracy under socialism was envisioned as a scheme in which industry was controlled by professional managers, who, in turn, were to be made accountable to the general population through supervision by a democratically elected parliament, local governments, and consumers' cooperatives.

They rejected the idea that socialism would involve ownership of all industry by the national government. Ownership should reside both in the national government and in any of a variety of smaller local or regional administrative units. The scope of an enterprise's activities and the portion of the population affected by these activities should, they believed, determine the nature of social ownership of any particular business firm.

In *A Constitution for the Socialist Commonwealth of Great Britain*, they proposed the creation of two separate, democratically elected parliaments. One was to handle political affairs and the other to preside over social and economic affairs. In addition, they advocated a system of local governments based on local units with fixed geographic boundaries. These local governments, however, were to be combined in various ways to form administrative units to supervise and control different economic and social services. The particular size, shape, and location of these administrative units was to depend on the nature of the service involved.

In general, it may be said that the Webbs wrote a lot about the nature of the socialist society they would have liked to have seen created at some future time, but very little about specific tactics for transforming existing society into that future socialist system. They believed labor unions should confine their activities to representing the economic interests of their members in the collective bargaining process and should not act as insurgents. In fact, they seemed to see little hope for political change coming from a broadly based movement of workers. Rather, they assumed that an intellectual appeal might ultimately change the general public's opinions in a manner that would lead to the election of members of parliament who were sympathetic to socialist ideas.

The Fabian Society gradually succeeded in gaining influence in the parliamentary Labour Party. By 1918, the Labour Party had adopted a socialist program that reflected the Fabian Society's views and attitudes. By the 1920s, the Labour Party had formed a government, and the cause of socialism via the voting booth seemed to many to be on the road to triumph.

The Fabians had never wanted to be a mass membership society. They were a small, select group, and most of their efforts were devoted to educating the middle class to accept socialism. They published innumerable tracts exposing the poverty and injustice they found in early twentieth-century England. Remedies for these evils would be forthcoming through paternalistic government actions and programs, they believed, once the government was made truly democratic and the people were made aware of these conditions.

However debatable their certainty that socialism could be achieved through education, it is undeniable that the Fabians offered an impressive group of teachers. Some of the most brilliant of the English intellectual elite were members of the society, including, in addition to the Webbs and Shaw, H. G. Wells, Sydney Olivier, and Graham Wallas. With such sponsorship the Fabians' reformist, evolutionary socialism became eminently respectable. One could espouse socialism and still remain completely secure in a comfortable middle-class niche in English capitalistic society.

THE GERMAN REVISIONISTS

The German counterparts of the English Fabians were the revisionists. At the turn of the century the Social Democratic party was nominally a Marxist party. A large portion of the membership argued, however, that the course of history had proved Marx wrong on many issues and that a "revision" of Marx's ideas was necessary to make them relevant to German economic and social life. The most famous of the revisionists was Eduard Bernstein, who presented a detailed critique of Marxist ideas in his best-known work, *Evolutionary Socialism*, published in 1899. Bernstein maintained that capitalism was not approaching any kind of crisis or collapse and, indeed, had never been more viable. Marx was also wrong, Bernstein declared, in predicting the concentration of all industries in the hands of a few giant firms. He argued that enterprises of all sizes thrived and would continue to do so (despite the fact that corporate concentration and the cartel movement were more extreme in Germany than in any other capitalist country). Even if large trusts did dominate the economy, Bernstein insisted, there would be a "splitting up of shares," making petty capitalists of a very large percentage of the population, including many workers. He believed the economy had already gone far in this direction: "The number of members of the possessing classes is today not smaller but larger. The enormous increase of social wealth is not accompanied by a decreasing number of large capitalists, but by an increasing number of capitalists of all degrees."[4]

Furthermore, even workers who received no profits, rents, interest, or dividends were rapidly becoming much better off. Improvements in the general standard of living and the democratization of the government had made revolution not only highly unlikely but also morally undesirable. The hopes of the working class lay more "in a steady advance than in the possibilities offered by a catastrophic crash."[5]

Bernstein's book contained much more than the simple substitution of "peaceful evolution" for "revolution": It was, in fact, a direct attack on nearly all of the intellectual foundations of Marxism. Capitalism was not, he asserted, characterized by two polarized, conflicting classes. Class struggle could hardly be the moving force of history when class distinctions were rapidly breaking down and frequently nonexistent. Workers were far from being a homogenous mass, he argued, and therefore "the feeling of solidarity between groups of workers . . . is only very moderate in amount."[6] Instead of two fundamentally antagonistic classes, Bernstein saw a multiplicity of interest groups that were often in conflict but even more often united in a collective "community."

From his rejection of the class nature of capitalist society, it follows that Bernstein would have to reject Marx's theory of historical materialism. He argued that as society developed, economic forces came to be less and less important and ideological and ethical forces became increasingly significant.

> Modern society is much richer than earlier societies in ideologies which are not determined by economics and by nature operating as an economic force. Science, the arts, a whole series of social relations are nowadays much less dependent on economics than formerly they were; or let us say, in order to leave no room for misunderstanding, the point of economic development that has now been reached leaves the ideological, and especially the ethical, factors greater scope for independent activity than used to be the case. Consequently, the interdependence of cause and effect between technological, economic evolution and the evolution of other social tendencies is becoming continually more indirect; and accordingly the necessities of the former are losing much of their power to dictate the form of the latter.[7]

[4]Eduard Bernstein, *Evolutionary Socialism* (New York: Schocken Books, 1961 [first published in 1899]), p. xii.

[5]Ibid., p. xiv.

[6]Ibid., p. 120.

[7]Quoted in Cole, op. cit., p. 280.

He similarly rejected Marx's theory of surplus value. Marx had asserted that surplus value was created in the process of production by living labor alone. Bernstein simply dismissed this theory by stating that surplus value "can only be grasped as a concrete fact by thinking of the whole economy of society."[8] This, he believed, was a most damning criticism of Marx because the theory of surplus value was seen as the scientific basis for Marx's socialism. Henceforth, Bernstein averred, socialism would have to be based on ethical and not scientific foundations.

Perhaps the most fundamental difference between Marx and Bernstein was their difference concerning the nature of government in a capitalist society. Marx had asserted (and Bernstein's contemporary Marxist adversaries continued to assert) that capitalist governments were primarily instruments of class rule. Capitalists maintained their economic status and privileges through capitalistic property relations. They used their wealth, in turn, to control the political process in order to ensure the continuation of governments that were, above all else, committed to the defense of these property relations.

Bernstein dismissed the Marxist view of capitalist government as "political atavism." The Marxist notion may have once been valid, but contemporary extensions of suffrage had, he believed, invalidated it. Universal suffrage could make all people equally powerful in selecting the government and could thereby destroy class conflict by making each individual an "equal partner" in the community. "The right to vote," he wrote, "in a democracy makes its members virtually partners in the community, and this virtual partnership must in the end lead to real partnership."[9]

Thus Bernstein, like the Fabians, rejected the notion that the government in a capitalist society had an inherent class bias. In a capitalist democracy each worker was seen as an equal partner with each capitalist, and they could all be induced, through moral appeals, to use peaceful political means to promote the general interests of the entire community.

THE FATE OF EVOLUTIONARY SOCIALISM

Throughout the period from the publication of *Evolutionary Socialism* until the outbreak of World War I, Bernstein's ideas evoked intense controversy in the Social Democratic Party and also throughout the entire worldwide socialist movement. The issue at stake was of the utmost significance.

The Fabians and the Revisionists argued that persistence in legis-

[8]Bernstein, op. cit., p. 38.
[9]Ibid., p. 144.

lating reforms would ultimately achieve socialism. No single reform would, by itself, threaten the capitalist structure, but eventually the cumulative effect of many reforms would be the peaceful abdication of the capitalist class.

Marxists continued to believe, however, that as soon as any reforms seriously threatened the privileges and prerogatives of property rights, the capitalist class would resort to intimidation, repression, and ultimately abolition of the democratic rights of workers rather than seeing their economic power and social status eroded. When this happened, the working class would have to be prepared for revolution. If it were not, all of its hard-won concessions and advances would be lost.

By the beginning of World War I, it was obvious that the conservatives in the socialist movement had won at least a temporary victory over the revolutionaries. Capitalism in both England and Germany had passed through a period of prosperity in which the plight of workers had improved and a general feeling of optimism prevailed. In England the Fabian philosophy had come to dominate the Labour Party, and in Germany the Revisionists had gained control of the Social Democratic Party.

The subsequent history of those two parties was to illustrate the basic weakness of socialism that relied entirely on legislative reforms. Even though many party leaders continued to propound socialist ideas for some time, it was found that the pressure to attain an electoral majority continually forced party policies toward greater conservatism. In the 1950s both parties officially announced that they had given up the quest for social ownership of the means of production, distribution, and exchange. They asserted that ameliorative legislative to improve the living standards of the poor was all that remained to achieve a good and just society.

SUMMARY

In the late nineteenth and early twentieth centuries, improved working conditions, living standards, and political rights led to a split in the socialist movement. While the Marxist revolutionary socialists continued to affirm the necessity of a socialist revolution, a new school of reformist, evolutionary socialists argued that socialism could be achieved through gradual, peaceful legislative reforms.

In England, reformist socialism found its ablest leaders in George Bernard Shaw, Sidney and Beatrice Webb, and the other members of the Fabian Society. In Germany, it was Eduard Bernstein and the Revisionists who led the movement toward reformism. Both of these parties were ultimately pushed, by the pressures of achieving electoral majorities, to abandon the most fundamental tenet of socialism—socialization of the means of production.

imperialism and revolutionary socialism

The idea that a democratic government in a capitalist country could be used to effect a gradual and peaceful transition from capitalism to socialism led to a controversy that split the European socialist movement.[1] However, the issue of imperialism was of equal if not greater significance in precipitating this division among socialists. During the late nineteenth and early twentieth centuries, European economic imperialism was most intensive. The nature and importance of an appropriate socialist response to imperialism were issues that created profound divisions among socialists—divisions that persist to this day.

EUROPEAN IMPERIALISM

India was one of the earliest and most dramatic cases of European imperialism. The East India Company had traded extensively in India for 150 years before the conquest of Bengal in 1757. During this period India was relatively advanced economically. Its methods of production and its industrial and commercial organization could definitely be compared with those prevailing in western Europe. In fact, India had been manufacturing and exporting the finest muslins and luxurious fabrics since the time when most western Europeans were backward primitive peoples.

[1]See Chapter 9.

But after the conquest the East India Company became the ruling power in much of India, and the trade of the previous 150 years turned to harsh exploitation. It has been estimated that between 1757 and 1815 the British took between £500 million and £1000 million of wealth out of India.[2] The incredible magnitude of this sum can be appreciated only when compared with the £36 million that represented the total capital investment of all the joint stock companies operating in India.[3]

The policy of the East India Company in the last decades of the eighteenth century and in the early nineteenth century reflected two objectives. First, in the short run the myriad of greedy officials sought personal fortunes overnight: "These officials were absolute, irresponsible and rapacious, and they emptied the private hoards. Their only thought was to wring some hundreds of thousands of pounds out of the natives as quickly as possible, and hurry home to display their wealth. Enormous fortunes were thus rapidly accumulated at Calcutta, while thirty millions of human beings were reduced to the extremity of wretchedness."[4]

A British observer described this ruthless quest for wealth in similar terms: "No Mahratta raid ever devastated a countryside with the thoroughness with which both the Company [East India Company] and, above all, the Company's servants in their individual capacities, sucked dry the plain of Bengal. In fact, in their blind rage for enrichment they took more from the Bengali peasants than those peasants could furnish and live. And the peasants duly died."[5]

The second was a long-run goal: to discourage or eliminate Indian manufacturers and make India dependent on British industries by forcing the Indians to concentrate on raw materials and export them to supply the textile looms and other British manufacturers. The policy was brutally and methodically—and successfully—executed.

The total effect of this was that the British administration of India systematically destroyed all the fibres and foundations of Indian economy and substituted for it the parasitic landowner and moneylender. Its commercial policy destroyed the Indian artisan and created the infamous slums of the Indian cities filled with millions of starving and diseased paupers. Its economic policy broke down whatever beginnings there were of an indigenous

[2]Paul A. Baran, *The Political Economy of Growth* (New York: Monthly Review Press, 1962), p. 145.
[3]Ibid.
[4]Brooks Adams, *The Law of Civilization and Decay, An Essay on History* (New York: 1896); quoted in Baran, op. cit., p. 146.
[5]John Strachey, "Famine in Bengal," in Robert Lekachman, ed., *The Varieties of Economics*, vol. 1 (New York: Meridian, 1962), p. 296.

industrial development and promoted the proliferations of speculators, petty businessmen, agents, and sharks of all descriptions eking out a sterile and precarious livelihood in the meshes of a decaying society.[6]

It was only later, however, after the period of extensive railroad construction beginning in 1857, that the British thoroughly penetrated the interior of India. British investors who sank money into these railroads were guaranteed a 5 percent return by the government, which enforced a provision that if profits fell below 5 percent the Indian people would be taxed to make up the difference. Thus Indians were taxed to ensure that British investors would have adequate transport for further economic exploitation of the Indian interior.

Despite such harsh measures, the age of European imperialism really did not get under way on a broad, pervasive front until the last quarter of the nineteenth century. Between 1775 and 1875 the European countries had lost about as much colonial territory as they had won. The opinion was widely held that colonies were expensive luxuries.

All this changed suddenly and drastically after 1875. By 1900 Great Britain had grabbed 4,500,000 square miles, which she added to her empire; France had gobbled up 3,500,000; Germany, 1,000,000; Belgium, 900,000; Russia, 500,000; Italy, 185,000; and the United States, 125,000. Imperialism ran rampant as one-fourth of the world's population was subjugated and put under European and American domination.

Imperialism in Africa

By 1800, the Europeans had hardly penetrated beyond the coastal areas of Africa. By the early twentieth century, after a 100-year orgy of land grabbing and empire building, they controlled over 10 million square miles, or about 93 percent of the continent. In that gigantic rape, various European powers sought to acquire the abundant minerals and agricultural commodities of the Dark Continent.

The brutality of the European exploitation of Africa was perhaps most severe in the Belgian Congo. Belgian King Leopold II had sent H. M. Stanley into central Africa in 1879. Serving a private, profit-seeking company headed by Leopold and some of his associates, Stanley had a network of trading posts constructed and also duped native chiefs into signing "treaties" that established a commercial empire stretching over 900,000 square miles. Leopold set

[6]Baran, op. cit., p. 149.

himself up as sovereign ruler of the Congo Free State and proceeded to exploit the natural and human resources of the area for the profits of his company.

The exploitation was ruthless. Natives were forced, through outright physical coercion, to gather rubber from the wild rubber trees and ivory from the elephants. Leopold confiscated all land that was not directly cultivated by the natives and placed it under "government ownership." Atrocities of the worst sort were committed to force the natives to submit to a very burdensome tax system that included taxes payable in rubber and ivory as well as in labor obligations.

By the twentieth century the Congo had also become a rich source of diamonds, uranium, copper, cotton, palm oil, palm kernels, and coconuts. In general, it can be said that the Congo was one of the most profitable of European imperialistic exploits as well as one of the most scandalous.

The British grabbed the most populous and also the richest holdings in Africa. In 1870, Cecil Rhodes went to South Africa for his health. Within two years, his genius for organizing and controlling joint stock companies and his ability to corner the market on diamonds had made him a millionaire. In later years, the British South Africa Company, which Rhodes headed, came to control South Africa completely. Although it was a private, profit-seeking company, it had all the power of a government, including the authority (given in its charter of 1889) to "make treaties, promulgate laws, preserve the peace, maintain a police force, and acquire new concessions."

The expansionist policies of the British South Africa Company led to the Boer War (1899–1902), which crushed the Dutch republics (the Orange Free State and the Transvaal republic) and gave Britain complete control over all South Africa. South Africa proved to be a rich mining region. But the legacy of British and Dutch Imperialism is most vividly seen today in the suppression of the blacks, who constitute the vast majority of the population.

The other instances of imperialism in Africa are no less deserving of study. It must suffice in this short account, however, to mention that on the eve of World War I France held about 40 percent of Africa (much of it within the Sahara desert), England controlled 30 percent, and the remaining roughly 23 percent was divided among Germany, Belgium, Portugal, and Spain.

Imperialism in Asia

The results of the British takeover of India were evident by the turn of the twentieth century. In 1901 the per capita income was less than $10 per year; over two-thirds of the population were badly undernourished; most native Indian manufacturing had been either ruined or taken over by the British. Nearly 90 percent of the population struggled to subsist in villages where the average holding was only 5 acres and farming techniques were primitive. Much of the meager produce was paid out in taxes, rents, and profits that accrued to the British. Famine, disease, and misery were rife. In 1891 the average Indian lived less than 26 years and usually died in misery.

Much of the rest of Asia was also subjugated during this period. In 1878 the British overran Afghanistan and placed it under the Indian government, and in 1907 Persia was divided between Russia and Britain.

In 1858 the French had used the murder of a Spanish missionary as the rationalization for invading Annam, a tributary state of China. They soon established a French colony in what is now Vietnam. With this toehold the French succeeded, through war and intrigue in bringing all the territory of Indochina under their domination by 1887.

The Malay Peninsula and the Malay Archipelago (which stretches for nearly 3000 miles) were also carved up. The British grabbed Singapore and the Malay States, the northern part of Borneo, and southern New Guinea. Another part of New Guinea was taken by the Germans, and most of the remaining islands (an area comprising about 735,000 square miles) went to the Dutch.

AMERICAN IMPERIALISM

Throughout much of the nineteenth century American imperialism channeled all its energies into conquering the continent and exterminating the native American Indian population. The Samoa Islands were America's first overseas imperialist acquisition. In 1878, the natives of Pago Pago granted the Americans the right to use their harbor. Eleven years later, the islands had been conquered and divided between the United States and Germany.

Similarly, Pearl Harbor became a U.S. naval station in 1887. In a very short time American capitalists controlled most of Hawaii's sugar production. The tiny minority of white Americans soon revolted against Queen Liliuokalani's rule and, with the help of U.S. Marines, subjugated the native population. In 1898, Hawaii was officially annexed by the United States.

It was also in 1898 that the United States used the convenient sinking of the battleship *Maine* as an excuse to declare war on Spain and "liberate" the Cubans from Spanish oppression. Recognizing that it was no match for the United States, the Spanish government accepted every American demand, but the United States declared war anyway as a "measure of atonement" for the *Maine*. The

American victory gave it Puerto Rico, Guam, and the Philippine Islands outright, and the newly "independent" Cubans soon found American capitalists taking over most of their agriculture and commerce. Cuban independence had been restricted by a provision that the United States could intervene at its own discretion into Cuba's internal affairs "for the protection of life, property and individual liberty," a slogan that has been used to justify imperialism more than a few times. American troops invaded Cuba in 1906, 1911, and 1917 before secure control was finally established.

The Filipinos, who had been fighting for their independence from Spain, discovered the American brand no better than Spanish domination. President McKinley had decided that Americans were obligated "to educate the Filipinos and uplift and Christianize them"; but the Filipinos, who had been Roman Catholics for centuries, resisted American "Christianization." It took 60,000 American troops, as well as endless atrocities and concentration camps, before the Filipinos were finally "uplifted" and "educated."

In 1901, when the republic of Colombia refused to sell a strip of land (on which the Panama Canal was to be constructed) to the United States, President Roosevelt took action. A Panamanian insurrection was organized wtih American approval and help. United States warships were strategically placed to prevent Colombian troops from moving in to suppress the rebellion. The revolt started on November 3, 1903; on November 6, the United States extended diplomatic recognition to the "new nation"; on November 18, the United States had the Canal Zone on much more favorable terms than it had originally offered.

In 1904, President Roosevelt announced that the United States believed in the principle of self-determination for nations that acted "with reasonable efficiency and decency in social and political matters." He added, however, that "chronic wrongdoing, or any impotence which results in a general loosening of the ties of civilized society, may in America, as elsewhere, ultimately require intervention by some civilized nation. . . ."[7]

In 1909, U.S. Marines invaded Nicaragua to overthrow José Santos Zelaya, who had threatened American economic concessions there. American troops were back in Nicaragua in 1912. In 1915 American Marines invaded Haiti, and in 1916 American troops overwhelmed the Dominican Republic and established a military government there.

By World War I the United States had seized or otherwise controlled Samoa, Midway Island, Hawaii, Puerto Rico, Guam, the

[7]Quoted in G. C. Fite and J. E. Reese, *An Economic History of the United States,* 2d ed. (Boston: Houghton Mifflin, 1965), p. 472.

Philippines, the island of Tutuila, Cuba, Santo Domingo, Haiti, Nicaragua, and the Panama Canal Zone.

IMPERIALISM AND
EVOLUTIONARY SOCIALISM

The Boer War jolted British public opinion and resulted in strong conflicts among many radicals and socialists. On the one hand, it produced an abundance of jingoist sentiment and imperialist ideology that influenced some socialists; but on the other, J. A. Hobson's *Imperialism: A Study* caustically ridiculed this sentiment and ideology and advanced a theory of imperialism that was to have a profound influence on Marxists and many non-Marxist socialists.

Imperialism, according to Hobson, was a struggle for political and economic domination of areas of the world occupied by "lower races." Its "economic tap-root" was the necessity for advanced capitalist countries to find markets for goods and capital produced domestically but for which there was inadequate domestic demand. Evoking traditions of nationalism and militarism, it could "appeal to the lust of quantitative acquisitiveness and of forceful domination surviving in a nation from early centuries of animal struggle for existence."[8]

The basic cause of the deficiency in domestic demand was, Hobson believed, a severely inequitable distribution of income that resulted in a distorted allocation of resources, which led, in turn, to the quest for foreign markets. Hobson argued that the imperialist tendencies of the late nineteenth and early twentieth centuries could be reversed only by reform radical enough to effect a more equitable distribution of income. He summarized his position succinctly in the following passage:

> There is no necessity to open up new foreign markets; the home markets are capable of indefinite expansion. Whatever is produced in England can be consumed in England, provided that the "income," or power to demand commodities, is properly distributed. This only appears untrue because of the unnatural and unwholesome specialization to which this country has been subjected, based upon a bad distribution of economic resources, which has induced an overgrowth of certain manufacturing trades for the express purpose of effecting foreign sales. If the industrial revolution had taken place in an England founded upon equal access by all classes to land, education, and legislation, specialization in manufactures would not have gone so far. . . . ; foreign

[8]Quotations in this paragraph are from J. A. Hobson, *Imperialism: A Study* (London: Allen & Unwin, 1938 [first published in 1902]), p. 368.

trade would have been less important though more steady; the standard of life for all portions of the population would have been high, and the present rate of national consumption would probably have given full, constant, remunerative employment to a far larger quantity of private and public capital than is now being employed.[9]

The issue of whether publicly to denounce English imperialism bitterly divided the Fabians. Sydney Olivier's insistence that the society's executive committee issue a pronouncement condemnnig the Boer War in particular and imperialism in general was rejected by one vote, but the committee agreed to the demand that the issue be put to a general vote.

Led by George Bernard Shaw, the pro-imperialist faction argued that small, backward nations could not manage their own affairs and should not be considered as nations at all, and that the advanced European nations thus had a duty to police and manage the internal affairs of these backward peoples for their own welfare. The debate was bitter. Finally, 45 percent of the membership voted to condemn English imperialism, and 55 percent opted to approve of or ignore imperialism. Immediately, 18 members of the society, including several of its most prominent personalities, handed in their resignations.

The sentiments of the German Revisionists were similar to those of the Fabians, the majority either approving of European imperialism or not considering it a proper issue on which to take a stand. Bernstein, for example, wrote: "Only a conditional right of savages to the land occupied by them can be recognized. The higher civilization ultimately can claim a higher right."[10] Orthodox Marxists, however, were virtually unanimous in condemning imperialism, which they analyzed as only the latest stage in the historical development of capitalism: Capitalists were forced by the mounting contradictions of the economic system to turn frantically to economic exploitation of more backward areas.

ROSA LUXEMBURG'S
ANALYSIS OF IMPERIALISM

Rosa Luxemburg was one of the most important political leaders and exponents of orthodox Marxism. Her book *The Accumulation of Capital* contained a description and analysis of imperialism that

---

[9]Ibid., pp. 88–89.
[10]Eduard Bernstein, *Evolutionary Socialism* (New York: Schocken Books, 1961 [first published in 1899]), p. xii.

was to exert a strong influence on subsequent generations of socialists.

Luxemburg began her analysis by a review of Marx's analysis of the process of *capitalist commodity production*,[11] the process in which capitalists started with some given amount of money and purchased one commodity—labor power—and then sold a different commodity—that produced by labor in the production process. From the sales of the products of labor, they received a greater value than they laid out in expenses for raw materials, goods in process, and labor; that is, they received surplus value, or profits. The money they received in sales, however, had to be spent by purchasers of their commodities.

These purchasers of their commodities could be the laborers spending their wages for the means of subsistence, or other capitalists buying the raw materials and goods in process necessary for production. But we have already said that in order for surplus value to exist the proceeds from sales of commodities must exceed wages and expenditures on raw materials and goods in process. Part of the difference might be made up by capitalists' expenditures on consumption. Luxemburg observed, however, that capitalists' consumption expenditures typically make up only a small part of the surplus value they receive.

Another part of the deficiency in expenditures could be made up by capitalists purchasing capital goods that were not necessary to maintain the current level of production but were desired so that future production could be expanded. But the desire to expand production would have to be predicated on the expectation of greater demand for consumption goods, and it was the insufficiency of this demand for consumption goods that represented the crux of the problem. Capitalists would accumulate capital goods not for their own sake but only in the expectation that this accumulation would increase their profits. The inescapable conclusion, for Luxemburg, was that from within the internal sphere of a capitalist economy the expenditures of capitalists and workers could not for any lengthy period be sufficient to permit continuous realization of the surplus value generated from expanding commodity production.

But capitalism had been more or less continually expanding for well over a century, and Luxemburg sought to discover the source of the necessary additional expenditures that made this expansion possible. This source she found in the historical tendency of the capitalist mode of production to continually expand into noncapitalist areas, bring these areas under its control, and incorporate them within the domain of capitalist relations. The expenditures of these

[11]See pp. 79–81.

noncapitalist areas in the purchase of commodities produced in capitalist areas would represent the additional necessary demand:

> From the aspect both of realizing the surplus value and of procuring the material elements of constant capital, international trade is a prime necessity for the historical existence of capitalism —an international trade which under actual conditions is essentially an exchange between capitalistic and non-capitalistic modes.[12]

Luxemburg therefore believed that "imperialism is the political expression of the accumulation of capital in its competitive struggle for what remains still open of the non-capitalist environment."[13] The continuous diminution of the size of the unexploited noncapitalist areas of the world had led to a situation in which "imperialism grows in lawlessness and violence, both in aggression against the non-capitalist world and in ever more serious conflicts among the competing capitalist countries."[14]

Within this theoretical framework Luxemburg wrote penetrating and insightful descriptions of the way in which the development of capitalism necessitated the growth of nationalism, militarism, and racism. In her analysis of military spending, for example, she understood the dual function such spending served in protecting capitalist empires around the world while providing the necessary stimulation of aggregate demand at home:

> . . . the multitude of individual and insignificant demands for a whole range of commodities . . . is now replaced by a comprehensive and homogeneous demand of the state. And the satisfaction of this demand presupposes a big industry of the highest order. It requires the most favorable conditions for the production of surplus value and for accumulation. In the form of government contracts for army supplies the scattered purchasing power of the consumers is concentrated in large quantities and, free of the vagaries and subjective fluctuations of personal consumption, it achieves an almost automatic regularity and rhythmic growth. Capital itself ultimately controls this automatic and rhythmic movement of militarist production through the legislature and a press whose function is to mould so-called "public opinion." That is why this particular province of capitalist accumulation at first

---

[12]Rosa Luxemburg, *The Accumulation of Capital* (New York: Monthly Review Press, 1964) p. 359..
[13]Ibid., p. 446.
[14]Ibid.

seems capable of infinite expansion. All other attempts to expand markets and set up operational bases for capital largely depend on historical, social and political factors beyond the control of capital, whereas production for militarism represents a province whose regular and progressive expansion seems primarily determined by capital itself.

In this way capital turns historical necessity into a virtue.[15]

This passage was written in 1913. This level of clear understanding of the role of military expenditures was not widely achieved among economists until about a half-century later, when the forces Luxemburg was describing had developed well beyond what they had been on the eve of World War I.[16]

Despite such brilliant insights, Luxemburg's analysis of imperialism rested on a faulty theoretical structure. Noncapitalist consumers are not automatically a source of increased demand. If products are to be sold to them, products must also be purchased from them—otherwise they would have no foreign currency with which to make the purchases. The net result on aggregate demand from this buying and selling cannot be determined in advance. Moreover, in less developed countries capitalist investments are soon yielding surplus value of their own. This tends to worsen rather than solve the problem of adequate demand.

Luxemburg's problem was that she focused on the wrong problem—underconsumption. The real driving force of imperialism was the search for profitable investment outlets to which the advanced capitalist countries could export capital. These deficiencies in the Marxist analysis of imperialism were corrected by Lenin.

LENIN'S ANALYSIS OF IMPERIALISM

The most famous and influential socialist analysis was contained in Lenin's pamphlet *Imperialism: The Highest Stage of Capitalism*, published in 1916. Lenin attempted "to show, as briefly and as popularly as possible, the principal economic characteristics of imperialism."[17] The most important was that in the imperialistic phase of capitalist development the capitalist economies were thoroughly dominated by monopolies, a development Marx had correctly foreseen. By monopolies Lenin did not mean industries consisting of only one firm (the modern economic definition of monopoly); rather, he

---

[15]Ibid., p. 466.

[16]For a further discussion of the importance of military expenditures in increasing domestic aggregate demand, see Chapter 11.

[17]*Imperialism: The Highest Stage of Capitalism* (London: Lawrence & Wishart, 1939), p. 1.

referred to industries dominated by trusts, cartels, combinations, or a few large firms.

Drawing heavily on the German experience, Lenin argued that the development of monopolies was closely related to important changes in the banking system. Banks had assumed a position of central importance in the drive toward cartelization and had come to exercise considerable control over many of the most important industrial cartels. This control was so extensive that Lenin spoke of the imperialistic phase of capitalism as the age of "finance capital."

Banks were able to mobilize huge sums of money for investment, but persistent downward pressures on domestic profit rates dictated that investment outlets be sought outside the home country. Lenin, unlike Hobson, did not believe the necessity to export commodities was the most important economic cause of imperialism. Rather, it was the necessity to export capital. Backward areas offered a large and inexpensive labor force and lucrative investment prospects.

In the imperialist phase of capitalism the various governments fought to gain access to privileged and protected markets for the combines and cartels within their own political boundaries. At the same time, these national combines and cartels sought to partition the world markets through international cartels. Deep-seated rivalry and competition, however, were more important than opportunistic short-run collaborations. Persistent national conflicts and wars were the inevitable result. In Lenin's words,

> The epoch of the newest capitalism shows us that certain relations are being established between capitalist combines, *based* on the economic division of the world; while parallel with this and in connection with it, certain relations are being established between political alliances, between states, on the basis of the territorial division of the world, of the struggle for colonies, of the "struggle for economic territory."[18]

Such a situation was, Lenin believed, inherently unstable. Imperialism would lead to wars among the advanced capitalist countries and to rebellions and revolutions in the exploited areas. As long as the capitalist system could support its imperialistic thrust, however, it would prolong its existence by providing outlets for excess investment funds. The extra profits that imperialism secured for the home country meant that the wages paid its workers could be raised. Thus, because it shared in the spoils, labor would be at least temporarily sapped of its revolutionary potential and controlled by right-wing labor leaders, "justly called social imperialists."[19]

18Ibid., p. 69.
19Ibid., p. 99.

If imperialism expanded the domain of capitalism and in doing so prolonged the system's existence, the tensions and conflicts it engendered were, Lenin believed, more severe than those of the competitive capitalism about which Marx wrote. Capitalism was still doomed, and socialism was still the wave of the future.

SUMMARY

The late nineteenth and early twentieth centuries witnessed the imperialistic carving up of most of the world's economically underdeveloped areas. The inhabitants of these areas were harshly and cruelly exploited for the profits of large corporations in the advanced capitalist countries.

The issue of imperialism split the evolutionary socialist movement. Many of the reform socialists, such as George Bernard Shaw and Eduard Bernstein, were strongly pro-imperialist. Others, among them J. S. Hobson, were strongly anti-imperialist. Hobson's analysis of imperialism stressed the maldistribution of wealth and income as the causes of this socioeconomic phenomenon. He advocated reforms to redistribute income and wealth within the capitalist framework.

Virtually all Marxist socialists opposed imperialism. Rosa Luxemburg saw the root problem as inadequate aggregate demand. Although her theoretical framework had some weaknesses, she had brilliant insights into the nature of imperialism, nationalism, racism, and militarism. Her weaknesses were corrected in Lenin's *Imperialism: The Highest Stage of Capitalism*. He stressed the importance of investment outlets and the capitalists' need to export capital. His analysis has remained the most influential Marxist critique of imperialism.

keynesian economics and the great depression

While the period from the Civil War to 1900 was one of rapid economic expansion in the United States, these accomplishments were dwarfed by the growth that occurred between 1900 and 1929. The following figures show the percentage increase in manufacturing production in several key industries between 1899 and 1927.[1]

Chemicals, etc.	239%
Leather and products	321
Textiles and products	449
Food products	551
Machinery	562
Paper and printing	614
Steel and products	780
Transportation and equipment	969

It has been estimated that U.S. wealth (the market values of all economic assets) reached $86 billion by 1900; in 1929, it stood at $361 billion.

This spectacular growth gave the United States a huge edge over all other countries in manufacturing output. The American prosperity of the 1920s was based on high and rising levels of output—though there were recessions in 1923 and 1927. The gross national product, the value of all goods and services produced, increased by

[1]Figures taken from Leo Huberman, *We the People* (New York: Monthly Review Press, 1964), p. 254.

62 percent from 1914 to 1929. Only 3.2 percent of the labor force was unemployed in 1929, and labor productivity rose during that decade at least as fast as wages. Between 1921 and 1929, total automobile registrations increased from less than 11 million to more than 26 million; consumers spent tens of millions of dollars on radios, refrigerators, and other electric appliances that had not been available before. American manufacturing seemed to most people a permanent cornucopia destined to create affluence for all.

This leadership in manufacturing was associated with financial leadership in the world economy. The American economic empire began to rival that of England. By 1930 American businessmen owned large investments around the world. The following figures give the values of these investments in 1930.[2]

Canada	$3,942,000,000
Europe	4,929,000,000
Mexico and Central America	1,000,000,000
South America	3,042,000,000
West Indies	1,233,000,000
Africa	118,000,000
Asia	1,023,000,000
Oceania	419,000,000

THE GREAT DEPRESSION

But this era of rapid growth and economic abundance came to a halt on October 24, 1929. On that "Black Thursday" the New York stock market saw security values begin a downward fall that eventually was to destroy all faith in business. Their confidence undermined, businessmen cut back production and investment. This decreased national income and employment, which, in turn, worsened business confidence even more. Before the process came to an end, thousands of corporations had gone bankrupt, millions were unemployed, and one of the worst national catastrophes in history was under way.

Between 1929 and 1932 there were over 85,000 business failures; more than 5,000 banks suspended operations; stock values on the New York Exchange fell from $87 billion to $19 billion; unemployment rose to 12 million, with nearly one-fourth of the population having no means of sustaining themselves; farm income fell by more than half; and manufacturing output decreased by almost 50 percent.[3]

America had plunged from the world's most prosperous country

---

[2]Ibid., p. 251.
[3]Figures taken from Louis M. Hacker, *The Course of American Economic Growth and Development* (New York: Wiley, 1970), pp. 300–301.

to one in which tens of millions lived in desperate, abject poverty. Particularly hard hit were the blacks and other minority groups. The proportion of blacks among the unemployed was from 60 to 400 percent higher than the proportion of blacks in the general population.[4] Certain geographic areas suffered more than others. Congressman George Huddleston of Alabama reported in January 1932:

> We have about 108,000 wage and salary workers in my district. Of that number, it is my belief that not exceeding 8,000 have their normal incomes. At least 25,000 men are altogether without work. Some of them have not had a stroke of work for more than 12 months, maybe 60,000 or 75,000 are working one to five days a week, and practically all have had serious cuts in their wages and many of them do not average over $1.50 a day.[5]

Many cities reported that they could give relief payments for only a very short time, often one week, before people were forced to their own devices to subsist. The executive director of the Welfare Council of New York City described the plight of the unemployed:

> When the breadwinner is out of a job he usually exhausts his savings if he has any. Then, if he has an insurance policy, he probably borrows to the limit of its cash value. He borrows from his friends and from his relatives until they can stand the burden no longer. He gets credit from the corner grocery store and the butcher shop, and the landlord forgoes collecting the rent until interest and taxes have to be paid and something has to be done. All of these resources are finally exhausted over a period of time, and it becomes necessary for these people, who have never before been in want, to ask for assistance. The specter of starvation faces millions of people who have never before known what it was to be out of a job for any considerable period of time and who certainly have never known what it was to be absolutely up against it.[6]

The abject despair of these millions of people is at best suggested by a 1932 report describing the unloading of garbage in the Chicago city garbage dumps: "Around the truck which was unloading garbage and other refuse were about 35 men, women and children. As

---

[4]See Lester V. Chandler, *America's Greatest Depression* (New York: Harper & Row, 1970), pp. 40–41.

[5]U.S. Congress, Senate, Hearings before a subcommittee of the Committee on Manufactures, 72d Cong., 1st sess., p. 239.

[6]Quoted in Chandler, op. cit., pp. 41–42.

soon as the truck pulled away from the pile all of them started digging with sticks, some with their hands, grabbing bits of food and vegetables."[7]

What had happened to reduce the output of goods and services so drastically? Natural resources were still as plentiful as ever. The nation still had as many factories, tools, and machines. The people had the same skills and wanted to put them to work. And yet millions of workers and their families begged, borrowed, stole, and lined up for a pittance from charity, while thousands of factories stood idle or operated far below capacity. The explanation lay within the institutions of the capitalist market system. Factories could have been opened and men put to work, but they were not because it was not profitable for businessmen to do this. And in a capitalist economy production decisions are based primarily on the criterion of profits, not on people's needs.

THE ECONOMICS OF KEYNES

The socialist cause gained many enthusiasts in the 1930s. While the capitalist world was suffering what was perhaps its most severe depression, the Soviet economy was experiencing rapid growth. When the depression struck, it was a traumatic shock to many Americans, who had come to believe their country was destined to achieve unparalleled and unending increases in material prosperity.

The capitalist economic system seemed to be on the verge of total collapse. Drastic countermeasures were essential, but before the system could be saved the malady had to be better understood. And to that task came one of the most brilliant economists of this century: John Maynard Keynes (1883–1946). In his famous book *The General Theory of Employment, Interest and Money*, Keynes attempted to show what had happened to capitalism so that it could be preserved.

Keynes began his analysis by looking at the process of production. In a given production period a firm produces a certain dollar volume of goods. From the proceeds of the sale of these goods, it pays its costs of production, which include wages, salaries, rent, supplies and raw materials, and interest on borrowed funds. What remains after these costs are paid is profit.

The important point to remember is this: What is a cost of production to the business firm represents income to an individual or another firm. The profit is also income—the income going to the owners of the firm. Because the value of production is exhausted by the costs of production and profits, and all these are income, it fol-

[7]Quoted in Huberman, op. cit., p. 260.

lows that the value of what has been produced must be equal to the incomes generated in producing it.

In terms of the entire economy the aggregate picture is the same as that for the individual firm: The value of everything produced in the economy during any period is equal to the total of all incomes received in that period. Therefore, in order for businesses to sell all that they have produced, people must spend in the aggregate all their incomes. If an amount equal to the total income in society is spent on goods and services, then the value of production is realized in sales. In that case profits remain high, and businessmen are willing to produce the same amount or more in the succeeding period.

Keynes called this a *circular flow:* Money flows from businesses to the public in the form of wages, salaries, rents, interests, and profits; this money then flows back to the businesses when the public buys goods and services from them. *As long as businesses sell all they have produced and make satisfactory profits*, the process continues.

But this does not happen automatically. When money flows from businesses to the public, some of it does not flow directly back to businesses. The circular flow has leakages. To begin with, all people do not spend all their incomes. A percentage is saved, usually in banks, and therefore withdrawn from the spending stream. This saving may be offset by other people, who borrow money from banks and spend more than their income. Keynes, however, pointed out that at the peak of prosperity saving is usually greater than consumer borrowing; thus there is usually net saving, or a net leakage, from circular income-expenditure flow.

Keynes also identified two other leakages: (1) People buy goods and services from foreign businesses, but the money spent on these imports cannot be spent on domestically produced goods. (2) The taxes people pay are also withdrawn from the income-expenditure flow.

These three leakages (saving, imports, and taxes) may be offset by three spending injections into the income-expenditure flow: (1) Imports can be offset by exports. They are exactly offset when foreigners buy goods produced in the United States in amounts equal to foreign imports purchased by Americans. (2) The government uses taxes to finance the purchase of goods and services. If it uses all taxes for this purpose and balances the budget, then government expenditures will exactly offset taxes in the spending stream. (3) If businessmen wish to expand their capital, they can finance investment in capital goods by borrowing the funds that were saved. Investment, then, may exactly offset the saving leakage.

If these three injections into the income-expenditure flow are just as large as the three leakages, then spending equals the value of production. Everything that has been produced can be sold, and prosperity reigns.

Keynes, however, believed it was unlikely that the process could continue uninterrupted for very long. Investment, which is necessary to absorb savings, enlarges the capital stock and hence increases the economy's productive capacity. In order to utilize the new productive capacity fully, production and income must increase in the next period. But with the higher income there will be more saving, which necessitates more investment; and this investment is by no means automatically forthcoming.

Keynes saw that individuals with higher incomes saved a higher percentage of their incomes than those with low incomes. He concluded that this pattern would hold for the whole society. As the aggregate income of society increases, total savings increase more than proportionately. In other words, at each new higher level of income a larger percentage of income is saved.

Thus investment would have to increase at a faster rate than income if it were to continually offset saving. Only this rapid increase would permit businesses to sell everything they produced; but the faster investment grows, the more rapid is the increase in productive capacity. Because of this, the economy must invest ever-greater amounts (both absolutely and relatively) in each successive period if the balance is to be maintained. However, according to Keynes, in any mature private enterprise economy the number of profitable investment outlets is limited. Hence, as the process of economic growth continues, the difficulty of finding sufficient investment outlets becomes more and more acute.

If it becomes impossible to find enough investment outlets, then investment falls short of saving and total expenditures for goods and services fall short of the value of those produced. Businesses, unable to sell all they have produced, find that their inventories of unsold goods are increasing. Each business sees only its own problem: that it has produced more than it can sell. It therefore reduces production in the next period. Most businesses, being in the same situation, do the same thing. The results are a large reduction of production, a decrease in employment, and a decline in income. With the decline in income, however, even less will be spent on goods and services in the next period. So businessmen find that even at the lower level of production they are unable to sell all they have produced. Again they cut back production, and the downward spiral continues.

Under these circumstances businesses have little or no incentive to expand their capital goods (because excess capacity already exists), and therefore investment falls drastically. Expenditures of all types plummet. As income declines, saving declines more than proportionately. This process continues until the declines in income have reduced saving to the point where it no longer exceeds the reduced level of investment. At this low level of income equilibrium is restored. Leakages from the income-expenditure flow are again equal to the injections into it. The economy is stabilized, but at a level where high unemployment and considerable unused productive capacity exist.

Keynes' analysis was not, in its essentials, drastically different from those offered by Marx (Chapter 6) and Hobson (Chapter 10). The principal cause of a depression was, in the opinion of all three thinkers, the inability of capitalists to find sufficient investment opportunities to offset the increasing levels of saving generated by economic growth. Keynes' unique contribution was to show how the relation of saving to income could lead to a stable but depressed level of income with widespread unemployment.

Marx (and Lenin) had believed the disease incurable under capitalism. Hobson had prescribed measures to equalize the distribution of income and thereby reduce saving as a cure. Could Hobson's prescription work? This probably is not a very meaningful question. In most industrial capitalist countries wealth and economic power determine political power, and those who wield power have never been willing to sacrifice it to save the economic system.

In the United States, for example, of the 300,000 nonfinancial corporations existing in 1925 the largest 200 made considerably more profit than the other 299,800 combined. The wealthiest 5 percent of the population owned virtually all the stocks and bonds and received over 30 percent of the income. Needless to say, this 5 percent dominated American politics. In these circumstances speculating about what would happen if the income and wealth were radically redistributed amounts to mere fanciful daydreaming.

Keynes' answer to the problem was more realistic. Government could step in when saving exceeded investment, borrow the excess saving, then spend the money on socially useful projects. These projects would be chosen in order not to increase the economy's productive capacity or decrease the investment opportunities of the future. This government spending would increase the injections into the spending stream and create a full-employment equilibrium. In doing so, it would not add to the capital stock. Therefore, unlike investment spending, it would not make a full-emplopment level of production more difficult to attain in the next period. Keynes summarized his position thus:

Ancient Egypt was doubly fortunate, and doubtless owed to this its fabled wealth, in that it possessed *two* activities, namely, pyramid-building as well as the search for precious metals, the fruits of which, since they could not serve the needs of many by being consumed, did not stale with abundance. The Middle Ages built cathedrals and sang dirges. Two pyramids, two masses for the dead, are twice as good as one; but not so two railways from London to York.[8]

What types of expenditures ought the government to make? Keynes himself had a predilection toward useful public works such as the construction of schools, hospitals, parks, and other public conveniences. He realized, however, that this would probably benefit middle- and lower-income recipients much more than the wealthy. And because the wealthy have the political power, they would probably insist on policies that would not redistribute income away from them. He saw that it might be politically necessary to channel this spending into the hands of the large corporations, even though little that was beneficial to society would be accomplished directly. He wrote:

> If the Treasury were to fill old bottles with banknotes, bury them at suitable depths in disused coalmines which are then filled up to the surface with town rubbish, and leave it to private enterprise on well-tried principles of laissez faire to dig the notes up again . . . there need be no more unemployment. . . . It would indeed be more sensible to build houses and the like; but if there are political and practical difficulties in the way of this, the above would be better than nothing.[9]

The depression of the 1930s dragged on until the outbreak of World War II. From 1936 (the year Keynes' *General Theory* was published) to 1940, economists hotly debated the merits of his theory and policy prescriptions. When the various governments began to increase armament production rapidly, however, unemployment began to melt away. During the war years, under the stimulus of enormous government expenditures, conditions in most capitalist economies were rapidly transformed from a situation of severe unemployment to one of acute labor shortage.

The American armed forces mobilized 14 million people, who had to be armed, quartered, and fed. Between 1939 and 1944 the output of the manufacturing, mining, and construction industries doubled, and productive capacity increased by 50 percent. The American economy produced 296,000 planes, 5,400 cargo ships, 6,500 naval vessels, 64,500 landing craft, 86,000 tanks, and 2,500,000

---

[8]J. M. Keynes, *The General Theory of Employment, Interest and Money* (New York: Harcourt Brace Jovanovich, 1936), p. 131.
[9]Ibid., p. 129.

trucks.[10] During the war period the most pressing problem was a *shortage* of labor, as contrasted with the 19 percent unemployment that existed as late as the beginning of 1939.

KEYNESIAN ECONOMICS AND IDEOLOGY

Most economists believed this wartime experience had proved the basic correctness of Keynes' ideas. Capitalism could be saved, they proclaimed, by wise use of the government's powers to tax, borrow, and spend money. Capitalism was again a viable social and economic system.

But viability alone was insufficient as an ideology for capitalism. The USSR did not have unemployment in the 1930s, and its spectacular rate of growth during this period had proved the viability of the Soviet economic system. This challenge elicited a resurgence of the older neoclassical economic ideology. These older theories were cast in an esoteric and highly elaborate mathematical framework. Typical of the new economists was Paul A. Samuelson, whose book *The Foundations of Economic Analysis* is among the technically most formidable treatments of economics.[11] In 1947 The American Economic Association awarded him the first John Bates Clark Medal for the most outstanding contribution to economics made by an economist under 40 years of age. The book was also instrumental in securing the Nobel Prize in economics for Samuelson in 1970.

Samuelson has made an even more significant contribution in terms of his influence on the dominant economic ideology of capitalism in the past 25 years. His introductory text, *Economics*, has undergone nine editions, has been translated into almost every major language, and has sold millions of copies.[12] The first edition set out mainly to explain and simplify Keynes' ideas. Each subsequent edition has tended to bring in more of the traditional neoclassical ideology of capitalism. In 1955 Samuelson offered his "grand neoclassical synthesis," an integration of Keynesian with neoclassical economics. The Keynesian theory would provide the knowledge necessary to maintain a full-employment economy, and the market system could operate within this Keynesian framework to allocate resources according to the time-honored principles of the neoclassical ideology. Almost every student of economics in the past 25 years has learned his elementary economics from Samuelson's textbook or from one of the many others that have attempted to copy his approach and content.

[10] All figures taken from Hacker, op. cit., p. 325.
[11] Paul A. Samuelson, *The Foundations of Economic Analysis* (Cambridge, Mass.: Harvard University Press, 1947).
[12] Paul A. Samuelson, *Economics* (New York: McGraw-Hill, 1948).

THE EFFICACY OF
KEYNESIAN ECONOMIC POLICIES

After 1945, Keynesian economics became orthodoxy for both economists and the majority of politicians. Almost 3 million veterans were
demobilized in that year. In 1946, another 11 million joined the
civilian labor force. Congress and many economists feared a new
depression and immediately took steps to apply the new Keynesian
ideas. Passage of the Employment Act of 1946 legally obligated the
government to use its taxing, borrowing, and spending powers to
maintain full employment. The act declared that "it is the continuing
policy and responsibility of the Federal government to use all prac-
ticable means . . . for the purpose of creating and maintaining . . .
conditions under which there will be afforded useful employment
opportunities, including self-employment, for those able, willing, and
seeking to work, and to promote maximum employment, production
and purchasing power." This was the first time the U.S. government
ever acknowledged responsibility for employment, and it is still not
really committed to full employment for all people.

Have Keynesian economic policies worked? The answer to this
question is very complex. Since World War II there have been no
major depressions in the United States, but there have been five recessions (the modern euphemism for a mild depression). In 1948–
1949, a recession lasted for 11 months; in 1953–1954, for 13 months;
in 1957–1958, for 9 months; and in 1960–1961, for 9 months. The
1969–1971 recession went on for over two years.

Because of these recessions, the economy's performance in the
1950s left much to be desired. The real rate of growth of GNP was
2.9 percent, which does not compare very favorably with the 4.7
percent for 1920–1929 or the 3.7 percent for 1879–1919. The bright-
est spot in the American economy's performance has been the
growth rate in the 1960s, which averaged around 5 percent.

Unemployment for the 1950s and early 1960s averaged 4.5 percent, although it dipped to 3.5 percent in the mid-1960s. Moreover,
inflation has been a persistent problem since World War II. From
1945 through 1968 the average annual increase in wholesale prices
was 3.8 percent (most of which occurred in the late 1940s); the rate
of increase from 1968 to 1970 was nearly 5 percent. The 1969–1971
inflation was accompanied by an economic recession in which unemployment soared to rates of over 6 percent. The simultaneous
occurrence of both high unemployment and a high rate of inflation
led to President Nixon's attempt to freeze wages and prices in late
1971, followed by government control over increases in wages and
prices.

Economists like Samuelson argued that Keynesian policies, reflected in enormous government spending, resulted in the impressive

growth performance of the 1960s; but they find the accompanying inflation quite mysterious. Before judging this performance, however, it is necessary to see what the American government substituted for the pyramids of Egypt and the cathedrals of the Middle Ages. In 1960 one observer wrote: "A central aspect of our growth experience of the past two decades is one which few spokesmen for the future candidly discuss. This is the fact that our great boom did not begin until the onset of World War II, and that its continuance since then has consistently been tied to a military rather than to a purely civilian economic demand."[13]

THE WARFARE ECONOMY

In 1940, military-related expenditures were $3.2 billion, or 3.2 percent of GNP. In 1943, at the height of World War II, military spending gobbled up almost 40 percent of GNP, while profits rose to unprecedented heights. The war provided capitalists with a clear example of how government military spending can end a depression and guarantee large returns to capital.

By 1947, military spending was back to only $9.1 billion, or 3.9 percent of GNP. During the rapid growth of the 1960s, military expenditures grew at approximately the same rate as GNP. If other expenses that are related to militarism but not included in the "defense" budget are taken into account, the total has been close to 15 percent in recent years.[14] The United States has spent and continues to spend more on militarism than any other country—more in absolute terms, relative terms, and per capita.

The result of these enormous expenditures has been the growth of the *military-industrial complex* as a necessary adjunct to economic prosperity. Its essential features have been described as follows:

> The warfare state we have constructed over the last two generations has a large clientele. At the top of the pyramid is the so-called military-industrial complex. It comprises, first, the Defense Department of the Federal Government, along with such satellites as the CIA and NASA. The admirals and generals, the space scientists and the intelligence men, like all government bureaucrats, are busily engaged in strengthening their influence. To this end they cultivate congressmen and senators, locate military establish-

---

[13]Robert Heilbroner, *The Future as History* (New York: Harper & Row, 1960), p. 133.

[14]See, for example, Daniel R. Fusfeld, "Fascist Democracy in the United States," *Conference Papers of the Union for Radical Economics*, December 1968, pp. 11, 34–35.

ments in politically strategic districts, and provide legislators with special favors. Former military men are drawn into the net of influence through the Army and Navy associations and through veterans' organizations. The military are supported by the industrial side of the complex. These are the large corporations on whom the military depend for the hardware of modern war. Some sell the bulk of their output to the military, like North American Aviation, Lockheed Aircraft, General Dynamics, McDonnell-Douglas, and Thiokol Chemical. Others are important military suppliers but make the bulk of their sales in civilian markets, such as Western Electric, Sperry Rand, General Electric, or IBM. Others, such as Dupont and General Motors, are only occasionally military contractors.[15]

The extent to which military production dominates the American economy is indicated by a recent survey showing that the five key military-related industries accounted for 7.9 percent of all employment in New York, 12.3 percent in New Jersey, 13 percent in Texas, 14.6 percent in Massachusetts, 15.7 percent in Maryland, 20.9 percent in Florida, 23.4 percent in Connecticut, 30 percent in Kansas, 31.4 percent in California, and 34.8 percent in Washington.[16]

Military expenditures operate in exactly the way Keynes believed pyramid building operated in the ancient Egyptian economy. For generals and most politicians, a tenfold overkill potential is twice as good as a fivefold overkill; two ABM (antiballistic missile) systems are twice as good as one but only half as good as four. And if the public cannot be easily convinced of this, the immense amount of research financed by the military-industrial complex comes to the fore. Weapons and delivery systems are rapidly superseded by new models. Horror stories convince the public that a further escalation of the arms race is necessary and that "obsolete" (and often unused) models must be scrapped.

Military spending keeps the capital goods industry operating near full capacity without raising the economy's productive capacity as rapidly as would be the case if they provided capital goods for industry. Demand does not tend to drop below supply as persistently as it formerly did; military spending increases demand without increasing productivity.

The neglect of these effects of the Keynesian military-induced prosperity is perhaps "the most important abdication of any by the economists."[17] This type of economic theory has led to "an ahistori-

[15]Ibid., p. 13.
[16]Ibid., p. 15.
[17]Sumner M. Rosen, "Keynes Without Gadflies," in T. Roszak, ed., *The Dissenting Academy* (New York: Random House, Vintage Books, 1968), p. 83.

cal, a technical or mechanical, a nonpolitical view of what the economy is and how it works."[18]

Very few Keynesian economists have been willing to come to
grips with the implication of militarism as a tool of economic policy.

> The arms economy has been the major Keynesian instrument of
> our times. But its use has been cloaked as "national interest," its
> effects have been largely undermined, its international conse-
> quences largely deleterious and destabilizing, its importance mak-
> ing for uncritical acceptance and dependence by large segments
> of the society, its long-run effects hardly glanced at. The arms
> economy has done much more than distort the use of scarce cre-
> ative scientific and engineering talent. . . . It has forced us to
> neglect a whole range of urgent social priorities, the consequences
> of which threaten the fabric of our society.[19]

SUMMARY

The severity of the Great Depression of the 1930s caused many
economists to become dissatisfied with the orthodox neoclassical
economists' view that unemployment was merely a short-run, ephemeral "adjustment" to a temporary disequilibrium situation. Keynes'
new ideas were rapidly accepted by most important economists.
World War II proved that massive government intervention in the
market economy could create full employment; indeed, Hitler's
Germany had already established this in the 1930s.

Since the war the United States has not had a major depression.
Most economists agree that massive government spending is largely
responsible for this improved performance of American capitalism.
Critics have argued, however, that the social price of this prolonged
prosperity has been the creation of a military-industrial complex that
currently threatens the entire fabric of American society.

If this view is correct, then it is possible to conclude that Keynes'
theories enabled the neoclassical ideology to come to grips with the
most important economic problem of the 1930s but have obscured
if not worsened other problems. Some of these problems and some
contemporary ideologies of capitalism will be examined in Chapter 12.

[18]Ibid., p. 85.
[19]Ibid., pp. 86–87.

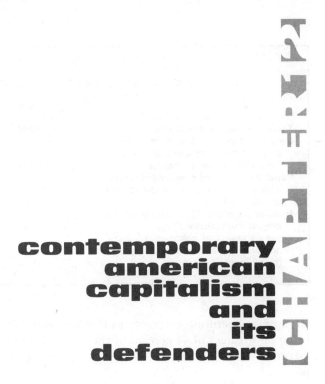

contemporary american capitalism and its defenders

Since World War II the American economy has experienced five mild recessions, albeit its growth has been fairly satisfactory by historical standards. Gross national product, in constant (1958) dollars, grew from $355 billion in 1950 to $727 billion in 1969. Disposable personal income, again in constant (1958) dollars, grew from $250 billion to $512 billion over the same period.[1] Although the growth rate was slightly below the historical average in the 1950s, it was well above average in the 1960s.

The technological advances of American capitalism have been particularly impressive. For several decades before World War I, the increases in output per man-hour in American industry had been about 22 percent per decade. After World War II, output per man-hour increased by 35–40 percent per decade.[2] This growth was made possible by huge expenditures on research and development, which increased from $3.4 billion in 1950 to $12 billion in 1960; fully half of these funds came from the federal government.

With these improvements in technology and increases in production has come a greater concentration of economic power in the hands of a very small number of corporations. In 1929, the 100

[1]Figures taken from *Federal Reserve Bulletin*, August 1970, pp. A68–A69.

[2]Louis M. Hacker, *The Course of American Economic Growth and Development* (New York: Wiley, 1970), p. 326. The increases in productivity in the 1920s had been even more impressive, however.

	1966	1967	1968
TABLE 12.1			
LARGE MERGERS AND ACQUISITIONS, 1966–1968			
Total number of acquisitions	1746	2384	4003
Number of acquired manufacturing and mining companies with more than $10 million in assets	101	169	192
Value of assets of acquired companies with more than $10 million in assets (in billions)	$4.1	$8.2	$12.6
Number of acquisitions made by 200 largest companies	33	67	74
Value of assets of companies acquired by 200 largest companies (in billions)	$2.4	$5.4	$6.9

largest manufacturing corporations had legal control (actual control being far greater) of 44 percent of the net capital assets of all manufacturing corporations. By 1962, this figure had increased to 58 percent.[3]

In 1962 there were 420,000 manufacturing enterprises. But a mere 5 of these enterprises owned 12.3 percent of all manufacturing assets; 20 owned 25 percent of the total. The total assets of the 20 largest firms were approximately as large as those of the 419,000 smallest companies combined. These 20 giants took a whopping 38 percent of all after-tax profits, leaving the smallest 419,980 to divide 62 percent. Furthermore, among the 180,000 *corporations* involved in manufacturing, the net profits of the 5 largest were nearly twice as large as those of the 178,000 smallest corporations.[4]

The rate of concentration has quickened. In every year since 1959, there have been more than 60 mergers a year involving the acquisition of companies with over $10 million in assets. The number of mergers increased throughout the sixties. Table 12.1 illustrates this trend.[5] From 1968 to 1970, the evidence points to an ever-faster rate of acquisition. The process of increasing economic concentration, which began about 100 years ago, continues unabated today.

[3]Gardiner C. Means, "Economic Concentration," in *Hearings Before the Subcommittee on Antitrust and Monopoly of the Committee on the Judiciary, United States Senate* (Washington, D.C.: GPO, July 1964), pp. 9–19.

[4]Willard F. Mueller, "Economic Concentration," *Hearings,* op. cit., pp. 111–129.

[5]Table constructed from data of the Federal Trade Commission, derived by Paul Sweezy and Harry Magdoff, in "The Merger Movement: A Study in Power," *The Monthly Review,* June 1969, pp. 1–5.

The post-World War II prosperity has not reduced the extremes of inequality in the United States. In the most complete study of the distribution of ownership of wealth ever undertaken,[6] it has been shown that the wealthiest 1.6 percent of the population owns over 80 percent of all corporate stock and virtually all state and local government bonds. Moreover, the concentration of ownership of these income-yielding assets has steadily increased since the early 1920s.

The distribution of income reflects the same extreme inequality. Despite the economy's impressive growth over the past three decades —and the much-publicized war on poverty of the early 1960s, which proved to be a half-hearted minor skirmish—poverty has remained an acute problem in the United States. In 1970, for example, 25.5 million Americans lived in families that had an annual income of less than $3900, the officially designated "poverty level."[7] The U.S. Bureau of Labor Statistics (BLS) reported that with the high prices that prevailed in 1970 it would require about $7100 for a family of four to live with "a sense of self-respect and social participation."[8] Thus most of these 25.5 million persons lived on less than half the amount necessary to generate "self-respect." Tens of millions more lived on less than $7100.

In stark contrast to this widespread poverty, the wealthiest 5 percent of the American population received over 20 percent of all income. At the top of this 5 percent was the elite 1.6 percent that owns most of the income-yielding stocks and bonds in the United States. The richest of the elite had incomes estimated between $50 million and $100 million per year (the latter amounts to about $275,000 per day).

Furthermore, taxes do little, if anything, to reduce the inequities in the distribution of income. It is commonly supposed that the U.S. tax system reduces inequality by taking a higher percentage of the income of the wealthy than is taken from the poor. The personal income tax does tend to reduce income inequalities, but the effect is much smaller than most people imagine. When economists analyze the total tax burden, however, they find that taxes actually increase inequality in the distribution of income because sales taxes, excise taxes, property taxes, and social security taxes all take a much larger percentage of the poor man's income than of the rich man's.

One economist, a recognized authority on taxes, has analyzed the total tax burden on incomes along the entire distribution spectrum. He found that families with incomes below $2,000 per year—certainly

[6]Robert J. Lampman, *The Share of Top Wealth-holders in National Wealth, 1922–1956* (Princeton, N.J.: Princeton University Press, 1962).

[7]*Los Angeles Times,* May 8, 1971, pt. I, p. 1.

[8]Ibid., December 21, 1970, pt. I, p. 18.

a level of abject poverty—paid out one-third of their income in taxes. As incomes got higher, people paid a lower percentage of their income in taxes. For example, families making between $10,000 and $15,000 paid out a proportion of their income that was nearly one-third lower than that paid by families with incomes below $2,000. Only among the wealthiest 5 percent of families did the total tax bite exceed that exacted from the poorest. The wealthy elite actually paid out, on the average, 36.3 percent of their income for taxes, a mere 3 percent higher than the poorest segment of society paid.[9]

Thus it appears that on the one hand American capitalism in the past three decades has proved fairly successful if judged solely by the criteria of economic growth and productivity (although there has been persistent unemployment and inflation). On the other hand, the extreme inequalities in the distribution of wealth and income have continued and even grown worse. It is not surprising, therefore, that these decades have seen numerous ideological defenses of American capitalism as well as socialist and radical critiques of the U.S. economy.

CONTEMPORARY
CLASSICAL LIBERAL IDEOLOGY

Neoclassical economics was the principal purveyor of the classical liberal ideology of capitalism during the late nineteenth and early twentieth centuries. Since the 1930s, neoclassical economics has become more and more complex mathematically, which has enabled modern economists to gain many new theoretical and scientific insights. Its most important assumptions, however, those on which the entire theory rests, are still metaphysical in character. They have not been established on a scientific basis, either empirically or theoretically.

The finest summary of contemporary neoclassical economics is C. E. Ferguson's *The Neoclassical Theory of Production and Distribution*.[10] The mathematical reasoning in this book is so complex that very few people other than professional economists who are thoroughly competent in higher mathematics can understand it. Professor Ferguson is aware, however, of the tenuous nature of many of the assumptions of this ideology, which, like the medieval religious ideology of feudalism, ultimately must be accepted on faith

[9]B. A. Musgrave, "Estimating the Distribution of the Tax Burden," in *Income and Wealth*, ser. 10 (Cambridge, England: Bowes & Bowes, 1964), p. 192.

[10]C. E. Ferguson, *The Neoclassical Theory of Production and Distribution* (London: Cambridge University Press, 1969).

alone. He admits this and asserts his personal faith: ". . . placing reliance upon neoclassical economic theory is a matter of faith. I personally have the faith; but at present the best I can do to convince others is to invoke the weight of Samuelson's authority. . . ."[11]

When the thrust toward esoterica removed classical liberal ideology from the level at which it could be widely understood, however, it also substantially reduced its effectiveness as a popular ideology of capitalism. To promote widespread popular acceptance of the ideology has been the task of numerous organizations. The best-known American organizations, which propagate a simplified, more popular version of the classical ideology, are the National Association of Manufacturers (NAM), the Foundation for Economic Education, the Committee for Constitutional Government, the U.S. Chamber of Commerce, and the American Enterprise Association.

A congressional committee found that out of $33.4 million spent "to influence legislation" $32.1 million was spent by large corporations. And of this $32.1 million about $27 million went to such organizations as those mentioned in the previous paragraph.[12] The NAM uses this money to publish a large amount of probusiness propaganda, including "an educational literature series, labor and industrial relations bulletins, news bulletins, a magazine of American affairs, and numerous studies on legislation, education, anti-trust laws, tariffs and unions."[13]

The Foundation for Economic Education reviews and distributes books that reflect the classical liberal ideology of capitalism and publishes and distributes, free of charge, a monthly journal, *The Freeman*, which propagates this ideology. The other organizations engage in numerous publishing and promotional activities designed to inculcate the same ideology as widely as possible.

The popularized statement of the classical ideology lays principal stress on the benefits of the free market. It is argued that the forces of supply and demand in a free market will always lead to results that are preferable to anything that could be achieved by the government or a central planning agency. The NAM, for example, asserts that the proper function of the government is to strengthen

---

[11]Ibid., pp. xvii–xviii. Professor Ferguson's candid admission was prompted by a rather esoteric debate among academic economists. The debate proved conclusively that some of the most fundamental tenets of neoclassical orthodoxy were untenable. For a summary of the conclusions of the debate, see E. K. Hunt, "Religious Parable Versus Economic Logic: An Analysis of the Recent Controversy in Value, Capital and Distribution Theory," *Inter-Mountain Economic Review,* (Fall 1971; also see sec. III of E. K. Hunt and Jesse Schwartz, *Critique of Economic Theory* (London: Penguin, 1972).

[12]R. Joseph Monsen, Jr., *Modern American Capitalism* (Boston: Houghton Mifflin, 1963), p. 19.

[13]Ibid.

and "make more effective the regulation by competition."[14] Almost none of its literature, however, suggests much concern with the concentration of corporate power. Rather, the main economic problems are the powers of big labor unions and the "socialistic" welfare measures of the government.

In essence, most of this literature uses a drastically simplified version of some of the classical and neoclassical economists' analyses. It supports the view that any conceivable threat to the operation of the free market, whether real or potential, is an evil to be avoided at any cost. These organizations have had considerable success in propagating this point of view, particularly among small businessmen. (Big business, however, generally continues to look with favor on government intervention because it usually benefits from such actions.)

CONTEMPORARY VARIANTS OF THE CLASSICAL LIBERAL IDEOLOGY

Most critics of the classical liberal ideology emphasize its failure to come to grips with the realities of the concentration of immense power in the hands of considerably less than 1 percent of all corporations. Several attempts have been made to construct an ideology that retains the competitive, private enterprise flavor of classical liberalism while recognizing the existence of concentrated corporate power. Two of these will be discussed: the *countervailing power* ideology, associated primarily with the economist John Kenneth Galbraith, and the *people's capitalism* ideology, associated primarily with Professor Massimo Salvadori.

In his famous book *American Capitalism, the Concept of Countervailing Power*, Professor Galbraith recognized the existence of large, special interest power blocks in the American economy but argued then that they should not be of much concern because "private economic power begets the countervailing power of those who are subject to it."[15] The result of this newly created countervailing power is "the neutralization of one position of power by another."[16]

Thus strong unions neutralize strong business firms in the field of labor relations, and strong buyers' associations neutralize the monopolistic or oligopolistic powers of strong sellers. The result, then, is a kind of market equilibrium or invisible hand that harmonizes the

---

[14]National Association of Manufacturers, Economic Principles Commission, *The American Individual Enterprise System, Its Nature and Future* (New York: McGraw-Hill, 1946), p. 57.

[15]John Kenneth Galbraith, *American Capitalism, the Concept of Countervailing Power* (Boston: Houghton Mifflin, 1956), p. 4.

[16]Ibid., p. 1.

interests of all. The harmonious whole is now simply made up of a few neutralized giants rather than numerous, atomistically competitive small firms.[17]

Another influential attempt to show the innocuous (or even beneficial) nature of corporate concentration was made by Professor Salvadori, who used the slogan "people's capitalism" to characterize what he believed to be the most essential feature of contemporary American capitalism: diffusion of ownership. The widespread diffusion of ownership of corporate stock, as well as other types of assets, means to Salvadori that capitalism is no longer a system where a tiny minority reaps most of the privileges but one in which the majority are rapidly becoming capitalists and getting a share of the privileges.[18] Salvadori has conveniently summarized his people's capitalism ideology:

> At present in the United States there are nearly half a million corporations; stockholders total about ten million (1959). Their numbers have increased rapidly in the post-war period. Standard Oil of New Jersey, for instance, had about 160,000 stockholders in 1946; twelve years later there were three times as many, close to half a million. As a rule, the larger the corporation the more widely spread the ownership. Large corporations in which a majority of shares are owned by an individual or by a family are fewer and fewer. It is already exceptional for a single individual to own more than four or five per cent of the stock of a given corporation. Unincorporated non-farm businesses number about four million; they belong to one or more individuals and this means millions of "capitalists." Nearly four million farmers (three-fourths of the total) are full owners or part owners of the farms they cultivate. Even considering that there is a good deal of overlapping among the three groups (shareholders, individual non-farm owners, farmers) one can say that at least one-fourth to one-third of all American families share the ownership of natural and artificial capital. There are also half a million independent professional people—lawyers, doctors, architects, engineers, accountants, etc.—whose other means of production are not only equip-

---

[17]It should be mentioned that Professor Galbraith has published several books since *American Capitalism, the Concept of Countervailing Power* appeared. Even a cursory reading of these books shows that he has altered his opinions fundamentally. Nevertheless, because the ideology of countervailing power has been very influential, and because most of this influence flows from his book, we are justified in associating this ideology with his name.

[18]This is curiously similar to socialist Eduard Bernstein's idea, discussed in Chapter 9.

ment of one kind or another but also skill and training, and whose income is related to the capital invested in acquiring professional efficiency; they are "capitalists" just as much as owners of natural and artificial capital. Most other families own durable consumer goods (houses, summer cottages, furniture, cars, electrical appliances, etc.), federal, state, and municipal bonds, insurance policies and savings to the extent that they can consider themselves "capitalists."[19]

Thus bigness of corporations does not, for Salvadori, appear to be an issue. Ownership is becoming more equitably distributed because most people are becoming "capitalists," and hence, by implication, none is powerful enough to exploit another. Disciples point out that by 1970 there were approximately 30 million stockholders. In this view the United States is becoming a nation where the majority are capitalists.

Even many defenders of capitalism concede that Salvadori's analysis serves only to obscure the nature of the concentration of economic power in the United States and that it neither eliminates nor justifies this concentration. A. A. Berle, Jr., a distinguished scholar of American capitalism as well as a corporation executive, has written:

> In terms of power, without regard to asset positions, not only do 500 corporations control two-thirds of the non-farm economy, but within each of that 500 a still smaller group has the ultimate decision-making power. That is, I think, the highest concentration of economic power in recorded history. . . . Since the United States carries on not quite half of the manufacturing production of the entire world today, these 500 groupings—each with its own little dominating pyramid within it—represents a concentration of power over economies which makes the medieval feudal system look like a Sunday school party.[20]

Contrary to the tone of this quotation, Berle is not a critic of American capitalism but one of the most important developers of a contemporary corporate, or collective, ideology of capitalism. Other conservatives have admitted that a very small percentage of all the millions of stockholders hold most corporate stock.

---

[19]Massimo Salvadori, *The Economics of Freedom* (Garden City, N.Y.: Doubleday, 1959), pp. 70–71.
[20]A. A. Berle, Jr., "Economic Power and the Free Society," in Andrew Hacker, ed., *The Corporation Take-Over* (Garden City, N.Y.: Doubleday, 1965), p. 97.

THE CONTEMPORARY CORPORATE
ETHIC AND CAPITALIST IDEOLOGY

The tactics of the late nineteenth-century robber barons led most people to reject the corporate ideology (discussed in Chapter 8). Their destructive competition and financial wheeling and dealing hardly supported the conclusion that they were becoming socialized stewards of the public welfare. And yet the classical liberal ideology had no real defense for the existing concentration of economic and political power. The Christian paternalist ethic, with its emphasis on the benevolence of the powerful, was still the only successful ideological defense of great inequalities of wealth and power.

It was simply not credible to cast the nineteenth-century capitalist in a kindly, paternalistic role. But some twentieth-century ideologists of capitalism have argued that capitalism has changed so drastically that capitalists have lost their importance in the system and have been replaced by a new class of professional managers. These theories envision this "new man," the professional manager, as the paternalistic steward of public welfare.

In 1932 A. A. Berle and G. C. Means published an important and influential book, *The Modern Corporation and Private Property*.[21] In it they argued that ownership of most of the colossal corporate giants had become so widely diffused that the owners of stock had lost or were rapidly losing control of these corporations. With no single owner holding more than 1 or 2 percent of the stock and with no effective ways of colluding, the owners were left with only the formal voting function when selecting the board of directors. Candidates for whom they could vote were selected by the existing board of directors. Thus the boards chose their own replacements and were essentially a self-perpetuating oligarchy. They wielded power but had no necessary connection with the owners of stock. They were not capitalists in the usual sense of the term.

In 1955 Berle wrote another book, *The Twentieth Century Capitalist Revolution*, in which he argued that corporations had developed a quasipolitical status. Managers were motivated primarily by the desire to promote the general public interest in their decision making, and any who were not so motivated would be forced by public opinion and the threat of government intervention so to act. This view has been widely accepted. Another economist, for example, wrote:

No longer the agent of proprietorship seeking to maximize return on investment, management sees itself as responsible to stock-

[21]A. A. Berle and G. C. Means, *The Modern Corporation and Private Property* (New York: Macmillan, 1932).

holders, employees, customers, the general public, and, perhaps most important, the firm as an institution. . . . There is no display of greed or graspingness; there is no attempt to push off onto workers or the community at large part of the social costs of the enterprise. The modern corporation is a soulful corporation.[22]

The corporation was "soulful," of course, because in this economist's opinion its managers were conscientious, paternalistic stewards of society's welfare.

The managerial ideology was spelled out in some detail in a series of lectures delivered by prominent corporation managers at Columbia University in 1956. According to the chairman of General Electric, the lectures were intended "to coax us businessmen out of our offices and into the arena of public thought where our managerial philosophies can be put to the test of examination by men trained in other disciplines."[23]

One of the dominant themes in these lectures was that because American capitalism is "new," the complaints men may once have had against capitalism are no longer justified. Thus the chairman of Sears Roebuck asserted: "The historic complaint that big business, as the producing arm of capitalism, exploited the many for the profit of the few and deprived the workers of the products of their own labor had a valid basis in the facts of European capitalism, but lacks substance when applied to American capitalism today."[24]

Another theme was the justification of bigness on the grounds of better efficiency and higher quality. "The American public," asserted the chairman of U.S. Steel, "has gradually become accustomed to larger and larger groups and has become convinced that big production groups are outstanding in reliability and in the quality of their products and services and are necessary to perform America's larger production tasks in research, in production, and in the procurement of raw materails."[25]

Finally, the businessmen all saw managers as "professional" men who are as much concerned with "customers, share owners. employees, suppliers, educational institutions, charitable activities, government and the general public" as with sales and profits. They believed that managers "all know that special power imposes special responsibilities on those who hold it." Most managers, they asserted, fully accept "their responsibilities for the broader public welfare."[26]

[22]Carl Kaysen, "'The Social Significance of the Modern Corporation," *American Economic Review*, May 1957, pp. 313–314.
[23]Quoted in Robert L. Heilbroner, *The Limits of American Capitalism* (New York: Harper & Row, 1966), p. 30.
[24]Ibid., pp. 31–32.
[25]Ibid., p. 32.
[26]Quotations in this paragraph are all from ibid., pp. 32–33.

Since 1942 this corporate managerial ideology has been assiduously disseminated by the Committee for Economic Development (CED). The CED readily accepted big business and also "the fact that government was big and was constantly growing bigger and that there was no returning to a simpler, happier past in this respect. It believed that the question was not *how much* government should do, but *what* it should do."[27] Government should not only accept all the duties assigned to it by the classical liberal ideology but also follow Keynesian policies to ensure stable full employment. Further, government should cooperate with corporate management in resolving conflicts and maintaining the tranquil, stable atmosphere within which management can effectively perform its public-spirited, paternalistic function of promoting the public welfare.[28]

Big business and big government are accepted by this ideology as not only inevitable but also necessary for maximum efficiency. Big labor unions are also accepted as long as they recognize that most of their legitimate interests are in harmony with those of business and management.

Another important propagator of the managerial ideology has been the U.S. Information Agency (USIA), the official government agency charged with the worldwide propagandizing of the "American point of view." The USIA operates on a grand scale. Its Voice of America broadcasts are heard around the world daily in scores of languages, and it publishes dozens of newspapers and magazines, maintains libraries, shows motion pictures, and engages in countless other propaganda operations.

Arthur Larson, who "was a semi-official ideolgist to the Eisenhower Administration and a former head of the U.S. Information Agency,"[29] published a book, *What We Are For*,[30] in which he explained the philosophy of USIA propaganda. In the modern capitalist economy, Larson argued, the government should do only what "needs to be done" and cannot be done "as well" by private businesses.[31] Modern capitalism has a multitude of powerful interest groups, such as big business, big unions, big government, and so forth, that have no major or basic conflicts. Rather, their interests harmonize, and they mutually support each other. Larson assumed both that business managers are motivated primarily by the desire to promote social welfare to meet the "basic political and economic needs of all people"[32] and that businesses operate more efficiently

[27]Karl Schriftgiesser, *Business Comes of Age* (New York: Harper & Row, 1960), p. 224.
[28]See Monsen, op. cit., pp. 25–29.
[29]Ibid., p. 42.
[30]Arthur Larson, *What We Are For* (New York: Harper & Row, 1959).
[31]Ibid., pp. 16–17.
[32]Monsen, op. cit., p. 45.

than government. There is therefore a built-in preference for a minimal role for government in the economy.[33]

CRITICISMS OF
CONTEMPORARY CAPITALIST IDEOLOGIES

Criticisms of capitalism have often gone hand-in-hand with criticisms of capitalist ideologies. In the remainder of this chapter
criticisms of the ideologies of capitalism will be examined. Some of
the principal criticisms of contemporary American capitalism will
be discussed in Chapter 13.

Criticisms of Neoclassical Ideology

Neoclassical economics completely dominated orthodox academic
economics in the late nineteenth and early twentieth centuries. From
the 1930s on, however, it came increasingly under attack. In 1938
Oscar Lange and Fred M. Taylor published their significant book
On the Economic Theory of Socialism.[34] Lange and Taylor accepted the neoclassical argument that a "purely" and "perfectly"
competitive economy will lead to an "optimum allocation of
resources," but they also showed that such an economy need not be
a capitalist one. They demonstrated that a socialist economy, in
which the means of production were collectively owned, could
also operate (through perfect planning or decentralized decision
making) in a state of "optimal economic efficiency." Private ownership had absolutely no formal or theoretical importance in the
neoclassical theory. Furthermore, under socialist ownership, they
argued, the inequities of income distribution under a capitalist
system would disappear.

The conclusion that many people drew from this book was that
the neoclassical liberal ideology could be used equally as well (if
not better) as an ideology of socialism. This was, indeed, a radical
undermining of neoclassical economics as an ideology defending
capitalism.

The classical liberal ideology was rejected by many, however,
because it seemed to present a severely distorted picture of the
realities of twentieth-century capitalism. Its basic assumption of
pure competition—that no buyers or sellers were large enough to
affect prices—was patently ridiculous. Moreover, it had little or
nothing to say about the important problem of pollution of the

---

[33]Larson, op. cit., p. 17.

[34]Oscar Lange and Fred M. Taylor, *On the Economic Theory of Socialism*
(Minneapolis: University of Minnesota Press, 1938). Lange had published his
essay two years eariler in *Review of Economic Studies*, October 1936, pp. 53–
71, and February 1937, pp. 123–142.

environment. Economists also established that simple countercyclical policies of the Keynesian variety were insufficient to obviate the problems of capitalism's cyclical instability[35] and cannot cope with inflation.

The *coup de grâce* came in J. De V. Graaff's tightly reasoned *Theoretical Welfare Economics*.[36] Graaff showed that economists had not really appreciated the long and restrictive list of assumptions necessary for the optimally efficient allocation of resources envisioned in the model of a competitive, free-market capitalism to be realized. He cited 17 such assumptions,[37] many of which were so restrictive and unrealistic that Graaff concluded that "the measure of acceptance . . . [this theory] has won among professional economists would be astonishing were not its pedigree so long and respectable."[38]

A few of Graaff's 17 conditions will suffice to illustrate his point. Neoclassical ideology requires that any individual's welfare is identical with his preference ordering. In other words, children, dope addicts, fiends, criminals, and lunatics, as well as all other people, always prefer that which is best for them. Neoclassical theory also requires that neither risk nor uncertainty is ever present. In the opinion of many, this book completely destroyed the basis for the economic analysis on which the classical liberal ideology was constructed.

Criticisms of the Managerial Ideology

The managerial ideology has also come under extensive criticism. Many economists (including several in the neoclassical tradition) argue that bigness on the scale of American big business cannot be shown to be related to efficiency or better service. Giant corporations are much larger than maximum productive efficiency would dictate. These economists contend that a drastic reduction in the size of many corporate giants would greatly increase productive efficiency.[39] Examples like the electric power industry's competition with the Tennessee Valley Authority (TVA), the oligopolistic airlines' struggle with small, unscheduled competitors, and the

[35]On this last point see Milton Friedman, "The Effects of a Full Employment Policy on Economic Stability: A Formal Analysis," in *Essays in Positive Economics* (Chicago: University of Chicago Press, 1953, and William J. Baumol, "Pitfalls in Counter-Cyclical Policies: Some Tools and Results," *The Review of Economics and Satistics*, February 1961, pp. 21–26.

[36]J. De V. Graaff, *Theoretical Welfare Economics* (London: Cambridge University Press, 1967).

[37]Ibid., pp. 142–154.

[38]Ibid., p. 142.

[39]See, for example, Walter Adams, "Competition, Monopoly, and Planning," in M. Zeitlin, ed., *American Society, Inc.* (Chicago: Markham, 1970), pp. 240–248.

challenge to the American steel industry from foreign competition are used to point out that private profits and monopoly power, not social welfare or social efficiency, are the prime motivations of big business.[40]

Critics also argue that managers have exactly the same motives as owner-capitalists. They cite an extensive study of the behavior of "management-controlled" giant corporations, which showed that managers were as profit-oriented as owner-capitalists. The author of the study concluded that "it would appear that the proponents of theories of managerial discretion have expended considerable time and effort in describing a phenomenon of relatively minor importance. The large management-controlled corporations seem to be just as profit-oriented as the large owner-controlled corporations."[41]

Many critics assert that modern managers have no more social conscience or "soul" than the nineteenth-century robber barons. The late Professor Edwin H. Sutherland, once known as the "dean of American criminologists" and former president of the American Sociological Association, conducted a thorough and scholarly investigation of the extent to which corporate executives were involved in criminal behavior. He took the 70 largest nonfinancial corporations, made only a few additions and deletions (due to special circumstances), and traced their criminal histories through official histories and official records.[42] There were 980 court decisions against these corporations. One corporation had 50 decisions against it, and the average per corporation was 14. Sixty of the corporations had been found guilty of restraining trade; 53, of infringements; 44, of unfair labor practices; 28, of misrepresentation in advertising; 26, of giving illegal rebates; and 43, of a variety of other offenses. There were a total of 307 individual cases of illegal restraint of trade, 97 of illegal misrepresentation, 222 of infringement, 158 of unfair labor practices, 66 of illegal rebates, and 130 of other offenses.[43] Not all of those cases were explicit criminal cases. But 60 percent of the corporations had been found guilty of criminal offenses an average of 4 times each.

From May 10, 1950, to May 1, 1951, a U.S. Senate Special Committee to Investigate Crime in Interstate Commerce, under the chairmanship of Senator Estes Kefauver, probed the connections of business and organized crime. Senator Kefauver, Democratic vice-

[40]Ibid.
[41]Robert J. Larner, "The Effect of Management-Control on the Profits of Larger Corporations," in Zeitlin, op. cit., p. 258.
[42]Edwin H. Sutherland, *White Collar Crime* (New York: Holt, Rinehart & Winston, 1961).
[43]These data are summarized by F. Lundberg in *The Rich and The Super Rich* (New York: Bantam, 1968), pp. 131–132.

presidential candidate in 1956, later wrote a book based on those hearings. Although he emphasized the fact that there was no evidence to link most big corporations with organized crime, he was nevertheless greatly alarmed at the extent of such connections:

> I cannot overemphasize the danger that can lie in the muscling into legitimate fields by hoodlums . . . there was too much evidence before us of unreformed hoodlums gaining control of a legitimate business; then utilizing all his old mob tricks—strong-arm methods, bombs, even murder—to secure advantages over legitimate competition. All too often such competition either ruins legitimate businessmen or drives them into emulating or merging with the gangsters. The hoodlums are also clever at concealing ownership of their investments in legitimate fields—sometimes . . . through "trustees" and sometimes by bamboozling respectable businessmen into "fronting" for them.[44]

In 1960 Robert Kennedy, who later became Attorney General of the United States, published *The Enemy Within*. He gathered the material for this book while serving as chief counsel of the U.S. Senate Select Committee on Improper Activities in the Labor or Management Field. Kennedy, like Kefauver, stressed the fact that he was not condemning all or even most businessmen. He wrote that

> we found that with the present-day emphasis on money and material goods many businessmen were willing to make corrupt "deals" with dishonest union officials in order to gain competitive advantage or to make a few extra dollars. . . . We came across more than fifty companies and corporations that had acted improperly—and in many cases illegally—in dealings with labor unions . . . in the companies and corporations to which I am referring the improprieties and illegalities were occasioned solely by a desire for monetary gain. Furthermore we found that we could expect very little assistance from management groups. Disturbing as it may sound, more often the business people with whom we came in contact—and this includes some representatives of our largest corporations—were uncooperative.[45]

Kennedy's list of the names of offending companies included many of the largest and most powerful corporations in the United States. Ferdinand Lundberg has described the extent to which corporate

[44]Estes Kefauver, *Crime in America* (Garden City, N.Y.: Doubleday, 1951), pp. 139–140.
[45]Robert Kennedy, *The Enemy Within* (New York: Harper & Row, 1960), p. 216.

leaders and management receive either very light punishment or no punishment at all when they become involved in improprieties or illegalities. Among the many cases he cites is that of

> the bribe of $750,000 by four insurance companies that sent Boss Pendergast of Missouri to jail, later to be pardoned by President Truman. . . . It was almost ten years before the insurance companies were convicted. Then they were only fined; no insurance executives went to jail. There was, too, the case of Federal Judge Martin Manton who was convicted of accepting a bribe of $250,000 from agents of the defendant when he presided over a case charging exorbitant salaries were improperly paid to officers of the American Tobacco Company. While the attorney for the company was disbarred from federal courts, the assistant to the company president (who made the arrangements) was soon thereafter promoted to vice president: a good boy.[46]

Critics of the managerial ideology do not cite such studies and examples to show businessmen to be criminals. Obviously most of them are not. The point they wish to make is that the power of monetary incentives and the quest for profits are no less pronounced among managers than among owner-capitalists. In fact, the pressure to acquire ever-increasing profits is so strong on many businessmen and managers that some persistently resort to illegal or improper means. With such pressures, the critics argue, society can ill afford to turn to the managerial class for paternalistic stewardship of the social and economic welfare.

SUMMARY

Since World War II the concentration of corporate power has become more extreme, and inequalities of income distribution have been reduced very little, if at all. Despite these facts, many contemporary ideologies continue to rely on the classical liberal defense of capitalism. Other ideologists continue to place the corporate ethic at the base of their defense of capitalism. The latter group stresses the "efficient, far-sighted policies" of the large corporations, and the "professionalism" as well as "broad, humanistic concerns" of corporate managers. Critics of this point of view argue that corporate managers are motivated by the same force that moved nineteenth-century capitalists: the quest for maximum profits.

[46]Lundberg, op. cit., p. 135.

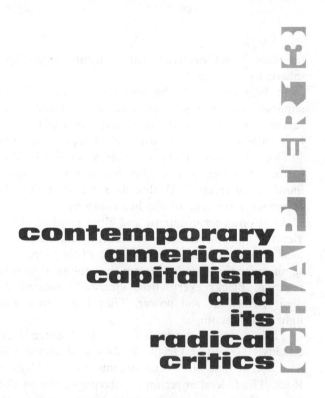

contemporary american capitalism and its radical critics

Radical criticism of American capitalism was widespread during the depression of the 1930s. During the late forties and early fifties, however, pervasive repression of dissent, combined with a relatively prosperous economy, effectively stifled most radical criticism.[1]

All this changed abruptly in the 1960s and early 1970s. The two most important galvanizers of this resurgence of radical criticism were the civil rights movement and the war in Vietnam.

THE CIVIL RIGHTS MOVEMENT

The struggle for equality for blacks in America really began in 1619, when the first black slaves were brought to the colonies. Since that time the struggle has been nearly continuous. In the 1950s, however, the blacks' quest for their basic human rights entered a new phase.

On May 17, 1954, in the case of *Brown* v. *Board of Education of Topeka*, the U.S. Supreme Court unanimously concluded "that in the field of public education the doctrine of 'separate but equal' has

[1]For a thorough description of the repression of this period, see Fred J. Cook, *The Nightmare Decade: The Life and Times of Senator Joe McCarthy* (New York: Random House, 1971). Also see Cedric Belfrage, *The American Inquisition, 1945–1960.* (New York: Bobbs-Merrill, 1973).

no place!" and declared that "separate educational facilities are inherently unequal."

In 1954 and 1955, the few black individuals who applied for admission to white schools were rebuffed and very often suffered severe reprisals. It began to appear that the Court decision would have little effect on the patterns of segregation that then existed. In December 1955, however, a black woman in Montgomery, Alabama, refused to give up her bus seat to a white man. She was immediately arrested. Within days the blacks of Montgomery had organized a boycott of the bus company.

After one year of intense and bitter conflict, the protest ended in victory. The 50,000 blacks of Montgomery succeeded in getting the local bus segregation law nullified. This victory had a symbolic significance that was far greater than the particular issue of bus segregation. Blacks everywhere vicariously shared a new sense of digiity, freedom, and power. They began to organize actively to fight white racism.

Their attempts met with fanatical resistance. In the fall of 1957 Arkansas Governor Orville Faubus used armed troops to bar the entrance of nine black students into Central High School in Little Rock. The federal government interpreted this as a blatant challenge to its authority and sent in paratroopers to enforce the federal court orders. Many southern communities chose to close their public schools rather than allowing them to be integrated.

In 1957 and 1960 Congress passed civil rights acts designed to extend voting rights to blacks. The Kennedy Administration urged young people, black and white, to concentrate on a massive registration drive to get southern blacks on the voting lists. Attracting both radical critics of capitalism and liberal young people who generally did not seriously question the basic social and economic system of capitalism, the civil rights movement was nationwide. In the early 1960s the liberals dominated the movement numerically. They believed that a massive protest against racism would open the public's eyes and that an aroused population would demand new laws that would improve, if not completely cure, the situation.

During this period civil rights activists organized sit-ins at segregated lunch counters and bus depots, pray-ins at segregated churches, and wade-ins at segregated beaches. Massive nonviolent demonstrations or nonviolent civil disobedience, they hoped, would reach the consciences of enough people to achieve integration.

Despite some successes in terms of new civil rights legislation, disillusionment began to affect large numbers of blacks as well as white civil rights workers. They began to realize that political franchisement had little effect on the vast economic inequalities blacks suffered. Of what use was the vote if a black man or woman could not secure a job, or if he or she was paid a salary that kept the family in a condition of poverty and degradation? Whereas in 1950 the average salary earned by a black was 61 percent of that earned by a white, by 1962 it had fallen to 55 percent. In the face of massive civil rights movement, the relative economic position of the blacks had actually deteriorated. Furthermore, whereas in 1950 the rate of unemployment among blacks had been slightly less than twice as high as that for whites, by 1964 it was significantly more than twice as high. In 1947, blacks constituted 18 percent of the poorest class in America; by 1962, they accounted for 22 percent of this class.

Many civil rights advocates became convinced that the most significant barriers to black equality were economic. They turned their attention to a critical analysis of American capitalism as a means of understanding the perpetuation, indeed the worsening, of the inequalities suffered by blacks.

THE WAR IN VIETNAM

The other major force that helped spark the resurgence of radical criticism was the war in Vietnam. Throughout the 1950s the U.S. government consistently fought against fundamental social and political change in less developed countries. In the guise of "protecting the world from communism," the United States had intervened in the internal affairs of at least a score of countries. In some, like Guatemala and Iran, U.S. agents actually engineered the overthrow of the legitimate governments and replaced them with regimes more to American liking.[2]

Most criticism was muted by the political repression of McCarthyism. The college students of the 1950s, the "silent generation," generally acquiesced in the national mood of anticommunism that provided the justification for political repression at home and extensive intervention in other nations' internal affairs. During the 1950s, American intervention in Vietnam attracted little special attention. It was merely one of many countries that were being "saved from communism." In the 1960s, however, all this was to change drastically. The Vietnam War became a powerful force in regenerating radical criticism of American capitalism. For this reason, a brief examination of the origins of the Vietnam War is needed here.

During the World War II occupation of Vietnam, the French colonial regime collaborated with the Japanese. Toward the end of the war the Japanese locked up the colonial administrators and estab-

---

[2]For a popular account of these interventions, see David Wise and Thomas B. Ross, *The Invisible Government* (New York: Random House, 1964).

lished a puppet regime under the Annamite Emperor Bao Dai. Throughout this period the Americans and the French had supported a resistance movement, the Vietminh, headed by Ho Chi Minh. When Japan surrendered, there was a peaceful transfer of political power to the Vietminh.

The French did not want to lose this part of their colonial empire but realized that they were too weak to inflict a quick military defeat on the new government. On March 6, 1946, they signed an agreement with the Ho Chi Minh government that read in part: "The government of France recognizes the Republic of Vietnam as a free state having its government and its parliament, its army and its finances, forming part of the Indo-Chinese federation and of the French Union."[3] This agreement clearly intended that the Ho Chi Minh government would enjoy a status similar to the governments of the members of the British Commonwealth. It legally established Ho Chi Minh's regime as the legitimate government of *all* Vietnam. Nothing that subsequently occurred changed this essential fact.

The French were confident, however, that they could make a subservient puppet of Ho Chi Minh. They failed completely in this task. Unable to reduce Ho Chi Minh to this role, they brought back Emperor Bao Dai, even though he had voluntarily abdicated his throne, changed his name, and retired to Hong Kong. They "installed" him as "chief of state" and declared the Vietminh to be outlaws. There followed six years of intense, bitter warfare. Finally, in 1954, the Vietminh decisively defeated the French. The Geneva Accords of July 1954, which arranged for the French surrender, called for a cease-fire and a *temporary* separation of opposing forces. Ho Chi Minh's followers were to move north of the seventeenth parallel, and Emperor Bao Dai's were to move to the south. This arrangement was to end within two years with a national election to choose the leader of all Vietnam. Shortly after these negotiations American-backed Ngo Dinh Diem ousted Bao Dai, proclaimed the existence of a "Republic of Vietnam," and appointed himself its first president.

There were no elections. The Americans and Diem simply asserted that there were now two Vietnams. The reason for refusing to have the election was candidly admitted by President Eisenhower in his book *Mandate for Change.*

I am convinced that the French could not win the war because the internal political situation in Vietnam, weak and confused, badly weakened their military position. I have never talked or

---

[3]Quoted in Leo Huberman and Paul M. Sweezy, "The Road to Ruin," *Monthly Review*, April 1965, p. 787.

corresponded with a person knowledgeable in Indochinese affairs who did not agree that had elections been held as of the time of the fighting, possibly 80 percent of the population would have voted for Communist Ho Chi Minh as their leader rather than chief of state Bao Dai.[4]

Obviously the substitution of Diem for Bao Dai did not change the situation.

This American-imposed solution was rejected not only by Ho Chi Minh and his followers in the North but also by people in the South. So the war of national liberation, which had been fought against the Japanese and the French, was continued against the United States.

Americans were repeatedly told that their government was fighting a war to protect the South Vietnamese from the armed aggression of North Vietnam. The North Vietnamese were pictured as violators of the Geneva agreements, determined to enslave the South Vietnamese.

Critics of American policy challenged this official version of the nature of the war. Their assessment of what was happening in Vietnam received widespread support in academic circles, and college campuses became centers of antiwar sentiment. From the early 1960s through about 1966, most opposition to the war was largely confined to the campuses. During the last years of the decade, however, people from all segments of society actively opposed the war. The antiwar movement had become a mass movement.

Finally, in 1968, U.S. Secretary of Defense Robert S. McNamara, himself becoming disillusioned with the official rationale for the war, ordered the U.S. Department of Defense to prepare an in-depth account of how the United States became involved. In early 1971 the report was completed. The 7000-page document was obtained by the *New York Times*, which paid researchers to determine whether new facts had been brought to light. The Defense Department admitted that (1) the Eisenhower Administration had played a "direct role in the ultimate breakdown of the Geneva settlement";[5] (2) from 1954 onward, the United States had engaged in "acts of sabotage and terror war are against North Vietnam";[6] (3) the United States "encouraged and abetted the overthrow of President Ngo Dinh Diem" when he was no longer considered to be of use; (4) for many years before 1965 the U.S. government undertook

---

[4]Quoted in ibid., p. 789.

[5]Quoted in Neil Sheehan, "The Story Behind the Vietnam War, Based on a Pentagon Study," *New York Times News Service*, June 13, 1971.

[6]Ibid.

"the careful preparation of public opinion for the years of open warfare that were to follow."[7]

American involvement increased steadily until by 1968 the United States had an army of over 500,000 men on Vietnamese soil and were spending nearly $3 billion per month ($100 million per day!) in the attempt to impose a "suitable political solution" on the Vietnamese.

American battle casualties rose until hundreds of thousands of Americans were wounded and well over 50,000 Americans were killed. Young people everywhere began to question the morality of the war. Beginning in 1964, teach-ins protesting the war were mounted on college campuses around the United States. Most organizers and participants were convinced that American involvement in the war was a tragic mistake that would be rectified if the public could be made aware of the true facts of the situation.

The antiwar movement grew rapidly. President Johnson's landslide victory in 1964, as well as his decision not to seek another term in 1968, are often attributed, at least in part, to the powerful, widespread opposition to the war. After a few years of debate, however, antiwar critics were convinced that most Americans did now know the basic facts of Vietnam and wanted a hasty end to the war. Yet the American government, without giving any convincing reasons for its actions, continued to seek military victory.

Critics began to ask whether there was not some deeper motive than simple anticommunist sentiment propelling the American government. In particular, they began to search for an economic motive or rationale for the war. They began seriously to reexamine the older radical theories of capitalist imperialism.

THE WOMEN'S LIBERATION MOVEMENT

The women's movement, like the black movement, did not suddenly spring into being in the 1960s out of thin air. The earliest political activity of a significant number of U.S. women came in the 1820s and 1830s in the abolitionist movement to end slavery. Experience in the abolitionist movement made women aware of their own oppression and gave them the confidence to build a movement of their own, especially because they were ignored or dismissed by some of the abolitionists. The women's movement before the Civil War fought not only for the abolition of slavery, but also for ending the laws that made the man the sole controller of all property and all decisions in marriage (even giving men guardianship of the children in event of separation), as well as for the right to vote.

The aftermath of the Civil War gave the vote to blacks—or, rather, it gave the formal right to black *men*, but with no mechanism

[7]Ibid.

of enforcement in the South. Women, both black and white, were not given the vote. The women's movement fought a long, long battle until women were finally given the vote in 1920. The early movement had concerned itself with a broad range of issues, from poverty and divorce laws to working conditions, but the movement after about 1890 concentrated solely on the narrow issue of voting. By 1920 some 2,000,000 women were members of the leading woman suffrage organizations! Yet when the vote was given, most of these women thought the battle was won—so the women's movement collapsed and did not recover till the late 1960s.

A brief upsurge in the fight for women's rights occurred only in World War II, when millions of women were drawn into war work. The symbol of Rosie the Riveter replaced that of Jane the Housewife. Overnight it became fashionable for women to work in a war factory or a war office, and there was even discussion of child care to help working mothers. Moreover, the two political parties made considerable sympathetic noises in favor of the idea of an equal rights amendment for women in the federal constitution.

Unfortunately for women, the late 1940s and 1950s was a period of general repression on the American scene. People were happy to see the war's end and wanted nothing but smooth private lives of moneymaking, with no discussion or recognition of continuing social problems. All the radicals and liberals who advocated any social change were hounded by Senator McCarthy and a huge number of publicity-seeking inquisitors; one of those who made a successful career of red-witch-hunting was Richard Nixon. Women were told to leave their war jobs and get back to kitchen, children, and church (just as Hitler had told the German women). The media—and even conservative psychologists—painted a picture in which every woman was a happy housewife surrounded by hoards of gleaming children and gadgets.

Yet reality was quite different. Later studies have shown that most women who are nothing but housewives are dreadfully unfulfilled and unhappy. Moreover, even in the 1950s the number of women at work kept increasing, despite all the propaganda. By 1970, 4 out of every 10 workers were women—and a majority of all women between 16 and 64 now work! Yet they work in the poorest jobs, such as domestic servant or secretary, and are paid less than men even for the same job. The average full-time woman worker only makes 59 percent of what a full-time male worker is paid. Furthermore, in every area women who are fully qualified are denied promotion. Only a few of the thousands of corporate executives are women; only 9 percent of full professors are women; only 16 of the 435 representatives in Congress are women; and no woman has ever been President, Vice President, or a Supreme Court Justice.

In the 1960s women began to protest these conditions. The first result of protest was the Equal Pay Act of 1963. Then, in 1964, a provision for women was added to the Civil Rights Act, which prohibited discrimination in employment against minority groups. Yet the addition was made by a southern congressman who wanted to defeat the whole act by amending it to add the ban on sex discrimination—and its final passage was a political miracle. Even after it was passed, the agencies who were responsible for enforcing it treated the sex discrimination ban as a joke and made very little attempt to enforce it.

As a result, in 1966 the National Organization of Women was formed. It is a moderate organization that wished to see the laws against sex discrimination fully enforced and has worked to get other laws—like the Equal Rights Amendment—passed so as to give women fully equal rights at last.

In the meantime radical women gained a great deal of experience in the civil rights movement and the antiwar movement. Once again, recognition of the oppression of blacks made women conscious of their own oppression. They therefore began to work to direct the Left movement toward the fight for equality for women as well as for minorities. In this, however, they were rebuffed by many male radicals who were unenlightened on the subject of women. Thus when the subject of women's rights was broached by black women in the civil rights organization called the Student Nonviolent Coordinating Committee, its leader Stokely Carmichael said: "The only position for women in SNCC is prone."[8]

By 1968 many radical women were fed up with most of the Left organizations, so they organized their own separate movement. The radical women's movement has only women leaders and allows no men in it, even as members; but it does cooperate with other Left organizations when the need arises. It has no single national organization but has hundreds of local ones. Some of the organizations are purely feminist, seeing all men as the enemy. Others are socialist, believing that capitalists are the main enemy and that socialism is a necessary precondition of women's liberation. The women's movement as a whole, including moderates, feminists, and socialists, is probably now the largest and most active single component of the Left movement in the United States.

CONTEMPORARY
CRITIQUES OF AMERICAN CAPITALISM

The civil rights, antiwar, and women's liberation movements led to a burgeoning literature critical of the basic institutions of American

---

[8]Quoted in Judith Hole and Ellen Levine, *Rebirth of Feminism* (New York: Quadrangle, 1971), p. 110.

capitalism. Like earlier critiques, this literature censured the grossly unequal distribution of income, wealth, and power in the United States. These critics, like the leftist Keynesians, deplored the extent to which post-World War II economic stability had been purchased at a cost of thoroughgoing militarism (discussed in Chapter 11).

On these points radical and liberal critics have been in agreement. Liberal critics believe political reform and electoral politics are sufficient to correct these perversions of the American economy. Radical critics, however, believe inequality and militarism are inherent in a capitalist economy and that it also necessarily involves (1) imperialistic exploitation of underdeveloped countries as a means of maintaining high output and large profits in the United States, (2) endemic discrimination against minority groups and women, (3) inability to control pollution and resources exhaustion, and (4) a degrading commercialism and social alienation. In the remainder of this chapter some of the literature in these four general areas will be described. Much of this literature has appeared in the *Review of Radical Political Economics*, published by the Union for Radical Economics (URPE). Its address is: Office of Organizational Services, Michigan Union, Ann Arbor, Michigan, 48104. URPE is the main organization of U.S. radical economists.

AMERICAN IMPERIALISM

One of the first and most influential of these critics was Paul A. Baran. His book *The Political Economy of Growth*,[9] first published in 1957, has undergone two editions, has been translated into several languages, and has sold very well in the United States and even better in most less developed countries. Baran argued that before a less developed country could industrialize it would have to mobilize its *economic surplus,* or the difference between what is produced and what has to be consumed in order to maintain the economy's productivity. It is the source of investment capital with which the country can industrialize. Under present institutional arrangements, most less developed countries either waste their surpluses or lose them to imperialistic capitalist countries.

"Far from serving as an engine of economic expansion, of technological progress and of social change, the capitalist order in . . . [underdeveloped] countries has represented a framework for economic stagnation, for archaic technology, and for social backwardness."[10] The peasant agriculture usually produces a sufficiently large surplus in these countries. In fact, Baran pointed out that the surplus

[9]Paul A. Baran, *The Political Economy of Growth* (New York: Monthly Review Press, 1962).
[10]Ibid., pp. 163–164.

is frequently as high as 50 percent of the total amount produced. "The subsistence peasant's obligations on account of rent, taxes, and interest in all underdeveloped countries are very high. They frequently absorb more than half of his meager net product."[11]

The problem is in the disposition of this surplus. Part goes to middlemen, speculators, moneylenders, and merchants—petty capitalists who have neither the interest nor the wherewithal to finance industrialization. A much larger part goes to the landowning ruling class, which uses its "share" to purchase luxury consumption goods, usually imported from capitalist countries, and the extensive military establishments needed to maintain their internal power.

Importing luxuries and military hardware necessitates sending exports to the industrialized countries. Exports usually consist of one or two primary agricultural products or mineral resources. The capitalist countries with which they trade have such monopsonistic buying power that the terms of trade are very unfavorable to the underdeveloped countries. The large, multinational corporations that purchase the raw materials are not interested in the industrialization of these countries. Thus foreign capitalist investment is limited to that necessary for the profitable extraction of resources.

An alliance between reactionary landowning class and foreign capitalists protects the interests of both by suppressing dissidence and keeping the masses at a subsistence standard of living. Thus landowners can maintain their position and capitalists are guaranteed cheap labor and large profits.

> Small wonder that under such circumstances Western big business heavily engaged in raw materials exploitation leaves no stone unturned to obstruct the evolution of social and political conditions in underdeveloped countries that might be conducive to their economic development. It uses its tremendous power to prop up the backward areas' comprador administrations, to disrupt and corrupt the social and political movements that oppose them, and to overthrow whatever progressive governments may rise to power and refuse to do the bidding of their imperialistic overlords.[12]

Baran believed the American government works hand in hand with American big business. Most U.S. economic and military aid provided to less developed countries is given, in his opinion, in order to prop up client governments. Often such governments are not strong enough to survive on their own, even with this aid. Under these circumstances the United States intervenes, either clandestinely

[11]Ibid., p. 165.
[12]Ibid., p. 198.

(through CIA sabotage and intrigue) or directly (through the use of military force).

Baran and like-minded critics see the interventions in Guatemala, Iran, Korea, Cuba, the Dominican Republic, Vietnam, and Cambodia as examples of American endeavors to protect business interests, both current and potential, against threats from more progressive social and political movements. They point to 53 different "U.S. defense commitments and assurances" that commit the United States to the use of military force to maintain existing governments, very often against their own people.[13]

The dependence of less developed countries on a small number of export commodities is documented in a study based on International Monetary Fund data. Each of the 37 countries considered earns 58 to 99 percent of its export receipts from 1 to 6 commodities.[14] Furthermore, the United States depends on imports as the principal source for most of the 62 types of materials the Defense Department classifies as "strategic and critical." For 38 of these, 80 to 100 percent of the new supplies are imported; for 14 more, 40 to 79 percent are imported.[15]

A large and increasing percentage of U.S. corporate sales and profits results from exports and sales of foreign subsidiaries (many of which, of course, are in less developed countries).[16] Moreover, detailed examination reveals that the foreign trade of the less developed countries is very lopsided. Raw materials and metals in their first state of smelting constitute 85 percent of exports; manufactured goods (mostly textiles), only 10 percent. But about 60 percent of their imports are manufactured goods.[17] Because most manufactured imports are consumer goods, such a pattern of trade cannot lead to development but only to continued economic dependence.

Critics of this point of view (i.e., defenders of American economic foreign policy) argue that although foreign trade and foreign investments are important to American corporations, they also benefit the less developed countries. The orthodox argument is expressed in a widely used textbook:

In general, a restrained optimism as to the future prospects for underdeveloped countries in their trading relations with the de-

[13]See Harry Magdoff, *The Age of Imperialism, The Economics of U.S. Foreign Policy* (New York: Monthly Review Press, Modern Reader Paperbacks, 1969), pp. 203–206.

[14]Magdoff, op. cit., pp. 99–100.

[15]Percy W. Bidwell, *Raw Materials* (New York: Harper & Row, 1958), p. 12.

[16]Magdoff, op. cit., p. 57.

[17]Pierre Jalee, *The Pillage of the Third World* (New York: Monthly Review Press, 1965), p. 8.

veloped countries seems to be warranted. The most encouraging sign is the growing recognition on the part of developed countries that opening their markets to the export products of underdeveloped areas is an essential part of their accepted program to assist underdeveloped countries to grow.[18]

But this position does not deal directly with radical critiques of American economic foreign policy. It simply assumes that all the underdeveloped countries need is *more* trade. Another orthodox scholar who has studied the problem more thoroughly admits that "increasing the flow of private capital to underdeveloped countries will probably require a *recasting of economic policies* in both underdeveloped and advanced countries."[19] He does not go on to analyze what obstacles prevent this "recasting of economic policies."

Conservative defenders of American policies grant that developed capitalist countries have had immense economic, political, and military power, which they have used to influence and control peoples around the world. They deny, however, that this "imperialism" is basically economic in nature. Thus the widely respected economic historian Professor David S. Landes writes:

> It seems to me that one has to look at imperialism as a multifarious response to a common opportunity that consists simply in disparity of power. Whenever and wherever such disparity has existed, people and groups have been ready to take advantage of it. It is, one notes with regret, in the nature of the human beast to push other people around—or to save their souls or "civilize" them as the case may be.[20]

One radical critic has answered this assertion by noting that the modern capitalist drive to save people's souls from communism and to civilize them is perfectly compatible with economic motives. He cites the following quotation from an officer of General Electric Company: "Thus, our search for profits places us squarely in line with the national policy of stepping up international trade as a means of strengthening the free world in the Cold War confrontation with Communism." The critic, Harry Magdoff, summarizes his position: "Just as the fight against Communism helps the search for profits, so the search for profits helps the fight against Communism. What more perfect harmony of interests could be imagined?"[21]

[18]Delbert A. Snider, *Introduction to International Economics* (Homewood, Ill.: Irwin, 1963), p. 548.

[19]Benjamin Higgins, *Economic Development* (New York: Norton, 1959), p. 593; italics added.

[20]David S. Landes, "The Nature of Economic Imperialism," *The Journal of Economic History*, December 1961, p. 510.

[21]Magdoff, op. cit., pp. 200–201.

Many books written in the 1960s attempted to explain contemporary American foreign policy—and the cold war between the United States and the Soviet Union—in terms of American economic imperialism.[22]

RACISM AND SEXISM

Radical critics also point to the pervasive effects of discrimination based on race and sex that exists in capitalist countries, particularly in the United States. Virtually everyone agrees that racism and sexism create severe discrimination. Defenders of American capitalism explain this discrimination in one of two ways. The more reactionary is to argue that job discrimination merely reflects the innate inferiority of women and blacks. Few, if any, intellectuals embrace this position, but it apparently is accepted by a large minority in the United States. The other contention is that racism and sexism are products of a fairly universal human bigotry and are not related to capitalism or any other economic system.

Critics of capitalism point out that the wages of blacks and women make up a significant part of capitalists' wage costs. In 1970, for example, the wages of American women averaged only about 50 percent of the wages of men doing the same jobs. On that basis it would appear that approximately 23 percent of all manufacturing profits are attributable to the lower wages paid to women. Profits made as a result of racial discrimination would certainly be smaller, but they would still be significant.

In one of the most influential socialist critiques, Paul A. Baran and Paul M. Sweezy have argued that it is necessary to

> consider first the private interests which benefit from the existence of a Negro subproletariat. (a) Employers benefit from divisions in the labor force which enable them to play one group off against another, thus weakening all. . . . (b) Owners of ghetto real estate are able to overcrowd and overcharge. (c) Middle and upper income groups benefit from having at their disposal a large supply of cheap domestic labor. (d) Many small marginal businesses, especially in the service trades, can operate profitably only if cheap labor is available to them. (e) White workers benefit by being protected from Negro competition for the more desirable and higher paying jobs.[23]

[22]See Magdoff, op. cit., D. F. Fleming, *The Cold War and Its Origins* (Garden City, N.Y.: Doubleday, 1961); Gar Alperowitz, *Atomic Diplomacy: Hiroshima and Potsdam* (New York: Simon & Schuster, 1965); David Horowitz, ed., *Corporations and the Cold War* (New York: Monthly Review Press, 1969); and David Horowitz, *Empire and Revolution* (New York: Random House, 1969).

[23]Paul A. Baran and Paul M. Sweezy, *Monopoly Capital* (New York: Monthly Review Press 1966), pp. 263–264.

They also assert that, in addition to increasing profits, discrimination increases social stability in a capitalist economy. The class structure of capitalism, they hold, leads to a situation in which

> each status group has a deep-rooted psychological need to compensate for feelings of inferiority and envy toward those above by feelings of superiority and contempt for those below. It thus happens that a special pariah group at the bottom acts as a kind of lightning rod for the frustrations and hostilities of all the higher groups, the more so the nearer they are to the bottom. It may even be said that the very existence of the pariah group is a kind of harmonizer and stabilizer of the social structure.[24]

Although Baran and Sweezy's assertions pertain to racism, many critics argue that sexism performs much the same function in a capitalist society. These critics generally do not believe that capitalism is the original creator of racism and sexism but rather that capitalism perpetuates and intensifies racism and sexism because they serve valuable functions.

> Today, transferring the locus of whites' perceptions of the source of many of their problems from capitalism and toward blacks, racism continues to serve the needs of the capitalist system. Although an individual employer might gain by refusing to discriminate and agreeing to hire blacks at above the going black wage rate, it is not true that the capitalist class as a whole would profit if racism were eliminated and labor were more efficiently allocated without regard to skin color. . . . The divisiveness of racism weakens workers' strength when bargaining with employers; the economic consequences of racism are not only lower incomes for blacks but also higher incomes for the capitalist class coupled with lower incomes for white workers. Although capitalists may not have conspired consciously to create racism, and although capitalists may not be its principal perpetuators, nevertheless racism does support the continued well-being of the American capitalist system.[25]

Similarly, the critics argue that sex prejudice helps divide the labor, civil rights, and radical movements to the benefit of American capitalists.

---

[24]Ibid., pp. 265–266.
[25]Michael Reich, "The Economics of Racism," in David M. Gordon, ed., *Probelms in Political Economy: An Urban Perspective* (Lexington, Mass.: Raytheon/Heath, 1971), pp. 109–110.

ALIENATION

Many contemporary radical critics have refined and elaborated on Marx's theory of the human alienation inherent in the capitalist economic system.[26] Baran and Sweezy, for example, maintain that total alienation pervades and dominates contemporary American capitalism:

> Disorientation, apathy, and often despair, haunting Americans in all walks of life, have assumed in our time the dimensions of a prolonged crisis. This crisis affects every aspect of national life, and ravages both its socio-political and its individual spheres—everyman's everyday existence. A heavy strangulating sense of the emptiness and futility of life permeates the country's moral and intellectual climate. High level committees are entrusted with the discovery and specification of "national goals" while gloom pervades the printed matter (fiction and non-fiction, alike) appearing daily in the literary market place. The malaise deprives work of meaning and purpose; turns leisure into joyless, debilitating laziness; fatally impairs the education system and the conditions of healthy growth in the young; transforms religion and church into commercialized vehicles of "togetherness"; and destroys the very foundation of burgeois society, the family.[27]

The fact of alienation, like the facts of racism and sexism, is explained by many defenders of capitalism as an unfortunate but inevitable by-product of industrial civilization. They point to all the boring and dangerous work that must be done, as well as to the narrow and fragmented personalities of the enormous number of bureaucrats. An industrialized socialist economy would, they assert, create the same type of alienation. Few people, regardless of political and economic views, would be willing to forgo the advantages of industrialization in order to combat alienation. And even if people did want to return to preindustrial society, there is simply no practical way of turning back time to some imagined golden age.

Socialist critics reply that although some amount of alienation will surely exist in any industrialized society, capitalism significantly intensifies alienation and makes it more pervasive. Erich Fromm, a famous psychoanalyst, social philosopher, and author, argues that the most important single cause of alienation is the fact that the individual feels no sense of participation in the forces that determine social policy. He sees these forces as anonymous and totally beyond the sphere of any individual's influence. "The anonymity of the

[26]See Chapter 6.
[27]Baran and Sweezy, op. cit., p. 281.

social forces," writes Fromm, "is inherent in the structure of the capitalist mode of production."[28]

Fromm identifies several types of alienation created by the capitalist mode of production. Conditions of employment alienate workers. Their livelihoods depend on whether capitalists and managers are able to make a profit by hiring them, and thus they are viewed as means only, never as ends. The individual worker is "an economic atom that dances to the tune of atomistic management." Managers "strip the worker of his right to think and move freely. Life is being denied; need to control, creativeness, curiosity, and independent thought are being balked, and the result, the inevitable result, is flight or fight on the part of the worker, apathy or destructiveness, psychic regression."[29] The worker feels that the capitalist controls his whole life; both workers and consumers (and voters) feel weak and insignificant in view of the colossal power of the corporations over working conditions, prices, and even government policy.

And yet Fromm argues that the "role of the manager is also one of alienation," for he too is coerced by the ineluctable forces of capitalism and has very little freedom. He must deal "with impersonal giants; with the giant competitive enterprise; with giant impersonal markets; with giant unions, and the giant government."[30] His position, his status, his income—in short, his very social existence —all depend on making ever-increasing amounts of profits. Yet he must do this in a world in which he has little personal influence on the giants with whom he deals.

Fromm also maintains that the process of consumption in a capitalist society "is as alienated as the process of production." The truly human way of acquiring commodities, according to Fromm, would be through need and the desire to use: "The acquisition of bread and clothing [should] depend on no other premise than that of being alive; the acquisition of books and paintings on my effort to understand them and my ability to use them."[31] But in capitalist societies the income with which to purchase these commodities can come only through sales in the impersonal market.

As a consequence, those who have money are subjected to a constant barrage of propaganda designed to create consuming automata. Capitalist socialization processes make consumption-hungry, irrational, compulsive buying machines of us all. Acts of buying and con-

---

[28]Erich Fromm, *The Sane Society* (New York: Fawcett World Library, Premier Books, 1965), p. 125.
[29]Quoted in ibid., p. 115.
[30]Ibid., pp. 115–116.
[31]Ibid., p. 120.

suming have become ends in themselves, with little or no relation to the uses or pleasures derived from the commodities.

> Man today is fascinated by the possibility of buying more, better, and especially, new things. He is consumption-hungry. The act of buying and consuming has become a compulsive, irrational aim, because it is an end in itself, with little relation to the use of or pleasure in the things bought and consumed. To buy the latest gadget, the latest model of anything that is on the market, is the dream of everybody in comparison to which the real pleasure in use is quite secondary. Modern man, if he dared to be articulate about his concept of heaven, would describe a vision which would look like the biggest department store in the world, showing new things and gadgets, and himself having plenty of money with which to buy them. He would wander around open-mouthed in his heaven of gadgets and commodities, provided only that there were ever more and newer things to buy, and perhaps that his neighbors were just a little less privileged than he.[32]

Finally, the most severe alienation is the alienation of a man from his "self." A person's "worth" in a capitalist market economy is determined in the same way as the "worth" of anything else: by sales in the marketplace. In this situation

> man experiences himself as a thing to be employed successfully on the market. He does not experience himself as an active agent, as the bearer of human powers. He is alienated from these powers. His aim is to sell himself successfully on the market. His sense of self does not stem from his activity as a loving and thinking individual, but from his socio-economic role. . . . If you ask a man "Who are you?", he answers "I am a manufacturer," "I am a clerk," "I am a doctor." . . . That is the way he experiences himself, not as a man, with love, fear, convictions, doubts, but as that abstraction, alienated from his real nature, which fulfills a certain function in the social system. His sense of value depends on his success: on whether he can sell himself favorably, whether he can make more of himself than he started out with, whether he is a success. His body, his mind and his soul are his capital, and his task in life is to invest it favorably, to make a *profit* of himself. Human qualities like friendliness, courtesy, kindness, are transformed into commodities, into assets of the "personality package," conducive to a higher price on the personality market. If the individual fails in a profitable investment of himself, *he* feels that he

[32]Ibid., p. 123.

is a failure; if he succeeds, he is a success. Clearly, his sense of his own value always depends on factors extraneous to himself, on the fickle judgment of the market, which decides about his value as it decides about the value of commodities. He, like all commodities that cannot be sold profitably on the market, is worthless as far as his exchange value is concerned, even though his use value may be considerable.[33]

Thus socialist critics argue that the impersonal nexus of the capitalist market mediates all human relationships. It makes profit and loss the ultimate and pervasive evaluative criteria of human worth. This means human alienation must inevitably be extremely severe in a capitalist market economy.

ENVIRONMENTAL DESTRUCTION

Capitalism must either experience economic growth or else suffer depression, unemployment, stagnation, and all the attendant social problems. But economic growth can also create situations in which the pursuit of profits comes into direct conflict with the public welfare. Critics of capitalism have argued that corporate profit seeking is generally accompanied by very little concern for conservation or for a clean, livable environment.

Pollution is of concern to defenders of capitalism as well as to critics. Defenders argue that it is a problem common to all industrialized economies. Critics assert that the problem is worse in a capitalist economy. Furthermore, they maintain that it would be virtually impossible to control pollution effectively in a capitalist system. This is so, they argue, because the basic economic cause of pollution in a capitalist economy is that business firms do not have to pay for *all* the costs incurred in the production process. They pay for labor, raw materials, and capital used up in production. But they use the land, air, and water for the disposal of waste products that are created in the process of production. Generally they pay little or nothing for the use of the environment as a garbage disposal.

It has been estimated[34] that each year businesses are responsible for over 25 billion tons of pollutants being spewed into the air and dumped into the water and on the land. This is about 125 tons of waste per year for every man, woman, and child in the United States. Included in this figure are about 150 million tons of smoke

---

[33]Ibid., pp. 129–130.

[34]These estimates are taken from an important and impressive study on pollution: R. C. d'Arge, A. V. Kneese, and R. V. Ayres, *Economics of the Environment: A Materials Balance Approach* (Baltimore: Johns Hopkins Press, 1970).

and fumes that blacken the skies and poison the air, 22 million tons of waste paper products, 3 million tons of mill tailings, and 50 trillion gallons of heated and polluted liquids that are dumped into streams, rivers, and lakes each year.

Critics argue that it is extremely difficult if not impossible for a capitalist economy to deal with these problems because those who receive the profits from production do not pay these social costs, and those who do pay the social costs have little or no voice in the operation of the businesses.

In response to the widespread public demand for control of pollution and polluters, the government has given contracts to many corporations to devise new methods of combating pollution. In effect the government is asking private corporations to act as the controllers of other private corporations. Radical critics are convinced that this corporate integration of polluters and controllers will never lead to any substantial improvement. Most of the important pollution control companies have become subsidiaries of the giant corporations that do most of the polluting.

One radical critic has analyzed the effects of this corporate control.

It is the chemical industry . . . that best illustrates the consequences of the incest between the pollution control business and the industrial polluters. First, the chemical industry is in the enviable position of reaping sizable profits by attempting to clean up rivers and lakes (at public expense) which they have profitably polluted in the first place. To facilitate this practically every major chemical company in the U.S. has established a pollution abatement division or is in the process of doing so. . . . A second consequence of placing the "control" of pollution in the hands of big business is that the official abatement levels will inevitably be set low enough to protect industry's power to pollute and therefore its ability to keep costs down and revenues high. According to a recent study by the FWPCA (Federal Water Pollution Control Administration) if the chemical industry were to reduce its pollution of water to zero, the costs involved would amount to almost $2.7 billion per year. This would cut profits almost by half.[35]

Under such circumstances the critics do not expect much progress in cleaning up the environment unless fundamental social, political, and economic changes occur first.

[35]Martin Gellen, "The Making of a Pollution-Industrial Complex," in Gordon, op. cit., pp. 469–470.

LIBERAL VERSUS RADICAL CRITIQUES OF CAPITALISM

The glaringly unequal distribution of wealth, income, and political power and the facts of militarism, imperialism, vicious discrimination, social alienation, and environmental destruction are all recognized and decried by both liberal and radical critics of capitalism. There is, however, an immensely important difference between the positions of liberals and radicals.

Liberals tend to see each of these social and economic problems as separate and distinct. The problems, they believe, are the results of past mistakes, inabilities, and ineptitudes or the results of random cases of individual perversity. Liberals also tend to consider the government as detached, disinterested, and motivated by a desire to maximize the welfare of all its citizens. Hence liberals generally favor government-sponsored reforms designed to mitigate the many evils of capitalism. These reforms never threaten the two most important features of capitalism: private ownership of the means of production, and the free market.

Radicals, however, see each of the social and economic problems we have discussed as the *direct consequence* of private ownership of capital and the process of social decision making within the impersonal cash nexus of the market. The problems cannot be solved until their underlying causes are eliminated, but this means a fundamental, radical economic reorganization. If private ownership of capital is eliminated and if significant restrictions are placed on the areas in which the market determines social decisions, the resulting system would no longer be a capitalist economic system. It would of necessity be some type of socialist society.

SUMMARY

From the late 1950s to the early 1970s, the civil rights movement, the women's liberation movement, and the antiwar movement generated a resurgence of radical criticism of American capitalism. The radicals argue that inequality, discrimination, alienation, environmental destruction, militarism, and imperialism are integral parts of a capitalist economy. Unlike liberals, who believe that these evils are accidental and that the system can be reformed, radicals contend that these evils cannot be overcome unless the basic structure of capitalism is fundamentally changed.

The principal obstacle to the achievement of such reforms is the fact that political power is derived from economic power. Radicals see capitalist governments as plutocracies hidden behind phony façades of democracy. Both political parties, they point out, spend many millions of dollars on each election. As a consequence, both political parties are almost completely controlled by the wealthiest 2 percent of the population, which owns most of the income-producing capital.[36] In this situation one would not expect the wealthy elite to support any government that threatened to destroy the basis of their wealth, privileges, and power. Therefore fundamental reform seems unlikely unless a reform movement can establish a base of power independent of wealth. This explains the popularity at radical gatherings of the slogan "Power to the People!"

[36]For detailed evidence for this point of view, see G. William Domhoff, *Who Rules America* (Englewood Cliffs, N.J.: Prentice-Hall, 1967), and Domhoff, *The Higher Circles: The Governing Class in America* (New York: Random House, 1970).

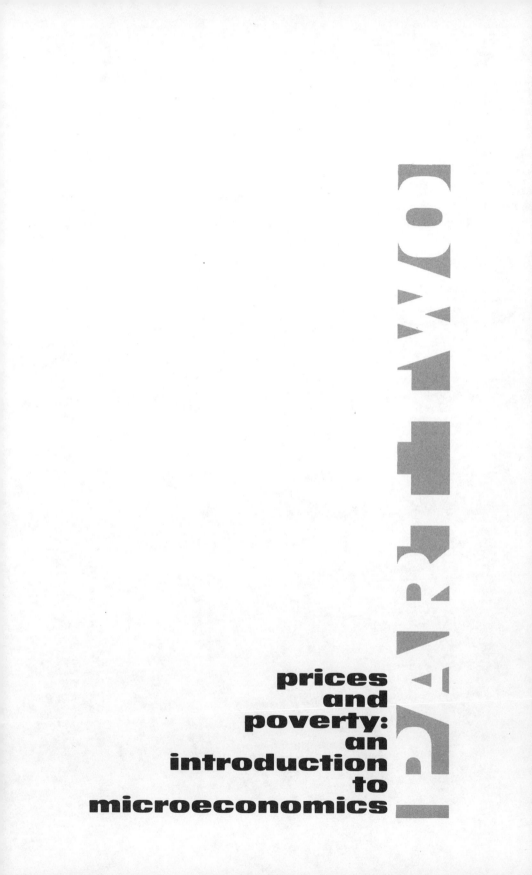

PART TWO

prices
and
poverty:
an
introduction
to
microeconomics

market allocation of resources: efficiency versus fairness

Part One of this book sketched some of the highlights in the history of economic thought and in the evolution of the private enterprise, or capitalist, system. In Parts Two, and Three, the actual working of the capitalist system is discussed. Part Two will concentrate on *microeconomics*, the economics of individual enterprises and individual workers and consumers; Part Three will deal with *macroeconomics*, the operation of the economy as a whole. Thus in Part Two, we shall discuss, among other things, how enterprises set prices and make profits under competition and monopoly, how workers' wages are determined, how the government affects the distribution of income, and the economics of racial and sexual discrimination.

A private enterprise economy is one in which the factories, tools, and stocks of goods with which production is carried on are owned by private individuals. Individual ownership includes, of course, the corporate form of ownership. In the corporation, individuals own the whole capital, but each person's ownership is specified in the form of the stock or shares that he holds.

Most modern private enterprise economies are distinguished by socially and technologically complex methods of production and distribution. It is possible to imagine an economy of small farmers and artisan-producers in which each individual owns his own means of production and is a fairly independent producer. In the reality of the modern private enterprise economy, however, this type of individual independence is completely impossible. The factory system, which the Industrial Revolution ushered in, has made individual producers completely dependent. A worker in an automobile factory, for example, owns no tools of production. He cannot, by himself, produce anything. He depends for his continued existence on being able to sell his labor time to a company that employs hundreds of thousands of people just like him. His work generally consists of one small, insignificant, and tedious operation (such as screwing a particular nut onto a particular bolt) that he repeats endlessly for eight hours.

In the American economy about 1.8 percent of the population owns 80 percent of all corporate stock. Most of the remaining 98.2 percent own little or no capital and depend on the *market* for their labor services to earn a living. When a worker succeeds in selling his labor services, he is paid a wage that is then spent in the market for goods and services. By purchasing these goods and services, he is playing a small (usually *very* small) role in creating the demand that provides jobs for the other workers who produce these goods and services. In fact, in the U.S. economy the continued employment of any individual may depend on the actions and behavior of hundreds of thousands or even millions of other people. All these people are related to this individual through only one social institution: the market. It is therefore vitally important to understand how the market functions.

In a private enterprise economy the market determines what is to be produced. Capitalists, or their hired managers, are motivated primarily by their drive to maximize profits. They go to the market to hire labor and buy raw materials, which they combine with the factories, machinery, and tools they own in order to produce an output. (Many capitalists are strictly middlemen and financiers and are not directly connected with productive output, but for our present purposes we shall ignore them.) They then sell their output in the market.

Their objective is to maximize the difference between their sales proceeds and their money expenses incurred in buying raw materials, hiring labor, and replacing used-up capital. This difference is, of course, profits. They constantly search for commodities that can be produced and sold profitably.

The capitalists' costs of production represent income to laborers and the owners of raw materials. Profit is the income that accrues to the capitalist. The recipients of these incomes spend them in the market for the goods produced by the capitalists' business firms. Thus money circulates from the business firms to the general public in the form of incomes generated in the production process. The money then returns to the business firms when the public purchases the goods and services these firms sell in the market.

There is thus an amazingly complex circulation of money from hundreds of thousands of business firms to hundreds of millions of people and back into the hands of the business firms. At all points the guiding force is the capitalists' constant search for profits. The decisions concerning what goods to produce (or even whether to produce), what inputs to buy, what wages to pay, and so forth are all determined by the criterion of profitability. All economic relations between people are mediated by the institution of the market. The market is obviously one of the most important social institutions in a private enterprise economy. In this and the several following chapters, we shall attempt to achieve a clearer understanding of what markets are and how they function.

It is important to begin by distinguishing a particular market and the market system (or, as it is often referred to, *the* market). Historically, a market was an area, usually near the center of a village or town, where producers and traders would meet and exchange goods. Later, any place where a merchant habitually sold his wares was a market. Today we sometimes refer to a grocery store as a market, but the word *market* is more generally used as an abstract concept. It refers, in general, to the negotiation of exchange transactions that generally involve money, and the determination of the prices at which these exchanges are transacted.

We speak of the stock market, the labor market, or the automobile market when we are referring to the buying and selling of stocks, labor services, or automobiles. We speak of the market or the *market system* when we wish to refer to monetary exchange and price determination in general. It is obvious that any market system that successfully facilitates price determination and exchange must contain complex systems of customs and traditions, laws, and agencies of law enforcement as well as the physical buildings in which business is transacted.

In this part of the book, physical settings of markets and many of the customs and laws that enable markets to function will be ignored. We shall concentrate on exchange (buying and selling) and the determination of price.

A market is basically a two-sided phenomenon with buyers facing sellers. Buyers have money they wish to exchange for goods, and sellers have goods they wish to exchange for money. The amount of a good that buyers would like to purchase at any given time is referred to as the *demand* for that good. Similarly, the amount of the good that sellers would like to sell is referred to as the *supply* of the good.

It should be stressed that demand is not necessarily related to need or desire. A penniless child longingly gazing through the window of a candy store adds nothing to the market demand for candy. Similarly, in the Great Depression of the 1930s millions of people went hungry while tons and tons of wheat and thousands of cattle and sheep were destroyed and wasted because of the lack of any market demand for them. The problem, of course, was that, like the child at the candy store, the unemployed millions had no money to exchange for food.

DEMAND AND SUPPLY

Restated more formally, the definitions of demand and supply are as follows: *Demand for a good refers to the amount of that good buyers would like to purchase during a given period and at a given price.* Obviously demand must be expressed in terms of a given period if it is to have any meaning. The number of automobiles people wish to purchase is certainly very different over the course of a week as opposed to a year. Similarly, a given price must be specified. Clearly the number of Ford cars people would like to buy will be very different if the price is $500 than if it is $5,000. An important point is that a demand for $100 worth of a good is simultaneously a willingness to supply $100 in money.

The definition of supply is very similar to that of demand. *Supply of a good refers to the quantity of that good sellers would like to sell during a given period and at a given price.* The supply of $100 worth of a good is simultaneously a demand for $100 in money.

If the reactions of buyers and sellers at different prices are considered, it becomes possible to define a demand schedule and a supply schedule. A *demand schedule* relates *various prices* of that good with the *amounts* of that good people would like to buy at each of the various prices. If the people of the United States were polled in order to determine the number of Ford Pintos they would like to buy at various prices, the results might be similar to those given in Table 14.1.

The information contained in this demand schedule can be shown on a graph as a demand curve. (See Figure 14.1.) A *demand curve*,

TABLE 14.1

NUMBER OF FORD PINTOS DEMANDED AT VARIOUS PRICES

Price	Quantity Demanded per Year (in 100,000s)
$1000	10
1500	8
2000	6
2500	4

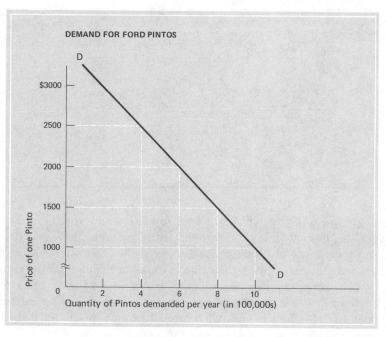

Figure 14.1

like a demand schedule, relates prices to quantities demanded. The *DD* curve makes it possible to select any price and ascertain the quantity buyers would like to purchase at that price.

Why does the demand curve usually have a downward slope? At higher prices, people have a small demand—both because other goods appear more attractive and because they just don't have enough income to buy at those prices. As prices decline, people demand more —both because they can afford more and because these goods are now cheaper relative to other alternatives. We discuss these issues in more detail in later sections.

In a similar manner it is possible to find the number of Pintos the Ford Motor Company would desire to sell at various prices. Table 14.2 summarizes this hypothetical information. In Figure 14.2 the same information is expressed in the form of a supply curve, demonstrating the quantities sellers would like to sell at various prices.

Why does the supply curve usually slope upward? Ford is in business for profit. At higher prices it can make more profit, so it is willing to supply more Pintos at higher prices. This issue is also discussed more fully in later sections.

Market prices are determined by the forces of supply and demand. Sellers wish to exchange products for money, and buyers wish to exchange money for products. When a particular price is established,

TABLE 14.2

NUMBER OF FORD PINTOS SUPPLIED AT VARIOUS PRICES

Price	Quantity Supplied per Year (in 100,000s)
$1000	2
1500	4
2000	6
2500	8

a specific quantity will be offered for sale and a specific quantity will be demanded. If these two quantities are equal, both sellers and buyers are able to conduct transactions in the desired quantities. For example, in Figure 14.3 the demand curve for Pintos (from Figure 14.1) is superimposed on the supply curve (from Figure 14.2). If a price of $2,000 is established, the point at which the curves intersect indicates that buyers and sellers want to buy and sell 600,000 cars.

When the desires of buyers and sellers are consistent and both are able to conduct their desired exchanges, the market is said to be in *equilibrium*. The notion of equilibrium is central to most economic theories. It generally means that supply and demand are equal and that the exchange desires of buyers and sellers are mutually consis-

Figure 14.2

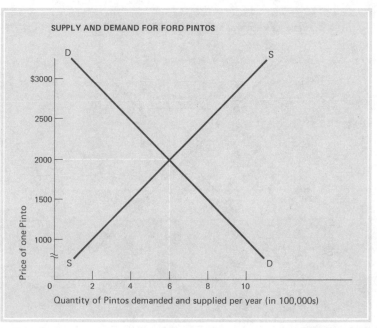

Figure 14.3

tent. At equilibrium prices everyone is able to buy or sell all that he chooses to buy or sell within his budget.

If a price that is higher than the equilibrium price is established, then supply will exceed demand. This is called a situation of *excess supply*. In Figure 14.4, if the price of Pintos is set at $2,500 an excess supply exists. Ford would like to sell 800,000 Pintos at that price, but buyers would like to buy only 400,000. There is an excess supply of 400,000.

In many markets there is a tendency for the forces of supply and demand to cause price changes that will eliminate excess supply and equilibrate the market. In the situation illustrated in Figure 14.4, thousands of Pinto dealers will find that at the established price of $2,500 they are unable to sell the quantity of cars they had anticipated. As unwanted inventories of unsold cars accumulate, the dealers cut back or eliminate entirely their orders with the Ford Motor Company. With production geared for the 800,000 cars the manufacturer had hoped to sell, it is not long before large unwanted inventories pile up at the factory.

In order to reduce these inventories and stimulate sales, the manufacturer *may* reduce the price, which definitely would improve the imbalance between supply and demand. As long as the price remains above $2000, however, the excess supply will persist, and the motive

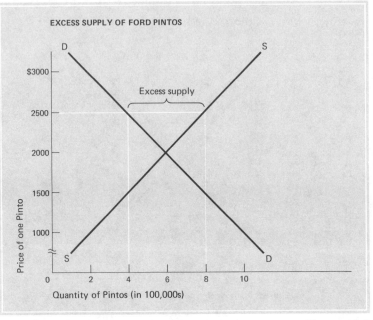

Figure 14.4

to cut the price further will continue to exist. Only at the equilibrium price of $2000 will excess supply disappear and the market be cleared.

At a price below $2,000 demand would exceed supply. (See Figure 14.5.) Dealers would find long lines waiting to buy the few available cars. Orders sent to Ford would go largely unfilled because these orders would far exceed the number of Pintos being produced. Figure 14.5 shows that at the low price of $1000 Ford will offer to supply only 200,000 cars but consumers wish to buy 1,000,000 cars. There is therefore an excess demand of 800,000 cars.

Under these conditions it would be obvious to the dealers and the manufacturer that more cars could be sold at higher prices. The search for higher profits would dictate that the price be raised. As the price is raised, the amount of excess demand declines. But at any price below $2000 there will continue to be some excess demand. There will therefore continue to be an upward pressure on the price until it reaches the equilibrium level of $2000.

The rate at which price changes bring the market into equilibrium varies greatly from market to market. In some markets sellers are very sensitive to unwanted changes in inventories, so adjustments in price occur very quickly. The New York Stock Exchange is highly sensitive to hour-by-hour fluctuations in supply and demand.

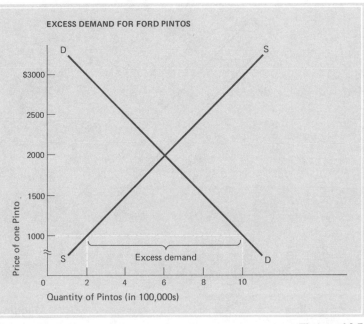

Figure 14.5

Frequent price changes serve to keep the market very near equilibrium at all times.

At the other extreme, what is for most people the most important of all markets—the labor market—may go for years in a situation of disequilibrium. With only a few exceptions (mostly in time of war), this market has had a persistent excess supply, which means, of course, involuntary unemployment for some people. This is a subject that will receive considerable attention in Part Three.

There are also many cases in which control of supply or demand gives an individual or group of individuals the power to *fix* prices. In this case excess supply or demand may not lead to price changes if those changes are not in the best interests of the price fixer. We shall examine this fact and its implications in later chapters (17 and 18) on imperfect competition, *oligopoly* (when a few firms control supply), and *monopoly* (when one firm controls supply).

CHANGES IN DEMAND

There are three main factors that can change the demand for a particular commodity: (1) price changes, (2) changes in tastes or preferences, and (3) changes in income that consumers have to spend.

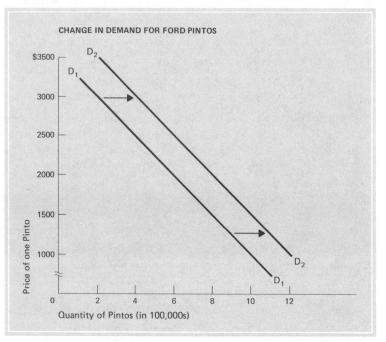

CHANGE IN DEMAND FOR FORD PINTOS

Figure 14.6

We have already discussed price changes. With a given demand schedule, a lower price means more demand, while a higher one means less demand.

Suppose there is a change in preferences, with consumer preferences shifting from big, gaudy cars to small, economical ones like the Pinto. What happens to the demand schedule? At any given price, more will be demanded. This upward shift in demand is illustrated in Figure 14.6. The old demand curve, D_1D_1, is replaced by a new and higher demand curve, D_2D_2.

Now consider another influence on demand. Suppose that there was a general increase in the incomes of all people consuming Pintos. Wtih the new, higher incomes individuals will probably buy *more* Pintos at *every* possible price. The higher incomes cause a *shift* in the demand curve. This produces a *new demand curve* (line D_2D_2). *At any price* the new demand curve shows that people wish to buy more at that price than they formerly did (when line D_1D_1 was the demand curve).

This increased demand is the result of the increase in income. In general, whenever there is a change in any of the factors (other than price) that affect demand, this change will be shown as a shift in the demand curve.

A bit of terminology here will make you sound like a sophisticated economist and may save you some confusion later on. Whenever an economist says flatly "demand has changed," he means *the whole demand curve has shifted*. An increase in demand means a shift of the curve outward (to the right, from D_1D_1 to D_2D_2); it means *more* Pintos are demanded at any given price. A decrease in demand means a shift of the curve inward (to the left, from D_2D_2 to D_1D_1); it means *fewer* Pintos are demanded at any given price.

When everything else stays the same (i.e., the curve does not shift) and only the price changes, the economist will *not* say "demand has changed." He will just say there has been *"movement along* the demand curve," or a change in quantity demanded. He will say, "at a higher price, less quantity was demanded" or "at a lower price, more quantity was demanded," but with no change or shift in the demand curve as a whole. In other words, with no shift in demand Ford could sell more Pintos only by lowering the price (and if Ford raises the prices it will sell fewer Pintos).

Of course, in reality both things often happen at once: (1) Prices of Pintos change, and (2) income and other factors affecting demand change. As a result of both (1) and (2), the quantity of Pintos demanded has changed. But it is impossible to be sure how much of the demand change was a result of the price change (movement along the demand curve) and how much was a result of changes in income and other factors (shift in demand curve). In other words, reality does not draw curves; only economists draw curves to try to analyze what is going on.

CHANGES IN SUPPLY

The explanation of shifts in demand and movements along demand curves may be repeated for changes in supply. The student should work this through himself in Figure 14.7. Consider, for example, the way higher or lower prices per car would cause Ford to move along the supply curve (S_1S_1), offering more or fewer Pintos to the consumer market at different prices. But also consider the way lower costs per car (such as a lower price of steel per ton) might motivate Ford to offer more Pintos at each given price consumers would pay (i.e., a shift from supply curve S_1S_1 to S_2S_2).

CHANGES IN SUPPLY AND DEMAND

Finally, by putting the changes in supply and demand together it is possible to explain how prices are forced to change. The effect on the price of Pintos of an increase or decrease in demand (with supply conditions remaining unchanged) is shown in Figure 14.8.

Figure 14.7

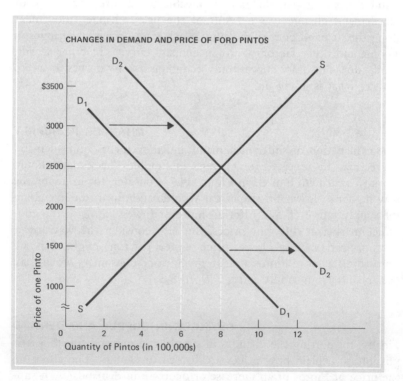

Figure 14.8

An increase in demand for Pintos can be explained as a shift up from curve D_1D_1 to D_2D_2, or as a movement along the supply curve *SS* up and to the right. Either description is correct. Either way, the fact is that Ford can sell *more* Pintos at a *higher price*. The quantity sold went from 600,000 to 800,000; the price went from $2,000 to $2,500. Of course there is nothing mysterious about that delightful result for Ford. It happened because it was assumed that demand shifted to Pintos (from Chevrolets or Volkswagens, perhaps). In the example in which Ford could sell more Pintos only at a lower price, it was assumed that there was *no* shift in demand to Pintos.

Similarly, in Figure 14.8 a decrease in demand for Pintos means a shift down from curve D_2D_2 back to D_1D_1. Suppose consumers shift demand from Pintos to Volkswagens. Then Ford will sell *fewer* Pintos at a *lower* price per car, assuming that the supply curve remains as drawn.

Now, on the other side, consider the changes in the supply of Pintos while the demand remains the same. (See Figure 14.9.)

An increase in supply means a shift over from curve S_1S_1 to S_2S_2. For some reason, perhaps lower costs per car or competition from Volkswagen, Ford is offering to supply more Pintos at every price at which consumers might demand them. There is an outward shift in the supply curve or a *movement* out *along* the demand curve.

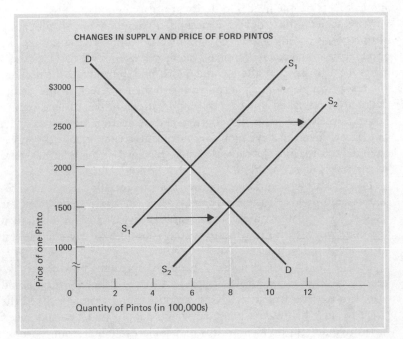

CHANGES IN SUPPLY AND PRICE OF FORD PINTOS

Figure 14.9

With demand unchanged, Ford is selling more Pintos by lowering their price. Whereas it previously sold 600,000 Pintos at $2,000 each, it now sells 800,000 at only $1,500 each.

A decrease in supply means shifting back from S_2S_2 to S_1S_1. Suppose, for example, that Ford's production costs rise for some reason. It may then charge higher prices *and* sell fewer cars. The supply curve has shifted, moving back along the demand curve, so that prices have gone up and fewer Pintos are being sold.

Of course in reality *both* curves may shift in the same period. Because of this possibility, it is usually impossible to tell which curve has shifted and which has remained stationary (or by how much each has moved) in the real world.

THE MARKET AS AN ALLOCATIVE DEVICE

One of the central problems with which economics deals is the allocation of scarce resources. Perhaps the most universal of social and economic problems faced by all societies is the fact that no society's capacity to produce or secure goods has yet been sufficient to satisfy all the wants, needs, and desires people have for these goods. Any good is considered by economists to be a *scarce good* when demand would exceed supply *if the good were to be given away freely in any desired quantity with no price charged for it*. It is obvious that most objects people need and desire are scarce goods.

Any society must devise a method of dividing up or allocating scarce goods among its citizens. In a slave economy, the slaves, like productive domesticated animals, were given enough to keep them fairly healthy so that they could work and reproduce themselves; the rest of the economy's output went to their masters. In the feudal economy (described in Chapters 1 and 2), conditions of land tenure largely determined the distribution and allocation of goods. The feudal serf, like the slave, got a minimal subsistence income, whereas the feudal lord, like the slave's master, received a much larger share in the fruits of production.

In a private enterprise economy, the market allocates scarce resources and goods. If the needs and desires for a particular good far exceed the available supply (as is the case with most goods), then the good goes to those who are willing and able to pay the highest price for it in the market.

It may be the case that many people desperately need a car like the Pinto but cannot afford its present price, although they could afford to pay a lower price. Now suppose the government fixed the price by law below the point at which supply and demand meet. There would still be two groups of people excluded from the consumption of Pintos: (1) Those who could not afford to pay even the lower price would again be excluded; (2) those who did not get their places in line before the supply of Pintos was exhausted would be excluded, in spite of the fact that they would have been willing and able to pay even the higher price. This kind of shortage may become a common situation in America if the wage-price controls begun in late 1971 are continued for a long period. In some socialist countries, such as the Soviet Union, price fixing of this type is fairly common. This explains the frequent reports of "shortages" and long queues in these countries.

Obviously, to the extent that markets tend to be self-equilibrating in a private enterprise economy and that there is no government price fixing, there will be a tendency for these shortages to be eliminated. It must be emphasized, though, that economists use the term *shortage* in a way that has no necessary relation to the abundance or lack of abundance of a good relative to people's need for it. The shortage is only relative to the demand *in money terms* by paying customers.

For example, imagine two economies, one in which an efficiently self-equilibrating market exists and another in which goods are all given away free on a first-come, first-served basis. In the first economy, there may be an extreme paucity of provision with only a tiny elite minority receiving most of the meager supply of available goods. If the markets are all equilibrium, there are no shortages in the economist's sense, despite the fact that many may be dying of starvation. In the second economy, there may be an abundance of goods that are given away at no charge. Even though virtually everyone might be very well off relative to even the richest citizens in the first economy, if some people want more than is available to them there will be an economic shortage.

It is important to understand clearly the economist's meaning of the word *shortage* because the assertion that a market economy has fewer shortages than a nonmarket, or planned, economy is often misconstrued to imply that the material welfare of people in a market economy must be higher than that of people in a nonmarket economy. This welfare may or may not be higher, but it has nothing to do with the existence or nonexistence of economic shortages. In fact, in economies where the decision has been made *not* to use the market as the primary device to allocate scarce resources, the people have chosen to divide the produce of society by some nonmonetary means. They will no longer exclude those who cannot afford to pay the market price for a scarce good but must use some other principle of distribution.

How can market versus nonmarket means of allocating scarce goods be evaluated? Such an evaluation would require the weighing of many diverse considerations. The market tends to allocate scarce goods with a minimum of inconvenience and bureaucratic red tape. The whole process is generally quite efficient and impersonal. By contrast, look at two widely used nonmarket allocative mechanisms. First, there are rationing coupons like those used by the United States during World War II, which limit the amount of a scarce good any individual can purchase, regardless of the amount of money he has. Second, there is the first-come, first-served technique, in which those at the end of the queue are automatically eliminated when the supply of the good in question is exhausted.

The first of these nonmarket allocative mechanisms involves the high cost of extensive record keeping and some inevitable bureaucratic inefficiencies in the control and distribution of the coupons. The second method causes much wasted time as people wait in queues. If often leads to bitterness and resentment because people who can afford to buy the scarce commodity wait in line for a long time, only to find the supply exhausted when they finally work their way to the head of the line.

Thus it can be said that, in terms of convenience and efficiency, the market is probably superior to these two nonmarket allocative mechanisms (the superior efficiency relates only to the allocative process and implies nothing about technological efficiency in the production of goods and services in private enterprise versus nonmarket economies).

The market is frequently criticized, however, on the grounds that the resultant allocation of scarce goods is inequitable, unfair, and unjust. It is argued that in a private enterprise economy like the United States, where a few people receive the overwhelming bulk of all profits generated by the economy, an unjustly lopsided concentration of income and purchasing power is created. Many economists feel that as a consequence of this concentration of purchasing power the private enterprise economy emphasizes production primarily for the wealthy. In allocating scarce medical care, for example, the private enterprise system places more importance on psychiatric care for the neurotic pets of the wealthy than it does on the provision of minimal health services for the children of the poor.

To illustrate this last point, imagine a hypothetical island economy that is periodically struck with an epidemic of a disease that affects only children. From past experiences the islanders have found that when the disease strikes it randomly affects 80 percent of the children. They have also discovered a preventive antidote that reduces the chances of death if it is taken before the disease strikes. A child who has taken no doses of the antidote has a 90 percent chance of dying when he contracts the disease. With one dose of the antidote, the chance of death is reduced to 10 percent. Two doses reduce the chance to 8 percent; three doses reduce the chance to 6 percent; four doses reduce the chance to 5 percent. Beyond four doses, the anti-dote has no further effect, and the chances of death remain at 5 percent.

Suppose that the island has 1000 children and that at the first sign of a new outbreak of the dreaded disease the people have produced and accumulated 1000 doses of the antidote. The antidote must be used immediately if the children's lives are to be saved. What system of allocation should the people use to distribute this extremely important scarce good? If the government on the island issues rationing coupons so that each child gets one dose of the antidote, then the following results could be expected: 800 children will get the disease, but since each has had one dose of the antidote, only 80 children will die; 920 children will survive the epidemic.

On the other hand, suppose the relative distribution of income and wealth that exists in the United States today. According to this income distribution, the islanders leave the allocation problem to the private-enterprise, free market system, with the following results: the 250 children who have the wealthiest parents will each take four doses of the antidote; of these 250, about 200 will get the disease and about 10 will die; of the remaining 750 children, 600 will get the disease and about 540 will die.

Using a nonmarket allocative mechanism, the islanders were able to save 920 children while 80 died. Given the unequal distribution of income and wealth that exists in the private enterprise market alloca-tion, they saved 450 children while 550 died. This is admittedly a farfetched example with hypothetical percentages chosen to illus-trate our point dramatically. But the point is there, and perhaps exaggeration is the most effective method of illustrating it. The student is urged to read *Don't Get Sick in America*,[1] a frightening but scholarly study that shows that this example is by no means as distorted as it might appear at first glance.

In ending this discussion on market allocation, it should be noted that one's view of the desirability of the market system depends on whether one is more impressed with the efficacy and impersonality of this allocation mechanism or with its lopsided results. Thus one defender of capitalism writes: "The case for capitalism is at its strongest on the simple thesis that the market knows best how to allocate and use the scarce resource of capital."[2] A critic of capi-talism sees it differently: "The main reason that freedom of contract has never been as free as advertised—and it is a painfully obvious reason—is that sellers and buyers are not equal in bargaining power.

---

[1] D. Schorr, *Don't Get Sick in America* (Nashville, Tenn.: Aurora Pub-lishers, 1970).

[2] Simon Webley, "The Utilization of Capital," in M. Ivens and R. Dunstan, eds., *The Case for Capitalism* (London: Michael Joseph, 1967), p. 41.

So the terms of sale will simply reflect the power, or lack of it, that each party brings to the market place. So a market is also a financial slaughterhouse, where the strong chop up the weak."[3]

Even the "efficiency" of the capitalist market has been criticized as a very narrowly limited concept. As will be seen in Chapters 17, 18, and 19, such efficient allocation of resources would operate only under pure competition; America, however, is characterized by a high degree of monopoly power. In Chapter 21 we explore the fact that if there is discrimination the market will reflect it and may reinforce it. In examining the aggregate economy in Part Three, we shall demonstrate that "efficient" use of resources applies only to employed resources but that the market system may leave many resources, both machines and human beings, unemployed. In Part Three we also note that private efficiency may ignore social costs such as pollution. This list of qualifications to market "efficiency" will be lengthened still further in Part Three, particularly when we consider the international market mechanism that includes the less developed two-thirds of the world.

SUMMARY

In a competitive market economy prices are determined by the conditions of supply and demand. Demand is based on consumers' desires and incomes. No cash, no sale. If there is pure competition, the market mechanism will allocate resources to each industry according to the cash demand for its product. Supply is based on the firm's costs of production. Thus, as costs go up, higher prices are required in order to induce the firm to supply more. As the price goes up, however, consumers will demand less. The equilibrium price will be the point at which supply and demand just balance. Its defenders claim that this system of production for private profit is efficient, even if it is not humane (but even its efficiency is very narrowly defined).

---

[3] D. T. Bazelon, *The Paper Economy* (New York: Random House, Vintage Books, 1963), p. 52.

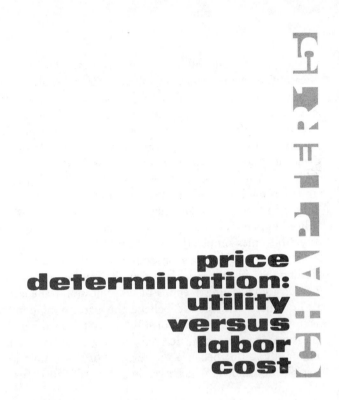

price determination: utility versus labor cost

In Chapter 14, we examined the ways in which competition in the market allocates all resources under private enterprise capitalism. We explored the mechanics of price determination by supply and demand. Now it is necessary to make a careful examination of the ways in which market supply and market demand are themselves determined by other forces. This will involve looking at consumer behavior in the market and then at enterprise behavior in the market. Finally, we will demonstrate the relationships between this understanding and the theories of value and price described in Part One.

UTILITY AND DEMAND

It has been demonstrated that the competitive market tends to allocate resources to produce things according to the pattern of consumer demand (wth each customer's desires weighted according to how much money he has to spend). The heart of neoclassical economics, from early theorists like Stanley Jevons to most present-day textbook writers, is the notion that consumer demand, in turn, is determined by the utility of each commodity to the consumer. *Utility* is defined as *the pleasure or satisfaction one receives from consuming a good*. Most textbooks state that utility alone determines how much people will be willing to pay for the good or how much of the good people will buy at various prices. However, several qualifications to this statement of the importance of utility must be made.

First, consumers often are persuaded by false and misleading advertising that they will receive a great deal more pleasure from a commodity than is attainable. On this basis they purchase the commodity, only to be disappointed and receive little or no satisfaction from it. Second, many actions are guided not by a search for pleasure, satisfaction, or utility but by habit, caprice, impulse, or any one of dozens of motives psychologists could list. Third, and most generally, a market society tends to inculcate a "buying mentality" in many consumers. The objective in making purchases sometimes becomes simply the spending of money per se rather than the satisfying of real needs or desires for the things purchased. This finding has been particularly emphasized in recent work in psychology concerning feelings of emptiness and alienation.[1]

For these reasons, we believe the pattern of consumer demand is forced into a particular form by many things other than the actual pleasure or satisfaction derived directly from consumption of each commodity. But because the term *utility* is almost always used to explain demand, it will be retained but redefined for our purposes. We conceive of utility as synonymous with desire. If we say that a particular good possesses utility for a particular person, we simply mean that that person *desires to buy* the good in question. The desire may be the result of any number of motives. It may be a healthy desire that will, if satisfied, increase the person's well-being, or it may be a perverted or morbid desire that will, if satisfied, lead to pernicious or harmful results. In other words, the satisfaction of any particular desire cannot be said, a priori, to be either morally good or morally bad until there is sufficient information available to make an independent moral judgment.

DIMINISHING MARGINAL UTILITY

Our examination of the theory of demand begins with the principle of *diminishing marginal utility*. The marginal utility of a good is defined as the strength of the consumer's desire to purchase *one additional unit* of the good. The principle of diminishing marginal utility states that *as more and more of a good is acquired, the marginal utility of the good diminishes*.

On a hot summer day, for example, a person may desire a malted milk very intensely. But if he has one malted milk, the intensity of his desire for another diminishes. If he has two malted milks, the intensity of his desire for a third will be very low. He may have no

---

[1]See the discussion by Erich Fromm in Chapter 13.

desire at all for a third. Another way of stating this is to say that the marginal utility of malted milks diminishes as one more is bought.

HOW CONSUMERS MAXIMIZE UTILITY

When consumers spend their income, they strive to maximize their utility. Suppose their income permits them to purchase a large number of different groups, or *bundles*, of commodities. They will try to choose the bundle that satisfies their strongest or most urgent desires; that is, they will attempt to maximize their utility.

The consumer comes to the market with (1) a set of preferences or desires and (2) a certain amount of money income. Because the consumer's desires are constrained by his income, he must pay attention to prices. It turns out that the consumer will maximize his satisfaction or utility when he spends his income so that *the marginal or additional utility derived from the last unit of each good purchased is exactly in proportion to the price paid for each good.* Another way to state this rule is to say that the consumer's satisfaction is maximized when an additional dollar spent for any one good yields exactly the same marginal utility as an additional dollar spent for any other good. This rule is explained further in a simple example whose calculations are shown in Appendix A to this chapter.

ELASTICITY OF DEMAND

Economists have developed concepts to describe demand curves in terms of how much the amount demanded reacts to a price change. If a small price change up or down causes a very big change in quantity demanded, the demand is said to be very *elastic*. But if a significant price change causes almost no change in quantity demanded, the demand is said to be very *inelastic*.

What kind of commodities have elastic demands (big reactions to price changes)? Mostly luxuries, such as movies or cake or Cadillacs. If the price is low enough, a consumer will be happy to buy a piece of cake or go to a movie or buy a new car. But if the price of one of these luxuries goes up while his income stays the same, the consumer will have to cut back on the luxury to buy things he needs more. Demand for luxuries is very sensitive to prices; it is elastic.

The demand curve for cake might look like the one in Figure 15.1. The demand is elastic because when price declines, the rise in quantity is more than proportionate, so the total expenditure (or revenue to the seller) actually rises. Thus, at $3 only 100 cakes are sold and the total revenue is $300. But if the price goes down to $2, then 300 cakes are sold and the total revenue rises to $600.

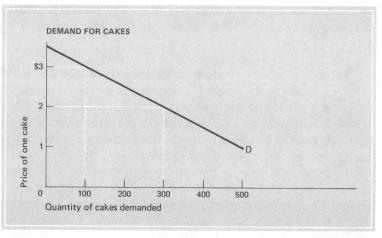

Figure 15.1

What kind of commodities have inelastic demands (small reactions to price changes)? Mostly necessities, such as medicine or basic foods. If you are diabetic and need insulin to stay alive, then you will still buy almost the same amount even if its price doubles. If you live in China and your main food is rice, then if the price rises considerably you will reluctantly look for a substitute; but you may still demand quite a bit. If the price of rice falls, you may demand more; but if it was already 80 percent of your diet, you will not demand much more.

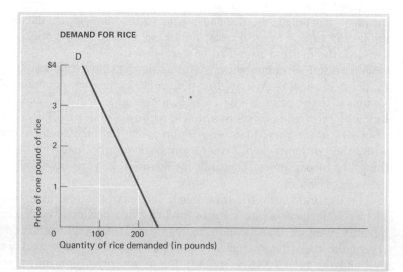

Figure 15.2

The demand curve for rice in China might look like the one in Figure 15.2. The demand is inelastic because when price declines, the rise in quantity is *less than proportionate*, so the total revenue declines. Thus, at $3 the quantity demanded and sold is 100 pounds and the total revenue is $300. But if the price goes down to $1, the quantity demanded only goes to 200 pounds and the total revenue *declines* to $200.

These, then, are the concepts of elastic and inelastic demand. They can be expressed in a general formula to measure elasticity. Elasticity may be defined more precisely as

$$\text{Elasticity} = \frac{\text{percentage rise in quantity demanded}}{\text{percentage cut in price}}$$

Of course it is just as easy to talk about a decline in quantity demanded due to a price rise or, in general, the percentage *change* in quantity demanded due to a percentage *change* in price. Exactly how to calculate elasticity is shown in Appendix B to this chapter.

SUPPLY AND MARGINAL COST

Consumer behavior and demand have been examined in great detail. In order to complete the picture, it is necessary to examine the behavior of business enterprises in supplying goods, but only in enough detail to supply the information necessary for an understanding of price determination in the competitive market. The details of business price and output behavior are very different for pure competition and for various degrees of monopoly power; these details will be discussed in the chapters on competition and monopoly.

A firm's decision regarding the quantity of its product it wishes to supply at various prices depends on many things. The most important factor, though, is usually its costs of producing different quantities of its product. Just as neoclassical economics emphasizes marginal utility in determining consumer demand, it emphasizes marginal cost in determining business supply to the market.

Marginal cost is the additional cost of producing one more unit of output. Suppose a firm owns a single factory with 100 machines. It can increase its output only by adding more raw materials and more workers. Here, however, there is a law of increasing marginal cost for firms that is similar to the law of diminishing marginal utility for consumers.

Assume a given factory and machines (and no time to add more or improve technology). Then the lowest cost per unit is reached at some particular flow of raw materials and some *given number* of workers. To make it simple, assume that raw material flow is always adjusted to the number of workers. As the number of workers is increased, the cost changes. If there are too few workers, they will not be able to handle the whole factory efficiently. But as the number of workers increases beyond some point, they add less and less to the product; or, the marginal cost of one more unit of output rises. For example, if there are only 100 machines and each machine needs only 1 man, what can more than 100 workers contribute? Certainly some are needed to bring in raw materials and to take them away, clean up, and repair. At some point, however, whether it is 125 or 150 or even 200, an additional worker could only add less than the previously hired worker.

Within these rigid assumptions it is hard to quarrel with this law. On this basis it is possible to picture marginal costs rising with output (after some minimal cost point is passed). Entrepreneurs will obviously not supply additional goods to the market at a price below their additional cost. Therefore, as the marginal cost of production rises for additional output, the prices at which additional supply will be offered must also rise.

In a perfectly competitive market the firm's supply curve is identical to its marginal-cost curve. (See Chapter 18.) The reason firms will supply goods at "cost" is that the traditional neoclassical definition of cost includes a "normal" profit. (The implications of this peculiar neoclassical definition will be examined in Chapter 18). With imperfect competition or monopoly, the amount a firm will supply is not determined solely by its costs. (This will be discussed in Chapters 17 and 18.) In the present context, however, it is sufficient to know that the firm's marginal cost is important in determining how much it will supply to the market.

THE PRICE AND OUTPUT OF AN INDUSTRY

Based on an understanding of the ways in which consumer desires (and income levels) determine demand and the ways in which enterprise costs determine supply to the market, it is possible to sum up the action of supply and demand for a whole industry. The mechanics of it were studied in Chapter 14. Here the main point is recapitulated in this new context.

Figure 15.3 shows the usual supply and demand curves. Supply SS is based on marginal cost; demand DD is based on marginal utility.

The point at which supply and demand meet determines both the price of the car and the number of cars produced. At any lower price level, there is excess demand, and therefore the industry can produce more cars *and* raise their price, hence making more profit.

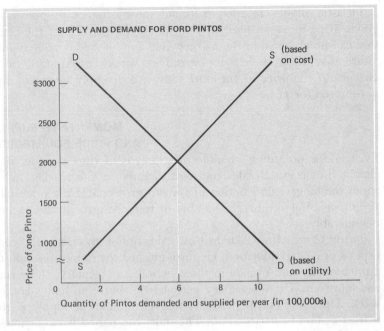

SUPPLY AND DEMAND FOR FORD PINTOS

Figure 15.3

At any higher price level, there is excess supply, and therefore the industry is forced to produce fewer cars and lower its prices.

The demand behavior is based on the marginal cost (always including a "normal" profit) of a Pinto to the Ford Motor Company.

This is a much oversimplified statement of the current view of price determination. Before it can be further refined and compared with earlier theories, one more tool is required: elasticity of supply.

ELASTICITY OF SUPPLY

It is not necessary to become involved in a detailed discussion of elasticity of supply because the concept is exactly analogous to that of elasticity of demand. Supply is elastic if it responds more than proportionately to a price change, and it is inelastic if it responds less than proportionately to a price change. More precisely,

$$\text{Elasticity of supply} = \frac{\text{percentage rise in quantity supplied}}{\text{percentage rise in price}}$$

Unlike demand, the quantity supplied moves in the same direction as price because a higher price means a higher profit (costs remaining the same), which induces a business to produce and sell more.

Inelastic supply reaction is found most often with perishable goods. Ripe tomatoes *must* be sold quickly, regardless of the price that can be obtained in the market. But durable goods such as furniture may show an elastic (sensitive) supply reaction to price changes. If the price of furniture falls, it can simply be stored and not offered for sale.

MOMENTARY SUPPLY
AND PRICE EQUILIBRIUM

Even in the preceding examples, the length of time considered is clearly important. Besides tomatoes already in the market, what about the longer-run reaction of tomato growers? If the price falls for a long enough time, the number of tomatoes grown *will* decline considerably.

In the 1890s Alfred Marshall used this notion to clarify the concept of price determination. He distinguished the supply reaction to a price or demand change in three periods: momentary, short run, and long run. The momentary period is so short (an hour, day, or week, depending on the product) that the amount of supply in the market cannot be varied at all. The short-run period is long enough for a factory to produce more or less for the market within its capacity but too short for any new factories to be built or put into use. The long-run period is long enough for as many new factories to be built as are necessary to bring the supply up to the demand.

How does this time factor affect elasticity of supply (and thus, indirectly, prices)? Assume that at a given moment Ford dealers have a certain supply of Pintos on hand. No matter what sudden change there is in demand, they cannot sell more until they receive more: Momentary supply is perfectly inelastic.

Assume now that the one Ford dealer in a town usually sells 10 Pintos a week and that the factory delivers 10 Pintos each Monday. One week he sells 6 Pintos up through Thursday. So on Friday he has 4 Pintos to sell. But that Friday 8 customers want to buy Pintos immediately (and are not willing to wait until Monday).

In this case the supply is fixed at 4, so the dealer will raise the price to take advantage of the higher demand. Suppose he has been selling at a price of $1,800. Because he cannot sell 8 at $1,800, he may try to sell the 4 he has at $2,000. (See Figure 15.4.)

The Ford dealer was ready for the usual demand D_1D_1, but the demand shifted that day to D_2D_2. Still, the supply is perfectly inelastic for that day; he simply cannot get more cars to sell in that period. So the higher demand reaches equilibrium with the fixed supply at a higher price.

Most of the early utility theorists (from the crude J. B. Say to the very sophisticated Léon Walras) concentrated on market exchange

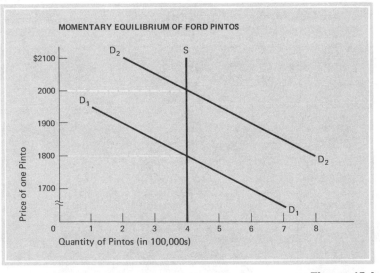

Figure 15.4

and gave litle consideration to changes in supply conditions. Consequently, it seems that this given momentary supply is the only case
they considered. They stated (and it is true in this case) that marginal utility determines demand and that demand changes largely
determine price changes. These theorists used this case to attack
the older theory (of Marx and the classicals—Ricardo and Smith)
that labor cost determines supply, which ultimately determines price.
Certainly *in this case*, where supply is perfectly inelastic, supply
cannot change and therefore cannot explain changes in price.

SHORT-RUN SUPPLY
AND PRICE EQUILIBRIUM

What price will bring an equilibrium of supply and demand in the
short run? Or how do supply and demand changes affect price in
the short run? These are the questions emphasized by Alfred Marshall and in every neoclassical beginning text to the present day.

Briefly, in the short run marginal cost tends to rise when a firm
tries to produce additional units of output beyond some point because the short run is, by definition, a period in which the firm has
a *given* factory and machinery and no time to expand it. Technology requires some particular number of workers to run the plant
at capacity (or at the cheapest cost per unit). When the firm tries to
produce more than the capacity for which the factory is designed
by adding more workers, the product per additional worker naturally declines; or, the marginal cost rises.

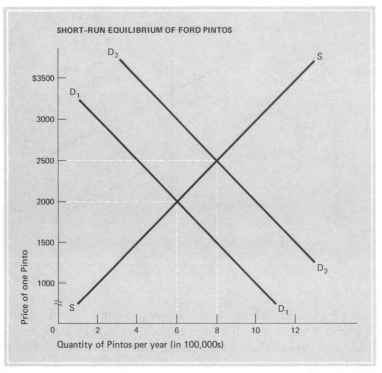

SHORT-RUN EQUILIBRIUM OF FORD PINTOS

Figure 15.5

Because supply will never be below marginal cost, the supply curve naturally rises (up and to the right, as in Figure 15.5) as output expands. In other words, with rising costs the firm will supply more goods only at higher prices; or, the supply curve is more or less elastic, depending on the product, but is certainly no longer perfectly inelastic.

A shift upward in demand will raise prices, as in the previous case, but now the new equilibrium price is clearly also affected by the movement along the supply curve.

Figure 15.5 shows that an increase in demand for Pintos raises *both* the price (from $2,000 to $2,500) and the quantity (from 600,000 to 800,000). The quantity rises because the supply curve is somewhat elastic. This reflects the fact that existing Ford plants have the capacity to turn out more Pintos, although at rising costs per car. It is clear in this case that both the quantity supplied and that demanded change and so together determine the new price equilibrium.

Alfred Marshall thus emphasized that supply and demand operate like the two blades of the scissors. Supply behavior is based on marginal costs. Demand behavior is based on marginal utility. It follows in the modern neoclassical view that both utility and cost together determine prices or values.

LONG-RUN SUPPLY AND PRICE EQUILIBRIUM

In the long run new factories can be built. Capital and labor can shift to industries where demand has risen. Therefore in the long run the quantity supplied can always rise as much as demand does.

Moreover, if Ford builds a new factory to produce more Pintos, the new factory need have no higher cost per car than the older factories. Hence the average cost (and the marginal, too) remain the same in the long run. Of course this is a rough approximation. In some cases, better technology may allow the new factory to produce Pintos at a lower cost per car. In other cases, expanded production with more use of a scarce raw material may drive the price of the raw material up, thus raising the cost per car. Here, for simplicity, the most common case—constant cost per car in the long run—is assumed.

If, however, marginal costs are constant in the long run, then the supply curve will also be constant. It will be flat, or a horizontal straight line on the graph. In short, supply will be perfectly elastic. Figure 15.6 illustrates this situation. In the long run what is the effect of an increased demand for Pintos? More factories are built, and the supply adjusts completely to the demand. Moreover, the new factories have about the same cost per car as the previous ones— assuming additional cost from greater use of resources is about canceled out by better technology.

In the long-run case, therefore, it can be asserted that the sole effect of an increase in demand is an equal increase in quantity produced. But the rise in demand has no effect on the price level. Of course at the initial moment of rise in demand, prices rose. However, that called forth more supply from existing factories in the short run, and therefore prices dropped a bit. In the long run, the entire rise in demand was met by an equal increase in supply from new factories. Since the new factories have the same cost per car as before, the price dropped back to its old level.

Therefore in the long run *demand determines the amount of production* (or the allocation of resources), *but supply alone determines the price level*. It can be said that the relative marginal utilities of different commodities determine the demand for them and the proportionate amounts of each produced. The long-run price level, however, is determined solely by the level of costs per unit—that is, the supply conditions.

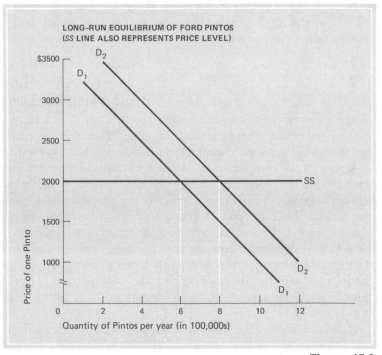

Figure 15.6

This is the case emphasized by the classicals and Marx. They were not so much interested in momentary or short-run market exchange and demand as in the long-run price or value of commodities. This they found to be determined solely by the cost of human effort or, as Marx put it, the total amount of human labor embodied in the product. He includes the labor involved in mining the raw materials and building the factories and machines used up in that production. This case, in which long-run labor cost determines price, is further explained in Appendix C to this chapter.

Marshall and the modern neoclassicals would agree that in this particular case of long-run supply and constant costs a change in marginal utility *does not* affect the price, but a change in the cost per unit *does* affect the price. The argument comes over the exact meaning of *cost*. The neoclassicals maintain that capitalists as well as workers put out an effort of some kind. The capitalist's "effort" may be a purely subjective "sacrifice" of immediate higher consumption for a later return on capital invested. Marx, however, insisted that it is only the workers' objective expenditure of labor that determines long-run price or value.

This dispute arises, of course, because these economists are concerned not only with the mechanics of price determination but also

with the equitableness of income distribution. If the contributions to
production by labor and capital are viewed differently, this obviously has much to do with how the distribution of income is viewed.
Should Ford workers or owners of Ford stock receive the income
from Pinto sales? This question of income distribution is discussed
in Chapter 16.

SUMMARY

Demand for a good is based on its utility, or the desires of the consumer plus the consumer's income. Supply is based on the cost of
production. At any given moment when supply is fixed, the changing demand sets the price. In a short run just long enough so that
a factory may produce more or less, both supply and demand
change and affect the price. In a long run long enough to build new
factories, the demand will still determine how much is to be produced—that is, the allocation of resources to different industries. In
the long run, however, any quantity that is demanded can be produced, so the price level will simply be determined by the cost
(including an average profit). In other words, in the long run twice
as much demand will mean twice as much production of the commodity; but if cost per unit stays constant, then the price will also
stay constant. The cost per unit is based on the total labor expended
to bring it to market, including both living labor and the labor
locked up in factories and machines used to produce it.

APPENDIX A
marginal utility and demand

Suppose that a person can spend his income on only three commodities: apples, bread, and cake. It is then possible to determine the quantities of each that he will buy in order to maximize his utility. Utility will be maximized if he buys the particular quantities of apples, bread, and cake that will leave the marginal utilities of each at a level at which the following condition holds:

$$\frac{\text{Marginal utility of apples}}{\text{price of apples}} = \frac{\text{marginal utility of bread}}{\text{price of bread}}$$
$$= \frac{\text{marginal utility of cake}}{\text{price of cake}}$$

The equality of these three ratios means that utility is maximized when the last dollar spent on apples yields the same utility as the last dollars spent on bread and cake. A numerical example will help explain this principle.

Table 15A.1 shows amounts of apples ranging from 1 pound to 6 pounds. The number of units of marginal utility for each pound of apples and the number of units of marginal utility per dollar for each pound of apples can be determined by reading across the table. The same kinds of assumptions are stated for bread and cake in Table 15A.2. Of course in reality it is not so clear that each consumer exactly measures or knows how many units of subjective

		TABLE 15A.1
Quantity (in Pounds)	Marginal Utility of Apples (in Units of Utility)	Marginal Utility of Apples per Dollar (Price: $1)
1	12	12
2	11	11
3	10	10
4	9	9
5	8	8
6	7	7

				TABLE 15A.2
Quantity (in Pounds)	Marginal Utility of Bread (in Units of Utility)	Marginal Utility of Bread per Dollar (Price: $2)	Marginal Utility of Cake (in Units of Utility)	Marginal Utility of Cake per Dollar (Price: $3)
1	24	12	30	10
2	22	11	27	9
3	20	10	24	8
4	18	9	21	7
5	16	8	18	6
6	14	7	15	5

utility he gets from each additional commodity. (Could you measure *exactly* the relative desire or utility to you of one more apple versus one more loaf of bread?)

Still, the theory does help elucidate consumer behavior in a rough sort of way. Now imagine that a consumer with an income of $24 dollars buys 6 pounds of cake for $18, 2 pounds of bread for $4, and 2 pounds of apples for $2. He has spent his entire $24 income, but he has not maximized his utility. The ratios of marginal utility to price are not the same for the three commodities. The ratios are as follows:

for apples $\dfrac{11 \text{ units of utility}}{\$1} = 11$ units of utility for last dollar

for bread $\dfrac{22 \text{ units of utility}}{\$2} = 11$ units of utility for last dollar

for cake $\dfrac{15 \text{ units of utility}}{\$3} = 5$ units of utility for last dollar

The utility he received from the last dollar spent on cake (5 units of utility) was considerably smaller than that of the last dollars spent on apples and bread (11 units each). Obviously this individual's utility could be increased if he shifted some of his purchases from cake to apples and bread.

If he gives up 3 pounds of cake, he will lose 54 units of utility but gain $9 to be spent on apples and bread. With this $9, the consumer purchases 3 more pounds of apples (thereby gaining 27 units of utility) and 3 more pounds of bread (thereby gaining 54 units of utility). Thus by shifting $9 worth of purchases the consumer gives up 54 units of utility and gains 81 units.

Obviously the second bundle of goods has more utility than the first. If the units of utility in the first bundle are added, they total 204 (6 units from cake = 135; 2 units from bread = 46; and 2 units from apples = 23). The total number of units of utility in the second bundle is 231 (3 units from cake = 81; 5 units from bread = 100; and 5 units from apples = 50). The ratios of marginal utility to price for the three goods in the second bundle are as follows:

$$\text{for apples} \quad \frac{8 \text{ units of utility}}{\$1} = 8 \text{ units of utility for last dollar}$$

$$\text{for bread} \quad \frac{16 \text{ units of utility}}{\$2} = 8 \text{ units of utility for last dollar}$$

$$\text{for cake} \quad \frac{24 \text{ units of utility}}{\$3} = 8 \text{ units of utility for last dollar}$$

Thus the maximizing condition holds; that is,

$$\frac{8}{\$1} = \frac{16}{\$2} = \frac{24}{\$3}$$

Purchases cannot be shifted among the commodities any further without losing some utility. The reader should experiment with such shifts in order to convince himself that this is a maximum.

With this information it is now possible to demonstrate why demand curves slope downward and to the right—that is, why the quantity demanded *increases* as the price *decreases*. (See Chapter 14.) Imagine an initial position at which all consumers are maximizing their utility—that is, they have equated the ratios of their marginal utilities and prices for all the goods. It is then possible to trace the effects of a decrease in price.

If the price of one good, say apples, were to decrease, consumers would find that the utility received for the last dollar spent on apples would be higher than that received for the last dollar spent on other goods. Consumers would immediately shift some of their purchases from other goods to apples. Thus the initial result of a decline in the price of apples is an increased quantity of apples demanded.

But what determines exactly how much demand will shift to apples? Exactly how much will the demand for them increase when the price declines? That depends on their marginal utility (the desire for an additional apple) relative to the marginal utility of other goods (the desire for more bread and cake). As consumers buy more and more apples, their desire for an additional one declines. (This is just one illustration of the law of diminishing marginal utility.) At the same time consumers are buying less of all other goods (less bread and less cake). So the *marginal* utility of other goods rises; at the margin, their desire for an additional piece of bread or cake is now increased. The process of shifting demand from bread and cake to apples stops when an additional dollar spent for more apples (even at the new, lower prce) yields just the same marginal utility as that spent for bread or cake (even at their old, unchanged prices).

APPENDIX B
elasticity of demand

Elasticity of demand was defined in words as:

$$\text{Elasticity} = \frac{\text{percentage change in quantity demanded}}{\text{percentage change in price}}$$

For those who prefer symbols to words, call elasticity E, quantity demanded Q, and price P, and let Δ mean "the change in." Then

$$E = \frac{\Delta Q/Q}{\Delta P/P}$$

The concept is important; the details of calculation are not. Nevertheless, the details may help you get the concept more firmly in mind.

Assume a move down the demand curve from some point 1 to point 2. The change in quantity demanded is $\Delta Q = Q_1-Q_2$. The change in price is $\Delta P-P_2-P_1$ because the price went down while quantity went up. The base for figuring the percentage could be either Q_1 or Q_2, with somewhat different results. As a convention economists always use the average, so $Q = (Q_1 + Q_2) \div 2$. Similarly, by convention $P = (P_1 + P_2) \div 2$.

The elasticity of demand for cake (shown in Figure 15.1) works out this way. Rise in quantity demanded is $300-100 = 200$. Average quantity, on which the percentage is based, is $(300 + 100) \div 2 = 200$. Fall in price is $3–$2 = 1. Average price is $($3 + $2) \div 2 = 2.5. Therefore

$$E_{cake} = \frac{200/200}{1/2.5} = \frac{1}{0.4} = \frac{100\%}{40\%} = 2.5$$

The percentage change in demand (100 percent) is much greater than the percentage change in price (40 percent); therefore the demand is elastic. More precisely, demand is elastic if E is greater than 1, and here E is 2.5.

Similarly, the elasticity of demand for rice (shown in Figure 15.2) works out this way. Rise in quantity demanded is $200–100 = 100$. Average quantity is $(200 + 100) \div 2 = 150$. Fall in price is $3–$1 = 2. Average price is $($3 + $1) \div 2 = 2. Therefore

$$E_{rice} = \frac{100/150}{2/2} = \frac{0.67}{1} = \frac{67\%}{100\%} = 0.67$$

Here the percentage change in demand (67 percent) is less than the percentage change in price (100 percent); therefore the demand is inlastic. Or, if you wish, it is inelastic because E is 0.67, which is less than 1.

To complete the concept, economists say that the demand curve is of *unitary elasticity* when E is 1. In this intermediate case the percentage change in demand is just the same as the percentage change in price.

At one extreme, a *perfectly inelastic* demand curve is shown by a vertical straight line. There is *no* change in demand when price changes. Thus E equals zero when demand is perfectly inelastic. However a *perfectly elastic* demand curve is shown by a horizontal straight line. When demand is perfectly elastic, E equals infinity. The firm can sell an infinite quantity of goods at the present price. Although these extreme cases are unrealistic, the concepts will be helpful later.

APPENDIX C
the labor theory of value

Most economists agree that in the short-run prices are best explained in terms of temporary movements of supply and demand curves. However, over a longer period there tends to emerge a relatively stable structure of prices. These long-run prices are what economists traditionally called "natural prices" or "normal prices." Economists have generally not considered explanations which rely on simple supply and demand curves as an adequate explanation of long-run or normal prices. They have advanced two types of explanations: several variants of the *utility theory of value* (of which we have examined one of the simplest) and the *labor theory of value*.

Theorists who hold a labor theory of value see the production process as necessary because the raw materials that make up the crust of the earth are not given to humans in easily usable forms. Raw materials must be transformed by human labor into more convenient and usable forms. This process of transformation is the process of producing commodities.

Karl Marx defined a commodity as any good or service which required the expenditure of labor to prepare it for the market and the production of which was motivated solely by the desire to sell it in a market. The value of a commodity has both a qualitative and a quantitative aspect. Quantitatively, it determines the rate at which the commodity can be exchanged for other commodities in the market. Qualitatively, the fact that an object of production has value reflects a particular stage in social history when specialization has isolated producers from one another, but where production remains a social act. The value of a commodity reflects the connection through the market that each isolated, individual producer has with every other.

Of particular importance in the evolution of commodity-producing societies is that stage of development where human exertion itself becomes a commodity—labor power—that is sold by one class of people (laborers) and purchased by another class of people (capitalists). At this stage commodity-producing societies become capitalist societies.

The labor theory of value can be illustrated with a simple example. (Table 15C.1.) Suppose in a small, simple commodity-producing society all producers make either blankets or apples. Suppose the looms on which to weave blankets and the trees on which to grow apples are communally owned and shared equally among all who wish to produce blankets or apples. On the average, it takes 3 weeks of labor time to produce 1 bushel of apples, while a blanket requires 1 week to produce. In such a situation, 1 bushel of apples will exchange for 3 blankets.

There are two ways in which a worker can get apples (or blankets): produce them directly, or produce blankets (apples) to sell in the market and use the proceeds to buy apples (blankets). The prices, $6 and $2, reflect the 3:1 ratio of labor embodied in the production of apples. At those prices it will not matter to a producer which of the commodities he specialized in producing. For a blanket producer to get a bushel of apples he must sell 3 blankets at $2 each. These blankets require 3 weeks work—the same amount with which an apple producer can acquire a bushel of apples. Similarly, an apple producer sells one-third bushel of apples for $2 and buys a blanket. The one-third bushel of apples requires 1 week to produce as does the blanket.

Suppose that apples were suddenly reduced in price to $4 per bushel. Now a bushel of apples could be gotten by working 3 weeks producing them directly, or by working 2 weeks, producing 2 blankets to be sold for $4, and buying the apples. Obviously, few pro-

			TABLE 15C.1
	Number of Weeks of Labor	Exchange Ratio	Price (If One Week is Valued at $2)
One Bushel Apples	3	1	$6
One Blanket	1	3	$2

ducers would want to produce apples when for only two-thirds as much work they could produce blankets and exchange them for apples. A large number of the apple producers would shift to blanket production. Almost immediately a shortage of apples would begin pushing the price of apples up, and the surplus of blankets would lead to a decline in the price of blankets. These changes will continue until the price ratio is, once again, 3:1. It might, for example, lead to prices of $1.50 for blankets and $4.50 for apples. These prices are proportional to the labor embodied in these commodities, and their establishment will once again make producers indifferent to whether they produce apples or blankets.

Surplus Value Under Capitalism

Now, suppose with prices of $6 and $2 prevailing, a sociolegal change takes place. The most cunning and unscrupulous member of society announces a new principle: private property in the means of production. He hires the strongest and most ruthless men as police to enforce the new laws of private property, and a group of clever academicians to devise theories designed to convince the public that these laws are natural and just. This man, then, becomes a capitalist. The first law of private property which he enunciates is this: no laborer shall use the weaving looms unless so directed by the capitalist who owns the looms. The capitalist himself owns the looms, of course, and this law merely means that he now has the power to determine if, and under what conditions, blanket makers can make blankets. The source of the power is, of course, the coercive power of the police whom he hired. He hopes, however, that the academicians do their job well, because no ruling or exploitive minority can maintain its position for long if it relies exclusively on coercive force.

In fact, under capitalist institutions, each capitalist makes profits from the blanket-making workers—and all workers—simply in the normal course of economic events. Marx explained that every capitalist sells his products for an extra value beyond the total paid out for present labor and the products of past labor (raw materials, supplies and machinery). This extra value is called *surplus value*. Where does the capitalist get this extra or surplus value?

The source of surplus value cannot be in mere buying and selling. A commodity must sell at, above, or below its value. If it sells at its value, then neither buyer nor seller has acquired surplus value through making an exchange alone. If a commodity sells above its value, the surplus value acquired by the seller is exactly offset by a loss of value to the buyer. Likewise, if a commodity sells below its value, the surplus value gained by the buyer is exactly offset by the loss of value to the seller. In each of these cases it is obvious that in net, for all of society, none of these exchanges can generate surplus value.

In order to understand the origin of surplus value, we must look at production. In the production process the capitalist buys one set of commodities—the means of production and labor power—and sells a different set of commodities—the final output produced by the laborers with the use of the means of production. The set of commodities which the capitalist sells has a higher labor value than the set of commodities which he buys and this surplus is what we call surplus value.

The source of the surplus value can be easily seen when one realizes that in an 8-hour work day the labor value of the commodity produced by a worker must, by definition, be 8 labor hours. But the 8 hours of labor power which the laborer sells to the capitalist is a commodity like any other commodity. We therefore must ascertain the labor value of the commodity called labor power. The labor value of labor power is simply that amount of labor that must be expended to keep the laborer selling his labor power and to reproduce his own replacements within his family. It is, as with all other commodities, the minimum amount of socially necessary labor to produce and reproduce labor power. In practice this turns out to be the amount of labor time necessary to produce the means of subsistence for a laborer and his family. For Marx and all other labor theorists, this subsistence was held to be socially as well as biologically determined. Therefore, labor theorists argue, on the basis of both theory and empirical evidence, that throughout the history of capitalism, and down to the present, most laborers have earned only enough to keep them and their families at a socially defined minimal standard of living and to establish the children at approximately the same class position as the parents.

The quantity of labor necessary to provide the laborer and his family with this subsistence turns out to be considerably less than the 8-hour day which he works; that is, the value of the labor power is considerably less than the value created by the labor power in the process of production. If it requires 6 hours a day to provide the necessities for a laborer's family for 1 day, then the labor value of 1 day's labor is 6 hours. But the standard work day is 8 hours. Therefore 1 day's labor power has a labor value of 6 hours but creates commodities having a labor value of 8 hours. The extra 2 hours is surplus labor, it produces surplus value, and is the source of capitalists' profits.

Redistribution of Surplus Value

Although surplus value is created only by labor, it is distributed among capitalists, through the competitive processes of the market,

in proportion to the total capital which they have invested. Therefore some capitalists receive as profits more than the surplus value
created by workers in their employ, while others receive less. But
overall total profits and total surplus value are equal. Competition
among capitalists merely redistributes surplus value; it neither increases nor decreases its magnitude.

To understand how competition redistributes surplus value—so
that the rate of profit on total capital is the same for all industries—
we must look more carefully at the components of capital. Capital
includes funds with which to pay wages, as well as raw materials,
goods-in-process, tools and machines, and factories. Marx called the
wage expenses of the capitalist *variable capital.* He gave it this name
because the worker creates surplus value with his labor and therefore the capital that the capitalist lays out in wages is variable in
value since it expands to replace itself plus to create profits. Marx
called the raw materials and the means of production *constant capital* because they merely reproduce their own value in a product and
do not create surplus value. Thus labor and not constant capital is
the source of surplus value.

On the other hand, the profits which capitalists receive are determined by the average rate of profit multiplied by the total of
both constant and variable capital. Competition among capitalists
ensures that the rate of profit on all capital will tend to be equal for
all capitalists. Under competition, if the rate of profit is lower in one
industry than in another, capital will move from the area of low
profits to high-profit areas. This will lower supply in the low-profit
areas, and raise supply in the high-profit areas. The prices rise in the
former and fall in the latter till profit rates are equal.

This means that if the proportion of constant capital to labor
differs from industry to industry, then the profit component in
prices will not necessarily reflect the amount of labor embodied in
each commodity. Furthermore, since the constant capital is comprised mostly of previously produced commodities, *their* prices will
differ from the labor embodied in them. The Marxist labor theory of
value shows that these deviations of prices from amounts of embodied labor follow a systematic, understandable pattern.

In Figure 15C.1 the rectangular bars are intended to depict constant capital and labor. The top bars reflect the final stage of production where the finished product is produced. The constant capital used at this stage of production consists of commodities produced
at an earlier stage of production. Therefore the bars immediately
below the constant capital bar reflect the ingredients used in that
prior period to produce the constant capital. The ingredients were,
of course, simply more constant capital and labor. But that constant
capital was itself produced in an earlier period and can be similarly

Figure 15C.1

reduced to its component inputs. Figure 15C.1 thus reflects a production process of four periods. Before that period, it can be assumed that only labor and raw materials began the process—or that the amount of constant capital has reached some arbitrarily determined order of smallness at which it can be ignored.

Since each stage of production (or level of bar graphs in Figure 15C.1) fully accounts for the constant capital of the next higher stage, we can reproduce Figure 15C.1 and show constant capital bars as dotted lines indicating that they have been dissolved into their component parts at an earlier stage of production. This is done in Figure 15C.2. When this is done it becomes clear what labor theorists mean when they say that production is a process of alteration of natural resources which is affected by labor and labor alone. All that remains in Figure 15C.2 is a series of *time dated labor inputs*.

Now we can show how the profits of the capitalist on his constant capital, as well as the profits on his variable capital, affect prices. We have already mentioned that the price of a commodity must include the value of constant capital plus a profit on constant capital. But the price of the constant capital itself reflected the value of prior constant capital plus profit earned on that prior constant capital. Thus the profit on constant capital is partly a profit made on the profit made on a prior constant capital. We are describing the phenomenon of compounding a growth rate. Profits are paid in one period and next period's profits include profits on those profits, etc.

From the foregoing it is obvious that prices depend not only upon

Figure 15C.2

the amount of labor embodied in commodities, but also upon the pattern through time that this expenditure of labor takes, and the rate of profit. The rate of profit is an integral and important part of the explanation. When the time patterns of labor inputs differ widely between two commodities, differences in the rate of profit can actually reverse the relative magnitudes of their prices. This means that with a low rate of profit one commodity will have a higher price than a second, while at a higher rate of profit the second commodity has the higher price, even though the amount of labor embodied in each, as well as the time pattern of labor has not changed.

This seems to some economists to refute the claim that the labor theory of value can show a systematic connection between the labor embodied in commodities and the prices of those commodities. This is not so, however, because the labor theory can explain the rate of profit in terms of the labor embodied in production. This being the case, it is obvious that the labor theory of value does, ultimately, fully explain prices in terms of the labor embodied in production.

distribution of income: marginal productivity versus exploitation

Different theories of the distribution of income lead to very different ideological positions vis-à-vis the evaluation of capitalism. Highly controversial issues are in question—for example, how capitalists make profits and whether workers are "exploited." Before these problems in theory are probed, it will be helpful to state the present factual situation to which they are relevant.

POVERTY

Everyone knows that much of the world lives in poverty, but it is more surprising to learn of the vast amount of poverty in the richest country in the world. In the United States in 1970, 14 percent of all families earned under $4000.[1] The official U.S. government definition of poverty, however, included any family living with a budget of less than about $3940.

Yet this official definition appears to be set much too low by contemporary U.S. standards. It is based on what the government admits is "an economy diet . . . meant for emergency or temporary use when funds are low—in other words a diet which over long periods of time does not meet minimum nutritional requirements."[2] Yet

[1]U.S. Department of Commerce, Bureau of the Census, *Statistical Abstract of the United States, 1972* (Washington, D.C.: GPO, 1972), p. 322.
[2]Donald Light, "Income Distribution," *Occasional Papers of the Union for Radical Political Economics*, December 1969, p. 2.

more than 25 million Americans were below that poverty line.[3] This means that most of them had not enough to eat of nutritional foods, lived in rat-infested slums, and obviously could not afford to give their children a good higher education.

The Bureau of Labor Statistics calculates that $6960 would be a "lower" budget for a city worker's family of four. (They also calculate "medium" and "higher" budgets.) This budget is certainly not extravagant: It assumes that clothes are replaced only after three years and that the worker has a used car or uses public transport. Furthermore, it assumes low-quality, low-rent housing. It assumes *no* money for recreation, nothing for college, and no saving for emergencies.[4] Yet 31 percent of all U.S. families fell below the income required for this pitiful budget. Moreover, 54 percent of all black families fell below this miserable "lower" budget.

INEQUALITY

Let us examine the full range of income in the United States, from very poor to very rich. This remarkable picture is shown in Table 16.1.

The poorest 10 percent of the families each made less than $2,700 a year, and all together received only 2 percent of all U.S. income. On the other hand, the richest 10 percent of the families each made over $20,000, and all together received 27 percent of all U.S. in-

TABLE 16.1

INEQUALITY OF U.S. INCOME DISTRIBUTION, 1970

Income Group of Family	Income Range	Percent of Total Income Received by Group
Lowest Tenth	$ 0–$ 2,700	2%
Second Tenth	2,700– 4,000	3
Third Tenth	4,000– 5,500	5
Fourth Tenth	5,500– 7,000	6
Fifth Tenth	7,000– 8,600	7
Sixth Tenth	8,600– 10,045	9
Seventh Tenth	10,045– 12,010	11
Eighth Tenth	12,010– 15,000	13
Ninth Tenth	15,000– 20,000	17
Highest Tenth	20,000 and Over	27

Source: U.S. Department of Commerce, *Statistical Abstract of the United States, 1972* (Washington, D.C., GPO, 1972), p. 324.

[3] U.S. Department of Commerce, op. cit., p. 330.
[4] U.S. Department of Labor, Bureau of Labor Statistics, *Three Budgets for an Urban Family of 4 Persons, 1969–70.*

come. These figures give some idea of the inequality in the United States. They indicate that the average family in the richest 10 percent received more than 13 times the income of the average family in the poorest 10 percent!

Moreover, income is still more concentrated in the very highest brackets. The richest 5 percent of families had over 14 percent of all family income. The richest 5 percent of unrelated individuals had 21 percent of all individual income. Only the top 2 percent of all taxpayers make over $30,000. Only the top one-tenth of 1 percent of all taxpayers make over $250,000 a year. About 2,000 taxpayers make over $1 million a year.

Because income is highly concentrated, saving is also. A small number of individuals and firms do most of the saving and investing of capital. In 1965 personal savings of individuals amounted to only $25 billion, whereas saving by businesses and corporations was $83 billion. Even within the category of personal savings, households in the lower two-thirds of the income range did no saving at all. On the contrary, most of this two-thirds consumed more than their total income; that is, they went into debt. More than half of all the personal savings available for investment was supplied by those in the upper 5 percent income bracket.

TRENDS IN INCOME DISTRIBUTION

Has there been any reduction of inequality in the distribution of U.S. income? The answer is shown in Table 16.2.

TABLE 16.2

HISTORY OF INEQUALITY OF U.S. INCOME, 1910–1970
(PERCENTAGES OF U.S. PERSONAL INCOME, BEFORE
TAXES, RECEIVED BY RICHEST 20 PERCENT AND
POOREST 20 PERCENT OF U.S. FAMILIES)

Year	Richest 20 Percent	Poorest 20 Percent
1910	46%	8%
1918	47	7
1929	51	5
1937	49	4
1947	48	4
1957	45	4
1965	44	4
1970	44	5

Sources: U.S. Department of Commerce, Bureau of the Census, *Statistical Abstract of the United States, 1972* (Washington, D.C., GPO, 1972), p. 324; also James Weaver, *Modern Political Economy* (Boston: Allyn & Bacon, 1973), p. 142.

The first thing we notice is how very little change there has been over this 60-year period. The most noticeable change is a fall in the share of the poorest 20 percent of Americans from 7 or 8 percent down to 4 or 5 percent, a fall by almost half. On the other hand, the share of the richest 20 percent of Americans has fluctuated in a narrow range, rising from 46 to 51 percent in 1929, then falling to 44 percent in 1970. Therefore we conclude that in spite of all the liberal outcry about inequality and all the government promises and programs to reduce it, there has been no improvement since 1910.

TYPES OF INCOME

Income is not randomly distributed among all individuals. On the contrary, distribution is closely related to type of income. Does most of a person's income come from labor (wages) or does it come from property (rent, interest, or profits)? If this fact is known, a good guess can be made about his income bracket.

Almost all the bottom 31 percent of families in 1970, those with less than the "lower" budget, were working-class families; and most of their income came from wages and salaries earned by their labor. But most of the income of the top 2 percent came from ownership of property in the form of rent, interest, or profit—in short, the income of the capitalist class. Moreover, the very, very rich elite (less than one-tenth of 1 percent of all taxpayers) collect 23 percent of all dividends and 37 percent of all capital gains. Fully 90 percent of the income in that top tax bracket is from property, and only 10 percent is from wages and salaries.[5]

Privately held wealth (the total someone owns at a given time) is even more concentrated than current income. In 1953, three American academic economists estimated that only 0.2 percent of "spending units" (i.e., 1 in 500 individuals or families reporting to the Internal Revenue Service) owned 65 to 71 percent of all publicly held stock.[6] In 1956, according to another conservatively calculated estimate, one-fourth of all U.S. privately held wealth was owned by only 0.5 percent of all Americans, and just 1.6 percent of the people held 32 percent of the wealth, including 82 percent of all stock.[7]

Notice the cumulative and self-reinforcing nature of the concentration of wealth and income. High concentration of stock ownership leads to a high concentration of income from profits. This in-

[5]U.S. Internal Revenue Service, *Statistics of Income, 1970: Individual Income Tax Returns* (Washington, D.C.: GPO, 1970).

[6]Keith Butters, Lawrence Thompson, and Lynn Bollinger, *Effect of Taxation on Investments by Individuals* (Cambridge, Mass.: Riverside Press, 1953), p. 400.

[7]Robert Lampman, *The Share of Top Wealth-Holders in National Wealth* (Princeton, N.J.: Princeton University Press, 1962), p. 24.

come is so concentrated that its recipients are in the highest income brackets. But it is only these highest income brackets that are willing and able to save significant amounts. Therefore they are the ones who make large investments, thus increasing their stock ownership. In other words, large ownership of stock leads to high income in the form of profits, but high income leads to more stock ownership.

The process of wealth and income concentration is self-reinforcing in other ways. For example, one vital prerequisite of upward mobility is education. But many careful studies have revealed that in a large percentage of cases "the father's income rather than the boy's brains determines who shall be college trained."[8] If you are poor, it is hard to support yourself through college even if you are of average intelligence. If you are rich but not bright enough to get into top universities, you can always find some private university willing to accept you for enough money.

Even with an education, though, the poor man can attempt to work his way up in business only from the point at which he is hired. The rich heir to a business may have little education and less intelligence but may still step into his father's shoes if he controls enough stock in the corporation. "It is very difficult to climb to the top. . . . It is easier and much safer to be born there."[9] In fact, many of the wealthy today merely inherited a great deal of stock. From 1900 to 1950 some 70 percent of the fathers of the very rich were big businessmen.[10] It is true that most of the very rich have "worked" as big businessmen; nevertheless, completely at-leisure coupon clippers increased from 14 percent of the very rich in 1900 to 26 percent by 1950.[11] The overall conclusion is that Horatio Alger's stories of poor boys rising into great wealth are myths. There is a certain amount of mobility from poor to middle-income status, but very little upward mobility from middle income into the richest elite groups.

There has also been a long-run trend toward less economic independence, with more people simply employees of businessmen. In 1800, perhaps 80 percent of the occupied population were self-employed entrepreneurs.[12] By 1870, the figure had fallen to 33 percent; by 1940, to 20 percent. This self-employed category includes all businessmen (big and small), all farmers (big and small), and all independent professionals. The percentage of those whose incomes came mostly from work for others thus rose from about 20 percent

[8]C. Wright Mills, *White Collar* (New York: Oxford University Press, 1956), p. 257. For precise data, see chap. 19.

[9]C. Wright Mills, *The Power Elite* (New York: Oxford University Press, 1959), p. 115.

[10]Ibid., p. 105.

[11]Ibid., p. 108.

[12]For this estimate and other facts in this paragraph, see Mills, *White Collar,* op. cit., pp. 63-64.

of the occupied population in 1800 to 67 percent in 1870 and 80 percent in 1940. This trend has continued in recent years.

THE MECHANICS
OF INCOME DISTRIBUTION

Adam Smith talked about *rent* going to owners of land, *wages* going to labor, and *profits* going to the owners of capital. What determines the share of each of these types of income in the net national income? Economists' answers to this fundamental question differ greatly according to their basic world views. In fact, there are really two closely related questions: (1) What determines the share of each type of income? (2) Is the present distribution of income among different types good or bad?

To simplify the question, in this chapter we shall ignore the rent of land. In the modern United States and most industrialized economies, it is a very small category and thus not essential to the argument. That leaves two of Smith's categories: wages and profits. We define *wages* to mean all labor income, including time and piece wages, monthly salaries, commissions, bonuses, and managerial salaries. We define *profits* to mean all the return on capital. For the purposes of this argument, profits are included both as the return on the entrepreneur's own capital (*dividends*) and as the return on borrowed capital (*interest*). For other purposes in later chapters, it will be necessary to distinguish between these two forms of profits. *Capital* is the factories, machinery, raw materials, and money with which production and commerce are conducted.

The modern corporation owns its capital goods: factory, machinery, and raw materials. It pays wages and salaries to workers (including managerial salaries and bonuses). The workers use the capital goods to produce a product. The product is owned and sold by the corporation. What is the difference between a corporation and an unincorporated business? The most important difference is that the individual capitalist owners are not liable for the debts of the corporation.

The owners of the corporation are its stockholders. They each own a number of shares of *stock*, which represent their portion of the value of the corporation. To get the stock, of course, they paid money to the corporation. It uses that money to buy capital goods and to pay for labor. It may also borrow money; usually it issues bonds, which show how much the lender is owed (and how much interest he gets). The stockholders receive dividends, which are all the profits of the corporation from sales less all of the costs paid out (including wages, depreciation of capital, and interest to bondholders). If the corporation is unable to pay its debts, it is ruled bankrupt by the courts. Those who have lent money to it will divide all its remaining assets. If there are any assets left over, they go to the stockholders. But if there are insufficient assets to cover the debts, that's just too bad; no one can sue the stockholders.

THEORIES OF INCOME DISTRIBUTION

In discussing how income is distributed between wages and profits, economists have advanced two distinct and opposing views. The conservative view has generally dominated and is still taught as gospel in most American textbooks. It is a justification and apology for the status quo of U.S. capitalism. According to the conservative theory, (1) profits result from the sacrifices and productivity of capitalists (as wages result from the labor of workers), and (2) therefore the present distribution of income, in which many high incomes are made from profits, is just and equitable. The radical view has been advocated for at least 150 years, but it is just now gaining prominence in the United States. According to it, (1) capitalists are unproductive and extract their profits from the product of labor, and (2) therefore we need a new economic system in which private profit is eliminated.

The Conservative Theory

The concept of profit as the reward to a capitalist for abstaining from immediate consumption was developed in the early nineteenth century by the economists W. Senior and J. B. Say. Each argued that provision of capital for production is a subjective cost, or disutility. The capitalist practices abstinence from consumption in order to invest capital and therefore is morally justified in making a profit from his investment. Similarly, wages result from subjective unpleasantness, or disutility, in providing labor.

In the 1870s Alfred Marshall[13] substituted *waiting* for *abstinence*. He argued that when the capitalist invests his capital in production he must *wait* to get the return from it until a future date. And the fact that he must wait to use all his wealth for consumption justifies his making a profit. Indeed, because he will not invest otherwise, a normal profit is simply a necessary cost of production.

The modern conservative theory of marginal productivity first appeared in full detail in John Bates Clark's *The Distribution of Wealth*, published in 1899.[14] It is dedicated to the propositions that workers and capitalists each receive in income exactly what they

[13]See Alfred Marshall, *Principles of Economics* (New York: Macmillan, 1953 [1st ed., 1890]).
[14]John Bates Clark, *The Distribution of Wealth* (Clifton, N.J.: Augustus M. Kelley, 1966 [first published in 1899]).

contribute as their marginal product and that this is an ethically just system. In other words, a worker's wage will just equal the additional (or marginal) product he adds to output. Likewise, the capitalist's profit just will equal the additional (or marginal) amount of product added by the piece of capital he adds to the productive process. This theory is gospel in all conservative textbooks, among them Paul Samuelson's famous work.[15]

The theory of marginal productivity is basically a very simple argument. Assume that there is a fixed amount of capital—that is, a particular factory and machinery. How many workers should be added by the rational capitalist to maximize his profits? Assume next that each additional worker adds something to the product, but that each additional workers adds less than the one before him. This is the case because there is a fixed number of machines for them to use; therefore workers can add very little beyond the optimum capacity of the given factory. Suppose that there are five machines and ten workers and that most efficient functioning requires two workers per machine. Table 16.3 demonstrates the contribution to the marginal product of additional workers in this hypothetical factory.

The capitalist should continue to add workers until he finds that the last worker's product just equals his cost, or wage. If the wage rate is $70 a week, he should hire only 13 workers (or 12). Because the thirteenth worker makes no additional profit for the capitalist, he should hire no more workers. The wage will just equal the additional (or marginal) product of the last workers.

Notice that what this theory has arrived at is a rule for capitalists to follow if they wish to maximize profits. If they do act this way (and they usually do), then the assertion that the wage is the same as the marginal product is at best a platitude: Workers are not hired if they produce a marginal product that is lower than the wage.

			TABLE 16.3
Number of Machines	Number of Workers	Total Product per Week	Marginal Product per Week
5	10	$1000	
5	11	1090	$90
5	12	1170	80
5	13	1240	70

[15]Paul Samuelson, *Economics,* 8th ed. (New York: McGraw-Hill, 1970 [first published in 1948]).

This is simply because by hiring additional workers profits would be reduced. But some conservatives believe that they have thereby proved that this is a just and ethical distribution of income.

The conservative theory does exactly the same thing for profits. Assume that the capitalist employs a fixed number of workers. How much new machinery should he add? Suppose each machine adds less than the one before it. This is the case because there is a fixed number of workers; therefore additional machines cannot be used efficiently. Even if the capitalist could enforce a speedup, 100 workers could not handle 1000 machines. Stated with these rigid assumptions, the theory of diminishing marginal productivity is likewise a truism. But in the real world the capitalist adds both workers and machines, and new technology to boot, so there may be no diminishing productivity.

In this simple example, however, each additional machine adds less to the product than the previous one (because workers and perhaps factory space are limited). Thus the capitalist should add machines until the additional product of one more machine will just equal its cost. Beyond that point more machines give no more profit, so no more machines should be bought. Therefore the cost of providing an additional machine (whether out of the capitalist's own capital or from borrowed capital) will just equal the value of its additional (or marginal) product. Conservatives conclude that what is paid to capital is *its own* marginal product and that profits are a necessary cost of production and may be ethically justified.

Of course this argument applies only under pure competition; it does not apply in our present situation of pervasive monopoly power. Even Samuelson's conservative textbook agrees that *extra profits* (beyond the marginal product of capital) *are made under monopoly* to the degree that monopoly power controls the market. (This point is emphasized in Chapters 17, 18, and 19.)

RADICAL CRITIQUE OF MARGINAL-PRODUCTIVITY THEORY

It is important to note the grain of truth in Samuelson's conservative argument. It does show that marginal-productivity theory provides a general notion of how to allocate resources. It tells the capitalist to keep hiring workers (or adding machines) as long as they produce extra profit. When the additional profit approaches zero (because the additional product drops to the cost level), then the capitalist should stop adding workers (or machines).

Samuelson also shows that these are useful rules even for socialist planners to follow in allocating resources among investment projects.

They must "introduce first those investment projects with the higher net productivity"[16] and use every additional worker and every additional machine in each project up to the point at which an additional unit would cost more than it adds to the product. In relation to the allocation of capital (factories and machines), this means that socialist planners must use something like a profit or interest rate to calculate which projects will bring the most return to society and which have returns too low to invest in.

Finally, Samuelson quietly adds a point about interest, or profits, under socialist planning that should be loudly and repeatedly stressed: "But, of course, no one necessarily receives interest income from them."[17] In other words, a planned socialist economy would have to calculate rates of return on different uses of capital to decide where to allocate it, *but it would not have to distribute any of these returns as income to any individual*.

We are concerned here, however, with the issue of how a capitalist system distributes income to individuals and groups. In relation to income distribution, radicals have attacked the marginal-productivity theory on several levels. They claim (1) that it is a tautology, (2) that the marginal product of capital cannot really be measured, and (3) that it confuses the productivity of capital and the productivity of the capitalist.

On the first level, it was indicated earlier that, given its assumptions, the analytic conclusions of marginal productivity follow practically by definition (but not its political-ethical conclusions). If it is assumed that the capitalist always acts to maximize profit, then he will never hire an additional worker who would cost more than he produces. He will only keep hiring workers who produce a surplus above their wages. If the product of the last worker hired is defined to be the marginal product, then it follows that his wage must be equal to that, neither more nor less. Similarly, a unit of capital will be utilized only if the additional product from its use equals the additional cost of its use. Given the assumption of profit maximization, these are tautologies in the sense that the conclusions are hidden in the definitions. It does tell the capitalist how to manipulate labor and other inputs to maximize profits, but it does not say whether this is good or bad for society.

Certainly in any society it may be correct to allocate machines so that the return, or profit, from adding one more machine to production equals its cost. But this useful rule does not prove that it is necessary to have a society in which private capitalists provide the

[16]Samuelson, op. cit., p. 580.
[17]Ibid.

money to buy the machines. Nor does it prove that the capitalist's profit is justified even if it equals the marginal product of capital. This theory provides a particular description of the process of allocation of capital, but it represents no advance beyond older ethical justifications of profit income in terms of the capitalist's abstinence or waiting. (Incidentally, these older theories have long been ridiculed by radicals on the ground that the capitalist makes very little sacrifice in abstaining from consuming his whole income or waiting for his profit return. Should we sympathize with the sacrifice of a fellow who sits on his yacht and decides to invest 50 percent of his $1 million income rather than consuming it all?)

The second radical criticism is that the marginal-productivity theory is unrealistic because it does not refer to anything measurable. What is meant by a *unit of capital?* If it means a particular machine, of what relevance is theorizing about transferring it to a more productive use? Particular machines are designed to do particular jobs. If we find that a marginal product is less than its cost in an industry, how can the machine be moved to another industry? It is not designed for other work. Furthermore, the theory assumes that small units of capital can be added or substracted at the margin. But most machines represent very considerable investments; they are not infinitely divisible.

Third, even admitting that the theory offers insights about how capitalists should invest and that it has some roughly definable meaning, still it pertains only to the production contributions of labor and physical capital. It says nothing about the capitalist's contribution. This is probably the most important point of criticism. Radicals admit that a machine may increase production, that workers need them, and that they increase the worker's productivity. In that sense Samuelson is right to say that "capital" has a "net productivity." But it is the physical capital that is productive (jointly with the worker), *not* the capitalist. The capitalist owns the capital, but he is not himself the machine. The machine does the work (with the worker); the capitalist gets the profit.

Radicals agree that machines are a necessary, or "productive," part of the physical productive process; they would even agree to the importance of managerial labor. Radicals argue, however, that this productivity of physical capital goods (created by another labor process in the past) is significantly different from the capitalist owners' ability to capture a certain portion of the product as interest or profit. "It is, of course, true that materials and machinery can be said to be physically productive in the sense that labor working with them can turn out a larger product than labor working without them, but physical productivity in this sense must under no circumstances be confused with value productivity."[18] In other words, "Under capitalism 'the productiveness of labor is made to ripen, as if in a hothouse.' Whether we choose to say that capital is productive, or that capital is necessary to make labor productive, is not a matter of much importance. . . . What is important is to say that owning capital is not a productive activity."[19] This is clear in the case of a mere coupon clipper (as most stockholders are today). The fact that some capitalists may otherwise perform productive labor through their own managerial work does not contradict the fact that they also make money through mere ownership of capital.

The Radical Theory

Inspired initially by Karl Marx's views, the radical analysis of income distribution argues first that the labor of humanity operating on nature is the ultimate source of all production. Radical interpretations of profit and wages emphasize the sociological fact that *the capitalist class owns all of the productive facilities and resources, while the working class owns only its own labor power.* Assuming these institutional conditions, the capitalists *must* be paid a profit or they will not invest their capital. Because the capitalists own the resources and productive facilities, they receive a large share of national income while putting forth no effort (or, as Marx phrased it, under these conditions they are able to extract, or "exploit," this profit from the workers' product).

This theory is not a quantitative economic theory of prices and wages but primarily a historical statement of the political-economic relationships of capitalism. Profit is traced not to a single "cause" but to the functioning of the capitalist economy as a whole within the given class and institutional framework. Profits are viewed as the residual product after wages are paid.

It is a fact that the average worker produces far more in a day than he is paid in wages and that the rest of the net product goes to the capitalist. The practical problem is to explain why long-run wages remain at a level that does not eat up the profits of capital. In empirical terms there was an amazing degree of agreement concerning the wage level among nineteenth-century economists. It is Marshall, not Marx, who stated: "If the economic conditions of the country remain stationary sufficiently long, . . . human beings would earn generally an amount that corresponded fairly well with their cost of rearing and training, conventional necessaries as well as

[18]Paul Sweezy, *The Theory of Capitalist Development* (New York: Oxford University Press, 1943), p. 61.
[19]Joan Robinson, *An Essay on Marxian Economics* (New York: St. Martin, 1960), p. 18.

those things which are strictly necessary being reckoned for."[20] In other words, the long-run price of labor power is the cost of "producing" the worker (with given traditions and under present cultural conditions).

Some evidence that wages in the United States are still set at or below the cost of subsistence of the workers is the fact that the one-third of family units with the lowest incomes go into debt in an average year. For wage workers as a whole, it may be claimed that the debts of some just about equal the savings of others. As noted previously, many workers' families earn less than the BLS "lower" budget. Thus it is true that in the long run 95 to 100 percent of wages ordinarily must be devoted to consumption spending.[21] To this extent Marx's theory of wages at "subsistence according to the cultural standard of the country" is proved. Admittedly, however, the "cultural standard" has been rising, so the average American wage is not what the rest of the world would normally consider a "subsistence" wage.

Modern radical criticism is concerned not with physical subsistence theories but with the fact that workers wages are less than the total product they produce. Radicals do not deny that as workers' productivity and total product have risen, wages have risen very significantly over the past 100 years. (Whether the *share* of wages in national income has remained constant or fallen is a controversial point among economic statisticians.) But profits have risen spectacularly and still grab a large part of the product. Compared with the very high incomes of profit recipients, workers' wages are low. (And, of necessity, workers still consume most or all of their income and save very little.)

Disagreement among economists has centered on the question of why the long-run wage level remains this low. Why do wages not rise to the point at which workers have the entire net product and there are no profits? To answer this question we must examine the factors of supply and demand on either side of the labor market.

On the supply side, the number of workers available at the going wage depends on the amount of population, on the laws (such as those about child labor and retirement benefits), and on sociological attitudes (such as those toward women working). Laws and basic attitudes about work change very slowly, so it may be assumed they are constant. The classical economists, like Malthus, emphasized the effects of population on wages. High wages would lead to more births and more survivals, and as population increased so would the

[20]Marshall, op. cit., p. 577.
[21]See Milton Friedman, *A Theory of the Consumption Function* (Princeton, N.J.: Princeton University Press, 1957), pp. 69–79.

supply of workers, which would hold down wages. Radicals have for the most part rejected population as a factor of primary importance in wage determination because (1) human beings do not react so directly to changes in income (at least, above the starvation level) and (2) population levels change slowly, whereas wage rates change fairly often and rapidly.

On the demand side, the marginal-productivity theory correctly concludes that demand for labor is much affected by technological change that may substitute machines for workers. But technology also changes fairly slowly, and thus this factor does not exert a sigiificant effect on wages. The theory may, to some extent, help explain long-run changes in wages, but it is of no help at all in understanding, for example, why wages decline in a depression.

Many radical economists believe it is most important to examine the overall demand for goods in the economy because that is the main determinant of the demand for labor. Workers are hired only while the capitalist expects to sell the goods they produce. When the overall, or aggregate, demand for goods is less than the supply in the market, production declines and workers are unemployed. Unemployment means that capitalists can set lower wages because workers compete for jobs. *Unemployment is the strongest factor holding down wages.*

The unemployment may be traced to lack of aggregate demand for goods (although it may be aggravated in the long run by a shift to machinery in the production of the goods). The reasons for lack of demand are very complex and will be discussed in the chapters concerned with depressions and unemployment. It should be noted here, however, that this theory means both that aggregate demand largely determines wages and that wages (or the distribution of income) help determine aggregate demand. It is a circular process in which (1) workers are unemployed because there is not enough demand for the goods they produce, but (2) there is not enough demand for goods partly because many workers are unemployed. In other words, demand itself is dependent partly on total income and partly on the distribution of income (because the poor must spend a much larger percentage of their income than the rich just to stay at minimum consumption levels).

Beyond the aggregate factors that determine the demand for workers, radicals emphasize that this is a world of monopoly, not pure competition. It will be seen that, within the broad limits allowed by aggregate supply and demand, the wage rate represents a bargain between labor and capital that is directly influenced by their relative power. On the one side stands the enormous economic and political power of the largest corporations. On the other side stand the vast numbers of workers, some unorganized and powerless, some organized into unions with a small amount of power. In Chapter 17 we begin the analysis of monopoly, eventually returning to its effects on wages.

TENTATIVE CONCLUSIONS

Of course many of these factors are recognized to a small extent by neoclassical economists, and many more are recognized by the liberal wing of Keynesian economists. Thus all economists share in a slight measure of agreement on *how* wages are determined, at least about broad analytic outlines; but they disagree, often violently, over the importance of different factors. When it comes to an interpretation of the facts, the conservatives still believe profits are justified. They talk about the productivity of capital and claim that capitalists must be paid profits or else they will not abstain from consumption and will not wait for their returns from investment. This position is, of course, supported by capitalists and their sympathizers.

The political or ethical view of the radicals is that profits are unjustified. They argue that capitalists merely own capital but that they themselves produce nothing. They use their monopoly of capital to exploit the workers by taking some of the workers' product as profits. In this view *any* profits are bad. This stand is endorsed by many workers and by radicals who sympathize with the workers' view.

It could be said that both sides are emphasizing different aspects of the same reality—or the aspects of reality consonant with their own conclusions. And it could be said that to some degree most economists choose according to their own biases. Even among economists, those who most loudly claim to be objective usually turn out to be the most partisan advocates when their masks are removed.

SUMMARY

There still exists a great deal of poverty in America. Moreover, distribution of U.S. income is very unequal. Most of the income of the rich is profit income; most of the income of the vast majority of the nonrich and poor is wage income.

According to marginal-productivity theory, workers receive the marginal product of labor and capitalists receive the marginal product of capital. This conservative theory tries to justify the present distribution of income. Critics admit that it says something about allocating labor and capital to different industries. But they claim that in relation to income distribution it explains nothing, is unrealistic and refers to nothing measurable, and confuses the product of capital with the product of the capitalist.

According to radical theory, workers produce the whole product but capitalists expropriate part of it in profits (by means of their control of all the resources and productive facilities). Radicals argue that private profits should be abolished and that resources and productive facilities should be taken from the small minority of capitalists and placed under the democratic control of the whole public.

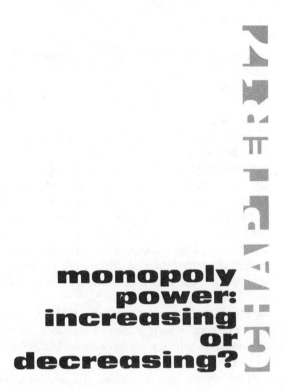

monopoly power: increasing or decreasing?

The world of numerous, small competitive capitalist enterprises, which Adam Smith thought would produce the best result for all concerned, is gone forever. Since the period of the 1890s and early 1900s, western Europe and the United States have been characterized by the domination of a relatively few giant firms. This new stage of monopoly has not ended capitalism, but it has intensified many old qualities and added some entirely new (and unpleasant) features.

In the monopoly stage of capitalism the setting of prices and outputs is quite different than under competition, and the profit result is equally different. The amount of waste, manipulation of the consumer, limitation of the worker's wages, and conflict between profit seeking and social needs (such as the need for a decent environment) exist on entirely new scales. If Adam Smith's harmony-of-interests theory ever had a grain of truth, it is surely not applicable to the monopoly stage of capitalism.

THE TREND OF CONCENTRATION

In a purely competitive economy each competing business unit would be so small that its actions taken alone could not appreciably influence the quantity of goods or the price in the market. Such, more or less, was the U.S. economy during the early nineteenth century. Small farms and small businesses produced most of the output, and there were no giant corporations dominating an entire industry (though there were many local monopolies). As late as 1860, there were still no incorporated business firms in many of the major urban industrial centers. Since that time, the picture has changed drastically.

In Chapters 7 and 8 the rise of big corporations in the post-Civil War period was discussed. By 1900 the share of manufacturing output produced by corporations had grown to two-thirds. Some of the big corporations developed by virtue of rapid internal growth; others arose through mergers of formerly independent firms.

Mergers have come in waves. The first massive movement, which lasted from the early 1890s to the outbreak of World War I, was characterized by *horizontal* mergers, in which a big corporation absorbed other corporations that were its direct competitors. The result of such mergers was, of course, industries dominated by fewer and much larger corporations.

The second wave came in the 1920s. It was characterized by *vertical* mergers, which occurred between firms producing goods in sequence, as when a giant corporation absorbs its suppliers or absorbs the firms to which it sells its output.

The 1960s witnessed a third and unique wave. Most of these mergers were of the *conglomerate* variety, in which giant corporations absorb other corporations that have no relation to it. The aim is simply to establish a colossal corporate empire that will give its controllers immense economic and political power.

From 1950 through 1959, there were an average of 540 corporate mergers a year. From 1960 through 1967, the average was 1100 a year. In 1968, there were 2655 mergers. More and more of these are conglomerate mergers between two giants in different industries. From 1948 through 1953, conglomerate mergers accounted for 59 percent of the total. From 1960 through 1965, they comprised 72 percent of the total. In 1968, conglomerate mergers accounted for 84 percent of all mergers.[1]

Today, there still are millions of very small industrial enterprises, but a few hundred corporate giants hold most of the wealth and do most of the producing.

Table 17.1 reveals the extremely high concentration of corporate assets in a comparatively few firms. At the bottom, a large number of small corporations (890,000, or 58 percent of the total) held a minuscule portion of total corporate assets ($30 billion, or 1 percent). At the top, a few giant corporations (1,041, or just 0.07 percent)

---

[1]All data in this paragraph are from the Federal Trade Commission and were cited in Federal Reserve Bank of Cleveland, *Economic Commentary*, May 12, 1969, p. 3.

TABLE 17.1

DISTRIBUTION OF CORPORATE ASSETS
(ALL U.S. CORPORATIONS, 1969)

Size (In $000s of Assets)	Corporations (Percent in Size Group)	Assets (Percent Owned by Group)
$ 0–100	58%	1%
100–500	30	5
500–5,000	10	9
5,000–250,000	2	30
250,000 and Over	0.07	55
Total	100.00%ᵃ	100%

ᵃData add to more than 100% because of rounding.
Source: U.S. Internal Revenue Service, *Statistics of Income, Corporation Income Tax Returns for 1969.*

held a majority of all assets ($1.218 *trillion,* or 55 percent). That some 1,000 U.S. corporations would hold more than $1 trillion in assets is incredible; that amount is more than the total value of all western European assets. Among those 1000 corporations, there is still a great concentration within just the top 200 or 300 corporations.

The figures for all corporations average out differences in various sectors. In the important sector of banking alone, for example, there are approximately 13,775 commercial banks, but a mere 14 of them hold 25 percent of all deposits, and the 100 largest banks hold 46 percent of all deposits.[2]

Another function of banks is to hold assets in *trust* for individuals and corporations. Banks exercise the voting power for these stocks, which gives them immense power without having legal ownership. Forty-nine of the largest banks hold over 5 percent of the common stock in 147 of the 500 largest industrial corporations in the United States. They also hold at least 5 percent of the common stock in 17 of the largest companies in the fields of merchandising and transportation. These banks are represented in the boards of directors of the majority of the largest corporations in the fields of manufacturing, merchandising, utilities, transportation, and insurance.

Finally, let us turn to the decisive sector of manufacturing taken alone. In the general category of manufacturing enterprises, there were 180,000 corporations and 240,000 unincorporated businesses

[2]The figures on the concentration in banking are taken from the Patman Committee Staff Report for the Domestic Finance Subcommittee of the House Committee on Banking and Currency, *Commercial Banks and Their Trust Activities; Emerging Influence on the American Economy* (Washington, D.C.: GPO, July 1968).

in 1962.[3] Ninety-eight percent of all manufacturing assets were owned by the corporations. Of the 420,000 manufacturing firms, the 20 largest (not 20,000, but 20!) owned 25 percent of total assets of manufacturing firms. The largest 50 firms owned 36 percent, and the largest 200 owned 56 percent. If adjustment is made for giant firms that are owned by even larger giants (i.e., if their ownership is added together), we arrive at a much higher percentage of control. The fact is that, after adjustment for ownership of subsidiaries, a mere 100 firms owned 58 percent of the net capital assets of all the hundreds of thousands of manufacturing corporations. Another index of the imbalance of economic power is the fact that the largest 20 manufacturing firms owned a larger share of the assets than the smallest 419,000 firms combined.

When profits earned are examined, the contrast is even more striking. The *net* profits of the 5 largest corporations were about *twice as large* as those of the 178,000 smallest corporations combined.

Between 1950 and 1962, the share of all manufacturing assets held by the largest 200 firms increased by 17 percent. Between 1962 and 1970, the rate of increase was even more rapid. Since 1959, big business has been absorbing other business firms with $10 million or more in assets at a rate exceeding 60 a year. Since 1950, 1 out of every 5 of the 1000 largest manufacturing companies has been swallowed by an even larger giant. In 1966, 101 companies, each with assets of more than $10 million, were absorbed by other companies; in 1967, the number was 169; in 1968, it was 192. Obviously oligopolistic business giants are far from satisfied with the immense size and power they already have. There is nothing to lead us to believe that these mushrooming industrial empires are about to discontinue merging.

Furthermore, the few large firms control most research and thus will continue to grow more rapidly. A 1960 survey showed that just 4 firms accounted for 22 percent and 384 firms accounted for 85 percent of all industrial research and development.[4]

If the individual industries, which are the arenas of most direct competition, are examined, the picture of economic concentration may be even more sharply drawn. Let an *industry* be defined so that there is easy substitution among the products of all firms within it, and very little possible substitution with products of outside firms.

[3]The data that follow are taken from Willard F. Mueller, "Economic Concentration," in hearings before the Subcommittee on Antitrust and Monopoly of the Committee on the Judiciary, United States Senate, 88th Cong., 2d Sess., pursuant to S. Res. 262, *Part I: Overall and Conglomerate Aspects* (Washington, D.C.: GPO, July 1964), pp. 111–129.

[4]See John K. Galbraith, *The New Industrial State* (Boston: Houghton Mifflin, 1967), p. 23 and sources cited therein.

The huge firms try to gain monopoly control of a whole industry to escape what they call the "rigors of competition" or "cut-throat competition"—meaning that they want the freedom to set their prices wherever they please without fear of competition. Their behavior and excuses are ironic because they tell everyone else how great the "free," competitive market is.

Finally, it is worth noting that much of the increase in concentration comes during depressions. In every depression millions of small businesses are driven to the wall and go bankrupt. Then the big fish eat the little fish, buying up most assets for a song. The result is that each recession or depression further increases monopoly power.

For all of these reasons, three or four giant monopolistic corporations control most of the production of most industries. Many small firms also exist in most industries, but altogether they produce a small percentage of the total output.

The economy of the United States has thus changed from a predominantly competitive to a predominantly monopolistic production situation. The monopolies are still growing through conglomerate mergers of giants in different industries. The apparent degree of concentration may not change in each industry, but the same conglomerate may now control a large firm in each of many industries. Thus the data on particular industries, which indicate that the shares of the 3 or 4 largest have not increased much for several years, severely understate the trend toward concentration of power in the 100 largest manufacturing firms.

THE REASONS FOR MONOPOLY
The fundamental cause of the emergence of the giant corporation is the economy of scale that can be derived from large-size production units that turn out cheaper goods by using more specialized machinery, more specialized workers, and mass production assembly lines. Small firms are driven out of business by the cheap goods produced through large-scale applications of technology. The large firm gains a monopoly by selling at a lower price while making more profit.

In addition to improved technology based on the economies of scale, there are other reasons for the greater profitability of huge firms like General Motors. These firms grow internally or via merger far beyond the technologically necessary minimum because they wish to exercise monopoly power over the market. With small competitors eliminated or dominated, the few remaining giant firms can restrict output and set higher prices to make higher profit rates. Moreover, they can plan with more certainty over a longer period with less risk.

This elimination of risk and uncertainty entails not only controlling their own industry's output but also (1) buying out raw material suppliers, (2) buying out dealers and outlets for the finished product, (3) vast nationwide advertising, and (4) linking up with banks and other financial sources. With these motivations there is no clear upper limit to desirable size. The motto seems to be "the bigger the better."

PRICES AND PROFIT MAXIMIZATION

What is the effect of monopoly on the price structure? The essence of the monopolist's position is his ability ot keep competitors out of the market by means of greater efficiency, control of natural or financial resources, control of patents, or any other legal or illegal methods. Thus he can charge what the market will bear, and there is no competitive mechanism to bring his higher profit back down to the average rate of profit in industry as a whole.

Although the monopolist can make a higher-than-average rate of profit, he cannot make profit out of thin air. Total profit still remains within the limits of total revenue minus costs. To some extent monopoly does not affect aggregate prices or aggregate profits but only redistributes aggregate profits. From a given amount of aggregate profits monopolists may take away part of the profits of small businessmen and farmers by competing for the consumer's dollar. They may also increase their share of profits through their power to buy raw materials and food at low prices and sell finished goods at high prices to these small entrepreneurs. However, monopolists may also increase total profits by using their power to raise prices or to restrict money wages in order to lower the workers' real wages.

As we shall see in detail in Chapter 18, monopoly price and quantity of production are set by the monopolist as he sees fit. In order to maximize his profits, however, he can only set the quantity at the point of greatest difference between total revenue (determined by demand) and total cost (determined by the cost of labor plus material costs). Once the quantity is set, even a monopoly can sell only at a price determined by the demand at that point. The difference between this and the competitive situation is that under monopoly the quantity supplied is set lower so that the price is higher. Therefore the short-run rate of profit is higher than the average under competition. The long-run rate of profit *remains* higher because capital cannot freely enter the industry.

Contrary to this view, many economists claim that modern businessmen do not always attempt to maximize profits. The capitalist today, however, is not the individual businessman but the corporation. Whether the businessman is rational and calculating in his private life is essentially irrelevant to the functioning of the system. In his company life there can be no doubt that the making and accumulating of profit hold as dominant a position today as they ever did. Like the individual enterprise of an earlier period, the giant corporation is an engine for maximizing profits, but it is not used merely as an enlarged version of the personal capitalist. There are two differences: (1) The corporation has a much longer time horizon, and (2) it is a much more rational calculator.[5]

Having said that much, it is important to avoid a dogmatic notion that every corporate decision is made in terms of immediate dollars-and-cents returns. Certainly corporate management may sacrifice short-run profits to ensure the security of their market control, to spur company growth, and even to act as dictated by the somewhat vague concept of prestige. Thus prices are not always set as high as the market will bear. It could be said that management maximizes a multiple set of objectives. Equally well (because the difference is only semantic) it could be emphasized that each of the other objectives is merely a rational way to achieve maximum long-run profits, which are the real sole objective.

WHO CONTROLS THE CORPORATION?

Liberals agree that monopoly is an evil aspect of capitalism, but they believe a remedy short of doing away with capitalism is possible. Some rely on stricter enforcement of antitrust laws. Others admit that these laws have clearly proved inadequate and advocate stricter laws. Still others claim that a process of internal change in giant corporations is automatically eliminating most of its negative qualities. Professor Galbraith is the leading spokesman of the latter view.

Galbraith[6] maintains that there is a great contradiction between the notion that the modern corporation is controlled most by the management and the fact that it nevertheless ruthelessly tries to maximize profits for its stockholders. Furthermore, he argues that the most important factor of production is no longer capital but the specialized talent of scientists and technologists, and that real power passes from stockholders and top management to the members of the *technostructure* (i.e., the technical personnel, including scientists and technicians). According to Galbraith, the members of the technostructure do not get the profits they are supposed to maximize. Because the technostructure supplies talent, not capital, why should they worry about the return to capital? He says that the modern

[5]In this respect see James Earley, "The Impact of Some New Developments in Economic Theory: Discussion," *American Economic Review*, Proceedings, May 1957, pp. 333–335.

[6]Galbraith, op. cit., chaps. 5, 6, 7, 8.

corporation has the capacity to shape society, but its resources are used to serve the deeper interests or goals of the technostructure, which possesses the real power.

Galbraith agrees that a few hundred giant corporations control the market, regulate output and prices, and exercise enormous political control. Yet with a wave of his hand he eliminates the corporate executive and puts the control of the corporation in the hands of scientists and technically skilled workers. He then finds that the technostructure really manages the corporation and that, for their own reasons, they manage it in the best interests of all society. In other words, Galbraith is very critical of capitalism, especially of the tremendous centralization of the means of production, but nevertheless is apologetic in the sense that he concludes that the industrial system has actually solved (or is solving) its problem.

The radical view is that Galbraith ignores the real position of modern corporate management. In the first place, the fact that so many top executives hold stock means their motivations cannot possibly be inconsistent with profit seeking. For example, in early 1957, 25 officers of General Motors owned an average of 11,500 shares each.[7] They might not be able to affect policy even with that amount of stock in General Motors, yet each owned roughly $500,000 in the company, and it is improbable that any was indifferent to profits. Further, among stockholders there are both more managers than representatives of any other group and a larger proportion of managers than in any other group.

Galbraith, of course, argues that it is not the motivation of the managers but the motivation of the technostructure that is decisive. Radicals counter that the goals of the technostructure would be the same as those of the managers: survival of the firm, growth, independence from outside control. All these demand profit-making activity. More important, it flies in the face of reality to believe that the technicians control the corporations. The managers hire and fire the technicians, not vice versa. In the end it is the boss rather than his hired hand who makes the decisions (and will use expert advice only to make more profitable decisions).

MONOPOLY PROFIT RATES
(AND INCOME DISTRIBUTION)

The monopoly structure of American capitalism has been examined and the price-setting behavior of its management investigated. How

[7] See Gabriel Kolko, *Wealth and Power in America* (New York: Praeger, 1962), p. 13.

do structure and behavior affect the performance of American capitalism? In this section the effect on profit rates is reviewed. First the sources, in theory, of monopoly profit are briefly recapitulated; then the facts of monopoly profit are presented.

The whole point of monopoly control of markets is, of course, to restrict output and charge higher prices. All consumers are hurt by higher monopoly prices. Workers may have a constant wage in dollars, but as prices rise their buying power falls. If we reduce the figure for money wages by the percentage of price increases, the result is called the *real wage*. For example, if money wages stay at $100 while prices rise by 7 percent, the real wage drops to $93. Therefore we may say that price increases by monopolies lower real wages and thereby increase their profits.

Purchasers of producer goods also suffer, so the profits of small businesses and farmers are lowered. Some large firms have extra market power as large buyers of commodities. Thus the large firm may also add to its profits by buying labor at a rate lower than the average wage. This factor may, of course, be somewhat offset by trade union action. In the modern world of monopoly, wages are not determined simply by automatic market supply and demand. They are determined by the bargaining strength of capital and labor, with monopoly capital usually in the stronger position. Workers are thus squeezed in from both sides by monopoly. On the one hand, the monopolies can pay lower money wages by exerting their power in the labor market. On the other hand, monopolies can charge workers higher prices as consumers.

Additional monopoly profits come from lucrative government military contracts, which are financed from the workers' tax money, thus again increasing total profits. Extra-high returns from foreign investments abroad also add to monopoly profits; that is, profits are extracted from workers in foreign countries (see Chapter 35).

Turning to the facts, we may investigate first how the profit rates of an enterprise are affected by its absolute size. The size of a business is indicated by the total amount of its assets, and the profit rate is the total profit divided by the capital investment of all the stockholders. Profit rates by asset size for all corporations since 1931 are given in Table 17.2.

In an economy of pure and perfect competition, all profit rates should be equalized in the long run. As Table 17.2 demonstrates, in the U.S. economy the long-run profit rate is not the same for all corporations. On the contrary, the smallest corporations have low or even negative profit rates, and the profit rate rises with the scale of the corporation, although the differences are quite small among the largest-size groups. This is a proof of the existence of monopoly power and imperfect competition.

TABLE 17.2

LONG-RUN PROFIT RATE, BY CORPORATE SIZE
(ALL U.S. CORPORATIONS, 1931–1961,
EXCLUDING THE WAR YEARS 1940–1947)

	Profit Rate (Profit Before Taxes Divided by Stockholders' Capital)
$ 0– 50,000	−7.1%
50,000– 100,000	4.1
100,000– 250,000	5.9
250,000– 500,000	7.4
500,000– 1,000,000	8.3
1,000,000– 5,000,000	9.3
5,000,000–10,000,000	9.7
10,000,000–50,000,000	10.4
Over $50,000,000	10.4

Source: Reprinted by permission from Howard Sherman, *Profit Rates in the United States* (Ithaca, N.Y.: Cornell University Press, 1968), p. 41.

Economic concentration, however, has another important aspect. The indicator of market power is a firm's relative size and importance in its own industry. A *concentration ratio* in each industry may be defined as the percentage of sales controlled by the eight largest corporations in the industry. Several studies have found a definite relationship between an industry's concentration ratio and its profit rates. Some evidence is presented in Table 17.3.

The very high concentration of production that exists in many industry groups reflects the fact that in the majority of U.S. industries the bulk of production is concentrated in a few giant corporations, with hundreds of smaller companies producing very little. Moreover, inspection of the table reveals a considerable rise in profit rates as the degree of concentration rises (the few noticeable exceptions are easy to explain from special cases). Thus in the 10 industry groups over the 50 percent concentration level, the average rate of profit is 20 percent; it is only 12.8 percent in the 10 industry groups under the 50 percent concentration level.

This analysis may be extended to the trend of aggregate profits under capitalism. It appears that the giant corporations have steadily reduced production costs per unit and that there have been powerful impulses toward innovation. Yet monopoly cannot be considered a rational and progressive system because although it reduces costs, it continues to set extremely high prices. Moreover, its increased productivity does not benefit everyone but only a few. Profit rates increase, and the share of profit in national income rises. Contrary to

TABLE 17.3

PROFIT RATES AND CONCENTRATION RATIOS, BY INDUSTRY GROUP
(ALL U.S. MANUFACTURING CORPORATIONS IN 1954)

Industry Group	Concentration Ratio (Percent of Sales by Eight Largest Sellers)	Profit Rate (Profit Before Taxes Divided by Stockholders' Capital)
Motor Vehicles and Parts	98.1%	27.1%
Tobacco	91.5	20.3
Transportation Equipment, Except Motor Vehicles	75.6	29.8
Rubber	74.2	17.8
Primary Metals	70.8	13.0
Chemicals	63.3	19.9
Electrical Machinery	60.8	20.7
Petroleum and Coal	57.7	7.7
Instruments	56.1	23.9
Stone, Clay, Glass	55.0	19.9
Food and Beverages	45.7	14.4
Machinery, Except Electrical	44.4	16.2
Fabricated Metal	40.3	15.6
Paper	39.4	17.3
Textile Mill	37.1	5.1
Leather	33.7	11.4
Furniture	23.8	12.8
Printing and Publishing	21.5	15.1
Apparel	20.5	7.6
Lumber	15.5	12.2

Source: Reprinted by permission from Howard Sherman, *Profit Rates in the United States* (Ithaca, N.Y.: Cornell University Press, 1968), p. 85.

the nineteenth-century economist's vision of falling rates of profit, under monopoly the rate tends to rise.

MONOPOLY AND WASTE

During the period since the U.S. economy has changed to a predominantly monopolistic structure, the rate of economic growth appears to have declined. Thus the GNP (in constant prices) grew by 4.31 percent per year in 1839–1879, by 3.72 percent per year in 1879–1919, and by 2.97 percent per year in 1919–1959.[8] It is impossible to say to what extent, if any, this decline is related to the high level of oligopoly power because so many other factors have been operative.

[8] U.S. Congress, Joint Economic Committee, *Staff Report on Employment, Growth, and Price Levels* (Washington, D.C.: GPO, 1961), p. 34.

We do know that production cannot reach optimum efficiency below a certain point, or quantity. Thus the fact that large firms account for most U.S. output means that most of the economy has the ability to produce at lower costs than ever before. Studies of cost data reveal the possibility of high efficiency at a fairly constant level beyond the necessary minimum scale of production.[9] Of course, because the very large firms also have disproportionately larger research facilities and control a very large percentage of all unexpired patents, they have the greatest potential for increasing efficiency. Moreover, many investment projects require resources beyond the means of small firms.

But the large, entrenched firm stands to lose most from the obsolescence of present machinery and from product improvements that reduce the number of units the customer need buy—for example, a longer-lasting light bulb. Therefore if the large firm has an oligopoly position and faces no serious competitive pressure for improvement, it may develop, patent, and not use important inventions. Monopoly power has paradoxical effects on innovation. Giant firms have a rapid rate of technological progress, but they retain a large amount of technologically obsolete equipment.

Monopoly power may also be used to restrict supply in order to raise prices. Thus, as will be seen in later chapters, monopoly power is one of the principal causes of inflation. Monopolies will expand production as rapidly as possible only in extraordinary periods of unlimited demand. This usually occurs only when government demand skyrockets, as in World War II. In wartime, monopolies can cease restricting output but still charge prices as high as the government will allow.

Moreover, the existence of economic concentration may have increased the severity and possibly the number of depressions because of (1) its destabilizing effects on remaining small businesses and (2) its lowering of workers' ability to consume. It would seem that this is another reason why the net effect of monopoly may be to lower the rate of economic growth.

On the other hand, breaking up large firms into smaller units would probably not increase economic growth. Reducing the American economy to small firms would certainly cause a major decrease in economic efficiency and most likely would have negative effects on investment. It is impossible to go backward to a competitive small business economy; the only answer seems to be to go forward to public and workers' control of the giant corporations.

The rate of growth (and waste) under monopoly is also affected

---

[9]See J. S. Bain, "Price and Production Policies," in Howard S. Ellis, ed., *A Survey of Contemporary Economics* (New York: McGraw-Hill, 1948), p. 140.

by the fact that the sales effort has greatly expanded. Once a relatively unimportant feature of the system, sales effort has become one of its decisive nerve centers. The impact of advertising and related expenditures on the economy is outranked only by that of militarism. In all other aspects of social existence, the influence of advertising is second to none. In an economic system in which competition is fierce and relentless but in which the small number of rivals rules out price cutting, advertising becomes to an ever-increasing extent the principal weapon of the competitive struggle. There is little room under atomistic competition for advertising; in monopoly it is the most important factor in the firm's survival.

Relatively large firms are in a position to exercise a powerful influence on the market for their output by establishing and maintaining a pronounced difference between their products and those of their competitors. This differentiation is sought chiefly by means of advertising, trademarks, brand names, distinctive packaging, and product variation. If successful, it leads to a condition in which consumers believe the differentiated products can no longer serve as close substitutes for each other.

Several studies have demonstrated that advertising involves a massive waste of resources, a continual drain on the consumer's income, and a systematic destruction of the consumer's freedom of choice between genuine alternatives.[10] Furthermore, advertising in all its aspects cannot be meaningfully dealt with as some undesirable excrescence on the economic system that could be removed if we would only make up our minds to get rid of it. Advertising is the very offspring of the monopoly form of capitalism, the inevitable by-product of the decline of price competition; it constitutes as integral a part of the system as the giant corporation itself. The economic importance of advertising lies partly in its causing a reallocation of consumers' expenditures among different commodities. Even more important, however, is its effect on the magnitude of aggregate effective demand and thus on the level of income and employment. In other words, it generates useless expenditures, both by capitalists and by consumers, which soak up part of its "overproduction" by getting consumers to spend money beyond their direct needs.

Advertising affects profits in two ways. The first effect is the fact that part of advertising and other selling expenses are paid for through an increase in the prices of consumer goods bought by productive workers. Their real wages are reduced by this amount, whereas total profit is maintained by the higher prices.

The other, more complicated, effect is that the profits and wages some capitalists and workers make from the business of advertising

---

[10]See, e.g., Galbraith, op. cit., passim.

constitute an expense for other capitalists. This component of the outlays on advertising and sales effort does not constitute an increase in total profit but does cause its redistribution. Some individuals living off profit are deprived of a fraction of their incomes in order to support other individuals living off profit, namely those who derive their incomes from advertising itself.

Furthermore, in making it possible to create the demand for a product, advertising encourages investment in plant and equipment that otherwise would not take place. The effect of advertising on the division of total income between consumption and saving is not measurable, but is clear in direction and probably very large. The function of advertising, perhaps its dominant function today, is to wage a relentless war on behalf of the producers and sellers of consumer goods against saving and in favor of consumption.

Actually much of the newness with which the consumer is systematically bombarded is either fraudulent or related trivially, and in many cases even negatively, to the function and serviceability of the product. Moreover, other products are introduced that are indeed new in design and appearance but that serve essentially the same purposes as old products they are intended to replace. The extent of the difference can vary all the way from a simple modification in packaging to the far-reaching and enormously expensive annual changes in automobile models.

In addition, most research and development programs, which constitute a multibillion-dollar effort in the United States are more closely related to the production of salable goods than to their much-touted mission of advancing science and technology. For example, if monopoly profit and dealers' markups are excluded, then the real cost of production of the 1949 automobile, built with the technology of 1960, would have been less than $700 in 1960 and far less in 1970. According to this calculation, useless automobile model changes alone amounted to about 2.5 percent of GNP by 1960. Thus the total amount of waste from all the time and effort devoted directly and indirectly to *selling* products under monopoly must considerably lower the rate of economic growth.

Not only does monopoly greatly increase the waste of capitalism but it also raises pollution and environmental destruction to a new level. In the competitive model, apologists could claim that consumer preference dictated what was produced and therefore that pollution was merely an unfortunate by-product of the demands of the public. The apologists argued that these unfortunate by-products of public preferences could be handled by some minor public action in beautifying the environment. Under monopoly, such apologetics are no longer possible; it is clear that consumer preference is manipulated and directed toward whatever products are most profitable to produce, and therefore "environmental damage becomes a normal consequence of the conflict between the goals of the producing firm and those of the public."[11]

So far only the unemployment, inflation, civilian wastes, and peacetime pollution caused by monopoly have been considered. Its full effect cannot be appreciated until its political power and militarist trend, international spread, and social effects are analyzed.

SUMMARY

In several waves of mergers since the late 1890s, the American economy has been converted from one of numerous small competitive industrial enterprises to one dominated by giant corporations. In each industry three or four corporations together make the decisive output, investment, and pricing decisions. All small businesses together produce a small percentage of total output and receive an even smaller percentage of profits. The high degree of concentration increases instability and unemployment in at least two ways: First, driven to the wall, small businesses reduce employment and sometimes set off depressions; many go bankrupt, thus worsening the depression. Second, the giant corporations keep their own prices and output high by restricting the supply of output and further reducing employment.

Giant firms increase their prices rapidly during prosperity, causing inflation by pushing profits up through the use of monopoly power over the market. Since the 1950s they have even had the power to continue raising prices during recessions (though more slowly than during expansions). The giant firms also mount giant advertising campaigns, wasting vast resources on the false claim that their products are better than others. Finally, the giant firms contribute giant pollution to the air, land, and sea; it is just not profitable to spend their money on purifying devices for their industrial processes or for their consumer products, such as cars.

[11]John K. Galbraith, "Economics as a System of Belief," *American Economic Review*, May 1970, p. 477.

pure competition and monopoly

In this chapter we wish to explore in detail how a firm maximizes its profit.[1] *Profit* is the difference between revenue (or sales proceeds) and costs. The revenue a firm gets in a given supply-and-demand situation depends on how much competition it faces in its industry.

An *industry* is the total of all firms selling a particular product. Thus, when we speak of the steel industry or the automobile industry, we are referring to all the individual business firms producing steel or automobiles. Industries fall within one of four categories: pure competition, monopolistic competition, oligopoly, or monopoly.

MARKET STRUCTURES AND THE DEGREE OF COMPETITION

A *purely competitive industry* is one in which four essential conditions are present: (1) The industry is made up of a very large number of firms, and there are also a large number of buyers of the product they sell. (2) Each seller supplies so small a percentage of the market that its actions have virtually no effect on the price at which the industry sells the product, and each buyer demands so small a percentage of output that his purchases alone also have virtually no

[1] Those readers who are merely looking for a general overview of economics may wish to skip the technical details—sections with symbols and graphs—that are explored in this and the following chapter.

effect on the price at which the industry sells the product. (3) It is very easy for new firms to get into the industry or for old firms to leave it. (4) Each firm produces a product that is so nearly identical to the product of the other firms that consumers are largely indifferent about which firm within the industry produced the product they buy.

A *monopoly* exists when there is only one seller of a product that has no close substitutes. In a monopolistic industry one firm *is* the industry. If the monopolist's position is to be maintained, he must erect barriers that prevent competitors from entering the industry. If he is successful in doing this, the payoff is generally very large. Because he has complete control over the price of his product (within the limits set by the demand schedule), he can set the price at the level that will maximize profits.

Between the extremes of pure competition and monopoly, economists make two further classifications. Closer to pure competition is *monopolistic competition.* A monopolistically competitive industry has a large number of small sellers who engage in some slight amount of *product differentiation.* A product may be differentiated in many different ways; for example, one seller packages his product more attractively or gives friendlier service. In any event, some consumers prefer one or another particular seller's product. For this reason, firms have a small degree of control over price, and a firm cannot enter the industry as easily as it can enter a purely competitive industry.

Closer to a monopoly (and often tantamount to it) is an *oligopoly.* An oligopolistic industry has a few giant sellers, each of which controls a significant share of the market. Entry into an oligopolistic industry is very difficult, often as difficult as into a monopolistic industry. There is generally, but not always, some product differentiation. The most significant feature of an oligopoly is the fact that, because of the interdependence of its members, no firm can make significant changes in price without reckoning with the reactions of its competitors.

In this chapter we discuss the profit-maximizing behavior of a firm in a purely competitive industry and a firm under conditions of monopoly. Profit-maximizing behavior of monopolistically competitive firms and oligopolistic firms will be examined in Chapter 19.

DEMAND AND PRICE FOR A PURELY COMPETITIVE FIRM

For a whole industry, a larger amount can be sold *only* at a lower price (or lower average revenue). This is not the case for a single competitive firm. In a purely competitive industry, each firm is so

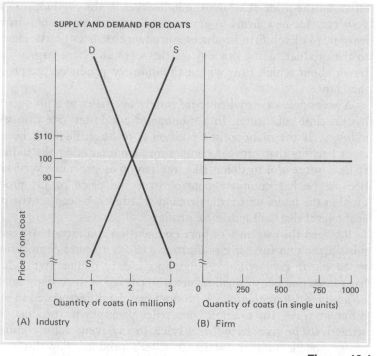

Figure 18.1

small that whatever quantity it chooses to sell will have a negligible effect on the supply for the entire industry. Therefore it can sell all that it wishes at the going price.

The situation for both a purely competitive industry and one firm within that industry is demonstrated graphically in Figure 18.1. Figure 18.1(A) shows the supply and demand for coats which is assumed to be a purely competitive industry. Figure 18.1(B) shows the price (or demand curve, since they are the same in this case) for the individual coat-making firm.

The price of a coat ($100) is determined in the industrywide market for coats by the intersection of the industry supply and demand curves. The graph shows that *at this price the individual firm can sell any quantity it wishes*. Because it has been assumed that the individual firm cannot affect supply for the entire industry, and because the market demand is equal to the industry's supply at the prevailing price ($100), the firm never experiences any problem in selling all it wishes to sell at this price.

Therefore the demand curve for the individual firm's output is a horizontal line at the industry-determined price. The firm sells any quantity it chooses at this price. Assume that it decides to raise its price in order to increase its revenue. Because the firms in a purely competitive industry all produce an identical product, no consumer will pay more than $100 for one firm's product when he can buy an identical product from a competitor for $100. Similarly, the firm will never sell any quantity at a price below $100. Because it can sell any quantity it chooses at $100, there would be no incentive for it to lower the price. Thus the firm in a purely competitive industry faces a given price; it cannot vary it upward, and it does not wish to vary it downward. (The situation is very different for a monopoly.)

SUPPLY AND THE COSTS OF PRODUCTION

A firm's decision regarding the quantity of its product that it wishes to supply at various prices will depend, to a large extent, on the costs of producing different quantities. In this section we shall analyze the firm's cost during the short run, when its output is limited to the productive capacity of current plant and equipment. Over a longer period the firm could construct a larger plant and install new equipment, thus expanding its scale of operations; but for the shorter period considered here, these capital goods are fixed in size and number.

Because the amount of a firm's plant and equipment is fixed in the short run, some of its costs must be considered fixed whether it produces nothing or operates at capacity. *Fixed costs* include the costs of maintaining plant and equipment, rent, and costs of watchmen, guards, and others. Obviously, if the firm produces more goods, then the *average* fixed cost will decline because the same cost is spread over, or divided by, more units.

Even during the short run, however, some costs—notably those of labor and material—are variable. The firm can produce more or less of its product by hiring more or fewer workers and using more or less raw materials.

The *average* variable cost for a unit of output is obtained by taking the total cost of labor and raw materials and dividing it by the quantity produced. If one laborer combined with a given amount of raw materials produced ten coats, and if each additional laborer combined with the same amount of raw materials continued to produce ten coats, then the average variable cost per unit produced would remain the same regardless of the amount the firm produced. The average-variable-cost curve would be a straight horizontal line, showing that the quantity of coats produced had no effect on its magnitude.

This situation does not obtain in most types of productive processes. Generally the firm's plant and equipment have been designed and constructed to operate most effectively at a particular level of output. The production of a single commodity usually involves numerous productive processes, which occur at different rates and are difficult to coordinate. For maximum efficiency no single process should be halted or stopped because it is outstripping the other processes; nor should other processes be stopped because this process cannot keep pace.

After engineers have calculated the various rates at which different productive processes will take place, the plant is constructed and equipped in such a way that there is some *optimal* level of production at which all productive processes can be effectively coordinated. Average variable costs are lowest at the optimum level of production but higher both below and above that level.

Because average fixed costs fall continuously, the total result is that average cost per unit may fall rapidly at first and continue to fall until the optimal point is achieved; then average cost may slowly rise. This usual short-run behavior of average costs (a U-shaped curve) is illustrated in Figure 18.2.

According to Figure 18.2, the quantity of 1000 coats is the production level at which all production processes are most effectively coordinated and plant and equipment are most efficiently utilized (the cost is only $75 per coat). At smaller quantities, bottlenecks occur and some equipment is *underutilized;* consequently, average costs are higher. At larger quantities, plant and equipment are being *overutilized* and various bottlenecks and inefficiencies are encountered; consequently, average costs are higher. The further a firm gets from the optimally efficient quantity (1000 coats in this case), the higher its average costs are. This is true whether the firm produces smaller or larger quantities than the optimal amount.

Figure 18.2

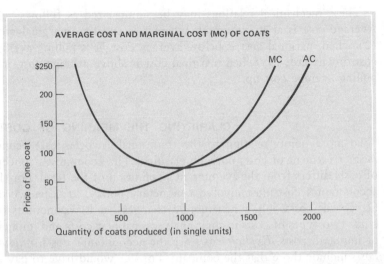

Figure 18.3

Because it is the basis of the supply curve, marginal cost is even more important than the average cost. *Marginal cost* is defined as follows:

$$\text{Marginal cost} = \frac{\text{increase in total cost}}{\text{increase in quantity}}$$

Because we may speak of decrease as well as increase, we may substitute the word *change* for *increase* in the definition to make it more general.

In Figure 18.3 marginal cost represents the increase in total costs of production attributable to an increase in output of one additional coat. If the change in cost attributable to producing one more coat is lower than the average cost of producing the product, then it may be said that the lower marginal cost is pulling the average cost downward. This is similar to the case of a person taking several tests. The last test score pulls the average score up or down, depending on whether it is higher or lower than the average. Thus it is possible to conclude that as long as the average cost is declining the marginal cost must be below it. When the average cost is rising, the marginal cost must be above it, pulling it upward. These relations between the average and marginal cost are illustrated in Figure 18.3.

Notice that at low production levels, those at which each additional coat is produced at less cost, marginal cost is very low (only $25 at 500 coats) and is well below the average. But at production beyond the optimal capacity, when the average cost of producing coats is rising, marginal cost rises rapidly to a high level ($150 at 1500 coats), and goes further and further above the average.

These mechanical relations may be summarized as follows: (1) Average cost is at its minimum when it is equal to marginal cost; (2) when marginal cost is below average cost, it is pulling average cost downward; (3) when marginal cost is above average cost, it is pulling average cost up.

CLARIFYING THE MEANING OF COSTS

Two more points relating to the traditional (neoclassical) economist's treatment of costs must be clarified. The economist's concept of costs differs from the accountant's definition of the term. For the accountant a cost must involve a monetary outlay. In other words, he records costs only when money changes hands. Economists include two types of costs in their analyses: explicit costs and implicit, or imputed, costs. *Explicit costs* are the accountant's costs; *implicit costs* include those that the company's owner would have to pay if, for example, he did none of the managerial work himself. Thus a normal wage for the managerial and other labor he performs is counted among implicit costs.

Assume, for example, that a man saves $20,000 and opens a service station. During the first year his accountant calculates that his total revenue was $32,000 and his costs $22,000. The accountant informs him that he has made a profit of $10,000. A traditional economist would assess his costs differently. Suppose that the owner worked 60 hours every week and that it would have cost him $3 per hour to hire a man to do this work. The economist would subtract the imputed wage of $9,360 and inform the owner that he had registered a profit of only $640 rather than $10,000. All economists agree that everyone deserves pay for his or her own labor, including managerial labor.

The traditional economist, however, would consider another, more dubious, implicit or imputed "cost." The man invested his own $20,000 in the station. He gave up the opportunity to invest it elsewhere—say, in 6 percent government bonds. Therefore the neoclassical economist says that he also had an implicit cost of $1,200 in interest forgone, so he "really" made a loss.

For neoclassical economists *profits* means only *excess* profits—that is, they are excess over all explicit and implicit costs, including a "normal" or average profit (or interest). Although this definition is useful in one way, it has a very conservative bias in another sense. It is useful in that the capitalist *does* require the bribe of an average rate of profit to get him to use his capital in production. He usually considers normal and necessary the rate that has been the average for the last few years. Thus only if an average profit is included with costs can it be said that supply behavior is determined completely by costs. This definition is employed here because it is convenient to be able to say, in agreement with all current economics books, that in pure competition the supply curve is identical with the marginal-cost curve—this point is examined later.

The neoclassical definition of costs sneaks in the idea that the capitalist *deserves* to receive an average profit as a cost of providing capital for production. It is true that physical capital goods are necessary for production, that in any society limited capital goods must be allocated to maximize returns, and that allocation is a social cost because it means other areas cannot use those capital goods. It is also true, given a private enterprise system, the capitalist entrepreneur must be bribed with the average profit to get him to furnish his capital. It was shown in Chapter 15, however, that the productivity of capital goods implies neither that the capitalist is productive nor that he deserves his profit. In other words, a socialist society would provide capital to itself out of public funds; it would consider provision of capital a cost of production; and it would calculate rates of profit in each industry to decide where to allocate capital. (See Chapter 38.) But a socialist society would not pay the profits to any private individual.

There is only one other essential point to be made in this discussion of costs. Total cost can be shown quite easily on a graph of per-unit costs. Because the average cost is the total cost divided by the quantity produced, it follows that total cost is given by the product of average cost multiplied by the quantity produced. In Figure 18.4 total cost is shown as a shaded rectangle. Taking any quantity

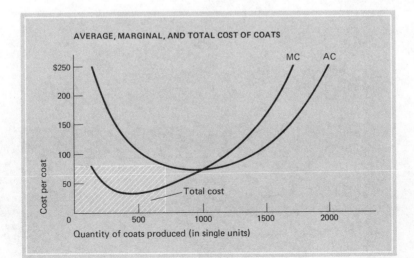

Figure 18.4

(for example, 700 coats in Figure 18.4), we go up to the average-cost curve and then over to the cost axis of the graph. Here the average cost per unit required to produce 700 coats is found: $80. We know that the total cost will equal 700 × $80. But because line 0-to-700 and line $0-to-$80 are adjacent sides of a rectangle, their product is equal to the area of the rectangle. Therefore the shaded rectangle in Figure 18.4 represents the total cost of producing 700 coats: 700 × $80 = $56,000.

MAXIMUM PROFIT UNDER COMPETITION

In an earlier section it was shown that once the price of the industry's product is determined, then the individual competitive firm faces a demand curve (or a given price) that is a straight horizontal line. It is also assumed that each firm has the U-shaped average-cost curve described earlier. In Figure 18.5 the demand curve has been superimposed on the cost curves in order to present the whole picture for the competitive firm.

In order to understand the firm's reaction to the market price ($100), it is necessary to ascertain what motivates the firm's owners (or managers). The answer provided by the vast majority of economists, from Adam Smith to the present, is that the one overriding objective of all capitalists, or their managers, is to maximize their profits. We accept this answer provisionally and treat each firm as a profit maximizer.

The manager whose cost and revenue curves are pictured in Figure 18.5 will maximize his profits by producing and selling 1200

Figure 18.5

coats. At this quantity the firm's marginal cost is equal to its price. The rule for maximizing profit under competition is to produce the quantity *that equates marginal cost and price*. There are two shaded rectangles in Figure 18.5. The combined area of the rectangles is equal to the firm's total income from sales or revenue (because it represents the price times the quantity the firm sells). The area of the lower rectangle is equal to the firm's total cost (because it is the product of the firm's average cost times the quantity it produces). The area of the upper rectangle is equal to the firm's profit (because it represents total revenue minus total costs, which is, by definition, profit).

In order to understand why 1200 coats is the quantity that maximizes the firm's profit, imagine that the firm produces and sells a smaller quantity of the product. For any quantity below 1200, the firm's price per unit is higher than its marginal cost. Consequently, if the firm produces and sells an additional coat, this last coat will add more to the firm's total revenue than it adds to the total cost. The last coat therefore adds to the firm's profit. As long as the firm is producing fewer than 1200 coats, it can add to its profit by producing and selling more coats.

However, imagine that the firm is producing more than 1200 coats. For any quantity above 1200 the firm's marginal cost exceeds its price per unit. If the firm were to produce and sell one less coat, the reduction in its costs would exceed the reduction in its revenue. Its profit would therefore increase. As long as the firm continues to sell more than 1200 coats, it can add to its profit by producing and selling less. It is now easy to see why the competitive firm maximizes its profit by equaling its maginal cost and its price.

For any price that prevails in the market, the marginal-cost curve will indicate what quantity the firm would like to sell. But a line showing the quantities a firm would like to sell at various prices is exactly what we defined a supply curve to be. Therefore *in pure competition a firm's marginal-cost curve is its supply curve*. Because the industry is simply the total of the firms within it, the industry's supply curve is the summation of the marginal-cost curves of all these firms.

EQUILIBRIUM FOR THE FIRM AND THE INDUSTRY IN PURE COMPETITION

In the purely competitive industry price is determined by the intersection of the industry supply and demand curves. The individual firm adjusts its quantity in order to maximize profit. Figure 18.6(A) shows an individual firm's cost and revenue curves.

In Figure 18.6 the firm and industry are in short-run, but not long-run, equilibrium. The industry is in short-run equilibrium

COMPETITIVE EQUILIBRIUM IN THE COAT MARKET

(A) Industry

(B) Firm

Figure 18.6

because it is producing at the point where its price and marginal cost are equal. But neither the industry nor the firm is making excess profit.

Two points should be made about the firm's excess profit: (1) It is assumed that all firms have access both to the same technology that this firm is using and to inputs of comparable quality. It can be concluded, therefore, that the cost curves of virtually all firms in the industry are nearly identical to those of the firm pictured in Figure 18.6(B). (2) It must be remembered that the firm's cost curves include an imputed cost covering an average return on the owner's capital; thus normal, or average, profit is included in the cost.

It must be concluded, therefore, that the firms in this industry are making excess profits above an average return on capital. Because it is easy to enter a purely competitive industry, capitalists who are making only an average profit in other industries will be attracted to this industry by the lure of excess profits.

An industry is said to be in long-run equilibrium when there is no tendency for firms either to enter or to leave it. The industry pictured in Figure 18.6 is not in long-run equilibrium because it is earning excess profits and therefore new firms will be entering it.

As new firms enter, their additional outputs must be added in order to derive the industry's new supply curve. This means that the supply curve will shift to the right. Figure 18.7 illustrates the original situation depicted in Figure 18.6 but also shows what happens as the supply curve shifts to the right (from the original position, S_2). When the supply curve shifts, it must ultimately shift to S_2. If it stops short of S_2, excess profits will continue and more firms

Figure 18.7

will be attracted, shifting the curve farther to the right until it reaches S_2.

With the greater supply provided by the new firms entering the industry, all excess profits have been eliminated. At the new, lower price of $75, the firm reduces its output from 1200 to 1000 coats in order to equate its marginal cost with the new price. This lower output maximizes the firm's profits in the new conditions. At that point, however, it is also true that the firm's average cost is just equal to its price per unit. The decline in price from $100 to $75 has eliminated the firm's excess profits (because its average cost is also $75).

With no excess profits there is no longer any incentive for new firms to enter the industry. The firms within the industry are receiving a normal, or average, rate of return on their capital and labor. Therefore there is no tendency for firms to leave the industry. It can now be said that when the new supply curve results in the establishment of a new price equal to the long-run average cost of each firm, then the industry is in long-run equilibrium because the number of firms within the industry has been stabilized.

Thus, when both the individual firms and the purely competitive industry are in long-run equilibrium, the following equality holds for each firm:

Price = marginal cost = average cost

The fact that price equals marginal cost indicates that the firm is satisfied that its current level of output is the most profiable one for it. The fact that price equals average cost indicates that there will be no tendency for firms either to enter or to leave the industry (because the average cost includes just an average rate of profit).

RELEVANCE OF
THE COMPETITIVE MODEL

The reader has probably wondered which industries in the contemporary American economy are purely competitive. Only one or two industries (out of many thousands) in the entire American economy present a factual resemblance to the model just worked through.

The most obvious choice of a purely competitive industry might be from agriculture. Traditionally, in the wheat industry, for example, each farmer produced a homogeneous product, and no farmer produced enough to affect the price significantly. Each would take as given the price determined in the market. Whether he sold all or none of his crop at this price was virtually irrelevant to the determination of price.

Over the past several decades, however, two important changes have occurred in agricultural markets: (1) The government has intervened extensively in the market through various schemes of subsidies and production controls. (2) The agricultural industry has been increasingly coming under the control of giant corporations that in no way resemble the small, relatively powerless firms pictured in the theory. These two developments have so fundamentally altered the agricultural market that the model of pure competition definitely does not explain or describe it.

If only one or two industries even resemble the model, then a question must be asked: What is the relevance of this analysis to the American economy of the 1970s? The answer is that such analysis reveals more about the thinking of many economists than it does about the functioning of the economy.

The model of pure competition is the basis of the neoclassical economists' claim that the unencumbered private enterprise market system results in a situation of optimum production and distributional efficiency. In Chapter 7 we saw that neoclassical economics arose as an apology for the status quo in capitalism. From the analysis just presented it can be seen that in pure competition each firm, in equilibrium, produces the quantity at which its costs are minimized and its production is most efficient. The firm receives only the socially defined normal rate of profit. No excess profits exist. The consumer gets the product at the lowest possible price. The theory also claims that every factor of production gets the value of what it contributes to production (although the theory says nothing about the inequitable ownership of factors of production that prevails).

Such is the economic ideal for the neoclassical, laissez faire econo-mists: a beautiful, well-ordered, just world. But examination of the contemporary American economy reveals that theirs is a totally illusory world.

A tiny minority of the neoclassical economists have honestly admitted the degree to which reality differs from their ideal.[2] But most persist in arguing that what exists bears a reasonably close resemblance to their model. Thus the neoclassical analysis is gener-ally used to show that the free-enterprise market economy is the best and most just of all possible worlds. Therefore the theory of pure competition is studied here primarily to understand the basis of a very important conservative ideology supporting capitalism. (The model of pure competition, in its simplest form, also provides analytic tools that can be used to study more realistic cases.)

DEMAND AND REVENUE FOR A MONOPOLY

A *monopoly* exists when a single firm constitutes the entire industry. The firm sells a product for which there are no close substitutes, and potential competitors are prevented in one way or another from entering the industry.

Under competition, the demand curve for a whole industry slopes down and to the right (because the quantity sold increases only when the price falls). The demand curve for a competitive firm, however, is a horizontal straight line (because the firm's output is so small, it can sell as much more as it wishes at the same price). A monopoly firm, by definition, is the only seller of a commodity; it *is* the industry. Therefore *the demand curve for a monopoly firm is exactly like the demand curve for a whole competitive industry:* it slopes down and to the right. The monopoly demand curve shows that, unlike the owner of a competitive firm, who faces a given price, the monopolist can *choose* to sell more goods at a lower price or fewer goods at a higher price (he is not a price taker but a price fixer).

Thus a market demand curve shows the maximum revenue per unit of the commodity that a monopolist will receive at any par-ticular level of sales he may choose. When they view it from this seller's standpoint, economists call the demand curve an *average-revenue curve*. It shows the average revenue per unit of the com-modity sold for any level of sales.

---

[2]See, for example, the chapter on Henry C. Simons in William Breit and Roger L. Ransom, *The Academic Scribblers* (New York: Holt, Rinehart & Winston, 1971), pp. 205–222.

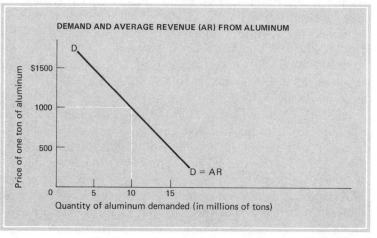

DEMAND AND AVERAGE REVENUE (AR) FROM ALUMINUM

Figure 18.8

Figure 18.8 shows a demand curve for a monopolized commodity —say, aluminum (for many years the Aluminum Company of America [ALCOA] had a pure monopoly of aluminum). It can be labeled a demand curve *or* an average-revenue curve. The curve in Figure 18.8 is labeled "demand = average revenue" to underscore this equivalence. At $1000 per ton, consumers wish to purchase 10 million tons. Alternatively, if the monopolist wishes to sell 10 million tons, then $1000 is the maximum price he can charge.

When ALCOA (assumed here to be a pure monopoly) decreases the price of aluminum and, hence, increases its sales of aluminum, two separate effects result in change in its total revenue: (1) the *quantity effect* and (2) the *price effect*. More aluminum can be sold only by lowering the price of aluminum. The decline in the price of aluminum multiplied by the quantity of aluminum sold at the old price is an amount of revenue that the firm loses in order to expand sales. Thus, when the quantity sold is increased by a lower price, the quantity effect always increases total revenue, while the price effect decreases total revenue. The net change in total revenue may be positive or negative, depending on whether the quantity effect or the price effect is larger.

Assume that ALCOA (or any monopoly) wishes to know how much total revenue will be increased if sales are increased by one ton. The information ALCOA is looking for is what economists call the *marginal revenue*, which may be defined as the change in the total revenue the firm will receive as a result of sale of one additional unit, in this case one more ton of aluminum. Marginal revenue is defined as follows.

$$\text{Marginal revenue} = \frac{\text{change in total revenue}}{\text{change in quantity sold}}$$

The average and marginal revenue of a monopoly are illustrated in Figure 18.9.

Notice that at any quantity of aluminum the marginal revenue is lower than the average revenue. Whenever the average revenue is decreasing, the marginal revenue must be lower than the average revenue. Again, this is similar to the case of a person taking a series of tests. If the average score declines as more tests are taken, it must mean that the marginal score (or the score on the last test taken) is below the average. In fact, it is the lower marginal score that pulls the average score down. Similarly, if the average revenue is decreasing, the marginal revenue must be below it and pulling it down.

When 10 million tons of aluminum are sold, marginal revenue is zero, or total revenue can be increased no further with the given demand: the quantity effect just offsets the price effect.

At quantities below (to the left of) 10 million, the quantity effect is more significant than the price effect, and therefore the marginal revenue is positive. As the quantity of aluminum sold increases, the price effect becomes more important and the quantity effect less important, until at 10 million they are equal. At higher quantities of aluminum (to the right of 10 million), the price effect is more important, and therefore the marginal revenue is negative. It is possible to conclude from this that a monopolist would always sell a smaller quantity than 10 million tons because if he expands sales to 10 million, the increase in revenue as a result of the last unit sold is

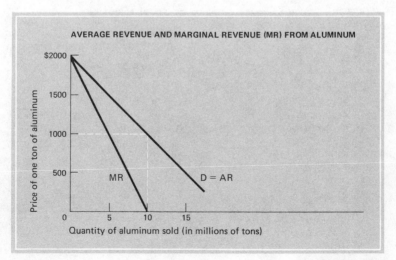

Figure 18.9

zero. If he sold a greater quantity, he would actually lose revenue because marginal revenue is negative at quantities above 10 million.

EQUILIBRIUM FOR THE MONOPOLY

In order to see the equilibrium price a monopolist will charge and the quantity he will sell, the monopolist's revenue curves must be superimposed on his cost curves. From the discussion in the previous section, it is known the average-revenue curve will slope downward and to the right and that the marginal-revenue curve will be below it and have a steeper slope. These curves are pictured in Figure 18.10. The profit-maximizing position is reached when the monopolist produces and sells the quantity (6 million tons) at which *marginal revenue equals marginal cost*. The reason for this is easy to comprehend. Below this level, one additional ton of aluminum brings in more revenue than its additional (or marginal) cost. Above this point, one additional ton of aluminum costs more than the average it brings in to ALCOA. Notice how the monopoly rule differs from the competitive rule that price should equal marginal cost. Because the monopolist has the entire market, his demand curve slopes downward, and therefore his marginal revenue is below the average revenue. In the competitive case, the firm is so small that the demand curve appears purely elastic in relation to it. Therefore the competitive price or average revenue *equals* its marginal revenue. Because the monopolist's marginal revenue is lower (and the more

EQUILIBRIUM FOR A MONOPOLIST SELLING ALUMINUM

Figure 18.10

general rule is that marginal cost equals marginal revenue), the monopolist chooses to supply less output to the market than would be the case in a competitive industry with similar cost and demand curves.

The average-revenue curve in Figure 18.10 indicates that $1500 is the maximum price at which 6 million tons can be sold. The shaded area shows the excess profits received at that price. For a monopoly, unlike a purely competitive firm, the making of excess profits is the usual and expected case. Nothing in the short or the long run tends to reduce these excess profits (except for changes in general business conditions as the economy undergoes cyclic fluctuations, a topic that will be examined in Part Three).

In addition to the high price the monopolist charges and the excess profits he makes, he almost never produces at the most efficient level of production. As shown in Figure 18.10, the monopolist stops producing before reaching the point at which his average costs are minimized. He does this, of course, because he is interested in maximum profits, not maximum efficiency. If he had produced the quantity that minimized his costs, he would have been forced to sell his product at a much lower price, and this would have reduced his excess profits. The reader can now easily see what is meant by the age-old charge that monopolies restrict output and sales in order to increase their excess profits. The reader can also see why, from the very beginning of the capitalist, private enterprise economic system, most businessmen have tenaciously fought to acquire monopoly power.

MODIFICATION OF
MONOPOLY ANALYSES

In the discussion of the market equilibrium for a monopolist, it was assumed both that the monopolist took his revenue and cost curves as given and that he maximized his profits by equating marginal cost and marginal revenue within the fixed constraints of externally determined revenue and cost curves. These assumptions enabled us to examine only one aspect of the monopolist's ceaseless drive for more excess profits. The monopolist can also increase excess profits by shifting his cost curves downward and his revenue curves upward.

Shifts in revenue curves can be effected in several ways. The first and most obvious method is through advertising. If the monopolist can persuade more consumers that they want or need his product, then he will be able to sell more of it at all prices along the demand curve—that is, the demand curve will shift upward and to the right. Thus we are literally bombarded with advertising. In a thousand

and one ways at least, businessmen endlessly attempt to convince us to consume ever-increasing amounts of their products.

Another way monopolists can increase the demand for their products is by convincing the government that it should erect and maintain protective tariffs to eliminate foreign competition. Although a firm or a group of firms often manages to achieve a monopoly within national boundaries, only very infrequently can a worldwide monopoly be achieved (however, many American-based multinational firms are working feverishly in that direction). To the extent that consumers buy a close foreign-made substitute for a monopolist's product, the demand for his product is reduced. Protective tariffs can eliminate foreign competition and thereby increase demand for the monopolist's product. Over the past several centuries businessmen have—generally with considerable success—sought the aid of governments in creating and protecting their firms' domestic monopolies by enacting protective tariffs. Such tariffs increase monopoly revenues at the expense of the consumer, who is forced to pay a higher price for "protected products." They are much like a tax levied by the government against all consumers, part of the proceeds of which is turned over to the monopolist to augment his excess profits.

Many large business firms are also able to increase the demand for their products through massive sales to the government. The bulk of these sales are connected with military procurement. For many of the largest U.S. corporations, these sales represent from 5 to 100 percent of their total sales. This topic is pursued in greater depth in Part Three.

There also are many ways business firms can shift their cost curves downward. They can press for government legislation that weakens labor unions; the Taft-Hartley Act of 1947 is an example of very restrictive legislation. They can also work to elevate "cooperative" and "reasonable" men to positions of leadership in unions, men who will not press very hard for wage increases that would disturb the status quo in the wage and profit distribution. They can also get President Nixon to appoint business-leaning "public" men to the wage and price control boards. These measures enable large firms to keep their wage costs to a minimum.

Monopolies also seek to achieve a monopsonistic position. A *monopsony* exists when a firm is the *only buyer* of a particular resource or intermediate product. A monopsonist can offer a very low price for the resource he is purchasing, and the seller must accept the offer or not sell his resource. Thus resource costs can be decreased if the firm can achieve monopsonistic buying power, which is no less actively sought than monopolistic selling power.

The immense political power that stems from their economic

power permits giant corporations to reduce costs in other ways. The government is often persuaded to allow them to use government-owned facilities for production connected with the armaments they are selling to the government. These facilities are generally used *free of charge*. And when the government has charged rent, it has reimbursed the corporations and given them extra profits on this rent; this is the so-called cost-plus contract. In other words, the government has actually paid the giant corporations to use government-owned facilities free of charge. Such a case was described by a U.S. Senate Committee report on pyramiding missile profits:

> Much of Western Electric's Nike production was done at two government surplus plants, which under the ordinary method of doing business with the government would have been supplied to Western Electric without cost. However, Western Electric instead of having the plants supplied free, rented them from the Government. Western Electric included the rentals as part of its overall costs and then charged the government a profit on these costs. The total rentals paid to the government by Western Electric for these plants amounted to over $3,000,000. When added to Western Electric's costs, the rentals generated additional profits to the company of $209,000. In such a situation, there could be little resistance on the part of Western Electric to having the government raise the rent, because as the rent went up, so did Western Electric's profit, since the complete amount of the rent was repaid by the landlord back to the tenant together with a profit.[3]

These are only a few of the ways large monopolistic corporations are constantly striving to use their economic and political power to maximize profits.

WHO ARE THE MONOPOLISTS?

Most introductory economics textbooks identify pure competition and monopoly as the extreme cases along the spectrum of industrial organization. They argue (and we agree) that there are almost no purely competitive industries. Most monopolies, they assert, are either local or regional in scope, ranging from the single grocery store in a small village to the single giant real estate developer in a large city. They maintain that national monopolies are as rare as purely competitive industries. According to these textbooks,

---

[3]U.S. Congress, Senate, Government Operations Subcommittee, *Pyramiding of Profits and Costs in the Missile Procurement*, Senate Report No. 970 (Washington, D.C.: GPO, 1964).

monopoly theory is of intellectual interest primarily as an extreme case with little actual or practical applicability at a national level in the American economy.

This view, we believe, is in error because it adheres strictly to the definition of monopoly as existing when there is only one seller. It interprets one seller to mean one firm. Admittedly, there are very few national markets where a single business firm is the only seller. Most important nationwide markets are dominated by a few giant corporations; they are oligopolies. In Chapter 19, however, we shall see that despite some distinct differences between oligopolies (a few firms) and monopolies (a single firm), most oligopolies act *as if* they were monopolies. We shall argue that our analysis of monopolies applies generally to oligopolies on questions of pricing, output, and the shifting revenue and cost curves. If our analysis is correct, so that we can redefine monopolies to include industries that behave as if they were a single seller, then monopolies dominate almost all the important national markets in the United States.

NATURAL MONOPOLIES
AND GOVERNMENT REGULATION

There are some industries that economists call *natural monopolies*. The technology used in these industries creates a cost curve on which the minimum average cost is not reached until a firm is producing a very large quantity. Generally, before the minimum average cost is reached a single firm can supply the entire market with the commodity in question. If two firms divided the sales between them, each would produce such a small quantity that its average cost would be much higher than that of a single firm supplying the entire market. In this circumstance a free market will always lead to one firm's acquiring a monopoly position.

The most common examples of natural monopolies are public utilities such as electric and telephone companies. Because each of these companies supplies a commodity that is a vital necessity for most individuals and most other business firms, they are almost always regulated by the government. This regulation generally takes the form of an imposed price ceiling (although the regulating agencies are often controlled by the monopolies, so the price ceiling is usually high enough to allow considerable excess profits).

The governing agency can reduce the monopolist's excess profits by lowering the price he will charge the public and/or increasing the quantity of the product he will sell. If the government wishes to increase the public welfare and still allow the monopolist to choose a profit-maximizing quantity to sell it, it will generally attempt to set the price at the level at which the monopolist's marginal cost is equal

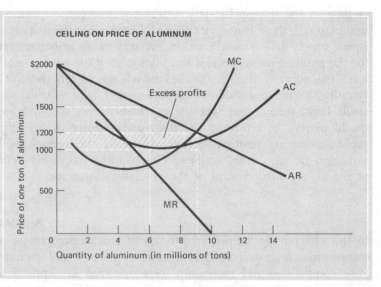

Figure 18.11

to his average revenue. This type of price ceiling is illustrated in Figure 18.11.

For quantities at which the price ceiling is below the firm's average-revenue curve, that ceiling becomes, in effect, an average revenue and a marginal revenue for the firm. The reasoning is analogous to that for a firm in pure competition, whose price is determined independently of its actions. The monopolist, unlike the purely competitive firm, however, cannot sell any quantity he wishes at that price. For quantities at which his original average-revenue curve falls below the price ceiling, the maximum price he can charge is determined by his average-revenue curve. In Figure 18.11, for quantities up to 7 million tons the price ceiling serves as an average-revenue and marginal-revenue curve. At quantities larger than 7 million tons, the firm reverts back to its original revenue curves. If the firm is not regulated, it will charge $1500 and sell 6 million tons. The price ceiling is imposed at the price ($1200) that will equate the firm's average revenue and its marginal cost (as under competition). The firm then treats the price ceiling as a marginal-revnue curve for quantities up to 9 million tons (where the price ceiling equals the average revenue and the marginal cost). He is then selling more at a lower price and receiving less profit.

Although the general public and other business firms are obviously better off after the price ceiling has been imposed, it is obvious that the monopolist is still making large excess profits (i.e., his average-cost curve is still below his average-revenue curve). But as long as the monopolist is left free to choose the quantity he wishes to sell, there is no price that will both clear the market (i.e., equate supply and demand) *and* in any way result in better service for the public. For example, if the price ceiling were set at a lower level, the quantity the firm wished to sell would fall short of the quantity the public wished to buy, so a market disequilibrium would result. If the price ceiling were set at a higher level, the government would merely be returning the monopolist nearer to his original profit-maximizing position at the expense of the general public's and other business firms' welfare. This happens frequently because of the monopolists' control of the regulatory agencies.

SUMMARY

In this chapter we defined four types of market structures: pure competition, monopolistic competition, oligopoly, and monopoly. Pure competition and monopoly were analyzed in depth. Purely competitive industries are almost nonexistent. They are studied because the analysis of pure competition is the foundation of the classical liberal, laissez faire policy prescription. Because a purely competitive firm will tend to produce at its most efficient, low-cost level of output, the level at which the firm earns no excess profits, pure competition is also sometimes used as a theoretical norm against which to evaluate and compare existing industries.

Monopolistic firms, however, almost never produce at the most efficient, low-cost levl of output. Furthermore, they generally receive large excess profits because of their control over the price they charge consumers. Even if the government were to attempt to control a monopolist in order to mitigate the exploitation of the general public, the monopolist would probably continue to make excess profits.

monopolistic
competition
and
oligopoly

In the United States today there are about 12 million business firms
(of which nearly 14 percent are corporations). If agriculture is
excluded as a special case not clearly fitting into any market
structure, well over 99 percent of the remaining firms fit into the
category we call monopolistic competition. Judged in terms of
number of firms, it is by far the most important category of industrial organization.

The overwhelming majority of business firms are, however,
minute firms in the fields of retailing, wholesaling, and the service
industries (e.g., small drugstores, hot dog stands, barber shops, and
so forth). In a very important sense the more basic industries (e.g.,
mining, agriculture, banking, transportation, manufacturing, and
communications) are the foundation on which the prosperity of the
nation depends. Those who control these industries dominate the
entire economy. Almost all the basic or fundamental industries are
completely controlled by giant oligopolistic corporations. Therefore,
judged in terms of economic power, oligopoly is by far the most
important category of industrial organization. Of the approximately
180,000 U.S. manufacturing corporations, for example, a mere 100
(0.004 percent) own 58 percent of total net capital assets.

If we were to describe America's industrial landscape, we would
begin with a vast plain of millions of tiny pebbles, representing all
the economically powerless, monopolistically competitive business

firms. At the center of this enormous plain would rise a few hundred colossal towers, representing the important oligopolistic corporations. These few hundred towers would be so large that they would dwarf into insignificance the entire plain below them.

EQUILIBRIUM FOR A
MONOPOLISTICALLY COMPETITIVE FIRM

Monopolistic competition exists in an industry made up of many small firms, each producing a slightly differentiated product. An example of a monopolistic competitor is the neighborhood gas station, which differs slightly, but only slightly, from its competitors. The differentiation may be merely in the packaging, the location of a retail store, or the service offered; but in any case it creates a certain amount of consumer loyalty, which creates demand curves that slope downward and to the right. If a firm raises its price, it will lose only a portion of its customers to competitors. Many will continue to buy the product at higher prices. But if a firm lowers its price, it will attract a few of its competitors' customers.

The monopolistically competitive firm maximizes its profits when it equates marginal cost and marginal revenue. In many cases, if the firm has recently substantially differentiated its product, it may make large, monopolistic, excess profits. Such a situation is shown in Figure 19.1(A).

A monopolistically competitive industry, however, has no significant barriers preventing the entry of new firms. New firms, seeing the excess profits, will begin producing and selling highly similar products and will drain the demand away from the firm pictured in

Figure 19.1

Figure 19.1(A). As a consequence, the original firm's average-revenue curve will shift downward and to the left. As long as excess profits remain, new firms will continue to enter and the average-revenue curve will continue to shift downward and to the left. Therefore the downward shift will come to a halt only after the average revenue curve just touches, but does not cross, the average-cost curve.

This situation is pictured in Figure 19.1(B). The average-revenue curve just touches, but does not cross, the average-cost curve. At that quantity the firm's marginal cost is equal to its marginal revenue; to maximize its profits, it produces at this point. It is also the quantity at which the firm's average revenue is equal to its average cost.[1] All the excess profits have been squeezed out by the entry of new competitors.

Notice, however, that the new equilibrium is always above the minimum point of the firm's average-cost curve. In Figure 19.1(B) the new demand curve, because it is still not flat as in pure competition, meets the average-cost curve above the minimum point. The price is above the minimum cost level, but there are no excess profits because at the actual production level costs are also higher than the minimum. In other words, the firm in monopolistic competition produces less output at a higher price and at a higher cost than the purely competitive firm in long-run equilibrium. We can therefore say that, in equilibrium, monopolistically competitive firms incur waste by never producing at their most efficient level. (In fact, only a purely competitive firm can be shown to produce efficiently in a private enterprise economy.)

The only way in which the firm can hope to regain some of its lost excess profits is to convince the public, usually through advertising, that its product has been more substantially differentiated from those of its competitors. But when one firm advertises and attracts new customers, its competitors generally retaliate by competitively advertising their own products. The net result often is that things are brought back to the point at which they were before the first firm began to advertise. Now, however, no firm is willing to curtail its advertising for fear of losing its customers to competitors who continue advertising.

Advertising becomes almost a pure waste that is locked into the system. We say "almost" a pure waste because we grant that advertising may occasionally impart useful information. Most advertising, however, is so notorious for its use of half-truths, emotional ap-

---

[1] It might seem to the reader that this result is attributable to the way in which we arbitrarily drew the curves in Figure 19.1. This is not so, but to prove it involves some knowledge of calculus, so we leave the proof to more advanced books.

peals, brainwashing, and psychological appeals to people's most basic frustrations that few people can tell when any genuinely useful information is being offered. Most of us consciously dismiss advertising as a totally unreliable source of information, even though we may unconsciously be affected by the constant barrage of advertising aggressively hurled at each of our senses.

Another waste of monopolistic competition is the tendency to duplicate needlessly the same service. For example, how many times have you seen four gas stations on the same street crossing on all four corners? This is totally inefficient from a social point of view.

Thus we have sketched the picture of monopolistic competition, a picture that fairly adequately describes the overwhelming majority of small businesses in a private enterprise economy. Millions of tiny, nearly powerless businessmen work feverishly to create or protect some amount of monopolistic excess profits. Millions of competitors try equally hard to take away those excess profits. No competitor is able to sustain the acquisition of excess profits for a very long period, but each perpetually struggles, worries, competes, connives, and battles in a never-ending war in which there are no victors. Millions of firms almost never produce at the most efficient, lowest-cost level of production; billions of dollars are wasted on the aggressive propagation of inane, mind-dulling, and obnoxious advertising.

OLIGOPOLY

An *oligopoly* exists when a few business firms dominate an industry. Unlike any of the industrial categories discussed up to this point, an oligopolistic firm does not face a definite, unambiguous demand curve for its product. The amount the oligopolist can sell at any price can be substantially affected by his rivals' actions. Furthermore, because his actions similarly affected his rivals, any time he changes his price he must assume that competitors will react in some way to this change. His rivals' reactions will, in turn, affect the customers' response to his initial price change. He must be prepared to respond to any unexpected moves by his competitors. Thus the fact of *interconnectedness* and *mutual dependence* of oligopolistic firms is the outstanding feature of an oligopolistic industry.

How can the effects of competitors' reactions be analyzed? First, their reactions to a price increase and to a price decrease can be differentiated. If a firm raises its price, it will automatically lose many of its customers to its rivals, who sell a highly similar product. Consequently, its action is not likely to provoke a reaction from its rivals. They are happy to acquire new customers.

However, if the firm lowers its price it will attract its rivals' customers if they do nothing to retaliate. Rather than losing their

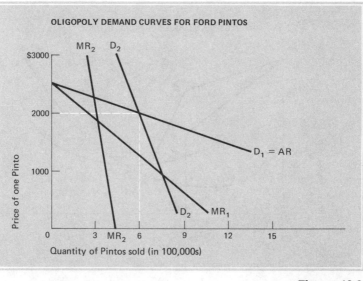

Figure 19.2

customers, they are likely to lower their prices by the same amount. It might seem that these price changes would cancel each other out, leaving each firm selling the same quantity at a lower price. This is not the case, however. When all the firms lower their prices, they attract new customers. Furthermore, old customers may buy more of the product sold by the industry.

Figure 19.2 provides two demand curves for an oligopolistic firm in an oligopolistic industry: Ford Motor Company (and our old friend the Pinto). Demand curve D_1D_1 is constructed on the assumption that rivals ignore price changes made by Ford. Demand curve D_2D_2 is constructed on the assumption that rivals follow suit and change their prices by the same amount. For demand curve D_1D_1, marginal-revenue curve MR_1 is constructed. For demand curve D_2D_2, marginal-revenue curve MR_2 is constructed. Demand curves D_1D_1 and D_2D_2 intersect at the price and quantity that prevailed before the price change.

From the discussion of oligopoly behavior it is assumed here that, beginning at \$2,000, Ford's rivals will not react if it raises its price. Therefore for all prices above \$2,000 (and quantities below 600,000 Pintos), the curves D_1D_1 and MR_1 are Ford's actual demand and marginal revenue curves. If Ford lowers its price below \$2,000, the rivals will lower their prices accordingly. Therefore for prices below \$2,000 (and quantities greater than 600,000 Pintos), the curves D_2D_2 and MR_2 are the firm's actual demand and marginal-revenue curves.

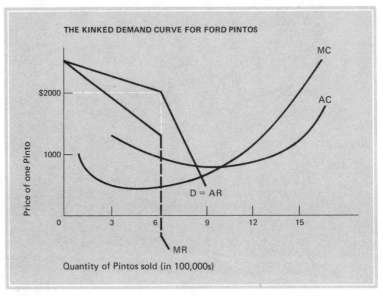

THE KINKED DEMAND CURVE FOR FORD PINTOS

Figure 19.3

By eliminating the irrelevant sections of the two demand curves, it is possible to construct the firm's actual demand and marginal-revenue curves. In Figure 19.3 these curves are constructed and the firm's cost curves superimposed upon them. Two things should be carefully noted: The average-revenue or demand curve is kinked (where the demand curve abruptly turns down), and the marginal revenue (at 600,000 cars) suddenly falls off into the negative quadrant of the graph.

It is clear from the graph that Ford will lose profits if it changes its price either upward or downward from the initial price of $2,000. It is also clear that it would be highly unlikely that the revenue curves could ever shift so far downward and to the left that Ford would lower the price it charged. An increase in costs or an increase in the revenue curves would have to be fairly substantial for the firm to raise its price, unless business conditions led rival firms to raise their prices as well.

This analysis helps explain the historically observed fact that prices in oligopolistic industries are very stable in the face of short-run small variations in demand. It also helps explain why, over the longer run, oligopolistic prices almost never fall. Rather, they show a persistent tendency to rise during periods of inflation and remain stable during periods of recession or deflation.

Oligopoly Prices

The analysis does not show, however, how the price charged by oligopolists is arrived at. Whatever price is established, a kink will develop at that price. But how is the price established in the first place?

Most textbooks develop elaborate models of oligopolistic behavior based on the assumption that regardless of how many times the actions of rivals upset their expectations, the rivals never learn that they are mutually dependent.[2] The German economist H. von Stackelberg developed a sophisticated analytic model of oligopolistic behavior that proved that oligopolistic rivalry will never result in the establishment of a stable price unless all the firms accept a single firm as a leader and all other firms accept positions as followers.[3] In other words, stability requires that a single firm (or any other single decision-makng body) make the decisions in the oligopoly and that the remaining firms accept the decisions made by the leader.

What type of decisions will be made by the oligopolistic leader in a private enterprise economy? The answer to this question is simple once the absurd assumption that oligopolistic firms do not recognize their mutual dependence is rejected. "If we assume that they recognize it [their mutual dependence], then they will set industry price at the monopoly price. The number of firms in the industry does not matter so long as they realize their interdependence."[4]

In other words, the large corporations prevent price competition, although they do compete through alleged quality differences and advertising. With no price competition the sellers of a given commodity have an interest in seeing that price or prices established are such as to maximize the profits of the group as a whole, so each product is priced *as if* it were sold by a single monopoly corporation. This is the decisive fact in determining the price policies and strategies of the typical large corporation. And it means that the appropriate price theory of an economy dominated by such corporations is not competitive price theory but monopoly price theory. What nineteenth-century economists treated as a special case is now the general situation.

It is true that there is little open collusion in the United States because of the antitrust laws. Yet some kind of tacit collusion prob-

[2]For a good, brief discussion of three such models, see Richard A. Bilas, *Microeconomic Theory* (New York: McGraw-Hill, 1967), pp. 213–219.

[3]H. von Stackelberg, *The Theory of the Market Economy*, trans. A. T. Peacock (New York: Oxford University Press, 1952), pp. 194–204.

[4]Bilas, op. cit., p. 219.

ably exists to a large degree in most industries, reaching its most developed form in what is known as *price leadership*. It is a mutual security pact in which no formal communication is necessary.

In this situation, when one firm raises or lowers the price, all the others will follow. When collusion is forbidden, the price leader calculates the share of the total market demand that his rivals will supply at various prices. He then chooses the price where the remaining demand (after the rivals have chosen their appropriate supply quantities) will maximize his profits. For the industry as a whole this solution approximates the pure monopoly solution. So long as all firms accept his solution, which is really nothing else but a corollary of the ban on price competition, it becomes easy for the group as a whole to feel its way toward the price that maximizes the industry's profit. In the appendix to this chapter we examine the exact mechanism of price leadership and other mechanisms by which oligopolies set a monopoly-like price.

There is the qualification that oligopoly prices do not in fact move upward or downward with equal ease, as they would in a pure monopoly. If one seller raises his price, this cannot possibly be interpreted as an aggressive move. The worst that can happen to him is that the others will stand pat and he will have to rescind (or accept a smaller share of the market). In the case of a price cut, however, there is always the possibility that aggression is intended—that the cutter is trying to increase his share of the market by violating the taboo on price competition. If rivals interpret the initial move in this way, the result may be a price war with losses to all. Hence everyone is more likely to be careful about lowering prices than about raising them. Under the present situation of oligopoly, in other words, prices tend to be stickier on the downward side than on the upward side, and this fact introduces a significant upward bias into the general price level in a capitalistic economy dominated by oligopolies.

OLIGOPOLY OR MONOPOLY?

In Chapter 18, four general classifications of market structures (pure competition, monopolistic competition, oligopoly, and monopoly) were described. We found that there were almost no purely competitive industries. In this chapter, it has been argued that, in their decisions regarding pricing, output, and sales, there is very little difference between oligopolies and monopolies.

Are there other differences of sufficient importance to make the oligopoly category a useful analytical tool? Or would it be better to drop oligopoly and simply refer to all industries that are dominated by a few giant corporations as monopolies?

The principal difference between oligopolistic and monopolistic firms is the rivalry that exists among the former. Although they have found by experience that this rivalry is mutually disastrous when it is extended to competitive pricing, they remain rivals. Their competition is generally confined to advertising, sales promotion, and cost reduction campaigns, and their actions do not differ substantially from the monopolist's behavior, particularly in attempts to shift revenue curves upward and cost curves downward.

It seems, therefore, that only when the passage of time results in a substantial shift of relative power within an oligopolistic industry are there important differences between a monopoly and oligopoly. During such a situation a struggle for the industry's price leadership might develop. Such a struggle might result, temporarily, in destructive price competition (or worse). But once a new leader emerged, the industry would generally return to the types of policies that make it hardly distinguishable from a monopoly.

Thus, the oligopoly category is useful for analyzing temporary situations during which destructive competition takes place. It might also be useful to differentiate between monopolies and oligopolies in analyzing differences between advertising and sales promotion techniques for firms that sell commodities for which there are close substitute (oligopolistic firms) and for those that sell products for which there are no close substitutes (monopolistic firms).

In almost any other situation or context, the differences between monopolistic and oligopolistic firms are insignificant. In most discussions it is quite appropriate to refer to all giant corporations as monopolistic firms, as is generally done in ordinary conversation. The economist's narrower definition of monopoly, while sometimes helpful, is so restrictive that it eliminates almost all existing business firms. Yet the formal analysis of a monopolist's pricing and output decisions forms the basis for understanding the behavior of most giant corporations.

SUMMARY

Most American business firms fit into the market structure of monopolistic competition. Our analyses has shown that although these firms do not generally receive excess profits, they incur waste by never producing at their most efficient level and by wasting enormous amounts of resources on competitive advertising.

A comparatively few powerful oligopolistic giants dominate the industrial landscape of American business. Oligopolies generally set prices as if they were monopolies (this point is developed further in the appendix that follows). Large excess profits and inefficiency characterize their operations.

APPENDIX

Price Determination in an Oligopoly

The simplest and most direct method of oligopoly pricing occurs when the oligopolistic firms form a formal cartel. A *cartel* is an association that acts as a monopoly. Within a cartel each firm is treated as if it were merely a separate plant owned by the monopoly.

Figure 19A.1 shows that a cartel's price determination is identical to that of a monopoly. The monopolist has a single marginal-cost curve; the cartel's marginal-cost curve is determined by adding together the various individual oligopolists' marginal-cost curves. The industry price is set at $2,000, and 3 million compact cars is the quantity sold by the industry. Each firm produces the quantity at which its own marginal cost is equal to the industry's marginal cost (and marginal revenue).

Cartels, as such, are illegal in the United States. But many oligopolistic industries have found several ways of engaging in covert collusion that enables them to cooperate in such a manner that their pricing and output decisions become almost tantamount to a formal cartel.

When this type of collusion is not possible, many oligopolistic industries rely on the price leadership of the dominant firm within the industry. The dominant firm may be either the largest or the most efficient; sometimes it is both. In this situation the dominant firm sets the price. The other firms take that price as given the same

Figure 19A.1

way a purely competitive firm accepts the industry price as given. They produce up to the point at which their marginal cost is equal to that price (which they take as their marginal revenue).

In order for the dominant firm to maximize its profits, it must know approximately what the marginal costs are for the other firms. For some time U. S. Steel was the price leader in its industry. Figure 19A.2 illustrates how price is determined in such an industry. *DD* is the industry demand curve; the demand curve for U.S. Steel is

Figure 19A.2

labeled $D_{uss}D_{uss}$. The summation of the marginal-cost curves for all firms other than the price leader is also shown.

The demand curve for the price leader (D_{uss}) is computed in the following manner: Whatever price the leader (U.S. Steel) selects, it knows the other firms will produce up to the point at which their marginal cost equals that price. U.S. Steel knows, therefore, that the other firms, taken collectively, will produce the quantity (in Figure 19A.2, 70 million tons) at which the summation of their marginal-cost curves equals the price it establishes. The demand for the leader's output will be the total market demand at that price minus the quantity the other firms sell. In others words, the leader's demand curve at any price will be equal to the difference between the market demand curve and the summation of the other firm's marginal-cost curves.

For example, if the leader establishes a price of $2000 the other firms will produce all that can be sold at that price (because at that point market demand equals the summation of the marginal-cost curves). At prices below $2000 the summation of the marginal-cost curves falls successively farther to the left of the demand curve. Therefore as price declines, the demand remaining for the leader increases.

The marginal revenue (MR_{uss}) is derived from U.S. Steel's demand curve. The leader will maximize its profit by producing the quantity (30 million tons) and establishing the price $1500) for the industry. The remainder of the firms will produce, among them, 70 million tons, and the entire industry will produce 100 million tons (equal to U.S. Steel's 30 million plus the others' 70 million).

It should be stressed that the follower firms only very superficially resemble firms in a purely competitive market. Although they take the price that has been established and adjust their output so that their marginal cost is equal to that price, their long-run normal position is one in which they also make monopolistic, excess profits. Because the oligopoly, like the monopoly, manages to keep new firms out of the industry, there are no market forces that would tend to erode profits.

A third method of establishing a monopoly price is through the creation of a government regulatory agency to supervise the industry. Although these agencies ostensibly exist to protect the general public's interests, very often they function as means of coordinating the industry and establishing a monopoly price (this was discussed in Chapter 8).

government
and
inequality

In Chapter 16, we examined the distribution of income in the United States and found a small number of very rich people, who are mostly recipients of profit income from capital. We also found a very large number of poor and low-income people, who are mostly wage workers or unemployed workers. In Chapter 17, we found that even in the corporate world there are a few very big fish and millions of small ones. Clearly economic power lies in the hands of a few thousand owners and executives of the major corporations.

In this chapter, the relationship of economic power to political power will be examined. First we shall explore the degree to which their vast economic power gives disproportionate political power to that same relatively small number of top corporate owners and executives. Then we shall see how the resulting government affects economic inequality via taxation, welfare, farm subsidies, antitrust laws, and education. In Chapter 29, government policies, particularly military spending, will be considered in relation to unemployment and inflation.

HOW ECONOMIC INEQUALITY
PRODUCES POLITICAL INEQUALITY

In spite of our formal political democracy, money talks in politics as elsewhere. Thus it is no surprise that many writers, not all radical, have alleged that those with economic power are dominant in U.S.

politics. While he was President of the United States, Woodrow Wilson wrote: "Suppose you go to Washington and try to get at your Government. You will always find that while you are politely listened to, the men really consulted are the men who have the biggest stake—the big bankers, the big manufacturers, the big masters of commerce, the heads of railroad corporations and of steamship corporations. . . . The masters of the Government of the United States are the combined capitalists and manufacturers of the United States."[1]

How far can Wilson's hypothesis be substantiated by the facts? Do the large number of low-income workers or the few high-income, upper-class capitalists dominate U.S. politics? The economics of class structure has been examined; now we must ask about consciousness of class background because this will affect political behavior. A careful study conducted in 1964 found, contrary to the myth of an all-middle-class America, that 56 percent of all Americans said they thought of themselves as "working class." Some 39 percent considered themselves "middle class." (It is true, though, that 35 percent of all those questioned said they had never thought of their class identification before that moment.) One percent said they were "upper class," and only 2 percent rejected the whole idea of class.[2]

An individual's political behavior is strongly influenced by class background. But that leads to a puzzle. If a majority identify with the working class, and everyone has one vote, why do parties favorable to the working class not win every election? Why do government policies usually further, not working-class interests but (as Woodrow Wilson asserted) those of the wealthy capitalist class? More precisely, given formal democracy and capitalism, exactly how does our extreme economic inequality tend to be translated into inequality of political power?

In the first place, there is the simple fact that the degree of political participation tends to vary with class background. "The average citizen has little interest in public affairs, and he expends his energy on the daily round of life—eating, working, family talk, looking at the comics [today, TV], sex, sleeping."[3] More exactly, 86 percent of those identified in another 1964 study as middle class voted, but only 72 percent of the working class voted. Similarly, 40 percent of

[1]Woodrow Wilson, *The New Freedom* (Garden City, N.Y.: Doubleday, 1914), pp. 57–58.
[2]This study is reported in Marian Irish and James Prothro, *The Politics of American Democracy* (Englewood Cliffs, N.J.: Prentice-Hall, 1965), p. 38. To avoid the imputation of a radical bias, we have taken all of the data in this section from their widely used traditional textbook. In turn, all of their footnotes refer to well-known conventional political scientists.
[3]Ibid., p. 165.

the middle class had talked to others about voting for a party or candidate, but only 24 percent in the working class had talked about it. Among the middle-class people interviewed, 16 percent gave money to a political cause, 14 percent attended political meetings, and 8 percent worked for a party or candidate; in the working class, figures on the same activities were only 4 percent, 5 percent, and 3 percent, respectively.[4]

Thus political participation of all kinds increases with income. Some of the reasons are obvious. Lower-income workers have less leisure, less money above minimum needs, more exhausting jobs. Furthermore, detailed studies show that because workers have less education and less access to information, they have less knowledge of the importance of various issues, which accounts, in part, for their lower participation. The same studies show more cross-pressures on workers—for example, the racial antagonisms that conveniently divide and weaken their working-class outlook.[5]

Unequal political power is also achieved through control of the news media. Even if the average worker "had an interest in politics, he would have great difficulty getting accurate information; since the events of politics unfold at a great distance, he cannot observe them directly, and the press offers a partial and distorted picture."[6] Even the quantity of news is limited. Although 80 percent of Americans read newspapers and 88 percent have television sets, only 2.8 percent of total newspaper space and even less television time is devoted to political news.[7]

If the quantity of political news is deplorable, its quality is abysmal or worse. The first problem is that only one view is available to most people because of increasing concentration of newspaper ownership. In 1910, some 57 percent of American cities had competing daily papers; but in 1960, only 4 percent had competing dailies. Furthermore, news media tend to have a conservative bias because (1) they do not want to offend any powerful interests; (2) they especially do not want to offend major advertisers, all of which are big businesses; and (3) most important, "Since the media of communication are big businesses, too, the men who control them quite naturally share the convictions of other businessmen."[8]

Economic power also worsens the substantial inequality of political power available to different pressure groups. Thus a standard political science textbook points to *status* as the most important factor in determining the influence of a pressure group. After listing

[4]Ibid., p. 38.
[5]Ibid., p. 193.
[6]Ibid., p. 165.
[7]Ibid., p. 183.
[8]Ibid., p. 184.

other sources of status, it concludes: "Finally, since status is so closely tied to money in the United States, the group with greater status will almost automatically be able to command greater financial resources. And it costs money to engage in pressure politics. . . ."[9]

The fact of economic power weighs all the more heavily because advertising is now a vital component of politics. ". . . Pressure groups . . . are now spending millions of dollars every year on *mass propaganda*. Not only broad groups like the National Association of Manufacturers, but even individual companies maintain elaborate bureaucracies to sell 'correct' ideas on general policy questions along with favorable attitudes to the company."[10]

The vast amount of business advertising reinforces the general ethos of capitalism. What is its message? Ours is a lovely country; material luxuries represent the *summum bonum;* everyone can have these material luxuries. A certain percentage of business advertising is devoted to specifically political issues. Yet the government permits *all* business advertising to be counted as a cost, which can be deducted from income when taxes are computed. Of course labor unions are not allowed this tax deduction for political advertising.

WATERGATE AND THE PRESIDENT

There is no great mystery about how economic power gains dominance over the President. Money, big money, is required for presidential campaigns. For example, just in the few months of primary campaigns in 1972, Edmund Muskie spent about $2 million. It is estimated that President Nixon spent $29 million in the 1968 campaign and about $55 million in the 1972 campaign. Two traditional political scientists admit that "because campaigns are exceedingly costly, the wealthier a person is, the more strategic his position for bringing pressure to bear on politicians."[11]

In return for the money showered on him, Nixon has appointed conservative businessmen to most cabinet and subcabinet positions; to almost all committees and agencies; to most high posts in the Republican party; and to many ambassadorships (including 16 of the 19 in Western Europe). Obviously these positions are desired and used in furthering the interests of these individual businessmen and of all business; an example is the business favors done by Nixon's friend, John Mitchell, who became Attorney General. This process, by which the President is elected by economic power and then appoints economically powerful people to positions from which they

[9]Ibid., p. 245.
[10]Ibid., p. 249.
[11]Robert Dahl and Charles Lindblom, *Politics, Economics, and Welfare* (New York: Harper & Row, 1953), p. 313.

can further extend and defend economic power, may be called a feedback mechanism. In later sections we shall look at how the political feedback mechanism operates on education, farm subsidies, tax loopholes, military spending, and so forth.

More direct feedback mechanisms to influence the political process itself include police to stop demonstrations, the use of the CIA and FBI to attack "radicals" (meaning anyone opposed to the administration), and the use of the President's prestige in TV and press announcements to promote big-business policies. Last but not least, the Watergate scandal has exposed the joint use of economic power and the President's political power to do political espionage, possibly so extensive as to prevent the opposition party from winning an election. If it could be used to such an astounding degree against liberal Democrats, how much must it be used against socialist radicals? Notice that Watergate involved economic power in several ways. On the one hand, at least $2 million was required for the actual conspiracy, of which about $800,000 apparently came from Texas oil men anxious to be given presidential favors. On the other hand, it reflects all the money that went into electing Nixon the first time.

One more word on Watergate. It mirrors the fact that when conservatives talk about "law and order" they mean primarily the protection of private property here and abroad—by any means available. Thus, letting the police shoot a black or Chicano unemployed worker in the back because he stole a $5 item is "law and order." Breaking into and bugging the Watergate Democratic headquarters (or breaking into and robbing a psychiatrist's office in the Pentagon Papers case) is "law and order" because it protects the administration that protects private property. Bombing Cambodia—even though it is unconstitutional because Congress did not authorize it— is "law and order" because it protects the friends of capitalism abroad. Thus the conservative view of "law and order" is always to protect property (or "national security," which is the same thing) but not people. *This function of "law and order" (or protection of private property) is the main function of the U.S. government.*

CONGRESS AND ECONOMIC POWER

Nor is Congress immune to the lure of economic power. Congressmen need money to get elected and reelected; they need it for advertising, to pay for TV, to pay air fares, and for many other basic necessities of political life. Lincoln is said to have spent only 26 cents on his campaign, but in the 1950s congressmen spent about $15,000 to $25,000, and in the 1970s many congressmen were spending over $100,000 on each campaign. In the 1970 Senate race in New

York alone, Goodell spent $1.3 million, Buckley $2 million, and Ottinger $4 million.

The Republican and Democratic parties together spent about $140 million in 1952, $155 million in 1956, $175 million in 1960, $200 million in 1964, $300 million in 1968, and some record sum in 1972 (not yet estimated in detail).[12] One investigation found that the Democratic party's money comes about 55 percent from corporations, 20 percent from big labor, 15 percent from racketeers and gangsters, and 15 percent from middle-class Americans in small contributions. The Republicans usually collect about twice as much in total, most of which comes from big business. Conservative Senator Russell Long guesses that "about 95 percent of congressional funds are derived from businessmen."

Congressmen are also indirectly affected by economic power through the strong influence of the President (or the Presidents' agents, such as Haldeman or Erlichman). Furthermore, big business can threaten to open or close plants in a particular congressional district. Business can give a congressman free time on radio or TV or a free plane ride. In addition, there are about 5000 fulltime lobbyists in Washington, about 10 for each congressman (and many are ex-congressmen or good personal or business friends of congressmen). Except in emergencies, lobbyists do not directly buy votes. They merely serve as the main channel for the largest campaign contributions, buy lunches and dinners, and supply petty cash, credit cards, profitable investment opportunities, legal retainers to congressmen (most of whom are lawyers), lecture fees, poker winnings (congressmen *always* win), vacations, and fringe benefits ranging from theater tickets to French perfume. The two largest lobbies are the oil interests (which make billions in special tax loopholes) and the military armaments industry. All of this power is so strong —and so necessary for election—that even liberals like Senators Fulbright, Mansfield, and Pastore will be found voting consistently for the direct needs of business interests in their districts—no matter how they may vote on broader issues.

Most congressmen, however, need little prompting to vote as economic power directs because most are so selected that this is their natural inclination. In the next section we shall note that few congressmen are black or Chicano or women or poor; most are white, male, and affluent. Thus one friendly senator, Boies Penrose, said to a meeting of businessmen (back in 1900, when such things were said more frankly): "I believe in a division of labor. You send us to Congress; we pass laws under . . . which you make money;

---

[12]M. Cummings and D. Wise, *Democracy Under Pressure* (New York: Harcourt Brace Jovanovich, 1971), pp. 304–305.

... and out of your profits you further contribute to our campaign funds to send us back again to pass more laws to enable you to make more money."[13]

ECONOMIC BACKGROUND
OF POLITICAL LEADERS

Upper-income members of the capitalist class hold a disproportionate percentage of the top political positions. From 1789 to 1932, the fathers of U.S. presidents and vice presidents were 38 percent professionals, 20 percent proprietors and officials, 38 percent farm owners, and only 4 percent wage earners or salaried workers. Similarly, from 1947 to 1951, the fathers of U.S. senators were 22 percent professionals, 33 percent proprietors and officials, 40 percent farm owners, and only 4 percent wage earners or salaried workers. Finally, from 1941 to 1943, the fathers of U.S. representatives were 31 percent professionals, 31 percent proprietors and officials, 29 percent farm owners, and only 9 percent wage earners or salaried workers.[14]

Data for 1970 show that 266 of the 435 members of the House of Representatives (about three-fifths) had outside financial interests providing over $5,000 in income per year beyond their congressional salaries.[15] This figure may be an underestimation because income of wives and children was not listed (nor was income under $5,000 listed). To make $5,000 a year from stocks and bonds requires at least $70,000 or $80,000 in holdings. The congressmen were not required to reveal the extent of their holdings. Some voluntarily disclosed this information. Very wealthy men, with fortunes ranging from many tens of thousands of dollars up to the figure of slightly under $3 million listed for Representative Pierre Du Pont, sit in Congress.

What are the sources of their wealth? A total of 102 congressmen held stock or well-paying executive positions in banks or other financial institutions; 81 received regular income from law firms that generally represented big businesses. Sixty-three got their income from stock in the top defense contractors; 45, in the giant (federally regulated) oil and gas industries; 22, in radio and television companies; 11, in commercial airlines; and 9, in railroads. Ninety-eight congressmen were involved in numerous capital gains transactions;

[13]Quoted in Mark Green, James Fallows, and David Zwick, *Who Runs Congress?* (New York: Bantam, 1972, The Ralph Nader Congress Project), pp. 7–8.

[14]Cunnings and Wise, op. cit., p. 39.

[15]All of these data were taken from statements filed with the House Committee on Standards of Official Conduct in April 1971; they were discussed in an article in the *Los Angeles Times*, May 24, 1971, pt. I, p. 12.

each of them netted a profit of over $5,000 (and some as high as $35,000).

In the executive branch (excluding the President and Vice President), upper-income, business-oriented individuals have had a majority of all the important positions throughout U.S. history. This includes the members of the cabinet, their assistants and department heads, and heads of most regulatory agencies. They quite naturally, with no conspiracy, tend to consult big businessmen and groups as experts (such as the Committee for Economic Development or the Council on Foreign Relations). Wealthy families have also contributed a majority of federal judges, top military men, and top leaders of intelligence agencies. Finally, it should be noted that there is much crossing over at the top: Ex-generals often become corporate executives, and corporate executives often get to be cabinet members.

Of course no serious radical would state the thesis of big-business control of government quite as strongly as President Wilson did in his anger at the moment he wrote. There are many qualifications. For example, although there are many men of means in Congress, the influence of wealth is much, much less than in the cabinet and other executive offices. Similarly, in state and local governments the influence of the wealthy is very strong, but certainly they do not have exclusive control. Moreover, even among the members of the capitalist class in high positions there are many differences of opinion, mistakes in perceiving their own interests, and conflicts of interest between different business groups. Thus the rule of the capitalist class is by no means monolithic; it rules through the forms of shifting coalitions and liberal or conservative styles, as reflected in the Democratic and Republican parties. Finally, the working class (including farmers, industrial workers, intellectual and professional workers, the poor and unemployed, and workers from minority groups) can sometimes organize sufficiently to overcome the power of money by pure weight of numbers and exert pressure, elect representatives, and sometimes even prevail on particular issues.

EFFECTS OF GOVERNMENT
ON ECONOMIC INEQUALITY

Although everyone knows that there is extreme inequality in the United States, liberals argue that the inequality is much reduced by higher tax rates on the rich, welfare payments to the poor worker, subsidies to the poor farmer, public education for the poor, and antitrust laws, which decrease the concentration of income and power. Thus Paul Samuelson asserts that the U.S. government has reduced income inequality, though he admits that it has not been much of a change: "The welfare state, through redistributive taxation and through educational opportunity . . . has moved the system a bit toward greater quality."[16] Radicals object to this conclusion on several grounds.

First, radicals present the facts on the history of income distribution, which were given in Table 16.2. These facts show that (1) there was very, very little overall change in income distribution between 1910 and 1970; (2) the share of the poorest 20 percent of the population has actually declined; (3) the share of the richest 20 percent has fluctuated, going down very, very slightly by 1970. Therefore, in spite of many promises by liberal U.S. government administrations, there has been no reduction of inequality since 1910.

Second, the main function of the system is the preservation of "law and order," which means that police and armies and courts and prisons all protect the private ownership of vast fortunes for the rich. Government thus preserves capitalist control of land and factories. With the help of government in breaking strikes, the rich can continue to pay low enough wages to farm and industrial workers to continue to make the high profits by which they grow richer.

Third, radicals have shown that the administration of every program from taxation to welfare has been such that the rich have benefited more and the poor less than the law would seem to indicate at first glance. We look in detail at each program in the following sections.

Taxation

It is certainly true that income tax rates rise as income rises, so that in theory individuals in the higher income brackets not only must pay more taxes but also must pay a higher percentage of their income in taxes. Indeed the theoretical tax rate today seems to take most of an individual's income, once that income exceeds $1 million.

In practice rich taxpayers find many loopholes that allow them to pay much lower tax rates. Thus in 1957, the highest tax rate had risen to an apparently confiscatory 91 percent, yet that category of taxpayers paid only 52 percent to the government.[17] In 1969, the tax rate paid by all taxpayers with incomes reported over $1 million was only 34 percent, and since they don't have to report all of it the rate was actually only 20 percent.[18]

One kind of loophole for the rich is *capital gains*. This is the income derived from sale of a piece of property (including corporate stock) at a higher price than that at which it was bought. The increase in value of the property (held more than six months), or

---

[16]Paul Samuelson, *Economics*, 9th ed. (New York: McGraw-Hill, 1973), p. 804.

[17]For this and much of the following information, see Gabriel Kolko, *Wealth and Power in America* (New York: Praeger, 1962), chap. 2.

[18]John Gurley, "Federal Tax Policy," *National Tax Journal*, September 1967.

capital gain, is taxed at only one-half the rate for ordinary income. In 1957, 20 percent of incomes above $100,000 a year was in the form of capital gains. But it should be noted that this loophole does not save money for the poor. For taxpayers in the $3,500–$4,000 income bracket, capital gains accounted for only 0.3 percent of income.

Another large loophole is tax-free bonds. The interest on federal bonds cannot be taxed by states, and the interest on municipal bonds cannot be taxed by states or by the federal government. Of course to make a significant amount of money from bonds a very large investment is necessary, and bonds are typically sold in large lots that only the rich can afford. Other loopholes include homeowners' preferences, dividend exclusion, depreciation allowances, and depletion allowances (especially gas and oil).

As a result of these loopholes, some startling statistics have appeared. In 1965, a certain taxpayer had an income of $20 million but paid no taxes. In 1959 (the last year for which full data are available), some 21,317 people earning more than $20,000 paid no federal taxes—and that included 56 people with incomes over $1 million in that single year. *It has been estimated that the total loss of government revenue from all loopholes in the income-tax laws is about $77 billion a year.*[19]

Whereas the rich, with their income from property, can find many tax loopholes, there are none for the average worker with wage income. Consequently, there is in fact only the slightest redistribution of income as a result of the federal income tax. The data for 1962 indicate that the richest fifth (or top 20 percent) of the population had 45.5 percent of all income before taxes. After taxes, their percentage of national income had decreased by only 1.8 percent. The poorest 20 percent had increased their share by only 0.3 percent; the second fifth, by only 0.6 percent; and the third fifth, by only 0.5 percent. Thus *after* taxes the richest 20 percent still had far more income than the poorest 60 percent.

Even more important is the fact that the federal income tax amounts to only 40 percent of all taxes and is the only one that is progressive to even a slight extent (*progressive* means that the tax falls more heavily on the upper-income groups). The other 60 percent of taxes are mainly "regressive," according to most observers, in that they fall more heavily on the lower income groups. "We might tentatively conclude that taxes other than individual income taxes do not reduce, and probably increase, income inequality."[20]

[19]J. Lechman and B. Okner, "Individual Income Tax Erosion by Income Classes," in U.S. Congress, Joint Economic Committee, *Economics of Federal Subsidy Programs*, pt. I (Washington, D.C.: GPO, 1972), pp. 13–40.
[20]F. Ackerman et al., "Income Distribution in the United States," *Review of Radical Political Economy*, Summer 1971, p. 24.

What are these other taxes? Corporate income taxes account for a little less than 30 percent. But corporations do not really pay these taxes out of their profits. On the contrary, corporations consider them a necessary cost and pass most of them on to the consumer in the form of higher prices. There is a great deal of controversy over exactly how much of the corporate income tax is passed on to consumers. But it is striking that big changes in the tax rate do not seem to affect profit rates after taxes very much, if at all.

A little more than 30 percent of all taxes are state and local, such as the sales tax and the property tax. In terms of percentages these fall much more heavily on lower- and middle-income groups than on the rich. For example, a tax on gasoline or telephone service is spread quite equally among the population; therefore these taxes take a much higher percentage of a poor person's income. In 1958 people in the lowest income class ($9–2,000) paid 11.3 percent of their income in state and local taxes. But each higher income group paid a smaller and smaller percentage: 9.4 percent ($2,000–4,000 group), 8.5 percent ($4,000–6,000 group), 7.7 percent ($6,000–8,000 group), 7.2 percent ($8,000–10,000 group), 6.5 percent ($10,000–15,000 group), and 5.9 percent (over $15,000 group).[21] Thus the higher the income group, the lower its state and local tax rates.

It is also thought that wealth is redistributed by inheritance taxes. But inheritance tax rates are not very high, and federal and state laws are notorious for their immense loopholes. Thus large gifts can be given during the individual's lifetime, of which a considerable amount is free of any tax and the rest is taxed at a very low rate. Moreover, inheritances can be put into trusts so that one's descendants get the income immediately but direct control of the principal amount only after a fixed time. It is estimated that trusts can save up to 70 percent of inheritance taxes.

Finally, significant taxes are paid in the form of compulsory contributions by workers to social security. These taxes are highly regressive. In conclusion, the whole tax system redistributes very little, if any, income from rich to poor. It certainly does virtually nothing to mitigate poverty or reduce inequality.

Welfare

Liberals assert that absolute poverty is the only income problem left, ignoring the fact that extreme inequality of income creates a relative, or social, poverty as well. They argue that because a growing number of people are getting larger welfare payments, the poverty problem will be solved. But poverty is not defined simply as an absolute income level of less than $3000; it is *relative* to the society in which a person lives. The people in India live on a median income of

[21]All data from Kolko, loc. cit.

$100. There, a person earning $3000 per year might be considered wealthy. But there can be no doubt that an American family living on that income could afford neither the cultural nor the physical necessities of life. So even if one earns $3000, in a society as affluent as the United States he still lives in relative poverty. Therefore "brutalizing and degrading poverty will exist as long as extreme income inequality exists."[22]

Because taxation does not redistribute income, the question is whether welfare programs have a significant effect in that direction. In the first place, expenditures for welfare have been fairly small. In 1968 welfare spending under all federal, state, and local programs was only $26.9 billion. This included public aid, unemployment payments, workmen's compensation, health and medical programs, public housing, and educational aid to low-income students. These payments do help the poor somewhat, but the effect is small; it has virtually no effect in altering the relative positions of the poorest or the richest segments of society.

This $26.9 billion was only 3.82 percent of all personal income in 1968. Therefore, although it could make a few people better off, it could not change things very much.

What has been the historical trend of welfare payments? In 1938, welfare payments were 6.7 percent of personal income; in 1950, welfare was down to 3.86 percent; in 1960, it was down a little more, to 3.31 percent. Thus the 3.82 percent level in 1968 was back to the 1950 level and still just about half the 1938 level. Not only is welfare a small percentage of personal income but it also has actually decreased as a percentage in 30 years of much-touted new programs. Furthermore, there are qualifications. Some of that 3.82 percent does not go to the poorest groups. Welfare money spent on school lunches or university scholarships benefits middle-class children as well.

Moreover, the poor help pay for welfare, so the net amount received is even less. It is estimated that in 1968 the poorest 40 percent of the population (those with incomes below $7500) paid in taxes about $6 billion of the money budgeted for welfare. This estimate assumes that taxes fell equally on the entire population and were not regressive, as the total tax burden may well be. Thus net welfare to the poor (assuming that all the welfare payments went to the poorest 40 percent) was not $26.9 billion but $26.9 minus $6 billion, or $20.9 billion. The percentage of income paid in net welfare is even smaller than it looks at first. It is no wonder, then, that our tax and welfare systems have not resulted in any significant redistribution of income.

[22]Richard Edwards, "Who Fares Well in the Welfare State," in R. Edwards, M. Reich, and T. Weisskopf, eds. *The Capitalist System* (Englewood Cliffs, N.J.: Prentice-Hall, 1972), p. 244.

Interestingly, this pattern of small effects and no significant reduction in income inequality over many decades also holds true for the capitalist countries of western Europe. Even in Denmark and Sweden, where taxation and welfare programs are supposed to be very, very progressive, recent studies have shown little change in income distribution (after taxes and welfare) for several decades. A UN report reveals that for all western Europe "the general pattern of income distribution, by size of income, for the great majority of households, is only slightly affected by government action."[23]

The problem is that the social and economic conditions of a private enterprise economy lead to a psychology in which one works only if one has to work. Thus only by offering extremely unequal incomes for differing amounts of work done can work incentives be maintained under this system. It would take very different institutions with very different education and propaganda to change this psychology. Thus U.S. welfare programs are very carefully designed to go to those who do not work: children, the old, the blind. No welfare income goes to those who work hard but are paid low wages (who constitute about half of the poverty group) because that might lower their "incentive." A few programs give the low-paid worker minimum health and education so that he or she is able to work but very carefully do not provide any food, clothing, or shelter. This philosophy of welfare leads to extreme degradation of welfare recipients. In order to galvanize the working poor to ever greater effort, welfare recipients are kept in such a pitiful, dehumanized condition that anyone would rather work, even at the most disagreeable jobs and at the lowest pay.

The dole a welfare recipient receives is grossly insufficient for even the barest subsistence livelihood. Moreover, in return for this paltry sum the individual loses many basic civil rights supposedly guaranteed to everyone. The single woman supporting a family on welfare, for example, must permit welfare workers to search her house and subject her to a demeaning interrogation to ascertain if her personal sexual conduct is proper and fitting. This is only one of many ways welfare recipients are degraded and dehumanized. It is quite absurd to argue that programs like these will ever eliminate poverty.

Farm Subsidies

The rural poor have suffered the most pathetic poverty. For most of the twentieth century the incomes of small-farm owners and farm workers have lagged far behind other U.S. incomes. For that reason,

[23]U.N. Economic Commission of Europe, *Incomes in Postwar Europe: A Study of Policies, Growth, and Distribution* (Geneva: United Nations, 1957), pp. 1–15.

liberals have persuaded Congress to pass various bills aiding farmers with subsidies. What has been the practical effect of these subsidies?

First, the high economic concentration among the business firms engaged in farming should be noted. At present the richest 10 percent of all farms produce over 50 percent of total agricultural output. The poorest 50 percent of all farms produce only 5 percent of farm output. Concentration in agriculture has greatly increased in the period since subsidies were initiated.

Second, the farm support programs benefit mainly the richest farmers and give very little support to the poorest farmers. In 1963–1965, the poorest 20 percent of all farms received only 1 percent of the farm subsidies given in sugar cane, rice, and feed grains, 2 percent of those in cotton, 3 percent of those in wheat, 4 percent of those in peanuts and tobacco, and 5 percent of those in sugar beets. At the same time, the richest 20 percent of all farms (with the highest incomes before subsidies) received 83 percent of the farm subsidies given in sugar cane, 69 percent of those in cotton, 65 percent of those in rice, 62 percent of those in wheat, 56 percent of those in feed grains, 57 percent of those in peanuts, 53 percent of those in tobacco, and 51 percent of those in sugar beets.[24]

Third, it appears in fact that the net result of the farm program is to increase the percentage of total farm income going to the richest farmers and to decrease that going to the poorest farmers. Roughly, this can be seen from the fact that in 1963 the poorest 20 percent of all farmers and farm managers received 3.2 percent of farm income, whereas the richest 20 percent received 50.5 percent of farm income. Yet the data cited on subsidies showed that many of the farm programs gave less than 3.2 percent of the benefits to the poorest farmers and more than 50.5 percent to the richest farmers. Thus not only do most of the benefits go to the richest farmers but their share of the subsidies is *higher* than their share of the presubsidy income, so the disproportionate subsidies make farm income more extremely unequal than it would be without them. Clearly income inequality in farming is actually increased by the farm programs. In other words, it appears to be a regressive program, although we cannot say just how regressive: "the net effect of these programs may be less regressive than the data suggest—or possibly more regressive—but the pattern is clear."[25]

The discussion up to this point shows the effects of the farm programs on farmers who own their own farms. There is a fourth factor: what are the effects on farm workers, who own nothing but

---

[24]All data from James Bonnen, "The Effect of Taxes and Government Spending on Inequality," in *The Capitalist System*, pp. 235–243.
[25]Ibid., p. 242.

their power to labor? The answer is very simple. The main farm programs provide farm owners—mainly on the largest, richest farms —price supports to maintain prices at a certain level above costs, and payments to keep some land out of production in order to reduce the supply of farm goods. No money from these programs goes to farm workers. In fact the programs may hurt farm workers to the extent that the programs pay to keep land out of production, thereby increasing unemployment. "The State pays the *owners* of farm property not to produce, but pays virtually nothing to *farm workers* who become unemployed as a result of this dole to property owners."[26]

Finally, the net result of this program—to help farm workers not at all, to help poor farmers slightly, and to help rich farmers very much—is not at all surprising. Indeed it represents the continuation of a consistent pattern in U.S. history. Large corporations have always been the ones helped by government subsidies. In the nineteenth century, for example, three-fourths of all railroad construction was paid for by the government, and huge amounts of land were given to the railroads. Merchant shipping today gets large subsidies. Largest of all is the amount the government gives business for "research and development" ($17 billion in 1969 alone) both directly and indirectly through academic institutions.

Education and Inequality

Government-subsidized education is often thought to decrease the inequality of incomes. "The government gives free education to all," goes the argument, "so anyone can improve his station in life by going to school for a longer period."

Clearly there is a significant positive correlation between amount of education and level of income. Thus in 1968 those with only eight years of schooling had a median income of only $6,600.[27] The median income for high school graduates was $8,300, and that for college graduates was $11,800. In part, more schooling is the *cause* of better jobs and better pay for the individual. In part, however, better schooling is the *effect* of having a high income (and to some extent individuals from high-income families may get high-income jobs merely because their fathers own the businesses in which they work).

It is a fact that individuals from high-income families are able to get more schooling in the United States than individuals from low-income families. This may be seen in the following data from a sur-

---

[26]Howard Wachtel, "Looking at Poverty from a Radical Perspective," *Review of Radical Political Economics*, Summer 1971, p. 12.

[27]All data in this paragraph are from Ackerman et al., "Income Distribution in the United States," op. cit.

vey that classified students graduating from high school in 1966 according to their family's income in 1965.[28] Of those in the under-$3,000 income group, only 20 percent started college by February 1967. Other figures for the same period are 32 percent in the $3,000–4,000 group, 37 percent in the $4,000–6,000 group, 41 percent in the $6,000–7,000 group, 51 percent in the $7,000–10,000 group, and 61 percent in the $10,000–15,000 group. Fully 87 percent of those with family incomes over $15,000 started college. Thus the higher one's family's income, the greater one's chance of going to college.

Children of richer parents get more schooling mainly because they can afford to keep their children in school longer than poor parents can. They can pay high tuitions in private schools that admit students even with low grade averages. Even in the public universities, where the tuition may be much lower or nonexistent, there are still living expenses. Many students must drop out of college or not enroll simply because they have no money on which to live while in school.

Furthermore, children of richer families have a better chance to do well in school and learn more. Opportunities and encouragement provided in the home and community are much more likely to produce highly motivated children who know how to study. Cultural background is very important in performance on IQ tests and college entrance record examinations. These examinations, which purport to test general ability, in reality are designed to conform to middle-class, white, urban experience. A student from a poor or black or rural background will lack the necessary cultural references to understand the questions or have any intuition of the answers. This has been proved over and over again, but the tests are still used. They determine which "track" (discussed below) an elementary student is put into, and they determine who enters college. Thus it is no surprise that only 7 percent of all college students come from the poorest 25 percent of all families.

Another condition that hurts students from poor families and helps those from richer families is the fact that schools in different areas get very different amounts of money. Central-city slum schools often receive less money per student and almost always attract less competent teachers. Suburban township schools are apt to receive more money per student and attract better teachers.

Students in elementary and high schools are put into different *tracks*.[29] One track is vocational training, which prepares the poor for manual labor. Another track, college preparation, equips students

[28]Ibid.
[29]The best description of "tracking" is in Florence Howe and Paul Lautner, "How the School System Is Rigged," in *The Capitalist System*, pp. 229–235.

from upper-middle-class and richer families for college, in order to get high-income jobs (so that their children can go to college, and so forth). In elementary schools it is often called *ability grouping* of the bright and the stupid. But the degree of ability is determined by IQ tests that do not assess innate intelligence but, as noted previously, discriminate on the basis of class background.

The tracking system exists both within and between high schools. Within some high schools, counselors push the poor and the minority groups into vocational training and the rich into college preparation. Within others, such pushing is hardly necessary because of the vast differences among schools. Schools in the black slums provide only basic, or vocational, training. Schools in the richest areas give only college preparation. These different tracks are enforced both formally by the tests given and informally by counselors and teachers. One investigation in New York showed that middle-class white children were usually offered voluntary classes in how to pass college examinations, but that in Harlem even seeing the old tests was "against the rules."[30]

We may conclude with certainty that our educational system does not reduce inequality from generation to generation. On the contrary, the richer students have more opportunities to get a good elementary and high-school education, to get into college, to remain in college, and therefore to get a high-income job after college—and then to send their children to college. Thus the educational system seems to transmit inequality from one generation to the next.

Government and Business

In the United States the Industrial Revolution commenced after the Civil War. In more than a century of American industrial capitalism, the relationship between government and big business is seen by some observers as having been desultory and often contradictory. This is because many government programs and legislative acts were designed to promote big business, whereas some laws, particularly antitrust legislation, were ostensibly designed to curb the size and power of big business.

Thurman Arnold, former "trust-busting" head of the federal government's antitrust division, believes that these contradictory policies and laws have stemmed from "a continuous conflict between opposing ideals in American economic thinking."[31] The power of "economic thinking," taken alone, explains very little, however. A more

---

[30]Ibid., p. 234.

[31]Thurman Arnold, "Economic Reform and the Sherman Anti-trust Act," in J. A. Garraty, ed., *Historical Viewpoints: Volume Two, Since 1865* (New York: Harper & Row, 1969), p. 151.

realistic explanation of these seeming contradictions would be based on the two broadest objectives of government in its dealings with big business.

First, the government has been committed to the maintenance of the capitalist system and the promotion of the interests of big business. This commitment has generally dominated the relationship between government and business. The interests of various capitalists and business firms, however, are not always mutually compatible. Many conflicts are so intense that, if left unresolved, they could eventually threaten the very existence of the capitalist system. Government's second objective, therefore, is to act as the arbiter in these rivalries and to resolve the difficulties before they become so extremely serious.

The antitrust laws have given the federal government a measure of power to enforce its function as arbiter. Interpreted in this way, the government's policy toward business has not been contradictory. Nor has this policy been designed, as many liberals believe, to curb the immense power of giant corporations. Rather, it has always attempted to promote the general interests of all capitalists and all businesses. Sometimes the individual interests of capitalists have coincided, as, for example, in the late-nineteenth-century attempt to crush labor unions. But in instances of industrial or commercial rivalry between two giant corporate empires, the interests have been in conflict. In such cases the general interests of all capitalists would depend on at least partial restriction of one or both of the rivals.

American industrialization was aided significantly by the intimate association of government and business. Big business was supported by protective tariffs, which began with the Morrill Tariff of 1861 and were expanded significantly in 1890, 1894, and 1897. Thus large corporations were protected from foreign competition and could use fully their domestic monopoly powers to charge high prices.

The due process clause of the Fourteenth Amendment had been intended to give equal rights to blacks. In the late nineteenth century, however, it was not used to help blacks at all. Rather, it was interpreted to prohibit state regulation of corporations (who were considered legal "persons"). The courts denied state governments the right to interfere in any way with even the most abusive, malicious, and socially deleterious corporate behavior.

The railroad magnates were among the most important entrepreneurs in the American Industrial Revolution. Through bribery, chicanery, and fraud, they amassed great personal fortunes. Building railroads was never more than the vehicle from which they launched their financial schemes. The federal government responded by generously giving federal lands to the railroads. Between 1850 and 1871, the railroads were handed 130 million acres of land, an area as large as all the New England states plus Pennsylvania and New York. During the same period, state governments gave the railroads another 49 million acres. All this, and yet some economic historians still refer to the second half of the nineteenth century as an age in which government stayed out of business affairs!

Toward the end of the nineteenth century, the relationship between the federal government and big business became a symbiosis in which the government governed in ways big business wanted it to govern and big business furnished the money, organization, and power structure through which politicians could come to power in the federal government. When progressive elements of the Democratic party saw that Democratic President Cleveland's relationship with big business was hardly distinguishable from the Republican–big-business relationship, they captured control of the party and nominated William Jennings Bryan, a champion of the workers and farmers. William McKinley, the big-business Republican candidate, raised campaign funds estimated to total as much as $15 million, 50 times more than Bryan's $300,000. From that time on, the Democratic party has been more careful about picking a candidate of whom at least a large segment of big business approves.

Regulatory Agencies

Since the late nineteenth century the U.S. government has established many regulatory agencies, such as the Interstate Commerce Commission, supposedly designed to protect consumer and environmental interests. Thus telephone and electric companies are given monopolies, but public agencies are placed above them to regulate their profits. These commissions are commonly thought to be the watchdogs of the public interests, but they often turn out to be merely a legal way to give monopoly powers to an oligopoly. The commissions are generally dominated by those they are supposed to regulate, and neglect the public interest. For example, when the public does not give them careful attention, the public utilities commissions normally grant most price increases desired by the regulated companies. Similarly, when California passed a new law by voters' initiative (against strong pressure from the construction industry) to regulate building on the California shoreline in the interest of environmental protection, Governor Reagan appointed to the agencies responsible for enforcement mostly representatives *opposed* to the protection of the shoreline.

While public agencies have always been dominated by business interests, some of the most obvious cases have occurred during the Nixon administration. The Federal Power Commission is an important agency supposed to protect consumer and environmental interests concerning gas and electricity. All five of the members appointed by Nixon were either businessmen in the gas or electric businesses or lawyers for these firms. As is usual, the Senate went along with the appointments in the first four cases. In the fifth case, however, Robert Morris was rejected when, on June 13, 1973, the Senate finally asserted its power to turn down such openly biased appointments—mostly because the Watergate scandal had weakened the usual coercive influence of the President over Congress. Senator Magnuson said that in the case of Morris the Senate was "again asked to accept . . . one more nominee whose professional career has been dedicated to the furtherance of the private interests of that industry." He pointed out that Morris had represented Standard Oil of California for 15 years. In fact, from 1964 to 1971 he had spent most of his time lobbying for Standard Oil against public interests on natural gas matters before the Federal Power Commission!

Antitrust Laws

There have been four major laws designed ostensibly to decrease the monopoly power of big business. The first was the Sherman Antitrust Act of 1890, which forbade any contract, combination, or conspiracy to restrain trade.[32] In fact, it forbade any agreement not to compete, regardless of how the agreement was achieved. It also forbade monopolies or attempts to monopolize.

The Clayton Act of 1914 forbade corporations to engage in price discrimination—that is, to force some customers to pay more than others. It also prohibited *interlocking directorates* where this would lead to a substantial reduction of competition.

The Federal Trade Commission Act of 1914 outlawed *unfair* methods of competition and established the FTC to investigate the methods of competition used by business firms. Finally, The Celler-Kefauver Act of 1950 forbade the purchase of either the stock of a competing corporation (which had already been illegal) or the assets of competing corporations (hitherto a big loophole in the laws).

The most interesting feature of the antitrust laws is that they were designed to limit the concentration of economic power among corporations. Yet as one observer has written, "the fact that after the passage of the Sherman Act the country witnessed a spectacular merger movement, another wave after the passage of the Clayton Act (1914), and again after the Celler-Kefauver Act, indicates that the laws have been ineffective in 'limiting the concentration of control.' "[33]

[32]For a more detailed historical account of the Sherman Act and its early enforcement, see Chapter 8.

[33]Douglas F. Dowd, *Modern Economic Problems in Historical Perspective* (Boston: Raytheon/Heath 1965), p. 49.

For the first two decades after the passage of the Sherman Act, the antitrust laws were used almost exclusively to break the power of labor unions to strike against employers. Although there have been periodic convictions of business firms throughout the twentieth century, most observers agree that virtually all the important oligopolistic corporations are constantly violating most of the antitrust law sanctions. There is almost no price competition among the giants. There are many, many instances of interlocking directorates, and almost no one doubts the pervasive existence of illegal collusion among giant corporations.

Why, then, are a few corporations occasionally singled out for conviction for violations of which virtually all corporations are guilty? We believe that in these cases the government uses the antitrust laws to act as arbiter in the irreconcilable conflicts between various corporations. Antitrust convictions are generally mildly punitive government actions, taken when the government decides which group of corporations should be supported in a particular conflict of interest. This was most apparent recently when the U.S. government acted against certain conglomerate mergers in which "young newcomers" tried to take over old, established corporations.

The government does not really attempt to eliminate the pervasive illegal policies of corporations. Throughout American history the government has done everything it could to create and promote the interests of monopolistic businesses. For the good of all, a few must occasionally be slapped on the wrists. Antitrust laws make this possible. They therefore operate to blunt some of the traditional antimonopoly sentiment and to resolve some conflicts between different corporate interests.

Government Purchasing Policy

Federal, state, and local governments buy one-quarter to one-third of our national product. Profit rates of corporations selling to government are much higher than the average profit rate. The largest single government purchase is of military supplies, where the most spectacular profits are made. Through this mechanism, government purchasing policies tend to shift income to the corporations and to their rich stockholders. All government spending will be analyzed in detail in Chapter 29.

SUMMARY

The economic power of a comparatively few corporations and individuals, examined in previous chapters, was shown here to result in a disproportionate degree of political power for this group. This is not an accident but a perfectly natural result of their control over the press, television and radio, advertising, financing for political campaigns and for lobbying, foundations, and many other avenues of control open to those with wealth.

Because of this natural influence (not a conspiracy), government policies do not decrease inequality in the American economy. In fact, after considering only the policies that are supposed to reduce inequality (such as taxation, farm subsidies, and education), we can conclude that many of them actually increase the degree of inequality. If we had considered all government policies, the net effect would undoubtedly have been to substantially increase inequality. Given the present sources of political power, it appears very doubtful whether the government will ever take actions that would substantially reduce poverty and inequality.

economics of discrimination: eternal fact of capitalism?

Most elementary economics books ignore racial and sexual discrimination as social phenomena outside of economics. These phenomena, however, have political-economic roots and, in turn, affect the economy in important ways.

TYPES OF DISCRIMINATION

In the United States racism involves prejudice and discrimination against many minorities. The most common form is use of an ideology claiming that another race is inferior in order to justify profit-making activity and discrimination against them. For example, the white colonists in America declared that the Indians were inferior and then stole their land and almost eliminated them.

Ironically, each succeeding wave of white settlers was met by a form of discrimination called *nationalist* prejudice, which was directed at them by those who were already here. Thus all Eastern Europeans were held to be backward in culture; Italians were all lazy; Irish were all loud and uncouth. Against Chinese and Japanese immigrants there was a combination of nationalist and racist prejudice. During World War II all Americans of Japanese ancestry on the West Coast were confined to concentration camps. (German Americans never were.) Finally, nationalist and racist prejudice also combines to support discrimination against Americans of Mexican and Puerto Rican origin. (Both were incorporated into the United

States through imperialist expansion, one group in the war against Mexico and the other in the war against Spain.)

Religious bigotry is another form of discrimination closely related to national chauvinism and racial prejudice; indeed, all are similar both in cause and in effect. In Europe, Protestants and Catholics killed each other for centuries; and in America, the Catholic minority is still subjected to a certain amount of prejudice and discrimination. Much worse, of course, was the many-centuries-long oppression of the Jews, forcibly converted, limited to certain occupations, often taxed to bankruptcy, and periodically massacred. Yet in the late nineteenth and early twentieth centuries, it appeared that anti-Jewish sentiment was dying away; and it has never been as severe in America as in some other countries, although it certainly exists. But just as the Jews began to feel secure, Hitler's fascism unleashed the worst racist atrocity in the history of the world. More than 6 million Jewish men, women, and children were tortured, gassed, and burned to death.

Another racist atrocity was the enslavement of black Africans throughout three centuries and their shipment under horrifying, inhuman conditions to various places of prison and work, especially the American South. This enslavement was not done in the name of Aryan domination, as was Hitler's killing of the Jews and other "inferior" peoples, but in the gentle name of Christianity, it being the white man's burden to bring civilization and the true faith to the black man. One result of this enslavement is that blacks today constitute the largest single minority in the United States, and one of the most oppressed.

When blacks were slaves doing simple agricultural work in the South, racism played its usual function of explaining that blacks were inferior to whites, that slavery was their natural condition, that such simple labor was all they could do, and that they were very happy in this condition. Now that blacks are a large part or a majority in many American cities and do all the complex tasks required to run American industry and urban life, the prejudices have changed somewhat, but the discrimination is as fierce as ever.

Last but not least, there is sexist discrimination against women in America. It will be shown that both the attitudes and the actual discrimination against the female 51 percent of Americans is very similar in nature to the discrimination against racial, national, and religious minorities.

THE IDEOLOGY OF RACISM

The main point of racism is that minority groups are held to be biologically inferior. Racism is called an "ideology" because it is a systematic set of beliefs claiming the superiority of one group to others; it is a "prejudice" in that no amount of evidence can shake these beliefs—and even inconsistent beliefs do not bother the true believers.

Adolf Hitler and his Fascists carried racism to its ultimate in the 1930s, when he proclaimed that white, male, non-Jewish Germans (called "Aryans") were a master race, superior to all other groups. He created a stereotype, or ideal picture, of all Aryans as big, strong, blond, and superintelligent—even though Hitler himself was none of these. His stereotype of the Jew was small, dark, greedy, and cowardly. His stereotype of all other peoples was likewise physically weak and mentally inferior. His stereotype of women had them all stupid and good for nothing but sex and childbearing; Aryan women were also dumb sex-objects, but were beautiful as well. Such stereotypes were not mere harmless nonsense; on this basis Hitler killed millions of Jews and Russians, enslaved hundreds of millions of people, and particularly enslaved all women.

Similarly, slave owners in the U.S. South before the Civil War claimed that all blacks were biologically inferior. The stereotyped black was stupid and lazy, shuffled his feet when he walked, but liked to sing and dance (to celebrate his happy life as a slave). The stereotype also said that blacks were oversexed. This stereotype has long provided an excuse for white men to rape black women, while lynching black men for imaginary rapes of white women. Wear de whaat wimmen

There are still racists who claim that all blacks are mentally inferior. For example, Dr. William Shockley, a white male chemist, claimed in 1973 that in data "from Negro populations with average IQ's of 80 in Georgia and 90 in California that each 1 percent of Caucasian ancestry raises average IQ by one point for these low IQ populations."[1] So the blood of the "master race" raises intelligence! Yet over and over again anthropologists and psychologists have demonstrated that so-called IQ scores are related to socioeconomic status and cultural background (because of the way the tests are designed), but are *not* related to race, religion national origin, or sex.

Such unscientific stereotypes are common in everyday thinking and strongly affect and harm blacks in occupational and professional roles. The following incident illustrates the awful power of prejudiced stereotypes:

> A young Negro lawyer recently recalled his first case, in which he was called upon to defend a burglar. The thief, white, appeared before the judge dressed as he had been when apprehended by the police, in dirty work clothes, his hair mussed,

[1] United Press story in *Press-Enterprise*, October 23, 1973, p. A-2.

an unshaven face. The lawyer . . . was neatly dressed in a business suit, was wellshaven, and was carrying a briefcase. The judge looked at both men and asked, unjokingly, "Which man is the lawyer?"[2]

Can you imagine how much attention the judge paid to the black lawyer's arguments?

RACIST DISCRIMINATION

The current data[3] show that in 1972 the median family income of white Americans was $11,550, while that of blacks was only $6,860, or 41 percent lower. A total of 24.5 million Americans were below the official poverty level (understated at $4,275 for an urban family of four); this represented a slight decline for white families from the previous year's figure—but the number of blacks living in poverty rose to an amazing 7.9 million! In other words, 9 percent of white families and 33 percent of black families were living in poverty. At the other extreme, 2.8 percent of white families but only 0.4 percent of black families had incomes over $25,000.

The same dreary picture exists for unemployment statistics. In 1972, when white unemployment was officially at the figure of 5 percent, black unemployment was exactly double that figure, or 10 percent. Similarly, among teenagers 16 and 17 years old, white male unemployment was a hefty 16 percent, but black male teenagers (16 and 17) were 35 percent unemployed! Among teenagers 18 and 19 years old, white male unemployment was 12 percent, whereas black male teenagers (18 and 19) suffered 26 percent unemployment. Black unemployment is approximately double that of whites in every category.

Discrimination shows up in every aspect of American life. Even the very conservative *Time* magazine concluded that "black Americans pay more than whites for comparable housing, and are four times more likely to live in substandard housing."[4] In fact, 25 percent of blacks reported leaky ceilings; 26 percent, overcrowding; 29 percent, rats; 32 percent, faulty plumbing; 38 percent, cockroaches.

Time's survey found that in 1969 there were only 9 black representatives and 1 black senator in the U.S. Congress. Of the nation's 24,000 architects, only 450 were black. Of the 6,338 American radio stations blacks owned 11. Of the 690 television channels, blacks

[2]Quoted in Cynthia Epstein, *Woman's Place* (Berkeley: University of California Press, 1971), p. 190 n.
[3]U.S. Department of Commerce, *Statistical Abstract of the United States, 1973*, and U.S. Department of Labor, *Manpower Report of the President, 1973*.
[4]*Time*, April 6, 1970, p. 53.

owned none. Of the 300,000 American lawyers, only 3,000 were black. Only 5 percent of all reporters and photographers were black. Thirty-eight percent of the Atlanta population was black but only 10 percent of the city's police force; and 63 percent of the Washington, D.C., population but only 21 percent of the police force was black. Of the 459 federal judges, only 22 were black. Of the 12,000 city and state judges, only 178 were black. Blacks are arrested three to four times more often than whites; and of those arrested, a larger portion are jailed, convicted, and given stiff sentences. As of April 1970 more than 50 percent of those condemned to death and awaiting execution were black.

Consider health next.[5] Blacks constitute almost half of all American drug addicts. The suicide rate of the black ghetto is about twice the white rate. In 1967, per 100,000 Americans, there were 15.3 cases of tuberculosis among whites and 65.1 cases among nonwhites. The death rate from tuberculosis was 2.8 per 100,000 whites and 8.4 per 1000,000 nonwhites. At birth, the maternal death rate per 100,000 for whites was 19.7 but 37.5 for nonwhites. The death rate for infants in the first 28 days was 15 for whites but 25 for nonwhites. The death rate for infants 1 to 11 months old was 4.7 for whites but 12.5 for nonwhites. Life expectancy for whites was 71.3 years; for nonwhites, 64.6 years.

In education,[6] 73 percent of whites complete eighth grade, but only 58 percent of blacks. And in mid-1970 three-fourths of the blacks in the South still attended elementary schools that were at least 95 percent black, whereas half of the blacks in the North attended elementary schools that were at least 95 percent black. High school is completed by 62 percent of whites but by only 40 percent of blacks. Only 6.4 percent of all college students are black, and half of these are in all-black colleges in the South. Blacks constitute only 1 percent of all doctoral candidates, 3 percent of all law students, 3 percent of all medical students, and less than 1 percent of the faculty at 80 public universities. Moreover, even if blacks surmount all the barriers and get an equal education, they still face job and salary discrimination. Thus whites graduating from eighth grade have higher incomes than blacks graduating from high school. And whites graduating from high school have higher incomes than blacks graduating from college.

Finally, recent trades show the situation worsening rather than improving in several aspects.[7] The differences between black and

[5]Data from U.S. Department of Health, Education and Welfare.

[6]U.S. Department of Labor, *Manpower Report of the President for 1972,* p. 194.

[7]See data and analysis in Louis Ferman, Joyce Kornbluh, and J. Miller, eds., *Negroes and Jobs* (Ann Arbor: University of Michigan Press, 1968).

white incomes and between black and white unemployment rates have been increasing in the past decade. Moreover, blacks constitute a growing percentage of workers in "declining job categories"— that is, unskilled jobs and industries with no employment growth. Blacks also constitute an increasing percentage (now over 25 percent) of all the long-term, or permanently, unemployed. Furthermore, "patterns of residential segregation between Negro and white . . . are more pronounced than they were a decade ago."[8]

It is not necessary to detail the comparative facts for other minorities in America because they are quite similar. The degree of oppression is particularly intense in relation to the second-largest minority group, Americans of Mexican and Puerto Rican descent. Actually, although there might be some controversy over recent trends, most writers on the subject, conservative or liberal as well as radical, seem largely to agree on the present extent of discrimination. The argument comes over the causes and the solutions.

WHAT CAUSES RACISM?

The most conservative view is now, as always, that there are inherited biological differences, making the blacks (and Mexicans, Indians, Jews, Catholics, ad infinitum) intellectually and physically inferior. The inferiority is the cause of lower income, less educational achievement, and so forth. Moreover, they are lazy and like to live in squalor. Because these arguments are not backed by any scientific evidence and because refutations do not lessen the prejudice one bit, we may leave this view without further comment. Races are, of course, defined by their superficial physical differences, but there are no important biological differences among the races of humankind, much less any inherited intellectual differences.

Most sociologists are liberal enough to admit that blacks are not inherently inferior. They still insist that the problem lies in the minds of blacks and whites. Many still assume that all whites have racist attitudes. Many more assume that all blacks have attitudes making it more difficult for them to get good jobs. Blacks are said to have "a set of beliefs that favor a social dependency role for the Negro rather than one of independence; . . . and low aspiration patterns that set limited achevement goals."[9] The traditional sociologists' solution would seem to be that we have to employ an unprejudiced psychoanalyst (from Mars?) to change the attitudes of all whites and blacks through therapy.

Radicals agree that it is a fact that most whites have racist preju-

[8]Ibid., p. 194.
[9]Ibid., p. 108.

dices and that it is a fact that some blacks still have attitudes of inferiority that impede their progress. It must be emphasized that the discrimination caused by white racism is a thousand times more of a barrier to blacks at present than any remaining black attitudes of inferiority.

But the most important question is, Why do these attitudes persist? Hundreds of comparative studies of other societies show that whites are not born with attitudes of racial superiority and blacks are not born with attitudes of racial inferiority. These attitudes are inculcated by society. They are given to children by the older generation in the family; by the educational system (e.g., in stereotypes in textbooks); by the media (e.g., in stereotypes on TV, in newspapers, books, and magazines); and by political leaders like George Wallace.

This leads to the next question: Why does the establishment permit and encourage racist stereotypes? (Of course, the degree of open stereotyping has been reduced in recent years, but only under the pressure of the civil rights movement.) It is the contention of radicals that racism plays an important function in supporting the status quo and that the capitalist establishment benefits from it directly and indirectly.

WHO BENEFITS FROM RACISM?

Conservative economists agree with the conservative sociologists that no one benefits from discrimination, that it is merely a matter of irrational and inexplicable tastes or preferences. Gary Becker, whose work is considered definitive by conservatives, says: "Discrimination and prejudice are not usually said to occur when someone prefers looking at a glamorous Hollywood actress rather than at some other woman; yet they are said to occur when he prefers living next to whites rather than next to Negroes. At best calling just one of these actions 'discrimination' requires making subtle and rather secondary distinctions."[10] Becker seems to think that discrimination against blacks is as trivial as preferring apples to oranges. (Notice that he also has a sexist prejudice in assuming that a "glamorous Hollywood actress" is attractive on an absolute basis, when this simply reflects a stereotyped standard.)

Radicals point out that Becker is wrong to consider discrimination trivial, "just" a preference. First, employers, union leaders, and military and government leaders are white males who have *power* to discriminate. Second, employers choose by a double standard—they *assume* that white males are good, qualified workers while

[10]Gary Becker, *The Economics of Discrimination* (Chicago: University of Chicago Press, 1957), p. 5.

blacks and women are not; and the burden of proof is on blacks and women to show themselves to be qualified. Even where there are laws against discrimination, control of the power structure means (1) the laws are not enforced, (2) prejudiced propaganda is channeled through the media, church, and schools, and (3) blacks continue to receive inferior training.

Conservatives emphasize that discrimination by business is irrational because (so they claim) businessmen lose profits as a result.[11] They argue that if there is discrimination in other areas of the economy, then each capitalist is presented with a supply of qualified blacks willing to work for wages below the going wages. Since the capitalist can purchase these workers at lower wages, he could make more profit by doing so. Therefore, capitalists who are willing to hire blacks (below the going wage) will make more profits, while those who refuse to hire blacks at any wage will lose profits.

The conservative economists conclude that the capitalists who discriminate do so for irrational reasons and lose money because of the discrimination. They further argue that under pure competition capitalists who discriminate will eventually be put out of business because of their higher costs per unit. Thus competition will tend to end discrimination and push black wages ever closer to white wage levels.

Most liberal economists seem to agree with most of these premises, which flow from good neoclassical economics. They argue, however, that the U.S. economy is characterized by a high degree of monopoly rather than pure competition. By the exercise of their monopoly power in the labor market and in the commodity market, they can hold down all wages and pass on to consumers some of the cost of discrimination. In other words, the liberals agree with the conservatives that racism is an inexplicable attitude, but they contend that it costs the capitalist only a little to indulge his strange preference. Therefore, they believe it might be a long time, if ever, before capitalism automatically ended discrimination, so the government should pass reform laws to end discrimination.

Radicals, on the other hand, do not believe that capitalists lose money from discrimination or that their attitudes are inexplicable. How could discrimination continue for such a long time if capitalists lose from it? Capitalists *gain* in many ways from racist discrimination and hence have an interest in continuing it. They gain because (1) racist prejudice divides workers, making unions weaker and resulting in lower wages for all workers; (2) the same division makes capitalist politicians safer from attacks by labor; (3) racist discrimina-

[11]See, e.g., Milton Friedman, *Capitalism and Freedom* (Chicago: University of Chicago Press, 1962), pp. 108–118.

tion makes it easy to keep blacks as an unemployed reservoir of cheap labor for boom times; (4) racism provides white politicians with a scapegoat for many social problems; and (5) racism helps inspire soldiers when they are supposed to kill Asians in Vietnam. As a result white capitalists as a whole benefit from racism, though white workers as a whole lose from racism.[12]

Radicals maintain that in the pre-Civil War South racism was a useful apologia for slavery. It meant that the slave owners would have no guilty consciences, the slaves might accept their lot more easily, and the Northerners would not interfere. Racism declared that slavery was divinely ordained by God as a benefit to the inferior black. Thus its first function was to justify economic exploitation.

This function of racism continues today, when apologists contend that black and Chicano workers are poorly paid only because they are inferior workers. More important, to the extent that white workers believe the racist ideology, unions are weakened by excluding black workers—or accepting them reluctantly and keeping them from equal power in unions. White and black workers have frequently broken each others' strikes in the past, though they are now learning to work together. In the areas of strongest racism and weakest unions, such as the South, black workers' wages are very low, but white workers' wages are almost as low. For this reason, one honest liberal economist has concluded: "Far from being indifferent to the existence of discriminatory attitudes on the part of workers, the capitalist gains from them and may find it profitable to invest in their creation."[13]

Another reason that racism is profitable to capitalists is the provision of a handy, but disposable, labor force. If an employer has 10 black and 10 white workers, and must fire half for a couple of months, which will he fire? If "he is rational and seeks to minimize his labor turnover costs, he will lay off his ten black workers on the assumption that they will be unlikely to get permanent or better jobs elsewhere because of the discriminatory practices of other employers."[14] Thus the capitalist can (and does) fire black workers in each recession and easily hire them back in times of expansion. He also gains by not paying the fringe benefits due workers who stay on the job for a longer time.

Radicals assert that blacks are exploited within the United States, both as an internal colony and as workers. Blacks today constitute

---

[12]This point is fully discussed and proven statistically in Michael Reich, "The Economics of Racism," in David M. Gordon, ed., *Problems in Political Economy* (Lexington, Mass.: Raytheon/Heath, 1971).

[13]Morris Silver, quoted in Ray Franklin and Solomon Resnick, *The Political Economy of Racism* (New York: Holt, Rinehart & Winston, 1973), p. 23.

[14]Franklin and Resnick, op. cit., p. 20.

about one-third of the entire industrial labor force and an even larger percentage of unskilled manual laborers. Racial discrimination keeps them "in their place" as a large pool of unskilled and often unemployed workers to be used to hold down wages in times of high demand for labor; racial prejudice justifies that place. Thus racism is in this respect only one more added apologia for considerable extra profits extracted at the expense of the lowest-paid part of the American working class.

Because that exploitation is at the heart of the system, legal reforms cannot give much help to most blacks. Radicals claim that

> the system has two poles: wealth, privilege, power at one; poverty, deprivation, powerlessness at the other. It has always been that way, but in earlier times whole groups could rise because expansion made room above, and there were others ready to take their place at the bottom. Today, Negroes are at the bottom, and there is neither room above nor anyone ready to take their place. Thus only individuals can move up, not the group as such: reforms help the few, not the many. For the many, nothing short of a complete change in the system—the abolition of both poles and the substitution of a society in which wealth and power are shared by all—can transform their condition.[15]

Radicals maintain the political function of racism is to find a scapegoat for all problems. For example, the white is told that the dirt and violence of the modern city is all due to the black. Similarly, Hitler told German workers that unemployment was all due to Jewish bankers, and the middle class was told that all the agitation was due to Jewish communists.

The second political function of racism, according to radicals, is to divide the oppressed so the elite can rule. For example, no one is more oppressed or poverty-stricken than the white southern sharecropper. But he has always fought against his natural allies, the blacks. Instead, the poor white has given political support to the wealthy white southerners who not only monopolize southern state and local politics but also wield disproportionate influence in Congress because they succeed to and hold key committee chairmanships and leadership positions by virtue of seniority. The same kind of divide-and-rule tactic is used in northern cities.

Radicals also claim that racism is a particularly handy tool of imperialism. England especially has long used the strategy of divide and rule: Hindu against Moslem, Jew against Arab, Protestant

---

[15]Paul Sweezy and Paul Baran, *Monopoly Capital* (New York: Monthly Review Press, 1966), p. 27.

against Catholic, Biafran against Nigerian, black against Hindu in Guyana. And America is quite willing to use the same tactic: Vietnamese against Cambodian, Thai against Laotian. Moreover, "inferiority" (inherited or acquired) is still being given as a reason for lack of development—where imperialism is the real reason. Finally, national chauvinism, or patriotism, always asserts that aggression comes from the other, evil people and that "our" pure motives should not be questioned.

SEXIST IDEOLOGY: STEREOTYPES OF WOMEN

Just as the ideology of racism relies on stereotypes of blacks, the ideology of sexism relies on stereotypes of women. One stereotype of women is that they are all sentimental and impulsive, emotional and foolish; not hard-headed, hard driving, and logical, as in the stereotype of a man. For example, former Vice President Agnew, that great defender of law and order, says: "Three things have been difficult to tame—the ocean, fools, and women. We may soon be able to tame the ocean; fools and women will take a little longer."[16]

Yet the opposite stereotype of women also exists. She is narrow in vision; interested in little, material things; grasping and evil. For example, the men who wrote the Bible claim: "And the Lord God said unto the woman, What is this that thou has done? And the woman said, The serpent beguiled me, and I did eat." On this basis medieval men stereotyped all woman as sly, sharp, aggressive witches.

Of course these two stereotypes are contradictory. How can all women be greedy, sharp, and aggressive and at the same time sentimental and foolish? Such inconsistencies never seem to bother prejudiced people. Neither are racists and sexists bothered by conflicting evidence; they always see things the way they wish to see them: "Thus, an anti-Semite watching a Jew may see devious or sneaky behavior. But in a Christian he would regard such behavior only as quiet, reserved, or perhaps even shy."[17] Since prejudice distorts "evidence," no amount of evidence can change it.

As an example of how prejudiced stereotyping is much too stubborn for evidence, imagine an employer interviewing a series of people for an executive job. Suppose he believes in the usual stereotype of women. Suppose the first woman is sophisticated and careful before speaking. He thinks: She is too passive and "feminine"

---

[16]Quoted in Kirsten Amundsen, *The Silenced Majority* (Englewood Cliffs, N.J.: Prentice-Hall, 1971), p. 114.

[17]Philip Goldberg, in Athena Theodore, ed., *The Professional Woman* (New York: Schenkman Publishers, 1971), p. 168.

for the job. Suppose the second woman objects to something he says. He thinks: she is an aggressive bitch. Suppose the third person is a man; he gets the job. In many real cases like this imaginary one, prejudiced stereotypes are not harmless; they lead directly to discrimination.

Above all, sexist stereotypes are intended to justify the domination of women by men. This is very apparent in a statement by Napoleon Bonaparte:

> Nature intended women to be our slaves . . . they are our property, we are not theirs. They belong to us, just as a tree that bears fruit belongs to a gardener. What a mad idea to demand equality for women! . . . Women are nothing but machines for producing children.[18]

SEXIST DISCRIMINATION

Sexism, or the theory of male supremacy, is an ideology that serves to justify discrimination against the majority of Americans. Although sexism is similar in the pattern of discrimination and in ideology to racism, it is more pervasive, more deeply ingrained, and harder to combat. Clearly the black woman is held to be doubly "inferior" and suffers the most discrimination.

The facts bear out these generalities. In 1970 only 5 percent of all four-person U.S. families headed by white males were below the official poverty line. Of families headed by white females, 37 percent were below the poverty line. And of families headed by black females, 62 percent were below the poverty line.[19]

The problem is no longer that women are not allowed to work outside the home. In 1970 women constituted 40 percent of the whole civilian labor force. In fact, more than half of all women age 20 to 64 were in the labor force.[20] It might be good if still more women worked, but that is not the main problem. The point is that over 90 percent of these women work not by desire but by economic necessity and they face discrimination on the job.

Thus in 1970 the average woman employed full-time earned only 58 percent of the average male's salary. This, in fact, was a decline from the 64 percent of ten years earlier. Specifically, the median salary of full-time workers was $7870 for white men, $5314 for black men, $4584 for white women, and only $3487 for black women. Furthermore, women who surmount the barriers to their

[18]Quoted in "Know Your Enemy," in Robin Morgan, ed., *Sisterhood Is Powerful* (New York: Vintage, 1970).
[19]U.S. Bureau of the Census, *Statistical Abstract of the United States.*
[20]U.S. Department of Labor, *Manpower Report of the President.*

getting an education discover that an equal education does not give them equal jobs or equal pay. Women with college degrees make just a little more than men with eighth-grade educations. Among women with 4 years of college, 17 percent take jobs as unskilled or semiskilled workers. Even among women with 5 years or more of college, 6 percent take unskilled or semiskilled jobs.

Moreover, women constituted only 9 percent of all the elite professionals: 7 percent of the doctors, 3 percent of the lawyers, and 1 percent of the engineers. Women account for only 5 percent of all individuals with incomes over $10,000, only 2 percent of the business executives listed in *Standard and Poor's Directory*, less than 4 percent of all federal civil servants in the 6 highest grades, and 1 percent of the federal judges; there are none in the U.S. Senate.[21] In California, women with 4 years or more of college earned on the average less than California men with a high school same education. In fact, a 1961 poll of the National Office Managers' Association found that one-third of the members admitted that they systematically paid women less than men for the same jobs.

Furthermore, more working women are unemployed. In 1972 white men were 4.5 percent unemployed, white women averaged 6 percent unemployment, black men averaged 9 percent, and black women averaged 11 percent. It might be added that discrimination against youth is also reflected in the unemployment figures. Among teenage black women (ages 16 through 19) looking for jobs, unemployment was an incredible 38 percent! It should also be said that women face discrimination even in getting unemployment benefits; for example, in 37 states a woman who is fired because she is pregnant does not get the benefit of unemployment insurance.

Discrimination against women workers means a significant amount of extra profits to employers. In 1970 women's wages averaged about 42 percent less than men's wages for the same job. On that basis it can be calculated that the extra profits from employing women at lower rates amounted to about 23 percent of all corporate manufacturing profits.

WHAT CAUSES SEXISM?

The ideologies of racism and sexism are similar in many ways. Both are based on the supposed inferiority of some groups of human beings to others: "All discrimination is eventually the same thing— Anti-Humanism."[22] Even in the present "enlightened" age, the

[21]See Caroline Bird, *Born Female: The High Cost of Keeping Women Down* (New York: Pocket Books, 1969), pp. 82 ff. This book gives an excellent factual survey.

[22]Congresswoman Shirley Chisholm, "Racism and Anti-Feminism," *The Black Scholar*, January–February 1970, p. 45.

ideology of sexism continues in unabated fury. Thus the conservative view still justifies lower pay for women: "If a woman were more like a man, she'd be treated as such."[23] This view ignores the main point: that millions of women get less pay for doing the same work as men.

A more "liberal" statement of sexism comes from Dr. Edgar Benson, member of the Democratic party's Committee of National Priorities (and a close friend of former Vice President Hubert Humphrey), who says "that physical factors, particularly the menstrual cycle and menopause, disqualify women for key executive jobs."[24] Is it not fortunate that instead of nervous females, who might get us into wars and crises like Vietnam and Watergate, we have had our destiny in the hands of a series of calm, masculine politicians?

All tests show that men and women are equal in intelligence, although they usually progress at different rates in childhood learning, with women leading in the early years.

Radicals certainly admit that there are physical differences between men and women. With respect to working ability, however, the evidence indicates that male and female workers are equal on the average. In fact, in some primitive societies women normally carry heavier loads than men. The question is one of training and expectations. Listen to the lot of the slave woman of the American South as stated by the great black abolitionist Sojourner Truth: "Look at my arm! I have ploughed and planted and gathered into barns, and no man could head me—and ain't I a woman? I have borne thirteen children, and seen most of 'em sold into slavery, and when I cried out with my mother's grief, none but Jesus heard me—and ain't I a woman?"[25]

Even in social and sexual matters, in the radical view, it is not a given, eternal fact that man must always dominate. In some primitve societies men and women appear to have about equal social and sexual roles. This is especially true in societies in which the economic roles of the two are roughly equal in importance, as when women gather wild food and men hunt. In other primitive societies, in which women conduct agriculture and hunting is unimportant, women appear to play the dominant role. If nothing else can be said without controversy, at least modern anthropology makes clear that there are many types of family organization (including various kinds of group marriages), not just one eternal type.

Only with the coming of civilization—meaning economic stratifi-

[23]Angus Black, *A Radical's Guide to Economic Reality* (New York: Holt, Rinehart & Winston, 1970), p. 37.

[24]Quoted in the *San Francisco Chronicle*, July 27, 1970, p. 9.

[25]Quoted in Bird, op. cit., p. 25.

cation and the possession of property in land, cattle, slaves, or serfs—does the woman also become a piece of property. In fact, for purposes of clear inheritance of property the woman of the upper class in ancient civilizations was very well guarded; only the male could freely violate the theoretical monogamy system. This was the beginning of the double standard.

The particular attitudes of American men and women are carefully inculcated, not inherited. "Women are taught from the time they are children to play a serving role, to be docile and submissive. . . ."[26] These attitudes are taught by the family, the schools, the media, the church, corporations, and the government—in which white males are usually dominant.

It has often been said that the position of women in a society mirrors the general condition of human rights in a society. Even in the nineteenth century, the connection was pointed out to those radicals who wished to ignore it: "Every socialist recognized the dependence of the workmen on the capitalist . . . but the same socialist often does not recognize the dependence of women on men because the question touches his own dear self more or less clearly."[27] In the twentieth century, the ideology of women's inferiority reached its high point in Nazi Germany. The Nazi directive to women was to be with "children, kitchen, and church."

WHO BENEFITS FROM SEXISM?

As in the case of racism, conservative economists argue that capitalists actually lose by discriminating against qualified women. Such discrimination, they say, means paying men for a job that women could do equally well for less pay.

The Establishment economist Barbara Bergmann repeats this argument:

> We come . . . to the allegation, usually made by radicals out to discredit capitalism, that women's subjection is all a capitalist plot. Who benefits financially from maintenance of the *status quo?* The most obvious beneficiaries of prejudice against women are male workers in those occupations in which women are not allowed to compete. . . . It is not the male workers or their wives who do the discriminating, however. The employers of the male workers (almost entirely males themselves) are the ones who do the actual discriminating, although of course they are cheered on in their

[26]Marilyn Goldberg, "The Economic Exploitation of Women," *The Review of Radical Political Economics,* Spring 1970, p. 35.

[27]Statement by August Bebel, *Women and Socialism* (Berlin, 1892).

discriminatory ways by their male employees. The employers actually tend to lose financially since profits are lowered when cheap female help is spurned in favor of high-priced male help.[28]

So in her view it is not the capitalists but only the male workers who gain from discrimination. The poor capitalists, who actually do the discriminating, lose by it. But why do capitalists in business for profits systematically choose to lose money? She says they lose financially but gain psychologically: "It feels so good to have women in their place." Neither she nor any one else with this view answers the obvious question: If it causes financial losses (even small ones), why hasn't such discrimination tended to decline and disappear under capitalism?

The truth is, according to radicals, that capitalists do not merely gain psychologically while incurring losses from sex discrimination. On the contrary, capitalists gain from sexism both in power and in *profits*. Moreover, all workers, male as well as female, lose from sexist attitudes.

How do capitalists make profit from sexism? Obviously they use it as an excuse to pay women lower wages. More important, sexist prejudice divides male and female workers, making it more difficult to organize strong unions. In the United States one of every four men workers are unionized, but only one of every seven women workers. The prejudice of union men is apparent in the fact that women constitute 20 percent of all union members but less than 1 percent of all union executive board members. Even in unions like the International Ladies Garment Workers Union, which is over 75 percent female, only a few tokens are on the executive board. Furthermore, in the past unions have done little, if anything, for women's specific grievances and have even joined employers in agreements for lower wages and worse job categories for women.

Union men often pay for their prejudices in broken unions and lower wages. For example, "Standard Oil workers in San Francisco recently paid the price of male supremacy. Women at Standard Oil have the least chance for advancement and decent pay, and the union has done little to fight this. Not surprisingly, women formed the core of the back to work move that eventually broke the strike."[29] Because it reduces union bargaining strength, sexism causes lower wages for *both* men and women. The evidence shows that in areas where most of the labor force is female the pay for both men and women is lower than average, even though the workers in many of

[28]Barbara Bergmann, "Economics of Women's Liberation," *Challenge* 16 (May/June 1973): 14.
[29]Kathy McAfee and Myrna Wood, "Bread and Roses," in Roberta Salper, ed., *Female Liberation* (New York: Knopf, 1972), p. 156.

TABLE 21.1

EDUCATION AND INCOME OF CLERICAL WORKERS, 1960
(ALL DATA FOR FULL-TIME, YEAR-ROUND WORKERS; ALL
OCCUPATIONS LISTED HAVE AT LEAST 51 PERCENT WOMEN)

Clerical Occupation	Percent that median education in occupation is above median education of all U.S. male workers.		Percent that median wage in occupation is below (or above) median of all U.S. male workers.	
	Men	Women	Women	Men
Library Attendants and Assistants	+23%	−18%	−46%	−45%
Doctors, Dentists, Office Attendants	+12	+12	−47	−32
Bank Tellers	+14	+12	−37	−16
Bookkeepers	+14	+12	−36	−11
File Clerks	+12	+10	−41	−25
Office Machine Operators	+13	+12	−32	− 4
Payroll Clerks	+13	+12	−43	0
Receptionists	+13	+13	−29	−23
Secretaries	+15	+14	−29	+ 5
Stenographers	+14	+14	−30	+ 2
Typists	+13	+13	−36	−20
Telephone Operators	+11	+10	−33	+ 7
Cashiers	+ 8	+ 8	−47	−22
Other Clerical Workers	+12	+12	−34	− 1

Source: Derived from Valerie Oppenheimer, *The Female Labor Force,*
Population Monograph Series no. 5 (Berkeley: University of California, 1970).

those areas have higher qualifications (shown in more education) than the average worker. An excellent piece of research has shown this for all the clerical occupations in which women predominate. (See Table 21.1.)

The table shows that in these occupations women's education is far above the median of U.S. workers, but their wages are far below. Moreover, the same is true of the men in these predominantly female occupations; their education is much above, while their wages are much below the U.S. median. Therefore, *sexist discrimination not only hurts female workers but also hurts male workers*—and the lower wages produce higher profits.

In addition to weak unions, another reason for low wages in the predominantly female occupations is that women are systematically excluded from other occupations and pushed into these. Such segregation causes overcrowding or oversupply in the areas where women are allowed to work, thereby lowering wages in these jobs. Some economists admit that males in these occupations will be hurt, but argue that males in other occupations will have higher wages because the exclusion of women lowers labor supply. Thus they claim that some male workers may gain from sexism. This is partially true, but ignores the weakening of unions in all areas and the other unfavorable sociopolitical effects for all workers mentioned below. It might also be noted that the sectors employing mostly white males are sectors with strong monopoly power, where higher wages are passed along in higher prices to all consumers.

Again, like blacks, women have a much higher unemployment rate. This is partly because the boss knows they can't easily get other jobs because of discrimination. So he can keep a core of skilled white males but hire (cheaply) blacks and women from the army of unemployed when he needs them at peak seasons. Thus the capitalist also avoids paying women fringe benefits, which accrue only to workers employed for a long time.

The glorification of housework can also be profitable. In the words of one male advertiser, "properly manipulated . . . American housewives can be given the sense of identity, purpose, creativity, the self-realization, even the sexual joy they lack—by the buying of things."[30] Thus advertisers use the sexist ideology to instill "consumerism" in women. The sexist image of the good woman shows her in her kitchen surrounded by the very latest gadgets, with the best cake mix, made up with miracle cosmetics. Commercials imply that she is a failure if her floors are not the shiniest and her laundry the whitest in the neighborhood. This image helps business sell billions of dollars of useless (or even harmful) goods.

Sexism is also profitable because women's unpaid work in the home is crucial to provision of the needed supply of labor. Housework is equivalent to about one-fourth of the GNP, though it is not counted in the GNP. If business had to pay women in full to raise and clean and cook for the labor force, it would seriously reduce profits. The labor of women as housewives is vital to industry; there would be no labor force without it, yet it goes unpaid. Furthermore, women in the family are not only profitable to capitalism through their unpaid material labor but perhaps even more in the psychological jobs that women (under sexist conditioning) do in the family. The woman in the sexist family helps provide "good" workers: "A woman is judged as a wife and mother—the only role she is allowed—according to her ability to maintain stability in her family and to help her family 'adjust' to harsh realities. She therefore transmits the values of hard work and conformity to each generation of workers. It is she who forces her children to stay in

[30]Quoted in Betty Friedan, *The Feminine Mystique* (New York: Dell, 1963), p. 199.

school and 'behave' or who urges her husband not to risk his job by standing up to the boss or going on strike."[31] Moreover, as a result of their dependent role in the sexist family, women themselves are socialized to be passive, submissive, and docile as workers.

The last, but not the least important, profit to capitalism from sexism comes in its increased support for political stability. On the one hand, the woman's psychological role in the sexist family has the same effects politically as economically: (1) It tends to make her more fearful and conservative, and (2) she tends to influence her husband in this direction and (3) to pass it on to her son and, especially, to her daughter. Sexism is also used as a political divide-and-rule tactic much like racism. White politicians blame all urban problems on blacks. Secretary of the Treasury Schultz blames unemployment (and accompanying pressure for low wages) on the competition of women workers. Thus conservative politicians try to make women a scapegoat for men's problems instead of an ally against the system.

LIBERATION MOVEMENTS

Discrimination means terrible socioeconomic conditions for many minority groups. These poor conditions have led to strong protest and liberation movements by many minority groups, such as blacks, Chicanos, and Indians. There are reform groups, such as the National Association for the Advancement of Colored People, who believe laws against discrimination can achieve equality under capitalism. There are also radical groups, such as the Black Panthers, who do not believe full equality is possible under capitalism but want to see an entirely new, restructured system to achieve full equality in a democratic socialist society.

The same reformer-versus-radical split exists among groups favoring women's liberation. There are many reforms on which all of those fighting against sexism can agree. For example, we need free child care centers, equal pay for equal work, equal access to all education, equal access to equal kinds of jobs, free birth control information and devices so that women can determine when they wish to have children, and as a last resort, free and legal abortions when necessary.

The problem is that it is unlikely that these reforms will change basic attitudes, nor is it clear that all these reforms can actually be achieved under capitalism. It is a fact that the lower wages of women are a source of additional profit. Perhaps even more important, it is a fact that the submissive attitude of women, encour-

[31]McAfee and Wood, op. cit., p. 156.

aged by church and television alike, serves as an important prop
to the status quo. There are thus strong and vested interests in favor
of maintaining the ideology of male supremacy and the practice
of sexual discrimination so long as capitalism exists.

SUMMARY

National, religious, and racial discrimination exist in America against
blacks, Mexican and Puerto Rican Americans and other "ethnic
groups," American Indians, Japanese and Chinese Americans, Catholics, and Jews. The well-documented oppression against blacks is
very severe in housing, education, jobs, health, and every other area
of life and (even in death; there are segregated cemeteries). The
racist ideology against blacks originated as an apology for slavery,
but it continues as an apology for low wages, high ghetto rents,
exclusion of blacks from the political process in the South and elsewhere, and many other profitable reasons for maintaining racist
myths.

Prejudice and discrimination against women are much older,
having been present in many previous societies. American women
continue to suffer from fewer educational opportunities, fewer job
opportunities, lower pay for the same jobs, and a sexist ideology that
says they are inferior. The ideology and discriminatory patterns
continue to be supported, in part, because some important interests
find them very profitable.

Women as well as blacks, Chicanos, and other minorities have
organized liberation movements. They are achieving some limited
reforms under capitalism. Their more radical groups are also playing a major role in the fight for a better—equalitarian and socialist
—society.

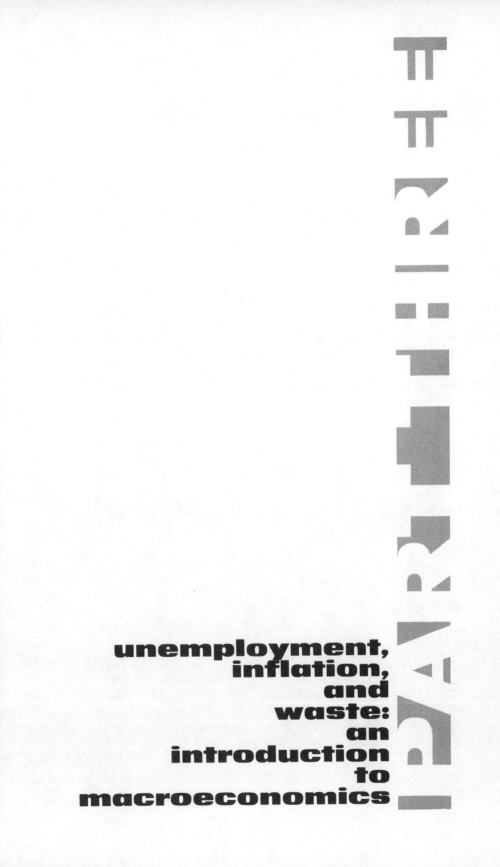

PART III

**unemployment,
inflation,
and
waste:
an
introduction
to
macroeconomics**

aggregate problems: unemployment, inflation, pollution, and underdevelopment

In this part the issues involved in aggregate or macroeconomics, the working of the economy as a whole, are examined. First, the historical evolution of the institutions of the private enterprise system and the theory of aggregate income determination are reviewed. The analysis then turns to why the economy continues to be subject to periods of substantial unemployment and why it continues to have those noticeable fluctuations of output and employment called *business cycles*. Next, the problem of inflation is considered, and the impact of monopoly power and of vast military spending on unemployment and inflation is investigated. Then the causes of retarded economic growth, as well as the human costs of economic growth, such as pollution, are discussed. Finally, the international relationships between the advanced and the less developed countries, and the barriers to growth in the latter (including imperialism) are examined.

THE PROBLEM OF UNEMPLOYMENT

The performance of the American economy is treated in detail in Chapters 28 and 29. It is sufficient to note here that there have been no major depressions since World War II. Nevertheless, there have been several minor depressions, which are defined as small declines in business activity on the order of 5 or 10 percent. It is now fashionable to call a minor depression a *recession* (*depression* has become a nasty word). Some authorities prefer even more euphemistic terms like *rolling readjustment*. Even in minor depressions, millions of people are unemployed and suffer extreme deprivation (e.g., cases of malnutrition have recently been found among the families of those long unemployed). In the recession of 1969–1970 there was an increase of 1.2 million in the number of Americans living in poverty.

The importance of the problem of periodic unemployment is quite apparent from both the social and the individual point of view. For the society as a whole, it means periods of unused resources, lower output and employment, and a much slower long-run rate of growth. Many attempts have been made to calculate the amount of loss to society from unemployment. One careful estimate put the total loss for the years 1953–1972 at 45 million man-years (valued at $1.8 *trillion* in 1970 dollars).[1] A *man-year* is the amount of work one person could produce in a year. If these calculations were extended back to cover all the depressions in U.S. economic history, the total loss would be tremendous.

Depressions and economic instability have other effects, however, which cannot be calculated in economic terms. There are sociological effects, as reflected in population growth, divorce rates, crime, physical and mental health, and even suicide rates.[2] If few resort to suicide, the total effect is nonetheless incalculably great on all who lose jobs, small businesses, or farms; who wander about on an enforced vacation with meager subsistence provided by private or public charities; who find all of their previous plans destroyed. Unemployment certainly amounts to vast social wastefulness as well as individual tragedies. Moreover, unemployment is not evenly spread but is highest among such economic groups as migrant farm workers and the untrained youth among such minority groups as blacks, and among women workers, generally the first fired and the last hired.

When a newspaper casually mentions that 5 million Americans want work but cannot find it, these are not just 5 million statistics but 5 million afflicted individuals. If a large firm closes down or moves to a new location, it leaves behind engineers and executives suddenly reduced from a useful job at $400 a week to unemployment compensation at $40 a week, as well as a large number of unskilled workers with no future prospects. At times whole mining towns seem to lose animation, and hundreds of miners' wives line up at soup kitchens and welfare departments for food allotments. In the "prosperous" year of 1959, a 38-year-old unemployed auto worker

---

[1] Leon Keyserling, "What's Wrong with American Economics," *Challenge* 16 (May/June 1973): 18–25.

[2] For the Great Depression of the 1930s, there is an immense literature on each area; for an overall study of the effects of earlier business cycles, see D. C. Thomas, *Social Aspects of the Business Cycle* (New York: Knopf, 1927).

represented millions of others when he said: "I've been looking for work all over but I can't get a job. I hate being on welfare. It's enough to make a man jump into the river."[3] When the majority of the people are working for good wages, very few really want to subsist as a useless stick of wood on a handout of a few dollars a week.

THE PROBLEM OF INFLATION

Inflation is defined as a rise in the general price level of all goods. A rise in one price offset by a fall in another is not inflation; this is constantly occurring as a result of shifting demand (e.g., from butter to margarine). Furthermore, we must distinguish the effects of a slow and gradual inflation from those of a very rapid, or galloping, inflation. If inflation results in the rise of prices by a few percent per year, then it is only a social irritant. It does work a great injustice on those who possess savings, who have made loans, who must live on a fixed income, or whose wages lag prices, because these groups find the value of their dollars steadily declining. In particular, the aged face an economic disaster when they retire. This decline of real wages and real savings exacerbates many economic and political conflicts. For a country as a whole, gradual inflation of domestic prices may reduce the volume of goods sold abroad; and for goods that still face competition, entire overseas markets may be lost.

The situation is much more serious, however, when the rate of price inflation reaches several hundred percent per year, as happened in Germany in the early 1920s. Rampant inflation brings such a rapid decline in the value of money that ultimately there can be complete dislocation and collapse of the economy, with correspondingly violent political reactions. At such times money and the market system fail completely. Productive effort is paralyzed, and exchange retrogresses to barter. In recent years there have been several underdeveloped countries, such as Brazil and South Vietnam, in which galloping inflation threatened to disrupt all normal economic processes.

Even in the United States, the magnitude of inflation is indicated by the fact that the consumer price level quadrupled between 1900 and 1958, and doubled between 1938 and 1958, alone.[4] During the 6 years from 1945 to 1950, wholesale prices rose 52.6 percent and consumer prices 33.7 percent. Nevertheless, inflation in the United States was in the very gradual category of 1 or 2 percent a year in most years from 1951 to 1965. After the escalation of the war in

---

[3]Reported in an excellent survey by A. H. Raskin, "People Behind Statistics: A Study of the Unemployed," *New York Times*, March 16, 1959, p. 1.

[4]See Willard L. Thorp and Richard F. Quandt, *The New Inflation* (New York: McGraw-Hill, 1959), p. 1.

Vietnam in 1965, however, inflation became progressively worse. It has been one of the major economic issues of the 1968 and 1972 presidential elections.

Since 1969, we have experienced strong and persistent inflation combined with rates of unemployment over 5 percent. Both inflation and unemployment have many harmful effects, and we wish to eliminate both. Unfortunately, some of the strongest policy weapons for full employment tend to produce inflation, and powerful measures to combat inflation sometimes tend to produce unemployment. As we shall see, traditional methods have failed to remedy this situation. In fact, by 1974 the rate of inflation was climbing rapidly; and the Gallup poll reported that 62 percent of Americans felt that it was the worst single national problem.

POLLUTION AND WASTE

No one who opens his eyes in Los Angeles can be unaware of air pollution—it is the yellow-brown smog in the air that makes you cry and rub your eyes. No one who swims in the lake near Chicago or Gary can be unaware of water pollution—it puts a blackish oil and metal film on your skin. Anyone who sees our vast acres of garbage, old-car dumps, or open-face mines will become aware of land pollution. Moreover, this result of industrialization is rapidly spreading around the world (you can cry as easily in Tokyo as in Los Angeles).

Not only are many industrial products harmful to the environment; some are useless as well. The widespread existence of useless production is primarily the result of advertising. For every bit of useful information in small print, there tend to be 999 neon signs filled with exhortations and lies. We shall also find that the effort to sell goods penetrates into production so that engineers spend millions of valuable hours putting tails on cars or even designing products with only limited durability, thus forcing the consumer to buy new ones.

The greatest waste, however, comes from military spending. An atomic bomb or a battleship does nothing constructive. A large portion of this part of the book will investigate the impact of the huge military waste on the economy—for example, how it may stimulate inflation and, moreover, who profits from it.

UNDERDEVELOPMENT AND IMPERIALISM

The human face of underdevelopment is the child with a bloated belly, suffering from various kinds of malnutrition. Over a billion people in less developed countries are on the margin of starvation.

Hundreds of millions have dread diseases. Housing is little and poor or even nonexistent. Clothing consists of rags. Why?

Why in a world of tremendous productive powers is this still the lot of the majority? Part of the answer is that these countries have suffered from two or three centuries of imperialism. The old colonial regimes first plundered them of all that was movable, such as the gold and silver of Mexico and Peru. Then they set up an unequal trade exchange, taking out raw materials at low prices and selling back finished goods at high prices. In every area, they exploited the abundance of cheap labor at the point of a bayonet. In Africa, they enslaved millions for labor elsewhere.

Why are these countries still making little or no progress? Part of the answer lies in the present low level of capital there, the present low level of human skills, and the overpopulation relative to their meager resources. Clearly these present evils stem in part from past colonialism. Yet another part of the answer is even more damning. It appears that the advanced capitalist countries continue to keep the less developed ones in a state of neocolonialism. Like the older colonial type of imperialism, the new neocolonialism involves dependent patterns of trade, removal of plunder (in the form of high profits on investment), and continued political domination (as in the "free elections" of October 1971 in Vietnam, in which American-backed President Thieu was the only candidate).

SUMMARY

This chapter is the introduction to Part Three. It briefly presents the main issues to be discussed: (1) how unemployment and inflation may occur in a capitalist economy; (2) the role of government, particularly the vast impact of its military spending; (3) the flow of wasteful and even harmful products, as well as the cost of growth in terms of environmental destruction; (4) growth in the less developed countries, with particular attention to the damage done these countries by Western colonization and imperialism.

To lay a systematic foundation for understanding these macroeconomic problems, we must begin (in Chapter 23) by tracing the operation of the institutions of the U.S. economy. Historically, to what exent have the basic institutions of capitalism allowed us to achieve stable economic growth without inflation or unemployment?

the
institutional
setting

Our economy experiences periods of prosperity and depression, or boom and bust. These are caused by the imbalance of *aggregate supply* and *aggregate demand*. Aggregate supply is defined as the total output that business produces and plans to sell. Aggregate demand is defined as the total dollar amount of goods that consumers, investors, and governments plan to buy. Sometimes the aggregate supply of produced goods is either too small or too great in terms of the aggregate demand for goods. Certainly if aggregate supply and demand were always equal, there could be no such periodic phenomena as overproduction and underproduction. Depressions occur when the aggregate demand is insufficient (in money terms) to purchase the whole supply.

The first question to be asked is simple but basic. In what kind of economy must total supply and demand always be equal? Under what economic institutions is it possible for demand to be greater or less than supply? Before an analysis of the historical facts can be undertaken, an obstacle must be removed from the path. That obstacle is the traditional theory of classical economics known as Say's law, named after the economist J. B. Say. We shall find that Say's law denies the possibility of widespread unemployment and depression, that it is relevant to some earlier societies, but has no application to modern industrialized, capitalist economies.

SAY'S LAW

In its most rigid form Say's law states that aggregate demand must always equal aggregate supply at any level of supply, including the full-employment level. This denies the possibility of either a deficiency or an excess of aggregate demand and therefore denies the possibility of depressions or inflations in general business activity. Say's law does *not* state that aggregate supply and aggregate demand are "identical" or are equal by definition: ". . . Though Say's law is not an identity, his blundering exposition has led a long series of writers to believe that it is one—and this in no less than four different senses."[1] Rather, *Say's law says that an increase of supply, through various automatic processes, calls forth an equal amount of demand.*

Aside from a few dissenters, whole generations of economists refused to accept the possibility that there could be involuntary unemployment or an excessive supply of goods. Furthermore, they never challenged the assumption that all commodities could always be sold at prices equal to their full, long-run costs. They admitted only the possibility of temporary, accidental maladjustments in one or a few industries. Such maladjustments were sure to be corrected as soon as competition could force capital to switch from one industry to another. In a typical statement Ricardo argued: "Too much of a particular commodity may be produced, of which there may be said to be such a glut in the market as not to repay the capital expended on it; but this cannot be the case with all commodities."[2]

The kernel of truth in Say's law is the platitude that every purchase constitutes a sale, and every sale means some money income to someone, which again may, and ordinarily will, be used for more purchases. Ricardo phrased the case for Say's law in this way: "No man produces but with a view to consume or sell, and he never sells but with an intention to purchase some other commodity which may be useful to him or which may contribute to future production. By purchasing them, he necessarily becomes either the consumer of his own goods, or the purchaser and consumer of the goods of some other person."[3]

This argument *must* be wrong as applied to modern private enterprise economies because observation reveals that such economies have never been without periodic depressions within the last cen-

---

[1]Joseph A. Schumpeter, *History of Economic Analysis* (New York: Oxford University Press, 1954), p. 618.

[2]David Ricardo, *The Principles of Political Economy and Taxation* (London: Gonner, Bell, & Sons, 1891 [reprinted from 1821 edition]), p. 276.

[3]Ibid., p. 273.

tury or more. Say's law is, indeed, true for certain earlier types of economies; the mistake was in taking these simpler economies as a model and then applying the conclusions to the modern private enterprise economy without considering the fact that entirely new institutions have evolved since the medieval period.

PRODUCTION FOR THE MARKET

It is characteristic of the private enterprise economy, which was fully developed in England by the end of the eighteenth century, that most production was directed solely toward its sale on the market. This was hardly ever true of earlier societies. In the most primitive societies, almost all productive activity is directed at production of food by gathering or hunting. These activities are necessarily carried out by the collective unit of all the males and/or females of the tribe. Generally, almost all of the produce is distributed according to some fixed scheme among the tribe's membership.

Even at a somewhat higher economic stage, production is still for use, and not for sale. None of the Indian tribes of the Americas, not even the Aztecs, bought or sold land or produced crops to sell for a profit to others. In fact, "for the red man soil existed only in order to meet the necessities of life, and production, not profit, was the basis of his economy. . . . Unemployment was certainly never a problem in the Indian communities of early America."[4] Because there was little division of labor within the tribe, there was little if any trade among its members. Furthermore, very little commerce was transacted between the most primitive tribes, and that "was virtually restricted to materials small in bulk and precious for their decorative or magical qualities."[5] We find that all over the world for thousands of years almost all economic systems, whether tribal or feudal, were based on relatively self-sufficient agricultural units.

In the Roman Empire, there was a great deal of trade, but most of it was in luxury goods.[6] This trade therefore did not affect the self-sufficiency of the basic agricultural unit, the slave-run plantation, although a lack of surplus food could bring starvation to large numbers of city dwellers. As one author says, ". . . Notwithstanding the phenomenal expansion of trade and industry, the vast masses inside the Empire still continued to win their livelihood from the soil.

---

[4]John A. Crow, *The Epic of Latin America* (Garden City, N.Y.: Doubleday, 1948), p. 54.

[5]Grahame Clark, *From Savagery to Civilization* (London: Cobbett Press, 1946), p. 96.

[6]See, for example, the brief account in F. W. Walbank, *The Decline of the Roman Empire in the West* (London: Cobbett Press, 1956), pp. 11–13.

Agriculture remained throughout antiquity the most usual and most typical economic activity, and land the most important form of wealth."[7]

The same was true of feudal England, where the primitive level of technology made impossible the supply of large urban populations and even greatly restricted trade between the villages. As a result, in the England of that day "towns developed slowly; each group of burgesses solved their local problems on their own initiative and in their own time. Even in 1377 not much more than eight per cent of the population were townsmen, and only a minority of these had independent dealings with continental markets."[8]

Of course in the later medieval period there were areas of more highly developed industrial production, such as Flanders and northern Italy; and even relatively backward England carried on a systematic wool trade with Flanders. Yet these were exceptions to the general rule of the feudal economy and may be considered early signs pointing to the end of that economy.

If there happened to be a surplus from the slave or feudal estate, then it might be marketed in return for foreign luxury items to be used by the lord of the estate. Finding a market, however, was not a matter of life and death for the economic unit. If the surplus found no market, the manor was still supplied with its necessities for that year, and it could and would continue the process of production for the next year's needs. What could disturb such economically self-sufficient societies were only the catastrophes that were more or less external to the economy—natural disasters such as droughts, plagues, or floods, or political troubles such as government interference, war, or revolution. These phenomena could and did depress production in various randomly spaced intervals, as well as seasonally because of the special seasonal sensitivity of agriculture.

This type of economy could not, however, conceivably face the problem of lack of effective demand for all commodities because the economic unit directly consumed most of the products of its own land and could do without trade altogether. Thus in discussing the business cycle of depression and prosperity, Mitchell observes that ". . . the total number of past business cycles may well be less than a thousand. For business cycles are phenomena peculiar to a certain form of economic organization which has been dominant even in Western Europe for less than two centuries, and for briefer periods in other regions."[9]

[7]Ibid., p. 18.
[8]Marion Gibbs, *Feudal Order* (London: Cobbett Press, 1949), pp. 7–8.
[9]W. C. Mitchell, *Business Annals* (New York: National Bureau of Economic Research, 1926), p. 47.

In the period of transition from feudalism to capitalism in the England of the sixteenth, seventeenth, and eighteenth centuries, the majority of the people still lived on the land and consumed their own products. As time went on, however, more and more products, both agricultural and industrial, were delivered to the market place. By the end of the eighteenth century, the private enterprise system of production for the market embraced most economic activity. By the nineteenth century, one business entrepreneur might own a factory producing millions of shoes, through his whole family could consume only a few pairs. The shoes had to be sold in order to buy other consumer goods for his family, pay wages to his employees, and replace and expand the plant and equipment of his business.

In the United States, the transformation to a market economy took place in the nineteenth century. In 1800, two-thirds of the U.S. population labored in agriculture, and most of the remainder were employed in commerce and shipping. Except for the foreign trade sector, markets were small and local. Many families and communities were almost self-sufficient. Native industry, which had a foothold in 1800, spurted during the War of 1812, when imports from England were cut off. By 1815, New England mills and factories were capable of supplying textiles and simple manufactures to the nation. Transportation networks were built to link communities and regions. This permitted farmers to specialize in commercial crops for cash income with which they purchased in the market the necessities of life. By 1840, a large national market for manufactures had been created. Families turned away from self-sufficiency and purchased cloth, flour, farm implements, and household items. Rapid industrialization followed. In 1860, the United States was producing more than one-fifth of world manufacturing output, and by 1913, American production had risen to one-third of the world total.

The process of industrialization, starting first in England and spreading to the rest of western Europe and the United States, had changed the character of production and employment. Production required a greater number of stages, or steps, as materials and products became less simple. Labor grew more specialized, and labor's employment came to be linked with the expanded use of capital.

In the modern market economy, every man's productive effort is related to sales in the market, and every man's income depends on the income of others. A man working in an automobile factory, for example, depends for his continued employment on millions of people buying cars each year. In turn, most of these car buyers depend on millions buying the products they produce. If consumers are unable to buy their cars, the automobile worker immediately loses his job. The car manufacturer needs less steel, less rubber, less paint, and so on. Each of these industries, in turn, lays off workers. The process goes on and on because of the interconnectedness of the market economy. Each time more workers lose their jobs, their income ceases. They can no longer buy the hundreds of goods and services they normally purchase, and the crisis widens and becomes more severe.

The sale in the market of privately produced goods and services generates all income. Decisions to purchase are made by thousands of small- and large-income receivers, and the total of these purchasing decisions makes up the total, or aggregate, demand. In previous economic systems, the self-sufficient economic unit—the craftsman producing a trickle of handmade items for known customers—could not possibly be troubled by lack of demand for his product. When almost all that was produced by the economic unit was consumed by it, Say's law had to be true. In the industrialized private enterprise system, however, *the businessman produces for the market and cannot continue production if there is no market demand for his products.* This, then, is the first major institutional feature of the private enterprise economy. Appearing in the eighteenth century and continuing to the present day, it is one of the factors that make business cycles possible.

REGULAR USE OF MONEY

Another institutional condition that opens up the possibility of a lack of aggregate demand is the regular use of money in exchange. The monetary system takes the place of the barter system of exchanging good for good. It was seen that production for the market makes cyclical unemployment possible. Use of money in the market exchange will be shown to be a second necessary condition for the emergence of business cycles.

The Uses of Money

Money replaced the barter system because it is much more convenient to use. What precisely are its functions in the modern economy? Traditionally, money is said to have four functions:

1. Money is the *unit of accounting*, or the standard of value—that is, it is a measuring stick for everything else. All contracts are drawn up in money terms, with so much money to be paid for a certain product at a certain time. We think of a coat or a table as being worth so many dollars.

2. Money is the *medium of exchange*, or actual intermediary between commodities (including services). Under barter, one commodity is exchanged for another commodity. In the monetary economy, a commodity is exchanged for money; then the money may be exchanged for another commodity.

3. Money is a *store of value,* or a device for hoarding. When money is received as an income, it need not be spent immediately. Instead, if it is in a nonperishable form such as gold, it may be buried or stored away and hoarded until the possessor chooses to use it. In the modern world money is deposited in a bank account, which is completely nonperishable; the money may even grow by earning interest while it is on deposit.

4. Money is a *standard of deferred payment,* or a unit of accounting for future payments on debts. In other words, I may buy something from you now but promise to pay for it later. My promise is always in terms of so many units of money, not, for example, in so many pairs of shoes. In the United States paper money is a legal tender (or legally acceptable unit) for the payment of any debt.

Our "money" today is (1) coin and paper currency in circulation plus (2) all demand deposits (checking accounts) in commercial banks. (In Chapter 30 the evolution of money, from commodities such as gold to its present complex forms in the U.S. economy, will be explored in detail.)

These are the four traditional concepts of the use of money, but they are grossly oversimplified and misleading. For one thing, a piece of paper cannot produce an automobile; only human beings can produce things. The piece of paper has power to command labor only because it faithfully reflects the human relationships on which our society is built. It is not really money but people who command and manipulate other people.

Moreover, the monetary system is often inadequate to fulfill these functions, which traditional views assume it will smoothly achieve. In Chapter 31, and briefly here, we shall see that it fails in all its functions during an inflation. In Chapter 28, and again briefly here, we shall see that the monetary system helps make depressions possible *and* tends to intensify them.

The Abuses of Money

Money does not serve its four functions equally well under all conditions. Imagine that there is catastrophic inflation, with prices doubling every hour, which means that the value of money falls by half each hour. Money then functions badly as a unit of accounting because the same product sells at such rapidly changing prices that neither consumers nor sellers can keep track of them. With rapid inflation money is also a poor medium of exchange: People may refuse to accept it at all because its buying power is so uncertain and may diminish further before it can be spent.

With rapid inflation money is also a very bad store of value because money hoarded away now will buy so very much less in the future. Instead of keeping money, everyone rushes to buy goods or real property that will be worth more and more units of money as the inflation continues. Anyone with cash savings in paper money or bank accounts or government bonds is badly hurt, so it may happen that no one will put money in banks or buy government bonds at almost any interest rate. Finally, with rapid inflation money cannot function as a standard of deferred payment because the standard itself keeps changing. If someone lends $100 today and it is worth only $1 when it is paid back tomorrow, then the lender is very badly hurt. When people refuse to accept the medium of exchange because they have lost confidence in it, economic activity falls to the level that can be maintained by barter.

The use of money, even in ancient times, brought many new complications onto the economic scene. In the Roman Empire, for example, vast amounts of money were needed by the government to support wars of expansion, large standing armies, police and bureaucracy, and an unfavorable balance of trade (due to import of luxuries from the East). The emperors were eventually forced to the expedient of debasing their coins by "clipping" (decreasing the metallic content of coins) or mixture with less valuable metals. As the government debased the coins and as production of goods declined in the later days of the empire, the amount that could be bought with the coins declined rapidly; in other words, a catastrophic inflation occurred.[10]

Despite their difficulties with it, the regular use of money did not lead to the modern type of depression because most of the Roman economy was still contained in self-sufficient agricultural units.[11] The luxury trade did suffer from the extreme inflation, but only as one more affliction in addition to colonial wars and slave revolts, the extreme inefficiency of employing slave labor, and the Roman citizens' attitude that any participation in the work process was degrading (because only slaves should work).

With the breakup of the Roman Empire, trade suffered a considerable decline. In early feudalism, the pattern was overwhelmingly that of the isolated, self-sufficient manor. Barter therefore grew in importance, and the use of money declined. On each manor, in return for the lord's protection, the serf provided all the services and consumer goods needed and required by the lord, his family, and his retinue. However, when technology began to improve, industry and commerce slowly began to revive in western Europe. The widespread trade of the later medieval period eventually led to the replacement of barter by a money economy; at the same time, follow-

[10]See, for example, Walbank, op. cit., pp. 42–43, 51–52.
[11]See ibid., p. 18.

ing the pattern discussed in the previous section, production was increasingly designed for sale in the market rather than use at home.

The modern private enterprise economy demands continuous use of money as the go-between in market exchange by the entire population. In a barter economy it is possible for one commodity to be brought to market in larger supply than there is demand for it; but it is impossible for "total supply" to exceed "total demand" because the two are identical; both are the same aggregate bunch of products brought to the market. The important point, however, is not the definitional identity of total supply and demand in a barter economy. It is that there may be a mismatch of particular supplies and demands, but no lack of *aggregate* demand. For example, those who bring cows to market may find more shoes and fewer coats produced than they desire; that is, they would rather "spend" their cows for fewer shoes and more coats than are available. The excess supply of shoes is balanced by the excess demand for coats. The result is only a temporary, or frictional, unemployment of shoe producers, which could be cured by a shift to coat production. It is true that in the actual medieval economy rigid feudal restrictions did not allow many such shifts in production or occupation, but it was just these restrictions that the classical economists wished to abolish.

The mistake made by the classical adherents of Say's law was to apply the impossibility of general unemployment in a pure barter economy to a money economy. They extended the argument by means of the general observation that money is merely the means of exchanging two commodities, so that the operation of the money economy is "essentially" the same as that of the barter economy. Thus we find Ricardo contending that "productions are always bought by productions, or by services; money is only the medium by which the exchange is effected."[12] One function of money is to facilitate the exchange of commodities, but it has other uses as well. In the modern economy, the seller obtains only money for his commodities, money that he may or may not use immediately or later to buy other commodities. Thus money functions as the means for the storage of value for future use. The wants of mankind may be infinite, but it is not always the case that all buyers have money to buy what they want. There is therefore *no inherent necessity in a money economy that sellers should find buyers for all commodities brought to market.*

The problem is not an aggregate lack of money in the economy. While those who wish to buy may have no money, those who have money may be taking it out of circulation and not using it in any way, or *hoarding* it. The chain of circulation may then be broken

---

[12]Ricardo, op. cit., p. 275.

at any point at which the flow of money is stopped or withdrawn from the system. In that case the reduction of the flow of circulation, like the reduction of the volume of water flowing in a stream, causes a slowdown in the movement of products being circulated by this means. While it is basically true that products exchange for products even after the introduction of money, the mere necessity of the money bridge makes all the difference in the world. If the bridge is absent, finished commodities may pile up in warehouses, while potential consumers are unable to buy them. Only money can make a possible consumer into an actual buyer in the private enterprise system.

An excess of supply in this economic system does not mean everyone is fully satisfied. People's wants are elastic; we may have as much of a particular commodity as we want at one time, but there is always an infinity of other things that we desire, things that still have use value or utility for us. Therefore the problem is not overproduction of the total commodities relative to what people want or desire. The problem is rather that there may be too many commodities on the market relative to the *effective demand*, which is limited by definition to desires that are backed by money in the marketplace.

CREDIT MONEY

In the United States at present, the largest part of the money supply, about four-fifths of the whole, is pure credit money. *Credit money* consists of demand, or checking, deposits at banks, which are dollar amounts owed by the banks to the holders of the accounts. Credit money is created whenever a bank makes a loan to a customer and "credits" his checking account with the amount of the loan. Except for the legal constraints on the lending of money, banks could go on creating money without limit as long as people had confidence in the acceptability of the money. Only the smallest portion of the money supply consists of coins and paper money issued by the U.S. Treasury. A somewhat larger portion is paper money issued by the Federal Reserve System (Fed). Technically, even these parts of the money supply are credits to the private sector because they are debts of government agencies that are payable on demand. Dollar bills, however, are no longer payable in gold, so a $10 bill presented to the Treasury or the Fed could be paid by any legal tender—say, two $5 bills. Thus the Treasury or the Fed may create money simply by using the printing press. Although Congress does impose a legal limit, it often raises that limit.

The use of credit intensifies all money problems; not only may a person sell something and not immediately purchase something else, but also it is possible to sell something and not receive the proceeds of the sale for some time. If Brown owes Smith, and Smith owes Johnson, and Johnson owes Martin, a break anywhere along this chain of credit circulation will be disastrous for all of the later parties in the chain. Moreover, the credit chain in the modern private enterprise economy is usually circular in nature, so that the reverberations reach the starting point and may begin to go around again. This does not, of course, explain why the chain should ever break in the first place.

It has been amply demonstrated that when money and credit institutions become the usual way of doing business, the business cycle of boom and bust becomes a possibility. Does this mean that these institutions are sufficient to explain the business cycle? We know that money and credit existed in ancient Rome and in the sixteenth to eighteenth centuries in western Europe, yet the financial disturbances of those times do not seem to have been the same phenomena as the modern type of business cycle. It is true that after the development of money and credit every catastrophic natural happening or violent political event might be reflected in a financial panic. For example, when the English fleet was burnt by the Dutch in 1667, and in 1672 when Charles II stopped payments from the Exchequer, there were sudden runs on the London banks. In the eighteenth century, financial crises resulted from the Jacobin conspiracy in 1708, the bursting of the South Sea stock speculation bubble in 1720, the fighting with the Pretender in 1745, the aftermath of the Seven Years' War in 1763, and the disturbances caused by the American Revolution.[13] These panics were unlike the modern business cycle, both in cause and effect, because they originated in external causes and resulted in only limited depressions in a few trades for brief and random periods. The first truly general industrial depression of the modern type appeared as late as 1793 in England.[14]

In summary, there is evidence of a long period of extensive use of money and credit with only temporary and externally caused financial panics. Conversely, in the nineteenth and twentieth centuries there have been depressions, as well as many minor recessions, that did not produce financial panics. There is no reason, all other things being equal, why money and credit should not flow steadily through the process of circulation, so long as business expectations remain optimistic. It may be tentatively concluded that the regular use of money and credit is a necessary prerequisite, but not a sufficient explanation, of business cycles.

[13]See discussion of all these events in W. C. Mitchell, *Business Cycles* (Berkeley: University of California Press, 1913), pp. 583–584.
[14]Ibid.

PRODUCTION FOR PRIVATE PROFIT

We have examined two conditions—production for the market and regular use of money—that must be present if business cycles are to occur. These are cycles in which demand fluctuates below the full-employment level of supply. But at least one more institutional condition is necessary before we can contend that total demand may not equal supply in this economy (or that Say's law does not hold true). It is the existence of private ownership of production facilities and production for private profit. Even in an economy characterized by exchange in the market through the medium of money, supply and demand can be kept in balance, or quickly brought back into balance, if both supply and demand are consciously planned by the same national agency.

A centrally planned socialist economy is one in which the government owns and plans the use of all means of production. Most business cycle economists admit that industrialized socialist economies do not experience the business cycle phenomena characteristic of industrialized private enterprise economies. This is the case because a socialist economy can make one unified plan for growth without concern for private profit. Thus all of the data on Soviet economic development indicate continuous full employment (except for retraining time or movement between jobs).

In a private enterprise economy, each individual enterprise makes its own plans on the basis of its own estimate of whether it will obtain a private profit by undertaking production. In the national plan of a socialist economy, *the same agency decides both the aggregate supply and the aggregate demand*. It sets the aggregate consumer demand by setting wages, and it controls the aggregate investment demand directly through the government budget.

Of course socialist planners may make mistakes in allocation of resources and new investment, especially because there are changes in technology and other new conditions each year. They may allocate resources to uses that are not as productive as others, or even order the production of one thing (say, automobiles) but not order enough production of other things going into it (say, rubber tires). In such cases there may be supply bottlenecks holding back production in some industries and temporary oversupply and unused capacity in others. Such mistakes may lower the rate of growth or even cause output to fall in one year (as happened in Czechoslovakia in 1963).

Moreover, much recent data on eastern Europe and the Soviet Union show a cyclical recurrence of slow-growth periods. Each time the economy starts growing rapidly, the bureaucrats get overoptimistic. They push production more rapidly than is physically possible, leading to supply bottlenecks. If they order too many new factories to be built at once, the result is half-built factories and little or no increase in current output. Nevertheless, there remain very important distinctions from a private enterprise economy. There need be no secondary effects, no cumulative collapse of production, because socialist investment is not based on private profit (and the economy does remain at full employment). Naturally, the fact that a socialist economy is not subject to cyclical unemployment does not prove by itself that it is better or worse than a private enterprise economy. For that overall judgment, we would have to consider all the criteria for comparing economies, including full employment, efficiency, growth, distribution of income, and political and social effects.

In an economy based on private ownership of individual competing units, the sum of decisions to produce may not equal the sum of decisions by other individuals and businesses to spend—that is, to consume and invest. If the sum of the outputs produced at present prices is greater than the sum of the monetary demand, then there is not enough revenue to cover the costs of production and also yield a profit for the private entrepreneur. This criterion is decisive because *if the private entrepreneur can make no profit, he will not continue production*, his machinery will stand idle, and all of his workers will be unemployed.

THE U.S. ECONOMY

Alternating periods of expansion and decline of output and employment have occurred regularly in the United States for over 150 years. The very earliest cycles were clearly tied to events abroad, but internally generated instability was evident by the 1840s. In its infancy, the American economy depended heavily on European trade. The country prospered with every quickening in the flow of ships and goods from Atlantic ports. When this flow was interrupted, distress in the coastal towns persisted until some new stimulus brought a return of strong demand for American shipping. Most profits came from commerce, and largely foreign commerce at that. It was in commerce and shipping that the most important capital investment was occurring. Therefore, between 1800 and 1815, a remarkably close correlation existed between demand for American exports and the health of the American economy as a whole.[15] In 1836, when European economic activity declined and the American expansion faltered, Europeans sold many of their holdings and

[15]See W. B. Smith and A. H. Cole, *Fluctuations in American Business, 1790–1860* (Cambridge, Mass.: Harvard University Press, 1935).

TABLE 23.1

TIMING AND DURATION OF BUSINESS CYCLES
IN THE UNITED STATES SINCE 1854

Standard Reference Dates			Duration (Months)		
Trough	Peak	Trough	Expansion (trough to peak)	Contraction (peak to trough)	Cycle (trough to trough)
Dec. 1854	June 1857	Dec. 1858	30	18	48
Dec. 1858	Oct. 1860	June 1861	22	8	30
June 1861	Apr. 1865	Dec. 1867	46	32	78
Dec. 1867	June 1869	Dec. 1870	18	18	36
Dec. 1870	Oct. 1873	Mar. 1879	34	65	99
Mar. 1879	Mar. 1882	May 1885	36	38	74
May 1885	Mar. 1887	Apr. 1888	22	13	35
Apr. 1888	July 1890	May 1891	27	10	37
May 1891	Jan. 1893	June 1894	20	17	37
June 1894	Dec. 1895	June 1897	18	18	36
June 1897	June 1899	Dec. 1900	24	18	42
Dec. 1900	Sept. 1902	Aug. 1904	21	23	44
Aug. 1904	May 1907	June 1908	33	13	46
June 1908	Jan. 1910	Jan. 1912	19	24	43
Jan. 1912	Jan. 1913	Dec. 1914	12	23	35
Dec. 1914	Aug. 1918	Mar. 1919	44	7	51
Mar. 1919	Jan. 1920	July 1921	10	18	28
July 1921	May 1923	July 1924	22	14	36
July 1924	Oct. 1926	Nov. 1927	27	13	40
Nov. 1927	Aug. 1929	Mar. 1933	21	43	64
Mar. 1933	May 1937	June 1938	50	13	63
June 1938	Feb. 1945	Oct. 1945	80	13	63
Oct. 1945	Nov. 1948	Oct. 1949	37	11	48
Oct. 1949	July 1953	Aug. 1954	45	13	58
Aug. 1954	July 1957	Apr. 1958	35	9	44
Apr. 1958	May 1960	Feb. 1961	25	9	34
Feb. 1961	Nov. 1969	Nov. 1970	105	15	120

Sources: National Bureau of Economic Research and *Business Conditions Digest*.

withdrew their funds, intensifying the major depression that followed.

After 1840, foreign influence persisted, but the course of the economy was increasingly shaped by the domestic environment. By midcentury, American business cycles were more clearly internally generated; a pattern of fluctuation characteristic of modern capitalist economies had set in.

The somewhat regular pattern of fluctuations has been traced and dated by the National Bureau of Economic Research. Table 23.1 shows the timing and duration of the aggregate cycle since 1854 in the United States. The 26 cycles have averaged about 50 months in length, but this includes several periods of war. Wartime expansions, of course, tend to be longer than peaceful expansions; they last at least as long as the period of mobilization and fighting. The 45 months' average duration for the 22 peacetime cycles better describes the historical pattern. Leaving out the wartime cycles, we find 13 cycles in which the depression phase lasted longer than the ensuing prosperity. There were also two cycles in which there were as many months of contraction of output as there were months of expansion. Remembering that this is the record of a young, vigorous economy experiencing rapid technological change (and rapid spread into new frontier areas in the nineteenth century), these frequent and often protracted declines in output point to the presence of serious instability.

During the period of American industrialization (1880s through 1920s), ". . . millions lived in abject poverty in densely packed slums. . . . They struggled merely to maintain their families above the level of brutal hunger and want for such little pay that their status was a tragic anomaly in light of the prosperity enjoyed by business and industry."[16] Prosperity *was* enjoyed by business and industry. Output, productivity, and profits all climbed impressively. Yet the last decades of the nineteenth century saw frequent periods of distress and depression. From 1873 to 1879, thousands of small businesses failed, farms were lost to foreclosure, and the accumulated savings of thousands of families, caught by bank failure, disappeared. Estimates of unemployment during the long depression that began in 1873 range from 1 to 3 million. When recovery came in the 1880s, output expanded more rapidly than at any other time in U.S. history, and yet the decade was interrupted by three years of depression. Vigorous expansion did not return to the economy until late in the 1890s; the depression of the early 1890s is generally regarded as the most severe on record prior to the Great Depression. Over 4.5 million workers were unemploped in 1894, or almost 20 percent of the labor force, and unemployment remained high until 1899.[17]

The inadequacies and deficiencies of the banking community and of the monetary system operated to aggravate the mild as well as the severe cyclic disturbances not only in the nineteenth century but also well into the twentieth century. As the economy matured, the frequency of banking crises accelerated. Precipitous monetary failures occurred in 1873, 1884, 1890, 1893, and again in 1907.

World War I brought economic expansion. It was followed, however, by the severe depression of 1920–1921. Production fell by 20

[16]Foster R. Dulles, quoted in Richard O. Boyar and Herbert Morals, *Labor's Untold Story* (New York: Marzani & Munsell, 1955), p. 34.

[17]See Stanley Lebergott, *Manpower in Economic Growth: The American Record Since 1800* (New York: McGraw-Hill, 1964).

percent and employment dropped 11 percent within a year. Furthermore, prices, which had been rising since the war years, fell to less than half their peak 1920 level.

The rebound out of the 1921 trough was a strong one, and notwithstanding the downturns of 1923–1924 and 1926–1927, the 1920s were growth years. Major advances in productivity took place, employment was high, and prices were steady or gently falling. Major new industries led the expansion. Automobile production tripled during the decade, making up one-eighth of the value of manufacturing by 1929. The automobile's stimulus to the construction, steel, glass, rubber, oil, retail trade, and service industries led to widespread increases in production. These were boom years for new construction of electric power facilities and for new housing and business construction as well. Radio was a growth industry, while production of other consumer durables reached record levels.

In October 1929, the stock market collapsed. It would be difficult to support a view that the stock market break was the basic cause of the depression of the 1930s. Manufacturing had begun to falter at least three months earlier, and the construction industry had been depressed for almost two years. But the collapse of the stock market *was* spectacular. Buyers for securities vanished as everyone rushed to sell. Debts that could not be paid encompassed the lenders in the downward spiral of asset values. Moreover, the loss of wealth was being matched by the loss of income as prices, sales, and production continued to fall. There were signs that the debacle had ended in early 1931, but instead of beginning to recover the downward momentum suddenly quickened. By 1933, at least 25 percent of the labor force was unemployed. The homeless, the hungry, and the desperate were never fully counted. The economy improved slightly until 1938, when it took another plunge downward. Full employment was restored only by the all-out war spending of World War II.

Since World War II, the American economy has been plagued by instability, although depressions approaching the seriousness of the Great Depression have been avoided. Several small recessions of the 1950s were followed by prolonged prosperity in the 1960s. After 1968, however, the problem became one of inflation as well as unemployment. The rate of inflation continued to rise into the early 1970s. By 1974, inflation was at 12 percent to 13 percent a year, while 6 percent to 7 percent of the labor force were unemployed and a recession was under way.

SUMMARY

According to Say's law, aggregate demand will always automatically adjust to aggregate supply. This was roughly true of earlier societies in which production was for self-sufficient isolated units, and the little exchange that existed was by barter. It is also roughly true in socialist economies, where production and investment are planned for social use. Say's law is *not* true for modern private enterprise, capitalist economies, in which (1) production is for the market, (2) exchange operates by means of money and credit, and (3) the aim of production is private profit. Thus, despite its impressive long-run growth, the American economy has been plagued by instability. The growth of large-scale, oligopolistic, corporate capitalism in the late nineteenth century only increased this instability. As a result, ever since the Industrial Revolution and the establishment of full-blown capitalist systems, western Europe and the United States have been subject to periodic depressions of "overproduction" in which output falls, factories are idle, and millions of workers are unemployed and on relief. This periodic unemployment means that every worker and small-business owner lives with uncertainty and great tension every single day. While society loses much product, millions of individuals lose jobs, are plunged into poverty, have a feeling of total helplessness and uselessness, and suffer greatly increased physical disease (including malnutrition) and mental disease (including rises in every indicator of ill-health from insomnia to suicide).

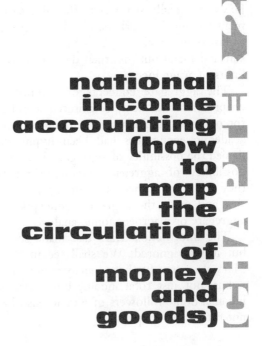

national income accounting (how to map the circulation of money and goods)

The Department of Commerce publishes detailed national income accounts (which are discussed in a lengthy appendix to this chapter). These accounts report the total flow of money and goods in the nation for a given period the same way private accounting reports the flow of money and goods through a single private enterprise. Many economists have labored to map this circulation of money and goods in the nation—just as biologists map the circulation of blood through the body. The two most famous economists who have labored at this task are Marx and Keynes.

J. M. Keynes made his major contribution in the midst of the Great Depression of the 1930s. He wanted to trace these flows in order to find out how it was possible for a nation to have a lack of demand for goods while millions of people were hungry, poorly clothed, and ill-housed. He found the answers by tracing how money may leak out of the system, how those who have money may hoard it and not spend it, while those who badly need goods have no money. He concentrated on the total or aggregate demand for goods coming from consumer spending on consumer goods and the demand from investors' spending on goods necessary for production.

Karl Marx wrote in the middle of the nineteenth century, when he had already witnessed a major depression each decade for several decades. In the midst of the misery of early British industrialization, he was especially sensitive to the effects of depression on unemployment among the workers. He also analyzed demand for goods from a class point of view, noting that workers account for most of consumer demand but that their demand is very much restricted by the limits of wage income.

The aggregate concepts of Keynes, which are stated in this chapter and the next, constituted a radical new way of thinking for orthodox, mainstream economists. Before Keynes, all orthodox academic economists had been hypnotized by Say's law, which denied the possibility of aggregate disequilibrium. Since there was no possibility of aggregate disequilibrium (depression or inflation), they had seen no need for aggregate concepts. Keynes changed all that and made the aggregate concepts the basis for a whole new aggregate or macroeconomic analysis.

The unorthodox Marx had made such an analysis long before, but it was ignored. We shall see in the following chapters how Marx also went further to analyze not total flows but flows by class —thus, not just total income but workers' income and capitalists' income. Some followers of Keynes also look at these facts, but it is not their usual emphasis.

THE CIRCULAR FLOW OF GROSS NATIONAL PRODUCT

Gross National Product (GNP) is defined as the total value of all the finished goods and services produced by a nation in a year's time. Each good or service is valued at its market selling price. The market pricing system thus provides a yardstick by means of which totally different and otherwise unrelated items can be compared and aggregated.

The national flow of production and income may be thought of as a circular flow of supply and demand between households and businesses. In this simplified picture of the economy, there is no foreign trade because if it were included, the circle of supply and demand would be broken at that point. The government sector also is not included for the sake of simplicity. Understanding the circular flow in this uncomplicated economy is essential to understanding the concepts of aggregate supply and aggregate demand. The same concepts underlie the construction of the national income and product accounts.

In a capitalist economy some households own property while others own only their power to work. The workers' households supply certain amounts of labor. The capitalist owners of property buy this labor and add to it the appropriate amounts of factories, machinery, and raw materials. At each given level of technology this will enable business to supply households with a certain amount of consumer goods and to supply other businesses with new *capital goods*. Capital goods are defined to include new factories and new machinery as well as raw materials supplied to business.

Consumer goods keep the households alive and ready for labor, and the new capital goods are available for further business expansion. Of course the services supplied by households to business as well as the products supplied by businesses to households are furnished for payment, not free of charge. In a primitive economy, services can be bartered directly for products, but a complex economy cannot be based on such a system of exchange. Payment must be made by means of money, which is the only type of effective demand in the U.S. economy.

In our simplified version of an economy (with no foreign trade and no government) the demand that calls forth the supply of business goods and services may be divided into two spending flows: private consumption and private investment. Thus *aggregate demand for the national product is equal to private spending for consumption and investment*. This concept of demand, based on consumer and investor spending, was Keynes' main analytic tool.

The payment for the supply of services from households may be similarly divided into various income streams: wages, rent, interest, and profits. Wage income includes hourly wages, piecework wages, salaries, and commissions. Profit income includes profits of both corporate and unincorporated business. Rental income includes the rent from land as well as buildings. Interest income includes all returns on borrowed money. It is assumed at this point that all of these business incomes are actually paid out to households.

The circular flow of supply and demand is depicted in Figure 24.1, which indicates how (1) money spending flows from households to business in return for (2) the flow of products from business to households. At the same time (3) the services and property of households flow to business in return for (4) the flow of money income from business to households. Notice that money moves in one direction around the circuit, whereas goods and services meet it in their equal and opposite movement. If there is no hitch, the supply and demand will flow smoothly and just balance each other in both sets of transactions.

Gross national product may be calculated in two different ways, corresponding to the money flow from households to business or the equal money flow from business to households. In the first, the aggregate money demand for all products, or the *flow of money spending* on consumer goods and investment goods, is examined.

$$\$ \text{ GNP} = \$ \text{ spending} = \$ \text{ consumption} + \$ \text{ investment}$$

CIRCULAR FLOW OF SUPPLY AND DEMAND

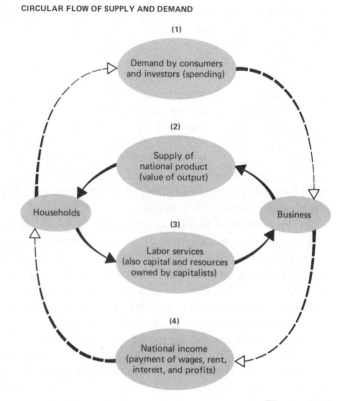

Figure 24.1

This flow of money spent for products must correspond to the equal and opposite flow of products to their final buyers. In the marketplace the money flow from purchasers is precisely the measure of the value of the GNP sold by business. Thus in Figure 24.1 the two upper loops, labeled (1) and (2), show the movement of money in one direction and the equal movement of goods and services in the the other direction. *The two are equal by definition* because the exchange price has been agreed to by both buyers and sellers. In the next chapter we will see how Marx and Keynes analyzed the problems that result when consumers and investors *intend* to spend *less* than the value of goods supplied at present prices.

The second way of calculating GNP is to add up the money paid out by businesses for all of their costs of production. Most of these costs of production constitute *flows of money income* to households. These incomes include wages paid for the services of labor, rent for the use of land, interest for the use of borrowed capital, and profit for capital ownership. Thus the two lower loops of Figure 24.1, labeled (3) and (4), depict the movement of goods and services to business in one direction and the equal movement of money as income to households in the other.

Actually businesses have other costs that have not yet been discussed. These costs make the second way of calculating GNP a little more complicated than suggested by the simple diagram in Figure 24.1. One of these costs is *depreciation,* or the funds set aside to replace the machinery and factory buildings that are used up or eventually worn out in the process of production. These funds are paid out not to any individual but to other businesses when it is time to replace the worn-out instruments of production. So when depreciation is added to the flows of money incomes, we get

$$\$ \text{ GNP} = \$ \text{ wages} + \$ \text{ rent} + \$ \text{ interest} + \$ \text{ profits} + \$ \text{ depreciation}$$

Marx emphasized this second way of looking at the flow of GNP. He agreed that the business pays out wages to workers. He also noted that business paid other businesses to replace the depreciated machinery. He stressed, in addition, the property incomes—rent, interest, and profit—that capitalists exploited from workers. Thus, he emphasized,

$$\text{GNP} = \$ \text{ wages} + \$ \text{ property incomes} + \$ \text{ depreciation}$$

We can calculate GNP, as Keynes did, in terms of all spending to purchase output; or we can calculate GNP, as Marx did, in terms of all the money flow through business to workers and capitalists (and for depreciation to other businesses). By definition the GNP calculated by either method must be equal to the same money value. Indeed, the U.S. Department of Commerce, which makes these calculations, always does arrive at the same amount by either method (after allowing for statistical mistakes).

GROSS NATIONAL PRODUCT IN REAL TERMS

To know whether a change in GNP reflects a change in national welfare, we must determine whether the change was due to a change in the economic measuring rod (prices) or a change in the *real* quantity of goods and services produced. If the national product doubles in money value but the price level has also doubled, then the real product—the goods and services available to the nation—has remained the same. Or, if GNP in current prices has risen 5 percent, but the overall price level has risen 3 percent, physical output has increased by only 2 percent.

In calculating GNP, the government must use current prices. But to make comparisons between years when price changes have occurred, the money value of GNP can be deflated by dividing the current value by an index showing how much prices have changed:

$$\frac{\text{Prices} \times \text{quantity produced} = \$\,\text{GNP}}{\text{Price index}} = \text{real (or deflated) } \$\,\text{GNP}$$

The Department of Commerce compiles price indexes for the many components of GNP. It also deflates each component by its index. Each index is constructed from the price changes that have occurred in the items that make up that component. By choosing a base year, such as 1929 (1929 = 100), against which all price changes are measured, deflated GNP data can be made comparable over the years.

POTENTIAL GROSS NATIONAL PRODUCT

Many times, part of the nation's productive capacity goes unused. Factories may stand idle or only partially used while millions of unemployed workers search for jobs. During such periods economists can calculate the approximate *potential* GNP that would obtain *if* the unemployed laborers could be put to work and *if* the factories not being utilized could be used to full capacity. The difference between potential and actual GNP is a widely used measure of the economic costs of recessions and depressions.

PER CAPITA GNP

We have noted that the actual GNP in real terms is used as a reflection of national welfare. But suppose we want to know the welfare not for the nation but for each individual. If China has the same national product as England, then the average Chinese is much worse off than the average Englishman because of the tremendous difference in population. Therefore to measure the individual welfare the GNP of a nation must be divided by the number of its population. This result is the per capita GNP. Notice, however, that per capita GNP is only an average; it does not say anything about how the GNP is distributed among individuals.

NET ECONOMIC WELFARE

Finally, suppose we have deflated GNP by price rises and by population increases. Is the resulting real per capita GNP a good measure of individual human welfare? More and more economists are coming to the conclusion that it is not a good welfare measure.

On the one side, there are some goods and services not included in the GNP because they are not given a value in the market. For example, the work of housewives is not counted in the GNP. Yet women work long, hard hours in the home, and their labor equals about one-fourth of the official GNP value. This exclusion is very inconsistent because a maid's labor is counted in the GNP to the amount of her salary, yet if she marries the house owner her labor is no longer counted and GNP is reduced. The reason for this exclusion is the sexist idea that women don't really work very hard, plus the capitalist notion that services are valuable only if they are sold in the market.

On the other side, many costs to the public are not subtracted from GNP, even though they are caused by the private capitalist production of GNP. For example, production and use of cars and trucks causes air pollution. This pollution costs the public in terms of health, such as eye and respiratory diseases, and even property damage, such as harm to trees and plants. Thus GNP should be reduced by the amount of this damage.

Moreover, some large portion of GNP is composed of wasteful or harmful goods that reduce or do not increase human welfare; this portion should not be included in GNP. For example, cigarettes are part of GNP, but they are harmful. Advertising "service" is part of GNP, but over 90% of it is pure propaganda or misinformation. The largest single waste is military spending, yet all of those billions of dollars spent to stockpile bombs and tanks are included in GNP.

It might also be noted that some projects benefit the public beyond the cost shown in GNP. For example, a dam built by the government for water and power (and counted in GNP at cost) may also produce recreation and beauty.

Therefore a new measure is needed, and some economists have argued for *net economic welfare* (NEW) to replace official GNP. NEW would equal GNP but in addition would (1) *add* housewives' labor, (2) *add* unpriced benefits (e.g., recreation from dams), (3) *subtract* unpriced costs (e.g., pollution from industry and cars), and (4) *subtract* all harmful and wasteful products.

SUMMARY

Goods flow from business to households, while labor services flow from households to business; money travels in the opposite direction around the circle. The gross national product is the money value of all the goods produced in a year. It should be corrected for inflation of prices or increase of population if it is to begin to measure welfare. But it should also be corrected to add housewives' labor and other benefits not priced in the market, and we should subtract from it all the harmful and wasteful products (including the military) plus all the costs of pollution and other environmental destruction. Only with these major corrections would a new measure of GNP reflect human welfare.

APPENDIX

We saw in Chapter 24 that if government and foreign trade are omitted, then GNP may be calculated as spending for consumption plus spending for investment.

We are now ready to bring government into the calculation of GNP and to admit that goods are sold and brought abroad. Government could be viewed as a giant household or business; but because government output of services is not sold in the marketplace, there is no obvious way to value the services it provides. The U.S. government is not to any appreciable extent an owner of any instruments of production; it receives its income by taxing the incomes of labor and of privately owned instruments of production. Yet government spending in the private sector is a very significant part of overall demand, and government employs about 18 percent of the labor force.

For our purposes the role of government in the economy will be simplified by assuming that it merely siphons money from the circular flow by taxing and injects it back into the spending stream by buying goods and services from businesses. The types of goods and services government buys and the uses to which it puts them will be considered in later chapters. Gross national product, with government spending in the economy and with foreign trade, when calculated from the expenditure side, becomes

$$\$ \text{ GNP} = \$ \text{ spending} = \$ \text{ consumption} + \$ \text{ investment}$$
$$+ \$ \text{ government} + \$ \text{ net exports} \qquad (1)$$

Net exports are the difference between what is sold and what is bought abroad. Exports bring a flow of dollars into the country in exchange for goods produced at home but sold abroad. Imports result in a flow of dollars out of the country for the purchase of goods produced abroad. If more is exported than imported, the net figure is an addition to the total amount of spending taking place for domestically produced goods and services. Foreign trade is also discussed in greater detail in a later chapter.

With governments in the picture another cost of doing business must enter the calculation of production costs: sales or excise taxes. These taxes include general sales taxes on all or most commodities, such as a 5 percent state tax on all sales. They also include special taxes, such as the tax on cigarettes, that affect only the purchasers of one commodity. In either case the government extracts the money at the point of purchase before it can be considered as income by business. These are sometimes called indirect taxes because they are not a direct tax on the income of any individual or business. From the income or cost side GNP is now calculated by adding the sales taxes as a cost of doing business. Thus

$$\$ \text{ GNP} = \$ \text{ cost of production} = \$ \text{ all wages} + \$ \text{ interest} + \$ \text{ profit}$$
$$+ \$ \text{ rent} + \$ \text{ sales taxes} \qquad (2)$$

Net National Product

Net national product (NNP) differs from GNP in only one respect: NNP does *not* include the amount of depreciation that has occurred during the year. *Depreciation* is defined as the amount of capital used up in the production process. The NNP is very useful as a measure of what part of the economy's total production is actually available for use. Certainly production that merely replaces machinery that has worn out and is no longer usable should not be considered as adding to the amount of capital available to the economy. Thus to compare useful production in two countries we would compare NNP, not GNP, because when we compare product actually available for use, we are not interested in the amount of depreciation or capital used up in producing the available product. To arrive at the figure for NNP, simply subtract depreciation from GNP.

$$\$ \text{ NNP} = \$ \text{ GNP} - \$ \text{ depreciation} \qquad (3)$$

In the national accounts depreciation is called *capital consumption allowance*. Unfortunately, the capital consumption allowance does not always reflect physical depreciation accurately because it involves many problems of estimation that are affected by the practices of accountants. These accountants must view not only the expected life of capital equipment but also the implications for tax liability. From the cost or income side NNP can be calculated by eliminatng depreciation (or the capital consumption allowance).

$$\$ \, NNP = \$ \text{ wages} + \$ \text{ rent} + \$ \text{ interest} + \$ \text{ profits} + \$ \text{ sales taxes} \tag{4}$$

If we were still excluding government, NNP and national income would be identical. *National income* is defined as the income of the nation in a year's time that is wholly derived from the production of final, usable goods and services. It is the income going to *all* the economic classes: wages to workers, rent to landlords, interest to lenders, and profit to capitalists. Sales taxes and all other indirect business taxes go to the government and do not become income to any class of citizens. When they are subtracted from NNP, the national income is simply

$$\$ \text{ National income} = \$ \text{ wages} + \$ \text{ rent} + \$ \text{ interest} + \$ \text{ profits} \tag{5}$$

or

$$\$ \text{ National income} = \$ \, NNP - \text{ sales tax} \tag{6}$$

Personal and Disposable Income

The government imposes various taxes on the national income but also adds to the income stream many kinds of welfare payments. Therefore the total of payments to all classes in production (i.e., the national income) is not the amount of income that households actually have at their disposal. Households' income comes from production *plus* various welfare payments *minus* various taxes.

In order to proceed from national income to the income that actually goes to people (i.e., *personal income*), various additions and subtractions must be made. First, some corporate profits are kept by corporations and are not paid out to individual stockholders. These profits, called *retained corporate profits*, must be subtracted from national income in the process of determining the personal income actually going to individuals. Second, the government collects taxes from corporations according to the amount of their annual profits; these *corporate profit taxes* are also subtracted from national income. Third, individuals pay out of their wage income certain compulsory contributions for social insurance to the government (these are payments for what is usually called *social security*); these also must be subtracted from the national income.

On the positive side, the government pays *interest on the national debt* to individuals; this must be added to the national income because it does become personal income. Finally, the government makes many *transfer payments*, or transfers from all taxpayers to various individuals for reasons other than current service rendered to the government. Typical transfer payments are unemployment compensation, farm subsidies, veterans' benefits, and social security payments by government to individuals. All such payments must be added to national income if we wish to calculate personal income. Totaling all the additions and subtractions from national income, the result is personal income. The procedure is indicated by the following unwieldy equation:

$$
\begin{aligned}
\text{\$ Personal income} = \ & \text{\$ national income} \\
& - \text{\$ retained corporate profits} \\
& - \text{\$ corporate income taxes} \\
& - \text{\$ contributions for social insurance} \\
& + \text{\$ government transfer payments} \\
& + \text{\$ net interest paid by government} \quad (7)
\end{aligned}
$$

Finally, there is *disposable personal income*, which is the amount of money actually at the disposal of individuals and households for spending on consumption or for personal saving. In order to find this quantity, *personal income taxes*, which are the taxes an individual or household must pay in proportion to its yearly income, must be deducted. The result is expressed as

$$
\begin{aligned}
\text{Disposable personal income} = \ & \text{personal income} \\
& - \text{personal income taxes} \quad (8)
\end{aligned}
$$

Consumers may now spend and save out of disposable personal income. If consumption expenditures are subtracted, we arrive at personal saving.

A simplified listing of the accounts discussed here is shown in Table 24A1.

An example of the actual figures in these accounts for one year is shown in Table 24A.2.

Saving and Investment

It is necessary to distinguish between the concepts of wealth, capital, and investment. *Wealth*, the broadest concept, is the total holding by everyone of all durable consumer goods plus natural resources) *plus* the total holding of the entire stock of capital. Wealth is not measured in the national income and product accounts. A high level of production certainly means that a large stock of

TABLE 24A.1

NATIONAL INCOME ACCOUNTS

Gross National Product
  − Depreciation (or Capital Consumption)
= *Net National Product*
  − Indirect Business Taxes (Mostly Sales Taxes)
= *National Income*
  − Retained Corporate Profits
  − Corporate Income Taxes
  − Contributions for Social Insurance
  + Government Transfer Payments
  + Net Interest Paid by Government
= *Net National Product*
  − Personal Income Taxes
= *Disposable Personal Income*
  − Consumption Expenditures
= *Personal Saving*

wealth exists in the form of productive capital. The national accounts, however, measure only the value of the flow of production, and hence income. They are not designed to measure the holding of wealth either as capital or, for that matter, in the form of claims measured in money, which would be called *financial wealth*. Capital is defined as the total value of all existing buildings and factories,

TABLE 24A.2

NATIONAL INCOME ACCOUNTS FOR 1973
(IN BILLIONS OF DOLLARS)

Gross National Product		$1289.1
− Depreciation (or Capital Consumption)	$110.0	
Net National Product		1179.1
− Indirect Business Taxes (Mostly Sales Taxes)	125.2	
National Income		1053.9
− Retained Corporate Profits and Corporate Income Taxes	81.2	
—Contributions for Social Insurance	92.1	
+ Transfer Payments	117.5	
+ Net Interest Paid by Government and Consumers	37.1	
Personal Income		1035.4
− Personal Income Taxes	152.9	
Disposable Personal Income		882.5
− Consumption Expenditures	827.7	
Personal Saving		54.8

Source: Federal Reserve Bulletin, May 1974. The Item Consumption Expenditures includes $22.5 billion in net interest paid by consumers.

machines and equipment for production, and inventories. *Inventories* are defined as the existing stocks of raw materials, goods in process, and finished goods stockpiled.

Investment may then be defined simply as the *change* in capital, its increase or decrease within a year or some other period. This means that any individual investment that does not increase the amount of capital, such as the purchase of old shares of stock by one individual from another, does not count as net investment for the nation. Even if a corporation sells new stock, the proceeds do not bcome net investment in the economy until the corporation actually uses the money to purchase new factories, equipment, or inventories. In other words, the investment discussed here is not mere financial dealing or individual investment of money, but the *real*, or physical, expansion of the nation's economic capacity. More specifically, this year's investment consists of new construction, new producer's durable equipment, and the change in business inventories.

Only one more distinction in this area of analysis need be made. The total investment in the economy is called *gross investment*. It includes both *net investment*, or investment to expand productive capacity, and *replacement investment*, or investment needed to replace the depreciation of present productive capacities.

There is, of course, a close connection between net and gross investment and net and gross national product. The connection can be easily stated through the spending approach to national product. Leaving aside government spending and net export spending, we find that

$ Gross national product = $ consumption + $ gross investment (9)

In this equation gross investment includes replacement investment, which is equal to depreciation. Similarly, without government or net export, we find that

$ Net national product = $ consumption + $ net investment (10)

Having defined investment, we must now define saving. Most of our national product goes for consumption—that is, the aggregate purchase of consumer goods and services by all U.S. households. *Whatever part of national income or product is not used for consumption is defined as saving.* Thus the following definition may be written (aside from government and foreign trade):

$ Net national product = $ consumption + $ saving   (11)

Aside from the government, there are only two sources of saving in the economy. These are (1) the personal saving of individuals and households and (2) the retained profits of businesses. Notice that the depreciation funds put aside by business, a form of gross savings, come of the gross national product. Therefore net saving is what remains from net national product after consumer spending, while gross saving is what remains from gross national product after consumer spending out of it.

Notice that both saving and investment are each by definition equal to national product (net or gross) less consumption. Therefore they must by definition equal each other. Leaving out government and foreign trade, we may write:

$$\text{\$ Consumption} + \text{\$ net investment} = \text{\$ consumption} + \text{\$ saving} \quad (12)$$

The equality between saving and investment is an accounting identity. Both are equal to national income minus consumption, by definition. Had we started from GNP, depreciation funds would have been included on both sides, making gross investment equal to gross saving of business and individuals. (The following equations will hold for net or gross amounts, so we do not distinguish between them.)

With government included, the identity becomes

$$\text{\$ Consumption} + \text{\$ investment} + \text{\$ government} =$$
$$\text{\$ consumption} + \text{\$ savings}$$
$$+ \text{\$ taxes} \quad (13)$$

This is so because national product is now the sum both of the three spending flows and of the three allocations between consumption, saving, and tax payments. The sum of investment spending and government spending is identical with the sum of private saving and taxation. If government spending and taxation are equal, the government budget in the national accounting framework is in balance. In practice, the difference between government spending and government taxation is called *government saving*, which may be positive if taxes exceed government spending or negative if there is a budget deficit.

When foreign trade is added, the identity becomes

$$\text{\$ consumption} + \text{\$ investment} + \text{\$ government}$$
$$+ \text{\$ exports} = \text{\$ consumption}$$
$$+ \text{\$ saving} + \text{\$ taxes} + \text{\$ imports} \quad (14)$$

This identity can be understood as representing, on the left side, the expenditures for goods and services by the four spending sectors and, on the right side, the uses of national income. The difference between exports and imports is often called *net exports*.

If it is positive, it indicates that foreigners cannot pay for all U.S. exports with the money spent on imports from them. Hence they are increasing the total demand for U.S. goods. Since they are putting money into the U.S. economy, net exports is also called *net foreign investment*.

By rearranging accounting terms and subtracting consumption from both sides, the overall identity between saving and investment can be written as follows:

$$\text{\$ Investment} + (\text{\$ exports} - \text{\$ imports}) = \text{\$ saving} \\ + (\text{\$ taxes} \\ - \text{\$ government}) \quad (15)$$

The sum of net domestic private investment and net foreign investment is identical to the sum of net private saving and governmental saving. Or, in brief, saving equals investment in the national accounts.

The Value Added Concept

The GNP of the United States includes only final products. It avoids counting the value of the same product more than once when this product appears at various intermediate stages of the production process. Suppose *both* the value of all the steel produced and the value of all the automobiles produced were counted in GNP. Since a great deal of steel is used in automobile production, we would be counting the value of that steel twice, once by itself and once as a principal ingredient in automobiles.

The correct procedure is to include only the *value added* by capital and labor (and land) in each industry—that is, the increase in the worth of the product in the production process of that industry beyond the worth of the raw materials bought from other industries. Therefore the value added by capital and labor (and land) to the raw material in the steel industry would be counted. Then the value added by capital and labor (and land) in making automobiles out of the steel would also be counted. But the value of the steel, or any other product from another industry, used by the auto industry would not be counted again. The whole calculation of gross product (using the cost of production, or income, approach) may be illustrated as follows:

$$\text{Gross product in steel and auto industry} \\ = \text{steel (wages + profits + rent + interest + depreciation)} \\ + \text{auto (wages + profits + rent + interest + depreciation)} \\ (16)$$

Notice that neither the cost of the iron or coal used in the steel industry nor that of the steel or rubber tires used in the auto industry is included; both are values produced by other industries and not values added by this industry. The value added is thus less than the price in each industry by exactly the amount of goods and materials bought from other industries.

SUMMARY

For the purposes of analysis economists try to keep accounts measuring all of national output. Everything put together is called the *gross national product*, the demand for which comes from consumers, investors, government, and foreign buyers. Although it is an important measure, we should not be mesmerized by the size of GNP because it includes many wasteful or even harmful goods and services (advertising, cigarettes, military). A second concept is the *net national product*, which equals GNP minus depreciation. Third, *national income* equals NNP minus sales taxes (and a few similar taxes). Fourth, *personal income* is what actually winds up in the hands of individuals; so it equals national income earned in the usual ways plus welfare and subsidies and interest payments from the government minus profits kept by corporations and corporate taxes and employees' social security taxes paid to the government. Fifth, *disposable income* is equal to personal income minus personal income taxes. Finally, *savings* equals disposable income minus consumption. Because investment is also defined as all income or output minus consumption, saving and investment are equal by definition in the national income accounts (but, as will be seen in the next chapter, what some people plan to save and others plan to invest may not be equal).

income
determination

In this chapter we discuss three very different analyses of how national income is determined, why unemployment and inflation occur, and what are the correct political policies to cure these problems. The first is the conservative position, presented by J. B. Say and almost all the classical and neoclassical economists. The second is the liberal position presented by J. M. Keynes and his followers. The third is the radical position, presented by Karl Marx and many other radicals.

THE CONSERVATIVE VIEW OF J. B. SAY

The conservative view, first presented by J. B. Say, is that unemployment and inflation are accidents caused by factors external to the economy. They are always minor and temporary; and the capitalist economy, if left to itself, will always automatically come back to full employment and stable prices in a short time. Say's law states that any supply of goods calls forth its own demand, so there can *never* be overproduction relative to demand for any length of time. J. B. Say had a very simple picture of the money flows in the economy, excluding government and foreign trade (Figure 25.1).

The picture in Figure 25.1 assumes that

CONSERVATIVE (SAY) VIEW OF INCOME FLOW

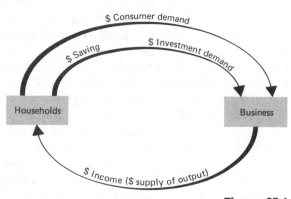

Figure 25.1

$$\$ \text{ Saving } = \$ \text{ investment demand}$$

and that

$$\$ \text{ Income} = \$ \text{ profit} + \text{rent} + \text{interest} + \text{wages} = \$ \text{ supply of output}$$

There is an important grain of truth in what J. B. Say claimed. It is true that output, which is supplied to the market and sold there, generates income. The capitalist pays out wages, rent, and interest. The residual from sales, whether positive or negative, may be called profits. These incomes all go to households (if we assume that corporations pay out all profits to stockholders). The households normally use all the money for consumption and investment. Since saving is defined as all nonconsumption, it is automatically equal to investment in this case.

Say and the other classical economists claimed that all income not spent for consumption would always be invested because if more money is saved than invested, competition among lenders will cause the rate of interest to fall. A lower rate of interest stimulates investment, which rises until it equals the supply of goods. Finally, if supply of goods is temporarily excessive, this causes very temporary unemployment. The unemployment causes competition among workers, which leads to lower wages. The lower wages stimulate capitalists to demand more labor (since it's cheaper now), which brings back full employment. Therefore the classical economists concluded that the capitalist system will automatically restore full employment with stable prices after any temporary dislocation. So the government should do nothing.

THE LIBERAL
VIEW OF J. M. KEYNES

Keynes (1883–1946) is perhaps the most important economist of the first half of the twentieth century. His background does not appear to be that of a radical or an earth shaker. Born into a respected English family and educated in the best British schools, Keynes worked for His Majesty's Civil Service and the Bank of England, edited the *Economic Journal*, and wrote careful treatises on Indian finances and formal logic as well as the general problems of money. Keynes was always considered one of the Establishment in cultural, governmental, and financial circles, yet he rocked the Establishment both in England and the United States by demolishing the myth of Say's law and automatic full employment.

Say's law had been attacked before by such unorthodox economists as Malthus and Marx. Keynes, however, attacked it in detail, using the respectable academic tools of the classical and neoclassical economists. In his most famous book, written at the depths of the Great Depression, he destroyed Say's law and proved that the equilibrium level of the economy might be either at a point of heavy unemployment or at overly full employment and inflation.[1]

EQUILIBRIUM OF
AGGREGATE SUPPLY AND DEMAND

Keynesian economists use the idea of an equilibrium of the forces of aggregate supply and demand as their important analytical tool for understanding the level of output and employment. *Aggregate supply* is defined as the total output that business produces and plans to sell.

Aggregate demand, a concept for which there is no direct statistical measure, is defined as the total dollar amount of final goods and services that consumers, businessmen, government, and foreigners *plan* to buy from the business sector. Equilibrium exists when planned aggregate demand equals planned aggregate supply.

It was noted in Chapter 24 that statisticians make supply and demand equal in the national income accounts, but that is only by including unwanted and unplanned accumulation of inventories as "demand" by definition. The situation is quite different if the demand that arises from planned (or intended) spending is examined. *Planned spending* is defined as all spending except the spending on unwanted increases in inventories. Planned supply and planned demand will be equal only when the economy is at equilibrium,

---

[1]John Maynard Keynes, *The General Theory of Employment, Interest and Money* (New York: Harcourt Brace Jovanovich, 1936).

LIBERAL (KEYNES) VIEW OF INCOME FLOW

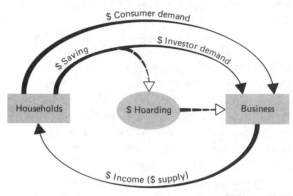

Figure 25.2

meaning that buyers' and sellers' desires exactly agree at present prices. If however, 1000 bushels of ripe tomatoes go unsold, then the supply at present prices is greater than the planned demand.

The problem may be explained another way by saying: there is equilibrium only if consumption plus planned investment are equal to consumption plus saving. *Saving* is defined to be the difference betwen income and planned consumption spending. Keynes argued that equilibrium is maintained only if saving out of income is just equal to planned investment spending.

The problem of economic equilibrium is illustrated in its simplest form in Figure 25.2. Business pays the national income to households. Then, if there is equilibrium, all of that income is spent by households to buy goods from business. This implies that all income that is not spent for consumption is saved in the form of investment spending. If some savings are not invested, but are diverted into hoards of money, then there will not be equilibrium of supply and demand.

The picture in Figure 25.2 assumes that

$ Saving = $ investment demand + $ hoarding or $ dishoarding

DISEQUILIBRIUM,
UNEMPLOYMENT, AND INFLATION

Say assumed that all output supplied to the market meant income and that all income is invariably spent, either for consumption or investment. Keynes, on the contrary, points out that some income may not be spent for either consumption or investment in a given period. "Hoarding" means *not* spending income. If all income is not spent, then some income drops out of the circular flow of money into inactive hoards. For example, money deposited in banks, if the banks do not lend it to anybody, is not spent.

Keynes pointed out that if all the money income—wages, profit, interest, and rent—from supplying goods to the market is not spent, then there may be disequilibrium. *Disequilibrium* here means simply that the total money demand for all goods is less than the value of all goods at present prices. When demand is less than supply, inventories accumulate and capitalists lose money, so they cut back on production and fire workers. The economy may reach equilibrium again only at a much lower level of supply, where vast numbers of workers are unemployed.

Keynes described this new situation of an unemployment level of equilibrium as one in which some savings are not invested but are hoarded, thus reducing demand. He pointed out that Say was wrong to think lower rates of interest would automatically stimulate investment. Investors invest only for profit, but suppose the outlook is for very little profit or even losses. No capitalist will be willing to borrow money even at very low interest rates because of the risk involved based on the poor profit expectations in the future—so saving may remain permanently higher than investment.

Moreover, Keynes argued that Say was wrong to think lower prices would automatically increase demand. He pointed out that lower prices will decrease wage and profit incomes, but the lower incomes mean less spending and even less demand. Further, Keynes argued that Say was also wrong to think lower wages would mean more demand for labor. Wages are the largest single component of consumer demand. If wages are lowered, demand for goods falls. Yet a falling demand for goods means capitalists' demand for labor may fall even further.

The opposite situation may result in inflation. Remember that inflation means rising prices (whereas deflation means falling prices). Suppose that planned demand is greater than supply or that planned spending is greated than income, or simply that planned investment is greater than saving. All of these words describe the same thing: At present prices, excess demand drives prices and outputs upward. At first, the only effect might be prosperity or rising output and employment. But when the barrier of full employment is reached, output can rise no higher, so a still-higher demand can result only in higher prices or inflation. In the case of inflation, according to Keynes, spending may be greater than national income because additional money moves out of hoards into investment, as shown in Figure 25.2. This movement of money out of hoards is called *dishoarding*. Spending can also exceed income if the spenders are borrowing from banks and the banking system as a whole is creating new money.

KEYNES AND CONSUMER BEHAVIOR

Having decided that inflation and depression are determined by the movements of aggregate demand relative to supply, Keynes' main enterprise is the explanation of those movements. He gives particular attention to deducing the psychological bases for the decision of households to save or consume at different economic levels.

Keynes[2] begins by classifying the elements of aggregate demand for net product into two categories: consumer spending and net investment spending. He first considers the behavior of consumer spending, which he believes is determined for the most part by the level of national income. His reasoning as to consumer behavior is based on certain broad psychological presumptions: (1) At a very low income level, the average individual still needs some minimum consumption and therefore will spend all his income on consumption and may even dip into savings or go into debt to spend more than his whole current income on consumption. (2) As his income rises, he needs a smaller percentage of it to cover his minimum needs, so at some break-even point he reaches an equality of income received and consumption spending. (3) As income rises to a very high level, consumption needs and desires may be filled through the use of a smaller portion of income, so an increasing percentage may be saved.

This usual behavior of consumers is illustrated in Figure 25.3. The line labeled Income (Consumption + Saving) shows the total income at each point; it is equal by definition to the income spent for consumption plus the income saved. *If* income exactly equaled consumption at every income level, then that line (at 45°) would also show consumer spending. In reality they are different. The line labeled Consumption shows how much consumer spending there actually is at each level of income. The space between these two lines obviously reflects the amount by which consumption differs from income. At low levels of income, consumer spending by the poor is greater than their income, so there is *dissaving* (using up of reserves or going into debt) by these consumers. At high levels of income, consumer spending by the rich is much less than their income, so there is saving by this group.

This Keynesian schedule of aggregate consumer spending at different income levels is called the *consumption function*. It tells us that in the short run consumption is not some constant proportion of income. Rather, as income rises, consumption rises, but saving rises too. Therefore *as income rises, the percentage of income spent on consumption declines*. The relationship between income and consumption is explored more thoroughly in Chapter 26.

[2]Ibid.

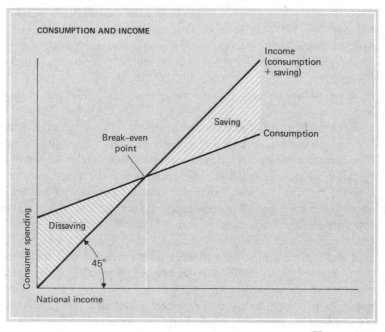

Figure 25.3

KEYNES AND AGGREGATE DEMAND

Consumption spending is the largest component of aggregate demand. In a simple economy, with no government and foreign transactions, consumption and investment together constitute aggregate demand. As has been seen, the demand may be greater or less than the aggregate supply of output that could be produced if everyone were fully employed. Consumption spending is generally considered the most stable component of aggregate demand. If consumption really behaves in a stable fashion, then, given any level of investment, our knowledge of consumer behavior enables us to derive the level of equilibrium income associated with that level of investment.

Take any arbitrary level of investment. Assume that this level of investment is constant (i.e., does not change when income changes). This investment is combined with consumer demand, according to Keynes' view of consumer behavior, in Figure 25.4. The aggregate-demand, or spending, line is derived by adding the constant amount of investment to the consumption schedule at every level of income.

The dollar amount of income is by definition equal to the dollar value of output. This is why the supply of output is shown as rising at a 45° angle, always remaining exactly equal to income received.

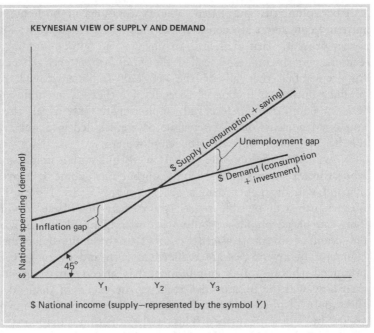

KEYNESIAN VIEW OF SUPPLY AND DEMAND

Figure 25.4

Figure 25.4 illustrates the economic results at three levels of income or output. If there is a relatively small labor force available, then full employment can produce only Income 1, a relatively low level of output. If there is a larger labor force, then full employment can produce Income 2. With a relatively large labor force, full employment can produce Income 3, a relatively high level of output.

It is clear that there is only one level of income at which aggregate demand (consumption plus investment) is equal to aggregate supply (output, or consumption plus saving): Income 2. This is called the *equilibrium level of income and output*. If full employment happens to produce this level, there is no problem.

Assume, on the contrary, that there is a large labor force, which at full employment produces Income 3. At this level it is obvious that the total of planned spending (aggregate demand) is less than the level of output (aggregate supply). The difference, labeled Unemployment Gap, represents goods and services produced that neither businesses nor consumers want to buy. These goods and services become unwanted inventories. In the next production period businessmen will cut back on production to avoid the continued buildup of unwanted inventories. This decrease in production (and in the number of workers employed) must continue until output at Income 2 is reached. At this point output is just equal to what will be voluntarily purchased. The expectations of both business-men and consumers are consistent at Income 2. There are no longer forces at work that will lead to changes in output and income. This is why Income 2 is called the *equilibrium* level of income. But remember that all of the workers fully employed *could* produce output or Income 3, so at level 2 there is unemployment. It is an equilibrium *below* full employment. Only if all the un-employed workers died of a plague or were killed in a war would this be an equilibrium with full employment.

Now assume the opposite case. If we begin with a much smaller labor force that can produce only output or Income 1, aggregate demand will be higher than aggregate supply. (See Figure 25.4.) Businessmen will be able to sell more than they have produced. This can be accomplished only with an unplanned and unwanted reduction of inventories—*disinvestment* to the national income ac-countant. In inventories are reduced to zero and no more can be produced (because full employment has already been attained), then how will the businessman react to the excess of demand over the supply of goods? Obviously, because he can produce no more goods, he will raise prices. This is the inflation situation (to be considered further).

If the businessman can find more workers (perhaps by import-ing foreign workers), he then will produce more in the next period. This process must continue until Income 2, the equilibrium level of income, is reached. Thus, if the national income is initially above or below Income 2, the forces of supply and demand will push it toward Income 2. At Income 2 the income level will tend to stabilize until something causes an increase or decrease in in-vestment. What happens when investment changes will be dis-cussed in Chapter 26.

In this example there is no reason to suppose that the equilibrium level of output and income is the level at which the entire work force is fully employed. As has been demonstrated, the level of output that could be produced (if the work force were fully employed) could be higher or lower than that produced at In-come 2.

If full employment of workers happens to produce output and national income at Income 3, then at full employment the aggregate supply will be greater than the aggregate demand. In other words, in this case, at full employment, saving (plus consumption) is *greater* than investment (plus consumption). This implies that the excess of money saved is being hoarded. Then there may be price declines or unplanned and unwanted increases of inventories. Out-put and national income therefore begin to decline toward Income 2 where aggregate demand and supply come into equilibrium. At

Income 2 the lower level of output implies a lower level of employment. In other words, the equilibrium level of output is below the full-employment level of output. Therefore unemployment is the result of the gap betwen aggregate supply and demand at the full-employment income level.

If, in the opposite case, full employment of workers can produce only output and national income at Income 1, the aggregate supply available at that level is less than the aggregate demand. In other words, in that instance saving (plus consumption) is *less* than investment (plus consumption). This implies that there is an excess of investment funds, which comes from dishoarding of previous savings or from an increased money supply. Then there may be unplanned declines in inventories and attempts to increase output beyond the full-employment level. Because output cannot rise beyond the full-employment level, prices must then begin to rise. Therefore the result of the gap between the demand for output and the smaller supply of it is price inflation. The inflationary tendency will continue until the *money* value of national output and national income approach the Income 2 equilibrium level (although *physical* output cannot go above the given full-employment level of Income 1).

The Keynesian analysis, in its simplest form, demonstrates how the nation's income is determined by the equilibrium betwen aggregate demand and aggregate supply. It shows that this level of income may be well *below* the level that could be generated by producing with the labor force fully employed, so the equilibrium level of a capitalist economy may be such as to cause large-scale unemployment. On the other side, the Keynesian analysis shows that the level of income and spending may be *above* the production possible with the labor force fully employed, in which case the equilibrium level of a capitalist economy may be such as to cause considerable price inflation.

THE RADICAL
VIEW OF KARL MARX

Keynes admits that capitalism may produce unemployment or inflation. Yet while he recognizes these problems (whose existence is not admitted by Say), he believes reformed government policies can solve these problems within capitalism. Karl Marx made the same critical attack on Say's law (long before Keynes was born) and proved that capitalism is subject to periodic attacks of mass unemployment. Unlike Keynes, however, he argued that the capitalist diseases of unemployment and inflation can be cured not by reforms but only by replacing capitalism completely with the

RADICAL (MARX) VIEW OF INCOME FLOW

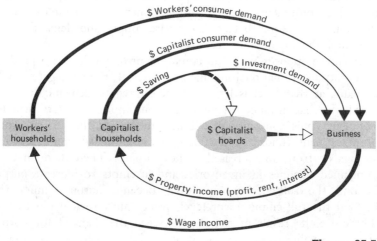

Figure 25.5

new economic system of socialism. These policy differences are discussed in later chapters.

Marx's distinctive contribution to income determination analysis is to point out the very different behavior of workers' wage income and demand from capitalists' property income and demand. This distinction is shown in Figure 25.5.

Marx divides income into two flows:

$$\$ \text{ Income} = \$ \text{ wage income} + \$ \text{ property income}$$

He assumes that workers are unable to save any of their low income:

$$\$ \text{ Wage income} = \$ \text{ workers' consumption}$$

But capitalists have high enough incomes from profit, rent, and interest so that they save as well as consume:

$$\$ \text{ Property income} = \$ \text{ capitalist consumption} + \$ \text{ capitalist saving}$$

Capitalists have so much saving that they may not see profitable ways of investing all of it. Then they may invest some and hoard the rest:

$$\$ \text{ Capitalist saving} = \$ \text{ capitalist investment} + \$ \text{ capitalist hoarding}$$

Thus Marx agrees with Keynes that saving may be greater than

planned investment (leading to unemployment), but he stresses
that this is a problem caused by capitalist behavior and the distribution of income. These problems of consumption and investment
are examined in the next two chapters.

SUMMARY

This chapter shows three views of income determination. The
conservative, J. B. Say, sees an automatic adjustment mechanism
keeping the circular flow of the economy uninterrupted at full employment. The liberal, J. M. Keynes, sees the flow interrupted by
hoarding, with no automatic return to full employment, but believes the capitalist government can correct the imbalance. The
radical, Karl Marx, agrees that capitalism often operates with unemployment; he separates the flows into workers' and capitalists'
income and spending, and finds the problem to be caused by the
basic relations of capitalism and unsolvable within capitalism.

consumption

The pattern of consumer behavior plays an important role in aggregate economics. This chapter looks at some factors influencing the relationship between consumption and income, the so-called consumption function, and examines the way in which this relationship affects the size of changes in the level of national income.

PSYCHOLOGICAL PROPENSITIES AND SOCIAL FACTS

Keynesian economists use certain shorthand terms to describe the relationship between consumption and income, The *average propensity to consume* (APC) is the portion of income spent for consumption, or the ratio of consumption to income at any particular level of income. Similarly, the *average propensity to save* (APS) is the ratio of saving to income at this particular level of income. (Remember that saving is defined as all income not consumed.)

Keynesian economists also speak of the *marginal propensity to consume* (MPC), which can be thought of as the portion that will be spent out of any additional increment to income. It is defined as the ratio of the change in consumption to the change in income. Similarly, the *marginal propensity to save* (MPS) is the ratio of the change in saving to the change in income. (Some of these relationships are explored further in the appendix to this chapter.)

The use of the word *propensity* to describe consumer behavior seems to imply that consumers follow some purely innate psychological laws. On the contrary, according to radical and Marxist economists, consumer behavior is determined not by any natural drives but by social conditioning. We are not born with a desire for television sets. Nor is there any innate compulsion to consume exactly 90 percent of our income and save 10 percent. Our desires for television sets, as well as our decisions on the ratio of consumption and saving to income, are determined by society's attitudes, ideologies, and institutions. Certainly family background has a significant influence on consumption habits, as do secular and religious educational systems. And last but not least, the vast volume of advertising in the U.S. economy affects the pattern and even the aggregate amount of consumption.

Thus consumer psychology is largely socially determined. Even more important than consumer psychology or desires, however, are the objective social facts of how income is distributed. Even if they have the very same psychological attitudes, an unemployed worker with a tiny income will not be able to save anything (and may dissave, or go into debt), whereas a businessman with a million-dollar income may consume only 10 percent of his income (and still have a very high consumption standard). Thus the data show that groups with very low incomes spend all (or more than all) their incomes on consumption. Groups with very high incomes spend only a small percentage (but more dollars) on consumption; the rest they save, in the form of either hoards or investments.

Obviously a change in the distribution of income will affect the percentage of income spent on consumption. Hence if society taxes the rich and gives to the poor, the percentage of income spent on consumption (the propensity to consume) will usually rise. But if society taxes the poor and gives to the rich, the percentage of income spent on consumption will usually fall.

Propensity to consume therefore depends mainly on just two factors (although it is influenced by many others): (1) consumer psychology as determined by social conditioning and (2) how society distributes income. In this context the term *propensity to consume* is perhaps misleading. A more neutral term, perhaps *consumption ratio*, might more easily include behavior based on both psychological desires and income distribution. Because most economic literature does use *propensity to consume*, we bow in this text to tradition, always remembering that it refers not to innate drives but to socially conditioned psychology and the objective facts of income distribution.

THE DISTRIBUTION OF INCOME

Comparative studies of family budgets show that families with higher disposable incomes save a much larger portion of their income than do lower-income families. Families in the very lowest income brackets are so poor that as a group they actually dissave. Of course there are exceptions: some families in the high brackets dissave, and many in the lower brackets save. On the whole, however, higher-income families consume a lower portion of their income.[1] Families earning profits (mostly in high income brackets) consumed only 40 percent to 50 percent of their income. Families living on wage income (mostly in low income brackets) consume 90 percent to 100 percent of their income. Thus, as noted previously, any change in distribution of income toward higher-income, profit-making families will lower the average propensity to consume. Any shift in income distribution toward low-income, wage-earning families will raise the average propensity to consume.

It is therefore instructive to examine the distribution of income in the United States. Until recently a majority even of Americans thought of the United States as an affluent society in which most people live in a nice, suburban home and have two cars, a color television plus one or two black and white televisions, a washer, a dryer, a dishwasher, and the thousand and one other conveniences of modern life. Many, including economists and other authorities, were surprised if not shocked to learn that a vast amount of poverty exists in the richest country in the world. In 1972 there were still 24.5 million Americans living below the official (understated) poverty level of income.[2]

Striking inequalities of income distribution were also described in Chapter 16. (See Table 16.1.) At one extreme are those who live in abject poverty, the lowest 20 percent of all families with only 5 percent of all family income (and the lowest 20 percent of all unrelated individuals with only 3 percent of all individual income). At the other extreme, the top 20 percent of all families had almost 42 percent of all family income (and the top 20 percent of all unrelated individuals had almost 51 percent of all individual income). Among the wealthy are the elite, the richest 2 percent, whose incomes range from $25,000 to an estimated $100 million per year.

Because these estimates are based on income tax returns, many economists argue that the statistics severely underestimate the extent of the inequality in the distribution of income. They main-

---

[1]Simon Kuznets, *Shares of Upper Income Groups in Income and Savings* (New York: National Bureau of Economic Research, 1953).

[2]U.S. Department of Commerce, Bureau of the Census.

tain that the number of very poor people is underestimated. Furthermore, these data do not include income from expense accounts and fringe benefits of various types, both of which accrue primarily to the upper middle class and wealthy because of their connections with large corporations. Specific tax allowances—for example, the notorious oil depletion allowance—increase the money received but not reported by the wealthy. Moreover, underreporting of income is most serious on income from dividends, interest, and rent—the primary sources of income for the rich—and least significant on income from wages and salaries—the source of income for middle- and low-income families. Taking all of these qualifications into account, income is unquestionably more unequally distributed than the statistics indicate.[3]

Furthermore, taxes do little, if anything, to reduce this inequality (this issue was more fully discussed in Chapter 20.) It is commonly supposed that the U.S. tax system takes a higher percentage of the income of the wealthy than of the poor. The income tax does tend to reduce income inequalities, although the effect is much smaller than most people imagine. However, analysis of the total tax burden reveals that taxes actually increase inequality in the distribution of income because sales taxes, excise taxes, property taxes, and social security taxes all take a much larger percentage of the poor man's income than of the rich man's.

B. A. Musgrave, a recognized authority on taxes, has analyzed the total tax burden on income along the entire distributional spectrum. He found that families with incomes below $2,000 per year, certainly a level of abject poverty, paid out one-third of their incomes in taxes. As incomes got higher, people paid a lower percentage in taxes. For example, families in the $10,000–$15,000 bracket paid a portion of their income that was nearly one-third lower than that paid by families with incomes below $2,000. Only for the wealthiest 5 percent of families did the total tax bite exceed that which the poorest were paying: The wealthy elite actually paid 36.3 percent of their income in taxes, a mere 3 percent more than that paid by the poorest segment of society.[4]

What accounts for these extremes of inequality? The answer is fairly simple. In the private enterprise system the vast majority of people work for wages and salaries. The poorest 20 percent of

[3]For sophisticated arguments supporting these points, see Selma F. Goldsmith, "Changes in the Size Distribution of Income," *American Economic Review*, May 1957, pp. 504–518, and Victor Perlo, "A Review of 'Shares of Upper Income Groups in Income and Savings,'" *Science and Society*, (Spring 1954, pp. 168–173.

[4]B. A. Musgrave, "Estimating the Distribution of the Tax Burden," in *Income and Wealth*, ser. X (Cambridge, England: Bowes & Bowes, 1964), p. 192.

the population is made up primarily of people who are disadvantaged in the competition to secure good jobs, or any job at all. They include the aged, the disabled, the fatherless families whose mothers must care for their children and get whatever money they can, the teenagers, the blacks, the Puerto Ricans, the Chicanos, and other groups that face discrimination in the labor market.

At the other extreme, the wealthiest 2 percent derive very little of their incomes from wages and salaries, and when they do work it is often in sinecures obtained through family connections. Most of this group's income comes from ownership of assets, from profits, dividends, interest, and rent. In the most complete study of the distribution of ownership of wealth ever undertaken, it was shown that in 1956 the wealthiest 1.6 percent of the population owned at least 80 percent of all corporate stock and virtually all of the state and local government bonds. Furthermore, the concentration of ownership of these income-yielding assets has steadily increased since the early 1920s.[5]

Thus it can be said that the extreme inequalities of income distribution are not attributable to differences in rates of wages and salaries, although there are large inequalities here to be sure. The very poor are largely those who cannot, for various social, political, and personal reasons, compete in the job market; and the very rich are largely those whose incomes derive principally from ownership.

Because the distribution of wealth changes very slowly if at all, and the problems of the poor persist decade after decade, it is not surprising that the relative distribution of income remains quite stable over long periods. It has been pointed out that studies that show a narrowing of the distribution of income contain errors of both omission and commission. Recent investigators conclude that it is narrowing extremely slowly, if at all.[6] In fact, in the 1960s the degree of inequality actually increased.

As noted earlier in this chapter, an income shift from the rich to the poor will tend to raise the propensity to consume (because the poor have to consume all of their income), and an income shift from the poor to the rich will tend to lower the propensity to consume (because the rich consume a much lower percentage of their income). Further, most of the income of the rich comes from ownership of property (profits, rent, interest, and dividends). But most of those whose income comes almost solely from

[5]Robert J. Lampman, *The Share of Top Wealth-holders in National Wealth, 1922–1956* (Princeton, N.J.: Princeton University Press, 1962).
[6]Goldsmith, op. cit., and Perlo, op. cit.

wages and salaries fall into that 59 percent of Americans who have *less* than the "moderate but adequate" income defined by the BLS. Thus the effects of shifts between property income and wage income are similar to those of shifts between rich and poor: If less goes to property owners and more to wage workers, the result is a *higher* propensity to consume because wage workers consume almost all their income. If less goes to wage workers and more to property owners, the result is a *lower* propensity to consume because property owners consume a small percentage and save a very large percentage of their income.

EMPIRICAL DATA ON CONSUMPTION BEHAVIOR

The changes in consumption and saving at different levels of income, as postulated in the consumption function, may be illustrated by actual data. In 1929, at the peak of prosperity, the level of consumer expenditure reached its highest point of the decade, as did national income. Personal saving was also at a record level of $4.168 billion.[7] By 1933, in the depth of the depression, aggregate income had fallen by half. Consumption had fallen swiftly, but not quite as disastrously, because people were spending on consumption *more* than their aggregate income by dipping into their stock of assets accumulated in previous years and by going into debt. As a result, personal saving was actually negative in 1933, at –$648 million (dissaving).

Empirical studies of consumption and income levels in other decades confirm the fact that total consumer spending rises when national income rises and falls when income falls. Consumption, however, neither rises nor falls as rapidly as income. Thus in prosperity a sizable portion of high incomes is usually saved, whereas in a depression, when income suddenly falls, all or more than all income is often spent on consumption. In other words, when national income rises in prosperity, the average propensity to consume (the ratio of consumption to income) generally falls, but when national income declines in a depression, the average propensity to consume generally rises.

There is, in fact, a great deal of evidence that indicates ". . . that as income falls in the business cycle, consumption will fall proportionately *less* than income; and again when income rises cyclically, consumption will rise proportionately less than income."[8]

[7]All data here are from U.S. Department of Commerce, Bureau of the Census, *Statistical Abstract of the United States, 1964* (Washington, D.C.: GPO, 1964).

[8]Alvin Hansen, *A Guide to Keynes* (New York: McGraw-Hill, 1953), p. 76.

Furthermore, this relationship is consistent with the fact that the ratio of additional consumption spending to additional income (the marginal propensity to consume) is far less than 1. Using the statistics for 1947 to 1958, it has been calculated that only 88 percent of additional disposable income is spent on consumption (and only 58 percent of additional GNP is spent on consumption).[9]

Empirical estimates for much longer periods are also available. One careful study estimated the average ratio of consumption to net national product by overlapping decades from 1869 to 1928.[10] Average consumer spending varied only between 84 percent and 89 percent of net national product. The average saving ratio consequently varied only between 16 percent and 11 percent of national product. Thus the propensity to consume out of national income did not change much, even though the average family income level rose tenfold in that period.

At first glance it may seem somewhat strange that the propensity to save did not rise over so long a period during which income was rising. Did Keynes not teach that it tends to rise at higher income levels? It is true that *at any given time*, higher-income groups save a larger portion of their income. For example, in 1948–1950 business owners (with relatively high incomes) saved 23 percent of their income, farmers saved only 12 percent, and nonfarm wage workers (with relatively low incomes) saved a mere 4 percent.[11]

The answer to the riddle of a constant or even falling propensity to save lies in the fact that what constitutes a basic, adequate standard of living is determined by social mores, not by biological necessities. The average man learns that in the long run everyone's income, including that of Mr. Jones next door, rises by the same percentage. Therefore the average man, in the long run, raises his own percentage of consumption to keep his standard of living up with that of the Joneses. In other words, if all income classes raise their income proportionally, then the propensities to consume and save stay about the same after a period of adjustment to new standards.

It would appear, then, that a person's position in the overall distribution of income is more important in explaining his consumption behavior than is the absolute level of his income.

[9]See Bert G. Hickman, *Growth and Stability of the Postwar Economy* (Washington, D.C.: Brookings Institution, 1960), p. 224.

[10]Simon S Kuznets, *National Product Since. 1869* (New York: National Bureau of Economic Research, 1946), p. 119.

[11]See Milton Friedman, *A Theory of the Consumption Function* (Princeton, N.J.: Princeton University Press, 1957), pp. 69–79.

RELATIVE INCOME

If consumption were determined by the absolute level of income alone, a doubling of all family incomes should result in a fall in the ratio of consumption to income. If, however, relative position on income scale strongly influences a family's consumption decisions, a doubling of the incomes of all families would leave the ratio unchanged because there would be no change in the relative living standards. Thus the comparative constancy over long periods of the propensity to consume can be explained in the following terms: (1) to a large extent minimal subsistence standards of living are socially determined, (2) the desire to emulate the patterns of those in higher income groups controls consumer behavior, and (3) the relative standing of different income classes have changed very little in the last 100 years.

The relative income hypothesis also helps explain why the propensity to consume falls in times of prosperity and rises in depressions. In the short run, when there are fairly sudden changes in national income, each individual sets his consumption in terms of his own previous level until he adjusts to the new national standards.[12] Thus if his income suddenly is higher, he can keep to the old average standard of consumption but save a higher percentage. If his income suddenly drops in a depression, however, he tries desperately to maintain his own previous peak consumption, or standard of living, and therefore the percentage of his income that is saved drops rapidly. It is for this reason that the average propensity to consume rises in a depression but slowly reverts to the long-run percentage as income climbs back toward the previous peak.

In the short run (over a period of a few years or so), the Keynesian consumption function, in which it is assumed that the average propensity to consume falls as income rises, is a reasonably accurate reflection of the relationship between consumption and income. Over longer periods, however, both theory and empirical evidence suggest that consumption remains, on the average, a fairly constant percentage of income.

INCOME DISTRIBUTION
AND CONSUMER BEHAVIOR

The relative income hypothesis is a good description of the psychological propensities of average consumer behavior in our present

[12]See James S. Duesenberry, *Income, Saving, and the Theory of Consumer Behavior* (Cambridge, Mass.: Harvard University Press, 1949).

society. We have noted, however, that consumer behavior is determined not only by consumer psychology (observed by Keynes) but also by the distribution of income among consumers (observed by Marx).

We shall see—in Chapter 28—that in every expansion period, when income is growing, consumer spending also rises, but not as rapidly. This falling propensity to consume could be partly explained—as Keynes argued—by the lagging psychological adjustment to higher incomes. Many other economists, particularly Marx, have observed that in each expansion period there is also a shift of income from wages to profits. Wages go to workers in low income brackets, while profits go to capitalists in high income brackets. Since capitalists save a very large portion of their income—while workers save almost none—there is naturally a much lower national "propensity to consume."

In fact, wages rise and fall proportionately less than aggregate income, while profits fluctuate more than the total national income. One conservative economist says: "Thus in a time of great activity, wages and salaries constitute a smaller fraction of increased national income than in a time of depression."[13] The aggregate data demonstrate that the ratio of wages to national income falls in prosperity but rises in depression. During the four business cycles from 1921 through 1938, wages (or aggregate employees' compensation) rose on the average in expansion periods by only 19.8 percent of their average value over the whole period. At the same time, the nonwage part of national income (profits, rent, and interest) rose by 23.3 percent. In these same four cycles, wage income fell on the average in contractions by only 13 percent of its average value, whereas nonwage income fell by 26.4 percent.[14] The differences, although small in percentages, are very significant in billions of dollars. These facts of income distribution are illustrated in Figure 26.1.

Furthermore, one of the single most important sources of saving today is corporate profits, either directly through corporate reinvestment or indirectly through dividend income. In the years 1921–1938 the average net profit of all corporations rose in expansions by an astounding 168.8 percent and declined in contractions by an equally startling 174.6 percent of their average value for the whole period.[15]

[13]John Maurice Clark, *Strategic Factors in Business Cycles* (New York: National Bureau of Economic Research, 1951), p. 155.

[14]Data derived from Wesley C. Mitchell, *What Happens in Business Cycles?* (New York: National Bureau of Economic Research, 1935), p. 79.

[15]Ibid., pp. 154–155, 324.

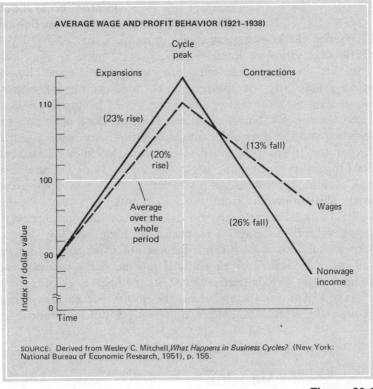

AVERAGE WAGE AND PROFIT BEHAVIOR (1921–1938)

SOURCE: Derived from Wesley C. Mitchell,*What Happens in Business Cycles?* (New York: National Bureau of Economic Research, 1951), p. 155.

Figure 26.1

The fact that wages rise and decline more slowly than national income is due to several factors: (1) The recovery phase of the cycle begins with large numbers of unemployed, and wages rates cannot rise appreciably until near the full-employment level. (2) Because the pressure of demand during expansion is met, in part, by a technological shift from labor to machinery, the derived demand for labor does not rise as rapidly as the demand for output. (3) In a world of unions and monopolies, the bargaining power of unions is greater in maintaining the status quo of wages against downward pressures than in raising wages to catch up to productivity increases. (4) It may be that workers have a "money illusion," which means that they bargain for money wages rather than real wages. In that case a rise in the price level during expansion would cause money wages to fall as a proportion of the money value of output. But a falling price level in depression would cause a rise in the proportion of money wages to money national output.

Interaction of Income
Distribution and Consumption Behavior

Combining the known facts about consumer behavior and income distribution yields an interesting picture. Assume, as is probably true, that profits rise and fall more rapidly than wages. Furthermore, assume that the propensity to consume out of wages is higher than the propensity to consume out of profits. Now in this case both the psychological influence of previous peak consumer spending and the shift in income distribution may help explain the fluctuations in the propensity to consume. In times of expansion, the propensity to consume begins to decline both because aggregate income approaches or passes its previous peak *and* because of the shift in income from wages to profits.

Figure 26.2 illustrates the typical behavior of consumption and saving as well as wages and profits at high and low incomes. *Saving* is defined as all national income not spent on consumption, and *profit* is defined as all national income not earned as wages (where *wages* include salaries and all other employee compensation).

As the national income rises, the profit percentage increases because of the pressures holding down wages. But the profit makers

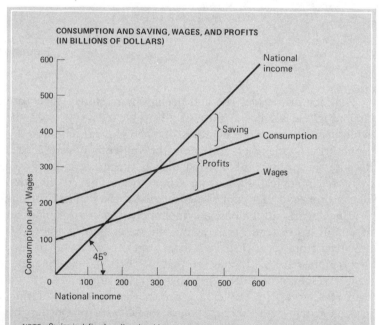

NOTE: *Saving* is defined as all national income not spent on consumption. *Profit* is defined as all national income not earned as wages (where wages include salaries and all other employee compensation). This is the typical picture according to underconsumptionist theory.

Figure 26.2

already had high incomes and high consumer spending, so their percentage spent on consumption from additional income is low and falling. Therefore, mainly *because of the shift of income from wages to profits, consumption is held to a much slower rise than national income*. Obviously the percentage saved also rises in times of expansion. The reader should spell out for himself or herself the reverse process, which takes place when national income contracts in a depression (wages decline more slowly than national income, therefore . . .).

SUMMARY

Consumer behavior is determined by both social conditioning and income distribution. Income is distributed very unequally, a few rich families having very high incomes, a large number of poor having a very low income. The poor (mostly wage earners) consume a very high percentage of their income. The rich (most profit and interest receivers) consume a small percentage of their income. For the most part people make consumption decisions on the basis of their perceptions of the general standard of living.

In expansion periods the average propensity to consume falls, partly for psychological reasons but partly because there is a shift of income from low-income wage earners to high-income profit makers. In depression periods the average propensity to consume rises, partly for psychological reasons but partly because there is a shift in the percentage of income going to low-income wage workers (though their absolute income levels are falling).

APPENDIX A

The Multiplier

Some economists believe that Keynes' most important conceptual contribution to macroeconomics is the consumption function and that the most important analytic tool to come out of the Keynesian dissection of consumption is the multiplier. The *multiplier* expresses the relation between an initial increase (or decrease) in one of the components of aggregate demand and the total increase (or decrease) in national income caused by it. The initial spending change may come from any one of the components of aggregate demand, but investment spending is the most volatile. Investment spending characteristically rises sharply or falls drastically during cyclical fluctuations. Its fluctuations are usually of much greater amplitude than those of consumption.

Obviously it is vital that government policy makers know how any change in spending, whether in direct government spending or in private investment encouraged by government spending, will affect national income. This question first received considerable attention during the 1930s, when New Deal politicians debated ways of combating the depression.

We leave government spending for a later chapter and concentrate here, as Keynes did, on the effects of changes in investment spending. In precise terms the *investment multiplier* may be defined as the ratio of change in national income to change in investment.

This is more than a definition; there is a causal relationship running from change in investment spending to change in income. Change in investment usually causes a larger change in income and output because some of the money spent on investment will be *respent* by its recipients for additional consumption.

Assume that during a period with some unemployment a firm decides to construct a large new factory. This sudden increase in investment spending will increase the incomes of the contractors who supply the necessary machinery and materials and provide jobs for previously unemployed workers. Now assume that the initial increase in spending and income is $1000. The recipients of this income will immediately respend most of it for consumer goods, which will result in new income for businessmen and workers in the consumer goods industries. These income recipients will, in turn, spend much of their new income on more consumer goods. Exactly how much additional spending occurs in each round will depend on the marginal propensity to consume of the income recipients. But it is already clear that any additional consumer spending must mean that the total income generated will be more than the original $1000 of investment spending.

The easiest way to see how the multiplier is supposed to work is to study a numerical example. In the example in Table 26A.1, only

TABLE 26A.1

HOW THE MULTIPLIER WORKS

1. Suppose an increase in investment of $1000.
2. Also suppose a marginal propensity to consume of 4/5, or 80 percent.

Number of Rounds of Spending	Increase in Investment	Increase in Consumption	Increase in National Income	Increase in Saving
0	$1000		$1000	$ 200
1	0	$ 800	800	160
2	0	640	640	128
3	0	512	512	102
4	0	410	410	82
5	0	328	328	66
6	0	262	—	—
—	0	—	—	—
—	—	—	—	—
—	—	—	—	—
—	—	—	—	—
—	—	—	—	—
Infinite Number of Rounds of Spending	Total Increase in Investment	Total Increase in Consumption	Total Increase in National Income	Total Increase in Saving
	$1000	$4000	$5000	$1000

some initial change in investment and a certain marginal propensity to consume need be assumed. One thousand dollars of investment becomes $1000 of income when it is spent. It is assumed that 80 percent, or $800, of that income is respent on consumption, which means another $800 of national income going to other individuals. They will then spend 80 percent, or $640, of *that* income, and so it goes. In the first round, 20 percent, or $200, leaks out into saving; and in the second round, 20 percent of the remaining income, or $160, leaks out into saving. The process ends only when the last $1 of the increased income is saved. At that point the whole $1000 of investment has been saved, but there already have been many rounds of consumption spending in between. In this example the total of all the rounds of consumption spending (or respending) will eventually approach $4000, and national income will approach a level that is $5000 higher than before.

If investment returns to its old level after completion of the factory, the entire process will then work in reverse. Therefore, when the multiplier is used as an analytical tool, it is necessary to distinguish between a one-time injection of new investment spending and a rise in the level of new investment spending that is sustained over a long period of time.

If the $1000 increase in investment is considered as a one-time injection of new spending, then the totals at the bottom of Table 26A.1 represent only temporary additions to consumption, saving, and national income. After these one-time increases are realized, however, total spending will eventually return to its original level. But if the $1000 increase is a new, stepped-up rate of investment spending that continues through several subsequent periods, the totals represent the rise from the old, lower levels to the new, higher levels of spending flows, which will persist in each future period.

From this description of how the multiplier works, it should be clear that if less is saved out of each increment to income, then each increment to consumption spending will be larger. In other words, if the marginal propensity to save declines, the subsequent increases in consumption and income will be larger.

The multiplier formula is just a shortcut for finding where the process of Table 26A.1 ends without repeating the calculation a great many times. Because the formula works equally well for an initial increase *or* decrease in investment, we shall speak generally of changes rather than increases or decreases. By definition:

$$\text{Multiplier} = \frac{\text{change in income}}{\text{change in investment}} \tag{1}$$

However, movement from one to another equilibrium position is assumed; therefore, at the end the change in saving must equal the change in investment. Substituting saving for investment, we get

$$\text{Multiplier} = \frac{\text{change in income}}{\text{change in saving}} \qquad (2)$$

or, by simple mathematical manipulation,

$$\text{Multiplier} = \frac{1}{\dfrac{\text{change in saving}}{\text{change in income}}} \qquad (3)$$

Lo and behold! The denominator of this fraction is nothing but the marginal propensity to save. So the formula to remember is just

$$\text{Multiplier} = \frac{1}{\text{MPS}} \text{ or } \frac{1}{1 - \text{MPC,}} \qquad (4)$$

because the marginal propensities to save and consume always add up to exactly 1.0.

Look again at the example in Table 26A.1. It has been established that *total increase in income = increase in investment × the multiplier*. In this example the increase in investment is $1000. What is the multiplier? The MPC is $\frac{4}{5}$, so the MPS is $\frac{1}{5}$. The multiplier must equal 1 divided by $\frac{1}{5}$, which is 5. So we may write

$$\text{Total increase in income} = \$1000 \times 5 = \$5000$$

This demonstrates how the multiplier is used to find the end result of investment spending.

Notice that if the multiplier is reduced, then the investment spending has less effect. At one extreme, if the multiplier is just 1, the change in income is just equal to the change in investment. At the other extreme, if the multiplier approaches infinity, any small change in investment will cause an infinite change in income.

Of course the value of the multiplier is controlled by the MPC or MPS. If MPC falls, so does the multiplier (because less is respent out of each increase in income). A multiplier of only 2 means an MPC of only $\frac{1}{2}$. A multiplier of only 1 means everything is saved and the MPC is zero. But a multiplier of infinity means all income is immediately respent for consumption, the MPC is 1, and the MPS is zero.

There are some obvious weaknesses or, at least, qualifications that must be kept in mind when the multiplier theory is used. First, so far the time element has been ignored; it takes a certain amount of time before income received is respent for consumption, and still more time before the second and third and later rounds of responding may occur. If the time lag happens to be very long or varies widely, a much more complicated multiplier will be needed to get a realistic answer to the change in income for one year.

Second, it has been assumed that MPC remains constant until the process is completed. In reality MPC often changes and is affected by many psychological and institutional factors. For example, the accumulated savings of World War II greatly increased the propensity to consume in the immediate postwar years.

Moreover, saving is not the only leakage from the income stream. Higher or lower taxes will also change MPC out of national income. Furthermore, if purchases of imports (e.g., Volkswagens) increase, there will be a leakage from domestic consumer spending. Thus the domestic MPC may change too often to permit accurate prediction of the multiplier for more than a few months in the future.

Third, the multiplier formula assumes that investment will remain the same while consumption and national income are expanding rapidly. Obviously the simple multiplier theory cannot be used if further changes in investment are to be considered.

For all of these reasons, we conclude that while the multiplier is a helpful explanatory device, it cannot be relied on for an exact estimate.

Summary

The investment multiplier measures the change in national income that results from a change in investment. The formula for estimating this multiplier is roughly 1 divided by the MPS. This formula is far from exact because it neglects (1) time lags; (2) leakages from increased saving, taxes, and foreign imports; and (3) further changes in investment.

APPENDIX B

Some Mysteries of the Consumption Function

The APC was defined as the ratio of consumption to income at any particular level of income. Similarly, MPC was defined as the ratio of change in consumption to change in income. Figure 26B.1 illustrates the consumption function and gives some definitions and identities. The reader should review them thoroughly to make sure he understands all the terms and concepts Keynesian economists use to describe the consumption function.

As the level of income rises, APC falls; that is, the ratio of C_2 to Y_2 is less than the ratio of C_1 to Y_1. Notice that the MPC is simply the slope of the consumption function. It is assumed for simplicity that MPC is constant, which means that equal additions to income will result in equal additions to consumption. In reality, though, MPC probably declines somewhat as income rises.

As the level of income rises, APS rises; that is, the ratio of S_2 to Y_2 is greater than the ratio of S_1 to Y_1. Because MPC is assumed to be constant, MPS also stays constant; that is, equal additions to income produce equal additions to saving.

Four simple identities result from these definitions. First, consumption plus saving (or dissaving) must always equal income. Second, the change in consumption plus the change in saving (or dissaving) must always equal the change in income. Third, because

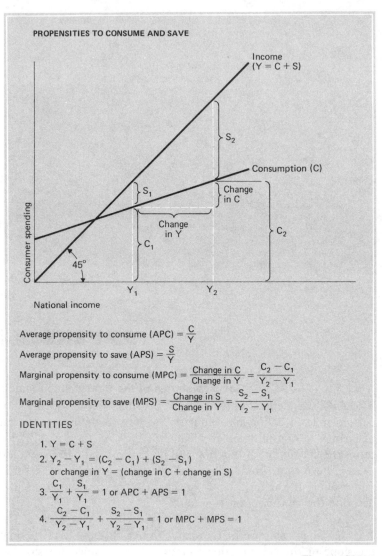

Figure 26B.1

consumption plus saving equal income, APC plus APS must always equal 1. Fourth, MPC plus MPS must always equal 1.

A numerical example may more clearly fix these definitions. Assuming that consumption for each level of income is known, then all the other quantities may be calculated according to their definitions. This procedure is illustrated in Table 26B.1.

In this table the simplest possible assumption is used: Consumption rises by $1000 with each $2000 rise in income. This is a constant

TABLE 26B.1

INCOME AND CONSUMPTION RELATIONSHIPS

Assumptions				Calculations	
Income (Y)	Con- sump- tion	Periods	Saving (S) = Y–C	Average Propensity to Consume = C/Y	Average Propensity to Save = S/Y
$ 0	$2,000	1	– $2,000	$\frac{2}{0}$ (or + in- finity)	$\frac{2}{0}$ (or – infinity)
$ 2,000	$3,000	2	= $1,000	$\frac{3}{2}$ (or 1.50)	$\frac{1}{2}$ (or – 0.50)
$ 4,000	$4,000	3	$ 0	$\frac{4}{4}$ (or 1.00)	$\frac{0}{4}$ (or 0.00)
$ 6,000	$5,000	4	$1,000	$\frac{5}{6}$ (or 0.83)	$\frac{1}{6}$ (or 0.17)
$ 8,000	$6,000	5	$2,000	$\frac{6}{8}$ (or 0.75)	$\frac{2}{8}$ (or 0.25)
$10,000		6	$3,000	$\frac{7}{10}$ (or 0.70)	$\frac{3}{10}$ (or 0.30)

MPC (and a constant MPS). Nevertheless, because it was assumed that consumption began above income (because some minimum consumption is necessary even at very low income levels), the table also reveals a falling APC with a rising APS.

investment

The classic study of the behavior of aggregate demand covers the four business cycles between 1921 and 1938.[1] During this period consumer spending averaged 82.3 percent and investment spending averaged only 17.7 percent of GNP. (In terms of percent, government and foreign trade effects were small and need not be separately investigated.) Because consumption is so much larger than investment, its absolute changes are also larger. Thus during these four cycles 59.6 percent of the expansion in GNP was in consumer goods, whereas 51.9 percent of the depression contraction in GNP was in consumer goods.

At the same time, changes in investment spending constituted only 40.4 percent of the expansion and 48.1 percent of the contraction in GNP. Yet it is striking that with investment averaging less than one-fifth of GNP, it still managed to represent close to half the change in GNP. Obviously this means that in percentage terms the fluctuations of investment are pretty violent. In fact, as a percentage of its own average value for the whole period, investment rose 55.4 percent in expansions and fell 49.3 percent in contradictions. Consumption, however, rose by only 15 percent and fell by only 9.9 percent of its average value. These facts are exactly what we would

[1]All data in this section are from Wesley C. Mitchell, *What Happens in Business Cycles?* (New York: National Bureau of Economic Research, 1951), pp. 154–155.

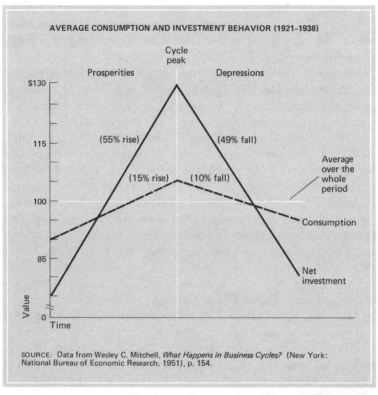

AVERAGE CONSUMPTION AND INVESTMENT BEHAVIOR (1921-1938)

Cycle peak

Prosperities   Depressions

(55% rise)   (49% fall)

Average over the whole period

(15% rise)   (10% fall)

Consumption

Net investment

Value

Time

SOURCE: Data from Wesley C. Mitchell, *What Happens in Business Cycles?* (New York: National Bureau of Economic Research, 1951), p. 154.

Figure 27.1

have expected from the theory developed in the last two chapters. They are illustrated in Figure 27.1.

The multiplier, which accounts for the magnified effect of fluctuations in investment on national income, was examined in Chapter 25. Our analysis turns now to the characteristically violent fluctuation of investment spending itself. Attempts to explain investment behavior constitute the heart of many business cycle theories. Economists have long realized, from the standpoint of understanding business fluctuations, that investment spending is the most important component of aggregate demand. Yet it is also the most difficult to explain and accurately predict.

GROSS AND NET INVESTMENT

In Chapter 24 *net investment* was defined as simply the change in capital within a given period. Obviously the stock of capital is steadily diminished through use, wear and tear, and obsolescence. However, the stock of capital grows as new capital goods are produced and purchased. *Gross investment* was defined as the total of all capital goods produced in a year. To determine *net investment*, the amount by which the capital stock has depreciated is subtracted from gross investment.

For example, in the crucial year 1929, $8.7 billion was invested in new construction and $5.8 billion in new producers' durable equipment, and there was a $1.7 billion increase in business inventories, or a total of $16.2 billion gross investment. Because allowances for depreciation (or capital consumption) amounted to $8.6 billion in that year, it can be assumed that $8.6 billion of the gross investment was for replacement. By definition the net investment must have been at the level of $7.6 billion.

Assume that the total amount of capital in the United States on January 1, 1929, was exactly $100 billion. According to the figures just given, there was an $8.6 billion depreciation during the year, just balanced by an $8.6 billion replacement. In addition, however, there was a net investment or addition to capital capacity of $7.6 billion during the year. It follows that on January 1, 1930, the amount of capital would have risen to $107.6 billion.

Although it was assumed that the amount of replacement investment can be measured by the estimated depreciation, the decision to replace depreciated capital goods is not automatic. In 1933 gross investment was only $1.4 billion, but depreciation was still $7.2 billion.[2] Therefore net investment was actually at the negative level of −$5.8 billion. The capital stock and hence the economy's productive capacity was rapidly diminishing. Gross investment could never be negative, for at worst no new capital goods would be produced. In that event net investment would be negative and equal to depreciation.

In an investigation of aggregate demand, it is gross investment that is important. *Any* investment spending is a part of the demand for currently produced capital goods. If growth of productive capacity is being considered, however, then net investment indicates by how much the capital stock has increased and thereby permits an estimation of the increase in the economy's capacity to produce.

DECISION TO INVEST

The businessman contemplating ordering and purchasing new plant or equipment will not decide to make the purchase unless the value of the profits he *expects* to receive from this investment is greater than, or at least equal to, the purchase price of the capital goods. Obviously profits are exceedingly important in determining the

[2]Ibid., p. 157.

level of investment—and hence output, income, and employment—
in the U.S. economy. Indeed the prime motivation for investment
in a private enterprise economy is the expectation of future profit
on the new investment. But because future profits cannot be known
with certainty, it is mainly on the basis of the present level of profits
and changes in profits that businessmen form their expectations.
Accordingly, high or rising profits will lead to optimistic expectations and new investment, whereas low or falling profits will lead to
pessimistic expectations and a decline in new investment.

The other and quite distinct reason for the importance of profits
is the fact that more profits provide the funds for more investment.
If there are no profits, the firm may lack funds to invest even if it
wishes to do so. Although the capital funds can sometimes be borrowed, more profits make it easier for the firm or its stockholders to
obtain credit. Moreover, most firms are quicker to invest from
internal sources, and in practice most expansion is financed with
retained profits. It is imperative, therefore, to inquire into the nature
of profits in the American economy.

PROFITS IN THE UNITED STATES

One of the most important determinants of profits in any industry
is the extent to which the industry is competitive, or the extent to
which economic power is concentrated in the hands of a few firms
within the industry. Many discussions of investment behavior (and
hence of business cycles and economic growth) have assumed or
implied an economy of pure or perfect competition. That would
be an economy composed of individual business units competing
with each other, where each is so small that its actions taken alone
could not appreciably influence the quantity of goods or the price
in the market. This more or less adequately describes the U.S.
economy of most of the nineteenth century, when small farms and
small businesses produced most of the output and there were no
giant corporations dominating an entire industry (although there
were many local monopolies). Since the 1890s or early 1900s, this
picture has not reflected reality and is thus irrelevant.

Today U.S. industry still has millions of very small enterprises,
but a few hundred corporate giants hold most of the wealth and
account for most of the production. In Chapter 7, we traced the
early development of monopoly power. In Chapter 8, we showed
the vicious tactics used by the giant firms to eliminate competitors.
In Chapter 18, we saw why theory predicts that the giant oligopolies
will restrict output, charge higher prices, and obtain higher rates of
profit. In Chapter 17 we examined the present results of incredibly
high levels of economic concentration.

At the bottom, a large number of small corporations hold a tiny portion of corporate assets. At the top, a few giant corporations hold a majority of all assets. The economy of the United States has thus changed from a predominantly competitive to a predominantly oligopolistic production situation.[3]

It also was demonstrated in Chapter 17 that monopoly (or oligopoly) finds many ways to make above-average rates of profit on investment. These are briefly reviewed here. First, the whole point of monopoly (or oligopoly) control of markets is, of course, to restrict output and charge higher prices, which squeezes extra points out of all consumers. Second, higher monopoly prices hurt all the farmers and small businesses that purchase producer goods; they must accept lower profits. Third, if a large firm has extra market power as a buyer of commodities (technically *oligopsony* power), it may also gain extra profits by buying at a lower price from small businesses and farmers.

Fourth, if a giant firm has extra market power as a large buyer of labor (again, oligopsony power), it may also add to its profits by buying labor at a lower rate than the average wage. Fifth, additional monopoly profits come from lucrative government military contracts (this will be discussed in Chapter 29). Sixth, additional monopoly profits come from concentrated ownership of investments abroad. In many cases foreign-based subsidiaries enjoy the same monopolistic advantages in the host countries. Furthermore, as was established in Chapter 17, the smallest corporations have low or even negative profit rates. Profit rates rise with the scale of the corporation.[4]

Another important aspect of economic concentration was discussed in Chapter 17. The indicator of market power is the relative size and importance of a firm in its own industry. The *concentration ratio* in each industry is the percentage of sales controlled by the 8 largest corporations in the industry. Several studies have found a definite relationship between an industry's concentration ratio and its profit rates.[5] When all industries were divided into 20 groups, a considerable rise of profit rates as the degree of concentration rises was found. Thus the average rate of profit on capital in the 10 industry groups over the 50 percent concentration level was 20 percent in one year. In the same year, the rate of profit on

[3]For convenience the terms *monopoly* and *monopoly power* are used in this chapter to include (a) concentration of a large part of all U.S. corporate assets in 200 or 300 giant firms and (b) oligopoly control of most individual markets. The meanings are differentiated where necessary.

[4]See Howard J. Sherman, *Profit Rates in the United States* (Ithaca, N.Y.: Cornell University Press, 1968), pp. 40–50.

[5]See, for example, J. S. Bain, "The Relation of Profit Rate to Industrial Concentration, American Manufacturing, 1936–1940," *Quarterly Journal of Economics*, August 1951, pp. 292–324.

capital was only 12.8 percent in the 10 industry groups below the 50 percent concentration level.[6]

MONOPOLY POWER AND
CYCLICAL INVESTMENT BEHAVIOR

How does economic concentration affect the amount of change in business performance from expansion to depression? There is considerable evidence that cyclical performance, as indicated by profit rates, is significantly different for big business and small business. Specifically, data on the profit rates of all corporations from 1931 through 1961 reveal that larger corporations had much more stable profit rates than smaller ones. The smaller the corporation, the greater the amplitude of rise and fall in its profit rate.[7]

Quarterly data on profit margins in U.S. manufacturing industries from 1947 through 1963 indicate that the industries with the lowest degree of concentration have the greatest cyclical changes in profit margins.[8] For example, apparel and lumber, two very competitive industries, have the highest cyclical changes in profit margins in times of both expansion and depression. But tobacco, one of the more concentrated industries, has the lowest cyclical changes in its profit margin both during expansion and contraction.

Investment behavior is closely related to profit rates and thus to monopoly power. It is known that the profit rates of small and competitive businesses are the first to turn at the peak of the business cycle. Moreover, the amplitude of fluctuation in investment is affected by corporate size and degree of concentration (the same way profit rates are affected). Thus one careful study found that small firms (with assets below $4.9 million) had more rapid rates of capital growth during periods of expansion but much higher rates of decline during recessions.[9] It also appears that investment tends to be more stable in industries with a high degree of concentration than in the more competitive industries. In other words, small businesses are hurt most by recessions and their investments decline the most (partly because their profits are taken away by the monopolies).

PSYCHOLOGICAL ATTITUDES

Because investment decisions are based on projections of sales and returns into the future, it would be easy to say that fluctuations in aggregate investment are caused by changes in investor confidence

[6]Such a difference is statistically significant—that is, it could occur by chance far less than 1 percent of the time.
[7]Sherman, op. cit., pp. 156–166.
[8]Ibid., Table 7–8, p. 171.
[9]John R. Meyer and Edwin Kuh, *The Investment Decision* (Cambridge, Mass.: Harvard University Press, 1957), pp. 163–167.

about economic conditions. Although it points to a vital aspect of economic behavior, such a "formula" actually explains nothing. There can be no denying the sensational effects of changes in expectations on real economic conditions in the private enterprise system. Between 1929 and 1932 children did not have enough to eat, men jumped from tall buildings, women pawned their fur coats. What caused the trouble? Pessimism?

To say that waves of optimism or pessimism strongly affect the economy is to make a very incomplete statement. *What causes the optimism or pessimism?* In 1929 most indexes of production, new investment, and profits turned down in the summer, but the stock market crash and the collapse of expectations did not occur until autumn. For example, the industrial peak was reached in June 1929, but stock prices did not peak until October 1929.[10] In a competitive, private enterprise economy, especially as it increases in complexity and interrelatedness, a single enterprise cannot accurately predict its future costs and receipts; therefore it tends to keep an optimistic outlook until it encounters obstacles. In fact, the usual order of events in depressions appears to be that first, production and financial indexes decline first, despite the most extreme optimism. It is only then, because of the change in economic conditions, that the optimism changes to pessimism, which reinforces the depression and may postpone the recovery. The reverse process seems to occur in economic expansions, when rises in production and profits are followed by a shift from pessimism to optimism.

Of course optimistic business expectations have a powerful uplifting effect, especially on new investment, which will be carried to much higher levels than it would otherwise have reached. Similarly, pessimistic business expectations cause a much greater decline in investment and even in consumption than the objective situation warrants. But the ultimate cause of pessimism in businessmen's attitudes is the fact that disequilibria in the market system lead to widespread adverse consequences that impede the search for profits.

INVENTIONS AND INNOVATIONS

Innovation is defined as the putting to use of inventories in the economy. It may lower costs on a given output, create more output with the same cost, improve the quality of old products, or create new products. Many argue that inventions and innovations act as random stimuli; by making investment more profitable, they prolong prosperity or bring an economy out of a depression.

---

[10]See U.S. Department of Commerce, *Historical Statistics of the United States, 1789–1945* (Washington, D.C.: GPO, 1949), p. 345.

Entrepreneurial expectations may vary widely as a result of economic prosperity or depression. Wesley Mitchell argues that in a depression every effort is made to find ways (inventions) to reduce costs, but that firms hesitate to make major new investments to innovate: "It is the season when alterations are planned; revival is the season when they are executed on the largest scale."[11] Thus the rate of innovation may be expected to decline drastically in a depression both because the rate of invention may decline somewhat and because business expectations usually become very pessimistic. In time of prosperity, however, innovation is greatly increased both by business optimism and, probably to a lesser extent, by more new invention.

By lowering cost per unit, innovations may improve profit expectations and thereby increase investment. By improving products or making new products, they may stimulate output demanded. Depression, however, is intensified not only by the drop in the rate of innovation but also by the fact that innovation may not be as stimulating in a generally pessimistic situation.

A cost-cutting innovation may also cause old machinery to become obsolete more rapidly, thereby tending to cause a temporary increase in replacement investment if business conditions make replacement desirable. If the innovation is in the quality of a product or is an entirely new product, then it may lead to a net increase in investment demand, although the innovating firm's final output of improved or new consumer goods must still compete for the consumer's dollar with the output of other industries.

THE ACCELERATOR

We have seen that the basis for investment decision making is the expected profit from the investment. But it is difficult to estimate expected profits, so economists and businessmen use crude substitutes to make rough guesses. The most widely used index on which to base guesses of the profitability of investments is changes in demand for output. This approach then investigates the ratio between increased output and increased capital investments.

If this ratio is known and stable, we could predict the change in capital (that is, investment) from a change in output demanded. The *accelerator* is defined as the ratio between investment decisions and changes in output demanded. In other words, the accelerator is the coefficient by which we multiply a change in output demanded to predict the level of investment.

[11]Wesley C. Mitchell, *Business Cycles and Their Causes* (Berkeley: University of California Press, 1959 printing, 1927 ed.), p. 190.

Notice that the businessman invests in (net) new machinery only to *increase* his output. So the accelerator coefficient relates invest-- ment decisions not to the level of demand for output but to the change (increase or decrease) in demand for output. Thus it helps explain why investment fluctuates more violently than total output. Furthermore, in spite of its many weaknesses, we shall see that the link provided by the accelerator between investment decisions and changes in output demanded is a crucial part of several theories of the business cycle.

What is the systematic reasoning that links investment to a change in output? With a given technology, a factory needs a certain amount of capital equipment to produce a certain output. Assume that there is an increase in demand for his products, so that the factory owner wishes to increase its output beyond the present capacity. If the technology stays the same, he must increase his capital equipment in proportion to the increase in output demanded. Therefore his demand for new capital (net investment) bears a precise relation to the increase in output.

This reasoning may be extended to the determination of net investment in the whole economy. At a given level of technology aggregate output can be increased only with a certain aggregate increase in capital (net investment). Therefore the demand for an increase in capital is in some ratio to the decision to increase output. That ratio is by definition the accelerator. Thus, in general, we may say that

$$\text{Change in capital} = \text{accelerator} \times \text{change in output}$$

By definition *capital* means the value of productive facilities. But the expenditure to increase productive facilities is by definition *net investment*. Because net investment is precisely the change in capital, we may write:

$$\text{Investment} = \text{accelerator} \times \text{change in output}$$

We may simply note the definition that

$$\text{Accelerator} = \frac{\text{investment}}{\text{change in output}}$$

and remember that this theory claims that the accelerator ratio is some precise and roughly constant number.

In the United States yearly output runs at about one-third of the value of all capital. Therefore it may be assumed that roughly three units of new capital are required to add one unit to national product.

The accelerator coefficient thus may be thought of as relating about three units of net investment to each added unit of output.

As an example, the output of shoes may be related to the investment in new shoe machinery. More demand for shoes means more investment in equipment. But if demand for shoes stays the same, there should be no further investment in shoe machinery. Finally, if demand for shoes declines, then the accelerator causes disinvestment. *Disinvestment* here means that some shoe machinery is allowed to wear out and is not replaced.

If the value of the accelerator is known, then what will happen to net investment for any movements of output can be predicted exactly. Table 27.1 picks some arbitrary changes in the output of shoes to see what will happen to investment in shoe machinery (given an accelerator set at 3).

The movements of shoe production are given arbitrarily; the rest of the table follows by assumption and definition. Thus from period 1 to period 2, output rises by $10, but because $3 of capital is required to produce $1 of output, capital must rise by $30. In other words, under this assumption a change in output of $10 causes net investment of $30. Similarly, in the next interval, a $20 rise in output causes $60 of investment. A *smaller* ($5) rise in output from period 3 to period 4 causes a *decline* in investment to only $15, and in the next interval, output does not change, so net investment, or the change in capital, must be zero.

From period 5 to period 6, output declines slightly, but investment must decline by three times as much. Next, a larger decline in output means a much larger decline in investment, and then a smaller decline in output causes a rise in investment to a less negative level. When output stops declining for a period, investment rises to zero. Finally, a small ($10) rise in output again leads to $30 of investment. Throughout, the level of net investment, or the change in capital, is related to the *change* in output. The desired new investment will always be the excess of desired capital over actual capital.

To illustrate the most important features of this process, the movements of output (shoe production) and net investment (increase or decrease in shoe machinery) may be graphed. The data in Table 27.1 are used as the basis for the graph in Figure 27.2.

Notice that in Figure 27.2 the movements of net investment in shoe machinery do not resemble the movements in the output of shoes; investment moves earlier and more sharply. However, the movements of investment in shoe machinery are exactly similar to the movements of the *change* in the output of shoes (multiplied by 3).

Several studies have indicated that in the long run, when productive capacity must grow if output is to grow, there is a roughly

TABLE 27.1

THE ACCELERATOR IN SHOE PRODUCTION (ASSUMING $3 MORE OF CAPITAL ARE NECESSARY TO PRODUCE $1 MORE OF OUTPUT)

Time Period	Shoe Production (Output)	Shoe Machinery (Capital)	Change in Output	Change in Capital (Net Investment)
1	$100	$300		
			$10	$30
2	110	330		
			20	60
3	130	390		
			5	15
4	135	405		
			0	0
5	135	405		
			−5	−15
6	130	390		
			−20	−60
7	110	330		
			−10	−30
8	100	300		
			0	0
9	100	300		
			10	30
10	110	330		

stable relationship between net investment and the change in output. In any short-run period, however, concern is focused on investment as an immediate psychological reaction to prospective changes in the amount of output demanded. It is easy to see that in the short run the rigid relationship between investment and change in output posited by the accelerator theory must be qualified in many ways.

First, even if the accelerator holds true for a 10-year period, does investment react exactly in that ratio to a change in demand in a 1-month period or even in a whole year? In reality the time lag between changed demand and net investment varies from industry to industry and even from phase to phase of the business cycle. A long and complicated process takes place before investment spending actually results. If demand improves, the corporate directors must come to *expect* increased future demand. But entrepreneurial expectations may also be affected by noneconomic psychological or political factors. Then the directors must appropriate funds for investment purposes and perhaps arrange outside financing. Next engineers must design new factories or new machines. Even after the construction actually begins, it is some time before all the investment funds are fully spent.[12]

[12]The timing of investment spending is discussed in detail in Howard Sherman and Thomas Stanback, "Cyclical Behavior of Profits, Appropriations, and Expenditures," *Proceedings of the American Statistical Association*, September 1962, pp. 274–285.

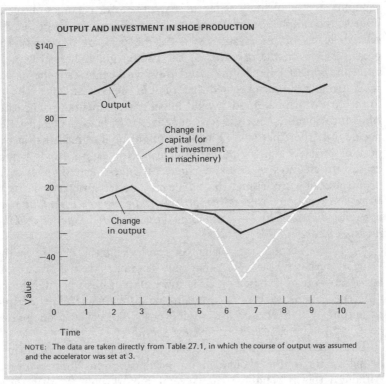

Figure 27.2

Second, the accelerator assumes that each industry faced with higher demands is already running at full capacity. That is not true, however, in a depression or in the early stages of recovery from a depression. During a depression there is much idle machinery and many empty, unused factories. Therefore in such periods any new demand can be met easily *without net investment*. Thus the accelerator is notably weaker whenever there is much unused capacity to produce.

Third, the accelerator ignores the physical limitations on the amount of investment or disinvestment in any given period. No matter how much the demand increases at the peak of prosperity, the investment goods industries can produce only so much in a given time. Therefore it must be assumed that these industries have just enough excess capacity to produce the investment goods called forth. Similarly, falling demand in a depression may indicate much disinvestment. But the whole economy can disinvest (or reduce its capital stock) in one year only to the extent of the depreciation of capital in that year. In other words, capital can be reduced in the economy as a whole only as fast as it wears out or becomes obsolete. Fourth, the simple accelerator ignores the effects of changes in the relative levels of prices and costs. At the peak of prosperity the great demand on the capacity of the capital goods industries may raise the *cost* of capital goods and thus weaken investment incentives. It might also be expected that a fall in the cost of labor relative to the cost of capital goods would impel entrepreneurs to substitute labor for capital in new projects; but there is little evidence that this occurs over short periods.[13] Finally, it might be imagined that at the peak of business activity the large demand for capital funds would cause interest rates to rise and choke off investment. However, if profits are high and rising, this effect may be felt primarily in new, large construction projects. *Empirical studies indicate that interest costs may not actually be of much quantitative importance in making investment decisions.*[14]

Of course because the change in profits and the change in the value of output will usually behave in the same way, the investment accelerator could be based on either one. Only if costs per unit move differently from prices will profits move differently from the value of output. The effects of a changing cost-to-price ratio on investment will be investigated in the next section.

Thus the accelerator principle says net investment is related in a definite ratio to the change in output during the business cycle. Although this is roughly true, several factors indicate that there is no reliable single fixed figure for the accelerator ratio. First, there is a long and varying time lag from the first indication of increased demand for output to the actual investment expenditure. Second, in a recession, the accelerator is greatly weakened. Third, investment cannot make as extreme swings as predicted because there is an upper limit, given by the capacity of the capital goods industries, and a lower limit, given by the amount of depreciation. Fourth, the simple accelerator is modified by changes in the relationship of prices and costs because these changes affect profits and, consequently, investments. There is no space here for a discussion of other modifications, such as the fact that the accelerator may work only in the aggregate and not at all in many individual industries. For all that, the accelerator does embody a large grain of truth and emphasizes the basic fact that new capital goods are built to meet new demand. It also explains, in part, why investment fluctuates so much more violently than consumer demand; it is related not to the level but to the *change* in demand. In Chapter 28 we shall combine the consumption function with the accelerator to explain a simple business cycle theory.

[13]See Meyer and Kuh, op. cit., pp. 181–189.
[14]Ibid., pp. 25–26, 189.

PRICE-COST
RELATIONS AND INVESTMENT

To this point we have spoken as if prices and costs per unit were constant, but in actuality prices do not stand still over the business cycle. For many decades before World War II prices varied systematically over the business cycle, almost always rising in times of expansion and declining during depressions. The best index of wholesale prices in the United States reveals that in 23 of the 26 cyclical expansions and contractions between 1890 and 1938, prices moved in the same direction as business activity and production. Thus part of the rise in demand during periods of expansion is taken up by higher output, but part is taken up by higher prices. Similarly, part of the decline in demand during times of contraction is met by lower output, but part is met by lower prices.

The greater volume of effective demand in expansion periods is financed both by a greater volume of money (as banks increase credit) and by a greater velocity of spending of money (as optimistic expectations speed up spending and reduce the percentage of money hoarded). Prices, however, are not isolated from costs; the price of one commodity may be part of the cost of another. Higher prices mean higher costs, which, in turn, cause higher prices; the process is cumulative. This cumulative expansion of prices, pushed up by higher costs and pulled up by more credit and faster spending, may be called the *normal inflation* of the average prosperity period.

Now costs may be divided into two main categories: (1) the cost of labor and (2) the cost of capital goods, including used-up raw materials, machines, and factories. We have seen that the total cost of labor rises less rapidly than the total revenue from output.

On the contrary, costs of capital goods rise faster than prices in times of expansion and decline facter during depressions. The reason is the acceleration principle, which states that the demand for capital rises as the demand for output rises. In periods of expansion the rapid increase of demand for output causes a high level of investment demand, which outruns the supply of capital goods and thereby causes a rapid rise in the price of capital goods. Moreover, demand for finished capital goods is transmitted to earlier stages of production in a further accelerated manner, so the prices of raw materials rise even more rapidly.

The theory of accelerated price increases in the earlier stages of production is borne out in a careful study of price behavior by Frederick Mills that includes data for many years on the prices of 22 consumer goods, 48 producer goods (i.e., capital goods except raw materials), and 32 raw materials.[15] Mills found that in the

[15]Frederick C. Mills, *Price-Quantity Interactions in Business Cycles* (New York: National Bureau of Economic Research, 1946), pp. 132–133.

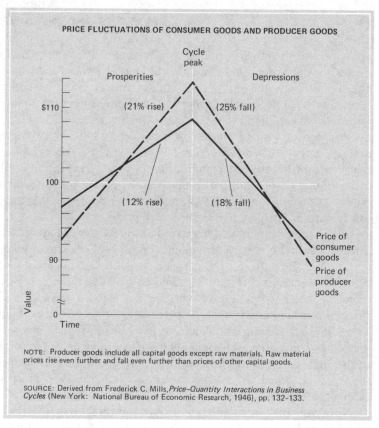

PRICE FLUCTUATIONS OF CONSUMER GOODS AND PRODUCER GOODS

NOTE: Producer goods include all capital goods except raw materials. Raw material prices rise even further and fall even further than prices of other capital goods.

SOURCE: Derived from Frederick C. Mills, *Price-Quantity Interactions in Business Cycles* (New York: National Bureau of Economic Research, 1946), pp. 132–133.

Figure 27.3

average expansion period, consumer goods prices rise by only 12 percent of their average value, but producer goods prices rise by 21 percent and raw materials prices rise by 23 percent. Similarly, in the average depression, consumer goods prices fall only 18 percent, but producer goods prices fall by 25 percent and raw materials prices by 26 percent. Some of these movements are illustrated in Figure 27.3.

In general, in the average business cycle consumer goods prices rise and fall the least, while producer goods prices rise and fall considerably more. Obviously as the peak of expansion is approached, the profit margin in consumer goods may fall while the profit margin in producer goods (and raw materials) may still be rising. But what does it matter if some industries make more profits while others make fewer profits, as long as the aggregate profit is unaffected?

It may make a great deal of difference if profits fall in one whole *stage of production.* The stage of production is a very useful concept in economics. It emphasizes that one group of industries must logically produce their products before another group can operate at all. Thus production of raw materials may be considered the first (or earliest or lowest) stage of production. The second stage would be production of producer goods such as machines and factories. The third and last stage would be the production of consumer goods.

We have been saying that prices in the third (consumption) stage rise and fall much less than those in the earlier stages. But prices of goods in the earlier stages (producer goods and raw materials) are costs of producing consumer goods. Thus as prosperity continues, prices are not rising as rapidly as costs in this whole range of consumer industry (which is by far the largest part of all industry). Therefore profit margins begin to fall in all of the consumer goods industries. Not only does this slow consumer goods production, but it must also (by the accelerator) result in a great decline of demand for all investment goods. Thus the squeeze on profit margins in consumer goods not only causes less production in the whole final stage of production of consumer goods but also reaches back to cause a decline in production of producer goods and raw materials. The point is that these earlier stages of production exist only for the ultimate purpose of providing the means of producing consumer goods. The decline of profit margins in consumer goods is enough to reduce aggregate investment and thereby end a boom.

The opposite process takes place in a depression. Consumer prices fall more slowly than the costs of producer goods and raw materials. The improvement of profit margins in consumer goods eventually leads to more investment and thereby begins a recovery.

SUMMARY

Investment shows violent fluctuations over the business cycle. In percentage terms consumption fluctuates much less. Investment depends on profit expectations. Profit expectations depend on expected revenues from sales and expected costs of production. Larger corporations and highly concentrated industries make higher profit rates than smaller corporations in more competitive industries. The giant corporations and concentrated industries also have more stable prices, profit rates, and investments. Small business is badly hurt and reacts strongly to even the slightest recession; many go bankrupt. Business investments rise and fall even more than the objective increases and declines in profit rates would indicate because of irrational and exaggerated psychological reactions ("confidence" or "lack of confidence").

The accelerator measures the reaction of investment to a change in output demanded. This theory tries to explain why small percentage changes in consumer demand usually result in huge changes in investment. Net investment may become negative in a depression. Yet net investment may rise very, very rapidly in a recovery.

The accelerator is not precise because it ignores many variables. One variable it ignores is the effect of changes in the cost of capital goods. In times of expansion, costs of capital goods rise faster than prices and output, so profits are squeezed and investment is damped. In times of contraction, costs of capital goods fall faster than prices, so profits do not fall as rapidly as they would otherwise and, eventually, investment recovers.

business cycles and unemployment

The *business cycle* may be defined as the movement of the economy between alternating periods of contraction (or depression) and expansion. In contractions, aggregate effective demand falls and production of total goods and services declines; the result is large-scale unemployment. In expansions, aggregate effective demand rises and production of total goods and services rises; the economy approaches full employment of workers and full use of capacity—though in some expansions there is still a significant amount of unemployment and unused capacity.

CONSERVATIVE NEOCLASSICAL THEORIES

Until the 1930s the main body of neoclassical economic theory did not try to explain, but rather tried to explain away, the business cycle. First, it was argued that the amount of general unemployment was exaggerated and that there were only partial and frictional fluctuations of production. Second, each depression was said to be the last. Indeed, in the 1920s they were said to be gone forever after more than 100 years of business cycle phenomena.

These attitudes are traceable, in the main, to the general social outlook of that period, which supported the status quo. In part, however, they may have resulted from the lack of much theoretical interest in the movements of aggregate demand. Neoclassical economists dealt mainly with demand for particular products based on the subjective utility to individual consumers. Individual desire, however, must obviously be limited and must begin to decline after some given quantity is consumed. Thus a typical neoclassical economist asserts: ". . . It is natural . . . that after the brisk demand of the . . . American public for motor cars in 1922–23, the intensity of the desire for these articles should fall away."[1] This approach leads naturally to thinking of the problem as one of absolute overproduction, of *too much* production. When, however, the entire economy is examined, and not just each individual product, it becomes clear that the problem in a major depression is not that more is produced than people subjectively desire to consume. On the contrary, there is not nearly enough produced to fulfill the desires or even the minimum health needs of the population; there is too much only *relative* to effective purchasing power.

As long as most economists accepted Say's law, which insists that there cannot be a general deficiency of effective demand relative to supply, there were only a few logically possible explanations for the fluctuations of aggregate output. One such explanation was that external, or noneconomic, shocks to the economy may limit supply or bring sudden demands. For example, sunspots may cause bad weather, and bad weather leads to bad harvests; unions may go on strike; governments may foolishly interfere with production activities; wars may stop the flow of raw materials or bring sudden demands for military production; and so forth. Thus one famous economist declares: "major depressions have been produced by a variety of different types of 'shocks,' not by a regular cycle-producing mechanism."[2]

Certainly such shocks as wars and bad weather do affect the economy; but such occurrences do not always coincide with the major swings in the economy, some of which occur in the absence of an apparent outside shock. Furthermore, noncapitalist economies have reacted quite differently to outside shocks. Therefore we may at least ask what mechanisms in the American economy give rise to cyclical movements as a result of these random shocks. We shall also try to understand how the internal operation of the economy might produce a business cycle even with no external shocks.

Before examining the internal functioning of the economy, we should mention the theory that explains depressions as a result of the shock of psychological pessimism. This theory argues that hoarding

---

[1]D. H. Robertson, *Banking Policy and the Price Level* (Clifton, N.J.: Augustus M. Kelley, 1949), p. 10.
[2]James S. Duesenberry, *Business Cycles and Economic Growth* (New York: McGraw-Hill, 1958), p. 11.

money is never rational. If money is not used for consumption, it is always most profitable to lend it at interest for further investment. Yet there may be temporary panics during which money is hoarded and credit is withheld. Typical of these explanations is the statement that "the chief cause of the evil is a want of confidence."[3] The defect of such theories lies in the fact that no one has ever demonstrated cycles of optimism and pessimism in businessmen independent of the economic cycle. In fact, the height of optimism is always reached, as in 1929, at the peak of the business cycle. Only *after* economic conditions have objectively worsened are there irrationally large reactions by businessmen, which intensify the economic downturn. Similarly, irrational optimism may intensify an economic expansion after conditions have objectively improved.

DESCRIPTION OF BUSINESS CYCLES

In 1913 Wesley Mitchell was one of the few relatively orthodox economists to view business cycle phenomena as other than accidental or external to the economy.[4] The thrust of all Mitchell's work is to demonstrate that the business cycle is a self-generating series of normal phases of business, each leading into the next under the conditions given by present economic institutions. Thus a contraction is the direct result of the preceding expansion, while every contraction prepares the way for a new expansion.

Mitchell showed that periods of expansion (which he called prosperity) are marked by rising production, relatively high rates of profit, high wages, high prices, and comparatively full employment. Periods of contraction are characterized by slower rises or actual declines in production, business losses, bankruptcies, relatively low wages, low prices, and large amounts of unemployment. A major contraction is called a depression; a minor contraction is called a recession.

Although Mitchell never formulated the comprehensive theory at which he was aiming, his immense empirical research forms the basis for all further scientific investigation of this field. Until the 1930s, however, few economists paid more than lip service to the facts presented by Mitchell. Those who mentioned these facts at all contended that they represented a special problem beyond the confines of the proper area of economics, which was to describe the process by which individual firms and individual consumers made minor ad-

[3]A. and M. P. Marshall, *The Economics of Industry* (London: Macmillan, 1881).

[4]Mitchell's first work on cycles was published in 1913. His last work, which argued the same basic position, was *What Happens During Business Cycles?* (New York: National Bureau of Economic Research, 1951).

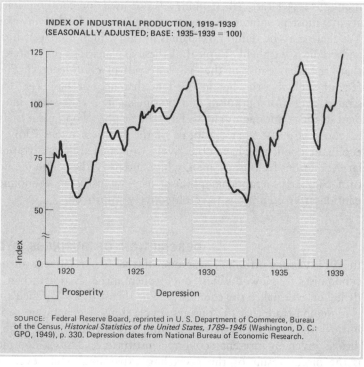

INDEX OF INDUSTRIAL PRODUCTION, 1919–1939
(SEASONALLY ADJUSTED; BASE: 1935–1939 = 100)

SOURCE: Federal Reserve Board, reprinted in U. S. Department of Commerce, Bureau of the Census, *Historical Statistics of the United States, 1789-1945* (Washington, D. C.: GPO, 1949), p. 330. Depression dates from National Bureau of Economic Research.

Figure 28.1

justments in a basically stable economy. In the Great Depression that complacency was forever shaken, although it raises its head anew in every expansion period.

In the early 1920s Mitchell made a thorough study, from every available source, of the business history of 17 countries.[5] He found that in none of these countries had periods of expansion continued for more than 5 or 6 years and that periods of expansion had always alternated with periods of depressed business activity. In the United States, from 1899 to 1959, there were recessions or depressions in 24 of the 60 years. From 1945 to 1959 alone, Americans experienced economic recession during about 23 percent of the time—or 40 out of 168 months. Many economists believe that only the Vietnam War prevented a recession from 1965 through 1968. There were new recessions, however, in 1969–1970 and in 1974, resulting in large amounts of unemployment.

Mitchell's comprehensive analysis of 794 different economic series (up to 1939) revealed that a very large percentage always move in

[5]W. C. Mitchell and W. L. Thorp, *Business Annuals* (New York: National Bureau of Economic Research, 1926).

the same direction as general business activity, though a few move contrary to it.[6] About 89 percent of Mitchell's economic series are dominated by the business cycle, and only 11 percent move irregularly with reference to it. It seems that the business cycle is a problem presented by real life and not by fancy, although the difficulty of having "too great" a supply of all goods does seem more appropriate to Alice in Wonderland than to an actual economy.

Figure 28.1 provides the index of U.S. industrial production in the "normal" peacetime period between the two world wars, from 1919 to 1939. This period has been studied intensively, and most modern business cycle theories are strongly influenced by the facts of these years. Here we see the minor depressions of the 1920s and the Great Depression of the 1930s. Notice that even in this so-called normal period the pattern is not simple but includes many minor fluctuations.

Since World War II the U.S. government has played a major role in the economy. For this and other reasons, the business cycle has been more moderate and has shown very different characteristics.

LIBERAL KEYNESIAN THEORIES

The economist whose name is connected with the theoretical revolution of the 1930s is Keynes (discussed in Chapters 11 and 25). As has been seen, Keynes' contribution was the demolition of Say's law. He recognized the possibility that the economy as a whole may be in equilibrium at other than full employment—that is, that more or less may be demanded than is supplied at full employment at the present price level. Most of his theory is to be found in some form in the work of earlier, but less orthodox, economists such as Marx (see Chapter 6) or Hobson (see Chapter 10). Furthermore, one of his most prominent followers comments that "Keynesian economics, in spite of all that it has done for our understanding of business fluctuations, has beyond doubt left at least one major thing unexplained; and that thing is nothing less than the business cycle itself."[7] Keynes' popularity perhaps is attributable to his having said, in a striking manner, the right thing at the right time, for he not only explained the possibility of depressions and inflations but also laid down possible solutions for these problems within the bounds of the private enterprise economic system.

The simplest Keynesian theory of the business cycle was stated by Alvin Hansen and Paul Samuelson.[8] It provides only a bare

[6]Mitchell, op. cit.
[7]J. R. Hicks, *The Trade Cycle* (Oxford: Clarendon Press, 1950), p. 1.
[8]See Paul Samuelson, "Interactions Between the Multiplier Analysis and the Principle of Acceleration," *Review of Economic Statistics*, May 1939, pp. 75–78.

sketch of reality, but it is an excellent means of illustrating the analytical framework on which more realistic theories may be built. The theory, sometimes called the *multiplier-accelerator* theory, consists of just three relationships. First, aggregate demand is composed of consumption spending plus investment spending. Of course this demand may be greater or less than the full-employment supply of output.

How much income is spent for consumption depends on the second relationship: Consumption is determined by some given propensity to spend out of last year's income. How much income is spent for investment depends on the third relationship: Investment is determined by the change in income during the previous year. If these three statements are accepted as reasonable approximations of reality, what kind of cyclical behavior results?

Assume that national income is expanding in the prosperity phase of the business cycle. The increase in income causes an even greater demand for new capital goods, or net investment. But an initial increase in investment spending causes a further increase in consumer spending and in national income. Then the process continues because the increase in income leads to more investment, which leads to more consumption and income, causing still more investment, and so forth. The consumption and investment relations together thus spell out a cumulative process: An initial expansion in the economy leads to continuing expansion.

Assume now that national income is contracting in the depression phase of the business cycle. The decrease in income causes (according to the accelerator) a much larger disinvestment of capital. The vast decrease in investment spending means much less income and less consumption. The further decrease in income leads to further disinvestment, which causes a further lowering of consumption, and so forth. Thus the combination of consumption and investment relationships also explains the cumulative process of contraction in the depression. An initial decline leads to continuing decline.

What is more difficult to understand is why the economy ever passes from the process of continuous expansion to the continuous contraction of depression, or, for that matter, how we move from depression back to expansion. The same theory can also explain these turning points, although not as persuasively as it explains cumulative expansion or contraction.

It is true that at the peak of expansion income, consumption, and investment are all increasing. Yet the careful observer can begin to discern strains and even cracks in the impressive facade of prosperity. Consumption increases, but the propensity to consume begins to decline as the portion of income saved increases. As a result, the aggregate demand out of national income rises more and more slowly. But a *smaller* increase in national income means, according to the investment relationship (the accelerator), an absolute decline in net investment. A decline in net investment, however, means an absolute fall in consumer spending and national income. Thus begins the process of contraction into depression.

Similarly, at the lowest point in a depression (the trough) it is true that income, consumption, and investment are all contracting. Yet as total consumption declines, the propensity to consume rises. As a result, the aggregate demand out of national incomes falls more and more slowly. But a *smaller* decline in national income means, according to the accelerator, an absolute rise in the level of investment (or at least less disinvestment). This causes a rise, no matter how small, in aggregate spending. Then the rise in spending means more income and a rise in consumption. Thus begins the process of recovery and expansion. Some readers may gain understanding from an arithmetic example of the whole process of expansion, downturn, depression, upturn, and again prosperity. Such an example can be constructed from the simple assumptions about consumption and investment behavior. Assume that net investment always equals the preceding change in income (that is, the accelerator is exactly 1). Also assume that the marginal propensity to consume is 0.90, or 90 percent of the previous period's income, to which we must always add some arbitrary minimum consumption (say, $96 billion). The resulting cyclical process of expansion and contraction is shown in Figure 28.2.

The time periods here may be taken as 2 or 3 months. Notice that after the initial rise the national income falls for 10 periods (from $1 trillion to $920 billion), then rises for 10 periods (from $920 billion to $1 trillion), and then begins to fall again. This same fluctuation will continue forever, or as long as we keep the same assumptions. Consumption is always determined by the preceding national income, and net investment is always determined by the difference between the two preceding national incomes. National income itself is always the sum of the consumption plus the net investment of the same period. Thus does the simplest (or multiplier-accelerator) theory give a consistent picture of how the economy produces depression out of expansion and expansion out of depression in a continuing business cycle.

THE UNDERCONSUMPTIONIST
VERSION OF LIBERAL THEORY

All economists agree that the simplest liberal Keynesian multiplier-accelerator theory is too simple to explain many of the facts. The liberal economist John Hobson argued that consumer demand is too

ARITHMETIC EXAMPLE OF SIMPLEST BUSINESS CYCLE THEORY[a,b]

(Assumes that consumption is always $96 billion plus 90 percent of the previous period's income, and that net investment is always equal to the change in income to one period ago from two periods ago. Also assumes that national income is expanding from $996 billion in first period to $1000 billion in second period. All figures in billions of dollars.)

Time period	Consumption	National income	Net investment
1		$ 996	
2		1000	
3	$996	1000	$ 4
4	996	996	0
5	992	988	−4
6	985	977	−8
7	975	965	−11
8	964	952	−12
9	953	940	−13
10	942	930	−12
11	933	923	−10
12	927	920	−7
13	928	925	−3
14	928	933	5
15	936	944	8
16	945	956	11
17	957	969	12
18	969	982	13
19	978	991	13
20	987	996	9
21	995	1000	5

[a]Some of the numbers are not exact because of rounding.

[b]The arrows show lines of influence. Only the first few arrows are shown. The student should fill in the rest of the arrows. The result will show how the pattern is repeated in every period.

Figure 28.2

restricted because wages are too low. He believed unemployment cycles could be cured under capitalism if workers were given higher wages—a theory that appeals to many trade unionists.

Hobson did *not* say that workers' wages—or even their share of income—are always declining. That could explain how capitalism gets into a depression but not how it gets out of it. What Hobson argued is that while total wages rise in the expansion period, the *share* of wages in national income falls. We saw in Chapter 26 that it is true that the wage share declines—while the profit share rises—in every expansion on record (and that the opposite happens in most contractions).

Hobson asked, What is the effect on consumer demand of this shift from wages to profits? He argued that profit makers have much higher incomes than wage workers. Therefore they save more and have a lower propensity to consume. Since they now have a larger share of national income, the national propensity to consume will decline. Again, we saw in Chapter 26 that this is a true statement.

Hobson concluded that in every expansion period the propensity to consume tends to fall, mainly because of the shift from wages to profits. Hobson thought this was sufficient to explain how inadequate consumer demand at the cycle peak causes a depression, while the opposite process would initiate a recovery.

Critics noted that this argument is not sufficient. Though there may not be enough consumer demand to buy all new production, investor demand may fill the gap. As one conservative economist says, "It will not do to explain insufficiency of investment by the insufficiency of effective demand because effective demand would be sufficient if aggregate investment were."[9] Of course if consumption were not rising at all, more investment could only mean the production of factories to produce more factories to produce more factories, and so on.

Later underconsumptionists completed the argument by explaining investment with the help of the accelerator principle. As we saw in Chapter 27, the accelerator principle says that investment is determined by the increase in aggregate demand. But consumer demand is the largest component of aggregate demand. When consumer demand rises more slowly at the peak, it means aggregate demand also increases more slowly. When the increase in aggregate demand is less and less, the accelerator says investment will actually fall. This sets off a depression. (The opposite process at the bottom of the depression initiates a recovery.) The process is depicted in Figure 28.3.

THE OVERINVESTMENT
VERSION OF LIBERAL THEORY

While some liberals argue that wages are too low, leading to underconsumption and depression, some conservative economists argue that wages are too high. They claim that *too much investment* leads to a fantastic demand for labor at the cycle peak. The rising cost of labor squeezes prices and sets off a depression. The only trouble with this theory is that it is contrary to the facts; wages rise much more slowly than prices or profits.

There are other versions of the notion that too much investment —or overinvestment—lands the economy in trouble (or "overheats"

[9]William Fellner, "The Capital-Output Ratio," in *Money, Trade, and Economic Growth: Essays in Honor of John Henry Williams* (New York: Macmillan, 1951), p. 121.

UNDERCONSUMPTION VIEW OF CRISIS AT CYCLE PEAK

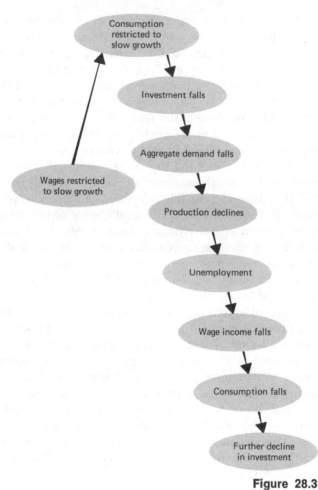

Figure 28.3

the economy). The most interesting and accurate idea relies on the rising costs of capital goods. The argument is that at the cycle peak investors try to buy more capital goods than are available; their demand is based on the accelerator principle.

As a result, *the price of capital goods rises more rapidly than other prices*, particularly faster than consumer goods prices. In Chapter 27 we saw that this is true of the average expansion period. Since prices of consumer goods rise more slowly, the profits of capitalists in this sector are squeezed by the rising costs.

The overinvestment theorists argue that such a profit squeeze will reduce capitalists' investments in production. Investments are reduced by lower rates of profit because (1) there is less expectation of future profits and (2) there are less funds available to the capitalists. Facts bear out this relationship, as we saw in Chapter 27. One

OVERINVESTMENT VIEW OF CRISIS AT CYCLE PEAK

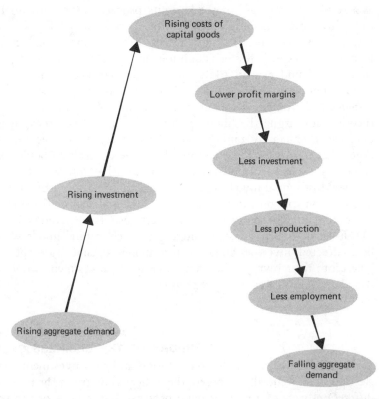

Figure 28.4

study of investment behavior, utilizing quarterly data for each of fifteen manufacturing industry groups, discloses a significant correlation between total profits and investment decisions in almost every industry.[10]

The overinvestment theory seems paradoxical. The cause of the crisis at the peak of the cycle is *too much* investment, which leads to high costs and small profit margins, which *reduces* investment and sets off a depression. Yet this theory does reflect an aspect of reality and seems to make sense when we carefully summarize it. (The chain of reasoning is also shown in Figure 28.4.)

To summarize the overinvestment theory: In expansion, rapidly rising demand for investment goods (overinvestment) causes a rapid rise in the cost of these goods to investors. The prices of consumer goods rise more slowly, squeezing profit margins in that sector, and

[10]See Howard J. Sherman and Thomas M. Stanback, Jr., "Cyclical Behavior of Profits, Appropriations, and Expenditures: Some Aspects of the Investment Process," *Proceedings of the American Statistical Association*, September 1962, pp. 274–286.

as a result, the increase of total profits proceeds more slowly. Because investment is determined by the increase in profits, less increase in profits causes less investment. Less investment causes less income which causes less consumption, and so forth until the depression is well under way. (The opposite process takes place in the contraction period and eventually leads to recovery.)

Since the problem is a profit reduction due to higher costs, these theorists also argue the liberal position that the government could cure the problem by taking appropriate steps. A few economists argue that profits could be restored by wage controls to hold down wage costs—a road the Nixon administration has followed to some extent. Most would lower costs of capital to investors through more indirect controls on interest rates. They would manipulate money and credit supplies so as to lower interest costs (see Chapters 30 and 31). Even though the costs of buying physical capital goods would be unaffected, investors could borrow money capital more cheaply. Therefore their own profits would be higher, investment would be stimulated, and the economy would recover.

A GENERAL (RADICAL)
THEORY OF THE BUSINESS CYCLE

Although the liberals' underconsumption and overinvestment theories appear superficially opposed, the radical view treats them as two different aspects of a more general process. At the peak of prosperity, the limited consumer demand *and* the rising cost per unit act together to squeeze profits and choke off economic circulation. At the trough of the depression, the end of decline in consumer demand *and* the falling costs per unit increase profits and stimulate economic activity.

The theory that depression is caused by *both* limited demand (underconsumption) and high costs (overinvestment) is a radical one because it shows that cycles of expansion and depression are inevitable under capitalism. Some liberals believe they could prevent depressions by higher wages, but that ignores the cost problem. Some conservatives would prevent depressions by lowering wages and interest rates, but that ignores the demand problem. Actually most traditional economists now agree with radicals that cycles of boom and burst are inherent in unregulated capitalism. They have fallen back to the second line of defense: that depressions can be prevented by the monetary and fiscal policies of the U.S. government (an issue discussed in the next three chapters).

The general radical theory may be stated here, very briefly, within the same framework we used earlier. Demand for output consists of consumption plus investment. Cost of output consists of wages plus plant, equipment, and materials used up. Total profit is the difference between the value of output demanded and the cost of output produced.

We assume the underconsumptionist version of consumer behavior. Consumption is a function of wage income and profit income. There is a high propensity to consume out of wage income and a lower propensity to consume out of profit income. Furthermore, we may assume with the underconsumptionists that wages rise (and fall) more slowly than national income. Thus as income rises in prosperity, the portion of income spent for consumption *must decline* because there is a shift of income from the wage earners, who have a high propensity to consume, to the profit takers, who have a significantly lower propensity to consume.

On the overinvestment side of the picture, we may assume that unit costs of capital goods rise faster than general prices, thereby reflecting the excessive demand for capital goods caused by overinvestment. (Wages are important because they are the largest single element of cost. But wages do not rise as rapidly as prices.) Costs of capital goods rise more rapidly than prices, and it may be that this element by itself causes total unit costs to rise more rapidly than prices at the peak of prosperity. Thus we may admit that total wages are rising absolutely in times of expansion but still argue (as do the modern underconsumptionists) that the wage share has been a declining *percentage* of national income in most past cyclical expansions. To complete the picture we need only add that it is consistent with both theories and with the facts to assume that aggregate investment is determined by the change in aggregate profits. This chain of reasoning is depicted in Figure 28.5.

According to our assumptions, the usual business cycle will appear phase by phase as follows: In the expansion period, national income and profits are rapidly rising. As income rises, wages and capital costs must also rise. As wages and profits are both increasing, aggregate consumption must increase. But the shift from wages to profits means a lower propensity to consume, which means that eventually aggregate consumption rises more slowly than aggregate income. For a while, however, investment increases quickly enough to fill the gap between aggregate output and consumption.

At the height of expansion, the maturation of these very tendencies causes the economy to reverse direction. Wages lag further and further behind aggregate income, and the propensity to consume continues to decline; therefore consumer demand lags behind output. At the same time, profit rates are squeezed from the other side by the rising costs of capital. As demand for output rises more slowly

RADICAL VIEW OF CRISIS AT CYCLE PEAK

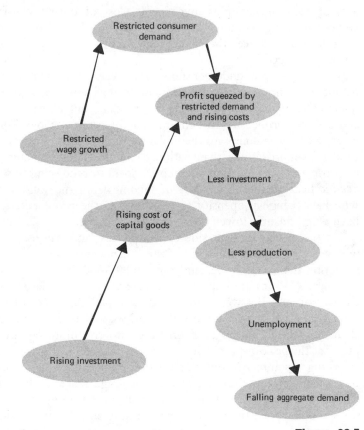

Figure 28.5

and costs rise faster than prices, the profit margin stops rising and may actually decline in many industries. With profits no longer rising rapidly, investment cannot stay at a high level, let alone rise sufficiently to fill the gap between output and consumption. Total demand falls short of supply, the contraction commences.

In the first stages of contraction, aggregate output, consumption, investment, wages, and profits all fall rapidly. Eventually, as wages fall less than profits, consumption falls less than national income and demand is relatively improved. On the other side, costs per unit decline more than prices until profits stop falling so rapidly (and actually begin to rise in some industries). With both the demand and cost picture looking less gloomy, investment picks up again. Rising investment means more employment, more wages, more profits, and a stimulus to consumption. Thus the recovery begins, and we arrive back in the expansion period, where the cycle begins again.

FACTORS INTENSIFYING
CYCLICAL UNEMPLOYMENT

We have now stated the basic theory of business cycles, but it is still quite abstract. To get closer to reality we must examine many other factors that do not cause, but do seem to intensify, cyclical upswings and depressions. Among these factors are (1) monopoly rigidities in the economy, (2) irrational optimism and pessimism, (3) foreign trade and investment, (4) postponement or hurrying of major inventions and innovations, (5) depreciation and replacement cycles, (6) panics and expansions in money and credit, and (7) inventory cycles. We shall investigate each of these briefly.

It was shown earlier that the U.S. economy is now dominated by oligopoly and monopoly power. How has this affected business cycles? The early apologists for monopoly claimed that by eliminating competition the big corporations would make the economy more stable and end depressions. That has not happened; the depression of 1929 (with monopoly already dominant) is the worst on record.

What we find is that the major monopolies are *themselves* quite stable in the sense that they are able to prevent their own prices, profits, and investments from dropping in a depression. *But these rigidities caused by monopoly hurt the economy as a whole.* Thus their higher prices are achieved by restricting supply of output, which means more unemployed workers. Their high profits come from the pockets of workers by lowering wages and charging higher prices. They also squeeze small farmers and small business by charging high prices for supplies of machinery and raw materials, but paying low wholesale prices for farm products. As a result of lower employment and lower real wages, there is still less consumer demand. As a result of the profit squeeze on small farmers and small business, there are thousands more bankruptcies.

The second factor intensifying business cycles is changes in psychological expectations. It appears to be the usual order of events in depressions that, first, production and financial indexes decline in spite of the most extreme optimism. Then, because of the change in economic conditions, the optimism changes to extreme pessimism and the extreme pessimism reinforces the depression and may postpone the recovery. The reverse process occurs in economic expansions, when rises in production and profits are followed by a shift from pessimism to optimism. These psychological expectations of economic conditions are not random. Specifically, *after* prosperity begins, optimism greatly intensifies the expansion. And *after* depression sets in, pessimism greatly intensifies the business contraction.

A third intensifying factor is changes in foreign trade and investment. The establishment of new colonies or new major areas of investment abroad, or the loss of colonies or confiscation of investment abroad, are random shocks that are apt to affect the level of economic activity. Like other random factors, they cannot account for the systematic fluctuation between long periods of expansion and long periods of contraction. For a small country, the loss of a colony might be a major disruption. But for the United States, even the loss of all its investments in Cuba had little aggregate effect (although it affected several individual corporations quite adversely). There is litle evidence to indicate any direct and systematic causal connection between investment abroad and domestic business cycles. This is not to say that foreign investments are unimportant to American corporations. On the contrary, they appear to be increasing in importance, as will be seen in Chapters 34 and 35.

A fourth intensifying factor is the postponement of major inventions and innovations in depressions and their hurried introduction in periods of expansion. There is no apparent reason to assume that the whole mass of investors should have ideas in bunches.[11] Of course one major invention is likely to lead to many others in that field or in closely related fields, but unusual inventive activity in one area may be canceled *on the average* by unusual lack of activity in some other area. There would still be some random variation in the rate of invention; but it would be within moderate limits around the given rate, certainly not enough by itself to set off a major depression or recovery.

However, the rate of invention may be influenced by the state of the economy. In a period of prosperity increased demand for output means increased desire for better technology with which to expand output rapidly. And more funds may be available for research. By contrast, research expenditures dropped in the severe depression of 1929–1933.

The rate of innovation (putting inventions to an economic use) does have its random movements. But the only movements great enough to cause significant intensification of the business cycle are the declines in innovation registered after depressions have begun and the rise in innovations registered after expansions have begun. It thus appears that changes in the rate of innovation are determined mostly by changes in business conditions; they are not an outside factor that causes business cycles, although in the long run innovations are an important factor leading to economic growth.

A fifth intensifying factor is the postponement or hurrying of in-

[11]For the opposite argument, that inventions and innovations inevitably tend to appear in waves and that business cycles "are due to the intermittent action of the 'force' of innovation," see Joseph A. Schumpeter, *Business Cycles* (New York: McGraw-Hill, 1939), p. 175, passim.

vestment to replace depreciated capital equipment, which is normally more than 50 percent of all investment.[12] If replacement spending is greater or less than current allowances for depreciation, then total demand is greater or less than it would have been. Furthermore, most changes in the difference between replacement and depreciation are not random with respect to the business cycle. During a depression, when there is no desire to maintain a high level of output, many necessary replacements may be postponed. Yet depreciation allowances continue, and thus this source of saving may be far greater than the replacement investment during such a period. In fact, because depreciation is related to aggregate capital accumulated in many previous years, it declines only very slightly except in very long depressions.[13]

Replacement expenditures are often postponed because they are not "needed" during depressions, so the continued saving of funds for *eventual* replacement of depreciated machinery means a net loss of demand. This reduction of demand intensifies the depression. On the other hand, when a long period of prosperity begins, firms spend replacement funds sooner than necessary; the latest innovations are made as "replacements" long before the old machinery has finished its useful life. This extra investment demand then adds fuel to the expansion under way.

A sixth factor intensifying depressions is the monetary panic that has often closed (and bankrupted) banks and further restricted demand in crises, as in 1907 and again in 1929. The stock market crash of 1929 still further contracted available funds. A closely related factor is the credit policies of financial institutions. They charge high interest rate at the peak of the crisis, pushing many small businesses to the wall. On the other hand, they are free and easy with credit during expansion, encouraging much speculation. Therefore expansion of money and credit supplies during prosperity intensifies economic expansion, while collapse of money and credit in crises worsens depressions. So money and credit, like the other factors just discussed, do not cause depressions by themselves, but their reactions can turn mild downturns into awful depressions.

The seventh and final intensifying factor to be considered here is the rise and fall of inventories. Inventories are stocks of goods held by producers, wholesalers, or retailers. Cycles are caused partly by fluctuations in investment in producers' equipment and factories but also by fluctuations in investment in inventories. Changes in inventory investment play a very important role in most business cycles.

[12]See Simon S. Kuznets' data, discussed in R. A. Gordon, "Investment Opportunities in the United States," in *Business Cycles in the Post-War World* (New York: Oxford University Press, 1952), p. 293.
[13]See Mitchell, op. cit., p. 142.

For example, in the five business cycles from 1919 through 1938, the average change in inventory investment accounted for 23.3 percent of the average rise in GNP in expansions and 47.5 percent of the decline in GNP in contractions. In the same period, changes in construction and producers' durable equipment together accounted for an average of only 20.5 percent of the rises and 37 percent of the declines.[14] This finding was confirmed for the postwar period when changes in inventories again constituted very large percentages of the cyclical changes in GNP.[15] If the longer and more severe, or major, depressions or expansions are examined, it appears that much of the decline or rise occurs in investment in plant and equipment. Examination of the shorter, less severe, minor recessions or expansions reveals, however, that most of the decline or rise is in inventory investment.

In the upswing of the cycle, when sales are rising and businessmen are optimistic, there is a high level of inventory investment. Businessmen try to keep their inventories in some desired ratio to sales but are never able to keep enough on hand during rapid expansions. The high and rising level of investment in inventories is one more factor pushing demand upward during the expansion.

Only after the peak of the cycle is passed and a depression begins do business inventories finally catch up with sales expectations. Then, shortly, as sales are falling and businessmen become pessimistic, they start to lower the level of inventory investment. By the trough of the cycle, businessmen believe they have far too many goods on hand to sell in a reasonable time, so they frantically try to reduce their inventories. Then inventory investment becomes quite negative—that is, it is less than what is sold. Thus inventory investment reacts to the same factors as plant and equipment investment (falling consumer demand, relatively high costs), and the precipitous decline in inventory investment makes the depression that much worse by further lowering the demand for goods.

SUMMARY

Our basic business cycle theory has been modified to a considerable degree. The rigid consumption function and investment accelerator mechanisms, basic to all the theories of the cycle examined in this chapter, are not by any means the full explanations of the history of economic expansions and contractions. We saw in the underconsumptionist theory that it is not enough to consider how consump-

[14]See Moses Abramowitz, *Inventories and Business Cycles* (New York: National Bureau of Economic Research, 1950), p. 5.

[15]See Thomas Stanback, Jr., *Post-war Cycles in Manufacturers' Inventories* (New York: National Bureau of Economic Research, 1962), p. 6.

tion is determined by the level of income. Income must be separated into wages and profits; and the shift from wages to profits in prosperity, with a return to a lower profit ratio in depression, must be considered. There is a higher propensity to consume out of wages, so a shift to profits means a lower national propensity to consume.

We also examined overinvestment theories, which stress changes in costs of capital goods and raw materials and their effects on profit margins. Then we looked at the impact of monopoly, noting that rigid monopoly prices make adjustments to depression more difficult, raise unemployment, and cause low profits and bankruptcies among small businesses. Finally, we found that both booms and busts are intensified by many other secondary factors, including irrational psychological reactions, money and credit panics and speculation, postponements (or speedups) of innovations, postponements (or speedups) of replacements for depreciated capital, and inventory investment or disinvestment.

government: welfare or warfare?

In American society the economy is powerfully influenced by the government, though the government is dominated to a large extent by economic power. The U.S. government has always affected the economy in many ways, from the inflationary spending of the Revolutionary War period through the deficit financing of the 1930s. An essentially new relationship has emerged, however, in recent years. Since 1941 the government has become far and way the largest single source of demand. The newly emerged economic structure is dominated not only by large private firms but also by pervasive governmental activity, mostly centered around military production. It follows that the actions of the U.S. government now form an integral part of the American economy. The following sections present a very brief introduction to each of the areas in which the governmental activity has affected economic growth and stability. (Earlier, in Chapter 20, we discussed the role of government in relation to the distribution of income.)

GOVERNMENT AND THE EARLY ECONOMY

The history of U.S. government activity is a record of the conflicts between the interests of sectors, regions, and groups, and most often these interests have been economic. As Madison said,

But the most common and the most durable source of faction has been the various and unequal distribution of property. Those who hold and those who are without property have ever formed distinct interests in society. Those who are creditors, and those who are debtors, fall under a like discrimination. A landed interest, a manufacturing interest, a mercantile interest, a moneyed interest, with many lesser interests, grow up of necessity in civilized nations, and divide them into different classes, actuated by different sentiments and views. The regulation of these various and interfering interests forms the task of modern legislation. . . .[1]

From the Revolutionary War through the nineteenth century, the government was concerned primarily with the protection of property, the promotion of business, and the establishment of the necessary institutional framework for a commercial, industrial economy.

One of the earliest demands on the national government was for tariff protection. American shipping and young, inefficient manufacturing industries wanted protection from European competition. From the very first, U.S. tariff policy was generally designed to serve American business interests and to ensure high profits by reducing foreign competition. Even when businessmen held the doctrine of laissez faire in the very highest esteem, they continued as a group to advocate tariffs. Allowing for a few brief, exceptional periods, the government gave them their tariffs and protected their internal monopolistic powers.

Just as important to the economy was a sound currency. The government actively pursued a policy of providing a stable and adequate money supply, and eventually central control over the monetary system, called for in the Constitution, was realized. The *proper amount* of money was a matter of considerable dispute throughout the nineteenth century. Many interests argued for more abundant, or easy, money; others argued for restricted, or tight, money.

Many sophisticated arguments were given in defense of easy and tight money. These arguments, however, often only thinly veiled the pleading of special interests. The advocates of easy money were the farmers and small businessmen, particularly along the frontier, who needed credit to buy and develop land. The eastern capitalists, who were generally creditors, did not enjoy the prospect of lower interest rates or plentiful dollars. Usually the federal government was accused of aligning with the eastern money interests. This widespread view helped Jackson kill the second United States Bank, which would have established a uniform banking and monetary system.

[1] James Madison, *The Federalist*, no. 10.

TABLE 29.1

STATE GOVERNMENTS' USES OF BORROWED MONEY IN 1838

Banking	$ 52,640,000
Canals	60,201,551
Railroads	42,871,084
Turnpikes	6,618,868
Miscellaneous	8,474,684
Total	$170,806,187

Source: Tenth Census of the United States, vol. VII (Washington, D.C.: GPO), p. 526.

The conflict became particularly intense in the last third of the nineteenth century, when the average price level fell continuously. This was very damaging to debtors who borrowed money when it was worth less and paid it back when it was worth more. Farmers in particular became a disgruntled class. With the advent of mechanized agriculture, they had gone deeply into debt. Agricultural prices fell precipitously, but freight rates failed to decline substantially. As money became worth more and more, they were continuously and ruthlessly squeezed. During this period agricultural and labor interests united to demand currency reform and the abolition of the gold standard. This cry for easy money was one of the unifying forces in the Populist political movement.

Another important function of the government in the eighteenth and nineteenth centuries was the creation of efficient transportation networks, a primary prerequisite for the growth of a commercial, private enterprise system. The importance of a stable currency and efficient transportation can be seen by examining the projects state governments financed through borrowing. Table 29.1 gives a breakdown of the nearly $171 million of state government debts in 1838.

Although the market was potentially national in size, a huge investment in transportation was necessary before regional markets could be united. Between 1815 and 1860, federal and state governments made 73 percent of the total investment in canal development, and governments were large suppliers of capital funds for railway construction before the Civil War.

After the Civil War, the railroad boom became even more important to the American economy. Between 1865 and 1914, railroad mileage increased from about 37,000 to almost 253,000 miles. During this period, the federal government became a major source of railroad financing. Earlier, between 1850 and 1871, the U.S. Congress had given away 175,350,000 acres of choice public lands to the railroads—a gift to private enterprise of taxpayers' property worth about $489,000,000.[2] In addition, in the same period, the government had granted the railroads $65,000,000 in special low-cost credit.

Thus throughout the period during which American capitalism was developing into an industrial giant, the government was instrumental in providing the institutional and economic framework in which profitable business could be conducted. Private enterprise profited handsomely as taxpayers subsidized many of the business and industrial ventures that helped provide these necessities.

FISCAL POLICY

The economic role of government that most directly influences the level of output, income, and employment is its taxing and spending of money, or *fiscal policy*. During most of American history the federal government has based its taxing and spending decisions on the political value of the project on which the money was to be spent. The effects of fiscal policy on output, income, and employment were ignored until the depression of the 1930s.

The prevailing economic philosophy was that taxes should be used only to finance necessary government expenditures. It was thought to be an unsound financial practice for governments to borrow money. If a balanced budget, in which expenditures equaled taxes, could not be achieved, it was thought to be preferable to have taxes exceed expenditures so that any debts incurred in the past could be retired. Only the Great Depression and the World War II experience forced a change in this policy. The trend since that time has been for government spending to rise much more rapidly than taxes.

Federal government spending in the United States in 1921–1929 was only 1 percent of GNP. In 1930–1940, as the New Deal responded to the Depression, it had increased to 4 percent of GNP. With World War II, government spending rose to the incredible height of 41 percent of GNP in 1943 and 1944. After the war it fell somewhat, but it bounced up again in the Korean war, so federal spending averaged 11 percent of GNP in 1945–1959. In 1960–1970, partly owing to the Vietnam War, federal spending averaged 13 percent of GNP—about two-thirds or more being military.[3] Total government spending—including state and local as well as federal—has averaged about 25 percent of GNP ever since 1945.

[2] G. C. Fite and J. E. Reese, *An Economic History of the United States,* 2d ed. (Boston: Houghton Mifflin, 1965), p. 330.

[3] James Cypher, *Military Expenditures* (Ph.D. dissertation, University of California, Riverside, 1973), chap. 6.

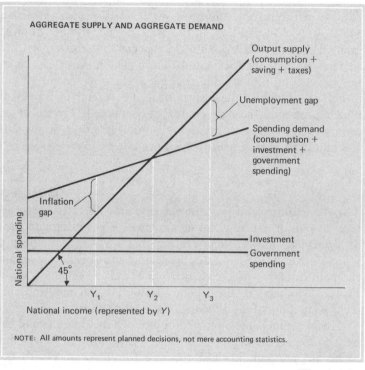

Figure 29.1

GOVERNMENT EXPENDITURES
AND AGGREGATE DEMAND

In the income determination model discussed in Chapter 25, we assumed an economy in which there was no government economic activity. We now move a step closer to reality by considering government spending and taxes.

Taxes, like saving, are a leakage from the income stream. Government expenditures, like investment, are an injection into the spending stream. Aggregate supply is now the total of consumption, saving, and *taxes*. Aggregate demand is the total of consumption, investment spending, and *government spending*. The equilibrium of aggregate supply and demand is depicted in Figure 29.1.

Figure 29.1 is exactly like earlier pictures of supply and demand except that government expenditures and taxes have been added. In this picture Income 2 is the equilibrium level of income, where aggregate supply and demand just happen to balance. Suppose that full employment will produce some much higher level of output and income, such as Income 3; then there is a lack of aggregate demand at that higher level, only Income 2 is actually produced, and there is vast unemployment. On the other hand, suppose that we have many fewer workers or less technology so that only a much lower level of output and income can be produced, such as Income 1. At that low level of output, there is a great excess of money demand for goods, but no more can actually be produced, so prices must rise and there is inflation until Income 2 is reached in money terms.

All of this duplicates what was said in Chapter 25 on income determination (which the student should review). What is new is that with government in the picture something can be done about either the unemployment or the inflation, assuming we don't have both at the same time. If there is unemployment—because we could produce at Income level 3, which is far above equilibrium—then the government can add to demand in one of two ways. It can directly increase government spending, which is a component of demand, and/or it can lower taxes, which increases the income available to be spent for consumer or investor demand.

On the other hand, if there is inflation because demand is at too high a level (perhaps because of vast government military spending), then the government can reduce demand in one of two ways. First, it may lower the level of government spending. Second, it may raise taxes, which reduce the amount people have left over for consumer or investor spending. These are the simple mechanics of fiscal policy; we will now proceed to its problems.

AUTOMATIC STABILIZERS

Excessive or deficient demand can be combated in two ways: with *automatic* fiscal devices and with *discretionary* fiscal policies. Automatic fiscal policy is built into the present structure of governmental taxing and spending to react automatically to inflation or depression. Discretionary fiscal policies are changes in the fiscal structure made by current and conscious government decisions. Since World War II the government has placed more reliance on automatic than on discretionary fiscal measures. The fiscal structure is supposed automatically to expand net government demand in depressions and to decrease net government demand in inflations.

To understand the working of the automatic stabilizers, we must glance back at the circular flow of income and spending. The circular flow, with the addition of government income and spending, is illustrated in Figure 29.2. Note that some government money flows *to* business (demand for goods and services) and households (welfare payments). The government receipts flow *from* business (sales taxes, corporate profit taxes, and social security taxes) and households (personal income taxes). An automatic stabilizer is a government device built into the fiscal system that automatically increases or decreases government flows to or from the rest of the economy in response to changes in economic conditions.

CIRCULAR FLOW OF INCOME

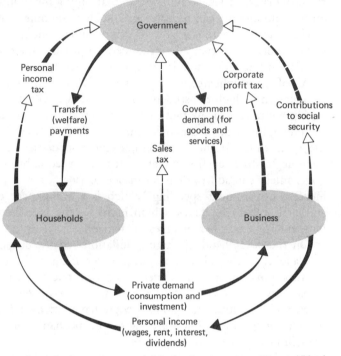

NOTE: International transactions are excluded, otherwise net exports would be an additional demand for products.

Figure 29.2

In a depression, when GNP tends to drop, the stabilizers should automatically increase government money flows to businesses and households and/or decrease money flows from businesses and households to the government. This will prevent disposable personal income from dropping as rapidly as otherwise, and thus investment and consumption expenditures can be maintained at a higher level. Similarly, in an inflation, the automatic stabilizers are supposed to decrease the amount given and increase the amount taken away from business and households, thus decreasing the total amount of consumer and investor spending. In either case the net changes in government flows should have a multiple effect.

Now what are the magic devices by which the government is supposed to keep the economy automatically stable? First, there are government taxes that automatically fall and rise faster than national income. The most important of these is the personal income tax. Most property taxes, sales taxes, and corporate taxes do *not* fall or rise faster than national income. But the personal income taxes paid to the federal government and to many states are a *progressive* tax system, which means that tax rates are higher in higher income brackets and lower in lower income brackets. Therefore as national product falls in a depression, personal income taxes fall faster because income falls into lower tax brackets. As a result, consumer and investor spending may fall less rapidly than they would otherwise. However, as the money value of national income rises in an inflation, the average tax bracket moves upward, and personal income taxes rise faster than national income, thus restricting the amount of private spending.

At the same time, on the spending side of the ledger, the government makes many types of welfare payments that automatically increase in depression and automatically decrease in inflation. For example, as full employment is approached, there will be very little unemployment compensation; but in a depression, with growing unemployment, this may become a significant source of buying power. Furthermore, many other kinds of relief to children or unwed mothers may have to be greatly increased in a depression but may become much less necessary in prosperity. Of course the individuals receiving unemployment compensation or relief benefits will have very high propensities to consume, and thus the spending multiplier from these payments will be very high. Finally, because farm prices usually drop much faster than other prices, the farm subsidies necessary to maintain parity prices are a major automatic source of spending power in depressions.

As a result of the automatic stabilizers, total government spending will automatically rise in a depression while taxes fall *if* discretionary spending and tax rates remain unchanged. In an inflation, total government spending will automatically decline while taxes rise *if* discretionary spending and tax rates remain unchanged. In this way some of the lack of demand in a depression may be automatically taken up by the rise in net government spending. Inflation may be automatically restricted by less net government demand and should be characterized by accumulation of tax surpluses. In other words, the desired effect of the automatic stabilizers is to increase greatly the ratio of consumer spending to national product in a depression and to reduce the ratio of consumer spending to national product in an inflation. Because this means that the change in demand is much less than the change in national product, it should also mean that investment will react less strongly to a change in national product. As a result, there should be a higher amount of investment during a depression and a smaller amount of investment during an inflation than would otherwise be the case. Obviously the effect of these changes would be to moderate the business cycle fluctuations.

The effects of the automatic adjustments are, however, conceded to be limited even by their staunchest supporters. They may have mitigated the postwar recessions, but recessions still do occur on a significant scale, one after the other. The simple fact is that the magnitude of the spending flows induced by the automatic stabilizers does not approach the level required to close the unemployment gap in most peacetime stiuations. The periodic deficiency in aggregate demand requires massive discretionary government expenditures if unemployment is to be kept at a satisfactorily low level. Moreover, it is clear analytically that if a longer and more severe depression should occur, the effect of the automatic compensatory devices would be greatly reduced. For example, tax rates can fall only to their minimum; then they must level off. Furthermore, unemployment compensation is limited not only in amount but also in the length of time it may be received.

Another problem lies in the fact that the automatic anticyclical devices may have worked all too well in choking off the upswings of the economy in the postwar period. Even if they do not set off a depression, they may be partly responsible for the economy's slowed rate of long-run growth and for the chronic unemployment, which has run at an official 5–6 percent in recent years even in times of prosperity. For the automatic devices do not begin to work only when the economy reaches full employment and heads for inflation; rather, these devices begin automatically to retard demand the minute income begins to recover from a depression. In other words, by restricting the amount of new investment in each period of expansion, they may reduce the rate of creation of new capital and thereby hold down the long run of economic growth. For these reasons, we can conclude that the automatic stabilizers probably result in as much economic harm as benefit.

DISCRETIONARY FISCAL POLICIES AND SOCIAL PRIORITIES

Because the automatic devices have failed to fully stabilize the economy or to help it grow, liberal Keynesian economists maintain that discretionary fiscal measures are necessary both to eliminate depression and inflation and to foster a higher rate of long-run growth. They contend that the legislature merely needs to increase spending and lower taxes in depression, and lower spending and increase taxes in inflation. But these measures also are subject to political and economic complications.

There are three different policy views of what government discretionary fiscal policy ought to be. The most conservative economists, such as Adam Smith or the contemporary American Milton Friedman, argue that no discretionary fiscal measures are needed. The government should stay out of the economy. Friedman agrees with Adam Smith that the less government the better. He attributes many of our economic problems to too much government interference with private enterprise, which would otherwise automatically adjust to all situations in a near-perfect manner. To the extent that conservatives admit any need for government policy, they say that only monetary measures are necessary. (Such policies are discussed in Chapter 31.) Conservatives favor measures affecting the money supply (via interest rates, for example) rather than any fiscal measures of spending or taxation because they feel that monetary measures do not directly interfere with business. They view an adequate money supply merely as one of the prerequisites for a private enterprise economy. Other prerequisites, which they believe government should provide, include police and armies to maintain "law and order," primarily to protect private property from its domestic and foreign enemies.

The second, the liberal, view is that of such economists as John M. Keynes or the contemporary American Paul Samuelson. Liberals admit that capitalism has real problems, such as general unemployment and inflation. Liberal Keynesians argue that adequate government measures of increased or decreased spending and increased or decreased taxation are necessary to correct these problems. Finally, they used to maintain that such measures can *always successfully bring about full employment* with stable prices. Some of them now, however, define full employment as "only" 4 or 5 percent unemployment and stable prices as "only" 2 or 3 percent inflation per year.[4] Others, including Samuelson, simply admit that ending inflation *and* getting full employment at the same time is one little thing not yet solved by establishment economists: "Experts do not yet know . . . an incomes policy that will permit us to have *simultaneously* . . . full employment and price stability."[5]

The radical view is expressed by Karl Marx or the contemporary American Paul Sweezy. Radicals argue that problems like periodic unemployment are deeply rooted in the capitalist system and cannot be cured by any amount of monetary or fiscal measures. They contend that the *U.S. economy has reached full employment only during major wars.* In normal peacetime years, they believe unemployment and/or inflation is the usual state of capitalism. They argue that the necessary drastic fiscal measures cannot be taken by capitalist governments because powerful vested interests oppose each such step, aside from military spending.

---

[4]See, for example, James Tobin and Leonard Ross, "Living with Inflation," *New York Review of Books*, May 6, 1971.
[5]Paul Samuelson, *Economics*, 9th ed. (New York: McGraw-Hill, 1973), p. 823.

All economists know and agree that government intervention can theoretically prevent large-scale unemployment or runaway inflation. The basic fiscal formula, to which may be added certain monetary measures, is to raise taxes and lower spending during inflations and lower taxes and raise spending during depressions. Moreover, corporate executives and congressmen alike are by now well aware of and receptive to these techniques. But that by no means settles the issue (even aside from the problem of simultaneous unemployment and inflation discussed in Chapter 31).

The problem remains one of finding suitable ways of spending the amounts of money necessary to maintain full employment. Many outlets that would be socially beneficial conflict with the vested interests of large corporations or wealthy individuals. Larger welfare payments tend to raise the wage level; government investment in industrial ventures or in public utilities tends to erode monopolistic privileges. The issue is the political constraints to economic policies.

In the years immediately after World War II, the problem was to spend $15–20 billion annually. This might have been a very agonizing social and political issue except for the advent of the Cold War.

Dollars for Cold War armaments did not violate any vested interests. Military spending is considered an ideal antidepression policy by big business for three reasons. First, such expenditures have the same short-run effect on employment and profits as would expenditures on more socially useful projects. Second, military spending means big and stable profits, whereas welfare spending may shift income from rich taxpayers to poor recipients. Third, the long-run effect is even more favorable because no new productive equipment is created to compete with existing facilities. During the past 25 years, the main change has been that the necessary addition to the income stream has risen to at least $70–80 billion a year. If it were politically possible, the whole amount could be spent on public commodities, such as housing or health or education, rather than on military waste. So the problem with stability under American capitalism is primarily in the political sphere, rather than in any lack of economic analysis.

One popular cure for depression is reduction of taxes to allow more money to flow into private spending. Given the composition of the U.S. government, however, tax cuts always end up benefiting mainly the rich and the corporations. Even in the liberal Kennedy administration, the taxes of the poor were reduced very little and of the rich very much, resulting in a redistribution of income to the deserving members of the wealthy class. Especially in a depression, however, the wealthy will not spend their increased income. The consumption of the wealthy remains at adequate levels even in a depression, and they have no desire to invest in the face of probable losses. Hence the political restriction as to *who* gets the tax cuts makes this policy economically ineffective.

Similarly, all economists (and even most businessmen) may see a need for more and more vast government spending under capitalism. The prime political question, however, is spending on what, for it is here that vested interests come into play. Thus even small vital expenditures on medical care have sometimes been defeated by the American Medical Association. Powerful vested interests oppose almost every item in the civilian budget as soon as expansion proceeds beyond the necessary minimum. What kind of interests must be defeated to have the necessary spending to fill a $70–80 billion deficiency in demand? Constructive projects such as the Missouri Valley Authority could develop dams, irrigation, and cheap power, but these have been fought tooth and nail by the private power interests (and, indeed, might lower private investment by direct competition). There could be large-scale public housing, but private contractors have long kept such programs to a minimum.

There might be other welfare spending—for example, on hospitals and schools. The rich, however, see these as subsidies to the poor for things that the rich can buy for themselves out of their own pockets. Proposals to increase unemployment compensation or lower taxes paid by the poor encounter even greater resistance because they would transfer income from the rich to the poor. Likewise, billions could usefully be spent in aid and loans to the less developed world, where poverty and human suffering is so widespread. That, however, could be passed on a massive scale only over the bodies of hundreds of congressmen, who represent well the wishes of their self-interested constituents and have no concept of the long-run gain to world trade and world peace. If any of these measures are to some extent allowed, it is only after a long political fight, certainly not promptly enough to head off a developing depression.

We could list, one by one, all the areas in which powerful vested interests stand in opposition to the satisfaction of some of the nation's most basic social needs. These interests will not tolerate government competition with private enterprise, measures that undermine the privileges of the wealthy, or policies that significantly alter the relative distribution of income. They therefore tend to oppose all government nonmilitary spending—except direct business subsidies. The only major exception to this generalization is government spending on highways, which is actively promoted by the largest and most lucrative single industry after defense: the automobile producers.

MILITARY SPENDING
VERSUS WELFARE SPENDING

From all of the facts just given, we conclude that welfare or constructive spending on a large scale is opposed by too many special interests to be politically feasible. Our hypothesis is that *only large-scale military spending brought the United States out of the great depression of the 1930s, and only large-scale military spending has kept the United States out of a major depression.* The liberals like Samuelson are much more complacent; speaking about mass unemployment and galloping inflations, he says they are things of the past. He asserts that there are ancient problems that are solvable and have been solved: "For example, however true it might have been in the turn-of-the-century era of Lenin . . . , it is definitely no longer the case in the age after Keynes that prosperity of a mixed economy (i.e., capitalism plus government) depends on cold-war expenditures and imperialistic ventures."[6]

It is a fact, however, that our economy has boomed by spending immense sums of money to kill the people of Vietnam. How would Samuelson replace that crutch to the economy? He says: "Does building missiles and warheads create jobs . . . ? Then so too will building new factories, better roads and schools, cleaning up our rivers, and providing minimum income-supplements for our aged and handicapped."[7] Certainly it is true that jobs could be created in all these constructive ways rather than the destructive ways of warfare. *But*—and it is a big *but*—we are talking about *government spending*, so we must remember that vested interests will obstruct programs that might harm them. Yet for the government to build new factories means direct competition with private industry. For the government to build schools means to take money from rich taxpayers and transfer it to the education of poorer citizens. To clean up the rivers means both more use of tax money and forcing private industry to spend money on purifying its wastes. Giving to the aged and handicapped means again adding taxes and shifting income to the poor.

The political reality is that vested interests oppose each of these programs with violent rhetoric and successful political pressure. Thus Congress does not even talk about building government factories for peaceful use—in fact, government atomic energy plants have been given away free to private capitalists. President Nixon, who was elected with big-business support, has vetoed bills and impounded money intended to clean up the rivers. A vast howl was

[6]Ibid., p. 823.
[7]Ibid., p. 824.

raised against McGovern's modest proposals for increased welfare, and Nixon has vetoed almost all recent welfare bills.

Samuelson, to his credit, was writing his new edition while at the peak of his involvement in the McGovern campaign, so perhaps that is why he gives a naive rebuttal on this point. He says that radicals have asked: "Politically, will there be as much urgency to spend what is needed for useful, peacetime full-employment programs as there is urgency and willingness to spend for hot- and cold-war purposes?" And he answers: It was proper to ask this question back in the 1950s. But . . . experience since then has shown that modern electorates have become very sensitive to levels of unemployment that would have been considered moderate back in the good old days. And they do put effective pressure at the polls on their government."[8] But in the first place, the pressure is only to get jobs—not necessarily to get welfare rather than warfare jobs; so McGovern lost (partly because many people were worried about losing jobs in military industries) and Nixon continues military spending to avoid unemployment—and does not do constructive spending.

In the second place, Samuelson just assumes that "the people" make our governmental decisions, but we saw in Chapter 20 that the dominant power in governmental decision making in the United States is big business. It would have been nice to test what the liberal McGovern would have done in power. Perhaps he would have been able (with much popular support to overcome business pressure) to substitute a little more welfare for a little less warfare. But that was not the record of previous liberal administrations: the Kennedy administration vastly increased military spending, invaded Cuba, and expanded the Vietnam War; and the Johnson administration further expanded the Vietnam War on a vast scale.

Finally, even Samuelson admits that in reality we do not have full employment but a considerable level of unemployment. He argues, however, that this is not the old problem of capitalism's inability to create purchasing power but a new kind of problem in which unemployment is associated with simultaneous inflation. As we saw in the previous section, Samuelson concedes that this new problem of inflation plus unemployment is one for which establishment economists as yet have no answer.

We have seen that Keynesian liberals fail to see the political constraints that make military spending the only allowable solution to unemployment. The political nature of the problem has become even more apparent in the inflationary situation of the past 20 years.

[8] Ibid., pp. 824–825.

The Korean and Vietnam wars caused so much government demand for military supplies that inflation resulted, prices rising especially in 1950–1953 and 1967–1974. To cure inflation, the simple Keynesian prescription is to increase taxes and reduce spending.

But whose taxes, which spending? Major increases in taxes on the wealthy are not easily passed by our government. And there is not that much room for further taxes on the poor and the middle class without provoking rising discontent. So it is easier to reduce government spending. But not military spending; politicians and spokesmen for industry and the military continue to convince the nation that these are absolutely necessary. Thus welfare spending is cut. Already a tiny percentage of the American government budget, welfare has nevertheless been cut further as a tool to fight inflation. Hence the burden of inflation has fallen on the common man and woman in the forms of rising prices, rising taxes, and falling welfare spending all at the same time.

At different times since World War II, perhaps most notably in the late 1960s and early 1970s, the American economy experienced a "first" in the nation's history: simultaneous unemployment and inflation. This situation appears impossible, according to elementary Keynesian analysis, because inflation implies an excess of demand over supply, while unemployment implies an excess of supply over demand. The answer to the riddle lies in the monopoly power of American capitalism. In spite of a certain amount of unemployment, the largest corporations actually still have the power to continue to raise their prices, which might be called *profit-push* inflation.

No aggregate fiscal policy can remedy or prevent *both* inflation and unemployment in these circumstances. To end unemployment by increasing aggregate demand sufficiently to affect output in all sectors means to allow the monopoly sector to set off another inflation spiral. To end inflation by reducing aggregate demand sufficiently to affect monopoly prices means to cause considerable unemployment in the whole economy. The capitalist governments of America and Europe have generally chosen to combat inflation at the expense of more unemployment.

The question of social and political priorities often boils down to a conflict between the genuine needs of the majority versus the desires of the tiny minority that possesses immense economic and political power. Government spending cannot be put to use in clearing slums, providing adequate housing and medical care, fighting disease, combating pollution, or meeting any of the other pressing social needs unless some form of arms reduction and a drastic scaling down of defense spending is accepted. But given the present economic structure, any sudden move in that direction could be disastrous.

THE MILITARY ECONOMY

To measure the full extent of the military impact on the economy, we must recall that the U.S. Department of Defense is the largest planned economy in the world today outside the USSR. It spends more than the net income of all U.S. corporations. By 1969, it had 470 major and 6,000 lesser installations, owned 39 million acres of land, spent over $80 billion a year, used 22,000 primary contractors and 100,000 subcontractors—thus directly employing in the armed forces and military production about 10 percent of the U.S. labor force.[9] Some key areas of the economy are especially affected. As early as 1963, before U.S. entry into the Vietnam War, studies show that 36 percent of the output of producers' durable goods were purchased directly or indirectly by the federal government, mostly for military use.

How did the U.S. economy come to have such an enormous military sector?[10] Of course in World War II the United States had an enormous military production. It was assumed by every policy maker, including economists and businessmen and political leaders, that the United States would mostly disarm after the war. It was also assumed that this would lead to a depression: therefore every possible solution was considered, with most analyses leading to the sole suggestion of renewed military spending. It was in this atmosphere that the Cold War was born; it provided every possible increase in military spending. In fact, since the United States had a monopoly of atomic bombs, the USSR was very unlikely to be aggressive. Moreover, Soviet foreign policy was mostly very cautious and conservative (so much so that revolutionaries in other countries accused them of betrayal for *not* supplying arms). In reality, the USSR had its sphere of influence—Eastern Europe—which the United States has not invaded, while the United States has spheres of influence and imperial power in much of Latin America, Africa, and Asia, which the USSR has never invaded. Thus, despite the Cold War rhetoric, the two major powers have never clashed militarily (except by indirectly supporting others).

Therefore the armaments spending justified by the Cold War rhetoric was not militarily necessary. It was utilized, as in Southeast Asia, to protect U.S. investments abroad but also in large part to support the U.S. economy at home. Thus we find in both world

---

[9]These data come from U.S. Defense Department documents that are reported in Seymour Melman, *Pentagon Capitalism* (New York: McGraw-Hill, 1970).

[10]Most of the analysis and all of the facts in the rest of this chapter come from James Cypher, *Military Expenditures and the Performance of the Postwar Economy, 1947-71*, (Ph.D. dissertation, University of California, Riverside). This dissertation is a gold mine of information and the best discussion now available of military spending.

wars that the industrialists dictated to the government exactly how the procurement process should be run, completely dominated the Department of Defense, and made enormous rates of profit. This condition has continued ever since. We shall see that military spending has been manipulated so as to decrease in most booms and increase in most recessions; thus it is now our leading "automatic" stabilizer (since Congress and the President have automatically approved these countercyclical changes).

How big is U.S. military spending? It certainly includes all Department of Defense spending, but it goes considerably beyond that. How far is controversial, but the most careful study to date (by James Cypher) includes half of all "international affairs" spending, veterans benefits, atomic energy and space appropriations (all military-related), and 75 percent of the interest on the public debt (since at least 75 percent of the debt was used to pay for wars). Other things that are too hard to get exact data on are: major parts of the budget for research and development, the CIA, and other intelligence agencies—and of course the deaths, wounds, and alienation of young Americans. For the five quantifiable items in military spending, Cypher adds up the grand total of $1.7 *trillion* from 1947 through 1971—enough to buy our entire gross national product for 1969 *and* 1970.

Yet this amount of direct military spending (even if it included the things we can't quantify) still underestimates the impact of military spending on the U.S. economy. There is a very large indirect or secondary effect on (1) additional consumer goods from the spending of those who receive military dollars and (2) additional investment in plant, equipment, and business inventories by military industries. Economists measure the secondary effects of military spending by the government multiplier (discussed in detail in the appendix to this chapter), which measures the ratio of the total increase in all spending to every dollar of increase in government spending. Estimates of the multiplier from military spending range from about $1.85 to $3.50 of total spending for every dollar of military spending.

The most important measure of military spending is as a percentage of our whole gross national product (GNP). From 1947 to 1971 it ranged from a low of 10.1 percent of GNP in 1948 to a high of 21.9 percent in the Korean War year of 1952. It was at 13.5 percent and 13.2 percent in 1967 and 1968, during the Vietnam War peak, and slowly fell to 12.6 percent in 1969, 11.6 percent in 1970, and 11.1 percent in 1971 (with another major rise in 1972). For the whole 1947–1971 period, direct military spending averaged 13.2 percent of GNP. Now if we are quite conservative and assume a multiplier of only 2, it is apparent that direct and indirect military spending accounted for the demand for 26.4 percent of GNP. This means that if military spending and its indirect effects had not been present in this whole period and all other things had been the same (which is very unlikely), we would have had a depression greater than that in the 1930s—when unemployment was 24.3 percent. Of course if the military multiplier is actually 3, then total demand for GNP would fall by 39.6 percent, if we ended all military spending —always assuming we did nothing else. Actually we have seen that the U.S. government might increase welfare spending a little, but it is not politically feasible on the scale required.

It is worth noting just how military spending has affected the U.S. economy at various times. As late as 1939, it had very little effect, being only 2.6 percent of GNP. In World War II, it rose to about 40 percent of GNP, which brought full employment (and even a shortage of labor). After World War II, there were several times when the drop in military spending seems to have been the main catalyst setting off a recession. Thus in 1948, it fell by 11 percent, followed by a recession in 1949. In 1953, it fell by 17 percent and in 1954 by 30 percent; and there was a recession in 1954. In 1957, military spending grew only 2.6 percent, followed by a recession in 1958. In 1960, it fell 3 percent, followed by recession in 1961. In 1969, it grew by only 3 percent, and it fell by 2 percent in 1970, followed by the recession of 1971. All this suggests that military spending must keep rising at a considerable rate to prevent recessions and that when it falters it sets off a recession.

Obviously this is no simple case of cause and effect. In the first place, it holds true only when the economy does not have other sources of major new demands (but that has not occurred ever since the first rush of consumer spending after World War II). And there is still an underlying private cyclical mechanism that makes the economy react as it does. Moreover, it can be offset by other policies on the required scale. Thus, in addition to the years mentioned, there is one other time when military spending faltered but did not set off a recession. In 1965 military spending did not change at all, but this lack was offset by the massive tax cut of 1964–1965, which did stimulate some private spending.

On the other side, it should also be noted that military spending seems to have been used to get the U.S. economy out of recessions. Thus in the recession of 1949, military spending was immediately increased by 7.6 percent; in the recession of 1958, it was increased by 8.1 percent; and in the recession of 1961, it was increased by 6.6 percent. It was also increased by 7.6 percent in 1955, which may have helped us out of the 1954 recession. In 1971 wage-price controls were used in the new unemployment-inflation situation, but it appears that military spending did take another jump upward in 1972 to help with the continuing unemployment.

Thus our automatic and inherent pattern of business cycles has now been overlaid with a more politically motivated business cycle. When there is an all-out boom, business influence gets government to reduce military spending. This reduction is desired (1) to avoid inflation and (2) to avoid full employment, which means "uppity" workers and higher wages. Since, however, it is hard to time the military spending reductions exactly when desired and very hard to estimate exactly how much is needed, this always seems to do more than just limit the boom; it almost always seems to turn into a full-scale recession. Indeed, in Chapter 28 we saw why the capitalist economy never stands still but always has cumulative forces pushing it rapidly up or down once it gets going. Thus when vested interests reduce military spending a bit—in order to limit the boom—this action sets off a recession. As the recession gets worse and profits decline, the same political-economic power is used to start increasing military spending again, thus setting off another boom. This, of course, is much too sketchy and rigid a schema to encompass all the many factors effecting current econmic history, but it is an important framework for understanding.

Finally, we must note why big business is so happy with a normally high level of military spending. On the aggregate level, we saw that it is used to protect U.S. investments abroad and to get the economy out of recessions (as well as to prevent a major depression); but there is an additional incentive for the individual defense contractor. This incentive is based on the fact that the rate of profit is very high in military production and that most of these profits go to a few very large firms. Almost all military contracts go to some 205 of the top 500 corporations, and just 100 of them get 85 percent of all military contracts.

There are some studies of military profits, but all of them understate the profit rates. In reporting to the government the military firms overstate their costs—and since they do not operate under competition but in a cosy relation with the Pentagon, they probably overstate costs more than most firms. Thus they allocate costs of other parts of their business to military contracts and add in all sorts of other unrelated costs—some have even tossed in the costs of call girls to influence government inspectors (called "entertainment" in their accounts). They also make many hidden profits through the use of complex subcontracting procedures to subsidiaries, unauthorized use of government-owned property, and getting patents on research done for the government.

Still, a study by the General Accounting Office (GAO) of the U.S. government has definitely spelled out their high profit rates.[11] First the GAO asked 81 large military contractors by questionnaire what their profit rates were for 1966 through 1969. The replies, which were limited by self-interest, still admitted an average profit rate of 24.8 percent—much higher than nonmilitary profits in the same industries. But spot checks showed that these profit rates were still very much underreported. So the GAO did its own audit of the books of 146 main military contractors. The study found that the profit rate of these merchants of death was a fantastic 56.1 percent rate of return on invested capital!

SUMMARY

Military spending took the United States out of the Great Depression and has prevented a major depression ever since. It directly employs about 13 percent of the labor force and indirectly another 13 percent or more in most years. A decline of military spending has set off several recessions, while increases in military spending have encouraged recoveries from several recessions. Any constructive government spending tends to compete with private enterprise and to redistribute income from rich to poor. Military spending alone does not compete with private enterprise; it indirectly stimulates private consumption and investment and redistributes income from the poor to the rich (because of the very high profit rates paid to military producers). Therefore very powerful economic interests are against constructive or welfare spending but favor military spending.

While enough military spending can produce full employment, it seems a highly irrational economic system that can guarantee full employment only in this way—since it also implies high taxes, inflation, and death. The other question we have not yet considered is the wasteful effect of putting 13 percent of the people to work on military production. This negative effect on long-run growth will be considered in Chapter 32.

[11]Fully discussed in Cypher, chap. 5.

APPENDIX
the government multiplier

The obvious objectives of government fiscal policy are to increase *the net flow of demand during depressions* by increasing spending and lowering taxes, and to reduce the net flow of demand during inflation by reducing spending and raising taxes. Not only the direct effects but also the secondary effects of these policies are important. For example, in a depression it is hoped that increases in government spending will mean more income to businesses or individuals and that this, in turn, will lead to further increases in private consumption and investment.

The secondary effects of a government expenditure may be quantified in terms of the government multiplier. The *government multiplier* is the ratio of increase in national income to an increase in government spending. The reader will recall that the investment multiplier was defined as the ratio of an increase in national income to an increase in private investment.

Take the very simple assumption that consumption reacts in a given ratio to an increase in income (while investment remains constant). This means every increase in income automatically leads to a certain increase in consumption spending. This spending means a further, though smaller, increase in income, some of which will be spent for a second round of consumption, and so forth.

The formal apparatus for studying the government multiplier is exactly the same as that for the investment multiplier. It may help to review a numerical example in which we assume (1) a certain increase in government spending with a given marginal propensity to consume and (2) that the increase in government spending takes place without any change in tax receipts. Under these simple assumptions, the formula for the government multiplier is

$$\text{Government multiplier} = \frac{1}{\text{MPS}}$$

or

$$\text{Government multiplier} = \frac{1}{1 - \text{MPC}}$$

Remember that MPS stands for marginal propensity to save and MPC stands for marginal propensity to consume. Also remember that MPS is just 1 − MPC. And MPC is defined as the ratio of an increase in consumption to an increase in income. Thus in Table 29A.1 the government multiplier is 5 and the national income increases by $5000.

Suppose, in different economic conditions, that only half of additional income is always consumed and fully half is saved. Then only half of new government spending will be respent for consumption. But half of that amount, as it becomes income, will be spent in a second round of consumption. Then half of the second round

---

TABLE 29A.1

HOW THE GOVERNMENT MULTIPLIER WORKS

1. Suppose government increases its spending by $1000 (while private investment does not change).
2. Also suppose a marginal propensity to consume of 4/5, or 80 percent.

Increase in Government Spending	Increase in Consumption	Increase in National Income	Increase in Saving
$1000		$1000	
0	$ 800	$ 800	$ 200
0	$ 640	$ 640	$ 160
0	$ 512	$ 512	$ 128
0	$ 410	$ 410	$ 102
0	$ 328	$ 328	$ 82
—	—	—	—
—	—	—	—
—	—	—	—
Total Increase in Government Spending	**Total Increase in Consumption**	**Total Increase in National Income**	**Total Increase in Saving**
$1000	$4000	$5000	$1000

of consumption will be spent for a third round of consumption, and so forth. The end result is that if MPC is just $\frac{1}{2}$, the multiplier approaches 2. That is, the total additional consumption will just equal the additional government spending, so the total increase in income is just twice the initial increase in income received from the government. Thus if the government spends an extra $1 billion, a multiplier of 2 says that a total increase of $2 billion in national income will be generated, of which $1 billion will be the secondary consumer spending.

For similar reasons, if MPC rises to $\frac{2}{3}$, the government multiplier rises to 3. If, however, the marginal propensity to consume is zero, then the multiplier is 1. In this case, there are *no* secondary effects because *all* of the first round of spending is saved. In the other extreme case, if MPC moves toward 1, the multiplier moves toward infinity—that is, the secondary effects are infinite because all income is immediately respent for consumption.

Of course, the government multiplier ratio is an artificial concept because it does not take into account all the changing factors and complications involved. The first qualification is the fact that the second, third, and fourth rounds of spending do not occur instantaneously; it takes time before income is respent for consumption. Long or varying time lags make it much more difficult to speak of an exact multiplier. Second, the multiplier explained here assumes that investment is a given constant and is not affected by changes in income. As has been seen in earlier chapters, however, there is probably a close connection between investment and the change in income. If this is so, changes in government spending, as well as the secondary changes in consumer spending, may directly affect investment. However, government spending may have negative psychological effects on investment if it is thought to take away funds by taxation or to compete by means of cheaper products. At any rate government spending is likely to have some direct or indirect effect on investment, and as a result investment may not legitimately be considered a constant in this regard.

The third major set of qualifications to the government multiplier arises from the fact that MPC does not remain constant, yet it is the very rock on which the multiplier theory is founded. It does not remain constant because, for one thing, consumption is actually influenced by many factors other than income. The marginal consumption ratio also varies because there are different leakages from the process at different times. For example, the effect of an increase in government spending on national income may be partly siphoned off by the levy of higher taxes or merely by automatic movements into higher tax brackets. Furthermore, it may happen that increased spending for imports removes some portion of income from the domestic multiplier process. For all of these reasons, MPC may change too often for any accurate prediction of the multiplier beyond a short period of only one or two rounds of the process.

The fourth and last qualification has to do with how the government spending is financed. If the government takes back through taxation the same amount that it spends, then there is no net addition to consumer spending, only the initial government spending is added to the economy, and the multiplier will be only 1. The national income will increase by the amount of the increase in government spending.

If increased government spending is financed by sale of government bonds, or *deficit spending*, the effect on the private economy depends on how the bondholders would have used the money had they not lent it to the government. If they had used it all for consumption or investment anyway, then there would be no net stimulation to the private economy. If they had used only a small percentage of it for consumption or investment (which is often the case), then the government spending would have a very powerful net effect on the private economy.

Finally, the most inflationary method of financing government spending is to print new money because this withdraws nothing from the private sector either by taxation or borrowing. In a deep depression, a government may finance expenditures by printing money; at full employment, it will attempt to use only taxation; and with a small degree of unemployment, it may use borrowing.

Summary

Government spending has both direct and indirect effects. The indirect effects occur through the additional consumer and investment spending the government stimulates. These indirect effects are called multiplier effects. The multiplier measures the total change in demand resulting from a change in direct government spending. Economists estimate it with the formula, multiplier = 1/MPS, but this formula is very rough and inaccurate because it leaves out many factors.

money and banking

Aggregate demand is the total planned spending of money in exchange for the economy's current output of goods and services. In order to isolate what determines the level of this demand, we assumed that the money supply remained constant when we examined changes in investment or consumption spending. Using this approach, any fall in total demand implies a rising flow of money into hoards, and any rise in total demand, as would occur when planned investment exceeds the flow of saving, implies that dishoarding is occurring. Therefore in equilibrium there is neither hoarding nor dishoarding, planned investment equals planned saving, and the total money supply is being used recurringly in exchange for goods and services. In this case a constant sum is being held in money balances. More realistically, when total demand is rising, the money supply may also be rising because new money may be created by the commercial banking system. Conversely, when total demand falls, the money supply may shrink because new credit money is not created and loans are repaid to banks. Our purpose in this chapter is to examine the money supply and to investigate the money creation powers of commercial banks.

The present money supply consists of coins and paper currency outside of commercial banks and checking accounts (demand deposits) in commercial banks. In July 1973 the total U.S. money supply was $264.5 billion, $56.8 billion in currency and $205.1

	TABLE 30.1 THE MONEY SUPPLY AND ITS COMPONENT PARTS (IN BILLIONS OF DOLLARS)		
Date	**Total Money Supply**	**Currency**	**Demand Deposits**
December 1947	$110.5	$26.1	$ 84.4
December 1950	114.6	24.6	90.0
December 1960	141.1	28.9	112.1
December 1966	170.4	38.3	132.1
December 1968	199.6	42.6	157.0
December 1970	208.6	47.8	160.8
December 1972	255.5	56.8	198.7
December 1973	270.4	61.6	208.8

Source: Federal Reserve Bulletin, May 1974, p. A14.

billion in demand deposits. The recent growth of the money supply and its component parts is shown in Table 30.1.

Demand deposits, which account for a fairly constant percentage of the money supply (76.4 percent in 1947 and 77.2 percent in 1973), are the debts of commercial banks. When we say banks create money, we refer to the fact that banks have the ability to create demand deposits. After considering a conjectural history of money, we shall investigate a conjectural evolution of this money creation power. (It is conjectural in that it is not an exact history of one place but what we believe to have been the logical and approximate development in most places.)

A CONJECTURAL HISTORY OF MONEY

Money is defined as any widely accepted medium of exchange. A commodity that is used as money does not necessarily have any intrinsic value aside from its general acceptability in exchange and for the settlement of debt. If the law requires that it be accepted in the settlement of debt, it is also *legal tender*.

Among the most primitive tribes exchange was conducted by the barter system. *Barter* means that one commodity is directly traded for another in the market without the use of money. For example, we may find trade in this form:

1 coat = 2 hats

If this exchange ratio persists for some time, people may come to think of one coat as *worth* two hats, or they may think of one hat as worth half a coat.

The second evolutionary step was to the crudest kind of money, a stage in which some particular commodity was used as money. Any convenient or often-used commodity might eventually attain the status of money if it were relatively scarce and therefore valuable. For example, in a community in which the number of cows owned was a status symbol, we might find that cows played the role of money. Thus

$$2 \text{ coats} = 1 \text{ cow} \qquad 1 \text{ cow} = 4 \text{ hats}$$

People in this society would calculate all their production and wealth in terms of cows. They might also actually sell or trade coats for cows and then use the "cow money" to buy hats, or vice versa.

Cows, however, are not a very convenient money commodity. They are perishable and not easily divisible, problems that could be solved by using precious metals or stones. The need to have large numbers of pieces of money that are of equal value led to the third step of the evolution, the development of *metallic money*. Precious metals have several virtues as a medium of exchange: (1) They are valuable; one need carry only a small amount to buy other commodities. (2) They are easily divisible. Uniform coins of various values can be made by melting, and thus the exact amount necessary for any purchase can be used. (3) They are nonperishable and hence can be stored indefinitely.

The durability and portability of metallic money means it may be used not only for calculating value ratios but also in every exchange. Thus trade takes this form:

$$1 \text{ coat} = 1 \text{ oz. gold} \qquad 1 \text{ oz. gold} = 2 \text{ hats}$$

Any commodity (e.g., a coat) may be sold for metallic money. Then the metallic money is put away until its holder wishes to buy another commodity (e.g., a hat).

The next step in the evolution came when paper claims were substituted for metallic money such as gold, but they were still payable in gold. These claims were originally issued by goldsmiths, private bankers, and merchants. Governments soon followed suit, issuing their own paper money, which consisted of IOUs, or promises by the government to pay in gold on demand. Of course it was possible to issue more paper money than gold because not everyone demanded gold at the same time.

The modern issue of *inconvertible paper money* is the fifth step in the evolution of money. Paper money looks the same as before, but a government declares that it will no longer convert, or pay its paper IOUs in gold on demand. This method of money creation financed the American and French Revolutions and the U.S. Civil War. Almost all governments had recourse to this expedient in the monetary chaos following World War I and during the Great Depression. At the same time they usually prohibited private institutions from issuing paper money. One way governments made their paper money more acceptable to the populace was to accept it themselves for tax payments and to declare it legal tender. Of course the value of inconvertible paper money today has no direct connection with gold reserves.

The most recently evolved form of money is the checking account. Sums of money in checking accounts are bookkeeping entries called *deposits*. They are actually promises to pay—that is, they are debts of the bank. Checks written against these accounts are orders to transfer deposit funds to others' accounts or to convert some of the deposit account into currency. The owner of such an account may have brought currency to the bank or may have deposited a check. He may have signed a note and borrowed the money. In such a case the bank and the individual merely exchange IOUs. But the bank's IOU, the demand deposit, serves all the functions of money. Checks drawn against the balance make payment without the use of currency or coin. Although a check is not legal tender, the deposit is convertible into legal tender, and the deposit account is money. It is apparent that the distinguishing characteristic of a bank is that, unlike any other private enterprise, the evidence of its debt to an individual is accepted as money.

A CONJECTURAL
EVOLUTION OF MODERN BANKING

Perhaps we can illustrate the role of the modern banker by returning to conjectural history. Centuries ago, when the market system was evolving, goldsmiths had large quantities of precious metals. To protect them, secure storage facilities had to be constructed. Other individuals sought the same security for their money but did not have enough money to justify the expense of constructing such facilities. The local goldsmith began to accept their coin (the sole form of money at this time) and precious metals. As evidence of these deposits he provided the depositor with a receipt. The goldsmith earned income by demanding payment from the individual depositor for the safekeeping function he performed.

In time, goldsmiths who had developed reputations for honesty found that these deposit receipts began to circulate and could be used by the individuals holding them in payment of debt. For example, merchants, instead of carrying coin on business trips, would deposit it with a reputable and renowned goldsmith. The receipt could then be used to settle his accounts in distant lands. Hence as long as the goldsmith was willing and able to redeem these deposit receipts, or paper claims, on demand for coin, they performed the function of money. Here we see the initial stages in the development of both the banking system and paper claims as money. The validity of the paper claims as money was premised on their general acceptability as money, which depended on the confidence that the public had in the goldsmith's ability to convert the paper claims into coin on demand.

Thus far, however, the goldsmith has not performed the primary distinguishing function of a banker, the money creation function. All he has done is to match his metallic assets with paper claims. His balance sheet probably would resemble this:

Assets		Liabilities	
Coin in vault	$1000	Deposits	$1000
Total assets	$1000	Total liabilities	$1000

Sooner or later the goldsmith realizes that he can create debt (demand deposits and notes payable on demand) in excess of the coin he holds in his vault. Why can he do this? First, because the people have confidence in his ability to redeem their paper claims into coin on demand. Second, this confidence leads other people to accept the paper claims in settlement of their debts. Therefore at any given time only a small portion of the paper claims need to be converted into coin.

As long as the goldsmith-banker can readily meet this small portion of claims for coin, he is in a position to increase his total liabilities beyond the actual amount of coin he has in his vault. In other words, he is able to create money. And the total of coin, bank notes, and deposit receipts now in circulation exceeds the amount of coin that has been minted by the government authority. The bank notes (issued by the goldsmith-banker to those who borrow from him) and the deposit receipts are *money*, the same way coin is money, because people are willing to accept them in payment for any debt. If an individual receives payments in the form of either coin or bank note or a deposit receipt, it makes no difference to him at all as long as he can use these equally for making his own payments.

The goldsmith (who is now a banker because he creates money) will then keep in his vault an amount of coin large enough to meet the demands for coin that will be made upon him. Of course he can roughly estimate these demands from his experience. The banker-goldsmith's balance sheet probably would resemble this.

Assets		Liabilities	
Coin in vault	$ 800	Notes payable	$ 600
Loans	800	Deposits	1000
Total assets	$1600	Total liabilities	$1600

The banker's liabilities in this example clearly exceed the coin in his vault. What he has done is lend money to individuals, of which $200 has had to be paid out in the form of coin (reducing his coin from $1000 to $800). However, people are willing to hold the other $600 of loans in the form of bank notes. Thus the banker has created new liabilities while holding only half of his total liabilities ($800) in the form of coin. He now has an additional form of income: the interest he earns from the loans he makes. The banker has created money in excess of the coin in his vault to the amount of $800.

The banker's ability to create money is limited by the portion of notes and deposits he is forced to hold in the form of coin because of institutional or other considerations. In this case, because he has to hold 50 percent of his deposit and note liabilities in the form of coin, he can expand the money supply by only twice the amount of coin in his vault.

Here we see the development, in its initial stages, of the modern banking system. The banker now creates debts that circulate freely as money and that slowly come to form an increasing part of the total money supply. He has succeeded in converting his idle coin, which earns no interest, into loans for which he charges a rate of interest. The borrowing-lending function, formerly performed by the moneylender, is now performed by the banker. The uniqueness of the banker, however, lies in the fact that, unlike the moneylender, he can make loans in excess of the actual coin in his vault.

OPERATION OF
MODERN COMMERCIAL BANKS

The banker's business consists of taking the money deposited with him, on some of which he pays interest, and lending it out at higher rates of interest. Money deposited in time or savings accounts pays interest to the depositor, but it must stay frozen, or on deposit, for some definite time before the interest is paid (thus it is counted only as *near money*). Money deposited in checking accounts available on demand (and therefore counted as part of the *money supply*) pays no interest. In order to pay the interest on savings accounts, the banker must get higher interest rates on the money he lends to others.

TABLE 30.2

CONSOLIDATED BALANCE SHEET FOR THE BANKING SYSTEM
OF THE UNITED STATES ON OCTOBER 27, 1971

Assets (in Millions)		Liabilities and Capital (in Millions)	
Gold Certificates (Held by Federal Reserve)	$ 10,500	Total Deposits	$571,000
Treasury Currency	7,600	Capital Owned by Stockholders	70,200
Loans	489,300		
U.S. Government Bonds	133,800	Total Liabilities	
Total Assets	$641,200	and Capital	$641,200

Source: *Federal Reserve Bulletin*, November 1971, p. A19.

The banker is torn between two objectives. On the one hand, he wants to make as much profit as possible by lending out as much as he can (and the riskiest loans pay the highest interest rates). On the other hand, he wants safety; he wants to be able to pay off easily any depositor who demands his money. Technically the banker is said to seek *liquidity*. The most liquid assets are those most easily available in cash to pay off depositors. Thus the most liquid asset is money in paper currency and coins (or even gold), which pay no interest to the banker. The next most liquid assets are government notes and bonds, sometimes called near money, which pay low interest but can be cashed immediately (although at variable prices if cashed before maturity). Least liquid are risky private loans, which may pay high interest but cannot be cashed for a long time and may never be paid back if the individual goes bankrupt. The precise way in which the entire American banking system holds its assets is indicated in Table 30.2.

Bank liabilities consist mainly of deposits, or the amount that is owed to their depositors. The assets of the whole banking system include gold (held only by the government's Federal Reserve Bank), currency (a very small item), and U.S. government bonds. By far their largest assets, however, are the loans that banks will some day collect back from individuals and businesses. For purposes of analysis we shall often classify all assets merely as *reserves* of money and near money or as *loans* to businesses, individuals, and governments. We shall soon discover that modern banks are required by the government to keep a certain ratio of their deposits in the form of reserves, which limits their power to make loans.

THE FEDERAL RESERVE SYSTEM

On December 23, 1913, President Woodrow Wilson signed the Federal Reserve Act establishing the Federal Reserve System (Fed).

It was the government's answer to the banking failures and monetary panics of the early 1900s. The Fed is the central bank of the United States, corresponding to the Bank of England or the Bank of France. Its original purposes were to give the country a currency flexible enough to meet its needs and to improve the supervision of banking. Today, however, these form only a part of broader and more important objectives, which include maintaining price stability, fostering a high rate of economic growth, and promoting a high level of employment.

Federal Reserve functions are carried out through 12 Federal Reserve banks and their 24 branches, but there is also central coordinatin by the Board of Governors in Washington. The Board of Governors consists of seven members appointed by the President and confirmed by the Senate. One of the Board's duties is to supervise all Fed operations. The Board participates in all of the principal monetary actions of the Fed. It has full authority over changes in the legal reserve requirements of banks (within the limits prescribed by Congress). The Board "reviews and determines" interest rates of the individual Federal Reserve banks. And the members of the Board constitute a majority of the Federal Open Market Committee, which buys and sells government bonds in the open market. In addition, it is responsible for the regulation of stock market credit, and it has the authority to establish the maximum rates of interest member banks may pay on savings and other time deposits.

The Fed controls the money supply in order to achieve its purposes. The real bases of the value of the nation's money supply are the goods produced and confidence in the government. Until recently, however, the money supply of the United States had as its legal base the country's gold stock, which stood at $11.8 billion on August 26, 1970. Congress had required the Federal Reserve to hold an amount equal to 25 percent of its liabilities in the form of gold, but this was purely a congressional whim. The requirement was removed in 1968 with no significant effect on the efficiency with which money has performed its functions.

Although the Federal Reserve Banks still hold gold certificates, this is merely one of several types of assets. Gold certificates need bear no necessary relationship to Federal Reserve liabilities (i.e., they bear no necessary connection to the U.S. money supply). The other principal types of assets are government securities and loans to the member banks. The principal liabilities are Federal Reserve note currency, which constitutes most of the paper currency held by the public, and member bank reserves, which, as will be seen, form the basis for the creation of credit money by the banking system.

The Fed specifies exactly how much reserves each member bank must hold in relation to its deposits. Recently required ratios are given in Table 30.3. Bank reserves of money or "checking accounts

TABLE 30.3

RESERVE REQUIREMENTS OF MEMBER BANKS
(AS PERCENTAGE OF DEPOSITS)

Date	Demand Deposits (checking accounts) City[b] Banks	Country[b] Banks	Time Deposits (saving accounts) in All Banks
Dec. 1948	22.0%	16.0%	7.5%
Sept. 1949	18.0	12.0	5.0
Jan. 1951	20.0	14.0	6.0
July 1953	19.0	13.0	6.0
July 1954	18.0	12.0	6.0
Apr. 1958	16.5	11.0	5.0
Dec. 1960	16.5	12.0	5.0
Oct. 1962	16.5	12.0	4.0
Mar. 1967	16.5	12.0	3.0
Aug. 1970	17.5	12.5–13[a]	3.0
July 1973	18.5	8.0–13[a]	3.0

Limits Set by Congress Within Which the Federal Reserve May Set the Requirements.

Minimum	10.0%	7.0%	3.0%
Maximum	22.0	14.0	10.0

[a]The reserve requirement increases with size of bank.
[b]Any bank with over $400 million in deposits is a "city" bank; any other smaller bank is a "country" bank.

Source: Federal Reserve Bulletin, August 1973, p. A9.

at the Fed" may be kept either in the bank vault or in the nearest Federal Reserve Bank. If it is kept as a deposit in a Federal Reserve Bank, the member bank may even earn a small interest on its money reserves. Country banks are given a lower required reserve ratio, apparently on the theory that they may also fall back on loans from the larger city banks.

The first purpose of the reserve system is, of course, to ensure that the bank has sufficient funds to meet its depositors' withdrawals. Yet in the Great Depression thousands of banks failed because runs on the banks by depositors exhausted their reserves. This purpose is now more fully met by the Federal Deposit Insurance Corporation (FDIC), which guarantees all deposits up to $15,000. The more important purpose that the Fed now serves is to control the money supply as a tool of general economic control. This purpose will be discussed in Chapter 31.

HOW BANKS MULTIPLY MONEY

Exactly how much money can banks create with a given amount of new deposits? Obviously this depends in large part on what reserve ratio the Federal Reserve requires them to hold. Part of each new deposit must be held in reserve, and part may be lent out. For convenience assume that the Federal Reserve ratio is set at 20 percent for all kinds of deposits in all kinds of banks. Then if a bank receives a $1000 deposit, it deposits the $1000 at the Federal Reserve Bank, thus increasing its reserves by $1000. The reader may imagine that this would permit the bank to make new loans totaling $4000 and thereby created $4000 in new money. Its new reserves of $1000 would be 20 percent of the original $1000 deposit and the $4000 in new deposits created by the loans. It might thus appear that a single bank could expand the money supply by a multiple of each new deposit it receives.

This is not the case, however. Something called *adverse clearing balances* prevents this. Assume that recipients of the $4000 in new loans write checks, totaling $4000, drawn on their newly created demand deposits. Now, assume (for simplicity of analysis) that these checks are all deposited with another bank. This second bank will immediately deposit these checks in the account it maintains at the Federal Reserve Bank, which increases the reserves of the second bank by $4000 but simultaneously charges these checks against the reserve account of the original bank. This reduces the original bank's reserves by $4000.

The Federal Reserve Bank then sends the checks back to the original bank on which they are drawn. The bank reduces by $4000 the demand deposits of the writers of the checks. Thus the bank finds its reserves reduced by $4000 and its demand deposits reduced by $4000. Because it had reserves equal to 20 percent of its demand deposits and because it is required to maintain this ratio of reserves to demand deposits, it can afford to lose only 20 percent as much in reserves as it loses in demand deposits.

When the bank lost $4000 in demand deposits, this permitted it to lose only $800 (20 percent of $4000) in reserves. Thus it has lost $3200 in reserves that it could not afford to lose. Obviously it overextended its loans by $3200. If the bank had lent only $800 instead of $4000, it would not have experienced this difficulty.

To avoid these adverse clearing balances with the Federal Reserve Bank, a bank must restrict its loans to its *excess reserves*. When the bank received its new deposit of $1000, it was required to hold only $200 of it in reserves. This means it had excess reserves of $800 (the original $1000 it received minus the $200 it must hold as reserves). Thus it can be concluded that if a single bank received a new $1000 deposit, it must keep $200 in reserve but could lend out $800. It lends money by giving its customers a new demand deposit of $800, thus creating money.

Yet a single bank may reasonably claim it adds nothing to the money supply. When the customer actually uses the loan, he draws

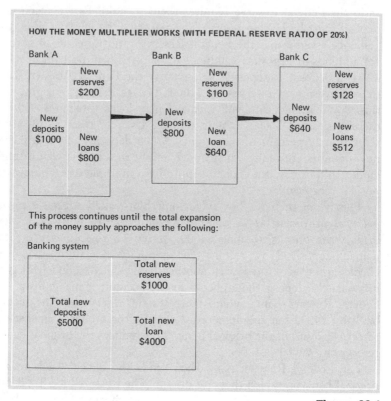

HOW THE MONEY MULTIPLIER WORKS (WITH FEDERAL RESERVE RATIO OF 20%)

Bank A

| New deposits $1000 | New reserves $200 |
| | New loans $800 |

Bank B

| New deposits $800 | New reserves $160 |
| | New loan $640 |

Bank C

| New deposits $640 | New reserves $128 |
| | New loans $512 |

This process continues until the total expansion
of the money supply approaches the following:

Banking system

| Total new deposits $5000 | Total new reserves $1000 |
| | Total new loan $4000 |

Figure 30.1

his deposit down to zero, while the bank merely pays out the $800 in cash. It is when the whole banking system is considered that a new deposit will generally lead to a multiple expansion of the money supply. How this expansion works can be seen in Figure 30.1 and in Table 30.4.

When the $800 loan from Bank A (in Figure 30.1) is spent, it becomes new deposits in Bank B, which are the basis for new reserves of $160 and new loans of $640. In the case of the whole banking system, the process will continue until all of the original new deposit ($1000) becomes required reserves in various banks. Because the new required reserves are then $1000 (or 20 percent of all new deposits), the new loans are $4000 (or 80 percent of all new deposits). Based on an initial new deposit of $1000 in money, the banking system has thus created a total increase in deposits of $5000 (assumed to be demand deposits and therefore counted as money).

For our analysis we use the concept of the money multiplier, which is analogous to, but not to be confused with, the investment multiplier of income determination. The *money multiplier* may be

TABLE 30.4

HOW THE MONEY MULTIPLIER WORKS

1. Assume an initial increase in deposits of $1000.
2. Assume a required Federal Reserve ratio of 20 percent.
3. Assume that banks are always fully loaned out.

Bank	Increase in Loans	Increase in Deposits (or Money Supply)	Increase in Reserves (Required)
Bank A	$ 800	$1000	$ 200
Bank B	$ 640	$ 800	$ 160
Bank C	$ 512	$ 640	$ 128
Bank D	$ 410	$ 512	$ 102
Bank E	$ 328	$ 410	$ 82
Bank F	$ 262	$ 328	$ 66
		$ 262	
—	—	—	—
—	—	—	—
—	—	—	—
—	—	—	—
All Banks	Total Increase in Loans	Total Increase in Deposits (or money supply)	Total Increase in Reserves (required)
	$4000	$5000	$1000

defined as follows:

$$\text{Money multiplier} = \frac{\text{total increase in deposits}}{\text{initial new deposit}}$$

A simple formula for deriving the money multiplier is

$$\text{Multiplier} = \frac{1}{\text{required Federal Reserve ratio}}$$

Assuming that each banker has to keep 20 percent of his deposit liabilities in the form of cash, the money supply can be expanded to five times the amount of cash that the banking system holds:

$$\text{Multiplier} = \frac{1}{0.20} = 5$$

Thus the initial new deposit of $1000 is multiplied by 5 to get a $5000 total increase in deposits (or in the money supply).

The analysis does not yet take into account several kinds of leakage that may occur in varying degrees over time. The assumption that banks are always fully loaned up is not consistent with the facts. There are often some excess reserves—that is, reserves above the legal requirement. Therefore the volume of expansion of deposits does depend on the degree to which bankers decide to make the maximum loans on their reserves. It also depends on the degree to which businessmen wish to accept these loans. Finally, the whole process takes time, and only a certain amount of the predicted expansion will occur in any given period.

It is nevertheless generally true that banks lend in some multiple of their reserves and that total expansion of the money supply will be greater, the smaller the required Federal Reserve ratio. In the next chapter we shall consider how the Federal Reserve uses the required reserve ratio and other tools to control the money supply. The relationship between money supply and price inflation will also be considered.

SUMMARY

In this chapter we examined the money supply and its probable evolution from barter to paper money to credit. We saw that today the most important component of the money supply is the demand, or checking, deposits and credits granted by the banks. We noted too that the Federal Reserve System was established to control the banks so they cannot go into an orgy of speculative lending that would end in monetary collapse. Finally, we examined how within these limits the banking system can still expand the money supply several times by giving credit to the allowed extent. This information will help us understand the problem of inflation and the monetary policies pursued by government.

inflation and monetary policy

Several varieties of price inflation have been discussed in previous chapters. Here it is time to summarize our knowledge of the theory and facts concerning the money supply and price movements. We begin by recalling the general monetary framework of the economy and then briefly recapitulating the problems of inflation within that framework. Then some of the tools the Federal Reserve can use to control the money supply will be examined.

A famous equation often used by economists is

Money supply × velocity of money = price level × transactions with products

The *money supply* is defined as the sum of coins and paper currency outside banks and demand deposits at banks (which form the largest part of the money supply). The *velocity of money* is defined as the speed (or number of times) with which money changes hands in a given period. The *price level* is the general index of the average of all prices in the economy. The *transactions* discussed here are simply the physical volume of sales of the national product.

NORMAL INFLATION IN PROSPERITY

In Chapter 28 it was demonstrated that the price level has generally risen in times of expansion and fallen during a depression. The reasons may be stated in terms of the monetary equation. In times of expansion transactions or sales of the national product rise considerably, but the flow of money (money multiplied by its velocity) rises even faster. Because the equation tells us that the price level equals the money flow divided by the products sold, in this case prices must rise.

Why does the flow of money rise so rapidly during a period of expansion? On the one hand, the money supply expands because banks give credit (in the form of demand deposits). Businesses want to borrow in order to take advantage of profitable opportunities, and banks want to lend because it appears that businesses can easily repay the loans with interest. The money multiplier process then assures that the money supply will increase several times.

On the other hand, the velocity of money increases as consumers and businesses both spend more rapidly. Consumers wish to get bargains before prices rise further and also because they feel assured of future income. Businesses likewise dig into their hoarded savings to make the investments that appear attractive. In times of expansion everyone wishes to spend in order to buy goods rather than hoarding money.

In a depression, by contrast, the money flow usually decreases even faster than the transactions with the national product. Banks call in their loans and businesses do not want to make new loans; therefore the money multiplier works in reverse to diminish the money supply several times over. Furthermore, individuals and businesses hoard their savings for the rainy days ahead, especially because there are no attractive opportunities for investment. As a result, the velocity of money circulation also falls considerably in a depression. For these reasons, depression is normally a time of price deflation.

MONETARY POLICY

One of the longstanding ways in which government has influenced the economy has been through the use of policies designed to expand or diminish the flow of money and credit. The main idea is that in a depression, an increased flow of money and credit will combat unemployment by increasing purchases of both consumer and investment goods. In times of prosperity, restriction of money and credit will reduce inflationary pressures by reducing the flow of demand. Monetary policy works mainly through its effects on the price for renting the commodity called money—that is, the rate of interest on loans. If the government can increase or reduce the supply of money while the demand for it remains constant, then interest rates may be lowered or raised. And if spending plans are financed by borrowed funds and if these plans react in any way to changes in the rate of interest, it follows that changes in the supply of money for loans will have some effect on total spending.

In an inflationary situation exactly how should monetary policy be applied and how effective is it? The supply of money and credit may be restricted by monetary policy through three major controls: (1) raising the required Federal Reserve ratio, (2) raising the interest rate the Federal Reserve charges banks, and (3) sale of government bonds by the Federal Reserve. Let us see how each of these controls is supposed to work.

First, in order to restrict credit the Federal Reserve may raise the ratio of reserves banks are required to hold against their deposits. Furthermore, as soon as one bank decreases its loans, the effect on all banks may be several times as great by virtue of the money multiplier. Thus in theory the raising of the Federal Reserve ratio from 10 to 20 percent would lower the multiplication of money by banks from tenfold to only fivefold. If all banks were fully loaned out, this would cause a great decrease of loans. A reduction in the volume of loans may then mean less money available for consumer and investor spending, thus reducing inflationary pressures.

Second, the Federal Reserve may also raise the interest rate banks must pay if they wish to borrow from the Federal Reserve Banks. Then a bank will either have to charge higher interest rates on loans to its customers or reduce the amount it lends in order to avoid borrowing reserves from the Fed. Either way, less money may be available for further consumption and investment spending, which may reduce demand and thus lead to a lower rate of price inflation.

Finally, the Federal Reserve may sell more government bonds to banks or rich individuals. The money to pay for the bonds must come from bank reserves or from individual bank deposits. In either case the ability of banks to make loans is reduced (manyfold, according to the money multiplier). Thus again consumer and investment spending may be decreased and inflationary pressures reduced.

These methods of reducing money spending in an inflation may encounter certain obstacles. First, each assumes banks had already made loans up to their maximum ratio of deposits to reserves. But banks often keep extra reserves above even the highest possible required reserve ratio and thus can keep lending until these reserves are exhausted. Second, these monetary controls assume that corporations must borrow from banks all the money they need for new investments. But corporations often keep their own internal savings, which they may decide to use regardless of bank policies. Third, in cases in which the government succeeds only in getting banks to raise their interest rates (by lowering money supply), there may be little effect on demand. If expected profit rates are rising even faster than interest rates, corporations may still be willing to borrow and invest more rapidly. In all of these cases the government may be able to restrict the money supply, but the velocity, or speed, of spending of the present money supply may increase even more rapidly.

Despite these weaknesses, monetary policy, if applied strongly enough (and rapidly enough because time is required for it to take effect), can choke off a general inflation. Of course too severe a remedy may cause instability in the bond and stock markets, loss of confidence by domestic and foreign investors, and eventually a business downturn. Finally, it should be noted that general monetary tools are of little help in an inflation caused by monopolistic price setting in particular industries. Monetary deflationary policies may even lower aggregate economic activity and increase unemployment if the inflation in particular industries occurs together with some amount of general unemployment (as appeared to be the case in the early 1970s in the United States).

In a depression exactly the opposite monetary policy may be applied. The supply of money and credit may be expanded by (1) lowering the required Federal Reserve ratio, (2) lowering the interest rate the Federal Reserve charges banks, or (3) purchase by the Federal Reserve of government bonds in the open market to put more cash into the hands of individuals and banks. These measures are designed to increase the volume of borrowing and thus the volume of spending by increasing the supply of money for loans and lowering interest rates.

Obstacles to monetary policies intended to combat depression include most of those met by counterinflationary policies and a few that are different and more difficult to surmount. First, the interest rate cannot go below zero, and in actual practice lenders will not go below a floor that is somewhat above a zero rate. Yet during a depression it may require a zero or even negative interest rate to stimulate borrowing. Second, neither consumers nor most investors seem much stimulated to borrow by slightly lower interest rates. Businessmen apparently consider the pessimistic outlook for smaller profits or even losses to be quantitatively much more important in investment decisions. Moreover, most businesses prefer to invest from internal funds; when their profits fall drastically in a depression, they are not much attracted by any kind of loan.

You can lead a businessman to the river of loans, but you cannot force him to drink. In terms of the money equation the government may increase the banks' supply of money, but consumers and businesses may reduce the velocity of their borrowing and spending even more rapidly. In short, monetary policies may have some effect in minor recessions, but when pessimistic expectations become general in a depression, monetary policy may be able to do little or nothing to expand the volume of spending.

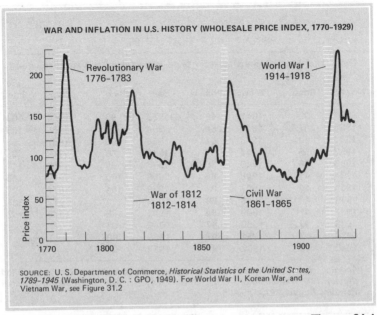

WAR AND INFLATION IN U.S. HISTORY (WHOLESALE PRICE INDEX, 1770–1929)

SOURCE: U. S. Department of Commerce, *Historical Statistics of the United States, 1789-1945* (Washington, D. C. : GPO, 1949). For World War II, Korean War, and Vietnam War, see Figure 31.2

Figure 31.1

INFLATION IN WARTIME

The usual inflation experienced during peacetime prosperity has been very slow and very slight compared with the rapid and spectacular inflation stimulated by wartime spending. Just how closely price inflation is correlated with war may be seen in Figure 31.1. Very rapid price inflation accompanied the Revolutionary War, the War of 1812, the Civil War, and World War I.

During wartime there is little production of consumer goods or private producer goods. In terms of the monetary equation the transactions included within the private portion of the national product decline, or at least are prevented from rising. At the same time there is full employment, with high wages and profits. The government finances the war production largely by increasing the money supply, either directly by printing money or indirectly by increasing the national debt. The debt is increased by issuing government bonds, which may be used to get more credit for banks or individuals. Furthermore, as prices begin to rise rapidly, people rush to buy goods before prices rise further, thus increasing the velocity of money.

COST-PUSH INFLATION

Turning to the modern period, we find all the varieties of inflation in developed countries well represented in U.S. price movements (see Table 31.1 and Figure 31.2).

TABLE 31.1

RECENT PRICE MOVEMENTS IN THE UNITED STATES

(Price is defined as the wholesale price index for all commodities, 1957–59 = 100)

Year	Price	Year	Price	Year	Price	Year	Price
1929	52	1941	48	1953	93	1965	103
1930	47	1942	54	1954	93	1966	106
1931	40	1943	57	1955	93	1967	106
1932	36	1944	57	1956	96	1968	109
1933	36	1945	58	1957	99	1969	113
1934	41	1946	66	1958	100	1970	118
1935	44	1947	81	1959	101	1971	122
1936	44	1948	88	1960	101	1972	126
1937	47	1949	84	1961	100	1973	143
1938	43	1950	87	1962	101		
1939	42	1951	97	1963	100		
1940	43	1952	94	1964	101		

Sources: U.S. Department of Commerce, *Statistical Abstract of the United States, 1964* (Washington, D.C.: GPO, 1964), p. 351, and *Federal Reserve Bulletin*, August 1973, p. A66.

Figure 31.2 records an initial large drop of prices during the Great Depression of 1929–1933. Then, with the recovery of demand, there was a rise until 1937. The recession of 1938 caused a price drop, which was followed by the slow rise of prices during World War II. This rise would have been much more rapid except that price control held down inflationary pressures. Immediately following World War II, the vast demand for consumer and investment goods burst the dam and flooded the market with purchasing power, resulting in the rapid price rises of 1946–1948. A recession lowered prices in 1949, and then the Korean War caused a second major round of inflation in 1950–1951. Another recession lowered prices at the end of the Korean War, after which they rose steadily until 1959. Prices remained fairly stable in the early 1960s but rose sharply from 1965 to 1971 because of the Vietnam War.

The surprising point is that the price index rose rather than declined in the recessions of 1958 and 1969–1971. During these recessions the prices of industries with monopolistic power actually *rose* in the face of declining aggregate demand.

It is such evidence that forces us to distinguish the inflations of the late 1950s and 1969–1974 from the ordinary *demand-pull* inflation, which is caused by the upward pull of aggregate demand. Here, instead, prices apparently are pushed upward by individual firms and industries. It is called *cost-push* inflation to indicate the belief that prices are pushed upward by either higher profit margins or higher

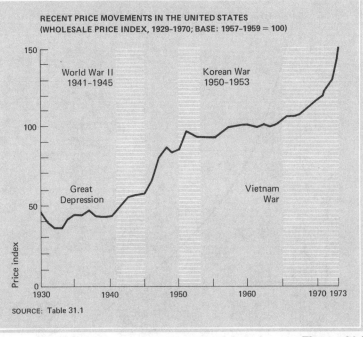

RECENT PRICE MOVEMENTS IN THE UNITED STATES
(WHOLESALE PRICE INDEX, 1929–1970; BASE: 1957–1959 = 100)

World War II
1941–1945

Korean War
1950–1953

Great
Depression

Vietnam
War

SOURCE: Table 31.1

Figure 31.2

wage costs. Many conservative economists argue that the monopoly or oligopoly power of firms is not responsible for spiraling prices but that the bargaining power of labor unions pushes wages up and that prices only follow wages.

It is true that in the nineteenth century, in the early stages of U.S. industrial development, there may have been a shortage of workers during some of the railway booms. These shortages temporarily caused an increase in wages and made immigration necessary to keep up with capital growth and to prevent wages from rising. Since that time, however, the opposite situation of labor surplus seems much more characteristic of the peacetime U.S. economy. Moreover, in all recent expansion periods profits have risen far faster than wages. Wage increases have been only a pretext for previously decided price increases; the cost-push theory of inflation has been used as a weapon against labor to hold down wages and increase profits.

Since World War II the United States has experienced long periods of expansion but also a number of short-term recessions. It is, of course, normal during a cyclical recovery to find prices rising as the demand for goods temporarily outdistances supply. The important point to note is that price rises take place long before full employment is reached. In fact, since 1953, even during the expansion

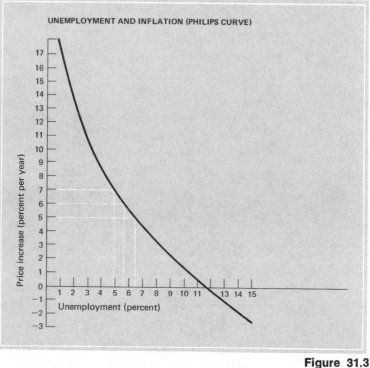

Figure 31.3

periods, there have been chronic excess capacity and chronic unemployment of at least 5 or 6 percent of the labor force, according to official statistics. True, the stage has been set for inflation by a fairly high level of demand. Demand, however, has still been below the full-employment level. Therefore it is *not* true that inflation has been caused by any real deficiency of labor supply relative to the demand.

The relationship of unemployment to inflation was first graphed by professor Phillips and is therefore called the *Phillips curve*. He used the actual statistics from history. For simplicity we present in Figure 31.3 a curve of the same variety, based on imaginary data (of roughly the same order as the real data).

This graph is merely a rough description of reality. The Phillips curve says that unemployment and inflation can and do exist together in the U.S. economy. It says that as unemployment decreases, inflation increases—or as unemployment increases, inflation decreases. That is generally true, since high unemployment means lack of demand, which makes it more difficult for businessmen to raise prices. At full employment there is generally ample aggregate demand, and price increases are much easier for businessmen to impose.

So far we have only stated the fact that considerable unemployment (as high as 6 percent) may exist in our economy at the same time as considerable inflation (as high as 12 percent). Now we come to the difficult question: How and why is this possible?

This strange and socially very costly phenomenon of unemployment *and* inflation is obviously not covered by the standard Keynesian analysis of inflation caused by the pull of excess demand. Yet the *wage-push* theory (wages rising faster than prices) is factually untrue. Only one explanation remains to be considered. Oligopolistic freedom of price fixing causes prices to rise in certain industries in the face of declining demand, with prices rising even during recessions in recent years. This phenomenon, which should be called profit-push inflation, results from the exercise of monopoly power.

PROFIT-PUSH
INFLATION AND MONOPOLY POWER

The relative stability of oligopolistic profit rates was emphasized in Chapter 27. Large corporations can afford to take a long view of profit maximization, and they have enough effect on the market through control of supply so that they can set their prices at levels different from those that would result in a competitive market. Their profit rates fall relatively little in recessions because *they maintain prices by restricting supply*. Yet neither do their profit rates rise spectacularly in periods of expansion. They increase production and retain their portion of the market in times of expansion, but they are cautious about raising prices to the full extent that might be feasible due to temporary increases in demand. This means that they normally leave considerable slack below the price level that would be most profitable in the short run. The reason for this cautious behavior is that their prices in expansion are already high enough for very high profits. By keeping prices a little lower than the maximum for short-run profits, they enlarge their share of the market, thus making even more profits in the long run.

As expansion continues, all firms are faced by rising costs for both labor and capital goods. The small firm whose price is set by competition can only watch its profit margin decline because the demand for its product is also limited. Not so the large oligopoly firm. Because it had intentionally set its prices below what the market would bear, it may now use up part of the slack to raise its prices, utilizing previous wage increases as an excuse. Higher wages may be part of the inflationary spiral, being themselves a response to earlier increases in price and profit. Higher wage costs, however, would have very little direct effect on prices if it were not for the oligopolistic structure of industry that allows freedom of price fixing within wide limits.

The market power of oligopolies to influence prices has been documented in several investigations. In the 1930s a famous study of price rigidity compared the lowering of prices by industries during the Great Depression with the ratio of concentration of production by the four largest firms in each industry. It was found that the prices of the more concentrated industries fell much less than competitive prices.[1] The evidence from expansions in the 1920s and 1930s is less clear, with fairly equal price rises in competitive and oligopolistic sectors or even a slightly greater rise in the competitive sector.

Empirical data for the period since World War II clearly document the pervasive effects of the increasing monopoly power. This increase reflects the accelerated trend toward concentration as well as the lucrative military contracts going to the giant corporations. During the 1948 recession, prices in the nine most competitive industrial groups fell by 7.8 percent, but prices in the seven most concentrated industrial groups fell only 1.9 percent.[2] In the recessions of 1953 and 1957, even the more competitive prices fell only slightly, but the prices in the more concentrated industries actually continued to rise. Of course this greater resistance of oligopoly prices to a decline is a major course of their more stable profit margins during depressions.

The expansions since World War II give even stronger evidence of the increase of monopoly power. From the trough of October 1947 to the peak of July 1953, the prices of the 7 most concentrated groups rose 23.3 percent, whereas prices in the 9 most competitive rose only 12.4 percent. Similarly, from the trough of August 1954 to the peak of July 1957, prices in the 7 most concentrated groups rose by 16 percent, whereas those in the 9 most competitive rose only 4.5 percent. Thus the cyclical pattern seems to have been changed (or exaggerated) by a long-run movement toward higher relative prices in the more concentrated industrial groups. This long-run change seems to be responsible for a persistent outward shift of the Phillips curve. (See Figure 31.3.) An outward shift of the Phillips curve means that the same level of unemployment is accompanied by increased rates of inflation; alternatively, the same rate of inflation is associated with higher rates of unemployment. This unprecedented combination of unemployment and inflation makes the problem of control within capitalism more difficult or even impossible.

[1]Gardiner C. Means, writing for the U.S. National Resources Committee, *Structure of the American Economy* (Washington, D.C.: GPO, 1939), vol. I, p. 142. Also see John M. Blair, "Means, Throp, and Neal on Price Inflexibility," *Review of Economics and Statistics*, November 1956, pp. 427–435.

[2]The data given here are all adapted from a table by Robert K. Lanzillotti in U.S. Congress, Joint Economic Committee, *Employment, Growth, and Price Levels*, (Washington, D.C., 1959), p. 2236.

What are the immediate policy implications for the U.S. government of the fact of profit-push inflation in the midst of unemployment? The Keynesian solution for unemployment is to increase aggregate demand (by spending more or lowering taxes), and the solution for inflation is to reduce aggregate demand (by spending less or raising taxes). These approaches are now clearly inadequate. A small increase in demand (usually through military production) does not necessarily stimulate output and employment but is used by the dominant large corporations to raise prices even more and thus extract higher profits. A small decrease in demand (usually by cutting welfare spending or raising taxes) does not reduce most prices but only leads to more unemployment.

WAGE-PRICE CONTROLS

On August 15, 1971, President Nixon announced a new economic policy designed to save America and increase corporate profits. Before arguing about what it has accomplished, we must be clear on exactly what has been the extent of these controls.

Phase 1 ran for 90 days from August to November 1971. All wages, prices, and rents were frozen. Profits were *not* frozen. In actuality all wage increases were prevented, but some prices continued to creep upward. Nixon explained that the controls were necessary because we had combined inflation and unemployment, and all other monetary and fiscal policies had failed.

Phase 2 lasted from November 1971 until January 1973. It had mandatory controls of wages, prices, and rents, but not of profits. Under this system inflation continued, though at a reduced rate of "only" about 4 percent per year. Unemployment fell from its highest level (in the official data) of about 6 percent in the 1971 recession down to about 5 percent. When one realizes that the official data leave out many people and do not even try to count part-time unemployment, this is still a very high level. Wages were successfully kept to a very, very slow increase in this period—but profits rose spectacularly (as we shall see in detail).

Phase 3 was supposed to "phase-out the economic stabilization program back to the free market, since the price target was being achieved," according to administration spokesmen. It removed all controls over prices in all industries except food, health, and construction, and substituted "voluntary" controls. The voluntary controls were no controls at all because they had no enforcement procedure; therefore business paid no attention to them, so prices skyrocketed rising at about 8 percent a year. In the end even the administration admitted failure in holding down prices and had to institute a new freeze. Phase 3 lasted only from January to June

1973. A striking feature of it was the pressure kept on the unions to abide by "voluntary" controls and the extent to which the unions did restrain workers from asking for wage raises, so that there was a very, very slight rise in money wages—and the earning power of workers declined! Again there were no controls on profits, which continued to soar.

Phase 3½ was a second freeze. All prices were frozen, *but* there were no controls on unprocessed food or on rents. Neither wages nor profits were frozen, but wages remained under Phase 3 controls. This phase lasted only 60 days, from June to August 1973.

Phase 4 began in August 1973 and ended in April 1974. It was again a mandatory system of controls over prices, wages, and rents but not over profits. It was very effective in holding down wages, but prices continued to rise at about 10 percent per year. In all of 1973, the actual buying power of workers declined by 4 percent, while profits rose rapidly. In the first half of 1974, unemployment rose to 6 percent, gross national product declined, and the rate of inflation rose to 12 percent. According to the usual definitions, the U.S. economy was in a recession in the midst of an unprecedented inflation. Nixon, however, denied it was a recession, preferring to call it a slight readjustment.

CONTROLS, INEFFICIENCY, AND CORRUPTION

Economists of all ideological views have criticized the controls, but for different reasons. The conservatives, such as Milton Friedman,[3] are horrified at the violation of the First Commandment of laissez faire economics: Thou shalt not interfere with the market process of setting wages and prices. They have always argued that resources, including capital and labor, cannot be efficiently allocated if prices are not set by competition in the market. If the government arbitrarily sets prices, how can a businessman calculate most efficiently what to produce or what technology to use? If a businessman does follow the arbitrary prices set by the government, then he will not produce what consumers desire, nor will he produce it in the cheapest possible way—it will not be produced as cheaply as possible because those prices do not correctly reflect the true scarcities of resources, and it will not be the combination of goods that consumers desire because those prices do not correctly reflect true consumer preferences. Thus wage-price controls doom a capitalist economy to inefficiency.

Radicals agree with the truth of this insight. Radicals—and some

[3]See Milton Friedman in *Newsweek*, August 30, 1971.

conservatives—go further along these lines to point out that a huge bureaucracy would be needed to really enforce these controls. Not only would that bureaucracy have enormous repressive power, but it would also be wide open to corruption. After all, if a businessman cannot freely raise his prices when opportunity arises, then he is better off spending his time and money bribing a bureaucrat to raise his prices than worrying about producing a better-quality product. At the same time, the controls do not end the money-grubbing aspect of capitalism. If capitalists cannot freely raise prices, then they will either bribe the bureaucrats as described or else evade the controls by selling illegally (that is, on a black market, the way much gasoline was sold during the "crisis"). In this sense comprehensive wage-price controls in a capitalist system combine the worst aspects of capitalism and Soviet-style socialism: a huge and inefficient bureaucracy *plus* private greed. Actually the bureaucracy has not grown very much because Nixon has not wished to enforce the controls over prices—though he has enforced wage controls.

CONTROLS AND INCOME DISTRIBUTION

When the conservatives, such as Friedman, argued against the controls, their own solution was an unregulated private capitalism. The liberals, such as Paul Samuelson,[4] pointed out politely that Nixon had already tried that solution, and that it was private capitalism that had resulted in our present unpleasant mixture of inflation and unemployment. Moreover, they pointed out that even the usual monetary and fiscal policies could not cope with inflation and unemployment at the same time. In fact, it was the liberals who first advocated the controls; they expected controls to hold down prices, while welfare spending would increase demand to eliminate unemployment. At first the liberals applauded Nixon's controls. Even in their naiveté, though, their initial reactions were a little doubtful on two points: Would Nixon actually hold down prices or just wages? And would he actually spend enough on welfare programs to end unemployment?

They were right to worry and wrong to applaud at all. Nixon has actually (1) held down wages, (2) allowed prices to continue to rise, and (3) done nothing to cure unemployment, except some military spending. The important thing to understand is that this was not accidental, nor would Nixon be the only President to do such a thing. It was shown in Chapter 20 that all U.S. governments have been strongly pro-business, for the very good reason that business money elects them (and many other reasons). Any wage-price

[4]See Paul Samuelson in *Newsweek*, August 30, 1971.

controls under a business-dominated government can be expected to favor business.

The only difference with Nixon is that (1) there is a great deal of evidence in his case that he accepted business bribes (such as those of the ITT and the dairy industry) beyond the usual legal election campaign contributions, and (2) he is much more blunt about his pro-business biases than most Presidents have been. For example, in his speech announcing the wage-price controls, Nixon said: "All Americans will benefit from more profits. More profits fuel the expansion. . . . More profits means more investment. . . . And more profits mean there will be more tax revenues. . . . That's why higher profits in the American economy would be good for every person in America."[5] Vice President Agnew repeated the theory, saying: "Rising corporate profits are good for the average man and are needed more than ever by the poor."[6] Can you think of some things the poor might need more than rising corporate profits?

Nixon and Agnew were really telling the truth this time. They succeeded quite well in their objectives of limiting wages and raising profits. Thus in all of Phase 1 and Phase $3\frac{1}{2}$ wages didn't rise at all. During all of the longer Phases 2 and 3, average hourly earnings rose only 5. 9 percent a year. At the same time the cost of living rose by about 4 percent yearly in Phase 2, about 8 percent yearly in Phase 3, and about 10 percent yearly in Phase 4. Since the cost of living rose faster than wages in 1973, for the first time on record in a year of economic expansion, the buying power of workers declined! In 1973, during Phases 3 and 4, wages rose by about 5 percent and retail prices about 9 percent, so "real wages" (that is, what the worker can buy) declined by 4 percent.

In Phase 2, during 1972, corporate profits (after taxes) rose by 16 percent from the previous year's figure. In phase 3, in the first quarter of 1973, corporate profits (after taxes) were up 28 percent over the first-quarter 1972 figure. In the second quarter of 1973, still during Phase 3, corporate profits (after taxes) were up by a spectacular 34 percent over the second-quarter 1972 amount. In Phase 2, at the same time that workers' wages were doing very poorly, compensation of top corporate executives jumped 13.5 percent from January 1972 to January 1973.[7]

One way Nixon achieved these results was by appointing a pro-business Pay Board to make wage decisions. The big unions first joined it, hoping to salvage some crumbs, then withdrew when they

[5]President Nixon, in TV speech, August 15, 1971.
[6]Vice President Agnew, at National Governors Conference, 1971.
[7]Most of these data are from government sources, but they have been neatly compiled in a pamphlet by the AFL-CIO, *The National Economy, 1973.*

found they were to be allowed nothing. The AFL-CIO said: "We joined the Pay Board in good faith, desiring—despite our misgivings—to give it a fair chance. . . . The so-called public members are neither neutral nor independent. They are tools of the Administration, and imbued with its viewpoint that all of the nation's economic ills are caused by high wages. As a result, the Pay Board has been completely dominated and run, from the very start, by a coalition of the business and so-called public members. . . . The trade union movement's representatives on the board have been treated as outsiders—merely as a facade to maintain the pretense of a tripartite body. . . ."[8]

THE CONTROLS AND UNEMPLOYMENT

It was shown in Chapter 28 that low wages are one part of the reason for recessions and unemployment. It was shown earlier in this chapter that inflation has been caused not by high wages but by high profits. Since Nixon and his appointees held the opposite view, they naturally did their best to hold down wages and encourage high corporate profits. They succeeded, and the results are as expected. First, inflation is gathering speed and the rate of price increase is increasing steadily. Second, income has been redistributed from wage workers toward profit-making capitalists.

Third, as a natural result, demand is decreasing and unemployment is spreading as of this writing. This is the "natural" result because most of our mass-produced goods must be bought by millions of wage and salary earners; the rich can buy only two or three TV sets per home, still leaving most to be sold to workers. Therefore when income shifts to the rich, there is less demand for most goods. Less demand for goods means less production, and that means unemployment.

In 1969, when Nixon entered the President's office, unemployment was at 3.5 percent. By 1971 the recession meant that unemployment had risen to about 6 percent by the official statistics. In phases 2 and 3, it dropped to about 5 percent but refused to go lower. The official data hide the widespread nature of unemployment. Thus in 1970, another year of "prosperity" and only 5 percent unemployment, a government investigation found that 14.6 million people were unemployed at some time during the year, and $4\frac{1}{2}$ million of these were unmployed for more than 15 weeks at a time. As this is written, unemployment is again rising. In addition to Nixon's encouragement for profits over wages, another reason for the high unemployment has been his refusal to spend much money for constructive

[8]AFL-CIO Executive Committee, in ibid., p. 7.

government projects; the only budget item to show major increases in this period has been military spending.

THE RADICAL POSITION

Wage-price controls have added to bureaucracy and corruption, economic inefficiency, worsening income distribution, and greater unemployment. Radicals argue that these are mostly inevitable results as long as a capitalist government administers such controls under capitalism. Since the combination of unemployment and inflation cannot be cured by monetary, fiscal, or even direct control policies, they argue that somethng more is needed for a solution. The radical solution is direct ownership of the monopoly corporations by the public. Control would be shared by democratically elected public representatives and democratically elected workers' representatives. Such public corporations could fully employ all workers and could set reasonable wages and prices. The profits of publicly owned corporations (after needed wage increases and necessary reinvestment) could be used for a wide expansion of social services. The details of operation of public or social ownership are discussed in Part Four of this book.

SUMMARY

The U.S. government uses the Federal Reserve to attempt to control inflation by (1) raising required bank reserve ratios, (2) raising interest rates on loans to banks, and (3) selling government bonds. All three of these monetary policies are intended to soak up money and thus reduce the amount in circulation. (Monetary policy is supposed to do the opposite during a depression.) Such policies may help somewhat to restrict mild price inflations; they may even help reduce somewhat the strong inflation caused by excess aggregate demand in wartime (which results from unlimited government demand for war supplies). Inflations caused by excess demand may also be met by fiscal policy—higher taxes or less government spending.

The present inflation, in the era of limited wars, is obviously very different because it is accompanied by significant unemployment. Since full employment does not exist, the inflation is not caused by excess aggregate demand. Instead it is a profit-push inflation caused by the ability of the monopolies to raise prices even without excess demand (but certainly aided by the strong demand in the military sector). Obviously control of this kind of inflation cannot be eliminated by traditional monetary policy—nor by traditional fiscal policy.

The Nixon administration tried direct price-wage controls to restrict cost-push inflation. Its problems are (1) inefficiency as prices no longer reflect demand and supply conditions; (2) pro-business bias, allowing for reduction of real wages through price loopholes and little attention to unemployment; and (3) continued monopoly profits based on old moneygrubbing, new loopholes, and new black markets.

economic growth

For the sake of simplicity it is assumed in this chapter that aggregate effective demand rises as rapidly as aggregate supply, that Say's law holds and that there are no depressions caused by lack of demand. Here we ask, How fast is it technically possible for the economy to grow? What is the maximum *potential* rate of growth of output obtainable by the economy? Because all problems of demand are assumed away, the remaining problem may be resolved into two questions: (1) How much of each input (land, labor, capital) can be procured under existing circumstances for use in production? (2) How much output can be obtained from these inputs in the production process?

PRODUCTION IS DETERMINED BY LABOR, CAPITAL, NATURAL RESOURCES, AND TECHNOLOGY

Many different physical inputs constitute an economy's production base. For convenience these may be grouped into three categories: capital, labor, and natural resources. *Capital* includes inventories of raw materials and goods in process as well as all plant and equipment. *Labor* means the number of man-hours available as well as the degree of skill of the available labor force. *Natural resources* include all useful materials (including land) known to be in the territory of the economy. Resources may be depleted by use or natural erosion but may be increased by new geological discoveries. *Technology* is the knowledge that determines how much output can be produced by a given combination of inputs. Therefore the level of potential output is a function of the currently available technology, natural resources, capital, and labor. A thorough analysis of the growth potential of any existing economy should consider each of these inputs in turn as well as the interrelations between them.

The actual long-run economic growth of the United States is summarized in a government report as follows:

It has been estimated that real gross national product grew 4.3 percent per year from 1839 to 1879; 3.7 percent per year from 1879 to 1919; and 3 percent from 1919 to 1959. . . . The growth of the labor force and of the capital stock partly explains our economic growth. In addition, more than half the growth is accounted for by improvement in the factors of production and technology.[1]

No one would deny the importance of improvements in technology or the quality of labor or capital; therefore no one denies the urgent need for such things as research, education, and public health measures. Recent studies, however, have shown that it is very difficult to get exact quantitative estimates of just how important the respective contributions resulting from the growth in the different factors of technology have been.[2]

Here we may leave aside the intricate factual questions involved in separating out the behavior and influence of each of the components of growth. The level of potential output may always be considered to be determined solely by the amount of any one factor (e.g., labor) and by the amount of output produced by a given level of that input (e.g., output per worker). Of course the amount produced by any one factor is influenced by the levels of all the others and by improvements in technology.

FULL-EMPLOYMENT GROWTH

In this section the labor force is assumed to be always fully employed. Potential growth of output is then determined by the growth of the labor force and by the amount produced per unit of labor.

---

[1]U.S. Congress, Joint Economic Committee, 86th Cong., 1st sess., *Employment, Growth, and Price Levels* (Washington, D.C.: GPO, 1959), p. xxiii.

[2]See, for example, E. D. Domar, "On the Measurement of Technological Change," *Economic Journal*, December 1961, pp. 709–729.

Productivity of Labor

The law of diminishing returns states that each additional worker adds less output than the worker hired before him. It holds true only if capital, natural resources, and technology remain unchanged and if some minimum scale of employment is reached. Given these assumptions, the law of diminishing returns is a truism; it cannot be other than true. All other things remaining the same, it is obvious that if enough workers are crowded onto a single plot of land or even the entire world, the crowding alone will eventually cause the product of an additional worker to decline. But many of the classical economists—Malthus, for example—went much further than the truism embodied in the law of diminishing returns. They predicted that diminishing returns per worker in the economy as a whole *would* come about in actual fact. Malthus reached this dismal conclusion on the grounds that population increase would be very rapid and would far outweigh the slow increase of capital, technology, and natural resources.

The gloomy long-run prediction based on this interpretation of the law of diminishing returns has not been borne out by the facts of historical progress. First, it is not even clear that the world population is at the minimum level at which further additions to the working force would bring diminishing returns, even if natural resources, capital, and technology were to remain constant. Second, labor itself improves in quality as scientific and technical education advance, although this may properly be classed as an aspect of technological improvement. Third, it was usual to argue that the earth is only so large and that its natural resources are slowly being depleted. The supply of *known* natural resources, however, is steadily expanding as a result of continual discoveries of new reserves. Furthermore, there have been important discoveries of new uses for previously neglected materials—for example, coal was once merely a hard black stone of no use for fuel or heating purposes. Moreover, better ways have been found to use available resources—for example, power production by atomic fission or fusion, or food production by hydroponic farming. Of course the last two means of resource expansion are also aspects of technological improvement.

Another reason why there have not been diminishing returns per worker in the economy as a whole is the increasing use of capital per worker, which allows a single worker to produce far more than previously. The final and most important reason for the defeat of diminishing returns is that development of technology in the past century has meant a much more efficient use of the available capital, natural resources, and labor. At the early date when Malthus wrote, it was still possible largely to ignore technological progress. Today even the blindest economist is forced to consider the starting advances continually made in productive know-how.

Empirically the evidence shows that population in the developed countries has not outraced technology, natural resources, and capital but that, on the contrary, product per person has grown enormously. In U.S. agriculture increase of output has far outrun increase of employment. In fact, between 1870 and 1940 employment in agriculture rose by only 34 percent, while output rose by 279 percent.[3] The United States thus has no problem of lack of food but rather a surplus relative to effective cash demand.

It may be concluded that *in the industrialized private enterprise economies slowed progress or retrogression is caused not by natural and technical problems but by man-made economic institutions that give rise to recurrent economic catastrophes.* The advent of atomic energy makes it especially clear that the natural sciences have given us ample power to obtain in the future fantastic levels of abundance or to blow to pieces the entire world.

Increase of Labor

The increase of the labor force is determined primarily by population growth, but it is also governed by changes in the age composition of the population and by the sociological attitudes and labor laws that determine the ages of beginning and retiring from work as well as the maximum hours of work. Many Malthusian-minded theorists mechanically project the present world rate of population growth into the near future and easily arrive at quite astronomical figures for total population. But it was demonstrated earlier that, to date at least, capital and technology have had no trouble keeping ahead of population growth; they probably could keep pace with even massive population growth in the coming years.

The mechanical prognostications of vast population growth, however, do not seem to have taken into account the best present knowledge of population growth patterns. Malthus described people breeding like animals and population exploding with only a few kinds of checks to its expansion. He spoke of "preventative checks" as those that cause lower birthrates. He recognized only abstention from sex or vice and sexual deviation and did not consider voluntary birth control through family planning and contraceptive methods. When preventative checks fail, according to Malthus, the result will be "positive checks" to population, where "positive' means a higher death rate. Thus positive checks include wars, famine, and disease.

[3]See Arthur Burns, *Frontiers of Economic Knowledge* (Princeton, N.J.: Princeton University Press, 1954), p. 4.

It is true that in many primitive economies at a low level of productivity, we often find very high birthrates. At this stage, however, population may be constant for centuries because it is held in check by equally high death rates, caused indeed by wars, disease, and starvation. A second stage of rapid population growth usually follows the beginnings of industrialization and the introduction of modern methods of public health sanitation. With better control of disease and enough food production, death rates decline. As long as birthrates remain high, the population soars. (This problem is examined in Chapter 35.)

At the third stage, however, as the economy matures, we find culture and education spreading to all the population. Knowledge of contraceptive devices for birth control also spreads, as well as the desire to use these means in order to keep the family to a manageable size. Thus all of the more industrialized countries have shown some tendency toward lower and lower birthrates during the past 100 years, although there have been some upward spurts in the rate for short periods.

FULL-CAPACITY GROWTH

So far we have concentrated on the increase of the labor force and output per worker. It is more convenient for our purposes, however, to estimate the potential growth of output in relation to the increase of capital and the output per unit of capital. Of course the output per unit of capital will reflect changes in technology, natural resources, and the labor supply.[4]

We may state a very simple relationship between output and capital at any given moment. The national product, or output, must equal the output per unit of capital times the amount of capital in use. Thus a simple formula may be written:

$$\text{Output} = \frac{\text{output}}{\text{capital}} \times \text{capital}$$

Of course this formula is always true by definition, and the only question is whether it is fruitful to think in these terms.

In the United States about $3 of capital goods are in use for each $1 of annual national product. So the ratio of output to capital is about 1:3. Therefore when the value of capital stock, including all machines and factories, was about $1500 billion, the economy produced annually an output of about $500 billion.

---

[4]This approach is detailed in E. D. Domar, "Expansion and Employment," *American Economic Review*, March 1947, pp. 34–35.

Now we may extend this analysis to a growing economy. The rate of growth of output is determined by the growth of capital and the changes in output per unit of capital. More precisely, the rate of *growth* of output is equal to the *increase* in output per *increase* in capital multiplied by the ratio of the *increase* in capital to output. Thus, we may write the equation of growth:

$$\frac{\text{Increase in output}}{\text{Output}} = \frac{\text{increase in output}}{\text{increase in capital}} \times \frac{\text{increase in capital}}{\text{output}}$$

This equation is true by definition, so it is always true. Notice that the formula is true not only for increases but also for decreases in output; we could substitute the word *change* for the word *increase* to obtain a more general formula.

The change (increase or decrease) in output as a ratio to present output is how we define the *rate of growth* of output. For example, if we produced $100 last year and we now produce $103, then the rate of growth is 3/100, or 3 percent per year.

The change in output as a ratio to the change in capital is defined as the *marginal* output/capital ratio. For example, if we invest $9 in additional capital and this results in a $3 increase in our output of national product, then we may say that the marginal output/capital ratio is 1:3. Finally, recall that an increase in capital is our definition of *investment*. Moreover, in this chapter it is assumed (for the sake of simplicity) that the amount of investment is just equal to the amount of saving. Therefore we may say that the *increase in capital* means the same thing as *investment*, or the same thing as *saving*. Then the ratio of increase in capital to output might be written as investment to output or saving to output.

If the equation of growth is put into these new terms, it may be written as follows:

$$\text{Rate of growth} = \frac{\text{change in output}}{\text{change in capital}} \times \frac{\text{saving}}{\text{output}}$$

We are merely affirming that how fast the economy grows depends on how much is saved and invested *and* how much is produced by new investments.

Consider an example of the use of this equation of growth. If the average ratio of saving to output is 9 percent and if the marginal output/capital ratio is 1:3, then we find that

$$\text{Rate of growth} = \tfrac{1}{3} \times 0.09 = 0.03, \text{ or 3 percent per year}$$

This has been approximately the performance of the U.S. economy over a long period.

The mechanics of the growth process may also be examined year by year. Table 32.1 assumes the same proportions as in the example just given of U.S. economic growth.

In Table 32.1 we have illustrated the arithmetic of a growing economy for a few years' time. The table begins at an arbitrary level of $100 for convenience in calculation. The table is purposely incomplete so the reader may finish it. Start with the output of the latest year. First, divide this output into 9 percent saving and 91 percent consumption (or a propensity to consume of 91 percent). Second, having found the amount saved or invested (the increase of capital), we can then find the increase of output for the next year by applying a marginal output/capital ratio of 1:3. For example, because saving or increase of capital was $9 in Year 1, the increase of output in Year 2 is one-third of that, or $3. The table is completed by merely repeating these two steps year after year. As long as the propensity to save and the marginal output/capital ratio remain unchanged, this economy will continue to grow at a steady 3 percent per year.

It is important to emphasize as many recent studies have done, that the most important factors in determining how much output will be produced by a given capital investment are the level of technology and the level of education of the labor force. It has been shown repeatedly that *the most profitable social use of resources* is in education—or production of *human capital*, as some cold fishes call it. Education not only raises the skills of workers in using physical capital but also leads to more research and creates higher levels of technology. Countries with a high level of resources in education have grown most rapidly.

AMERICAN GROWTH EXPERIENCE

What has been the actual long-run trend of the output/capital ratio in U.S. history? According to the best estimates, it has fluctuated around the level of $1 of annual national product to every $3 of the stock of capital.[5] There was a declining trend of product per unit of capital from the 1880s to World War I, but this was just about balanced by a rising trend in productivity from then until the 1940s. Other conflicting studies have shown as much as a one-third rise in capital productivity since the 1880s.[6] Because the data are very poor and there are very difficult problems of definition of *output* and *capital*, the recorded changes may not be very significant; therefore

[5]Fully discussed in Nicholas Kaldor, *Essays on Economic Stability and Growth* (New York: Free Press, 1960), p. 260.
[6]See, for example, Moses Abromovitz, "Resources and Output Trends in the U.S. Since 1870," *American Economic Review*, May 1956, p. 8.

TABLE 32.1

EXAMPLE OF ECONOMIC GROWTH

Assume $\dfrac{\text{increase in output}}{\text{increase in capital}} = \dfrac{1}{3}$ and $\dfrac{\text{saving}}{\text{output}} = 0.09$.

Year	Output (or National Product)	Saving = Investment = Increase in Capital	Increase in Output
1	$100.00 ————	$9.00 ————	➤ $3.00
2	103.00 ◄	9.30 ————	➤ 3.10
3	106.10 ◄	9.55 ————	➤ 3.18
4	109.28 ◄	—	—
5	—	—	—
6	—	—	—
7	—	—	—

it makes some sense to treat the marginal output per unit of capital as roughly constant in the simplest approximation to a long-run projection.

At first glance this seems a strange result because we might expect the product per unit of capital to rise as a result of great technological advances. However, that is not at all necessary because output per unit of capital is determined by two opposed trends. On the one hand, vast technological improvement has meant rapid growth in the output *per worker*. On the other hand, U.S. technology has been embodied in huge amounts of machinery per worker, and thus the growth of capital has been almost as rapid as the growth of output. Of course, it must be remembered that even if the ratio of output to capital in the U.S. economy has stayed roughly constant over a very long period, there are very wide differences among industries and also very wide differences between prosperity and depression when much capital may remain unused.

What has been the actual course of saving (and investment) behavior in the United States? We saw in Chapter 26 that the ratio of saving to national product has remained remarkably stable over a very long period. Thus in the United States the long-run propensity to save remains roughly between 9 and 11 percent.[7] Furthermore, the evidence indicates that the marginal output/capital ratio has fluctuated in about the neighborhood of 1:3. Assuming that these two ratios hold for the future, we may predict growth according to the growth formula. Taking one-third of 9 percent, we have a 3 percent rate of growth. This is approximately the rate of growth American GNP has achieved over a long period.

[7]See Simon S. Kuznets, *National Product Since 1869* (New York: National Bureau of Economic Research, 1946), p. 119.

SAVING AND GROWTH

There are two quite distinct points of view about saving. The classical economists, concerned as they were about economic growth, called for as much thriftiness and saving as possible. In early nineteenth-century England they observed that the savings of businessmen were being used to build more capital and drew the moral that more thrift and saving lead to more rapid increase of capital and, consequently, to more rapid economic growth.

Keynes pointed out that this conclusion is true only if we assume full employment and the rule of Say's law, that demand is always enough for any supply of goods and that all saving is automatically invested. Indeed we made this simplifying assumption when we asked how fast the economy would grow *if* there were always enough demand and *if* all saving were always invested. This assumption, however, is not true. During the Great Depression it was painfully obvious to all Americans that there was not full employment. In the Depression most saving was *not* being invested (except in the statistical sense of investment in unplanned and unwanted inventory pileups).

Keynes showed that, with unemployment and lack of investment opportunities, more saving may actually lead to *less* production rather than any economic growth. This finding constitutes the Alice-in-Wonderland theme of the *paradox of thrift*, which says that greater thrift and saving may sometimes lead to less investment, not more. If the economy is faced with a lack of money demand, then a higher propensity to save may simply lower consumer demand still further. The lower consumer demand may then lead to still less output and income and therefore less aggregate saving and investment than there was before individuals tried to save more of their income. Thrift may always be an individual virtue, as Ben Franklin preached, but it is not always a social virtue when there is a lack of paying customers in a private enterprise economy.

The Keynesian point may be made more obvious by means of a diagram. In Figure 32.1 we see growth represented as higher and higher levels of full-employment output. Assume that there is an increase in the labor force or that there is an improvement in the product per worker, which allows the same workers to produce more at full employment. If the growth of supply from FE_1 to FE_2 is met by an equal growth of demand from Demand$_1$ to Demand$_2$, then all is well. We return to an equilibrium at a higher level of full employment with greater saving and greater investment.

Assume, however, that output and income grow further, from FE_2 to FE_3, but that there is no further growth of demand. This means that at FE_3 the saving (plus consumption) is greater than the planned investment (plus consumption). Therefore at that level we

Figure 32.1

may speak of *too much* saving, which causes a lack of demand for output, which causes a decline of output back to the equilibrium level (now FE_2), far below the full-employment level (now FE_3). Thus the excess of saving causes a fall to a lower level of output, at which there is both less saving and less investment.

We may conclude that more saving at a given income level is a benefit to the economy if, and only if, there is an equal increase in investment. In other words, more saving, which could supply more capital to produce more output, is helpful only if businessmen expect demand to rise by an equal amount. Otherwise they will hoard the increased saving and precipitate a depression.

In the modern world we cannot afford to ignore either side of the problem. The U.S. rate of growth has not been as fast as desired. Setting aside more saving to invest in more capital makes it possible to raise the rate of growth. But this happy possibility cannot become a reality as long as significant unemployment of men and capacity continues, which shows that all of the savings now available are not being invested. More saving would only cause more unemployment in this case. First one must guarantee a solution to the Keynesian problem of finding profitable investment outlets for all existing savings. Then one can worry about the classical problem of generating a higher rate of saving to allow the possibility of more investment.

SUMMARY

This chapter began by discussing the quantity of output that may be produced. The quantity of output is determined by (1) the known natural resources, (2) the amount of capital available, (3) the level of technology, and (4) most of all, the labor force and its level of training and education. The potential rate of growth of output depends on the growth of these four factors. It was also seen that this potential is not realized to the extent that the capitalist system creates unemployment.

Let us repeat that economic growth is necessary if many social ills are to be solved. With the widespread existence of poverty here and abroad, no one can deny that a larger output of goods and services is needed if everyone is to enjoy a high standard of living. Yet excessive concern with growth for its own sake has often obscured many significant economic and social problems. In the next chapter we will see that human welfare could be improved even with no further growth if various kinds of waste were eliminated—and if more of the product went to the average person than to the few rich individuals. It will also be shown that the quality of economic growth (with a minimum of waste and pollution) is at least as important as the *quantity* of growth.

waste and pollution

This chapter explores all the wasteful aspects of production in the United States as well as the sources of pollution and environmental destruction. The wasteful products should not be included in a calculation of social welfare because they do not provide social benefit, even though they are included in the government's accounting of GNP. The pollution and other harm caused by some products should actually be *subtracted* from GNP as a social cost if we wish to compute the total national welfare from economic growth.

MILITARY PRODUCTION AND WASTE

We saw in Chapter 29 that most military "goods and services" (or evils and disservices) are not needed by the people of the United States. We saw that they serve the interests of the big businesses that produce for the military or have investments abroad that the miliary protect from foreign revolutions. We also noted that a dollar of military expenditure not only generates demand to that amount but also generates further spending by the workers and profit makers who receive the military spending. In other words, *if the system cannot reach full employment any other way, then military spending can produce full employment.* On the other hand, if military spending takes place when there is already full employment, then it competes with private spending for labor and resources and can only cause inflation.

It is a fact, however, that the U.S. capitalist system normally operates far below full employment. It is also a political fact of life —as we saw in Chapter 29—that no other kind of government spending can possibly be done on the scale needed to produce full employment. Therefore, within the present system's political and economic constraints, it is true that vast military spending is "necessary" to maintain full employment. Moreover, we have noted that such spending not only puts people to work producing military destruction but also has secondary effects of raising consumer and investor spending.

Obviously, however, military spending and wars also result in more taxes, inflation, wounds, deaths, and alienation and deterioration of life for millions. So whether or not it is wasteful to have military spending—$1.7 trillion from 1947 to 1971—depends on whether we could have a system in which it was possible to have full employment at peaceful pursuits without any military spending. Radicals believe that such a system is possible—that democratic socialism is such a system. Therefore radicals argue that all military spending is wasteful. If we had had as much employment as we did from 1947 to 1971, but all of the military spending had been put into productive plant and equipment for peaceful products, then (in our present state of technology, or ratio of productive facilities to output) the United States could be producing *every year* about $600 billion more in goods and services—or more than half again as much as we are now producing.

MONOPOLY AND WASTE

Production does not reach optimal efficiency below some crucial size. Thus the increase in importance of large firms does mean that most of the economy has the ability to produce at lower costs than ever before. The data on both costs and profit rates reveal the possibility of high efficiency at a fairly constant level beyond the minimum-size firm.[1] In addition, the very large firms also have disproportionately larger research facilities and hold a very large portion of all unexpired patents. Therefore they have the greatest potential for efficiency improvement. Moreover, many investment projects are simply too large for small firms.

But the large, entrenched firm stands to lose most by the obsolescence of present machinery. It also loses most from product improvements that will reduce the number of units the customer needs to buy. Therefore if the large firm has a monopoly position and faces no serious competitive pressure for improvement, it *may* hide away and not use many important new inventions. Monopoly power may also be used to restrict supply in order to maintain prices.

[1]See J. S. Bain, "Price and Production Policies," in Howard S. Ellis, ed., *A Survey of Contemporary Economics* (New York: McGraw-Hill, 1948), p. 140.

Monopolies will expand production as rapidly as possible only in the unusual periods of unlimited demand, such as World War II. Therefore although large monopolies have the potential to produce better goods more cheaply than small competitive firms, in many cases they do not use that potential but produce less useful goods sold at high prices.

Finally, we have seen that the existence of economic concentration may have increased the severity and possibly the number of depressions because of its destabilizing effects on the remaining small businesses. If this is so, then unless it has had a fully offsetting effect in increasing growth during prosperity, it would seem that this is another reason why the net effect of monopoly may be to lower the rate of economic growth. This is not to say, of course, that breaking up large firms into smaller units would increase economic growth; this would certainly cause a major decrease of economic efficiency in addition to probable negative effects on investment.

What should be done about monopoly waste? Conservatives argue that there is very little waste and nothing should be done. Liberals wish to break up monopolies in spite of the inefficiency of small firms. Radicals argue for democratic control of monopolies by workers and the public.

WASTEFUL SALES EXPENSES

In the United States a very large amount of human effort is put into the peculiar occupation of getting people to buy products they may not want. Obviously every society needs to distribute its goods from the factories to the consumers, but the U.S. economy goes far beyond that. It spends billions of dollars and millions of hours of labor time for sales workers to go around from door to door or to stand in a store and persuade other people to buy things. A huge percentage of this effort is not technically necessary and so may be called wasteful.

A second aspect of selling is advertising. Again, some small amount of advertising is needed in any society to supply useful information to consumers. Studies of the U.S. economy, however, indicate that more than 90 percent of all our advertising is not information but an attempt to persuade consumers that each of several identical products is better than the others. Therefore $15–20 billion a year (or more) is spent on advertising that should be described as wasteful.

A third aspect of selling is the giving of estimates. In many industries, such as construction, a tremendous amount of highly skilled effort by highly paid engineers consists in providing estimates on which their company may bid for a new job (e.g., a public school or road or military facility). In each of these cases the buyer of the construction has already had its own engineers furnish an estimate;

in addition, another ten or twelve sets of engineers may do this difficult work of cost estimation all over again.

A fourth aspect of selling reaches back into production. It is the
designing of new products or changes in existing products—not to
make them better and sometimes even to make them worse—in such
a way that they will be more attractive to consumers. One example
is women's skirts, in which the hemline is regularly raised or lowered
so that women wishing to keep in style will have to buy new skirts
or dresses. Another example is the yearly change of automobile
models. One year tails were put on cars, another year they were
taken off, (and men are told they must have the latest model to show
their masculinity—and their success—and attract women). In some
years it has been estimated that these automobile model changes took
up to 2.5 percent of the entire GNP in totally wasted effort.[2]

Last but not least, sales efforts take the even more despicable form
of "planned obsolescence." This means engineers are put to work
designing a product that will fall apart quicker than previous ones
so that the consumer will have to buy a new one.

ENVIRONMENTAL DESTRUCTION

One poetic observer writes: "America was once a paradise of tim-
berland and streams but it is dying because of the greed and money
lust of a thousand little kings who slashed the timber all to hell and
would not be controlled."[3] It is not, however, just a matter for poets
and far-off forests. If President Nixon looks out the window when
he flies to San Clemente, he will notice a large, brownish cloud
covering much of Southern California. And this cloud—called smog
—does not merely look bad and cut visibility but also menaces the
people's health. Ironically, many people in the 1930s and 1940s came
to Southern California because they had respiratory problems, because it was a place where the air was crystal clear, warm, dry, and
healthy. It seems almost incredible that in such a short time it could
become a place where a few minutes of outside work in the after-
noon is exhausting and the air itself causes thousands of cases of
respiratory diseases among children.

Let us list systematically the major forms of pollution.[4] First,

[2]Franklin Fisher, Zvi Grilliches, and Carl Kaysen, "The Costs of Automobile Changes Since 1949," *Journal of Political Economy*, October 1962.

[3]Garrett De Bell, ed., *The Environmental Handbook* (New York: Ballan-
tine, 1970), p. 3.

[4]The following list and most of the data in the rest of this chapter come
from Mathew Edel, *Economies and the Environment* (Englewood Cliffs, N.J.:
Prentice-Hall, 1973). This slender book is by far the clearest, best-written,
most careful, and most revealing study of the political economy of ecology
published to date. We highly recommend it as the best introduction to the field.

there are visible objects such as cans and waste paper, and smoke. Businesses spew over 25 billion tons of pollutants into the air and water and land every year. This includes about 150 million tons of smoke and fumes that blacken the skies and poison the air, 22 millions tons of waste paper products, and 3 million tons of mill tailings. This is not a new phenomenon but has increased with economic growth. It creates problems particularly in slums in central-city areas that get much of the smoke and act as dumping grounds for garbage; it has also gone to the extent of blocking some rivers with solid wastes.

Second, there are organic wastes, detergents, and fertilizers, including human and animal wastes, and materials such as nitrates and phosphates that lead to rapid growth of algae. Altogether, about 50 *trillion* gallons of heated and polluted liquids are dumped into our streams, rivers, and lakes each year. This amount has been rapidly increasing in recent years. When the organic wastes and algae cause exhaustion of the oxygen in the water, other life is unable to survive, and septic decay by anaerobic bacteria causes terrible odors and incubates many diseases.

Third, there is local air pollution, including smoke, carbon monoxide from auto exhausts, nitrogen oxides and sulfur oxides, and photochemical smog produced by hydrocarbons reacting chemically in the air. Automobiles are the worst offender, producing 86 million tons of pollutants a year, but industry and power plants produce another 43 million tons. Altogether, all sources in the U.S. economy introduce 72 million tons of carbon monoxide, 26 million tons of sulfur oxides, 13 million tons of nitrogen oxides, 19 million tons of hydrocarbons, and 12 million tons of particulate matter into the air each year. This pollution causes property damage, local weather changes, lung diseases, and many other diseases; in some temporary emergency situations (caused by local air inversions) even deaths have been caused.

Fourth, there is worldwide atmospheric pollution, including carbon dioxide and dust clouds, which may affect the climate. Increasing carbon dioxide in the atmosphere tends to trap heat and warm the earth, while dust reflects the sun's rays, so that it tends to cool the earth. If either trend became dominant, our climate would change drastically.

Fifth, there are persistent poisonous materials, including DDT and the heavy metals (lead, mercury, and cadmium), that threaten health. DDT remains in each animal until it is eaten by another, right up the food chain to humans, causing various health effects. The heavy metals tend to attack the central nervous system of any animal.

Sixth, there is increasing stray energy, including sonic booms, high-decibel sounds, heat from power plants, atomic contamination, and radioactive fallout. Increased heat can disturb the whole animal and plant environment; noise can do both psychological and physical damage; and radioactivity not only hurts the present body but carries over through genetic defects to the next generation.

Finally, there is the mere fact of congestion, which increases other forms of pollution and also does direct damage. Crowding not only has very bad effects on human psychology but also increases the probabilities of epidemic diseases.

CAUSES AND CURES OF POLLUTION

The diagnosis of what causes pollution leads each different theory to a different prescription of how to cure it. Each of these diagnoses and prescriptions is associated with a general political outlook: conservative, liberal, or radical.

The Conservative View

Many conservatives deny that the picture is as grim as we have painted. Thus President Nixon acknowledges that there is some environmental problem but gives it very low priority and vetoes most bills designed to do something about it. (Profits come first.)

The conservative economists who do take the problem seriously begin, as usual, with Adam Smith's analysis—that the "invisible hand" of competitive private enterprise will balance all costs and benefits to consumers and producers and will finally give the optimal social result. They acknowledge that to some extent the market does not seem to be workng well enough to prevent pollution. They argue that the reason is that pollution costs constitute a slight exception to Adam Smith's rule (that competition results in an optimal social result).

The reason that Adam Smith's rule is partially violated in this area, they say, is that some costs—like pollution—are costs to all of society but are not costs to individual firms. Moreover, the benefits of nonpollution go to all of society rather than to individual firms. Thus the costs of pollution do not lower their profits, nor do the benefits of nonpollution raise their profits. Therefore since the behavior of individual firms is determined solely by their expected profits, they ignore the fact of the pollution they create. This is the view of serious conservative economists, though they use slightly different rhetoric to describe the problem.

Since the problem is "merely" that pollution does not affect the competitive market producer, the solution is to make pollution marketable. One approach is to make air and water into private property so owners could sell or rent them. Then we could have competition between those who wish to buy them to pollute and those who wish to buy them to breathe. Of course if someone got a monopoly of air we might not be able to afford breathing. And how much a person could breathe or drink would depend on one's income.

To avoid a monopoly on air and water, the slightly less fanatic conservatives suggest that the government could auction off the "right to pollute" certain areas, or firms could pay for pollution damage, or we could all pay firms not to pollute by giving subsidies from local governments!

The Liberal View

Liberals argue that it could make capitalism slightly ridiculous and be highly inequitable to buy and sell air and water in this way. Mainly they argue that the problem is much broader than the conservatives acknowledge, so such minor patching could not work. They argue that these costs of pollution—which are external to private accounting and are therefore called *externalities*—pervade the whole system. They are not simply a minor exception to Adam Smith's model but are involved in almost all production of goods and services. Furthermore, they point out that many of the benefits of nonpollution of air or water are collective or public goods by nature—that is, there is no way to divide up clean air for sale to some people but not to others.

Therefore the liberals conclude that private enterprise cannot solve this problem by tinkering with new "property rights" in air and water but that the government must exercise its power to stop pollution. Thus the liberal Samuelson says: "Is reliance on spontaneous business efforts futile in the solution of a problem like this? Experience gives a pessimistic answer. . . . Since no one profit maker has the incentive, or indeed, the power, to solve problems involving 'externalities,' here is a clear case for some kind of public intervention."[5] So liberals advocate various laws to control the polluters.

POWER AND POLLUTION: A CRITIQUE OF THE LIBERAL VIEW

The liberal view asserts that the capitalist state can pass and enforce laws controlling pollution while preserving capitalism. They fail to see that the "right to pollute" is deeply imbedded in our present economic system and that all efforts to control it must meet the fiercest opposition. Thus even the *New York Times* (in an editorial on February 9, 1971) admits that "a corporate manager has his at-

---

[5]Paul Samuelson, *Economics*, 9th ed. (New York: McGraw-Hill, 1973), pp. 816–817. For a more thorough statement of the same view, see A. Freeman, R. Haveman, and A. Kneese, *The Economics of Environmental Policy* (New York: Wiley, 1973).

tention focused on the profit targets and production schedules. He has a *natural resistance* to taking into account environmental costs. . . . What is involved is a conflict of values. Nixon proposes many excellent environmental measures but he often talks the old fashioned language of the profit-first businessman."

We saw in Chapter 20 that the entire governmental apparatus always tends to put the interests of private property ahead of human values. Therefore the "natural resistance" of businessmen to pollution controls tends to be passed on to the government that it dominates. This is true of liberal as well as conservative governments but is perhaps more obvious in the case of a directly business-subservient government like Nixon's. There is no conflict of values but a conflict of interests; just enough must be said about the environment to get Nixon and his fellows elected by the public that demands controls, while he must also make sure that no such controls are put into effect so as to satisfy all the businessmen that give him his campaign funds.

For these reasons, as early as 1971 Nixon emphasized ecology in his State of the Union address. But when it came to proposing laws, the administration always argued for the words "taking into account the practicability of compliance." These words mean that no pollution control is "practical" or legal if it cuts down profits in any way! Since almost all controls do cut into profits, no controls would be practical in the administration's view.

Thus it is also quite understandable that the Nixon administration (and big business) opposes any increase of public transportation to replace the polluting automobile; it even opposes all research to find better automobiles to replace the present gas-eating monsters. For example, Senators Muskie and Magnuson proposed to allocate between $3.6 million and $5 million to do research on electric cars. This is a very tiny amount by comparison with the billions and billions spent by the military, but even this tiny amount of research money was opposed by the heads of the Departments of Commerce, Transportation, and Health, Education and Welfare. Undersecretary of Commerce J. Herbert Hollomon revealed their true concerns when he said: "The automobile contributes directly or indirectly to a substantial portion of our Gross National Product. It is a significant item in our trade relations with the rest of the free world. It involves a large segment of our work force and is a major factor in the production of some of our largest industries."

Indeed, the automobile and related industries are very important interests in our economy. When we add together auto production (the big three especially) plus gas and oil production (including 15 of the 60 largest corporations), plus highway builders, plus tire companies, and so on, they produce more than 12 percent of GNP and pack a tremendous political clout. When we ask why there is not more public investment in rapid transit systems or more public research into alternatives to the internal combustion engine, the answer seems to be the raw political-economic power of the auto, gas, and highway industries. In fact, private opposition and political constraints have reduced rides on public transit from 23 billion in 1945 to only 8 billion a year in 1967.

The highway lobby is probably second in power only to the military-industrial complex. There are lobbyists at Congress from the American Road Builders Association, the Associated General Contractors of America, the National Highway Users Conference, American Trucking Associations, the American Association of State Highway Officials, and the American Automobile Association—as well as representatives of many individual firms. So far this lobby has been able to prevent any use of the immense highway funds for public transit. (The same lobbyists have also been successful in preserving the oil depletion tax loophole.)

In addition to preventing the passage of pollution control laws (or better rapid transit or research for better cars), the same forces *In his opinion* have been quite successful in preventing effective use of the laws that have been passed. For example, there are antipollution boards in most states, but a careful survey shows that at least 35 of them are totally dominated by the very polluting firms they are supposed to control. In Chapter 20 the Federal Power Commission was found to be similarly controlled by the gas and electric power interests. Even brand new commissions suffer the same fate. For example, in California the construction industry spent millions of dollars to defeat a law for the preservation of the seashore; but when the law was passed anyway the Governor (Reagan) and local governments both appointed mostly representatives of the same polluting interests to the new boards designed to oversee the protection of the seacoast.

Since autos are the most important source of smog, we would expect many legal procedures to force the auto companies to institute controls. Their tremendous power, however, has been used to emasculate such law enforcement. For example, "throughout 1969, the Department of Justice in Washington held a secret hearing to discuss with industry lawyers its charge that automobile manufacturers have conspired to stifle the introduction of smog-control devices on automobiles. On September 11, the department announced that it had entered into a consent decree allowing the companies to escape federal sanctions by promising that they would not conspire any more."[6] Furthermore, in the general atmosphere of big business influence and corruption in the Nixon administration leading up to

[6]de Bell, op. cit., p. 269.

the Watergate scandal, it was easy for the auto companies to exert pressure on the Environmental Protection Agency. As a result, the EPA has postponed the enforcement of the standards set by the Clean Air Act passed by Congress (which itself had been watered down by auto lobbyists).

Even if the laws are enforced, the existence of the capitalist system brings about a clash between the environmental and economic interests of most people. For example, under the Clear Air Act a cement factory in the little town of San Juan Batista has been found guilty of terrible pollution of the air. The company admits this but says that it will "cost too much"—that is, it will lower profits—to install the proper purification machinery. Therefore the entire cement factory is closing and will move elsewhere. In this way the burden of environmental protection is made to fall on local workers and on the local people and governments.

This strategy is known as *divide and rule*. It has been very effectively used by polluting businesses to split the opposition to pollution. Thus in the case of the California shoreline protection law, the construction industry bosses got the construction unions to oppose it as well—for the very good reason that more of them would be unemployed if there were less construction. Similarly in the case of funds for highways the Teamsters union always supports these funds and new road building against community wishes—again because they wish to protect their jobs. "Because America does not guarantee workers jobs in their own communities, people must be concerned that investment take place near where they live."[7] So the conflict between jobs and ecology is built into our present capitalist system.

Another conflict utilized by the big polluters is that between the interests of different states. Given this conflict, the oil companies wanted the individual states to control "tidelands oil" rather than the federal government. Each state is relatively weak by itself compared to the industrial giants, so they can always threaten to take their business elsewhere. It is thus easier to take resources, such as oil, away from individual states or to be allowed to pollute individual states.

The same kind of conflict and threats can be utilized at the national level. Already many small countries have capitulated to a vast amount of pollution rather than losing business and jobs to other countries. Even the powerful United States is not immune. Since the environmental protection laws have been tightened, many of our own powerful multinational corporations have moved or threatened to move whole enterprises to less well-protected countries.

[7]Edel, op. cit., p. 130.

THE REVIVAL OF MALTHUSIANISM

In the early nineteenth century the Reverend Malthus studied population and poverty. He decided that population always increases in geometric progression—2, 4, 8, 16, etc.—because people breed like rabbits. He also decided that production could increase only arithmetically—1, 2, 3, 4, etc.—because of our limited land and resources. Therefore from this mechanical exercise he concluded that poverty is caused by too much population and that there is nothing we can do about it. The only alternatives are: abstain from sex altogether or wait until famine and disease remove the excess population. Malthus overlooked technology, which allows us always to produce more per worker. He also overlooked the fact that after industrialization more educated and sophisticated men and women would decide to have less children per family by practicing birth control. Therefore instead of ever-decreasing product per person, the developed countries have experienced ever-increasing product per person. Furthermore, we shall see in Chapter 35 that the less developed countries are kept that way not by population pressure but mainly by foreign imperialism.

In recent years many conservatives, some liberals, and even some radicals have brought back to life the old Malthusian argument: They conclude that rising population and rising production together doom us to ecological catastrophe and to eventual poverty as our resources are eventually depleted. The only way out, they tell us, is to have a zero rate of population growth and a zero rate of economic growth. Partly they are concerned with the very real problems inherent in growth under capitalism. The well-known liberal economist John K. Galbraith makes this perfectly correct point, saying: "I am not quite sure what the advantage is in having a few more dollars to spend if the air is too dirty to breathe, the water too polluted to drink, the commuters are losing out in the struggle to get in and out of the city, the streets are filthy, and the schools so bad that the young perhaps wisely stay away, and hoodlums roll citizens for some of the dollars they saved in tax."[8]

The problem comes when this correct point is pushed much too far. One commentator in the *New York Times* wrote: "There are, alas, a few 'iron laws' . . . The hard fact is: growth of production is the basic cause of pollution growth."[9] Even stronger are the doomsday statements made by the Club of Rome, a group of businessmen and management experts. On the basis of certain arbitrary assump-

[8]J. K. Galbraith, in congressional testimony, quoted in Michael Harrington, "Reactionary Keynesianism," *Encounter* 16 (March 1966): 51.
[9]Edwin Dale, *New York Times Magazine*, April 19, 1970, p. 27.

tions about resource and waste disposal variables, they "scientifically prove"—by putting everything into a computer—that in just a certain number of years hundreds of millions of people will die from either pollution or lack of food. On this basis some conservatives conclude that we can do nothing but live—and die—with pollution and poverty, while many liberals and some radicals argue that the only hope is to limit absolutely to present or lower levels the amount of economic growth and the amount of population.

We certainly agree that there is an enormous problem here. It is not true, however, that this fate is inevitable or that limiting growth and population are the only or even the best answers. In the first place, the link between pollution and GNP growth is not a simple one-to-one relationship. If we spend $10 for an evening at the theater, the accountants record $10 GNP growth; but very little pollution is created. If, on the other hand, we spend $10 for gas for pleasure driving, a great deal of pollution is created. It turns out that much of the worst pollution is associated with petroleum products, certain heavy industries, and military industry. If we eliminated the automobile and military production, most pollution would be gone.

The problem is not merely the fact that some GNP growth involves much more pollution than other growth; it is also the fact that much of this spending is on unnecessary or even harmful goods that could be eliminated—without reducing food, clothing, and shelter. Furthermore, some activities *should* grow—for example, growth of services combatting pollution—even though these will be treated as GNP growth by the accountants. Finally, much more of the GNP can be recycled.

In the second place, no-growth policies cannot be considered apart from income redistribution policies. Under the present capitalist system poor people rightly suspect that "no growth" means they would be frozen into poverty forever.

In the third place, international redistribution must be considered. At United Nations conferences, when affluent American delegates have argued for no-growth policies, the poor countries have rightly suspected that this means their whole countries would be frozen into poverty forever. In addition, when birth control is advocated by the U.S. government for these countries, they are rightly suspicious of nationalist and racist motives for reducing their populations but not the U.S. population. It is also a fact that the best way to get birth control and less population growth is by achieving an urban and industrialized society (which means more growth for these countries), since people then have the knowledge of birth control and the desire for fewer children.

In the fourth place, the theorists of no growth never consider whether a different political economic system could achieve much less pollution even with the same growth. Yet we have seen that, while some pollution is caused by any massive economic growth under present technology, it is capitalist greed for profits that causes many additional problems. It is a government dominated by capitalist economic power that is slow to legislate and slow to enforce pollution controls. It is a capitalist system that cannot guarantee workers other jobs when some jobs are prohibited because of pollution effects. It is capitalist systems that cannot willingly redistribute to poor people and poor countries the existing goods and services. It is the capitalist system that makes poor people and poor countries suspicious of birth control—though birth control would make very good sense under a non-profit-oriented system. Finally, it is impossible to conceive of a no-growth rule imposed on capitalism; how could private enterprise exist if it is prevented from growing? It would mean monopolies for existing industries, ever-higher prices, and no new competitors allowed—plus a very extensive government bureaucracy to give detailed instructions to prevent growth.

THE RADICAL VIEW

Obviously radicals agree that some pollution is likely in any highly industrialized and densely populated economy. But a very large part of pollution in the U.S. economy is due to the capitalist economic system for all the reasons given previously. "Look at the values which galvanize energies and allocate resources in the business system: pursuit of money, enrichment of self, the exploitation of man —and of nature—to generate still more money. Is it surprising that a system seeking to turn everything into gold ends up turning everything into garbage?"[10]

Radicals argue that the correct solution is a new economic system, one in which the people decide democratically how to run it, rather than having the decisions being made by a few people. Note that this is a classic definition of "socialism." It excludes the Soviet Union, however, because they also have an economic system dominated by a few undemocratically selected rulers.

Under a democratically run socialist economy, wasteful goods and services—such as vast military production, oversized private automobiles, and advertising signs by the millions—would be eliminated. Under a democratically run socialist economy, the national income would be shared much more equally than today, so most people could live better at any level of GNP than under our present system of unequal distribution. Under a democratically run socialist economy, there would be no private enterprises to push frantically

[10]Editorial, *Ramparts*, May 1970, p. 2.

for more growth to make more profits, and birth control information and devices would be freely available to all.

The Energy "Crisis"

Is there a crisis? The available data are very poor because the oil,
gas, and electric companies have tried very hard to keep them secret.
It seems, however, that the U.S. economy does have plenty of energy
reserves for the next few decades. For the short run the question is
only what the companies are willing to produce. For the long run,
there undoubtedly will be shortages if the system continues as it has.

If there is a shortage at present, who is to blame? In the first
place, the energy companies are to blame because they have purposely restricted production. The oil companies have plenty of crude
oil but have not built enough refineries. The electric companies have
also not built enough generating plants. Why not? Because these are
monopolies or oligopolies. By the exercise of their monopoly power,
they can restrict production. Restricted production means less supply
to the market, which causes a "shortage" that allows them to charge
higher prices. These higher prices result in greater profits per unit.
Of course if the companies reduced supply too far, their total profits
would fall; but they are very careful to reduce supply only far
enough to optimize profits for the whole industry.

This is quite apparent in the profit rate data. While consumers
were told to cut their heat and freeze a little to conserve energy—
while paying higher prices—the companies had zooming profits in
1973. The profits of Exxon alone rose from $1.5 billion in 1972 to
$2.5 billion in 1973. The profits of the nine largest companies rose
by 45 percent in the first 9 months of 1973[11] and still further in the
last quarter.

While their profits rose, they created a smoke screen of very extensive advertising propaganda—and all their advertising is tax de-
ductible. First, they argued that they couldn't expand faster because
environmental groups harassed them. Yet the data show that they
did not want to expand faster because they wanted a "shortage."
There is even some evidence that the oil companies asked the Arab
countries to hold back some of their oil.

Second, the oil companies argued that the one to blame is really
the consumer. Exxon sponsors ads to say that housewives should do
their errands all in one trip to save gas. It sponsors other ads to say
that we should all drive slower. The companies even tell us to lower
our house temperatures to save heating oil. But it is wrong to blame
the people or to ask them to make voluntarily sacrifices. It is the
companies who caused the shortage and are profiting from it.

[11]These data are from an excellent article by Frank Ackerman and Arthur
MacEwan, "Energy and Power," *Monthly Review* 25 (January 1974): 1–14.

Yet it is *not* the case that the companies are run by evil men who beat their mothers. They are simply part of the capitalist system acting the only way they can within that system. The system is planless. Thus the companies can restrict their production with no one to tell them no. At the same time, it is only good business practice to tell consumers to use more of their product. There have been gigantic advertising campaigns to tell us to use more gas in the home, more gadgets of every kind in the home, and larger energy-eating autos. Their profits are maximized, which is their duty to stockholders, only by restricting production while increasing demand. If a corporate executive did not follow these policies, either he would be fired by his stockholders or the whole company would go bankrupt.

Moreover, the system is characterized by monopoly in almost every industry. Monopoly means, according to all economists, restricted production, more advertising, and higher profits. This same system tends to squander all our resources, both by urging consumers to spend more money on everything and by its own wasteful advertising—and by all-out support for ever-larger military spending.

Finally, the system tends to oppose really basic research to find new, cheaper, and more plentiful sources of energy. Such research might destroy the cozy monopoly power of the large energy corporations. At any rate it is a risk because they might have to scrap a large amount of existing equipment and might not be able to establish monopolies over the new sources of energy. They are thus very conservative about fundamental new ideas and try to prevent the government from doing much basic research either. For all of these reasons, the business system is not only responsible for the present limited "shortages" but is likely to create very real shortages of every kind of energy in the future if we allow it to keep working as it has always done.

The blame must also be placed on the government. Besides the normal inefficiency, the real problem is that the government is on the side of the energy companies. Its highest goal is to create more profit for the companies. The main reason for this attitude is that, as the case of ITT and Nixon—or the case of the dairy industry and Nixon —shows, the politicians get most of their large contributions from the large corporations; in return, they are expected to do favors for those corporations. Thus Nixon stacked the Federal Power Commission with commissioners who are all representatives of the oil, gas, and electric companies. It has been observed that the Nixon administration has been the best that money could buy—but, again, that is normal for all political administrations in a society dominated by big business.

We noted earlier that the big oil and electric companies have benefited from the "crisis" through higher profits. It should be added that the Nixon administration also benefited from the energy crisis. While Nixon was under attack for the Watergate crimes, he could urge people to forget all that and to rally around him patriotically, as in a war, to solve the energy crisis. Like the companies, he has made speeches blaming the consumers and asking them to save energy, while never attacking the companies.

On the contrary, the administration and the companies have used the occasion to try to push through Congress various legislation they have always wanted. They have argued for a delay in the Clean Air standards to save on energy—and, incidentally, to protect the auto companies' profits. They have argued for loosening the antitrust laws so the government and all the companies could collaborate to save oil and gas—and to allow more profits by the companies. They have used the "crisis" as an excuse for pushing the Alaska oil pipeline, for keeping oil depletion allowances, and for numerous other pro-business measures.

Who has been hurt by the energy "crisis"? We noted that the large corporations and Nixon have actually benefited from it. Yet most people have been hurt. Tenants have had to pay higher rents while receiving less heat. Workers have been fired with energy shortages as an excuse. All consumers have had to do with less oil and gas. Moreover, most cutbacks to businesses have hurt small businesses because their quotas have not been enough to stay in business. Also hurt have been the small, independent oil companies. The shortage has thus resulted in further economic concentration.

What is a reasonable solution? It seems obvious that the resources of the United States should belong to all Americans. Yet it seems that the corporations have used their control of those resources to exploit their workers, restrict production, and charge high prices to consumers. Therefore it seems only just that we the people should take over the large monopolized energy companies. The public and the workers in these enterprises should each elect representatives to directing boards that would run the companies. This way we could extend our political democracy to democratic control over the energy industry. A democratically controlled industry could expand production and sponsor basic research while cutting some prices and reducing the profit margin.

SUMMARY

There are various kinds of economic waste: military production, monopoly misallocation, most advertising and sales expenses, planned obsolescence, lack of conservation, and pollution. There is pollution of land, air, and water. Extreme conservatives argue that non-pollution (such as clean air) could be given a price and bought and sold in the market, thus automatically solving the problem. Liberals believe that is insufficient; legal controls are needed to prevent pollution by private enterprise. Radicals don't believe controls will work under capitalism; a democratic socialist society is a necessary condition for an end to waste and pollution.

international
trade
and
finance

Throughout most of Parts Two and Three, we have discussed the American economy as though it existed in isolation. In this chapter, we shall consider some of the economic and financial relationships between different countries. Market transactions over national boundaries are similar in some respects to transactions within a single country. Goods and services are purchased from foreigners, investments are made in foreign countries, and profits are made in these countries and then repatriated in much the same way as they would be between two states within the United States.

There are also important differences between foreign market transactions and domestic transactions. The most obvious is that when international boundaries are crossed, different currencies must be used to make payments. A second and even more important difference is that various governments are involved, either directly or indirectly, in international transactions.

INTERNATIONAL ECONOMIC RELATIONS

In market transactions property rights are exchanged. We have already seen that it is through the system of property rights that those who are economically powerful derive and use their power. The essential feature of property rights is that there must be a government with the power to enforce these rights.

Within a single country, a fairly consistent set of property rights is protected by a single government. In the United States, about 1.5 percent of the population owns most of the income-producing assets. Ownership gives this small minority ultimate control of most of the political processes. It is through this control that they maintain governments that give the highest priority to the protection of the property rights on which the economic power of the wealthy elite rests.[1]

Across national boundaries, however, there are often widely different property systems with different governments enforcing the property rights. Very little international trade would take place if there were not some commonly recognized core of property rights with some government or governments having the power to enforce them.

At present, international transactions are concentrated in two large groups of countries, the socialist countries and the capitalist countries. Within each group there are generally fairly common sets of property relations and fairly definite power hierarchies. Although some trade does take place between capitalist and socialist countries (many of them are geographically adjacent to each other and have long histories of economic interaction), this trade is generally much smaller in volume than trade with other economies within a country's own ideological and social sphere.

The power hierarchies within each of these two blocks ensure a sufficient degree of stability and consistency in the enforcement of property rights so as to make extensive economic interaction possible. A given country finds its powers as well as its restrictions defined by its place within the hierarchy. Within the capitalist group, for example, the United States stands at the top of the power hierarchy. Canada, Japan, and the countries of western Europe are on the second level of the pyramid. At the bottom of the pyramid are the less developed countries of Latin America, Asia, and Africa.

The relationships between pairs of countries on different levels of the hierarchy are various and complex. Most of the countries are nominally sovereign, independent states. Their particular position in the world hierarchy of capitalist countries, however, modifies and constrains this sovereignty and independence in a multiplicity of ways. A country in the middle level of the pyramid may find control being exerted on it from above while at the same time it benefits and profits by exerting control on countries at a lower level. We can briefly examine Canada's position in order to illustrate the constraints that exist for a country in the middle level of the hierarchy. (Canada is perhaps an extreme case because American control there has ad-

[1] Evidence for this statement was presented in Chapters 20 and 29.

vanced beyond that which exists in any of the western European countries.)

THE CASE OF CANADIAN-
AMERICAN ECONOMIC RELATIONS

Canada invests hundreds of millions of dollars annually in less developed countries. With these investment dollars goes a large measure of Canadian economic power within many of these countries. However, a Canadian government report in 1968 showed that foreigners owned $33 billion of Canadian assets. The principal owners of these assets were the United States (approximately 80 percent) and the United Kingdom (approximately 12 percent). The bulk of this foreign ownership was direct or equity ownership (about 60 percent).[2]

The composition of this foreign ownership conformed perfectly with the time-honored explanation of economic expansionism: the securing of sources of raw materials and markets for manufactured goods. Fifty-four percent of all Canadian manufacturing industries were owned by foreigners, and 60 percent were controlled by foreigners. Foreign ownership of mining and smelting stood at 62 percent. The petroleum and natural gas industry was 64 percent foreign owned and 74 percent foreign controlled.

Within the manufacturing sector the industries that were oligopolistically organized were almost completely foreign owned. These figures are 97 percent of the automobile industry, 97 percent of the rubber industry, 78 percent in chemicals, and 77 percent in electrical apparatus. These industries were controlled almost exclusively by U.S. interests.

This control of oligopolistic industries was reflected in the fact that of the 414 corporations with assets above $25 million, 53 percent of these assets were in firms that were more than 50 percent owned by nonresidents; the figure for firms with assets below $25 million was 32 percent.

The immense profitability of American subsidiaries in Canada is grossly underestimated if one looks simply at the more than $1 billion a year in interest and dividends received from Canadian firms. Payments for management fees, royalties, franchises, advertising, rent, professional services, and so forth probably amount to nearly $500 million a year, although accurate statistics on these do not exist.

Very possibly an even larger source of profits (for which no statistics would be available) lies in the buying-and-selling policies

[2]*Canadian Privy Council Report of the Task Force on the Structure of Canadian Industry* (Ottawa: Queen's Printer, January 1968). These data and those that follow were taken from various pages of the report.

of parents and subsidiaries. Thus an American company controlling Canadian natural resources can pay a high price for these resources and show a large profit on the books of the subsidiary—or it may pay a low price and show the profits on its own books. Similarly, an American manufacturing firm that requires its Canadian subsidiary to purchase manufactured components from the parent company can follow pricing policies that can make the profits appear on either side of the border. This permits the company to use an optimum combination of tax loopholes in both countries.

It appears probable, however, that the greatest pressures exist for American corporate managers to maximize the parent company's profits. It is generally the profits of the parent on which these managers' personal careers depend. Thus a study of the National Industrial Conference Board showed that while manufactured component parts represented 35 percent of material costs for Canadian industries, they represented only 23 percent of material costs for American industries.

The results of this economic takeover have manifested themselves in the decreasing degree of independence both externally and internally in Canada's economic and political policies. Over the past ten years Canada has been under constant pressure to follow the U.S. "line" on Vietnam more closely. U.S. subsidiaries have openly refused employment to U.S. immigrants who appear to be draft dodgers; Canada has not refused American nuclear weapons; U.S. subsidiaries, by taking orders from the parent company, follow U.S. State Department guidelines and partially subvert the Canadian government's attempts to increase trade with certain communist states.

Moreover, American control of the composition of Canadian investment results in a far less than optimally arranged industrial structure. American firms have literally made a "little America" of Canada's economy. The result in many industries is a large number of units each producing at a smaller-than-optimum scale. Canada, with a population equivalent to roughly 10 percent of that of the United States, gives its consumers an array of brand names virtually identical to that faced by the American consumer.

Perhaps in the long run the worst evil of American ownership will be the complete elimination of the possibility for Canadians to achieve a more equitable distribution of wealth. Within a capitalist society the primary means of redistributing wealth (at least in theory, if not in deed) have been the use or potential use of death duties, inheritance taxes, taxes on gifts and bequests, and capital gains taxes. Because almost all Canadian assets owned by foreigners are owned by foreign corporations and because the foreign corporations almost never die or divest themselves of their Canadian holdings, these methods can never substantially redistribute wealth.

Thus an understanding of international economic transactions must be based on a knowledge of the relative power positions of the countries involved. A country's economic objectives and national policies will always be significantly influenced by its position in the international hierarchy of capitalist countries. (Socialist countries are discussed in Part Four.)

FINANCING FOREIGN TRANSACTIONS

In terms of volume a country's most important kinds of foreign economic transactions are importing (purchasing commodities from foreigners) and exporting (selling commodities to foreigners). Imports and exports involve the exchange of different currencies and are therefore more complex than ordinary economic transactions. If an American business firm decides to import German beer, it faces a problem. The importer sells the beer in the United States for American dollars, but the German exporter must be paid in German deutschemarks (DMs).

Similarly, assume that Coca-Cola exports its product to Germany. The German importer sells the Coca-Cola to Germans for DMs and with the proceeds pays its bill to the company. It pays in DMs, but Coca-Cola wants to collect in dollars.

Now assume that the importing of beer and the exporting of Coca-Cola were the only economic transactions jointly involving Germans and Americans, and that Americans buy DM4000 worth of beer and Germans buy $1000 worth of Coca-Cola. If the rate at which DMs exchange for dollars were DM4 = $1, then all of the transactions could be easily accomplished. We shall trace through these simple transactions to show how foreign sales and purchases are financed.

The American beer importer will take a $1000 check to his bank (say, the Bank of America) and exchange it for DM4000 (because we have assumed that $1 exchanges for DM4). With the DM4000 the importer can pay his debt to the German beer exporter.

Meanwhile the German importer will take a check for DM4000 to the Bank of America's German branch and exchange it for $1000, with which he pays his debt to Coca-Cola.

The Bank of America has engaged in two transactions. First it gave up DM4000 in exchange for $1000; then it gave up $1000 in exchange for DM4000. Thus the two transactions cancel each other and the Bank of America is left with the same amount of both dollars and DMs. (In this simple example we have ignored the fact that in each transaction the Bank of America will charge a fee for making the exchange and will thereby add to its profits.) No dollars actually left the United States; nor did DMs actually leave Germany. It worked out exactly as though the American beer importer had paid Coca-Cola and the German Coca-Cola importer had paid the beer exporter.

There are two reasons why our example worked out so neatly. First, the demand for *foreign exchange* (which is generally what foreign currencies are called) was exactly equal to the supply of foreign exchange. The demand for foreign exchange, it should be noted, arose from the import of foreign goods, while the supply of foreign exchange arose from the export of domestic goods. Second, the supply of and demand for foreign exchange were equal because the *exchange rate* at which dollars could be converted was $1 = DM4. There are, then, two important considerations in the financing of foreign transactions: (1) the number and magnitude of transactions giving rise to a demand for and supply of foreign exchange and (2) the rate at which dollars can be converted to foreign exchange, or the exchange rate between American dollars and the various foreign currencies. We shall consider each of these.

THE BALANCE OF PAYMENTS AND THE DEMAND FOR AND SUPPLY OF FOREIGN EXCHANGE

We begin by taking the exchange rate as given and examining the international transactions that give rise to a demand for and supply of foreign exchange.

Our previous example gives us two very important types of transactions that create a demand for and a supply of foreign exchange. The export of Coca-Cola created a supply of foreign exchange, supplied by the German importer. The import of beer created a demand for foreign exchange, with which the German exporter could be paid.

There are many other types of transactions that perform the same functions. The *balance of payments* is a systematic accounting of all such transactions for one country for a given period, usually one year. Transactions are aggregated into different categories. The *current account* records all sales and purchases of goods and services between Americans and foreigners.

Table 34.1 summarizes the current account for 1970. All items on the left side of the table are transactions that created a supply of foreign exchange. The transactions listed on the right side created a demand for foreign exchange.

From the current account transactions in 1970, the United States earned $6.9 billion more foreign exchange than it spent. Other transactions were involved in the overall balance of payments, however. These are summarized in Table 34.2.

TABLE 34.1

CURRENT ACCOUNT OF U.S. BALANCE OF PAYMENTS
FOR 1970 (IN BILLIONS OF DOLLARS)

Transactions that Created a Supply of Foreign Exchange		Transactions that Created a Demand for Foreign Exchange	
U.S. exports of merchandise	$42.0	U.S. imports of merchandise	$39.9
Foreign purchases of U.S. transportation, insurance, and other private services	9.8	U.S. purchases of foreign transportation, insurance, and other private services	9.5
U.S. income from private foreign investments	9.6	Foreign income from private investments in the U.S.	5.1
Total	$61.4		$54.5
Net balance	$ 6.9		

Source: *Federal Reserve Bulletin*, April 1971, p. 270.

The most important of these other types of balance-of-payments entries are military spending (and sales) and federal government grants and investments in foreign countries, on the one hand, and American private investment in foreign countries, on the other. Because our worldwide military expenditures far exceed our sales of

TABLE 34.2

REMAINDER OF U.S. BALANCE OF PAYMENTS
FOR 1970 (IN BILLIONS OF DOLLARS)

Transactions that Created a Supply of Foreign Exchange		Transactions that Created a Demand for Foreign Exchange	
Net balance carried forward from current account	$ 6.9	Remittances and pensions (net)	$ 1.4
Military sales	1.5	Military purchases abroad	4.8
Foreign investment in U.S.	4.4	U.S. government grants and investments abroad	3.5
		U.S. private investments abroad	6.4
		Change in U.S. liabilities to commercial banks abroad	6.5
		Errors and omissions	.9
Total	$12.8		$23.5
Net balance			$10.7

Source: *Federal Reserve Bulletin*, April 1971, p. 270.

military equipment and American capitalists always invest much more in foreign countries than foreigners invest in the United States, it is clear that these entries will create a net demand for foreign exchange. Since the early 1950s these items have created a *larger* net demand for foreign exchange than the net supply of foreign exchange generated in the current account. As a consequence, the United States has had a deficit in its balance of payments. Strictly speaking, the balance of payments always "balances." This is because the net deficit generated in Tables 34.1 and 34.2 must be financed somehow. It has been financed by either (1) using up America's gold stock or (2) borrowing from foreigners (of which we shall say more in the following pages). If we had included the transactions that depleted the United States' gold reserves and the transactions in which foreigners lent us enough to cover our deficit, then the balance of payments would have balanced. (The balance in this overall sense is merely a result of double-entry accounting. It should not confuse the reader. By saying that the balance of payments is in deficit, economists merely mean that the United States must use its gold or borrow from foreigners to finance its international transactions.)

From Table 34.2 we see that the $6.9 billion in foreign exchange earned in the current account was more than used up in these other types of transactions. In fact, in 1970 the United States incurred a deficit of $10.7 billion in its balance of payments. The deficit, considering only the transactions that were not part of the current account, was $17.6 billion. Of this sum, $6.5 billion was due to foreign commercial banks drawing down their balances in American banks. Military purchases abroad and U.S. government grants to foreigners accounted for $8.3 billion, and American businessmen invested $6.4 billion abroad (which increased the value of American-owned foreign assets and investments to $166 billion).[3] To finance the $10.7 billion deficit, the United States gave up $3.3 billion in reserve assets (gold and claims on other currencies) and foreigners accepted $7.3 billion in American short-term IOUs.

Since 1945 the United States has nearly always exported more than it has imported and therefore has had a favorable balance of trade (we have earned foreign exchange in the current account). This foreign exchange has been used to finance worldwide military ventures and corporate investments in other countries. But the financing of these transactions has used more foreign exchange than has been earned in current account surpluses. Thus Americans have had to come up with more money to finance military expenditures and foreign investments. The year 1970 was typical of what has hap-

[3]*Federal Reserve Bulletin*, April 1971, p. 280.

pened nearly every year since 1950. The United States built up a foreign exchange balance in current transactions, but militarism and foreign investment used much more foreign exchange than this balance would finance. The remainder was made up in two ways: The United States paid out gold, and foreigners were forced to extend low-cost loans to Americans. We shall examine each of these separately.

The drain on the U.S. gold stock is simple and easy to understand. When U.S. corporations and the government spend more than is earned from the export balance, some of the difference is paid out in gold. In 1957, the U.S. Treasury had $22.8 billion in gold stock. By 1969, this figure had fallen to $10.4 billion. In the 12 years between 1957 and 1969, about $12.4 billion of U.S. foreign investment was financed by exporting gold.[4]

The second source for financing excess foreign investments has been cheap foreign loans. To understand why foreigners *must* make these loans, we must discuss the role of the American dollar in the financing of international transactions.

THE AMERICAN DOLLAR
IN INTERNATIONAL FINANCE

Since every country has a different currency and some of the currencies have unstable values, it is necessary to have a currency with which to conduct international business. The American dollar is used far more extensively than any other currency for this purpose. The American dollar is, then, the currency of which other countries must keep a balance in order to facilitate their foreign financial transactions, just as the individual must keep a small balance of currency to finance his day-to-day transactions.

But the worldwide volume of international transactions has grown rapidly and continuously since World War II. This means other countries have been forced continuously to build up their American dollar bank balances.

We have already seen, in Chapter 30, how the U.S. banking system can expand the money supply without cost. American businessmen take these dollars and send them to other countries in payment for their foreign investments. If U.S. currency were not the international medium of exchange, foreigners would immediately demand that the dollars be taken back in exchange for more U.S. exports or for gold. These commodity exports or gold exports would represent the *real* payment for the foreign resources U.S. corporations have taken over.

[4]Figures taken from *Federal Reserve Bulletin*, September 1970, p. A75.

But because foreign countries must continuously build up American dollar balances if they are to continue to engage in international transactions, they are forced to keep them. This means they get no real payment for the resources they hand over to U.S. corporations. They are in effect extending low-cost loans that need never be repaid as long as the American dollar is the international medium of exchange. If the American dollar were not an important currency in international transactions, there would be no desire to hold American dollars, and the costs to American businessmen of borrowing abroad would be substantially higher.

Between January 1950 and June 1970 the increase in the American "liquid liabilities to foreigners" was $37.3 billion dollars.[5] A large amount of this represents foreign investment for which no real payment (in exports or gold) was made. Although many other types of transactions are also included in this total, nevertheless we estimate that over $30 billion was definitely in the category of *forced* foreign credit with which American corporations—almost without cost—financed foreign investments. In other words, America's role as world banker secured over $30 billion in loans for American foreign investment for which no payments in gold or commodity exports were ever made. Not only were there no net payments of these loans, but only the lowest, nominal interest charges were paid. It is obvious that being the world's banker has been lucrative for the United States.

THE DETERMINATION
OF EXCHANGE RATES

We began our discussion of the balance of payments by assuming that the rate at which American dollars are exchanged for other currencies is given and fixed. We turn now to an examination of how this rate is determined.

If there were a free market for all currencies and the value of any currency were free to fluctuate, then the foreign exchange rate would depend on the demand for and supply of foreign exchange. The value of an American dollar in relation to other currencies would increase when the foreign demand for dollars exceeded the supply of dollars available to foreigners. Similarly, the value of a dollar would decrease if the foreign demand were less than the supply of dollars in international finance. The exchange rate would be in equilibrium when the demand for and supply of dollars to be ex-

[5]Data for 1950 to 1960 were taken from S. E. Harris, ed., *The Dollar in Crisis* (New York: Harcourt Brace Jovanovich, 1961), pp. 308-309; data for 1961 to 1970 were taken from *Federal Reserve Bulletin*, September 1970, p. A76.

changed for other currencies was equal, or when there was neither a surplus nor a deficit in the balance of payments.

To illustrate this, imagine that exports and imports are the only transactions that enter into the balance of payments. Assume, for example, that in our original illustration of the United States and Germany trading Coca-Cola and beer, the exchange rate had been DM5 = $1. When the German importer of Coca-Cola purchased DM4000 worth of Coca-Cola, it would have bought him only $800 worth of Coca-Cola. However, had the American beer importer purchased $1000 worth of beer, he would have received DM5000 worth of beer. The American demand for foreign exchange (DM5000) would have exceeded the supply of foreign exchange (DM4000). The same thing can be stated in terms of dollars: The foreign demand for dollars ($800) would have been less than the supply of dollars to foreigners ($1000). The German balance of payments would show a surplus of DM1000, while the American balance of payments would show a deficit of $200.

If nothing happens to alter demand or supply in either Germany or the United States, then the deficit can be eliminated only if the value of a dollar (in terms of DMs) declines. Conversely, the value of the deutschemark in terms of dollars would have to increase. This change in the exchange rate would tend to create an international balance for both countries. If, for example, the rate went to $1 = DM4, the German Coca-Cola importer would find that $1 worth of Coca-Cola now costs him DM4 rather than DM5, and he is likely to increase his purchases of Coca-Cola. The American importer of beer will find that DM1 worth of beer now costs him 25 cents rather than 20 cents, and he is likely to buy less beer. If these changes in quantities demanded (in both countries) are sufficiently large, the American deficit and the German surplus will both be eliminated.

Many economists have expressed the faith that if there were freely fluctuating exchange rates, then changes in exchange rates would induce large changes in exports and imports. These changes would automatically eliminate surpluses or deficits in the balance of payments. Historically, however the exchange rates for most currencies have not been free to fluctuate. The governments of most countries have fixed their exchange rates and, as a rule, have changed them only infrequently. Proponents of fixed exchange rates argue that flexible exchange rates would result in day-to-day fluctuations in currency values, which would make international commerce very uncertain. For example, Coca-Cola might export $1000 worth of its product today, when $1 = DM4, but next week, when the German importer pays the bill, the rate could be $1 = DM8. If this happened, the German importer would become very reluctant to purchase more Coca-Cola in the future (because he had been forced to pay twice as much as he had anticipated).

With fixed exchange rates, a country cannot count on exchange rate changes to eliminate surpluses or deficits in its balance of payments. Therefore when a country experiences a surplus, it must accumulate large quantities of foreign exchange. But when it incurs a deficit, it must pay out large quantities of foreign exchange. Such fluctuations in foreign exchange holdings necessitate large reserves of foreign exchange. Large reserves have been the only way for a country to be certain that it will be able to finance any deficits that might occur in its balance of payments.

In recent decades most of these exchange reserves have been held in American dollars. We have already seen the advantage this bestows on the American economy and American businessmen. It is therefore not surprising that American bankers have always favored fixed exchange rates.

RECENT
INTERNATIONAL MONETARY CRISES

We have seen how the use of American dollars as the international medium of exchange has required that foreigners constantly increase their holdings of U.S. dollars to accommodate a constantly increasing volume of world trade. This has permitted the U.S. government to make enormous military expenditures in foreign countries and U.S. businessmen to purchase businesses and resources around the world in far greater quantities than could have been financed from current account surpluses alone.

Once the processes of worldwide militarism and worldwide economic domination were set in motion, however, they had a momentum of their own. Neither the government nor businessmen have attempted to limit these expenditures to an amount that could be financed out of current account surpluses plus the increase in foreigners' desired holdings of dollars. Cold War propaganda and the lure of larger profits from foreign investments have propelled the government and businessmen consistently to spend more dollars than foreigners have wished to hold.

In 1968, and again in early 1971, attempts by foreigners to convert their dollar holdings into gold or into other currencies created minor crises. Throughout the 1960s and early 1970s, it had been obvious that the size of the recurring American balance-of-payments deficit was too large. This meant U.S. currency was *overvalued;* that is, in order to make the deficit manageable, the value of the U.S. dollar should be decreased (or the value of undervalued currencies such as the German DM or the Japanese yen should be increased).

The problem was that in 1970 foreigners held $43.3 billion in American dollars.[6] If the value of the American dollar were decreased by 10 percent, these foreigners would suddenly lose the equivalent of about $4.33 billion dollars. This large amount of wealth would simply evaporate. Consequently, if foreigners received the slightest hint that the American dollar was about to be devalued, they immediately sought to exchange their dollars for gold or other currencies before the devaluation could take place.

In the 1968 and early 1971 crises, the governments of the United States and the western European countries succeeded in convincing dollar holders that the exchange value of the dollar would be maintained. This averted a major crisis, but the problem remained. If the United States continued to spend lavishly on a worldwide military empire and continued to attempt to extend its worldwide economic hegemony, then the pressure of foreigners attempting to convert unwanted dollar balances into gold or other currencies would constantly present the threat of a worldwide run on the dollar any time the fear of devaluation became widespread. Most economists agreed that if such a "run" on American dollars were to develop, the international monetary structure would collapse. If this were to occur, foreign trade would undoubtedly be drastically reduced, as it was after the international financial crisis of the early 1930s.

In the face of these dangers President Nixon took drastic action on August 15, 1971. The fact that America's exports were substantially less than its imports for the first time in many years precipitated extreme policy measures. In order to end America's persistent balance-of-payments deficit, the President did three things. First, he imposed a 10 percent tariff surcharge. In order to reduce demand for imports, Americans were forced to pay 10 percent more for all imported foreign goods. Second, the President announced a 90-day wage-price freeze (with wages frozen but leaving profits free to increase). This was designed mainly for domestic effects, but its foreign effect was to make American exports more competitive in foreign markets.

The third and most extreme measure taken by the President was to sever the direct link between the American dollar and gold. The American dollar had maintained a fixed exchange rate with other currencies by maintaining a fixed price of gold. Since the value of gold in terms of other currencies was also fixed, this fixed the exchange rates between any two currencies. For example, if gold costs 35 American dollars per ounce and also 15 British pounds per ounce, then the price (in American dollars) of one British pound would be fixed at $2.33.

[6]*Federal Reserve Bulletin*, April 1971, p. 270.

When the President cut the tie between gold and the American dollar, the United States no longer had a fixed exchange rate. The value of the dollar in relation to other currencies was allowed to fluctuate according to supply and demand.

It soon became apparent, however, that other countries were unwilling to allow their currencies to appreciate substantially in relation to the American dollar. The entire capitalist world was experiencing a recession during this period, and a decline in the value of the American dollar would stimulate demand for American exports (because they would now cost foreigners less of their own currency) and thereby add to aggregate demand in the United States and help us pull out of our recession. But by the same reasoning, an upward revaluation of foreign currencies in relation to the American dollar would decrease the exports of these countries to the United States (because they would cost Americans more dollars than before) and thereby decrease aggregate demand in these countries, worsening the problems of recession and unemployment.

By December 18, 1971, the American dollar had depreciated by over 10 percent. That meant, of course, that holders of American dollars had lost nearly $4 billion because of the dollar's depreciated value. Resistance to further depreciation had stiffened appreciably, so the United States returned to a fixed exchange rate on that date.

Over the next year and a half, it required extensive intervention in the foreign exchange market by various governments and central banks to maintain that fixed exchange rate. It became increasingly obvious that some fundamental realignment of currency values was needed. By early 1973, the economic situation in the capitalist world had changed from one in which recession and unemployment were the principal problems to one in which rapid inflation was the main concern. The United States took advantage of this economic change and in March 1973 announced that once again the dollar was to be allowed to fluctuate according to supply and demand.

Throughout May and June of 1973, the dollar dropped in value. By July 6, it had fallen by an average of about 15 percent, and even more in relation to the German mark. From July 1973 to the time of this writing (early 1974), the value of the dollar has remained fairly stable. This depreciation was allowed by foreign countries partly because it helped the antiinflation policies they were pursuing in their own economies and partly because of the enormous political and economic pressure the U.S. government put upon them. But the substantial losses that foreign holders of dollar reserves had suffered led to much stronger demands that the dollar depreciation be halted.

In July 1973, foreign central bankers met and agreed to increase the ceiling on their credit to the American Federal Reserve Bank from $11.7 billion to $18 billion. With this added foreign currency the United States intervened in the foreign exchange market to stabilize the dollar. It has remained relatively stable through early 1974. The present situation seems very precarious, however, because only a very delicate balance of appropriate international economic conditions and appropriate subordinating responses by foreign central bankers have made this stability possible.

Moreover, foreign holders of American dollar reserves have lost many billions of dollars through the devaluations of the American dollar over the two and a half years since August 1971. This seems certain to have an important impact in undermining the willingness of foreign businesses, governments, and banks to hold American dollars as a key currency. The American government will doubtless do everything within its power to maintain the international status of the dollar, but the era of nearly costless financing of America's military empire, and its global economic takeover, appears to be coming to an end. It may, however, take a considerable period of time before another currency (or currencies) is able to displace the American dollar.

The important issues, not yet resolved at this writing, are whether the United States will return to a fixed exchange rate once the dollar is devalued sufficiently and whether fluctuations in the demand and supply of American dollars will permit an orderly devaluation. Many economists and businessmen believe a freely fluctuating exchange rate may become unstable. If this instability becomes sufficiently severe, it could reduce world trade drastically.

The prospect of a significantly reduced volume of international trade raises the question of the merits of such trade. Why do nations engage in trade? In the next section we shall attempt to answer this question.

THE GAINS FROM INTERNATIONAL TRADE

The most obvious reason why nations engage in foreign trade is that many commodities cannot be grown or produced in certain regions of the world. Without foreign trade Americans would be unable to purchase coffee, cocoa, tea, coconuts, bananas, or any of a large number of commodities that cannot be produced in the United States. In addition to these consumer commodities, the United States depends heavily on imports for many of the most important minerals. In the late 1960s, for example, imports of iron ore were equivalent to 43 percent of the amount mined domestically; for copper, the figure was 18 percent; for lead, 131 percent; for zinc, 140 percent; for bauxite, 638 percent; and for petroleum, 31 percent. This partial listing alone indicates how crucial imports of agricultural products and minerals are to the American economy.

TABLE 34.3
PRICE PER GALLON OF BEER AND COCA-COLA IN THE UNITED STATES AND GERMANY BEFORE TRADE (IN DOLLARS)

United States		Germany	
Beer	$0.60	Beer	$0.75
Coca-Cola	0.40	Coca-Cola	1.00

The United States can also gain from importing manufactured commodities if the *relative* costs of producing two commodities differ between the United States and some other country. To illustrate this, let us return to the example of beer and Coca-Cola.

Assume that the United States and Germany each produce all the beer and Coca-Cola they consume domestically. Assume further that in the United States the average annual production per worker of beer is 5000 gallons and of Coca-Cola is 7500 gallons. Assume further that in Germany the figures are 4000 gallons (beer) and 3000 gallons (Coca-Cola). Table 34.3 shows hypothetical prices for the two commodities (German prices are given in dollars for easier comparison) in the two countries. These prices reflect ratios of labor productivity.

From these figures we see that the United States is more efficient in the production of both beer and Coca-Cola. Economists would say that the United States has an *absolute advantage* in the production of both commodities. It might seem that the United States would be better off not to import either beer or Coca-Cola from Germany because it can produce both more efficiently. This is not true, however. It would pay the United States to import beer and export Coca-Cola because the United States has a comparative advantage in the production of Coca-Cola and Germany has a comparative advantage in the production of beer.

The existence of a comparative advantage depends on the *relative* costs of the two commodities, not the absolute efficiency in producing them. In the United States, beer costs 50 percent more to produce than Coca-Cola, whereas in Germany, beer costs 25 percent less to produce than Coca-Cola. Therefore relative to the cost of producing Coca-Cola, Germany is more efficient in producing beer. Similarly, in the United States, Coca-Cola costs 33 percent less to produce than beer, whereas in Germany, Coca-Cola costs 33 percent more to produce than beer. Therefore relative to the cost of producing beer, the United States is more efficient in producing Coca-Cola.

Assume that the United States persuades Germany to exchange beer for American Coca-Cola at the prices prevailing in Germany. Some American workers will be shifted from beer production to

Coca-Cola production. For each worker transferred from producing beer to producing Coca-Cola, the United States will lose 5000 gallons of beer (which the worker will no longer produce) and gain 7500 gallons of Coca-Cola (which he will begin to produce). This Coca-Cola can be sold in Germany for $7500 (because the price of Coca-Cola is $1 per gallon in Germany). Then, paying the German price of 75 cents per gallon for beer, the United States can use the proceeds to purchase 10,000 gallons of beer.

The final result of this series of events will be that for every worker in the United States shifted from beer production to Coca-Cola production, the United States will lose 5000 gallons of domestically produced beer but gain 10,000 gallons of German-produced beer. Obviously the United States will be better off after the trade. But the prices at which the two countries traded are identical to the German prices before trade. This means that the United States received all of the gains from trade and Germany received no gains at all.

Assume now that Germany persuades the United States to trade at the prices prevailing in the United States. Then Germany will receive all of the gains from trade. When the Germans shift a worker from production of Coca-Cola to production of beer, the worker will produce 4000 gallons of beer (rather than 3000 gallons of Coca-Cola). This beer will be sold in the United States (at 60 cents per gallon) for $2400. With the proceeds of this sale the Germans can purchase 6000 gallons of Coca-Cola (at the rate of 40 cents per gallon). Thus if trade occurs at the U.S. prices, the Germans will shift men from production of Coca-Cola to production of beer, which they will export to the United States. In doing so, they will lose 3000 gallons of domestically produced Coca-Cola for every man so shifted, but they will gain 6000 gallons of American-produced Coca-Cola. Obviously this situation benefits the Germans.

From these examples two conclusions can be drawn: (1) If the relative costs of producing two commodities in two countries differ, then trade can benefit one or both of the countries, and (2) if the prices at which trade takes place are the same as those prevailing in one country before trade began, then that country receives none of the gains from trade and the other receives all of the gains.

We can draw a third conclusion, which is undoubtedly obvious from the preceding discussion: If the ratio of prices at which trade takes place lies somewhere between the price ratios in the two countries, then both countries will share in the gains from trade. If, in the beer-Coca-Cola example, the United States and Germany traded at the rate of one gallon of beer equals one gallon of Coca-Cola, then both countries would benefit from trade. The reader can calculate the gains in each country as workers are shifted to export production. Such a calculation will verify the fact that both countries would benefit from trade at a price ratio that lies between the two domestic price ratios.

When two countries engage in trade, the one that is able to exert the greater bargaining power will succeed in pushing the trade prices closer to the ratio of prices and production costs of the other country. In doing this, the more powerful country will reap most of the gains from trade. Many economists have collected evidence to show that in the trade that takes place between advanced, industrialized countries and less developed agricultural countries, the industrialized countries reap nearly all of the benefits.[7]

THE CASE FOR FREE TRADE

To what extent ought a country to engage in international trade? Nearly 200 years ago the classical economists (particularly David Ricardo) developed the analysis of comparative advantage and correctly identified the economic gains that two trading partners can secure. On the basis of this analysis they concluded that as long as anyone in either of the two countries desired to engage in further trade, then it was possible to reap more gains from trade. In practice this meant the government ought to place no restrictions on trade. People should be free to trade to any extent they wished. This conclusion was an integral part of the general laissez faire policy advocated by the classical economists.[8]

Over the past 200 years most orthodox economists have advocated free trade. They have extended and refined their analyses of comparative advantage and the gains from trade, but they have not altered the essential argument. They have consistently contended that any restrictions on international trade will reduce the volume of trade and that any reduction of volume will reduce the gains from trade. Therefore most economists have concluded that restrictions on international trade reduce a nation's economic welfare.

This consistent advocacy of free trade might seem surprising in view of the fact that only rarely during the past 200 years have the governments of the major capitalist countries pursued such a policy. Most of the time they have erected a wall of tariffs to keep out foreign goods. A tariff is a tax on an import that forces the importer to

---

[7]See, for example, U.N. Economic Commission for Latin America, *The Economic Development of Latin America and Some of Its Problems* (New York, 1949); Raoul Prebisch, "The Role of Commercial Policies in Underdeveloped Countries," *American Economic Review*, May 1959; and Hans Singer, "The Distribution of Gains Between Investing and Borrowing Countries," *American Economic Review*, May 1950.

[8]See Chapter 4.

charge a higher price to the general public in order to pay the tariff. Thus the tariff is really a tax paid by the consumer of the import.

Tariffs have usually been imposed for two reasons. First, in the nineteenth century the American government used the tariff as its chief source of tax revenue. Second, industries that must compete with foreign producers for the domestic market have lobbied for tariffs to protect their monopoly power from foreign competition. Because neither of these reasons would be particularly appealing to the general public, many arguments with greater popularity have been put forward. Historically there have been three very common arguments for tariffs in the United States. Economists consider them all fallacious. We shall examine each.

1. It is often argued that tariffs protect American workers from competition from foreign workers who are paid very low wages. This argument concludes that tariffs maintain higher wage rates for American workers. While free trade may hurt the workers in industries that are undersold by foreign competitors (the workers will probably have to transfer to new occupations), it should raise the overall wage level. This is because, as we have seen, the total output available for consumption increases after trade. It seems unlikely that workers would not share in this increase.

2. It is sometimes proposed that tariffs are ideal taxes because the foreign exporter pays the tax. As we have already noted, however, the American importer is forced to raise the price he charges his American customers. Therefore the American public pays most of the tax in the form of higher prices for the commodities it consumes.

3. Finally, there are the campaigns to "buy American products" to "keep money in the United States." This simplistic argument assumes that when imports are purchased, money leaves the country, and that if they had not been purchased, consumers would have bought American-produced commodities. It is argued that purchasing foreign products deprives American businessmen of sales and American workers of jobs. The problem with this argument is that it ignores the fact that when the United States engages in foreign trade commodities are *exported* as well as imported. The foreign demand for U.S. exports increases the sales of American businessmen and creates jobs for American workers.

There are other arguments for tariffs, some not so obviously fallacious as those we have discussed. Most economists agree, however, that in a powerful, industrialized economy like the United States, there are really no convincing arguments for tariffs. The few problems tariffs might help solve (e.g., industrial relocations, regional economic depressions, and general underemployment) could certainly be solved more efficaciously by other, more direct government policies.

What is true for industrialized countries, however, is not necessarily true for less developed countries. Many less developed countries have become suppliers of raw materials and agricultural products for industrial countries. They generally receive such low prices for their exports that their standard of living remains abysmally low. If they engage in free trade, small local manufacturing industries cannot hope to compete with foreign giants. As a consequence, industrialization takes place very slowly, if at all. These countries would certainly be justified in placing some kind of restrictions on imports as an aid to industrialization. The issues involved in the relationship between advanced, industrialized countries and less developed ones will be considered in the next chapter.

SUMMARY

International economic transactions differ from those within national boundaries. The two main differences are (1) different currencies are involved and must be exchanged and (2) differing economic and political relations exist among nations, with some dominant, others subordinate, and others in intermediate positions.

The balance of payments is an accounting of all transactions between the residents of one country and the rest of the world. It summarizes the country's sources of foreign exchange and the uses to which the foreign exchange is put. The fact that the American dollar has been widely used as an international currency has helped finance a worldwide military network as well as an ever-increasing private economic empire acquired through American investment abroad. However, recurring deficits in the American balance of payments forced President Nixon to take steps on August 15, 1971, that led to a devaluation of the American dollar in relation to other major currencies. This is likely to reduce the acceptability of the American dollar as an international medium of exchange.

Economists have shown that if the ratio of costs of production (or prices) differs between two countries then both countries can gain from trading with each other. Most arguments for tariffs in powerful, industrialized countries either are fallacious or fail to point out that economically more efficacious means can be used to achieve any end for which a tariff was intended. In the case of less developed countries, a stronger case can be made for trade restrictions.

economic underdevelopment: natural causes or imperialism?

In Chapter 32 the problems of economic growth in developed industrial economies were considered. In economies that have not industrialized, the problems of economic growth are substantially and qualitatively different from those examined in Chapter 32. Before meaningful growth in per capita output and income can take place in these economies, they must undertake industrialization.

The economic, social, and political obstacles to industrialization are different from the problems of advanced industrial countries. Economic growth in the developed countries means mere incremental additions to output within an established structure. Development of the less developed countries means basic social, political, and structural economic changes to lay the foundations for growth.

It is therefore necessary to devote an additional chapter to the question of economic development. The countries of the world are commonly divided into three groups: (1) socialist countries, (2) industrially developed capitalist countries, and (3) underdeveloped capitalist countries, or the *Third World*. It is with this third group that we shall be concerned in this chapter.

FACTS OF ECONOMIC UNDERDEVELOPMENT

There are at least two generally accepted definitions of a *less developed* country, one based on an economic index and the other based on certain distinguishing characteristics. The economic index generally employed is average income per person (GNP divided by population). According to this criterion, a country with an average income per person of less than some amount—say, $200 or $300 per year—is classified as less developed.

The phrase *less developed*, it must be emphasized, has misleading sociological connotations. For example, there is no correlation between level of income and level of cultural or social development. Obviously ancient Greece or Egypt or China had very highly developed cultures and very low average income levels. Further, an average may hide wide disparities in individual incomes. For example, Kuwait has one of the highest levels of average income per head; but most of the income is concentrated in the hands of a few very rich people, and there is an enormous gulf between the very rich and the very poor (despite Kuwait's much-publicized welfare handouts). The high average income per Kuwaiti is solely the result of this little country's oil resources, and therefore one cannot assume that it is highly developed in an overall sense.

Dissatisfaction with the use of a single, purely economic measure of underdevelopment has led some students of the subject to suggest a definition based on several distinguishing characteristics of less developed countries: (1) low income per person, (2) the existence of a very high portion (often 80 percent or more) of the population engaged in agriculture, (3) a low level of techniques used in production, (4) a low level of education, and (5) a low level of capital formation.

According to any definition of developed and less developed, the fact is that more than 50 percent of the population of the capitalist, or private enterprise, world live in countries that can be classified as less developed. The enormity of the problem is indicated by the estimate that to raise the incomes of the portion of the world's population living in these countries to an average of only $200 per person per year (less than one-tenth of the average American income), about $85 billion of aid per year would be needed.[1]

Among private enterprise, or capitalist, countries in the lowest category, with income per person less than $100 per year (and mostly agrarian and lacking in technology, education, or capital) fall India, most of Asia, and most of Africa. In the second category, with income per person between $100 and $300 a year (and still very underdeveloped in all other indexes), are most of Latin America, North Africa, Indonesia, and the Philippines. In the third cate-

---

[1]See Frederic Benham, *Economic Aid to Underdeveloped Countries* (London: Oxford University Press, 1961); all figures given here are in terms of the worth of the U.S. dollar in 1960.

gory ($300–600; still very poor, but slightly developed in some aspects) are a few Latin American countries, the Union of South Africa, Greece, and Spain. The fourth category ($600–1500; well developed in many aspects) includes Israel, Australia and New Zealand, Japan, and most of western Europe. In a category by themselves are Canada and the United States with over $2500 of income per person per year. (Kuwait and Qatar are also listed in this category, but these are tiny areas sitting on top of oil wells, with most of the income going to a few sheiks.)

In the advanced capitalist countries workers' wages have grown greatly in the past 100 years. But conditions in most of the capitalist world, its less developed part, have shown little or no improvement, and incomes remain at incredibly low levels. Most African and Asian incomes are less than one-tenth, and most Latin American incomes are about one-fifth, of the average income in the advanced capitalist countries. In fact, many of them are not only below poverty but also below subsistence levels. "Two-thirds of the inhabitants of the underdeveloped countries of the Third World do not get the essential minimum of 2,500 calories per day; the expectation of life for many of them is less than half that in the highly developed countries."[2]

The gap between rich and poor is reflected in the fact that in 1964 two-thirds of the world's population produced only about 25 percent of world output. At the same time, the United States alone (with only 6 percent of world population) produced about 30 percent of world output.

And the gap is widening.

In the whole period 1953–1964 the advanced capitalist countries showed rates of growth twice as rapid as those of the less developed capitalist countries.[3] Thus the advanced capitalist countries outproduced the less developed ones (in product per person) by 10:1 in 1950 but by 11:1 in 1960 and almost 12:1 in 1969.[4]

COLONIALISM AND NEOCOLONIALISM

It will help us to understand the current economic, social, and political conditions of less developed countries if we briefly examine some aspects of their history. In particular, we are interested in their relationships with the economically more advanced countries over the last several centuries.

[2]Perre Jalee, *The Pillage of the Third World* (New York: Monthly Review Press, 1965), p. 8.
[3]Ibid., p. 11.
[4]Jalee, loc. cit., and current UN data.

From the fifteenth century onward, the developing capitalist economies of Europe grew economically and militarily at a rate then unparalleled in human history. From the fifteenth to the nineteenth centuries, they slowly came to dominate much of the rest of the world. They plundered, enslaved, and ruled so as to extract the maximum from their subjects.

Such havoc was created that ancient and culturally advanced civilizations disappeared, as in Peru and West Africa, and progress was set back hundreds of years by the destruction of native industries, as in India. On the other side, the plunder was so great that it constituted the main element in the formation of European capital and provided the foundation for prosperous trade and eventual industrialization.

By the end of the nineteenth century, almost all of the present less developed countries were under the colonial rule of the more advanced countries. The imperialist countries invested in the colonial countries at astoundingly high profit rates, primarily because of a cheap labor supply and enforced lack of competition. The capital was invested mainly in extractive industries, which exported raw materials to the imperial country. In the imperial country, the cheap raw materials were profitably turned into manufactured goods, part of which were exported back (tariff free) to the colonial country.

The tariff-free imported finished goods generally completed through competition the destruction (often begun by plunder) of the colonial country's manufacturing industries. An example of this may be seen in colonial India, especially in its textile industry:

> Foreign trade statistics best show the effects of "reindustrialization." India, still an exporter of manufactured products at the end of the eighteenth century, becomes an importer. From 1815 to 1832, India's cotton exports dropped by 92 per cent. In 1850, India was buying one quarter of Britain's cotton exports. All industrial products shared this fate. The ruin of the traditional trades and crafts was the result of British commercial policy.[5]

The development of the colonial areas was thus held back by the imperialist countries, while the development of the imperialist countries was greatly speeded by the flow of plunder and profits from the colonies. The exception that proves the rule is Japan. Japan escaped colonialism as a result of several more or less accidental

[5]Charles Bettleheim, *India Independent* (New York: Monthly Review Press, 1968), p. 47. Also see Romesh Dutt, *The Economic History of England* (7th ed.; London: Routledge & Kegan Paul, 1950), pp. viii–x.

factors. Thus it was able independently to industrialize and develop its own advanced capitalist economy. Japan achieved this alone among the countries of Asia, Africa, and Latin America because the others had all been reduced to colonies and had their further development prevented.

The half-century from 1890 to World War II was the peak period of colonialism, when all the world was divided among the western European and North American powers. In the late 1940s and 1950s, a new era began, with formal independence achieved by hundreds of millions of people throughout Asia and Africa as a result of struggles fomented by the impact of two world wars, the Russian and Chinese revolutions, and long-pent-up pressures for liberation. The day of open colonialism is over, but the pattern still holds by which the ex-colonial countries export food or raw materials. In fact, the less developed countries are often dependent mainly on exports of just one product, and they still import most of their finished goods. Foreign investment still dominates their industries. Because of the continuance of the underlying colonial economic pattern, we are justified in describing this situation as *neocolonialism*, in spite of formal political independence.

In fact, formal independence has changed the essential economic relationships very little. On the one side are all the less developed, newly independent countries, still under foreign economic domination, still facing all the old obstacles to development. On the other side are the advanced capitalist countries, still extracting large profits from the dependent Third World. The imperialist group includes all the countries that extract profits by trade and investment. Thus it includes most of western Europe, Japan, and the United States. Neocolonial profits from the less developed countries flow even to countries like Switzerland that never held colonial power over any less developed country.

Although there are still cases of direct occupation (e.g., the Portuguese colonies in Africa), most neocolonial control comes through economic and monetary penetration. This ranges from blatant forms such as subsidies and military supplies to highly complex monetary agreements. It also seems to be characteristic to grant independence to small territories, tiny divisions of former colonial domains. Thus they have no political or economic power with which to resist continued domination.

It should also be noted that the economic control often is not direct but built up in a complex pyramid. For example, some American companies directly invest in northeast Brazil. More control of that area, however, is achieved through American domination of major southern Brazilian companies, which, in turn, buy controlling

interests in companies in the northeast. Still more control is achieved
through American domination of some western European companies,
which, in turn, own some major Brazilian firms or directly own some
of the local firms in the northeast.

OBSTACLES TO DEVELOPMENT

Is overpopulation the primary obstacle to economic development?
This view is widely held by the average man in the street, many
newspaper reporters, even some university professors. Little systematic evidence is presented to substantiate it. Generally proponents
merely point to the vast number of poor and starving people in
India as an example. Even such an eminent "economist" as Robert S.
McNamara (former president of Ford Motor Company and former
U.S. secretary of defense) asserts that "the greatest single obstacle
to the economic and social advancement of the majority of the peoples in the underdeveloped world is rampant population growth."[6]

The important point to note about McNamara's ideology is that
it tells the hungry people that the "greatest single obstacle" to their
development is their own animal sexual desires. The function of this
ideology is thus identical to that of the theory that underdevelopment is due to racial inferiority, the laziness and/or stupidity of "the
natives." It provides the perfect defense to the suspicion of these
peoples that their problems are due to antiquated social systems, rapacious ruling classes, and above all, foreign domination and exploitation.

If one turns to the facts, there is no evidence that high population
density is the prime cause of underdevelopment. More precisely,
there is no statistically significant correlation between high population density and low income per person. On the contrary, many
countries with high incomes per person also have high population
densities. For example, Belgium has 816 people per square mile, West
Germany has 624, and the United Kingdom has 588. India has only
406 people per square mile, and most of the less developed countries
have much lower population densities.

In fact, we find many cases of concomitant successful development with rapid population increase. The highest recorded rate of
population growth over a long period occurred in the United States
during the years 1850–1950; but because U.S. production also grew
at record rates, America not only became a developed country but

[6]Robert S. McNamara, "Introduction" to H. Gray and Shanti Tangri, eds.,
Economic Development and Population Growth, A Conflict? (Lexington,
Mass.: Raytheon/Heath, 1970). All of the Western experts in the collection
simply assume (or present inadequate proofs of) McNamara's ideology.

also had record growth rates of output *per person*, and thus individual welfare improved.

Of course if a country is standing still economically, any growth of population is a terrible problem. We do not deny that overpopulation can be a problem; we only maintain that it is always *relative* to growth of output. The basic problems are seen when we try to explain why output is rising so slowly in less developed countries. Although population is a problem, it is secondary to these larger problems, and exclusive focus on it tends to hide the more important problems.

Moreover, it turns out that the key to reducing population growth is development of industrialization and urbanization. A rural family with a primitive technology finds young children useful for many tasks. An urban family in an industrialized country sees children as an economic burden until they have undergone a long education. Furthermore, birth control information is much more effective in an urban setting in which a woman may find cultural interests outside the home and needs family planning to develop her own independent life. Thus all the developed areas from the United States to the Soviet Union have witnessed rapid declines in birth rates as the agrarian sector has shrunk and education and culture have spread as a result of economic development.

Another theory of underdevelopment claims that the less developed nations are all those that by accident have relatively few natural resources on their territories. Yet the less developed countries in 1965 provided 37.5 percent of the total output of raw materials in the capitalist world, including the bulk of many strategic materials. This is certainly a large enough absolute amount for a solid industrial base. But the less developed countries do not produce anything like 37.5 percent of manufactured goods. In fact, most of their raw materials are taken away to the advanced capitalist countries and are there manufactured into finished goods (some of them being sold back at a high profit to the less developed countries).

It appears, therefore, that the main obstacles to development are *not* natural or biological factors inherent in the less developed countries. The main obstacles are *not* sexual desires and procreation, laziness, low intelligence, or lack of natural resources. The obstacles reside in the present social relationships of man to man: the fact that all of the peasants' and workers' surplus over immediate needs is extracted from them by the landlords, moneylenders, tax collectors, and foreign corporations. We shall show that the native ruling classes use their high incomes for luxury consumption and that most of the foreign corporations' enormous profits are removed from the country.

As a result, there is a lack of capital for investment in development. The lack of capital (and lack of nonhuman power per person) *is* correlated with low income per person.[7] Lack of capital means not only little construction but also little new equipment and little technological improvement. It also means few funds available for education and training, let alone research. Lack of capital also means that millions of workers cannot be employed at a sufficient rate of profit and thus are left unemployed or underemployed. Thus it is the social relationships (and their consequences) that are the real obstacles to development.

As an example, consider the present revolution in agriculture in several less developed countries. In this "green revolution," new types of grains have been introduced, especially in India and Pakistan. They have brought much higher yields, and thus one of the technical barriers to feeding the population seems to be falling. To make efficient use of the new processes and output, however, requires large mechanized farms. Indeed, small peasants are being evicted in growing numbers to make way for large agricultural enterprises. The dispossessed peasants are swelling the ranks of the unemployed in the cities. At the same time, complaints are heard from the large farm owners that there is overproduction of grain relative to the small money demand of the poor. Thus the social relationships form a barrier to technological development.

It is a mere truism to say growth would be faster if the less developed countries had more capital, more technology, and more education and training. In fact, for many less developed capitalist countries, the problem is not a low rate of growth of income per person but no growth at all. Aggregate income does not grow much faster than (and maybe not as fast as) the population. Moreover, a complete change is needed from a rural, agrarian economy to an urban, industrialized economy. The issue, then, is how to *begin* to develop, how to start from little or no growth at all, and how to change the whole economic structure.

We shall argue that the obstacles are mainly institutional: (1) an internal ruling class that spends much of its income on luxuries and government revenues on unnecessary public monuments or military expenditures, (2) foreign trade on very poor terms, which creates an exploitative economic dependence and imports the wrong items for development, and (3) foreign investment in low-priority areas with high profits sent abroad. Notice that this is quite opposite to most Western views.

[7]See David Landes, *The Unbound Prometheus* (Cambridge, England: Cambridge University Press, 1969).

INTERNAL OBSTACLES TO DEVELOPMENT

Let us begin with the internal obstacles to development created by the less developed countries' social systems. The typical situation finds millions of peasants engaged in subsistence farming, obligated to pay high rents to landlords, high interest to moneylenders, and high taxes to local and national governments. From his original small net product, the peasant usually pays more than half to meet these obligations, thus retaining hardly enough for his bare subsistence and none for major improvement or investment.

The landlords and moneylenders take much of the surplus from the peasant and spend it on conspicuous luxury consumption. If they reinvest any, their extreme conservatism prompts them to invest in more land or to send it to some safe foreign country; little, if any, is invested in industry. The governments are mostly dominated by a small elite of wealthy landlords and merchants (in turn, often dominated by foreign elements), who have little motivation to invest government funds in constructive projects; in fact, the advent of industrial capitalism would undermine their power. Most government revenues are spent on military goods and services for the purpose of internal repression. Governments spend some on showcase projects (e.g., sports arenas) or, as in Venezuela, in beautification of the capital city. The little that is invested constructively is usually for roads or ports to serve the needs of foreign investors.

The reactionary ruling groups in the less developed capitalist countries are generally supported by the advanced capitalist countries (including the U.S. State Department). It is not that the U.S. State Department *wants* backwardness and governments dominated by reactionary landlords and military cliques. On the contrary, it would undoubtedly be happier with rapidly developing liberal capitalist countries (with American firms having most of the development investments). The problem is that these areas have only very few and very weak native capitalists who are linked by blood and marriage to the landlords and militarists. The countries are very much a part of the international commercialized capitalist market, but they have no steam to develop their own dynamic capitalism and thus remain appendages of the advanced capitalist countries.

Not only is there no strong group willing to build a liberal capitalism in these countries, but also the real political alternative is usually a left-leaning socialist government. Plans for rapid development have been an essential part of socialist programs, as with the socialist government of Cuba. But these socialist development programs have been violently attacked by the U.S. State Department. In Brazil and Greece and several other countries, very mild socialist governments (whose practical measures only *helped* native small capitalists and were not yet even contemplating socialism) were overthrown by military coups supported by the CIA. Thus the real choice in the less developed countries has not been between landlords and militarists versus liberal capitalists, but between landlords and militarists (and a few native capitalists) versus socialist movements (composed of workers and peasants and students). In every case so far the United States has chosen to support reactionary landlords and militarists such as Franco or Ky or Thieu.

THE EFFECTS OF FOREIGN TRADE
ON LESS DEVELOPED COUNTRIES

The colonial era left the economies of the Third World countries very dependent on foreign demand and consequently very sensitive to the foreign business cycle of expansion and depression. It is also a fact that international investments and trade in primary products (i.e., raw materials, both agricultural and mineral) show the greatest fluctuations. "It follows that any country whose economy is intimately dependent on foreign investment or whose trade is greatly dependent on primary commodities will be seriously affected by swings of business arising outside its own borders."[8]

This dependence is recognized in the less developed countries. The government of Ceylon states: "The economy of Ceylon depends almost entirely on its export in tea, rubber and coconut products. . . . About 80 percent of the people are employed directly or indirectly in the production and handling of these exports."[9] The government of Burma says explicitly: ". . . the most important source of unemployment in Burma is a decline in prices of raw materials caused by the depression generated elsewhere."[10]

The statistics for many countries, both developed and less developed, show that (1) a high portion of the demand for their national product is the demand for exports, and (2) exports to the United States constitute a high portion of the total export demand. Thus the United States often absorbs more than half, and always more than one-third, of the exports of Canada, Brazil, Chile, Mexico, the Philippines, and others.[11]

In addition to the special place of dominance of the United States vis-à-vis the less developed Third World, there are some data bearing on the trade relations of all the developed capitalist countries with

[8]League of Nations, *Economic Stability in the Post-war World* (Geneva: League of Nations, 1945), p. 103.
[9]United Nations, Department of Economic Affairs, *National and International Measures for Full Employment* (New York: United Nations, 1949), p. 42.
[10]Ibid., p. 21.
[11]See annual reports for all countries in International Monetary Fund, *International Financial Statistics* (Washington, D.C., published annually).

the Third World.[12] First, in the less developed countries there is rapid growth in production *only* of the raw materials and food products exported to the imperialist countries. Production of goods for internal use in the Third World grows very slowly, if at all.

Second, 73.5 percent of the total trade of the developed capitalist countries is with each other. The continued dependence of the less developed countries, however, is reflected in the fact that fully 74 prcent of *their* total trade is with the developed countries. Between 1948 and 1964 there were three important trends: "(1) The commercial growth of the imperialist countries was much greater in value than that of the Third World . . . , (2) the imperialist countries have come to depend less on the Third World for their exports, and (3) the latter has become more dependent on the countries of the capitalist group."[13]

These data also confirm the picture of the less developed countries as raw material exporters and finished-goods importers. Detailed examination "shows that the trade of the Third World is wildly out of balance: 85 percent of its exports consists of raw materials and another 5 percent of common metals, products of the first state of smelting. Only 10 percent of the total consists of manufactured goods, most of which are textiles. Imports, on the other hand, are predominantly manufactured goods (60 percent of the total)."[14] Because most of the manufactured imports are consumer goods, such a pattern can never lead to development but only to continued dependence.

The situation of dependence is still more exaggerated for each less developed country taken by itself. Each tends to export only one or two goods and to trade with only one or two buyers (so that the buyers can easily exert monopoly power). "For the vast majority of Third World countries the range of products is as narrow as possible; one, or two, or three products often providing three-quarters, or even more, of the trade of a country. The number of countries selling and buying is also very restricted; a single imperialist country usually occupies such a dominant position that it can exercise every kind of pressure."[15] It should be emphasized that the only cases where the former colonial master has not retained control of the Third World countries are cases where control has shifted to the United States—for example, all of Latin America, Vietnam, and parts of Africa.

In contrast, in recent years the developed capitalist countries' exports have consisted of only 30 percent of raw materials and 70 per-

[12]Jalee, op. cit., pp. 25–55.
[13]Ibid., p. 32.
[14]Ibid., p. 33.
[15]Ibid., p. 43.

cent of manufactured goods.[16] In fact, the international division of labor is becoming more and more pronounced rather than equalized. That is to say, the developed countries are producing a larger and larger percentage of the manufactured goods of the capitalist world, and the less developed Third World countries are producing a larger and larger percentage of the raw materials.

There is also a trend toward a worsening balance of trade for the Third World. This trend results from the fact that in the last 15 to 20 years international prices of most products have risen, but prices of most primary products have fallen. Because Third World countries export mainly primary goods, they are receiving lower prices, or less and less in each exchange of goods. The developed capitalist countries are receiving higher prices for their finished goods, or more and more in each exchange. Hence the foreign exchange of the less developed countries is drained off, their developmnt is retarded, and their balance-of-trade positions deteriorate further.

Another aspect of the worsening international payments situation arises from Western control of so-called invisible trade, or services. Over 90 percent of world shipping is controlled by the developed capitalist countries. Between 1951 and 1961 they increased the shipping rates paid by less developed countries by about 60 percent. The countries of Asia, Africa, and Latin America pay over $2 billion a year in shipping costs and insurance payments. Most of this money accrues to the developed capitalist countries.

We have noted that in recent years the value of the trade among the industrialized capitalist countries has grown much more rapidly than their trade with the Third World. As a result, the Third World's share in the trade of the developed capitalist countries fell from 32 percent in 1948 to 23 percent in 1964.[17]

Do the developed capitalist countries really need the trade of the less developed world as much today as previously? The percentage decline in trade suggests reduced importance. This was a period, however, of rapidly rising world trade; the absolute amount of trade between the two groups *rose* from $12 billion in 1948 to more than $25 billion in 1964. Furthermore, almost all of the increase in trade among countries in the industrialized capitalist bloc was in manufactured goods. While some of these exchanges are urgent, most of them merely increase efficiency; more expensive substitutes could easily be arranged (and, of course there is a heavy flow of luxury consumer goods, which could be ended without causing permanent damage).

The situation is quite different in the trade of the industrialized

16United Nations, *Statistical Yearbook* (New York, published annually).
17Jalee, op. cit., p. 53.

capitalist bloc with the less developed Third World. This trade is vital and irreplaceable. When developed capitalist countries import major food products and raw materials, they realize that these imports are very important. The food products are essential parts of the diets of Westerners, and the raw materials are indispensable for their factories. The manufactured goods that the underdeveloped countries buy are needed desperately because these countries do very little manufacturing themselves.

FOREIGN INVESTMENT

Much the same picture emerges if we look at American foreign investment. It is often argued that this investment channels American dollars into less developed countries. These dollars, it is claimed, can then be used to finance industrialization in the less developed countries. The data, however, do not confirm this argument.

The U.S. Department of Commerce has provided a partial breakdown of U.S. investment in different geographic areas. Interesting differences are documented for the period 1950–1965. In Europe, U.S. corporations made direct investments of $8.1 billion and transferred $5.5 billion of profit from their European investments to the United States, for a net flow of 2.6 billion U.S. dollars into this advanced capitalist area. Similarly, U.S. corporations invested $6.8 billion in Canada and extracted $5.9 billion of profit, for a net flow of 900 million U.S. dollars into this advanced capitalist area.

In the less developed Third World, the situation was different. In Latin America, American corporations invested $3.8 billion but extracted $11.3 billion, *for a net flow of 7.5 billion U.S. dollars from that area to the United States.* Yet profit rates were so great that at the same time the value of U.S. direct investments in Latin America *rose* from $4.5 billion to $10.3 billion. In fact in the period 1957–1964, only 11.8 percent of direct U.S. investment in Latin America came from the United States; 74.1 percent was reinvestment of profits or depreciation funds from Latin American operations. Similarly, in Africa and Asia in the period 1950–1965, American corporations invested only $5.2 billion but transferred to the United States $14.3 billion of profits, *for a net flow of $9.1 billion to the United States.* Yet enough profit remained for reinvestment so that U.S. direct investments in Africa and Asia rose from $1.3 billion to $4.7 billion.

Two facts are blatantly obvious from these data: (1) The rate of profit in U.S. investments abroad is several times higher in the less developed than in the advanced capitalist countries, and (2) the less developed neocolonial countries generously make a good-sized contribution to U.S. capital accumulation.

In addition to the basic fact that high profit rates squeeze more capital out of the less developed countries than foreign investment puts in, there is the problem that most foreign investment goes into areas that are least helpful to industrial development. We saw that in trade the less developed countries mainly export raw materials and import manufactured goods. This trade pattern is supported by the pattern of foreign investment.

On the whole the investment is mainly in the primary industries producing raw materials. But the materials are then shipped back to the developed capitalist countries for manufacture. On the one side, this discourages real industrial development. On the other side, it means the less developed countries are limited to production of the least valuable types of goods in international trade (since the relative price of raw materials has been declining). The fact is that the foreign capitalist firms in the less developed countries are located largely in the export sectors of the economy, exporting the goods that are easiest to sell in the international markets.

The International Monetary Fund report for 1963 states that "much of the foreign product capital investment in the underdeveloped countries takes the form of direct investment in primary production for export, especially in the oil industry."[18] The U.S. Department of Commerce figures show that in Latin America, Asia, and Africa a large majority of all U.S. investment is in the extractive industries, especially petroleum. Only in Europe and Canada is the majority of U.S. investment in the nonextractive industries, mostly in manufacturing.

It is true that in the past decade there has apparently been a strong shift in this pattern in some less developed countries. In several countries, such as Peru, there has been a sharp rise in the percentage of foreign investment going into manufacturing rather than agriculture or extraction of raw materials. These investments take advantage of the extraordinarily cheap labor to move part of U.S. and other foreign firms' operations within the less developed countries themselves (thus the "multinational" firms, to be discussed). Some economists—even radicals—argue that the trend toward more manufacturing investment is a fundamental change, an aid to development, and an attempt to integrate the less developed countries into the capitalist world.

Unfortunately, this change in the statistics has so far not been much of a help to development of the less developed countries (although it has meant that the foreign-directed multinational firms control ever more of their economies). There are three reasons for this. First, although it has increased, manufacturing is still a much

18International Monetary Fund, op. cit., 1963 report.

smaller percent of all foreign investment than agriculture and extractive industries. Second, almost all the manufacturing investment is in light or consumer goods rather than heavy, basic, producer goods. Third, most of the investment in consumer goods industries is not in production but only in assembly. Thus a U.S. firm may produce refrigerators or cars, ship the parts to Brazil, and have its subsidiary there assemble and sell them. This does not seem much of an aid to Brazilian industrial development.

MULTINATIONAL FIRMS

The ways in which American firms extract profits from less developed countries have changed since World War II. It used to be that most investment was in the form of loans or stock purchases in existing companies or the setting up of brand new companies (with or without native participation). Today such purely financial movements are less important. Rather, the capitalist corporation simply establishes branches of its own firm or completely subordinate satellite firms. The day of the multinational firm is here.

The very dramatic example of Exxon typifies the trend. By 1962 Exxon had 33 percent of its assets abroad (20 percent in Latin America and 13 percent in Europe and Asia). Furthermore, the importance of these areas is shown by the fact that Exxon's profit on investment in the United States amounted to only 7.4 percent; in Canada and in Latin America, 17.6 percent; and in Europe and Asia, 15 percent.

Not only does the giant multinational firm operate equally well in the United States and abroad, but also its board of directors, and its sphere of influence, usually reflect an inseparable mixture of financial and industrial interests. In the fantastic size and complexity of their structure, which includes both finance and industrial capital, and the multiplicity of their interests, which include both domestic and foreign sales, the giant corporations of today are very different from earlier banking or industrial interests.

Through multinational corporations American capital thus directly owns a large chunk of western European industry, and the capitalists of all the developed capitalist countries together own the major industrial enterprises of the less developed capitalist countries. "There are no reliable figures for the Third World as a whole which measure the extent of foreign economic intervention, but it is certain that many, perhaps even most, of the industrial undertakings of the underdeveloped countries are foreign-owned or controlled."[19] A careful investigation of one important neocolony concludes: "For-

[19] Jalee, op. cit., p. 22.

eign capital can . . . be said to share the control of the Indian economy with domestic capital on what is very nearly a fifty-fifty basis."[20]

It should also be stressed that most of these multinational firms are none other than our old friends, the few largest American corporations. In the last official survey by size of firm (using data for 1957), it was found that 45 giants (each investing over $100 million abroad) had 57 percent of total American direct foreign investment, that 163 firms had 80 percent, and that 455 firms had 93 percent.[21] Certainly any survey today would show increased concentration.

The concentration of profits is much greater. In 1966 more than half of American profits from abroad went to only 16 firms (all among the top 30 according to the *Fortune* listing.)[22] Moreover, these profits were not a small sum, even in terms of total American profits. From 1950 through 1969 profits from foreign investments were about 15 percent of total American corporate profits; so half of that was still a tidy sum for a handful of giant corporations.[23]

One of the most important recent trends is the differential growth of domestic U.S. sales and sales abroad. These sales abroad do not include export sales but are only the sales of the affiliates and subsidiaries of American corporations in foreign countries. From 1957 to 1962 total American domestic sales in manufacturing rose from $341 to $400 billion; the sales of foreign affiliates of the same manufacturing corporations rose from $18.3 billion to $28.1 billion. Hence foreign sales were and are growing much more rapidly than domestic sales.

Thus the United States is able to compete abroad not only with exports but even more importantly with the output of its foreign-based subsidiaries. This trend is reflected in the fact that the sales of American-owned plants abroad rose by 140 percent from 1950 to 1960, while exports from the United States went up by only 55 percent. And this trend has certainly continued since 1960, as may be seen in the fact that in 1961 only 460 of the thousand largest U.S. companies had a subsidiary branch in Europe, but in 1965 over 700 of them had a branch in Europe. This means, of course, that there is amazing concentration of capital in the few largest American firms, not only the capital of the United States but also that of the entire capitalist world.

[20]Bettleheim, op. cit.
[21]U.S. Department of Commerce, *United States Business Investments in Foreign Countries* (Washington, D.C.: GPO, 1960), p. 144.
[22]Arthur MacEwan, "Comment on Imperialism," *American Economic Review*, May 1970, p. 246.
[23]Ibid. Also data in Magdoff, op. cit., p. 183.

All of the largest American firms are on the road to being truly multinational, thinking from a viewpoint based on their worldwide investments. Therefore they are not merely interested, as was the earlier industrialist, in the export of commodities or, as was the earlier banker, in the export of capital. Rather, many have some of their major assembly plants in foreign countries and export a great deal from those subsidiaries. In fact, many foreign subsidiaries are large-scale exporters to the U.S. market. For example, in 1967 sales of all U.S. enterprises abroad totaled $32 billion, of which 11 percent was exported to the United States. That 11 percent constituted a total of $3.5 billion of goods, or 25 percent of total U.S. imports that year.

As noted earlier, this especially means that profits can be transferred around within the corporation, from a subsidiary in one country to a subsidiary in another. Therefore the reports of total profit remittances from the colonial areas to the United States can no longer be trusted as more than a general indicator. An entire corporation's total profits are the crucial point, and they often include hidden profits in one subsidiary by reason of another selling to it more cheaply, or hidden losses in one subsidiary by reason of another selling to it at prices above the market price. For example, it appears that in 1961 bauxite production in Jamaica, Surinam, and Guyana yielded to American corporations a rate of profit of from 26 to 34 percent. Yet this does not really give the total picture. Much of their costs "on materials and services" turn out to be exceedingly high payments to American corporations, also subsidiaries of the same major corporate group. On top of that, between 1939 and 1959 the price of bauxite in the United States almost doubled, but the price of bauxite exported from Surinam and Guyana remained almost the same throughout the whole period. Thus these firms' West Indian subsidiaries overpaid greatly for their materials and services and were underpaid for their finished product. (Notice that this also means more corporate taxes going to the United States but much less going to the West Indies.)

It follows that the multinational companies may have conflicting interests when it comes to terms, export subsidies, foreign investment, and so forth. They are absolutely united, however, in desiring there to be as many nations as possible whose laws and institutions are favorable to the unhampered development of private enterprise. Thus there is much intracorporate conflict over economic details, but there is no conflict over the main political and strategic issues concerning the defense of imperialism.

The United States, of course, is not alone in making foreign investments, yet its role has changed tremendously and is certainly dominant at present. Thus in 1914, the United States had only 6.3

percent of the capital-exporting countries' foreign investments; in 1960, it controlled 59.1 percent of all foreign investments. Canada's share has also increased, but most major Canadian industries are owned or controlled by American firms.

At the same time, the investments of the United Kingdom fell from 50.3 percent to 24.5 percent of the total (although Britain remains the largest foreign investor on a per capita basis). France's fell from 22.2 percent to only 4.7 percent, and Germany's, from 17.3 percent to 1.1 percent. Clearly total western European control of foreign investments has fallen drastically while American and Canadian investments have risen sharply.

What are the consequences of multinational firms? On the political side there is an important and expected change. Under the old system, there was conflict, direct and inevitable, between each of the investing countries. Under the new system at least some of that conflict is eliminated. Thus a multinational firm has the interests of many different countries and many different investment bases to consider. Still, most multinational firms have their home office in the United States. This, of course, greatly increases the dominance of the United States in the world scene.

NEOCOLONIAL "AID"

From 1951 to 1959, average annual donations from the advanced countries to the less developed ones amounted to $1.304 billion per year. The long-term public loans of capital amounted to $748 million per year. This gives a total of $2.052 billion per year.[24] Since these data include some aid and loans from the socialist countries, they overstate the amount provided by the advanced capitalist countries. For the year 1965, the Organization for Economic Co-operation and Development calculates that public aid from advanced capitalist (imperialist) countries to the less developed countries totaled $6.270 billion. Even including private investments and loan funds, which amounted to only $3.879 billion, the total comes to $10.149 billion for the whole year 1965. This is only 0.99 percent of the national income of the imperialist countries.[25] Furthermore this is a very generous estimate using extremely exaggerated figures. Such a small amount, certainly less than 1 percent of the national income of the countries giving the aid, could not be considered much of a burden. And also, unfortunately, it is not much of a help.

As we saw, the private investment part is itself more than offset by the profit and interest return on the investments. The small

[24]United Nations,*The International Flow of Long-Term Capital and Official Donations, 1951–1959* (Table 7).
[25]Jalee, op. cit.

public aid does not even offset the capital extracted by imperialism. The public aid that is (1) nonmilitary and (2) in the form of official donations or grants may be some help, but it is not a large total amount. Even this "help" has extreme qualifications in that it is often used to bolster repressive governments, to subsidize foreign investments "to subsidize foreign imports which compete with national products, to introduce technology not adapted to the needs of less developed countries, and to invest in low-priority sectors of the national economies."[26] The long-term public loans for nonmilitary purposes may also be some help, but the necessity to return principle and interest is rapidly becoming a main worry of the less developed areas. Thus the United States officially admits that for all less developed countries receiving U.S. aid, "the cost of maintaining such large indebtedness is at present eating up approximately 30 percent of all new assistance."[27]

It is the declared policy of all of the American agencies, such as the Agency for International Development, that the countries that receive the aid shall use it primarily to beef up the private enterprise sectors of their economies and shall not use it for public investment, which is often the most necessary in these countries for rapid development. Obviously it goes without saying that the aid of the United States is directed to shore up these countries against communism and is not given for any pure idealistic reason. In fact, the American aid agencies often point out that "(1) Foreign aid provides a substantial and immediate market for U.S. goods and services. (2) Foreign aid stimulates the development of new overseas markets for U.S. companies. (3) Foreign aid orients national economies toward a free-enterprise system in which U.S. firms can prosper."[28]

The U.S. Agency for International Development boasts that "Private enterprise has greater opportunities in India than it did a few years ago . . . fertilizer is an example of a field which is now open to the private sector, and was not in the past. This is largely a result of the efforts which we have made, the persuasion that we along with other members of the consortium have exerted on the Indian government."[29] A more blatant case of political pressure occurred in Brazil, where American aid fell from $81.8 million to $15.1 million from 1962 to 1964 because the United States disliked

[26]Theotino Dos Santos, "The Structure of Dependence," *American Economic Review* 60 (May 1970): 233.

[27]U.S. Congress, Senate, Committee on Foreign Relations, *Some Important Issues in Foreign Aid* (Washington, D.C., 1966), p. 15. Also see Magdoff, op. cit., pp. 52–57.

[28]Magdoff, op cit., p. 13.

[29]Reported in U.S. Congress, House, Committee on Foreign Affairs, *Hearings on Foreign Assistance Act of 1968*, p. 185.

the Goulart government. When "good" reactionary military officers overthrew Goulart, American aid jumped to $122.1 million in 1965 and $129.3 million in 1966.[30]

Nor are all the rewards of foreign aid purely ideological and in overseas areas. Just as the aid agencies claim, large parts of U.S. business benefit directly from the foreign aid program. Thus 24.4 percent of U.S. exports of iron and steel products are financed by the U.S. Agency for International Development. Similarly financed are 30.4 percent of the fertilizer exports, 29.5 percent of railroad equipment exports, 11.5 percent of nonferrous metal exports, and 5 to 10 percent of the U.S. exports of machinery and equipment, chemicals, motor vehicles and parts, rubber and rubber products, and textiles.[31]

IMPACT OF IMPERIALISM ON THE UNITED STATES

The impact of military spending on the United States was discussed in Chapter 29. Most U.S. military expenditures at home and abroad serve the aims of imperialism: protecting raw materials, foreign markets, commercial routes, spheres of influence of U.S. business, and U.S. investment opportunities (as well as capitalism in general). The profits from U.S. foreign trade and U.S. foreign investment, and from the military production to defend U.S. interests amount to about 25 to 30 percent of all profits. And recalling that most military and foreign profits go to the same few giant corporations, we begin to have some idea of the importance of American imperialism.

Conservative economists would object to lumping military profits with the profits from imperialism, but we believe it is impossible to separate the two. By 1969 the United States had a total of 1,517,000 military personnel in 1,400 foreign bases of all types, in 70 or 80 foreign countries (not including Korea and Vietnam).[32] The major reason for this multibillion-dollar allocation of resources is the need to maintain control over the vast American overseas investment empire. Note also that the decision to fight for a given area depends not only on the profits to be made from that area but

[30]Agency for International Development, Statistics and Reports Division, *U.S. Economic Assistance Programs, 1943–1966* (Washington, D.C., March 30, 1967), p. 28. Also see Magdoff, op. cit., pp. 39–47.

[31]Charles Hyson and Alan Stout, "Impact of Foreign Aid on U.S. Exports," *Harvard Business Review,* January-February 1968, p. 71. For a more recent and more complete analysis of foreign aid see Steve Weissman et al., *The Trojan Horse: A Radical Look at Foreign Aid* (San Francisco: Ramparts Press, 1974).

[32]Data from Harry Magdoff, "Militarism and Imperialism," *American Economic Review,* May 1970, pp. 237–242.

even more on its military-strategic importance to the structure of imperialism in a wider area. "Understood in these terms, the killing and destruction in Vietnam and the expenditure of vast sums of money that are not balanced in the eyes of U.S. policy-makers against profitable business opportunities in Vietnam; rather they are weighed according to the judgment of military and political leaders on what is necessary to control and influence Asia, and especially Southeast Asia, in order to keep the entire area within the imperialist system in general, and within the United States sphere of influence in particular."[33]

We may now make an evaluation of the costs and benefits of imperialism and militarism to the United States. On the benefit side, military production and military service do increase employment, assuming that the nation begins from a position of major unemployment. On the harmful side, the flow of capital to the United States (profits and interest from foreign investment less current investment) must have a negative effect on domestic profit rates and employment through the competition of more capital. Still, the net effect on employment is probably positive.

The public at large, the taxpayer, pays the direct costs, including $115 billion for six years of fighting in Vietnam.[34] Non-Vietnam military expenditures continued throughout the period at about $50 billion a year. Because America entered the war with a low level of unemployment, unemployment was not reduced (although *perhaps* a major depression was avoided at some point); but employment and demand remained high enough so that monopoly power brought about price inflation, which lowered the public's real income.

More than 45,000 Americans have been killed in Indochina and more than five times that many wounded. (About 1 million Vietnamese civilians have been killed, but that is presumably not a cost to America.)

The necessary climate of racism against the "inferior" Indochinese has also worsened racism at home (as racism learned and practiced by the soldiers in Vietnam is brought back to the United States). The need to limit opposition to the war has increased repression and denial of civil liberties and has especially undermined academic freedom in the colleges. The attempt to curb inflation by cutting all welfare spending increases the costs to the poor. For the public as a whole, therefore, the costs in blood and money are vast, and outweigh any slight employment benefits.

For the largest corporations, however, the balance is very different. They do pay some added taxes for the war, but they are

[33]Magdoff, op. cit., pp. 14–15.
[34]U.S. Bureau of the Budget.

able to pass on most of these to consumers and workers. They do have some higher costs from inflation, but their own prices rise faster. We speak here of the whole military-imperialist effort, not just the war in Vietnam. Some sections of big business found that the Vietnam War overheated the economy too much or was a tactically "bad" (that is, losing) war, and so opposed it. Aside from that specific tactical situation, their interests are clear: Profits from military production and from foreign investment represent about 25 to 30 percent of all corporate profits.

Furthermore, the largest 100 corporations receive more than half of that very large amount, or the difference between depression and very high profit rates. Therefore for the giant corporations the benefits of the military-imperialist effort clearly outweigh the costs (although whether some of these benefits dribble down to the very top strata of labor in order to keep labor content is still highly controversial). Because the same corporate interests are dominant in the capitalist state, it is no wonder that militarism and imperialism continue to be American policy, regardless of the tremendous cost to the American people.

SUMMARY

The less developed capitalist countries are not only poor but also are growing more slowly than the developed ones; the gap is increasing. While too much population is obviously a problem for less developed countries, the question is, What holds back their development? The most important barriers seem to be (1) reactionary ruling classes that waste much of the product in unproductive ways, (2) a trade pattern in which the less developed countries export mainly raw materials and import most of their finished goods, and (3) imperialist investment at such high profit rates that the profit outflow is greater than the current investment inflow.

Imperialism and militarism have both benefits and costs for the United States. Imperialist wars (as in Vietnam) and military spending for them do create some jobs, but they also create inflation, high taxation, reduction in welfare services, more racism, and thousands of dead and wounded Americans (and there are more rational and constructive ways of creating employment). On the other side, there are vast benefits for a small number of giant corporations that make very high profit rates on foreign investment and on military production.

PART FOUR

**socialist
economic
systems:
an
introduction
to
comparative
economics**

varieties
of
socialism

The word *socialism* has been used to mean a great many different things. To begin with, it refers to (1) a system of ideas, (2) a political movement, and (3) an economic system of actual institutions. In Chapters 5 and 6 the early socialist ideologies and the Marxist socialist theories were discussed. These were systems of ideas. To complicate matters, there are now many varieties of Marxist socialist ideas alone, not to speak of other socialist ideas. Different views within the general set of Marxist ideas are currently expressed by the Russians, the Chinese Maoists, the outlook of Cuba's Castro, and many others. We shall not develop each of these but shall refer to them from time to time when relevant.

In the second category, political movements, there is also a wide variety. In fact, most systems of socialist thought have generated socialist political movements. Today there are many parties calling themselves Socialist or Labor parties. Many of these, such as the Social Democratic party of West Germany specifically do *not* advocate a fully socialized economy but urge a mixture of capitalist and socialist economic forms (mostly the status quo, as it now exists in West Germany). The other main political branch of the socialist movement is tenanted by the parties calling themselves Communist. These parties do claim to advocate socialist economic systems. Finally, there are many radicals in the United States and elsewhere

who advocate socialism but do not belong to any of the Socialist
or Communist parties.

Socialist *ideas* are ideas put forth by the various socialist movements. Socialist *movements* include all the Socialist, Communist,
and radical parties and individuals who favor some variety of
socialist system. What is a socialist economic *system?* A capitalist
economic system is one in which there is private ownership for
private profit of all the means of production (factories, equipment,
land). *A socialist economic system is one in which there is public
(or social) ownership for the public good of all the means of
production.*

The words *public ownership*, however, are very ambiguous. We
must ask three very basic questions to clarify this definition: (1)
What is the political form (or system) of public decision making? (2) At what level, national or factory or other, are decisions made by the "public"? (3) Who owns the product of this
"public" production?

DEMOCRACY AND SOCIALISM

Who is the "public"? The classical socialist vision assumed that
public ownership meant extension of political democracy into the
economic sphere. Under capitalism, a few powerful individuals own
and control the economy. Under socialism, the public, through its
democratically elected representatives, would own and control the
economy. This control by the masses of the people—by the multi-
tudes of working men and women rather than the few plutocrats—
was seen as the heart of socialism.

Unfortunately, the end of private ownership of productive
facilities came first in the less developed countries of eastern Europe,
the Soviet Union, and China. In these countries there was little or
no democratic tradition or institutions; their socialist governments
were born in the midst of civil and world wars; and survival and
rapid growth were their main problems. Therefore, contrary to
every socialist dream, they emerged as one-party dictatorships.
Political and economic power are held by tiny, self-appointed elites.

Can this be called socialism? There is, by law, only "public"
and not private ownership of the productive facilities. But the
"public" decisions are made by a small, nonelective elite. Communists claim that this is socialism, but most other socialists claim that
it is not. In the next two chapters we shall discuss the development and functioning of the Soviet Union (and to a lesser extent,
China) as an example of an economy with government ownership
with decisions made by a one-party political dictatorship. For convenience we shall call this economy socialist, but readers must de-

cide for themselves whether it really meets the definition of socialism as public or social control of the economy.

CENTRAL PLANNING AND SOCIALISM

As we shall see, during the period of Stalin's control of the Soviet Union, it was taken for granted by most people that socialism means central planning. Indeed in the Soviet Union Stalin and a small elite around him decided on the economic direction, and a small group of economic planners in Moscow developed a plan to carry out his decisions. That plan was law, and it governed all Soviet enterprises in considerable detail. In Chapter 39, however, we shall see that even in the Soviet Union there has been a considerable loosening and decentralization since the late 1960s wherein individual managers have been given more decision-making power on the day-to-day operation of their enterprises.

In eastern Europe this process has been carried much further with individual enterprises acting as independent units in the market in several countries. It has gone furthest in Yugoslavia, where the manager of the enterprise is no longer appointed by the government but by a council elected by all the workers in the enterprise. The Yugoslavs claim that this is an essential feature of "real" socialism, but others claim that this is a retreat from public or national ownership back toward capitalism. Again, the reader will have to decide.

SOCIALISM AND COMMUNISM

To explain the definition of socialism, we first asked whether it implies a democratic political system. Next, we asked whether it means national control by the "public" or local control by workers in each enterprise (or by regions or even by local communes). Our third question is, Who should own the public product? In other words, how do individuals acquire consumer goods and services? As a matter of definition it is generally agreed that *socialism* means public ownership plus the payment of wages according to work done, which wages are used to buy consumer goods and services. But a pure *communist* economy would be one in which there was public ownership plus distribution according to need. In other words, there would be no wages or prices, and people would take goods and services without paying as they needed them.

No present government or major political party advocates complete and immediate communism. But the Chinese Communists have gone much further than anyone else in moving toward equal wages and in expanding the sector of free goods and services. The Soviet

Union continues to have a very wide range of wages, but it does have a considerable sector of free goods and services; mainly, all medical and educational services are free to the public. Even the United States has a few free goods and services, such as our public parks and highways. We shall return to this issue in our evaluation of socialism in the last chapter of the book.

socialist development in russia and china

Marx and most of his nineteenth-century disciples believed the end of capitalism was near, at least within the next several decades. The capitalist system proved to have considerably more staying power than they imagined. Lenin attributed much of this prolonged viability to the gains made through imperialism. Ironically, the same imperialism led, indirectly, to the demise of a great European power, Russia. A socialist revolution overtook the fallen giant, and power was seized, in the name of Marxism, led by Lenin and the Bolsheviks.

THE BOLSHEVIK REVOLUTION AND THE CIVIL WAR

The general competitiveness of nineteenth-century imperialism created an international climate of tensions and distrust. With the crumbling of the once powerful Ottoman Empire, the major European powers scrambled to seize territory over which the Turks were no longer able to maintain hegemony. The predictable result was open armed conflict: World War I. The war so weakened the economic and political structure of Russia that the tsarist government collapsed in 1917. It was replaced by a provisional government, which also proved unable to cope with the chaotic situation.

Finally, in October 1917, the Russian Bolsheviks seized power in an almost bloodless coup. For the first time socialists had the reins of power and could attempt to create a society without the many evils of capitalism they had consistently denounced. The problems that had overcome the tsar and the provisional government, however, were of an overwhelmingly magnitude, so the Bolsheviks, who were mostly political activists without experience in governing, had no easy road to tread.

The new government found itself in the midst of a war that had devastated the foundations of the economy, slowed transportation and communication almost to a halt, and created something approximating social anarchy. One of the chief sources of Bolshevik power was the support of the mass of peasants who were revolting against centuries of ruthless exploitation. In an elemental revolutionary thrust, the peasants seized the holdings of wealthy landlords and rich peasants. They divided the land up into millions of tiny plots. When, as one of their first acts after taking power, the Bolsheviks announced a land reform, they were merely putting an official stamp of approval on an event that was a *fait accompli*, about which they could have done nothing even if they so desired. Nevertheless, the new, small and inefficient peasant holding made it exceedingly difficult for the Bolsheviks to secure the food to feed their armies and urban dwellers. Moreover, the newly independent peasants wanted to consume the little they produced.

In the cities, most important enterprises and industries were in the hands of capitalists who were hostile to and distrusted the Bolsheviks. A very large percentage of the physical capital of these enterprises had been destroyed, and the allocation of raw materials and supplies had been severely disrupted. The Soviets had hardly begun to extricate themselves from the war with Germany when a group of reactionary pro-tsarist and pro-capitalist generals launched a military drive to destroy the new government.

The reactionary forces were supported by the major capitalist powers. Not only did their army (called the *White Army*) receive financial and material aid, but also most of the major capitalist governments sent armed troops to destroy the Soviet government. Few Americans realized it at the time, but President Wilson sent thousands of American soldiers and spent millions of tax dollars on a war that, like the Vietnam War nearly a half-century later, was undeclared.

WAR COMMUNISM

Thus in a period of bitter and extensive warfare, while the economy and whole society were approaching a state of total anarchy, the Bolsheviks were forced to take extreme measures in order to survive. The policies followed during the period from 1918 to 1921 were called *war communism*. The Communist government was driven under the exigencies of war, hunger, and chaos to attempt to impose centralized control on all economic processes. (The Bolshevik Party changed its name to Communist at this time.)

In May 1918, the government gave one of its agencies the power to obtain and distribute food. It became necessary to use brute coercion to wrest food from some of the richer peasants. Workers' detachments were sent to find and confiscate hoards of grain. Poorer peasants also attacked the richer ones and confiscated their hoards. The richer peasants resisted bitterly, and the result was almost a second civil war. Ultimately, however, the threat of a triumph of the White Army and a return of the old landlord class kept most peasants loyal to the Communists; their support was instrumental in the Communist victory in the civil war.

Being unable directly to secure sufficient resources to keep the economy going and fight the civil war, the government created large sums of money with which to buy resources in the market. The result was an inflation so drastic that money became almost worthless. Many state enterprises ceased using money in transactions among themselves. In 1919 and 1920, most workers' wages were no longer paid in money but rather in products or services. Many essential commodities, including municipal services such as public trains and tramcars, were free to workers.

The government was forced to nationalize almost all industry, from the largest factories down to enterprises employing only a few people. This was the only way in which they could gain the required amount of control over industry. It was made necessary not only because of the confusion but also because most capitalists and managers had a deeply ingrained hostility toward the Communists, and many actively attempted to sabotage the government's efforts. The nationalization drive ultimately became an attempt to eliminate all privately owned manufacturing enterprises.

There was also a drive to ban all private trade. Middlemen and tradesmen were said to be parasitic and to depend on exploitation of both producers and consumers for their profits. All trade and selling was to be transacted by governmental agencies. The government was never very effective at enforcing this ban especially in a number of critical areas in which severe shortages existed.

By 1920, when it became obvious that the White Army would be defeated, many more peasants began to resist the government's confiscation of their surpluses. Other pressures against the total regimentation of economic life began to assert themselves. In early 1921, the sailors at the Kronstadt Naval Station revolted against the miserable conditions of their life. (Ironically it had been a revolt of the sailors at the same naval station that had helped the Bolsheviks seize power three and a half years earlier.)

THE NEW ECONOMIC POLICY

Under these pressures the government abruptly abandoned many of the policies of war communism and inaugurated what was called the *new economic policy* (NEP). The government continued to own and operate heavy industry, power, transportation, banking, and some wholesale trade. Many small businesses and most retail and wholesale trade, however, were returned to private ownership and private profit making. Peasants were allowed to sell their goods in the market, and confiscation was ended.

The economy responded very rapidly to NEP policies. By 1928, the crises were over and the economy had been restored to its prewar levels of output in most industries. But the prewar levels were woefully inadequate. The USSR was still primitive and backward by Western standards. Furthermore, "instructed" by the earlier armed intervention by the great Western powers and the continuing barrage of anticommunist pronouncements and propaganda from most Western governments, the Communists felt threatened by the West. Believing that the USSR would eventually be attacked by hostile Western powers unless it achieved such strength that they would be reluctant to do so, the Communists accepted the fact that rapid industrialization would be absolutely necessary. Moreover, their socialist goals also required an industrialized economy.

THE INDUSTRIALIZATION DEBATE

With all Communists accepting the necessity of rapid industrialization, a debate raged in the late 1920s over the most efficient method of financing this industrialization. In order to feed and clothe the workers producing capital goods and to spare the material resources necessary for the construction of factories and machinery, large surpluses had to be appropriated by the government. Foreign capital goods could also be purchased if the surpluses could be marketed in the West. With the overwhelming majority of the Soviet work force employed in agriculture (and a large percent of these in subsistence agriculture), it was obvious that most of the surplus would have to come from agriculture. But Soviet economists and political leaders were divided on the question of how best to appropriate this agricultural surplus.

One group of conservative Communists (or *right-wing deviationists*, as Stalin called them) was led by the economist Nikolai Bukharin. He believed industrial planning should emphasize increased production of agricultural machinery and consumer goods to be sold to the peasants. The peasants should be paid high prices for their grain and should be offered consumer goods and agricultural machinery at low prices to induce them to expand output and market a continually larger surplus. Industrial development, Bukharin believed, was limited by the rate of expansion of agricultural production.

A second group, consisting of *left-wing* Communists, was led by Leon Trotsky, ex-commander of the Red Army and Lenin's chief lieutenant during the civil war, and Eugene Preobrazhensky, the leading Marxist economist of the period. They favored extracting a maximum surplus from agriculture by paying peasants low prices for produce (with heavy taxes) charging them, high prices for manufactured goods. Agriculture should be more efficiently organized, they believed, by the formation of large-scale collective farms. Many sectors of the economy should be purposely neglected or short-changed in order to devote a maximum of resources and manpower to the rapid expansion of heavy industry, which, when fully operational, would efficiently produce the capital necessary to catch up in the industries neglected in the initial phases of industrialization.

Joseph Stalin used the antagonisms created in the debates as a means of achieving power for himself. At first he aligned himself with the conservatives to form a coalition that ousted Trotsky and his left-wing sympathizers. He then turned on Bukharin and his followers and successfully stripped them of their power, leaving himself in full control. Having thus gained power, he began to move along lines that had been advocated by Trotsky and Preobrazhensky, although he moved more rapidly and more harshly than they had ever advised.

COLLECTIVIZATION

In November 1929, the government announced a policy of promoting collectives as a means of increasing agricultural production. At first the collectivization was to have been voluntary. Suddenly, however, in early 1930 the government decided to force collectivization as widely as possible and eliminate the richer peasants *as a class* by turning their holdings over to collectives. The resulting change was so profound that a careful expert could say: ". . . The events of 1929–34 constitute one of the great dramas of history."[1]

Only the poor peasants could be persuaded to join the collectives voluntarily; but they owned so few animals and so little capital that collectives could not succeed with them alone. The middle-income and rich peasants resisted forced collectivization with bitterness and ferocity. At times this resistance was so widespread as to constitute what could almost be called a second civil war. When the richer

---

[1]Alec Nove, *An Economic History of the USSR* (Baltimore: Penguin, 1969), p. 160.

peasants realized they could not defeat the government directly, they began to burn buildings, destroy equipment, and slaughter animals. By 1931, one-third of Russia's cattle, half of its sheep and goats, and one-fourth of its horses had been slaughtered.

The drama of the battle over collectivization was one about which many books have been written. Here it will suffice to say that an immense social cost was incurred but that it did bring about the revolution in Soviet agriculture that made industrialization possible. Collectivization succeeded in drastically increasing the government's collections of grain. The 22,100,000 tons from the 1930–1931 harvest amounted to more than twice the tonnage collected by the government in 1928–1929.

INDUSTRIALIZATION

When collectivization placed a large economic surplus in government hands, Soviet industrialization proceeded at a striking rate on the basis of successive Five-Year Plans during the 1930s. Industrial growth at such a rapid pace was unprecedented in history. Official Soviet figures for the 1930s show an average annual growth rate in industrial production of about 16 percent. Studies by Western economists using different methods of arriving at indexes of industrial production show somewhat lower rates (ranging from about 9 percent to about 14 percent), but by any of these estimates the performance was without historical precedent.[2]

The major Soviet achievement was not simply a higher rate of industrial growth; it was a significant transformation of the whole society so that industrial growth could begin and continue. Before 1928, the USSR was overwhelmingly agricultural with tiny islands of industry; by 1938, it was a major industrial power with agriculture playing a secondary role. Before 1928, the USSR was mostly rural; by 1938, the urban population had tripled—there was a constant flow of people from country to city and a flow of ideas from city to country. Before 1928, there was 80 percent illiteracy; by 1938, over 90 percent could do some reading and writing, there was a very large adult education movement, and all young people were in school. In other words, the Soviet Union changed from a less developed country in 1928 to one of the main developed countries in 1938.

This spectacular rate of growth was interrupted by World War II, during which the Soviet Union suffered unparalleled losses.

[2]For a short discussion of various estimates of Soviet industrial production, see Howard J. Sherman, *The Soviet Economy* (Boston: Little, Brown, 1969), pp. 79–99.

Estimates of the number of Soviet citizens killed in World War II are generally around the 20 million figure, although some experts place the figure at 30 million. Early in the war, Hitler rapidly conquered an area that contained over half of the USSR's prewar productive capacity. The German-occupied territory had accounted for 70 percent of Soviet coal mining, 60 percent of iron ore production, 50 percent of steel capacity, and 33 percent of the area sown in grain.

When the Soviet army retreated, it destroyed many productive facilities to prevent their use by the Germans. When the Germans were subsequently pushed back, they also pursued a scorched-earth policy, destroying everything of value as they retreated. Especially hard hit were factories and houses. In addition to killing more than 20 million Soviet people, the Germans destroyed the homes of another 25 million, totally razing about 2,000 towns and 70,000 villages.

The destruction of these millions of people, homes, factories, untold millions of animals, and railroads, transportation, and communications systems left the USSR an almost totally devastated "victor" in World War II. The economic progress of the 1930s, which had been purchased at a high social and human cost, was in large measure erased by the fascist attempt to conquer the Soviet Union.

Despite these losses, however, the Soviets retained their economic organization and general skills, and with their experience with economic planning gained during the 1930s they recovered with miraculous speed. By 1950, gross industrial production was actually substantially higher than it had been in 1940, and agricultural production had recovered almost to its prewar level.

THE POST-WORLD WAR II SITUATION

During the 1950s, the Soviet economy continued to grow at an impressive rate. From 1950 through 1958, its average growth rate was over 3.5 times that of the United States, according to official Soviet estimates, and nearly 2.5 times the U.S. rate, according to most American estimates.[3] The growth rate slowed during the late 1950s and early 1960s, but the Soviet economy still appears to have done better in its leanest years than the American economy did in the booming prosperity of the early and middle 1960s. This Soviet slowdown led to a series of reforms launched in 1965 and improved performance in the late 1960s.

The Soviet experience has proved that their model of central planning can achieve industrialization at a very rapid pace. But has their record led to any conclusions about the ability of a socialist

[3]See Sherman, op. cit., p. 105.

economy to overcome the difficulties socialists have traditionally attributed to capitalism? The question is very difficult to answer because most socialist criticisms of capitalism have assumed that socialism, when it came, would be superimposed on the productive structure of an industrial capitalist economy. Many of the worst evils found in the USSR during the past 50 years represent the social costs of industrialization and should not be compared with conditions under capitalism during the same period. A more appropriate comparison would be with England during the Industrial Revolution.[4]

Conditions of work were harsh and the worker's standard of living was low throughout the 1930s. After the first Five-Year Plan had provided the impetus toward industrialization, many leading Communists argued that more attention should be given to the working and living conditions of the laborers. Increasingly as the decade passed, the regime became less and less tolerant of such requests. Protests against prevailing conditions were often met with repression and terror.

The Stalinist purges of the late 1930s constitute one of the bleakest chapters in Russian history. They are certainly the nadir in the history of the Soviet Union. Stalin's paranoid excesses were barbarously harsh. Framing any real or imaginary opponent as a traitor, Stalin eliminated three-quarters of the men who had been elected to the Party Central Committee in 1934, 90 percent of the Soviet Army's generals, and many others of lesser status. In all, probably 500,000 persons were jailed or executed in the purges, in addition to the recalcitrant peasants who were dislocated and often sent to forced-labor camps in the collectivization drive.

In 1953, Stalin died. By that time, economic progress had made political liberalization possible. Since the execution in late 1953 of Stalin's chief executioner, Beria, violence has not been used to settle political issues in the Soviet Union. Leaders have come and gone, but no one has been executed as a consequence of political differences. Accompanying this decrease in coercive force has been a general increase in political and intellectual freedom. The increase has been very uneven and sporadic, however, and the Soviet society remains a substantial distance from the traditional ideals of socialism.

RECENT ECONOMIC REFORMS

In the more liberal atmosphere that has prevailed since the mid-1950s, Soviet literature on the problems of economic planning under

[4]See Chapter 5.

socialism has increased immensely. The basic problem under investigation has been the question of evaluating various output mixes and input costs. One of the most important issues with which the Soviets have been dealing is that of the relationship between the market and the plan. Specifically, the economists have debated the issue of the appropriate extent of centralized versus decentralized economic decision making. In 1962 the economist Evsei G. Liberman published an article in *Pravda* that initiated a debate on decentralization. This "great debate" eventually led to a series of economic reforms beginning in 1965.

The *Kharkov incentive system* (which was what Liberman named his plan) called for important changes in the planning process only at the level of the firm. For the entire economy, "the basic levels of centralized planning—prices, finances, budget account, large capital investments . . . all the value, labor and natural indices of rates and proportions of production, distribution and consumption will be determined entirely at the center."[5]

Liberman proposed that enterprises be assigned only their final output mix. The appropriate technology was to be determined by each firm. The more efficiently a firm used its inputs, the lower would be its costs. The lower its costs, the higher would be its net revenue, or profits (total sales revenues minus total costs). Therefore the size of a firm's profits would be an index of its efficiency. Bonus payments were to be given to firms that made profits above some profitability norm established for the industrial sector in which the firm was a part.

From 1962 to 1965 the Kharkov system was supported and attacked in a lively and penetrating debate. Critics pointed out that cost and profit calculations do not mean a thing if prices and costs do not accurately reflect a normative, or ethical, evaluation of social values and social costs. The Liberman proposal did not contain any new insights into the solution of this problem. Supporters argued that giving the individual firms more autonomy and responsibility would result in greater economic maneuverability and stronger individual initiatives. These, they asserted, would lead to greater efficiency regardless of whether prices accurately reflected social values. The greater individual freedom in making production decisions and the lure of profit bonuses would lead to more enthusiastic and conscientious application of productive effort.

Critics countered by pointing out the long socialist tradition that

[5]E. G. Liberman, "Plan, Profits and Bonuses," in M. E. Sharpe, ed., *The Liberman Discussion: A New Phase in Soviet Economic Thought* (White Plains, N.Y.: International Arts and Sciences Press, 1965), p. 79.

rejects, on moral grounds, any economic system that depends on acquisitive, greedy, pecuniary motives. They insisted that Marx's analysis of alienation proved that the root cause of alienation was the use of human beings by other human beings as mere objects to be utilized in the quest for more profits. What, these critics wondered, would differentiate a socialist factory manager, who hired laborers solely to maximize the factory's profits, from his capitalist counterparts?

In September 1965, however, it became obvious that, for the time at least, the Liberman supporters had won the day. The Soviet government proposed a major organizational reform, which was adopted as law by the Supreme Soviet on October 2 of that year. Although the reform did not make profits the only criterion of productive efficiency (as Liberman had proposed), profits did become the principal one among several criteria. Firms were given much more autonomy in purchasing and organizing inputs in the productive process. And bonuses were paid out of profits to managers who were successful under the new system. (The debate and the reforms are considered in more detail in Chapter 39.)

SUMMARY OF THE SOVIET EXPERIENCE

The Soviet Union industrialized with truly phenomenal speed, despite obstacles many economic and political systems probably could not have surmounted. Judged strictly from the goal of rapid industrialization, Soviet socialism has been a spectacular success.

But most socialists, in the nineteenth and early twentieth centuries at least, envisioned a socialist society that would be superimposed on the productive base of an advanced, industrialized capitalist economy. Capitalism was objectionable in their eyes because production was undertaken for profits and not for human welfare. Prices in a market economy merely reflected, for them, an index of the capitalists' ability to exploit workers and consumers in order to maximize profits. Such a system was, in their opinion, thoroughly irrational from top to bottom. They wanted it to be replaced by a socialist system in which human beings would live to their fullest potential in a decent environment. The problems involved in assessing social values and social costs in order to plan rationally were hardly touched upon by these socialists. Their goal was the replacement of capitalism with a humanist socialism. The problems of rational planning they left to be solved after socialism was achieved.

During the reign of Stalin, the goal of rapid industrialization overrode all others. The harsh intellectual repression, commencing with the purges of the late 1930s and lasting until Stalin's death in 1953, resulted in a nearly total eclipse of meaningful intellectual endeavors to solve the economic and philosophical problems of humanistically oriented socialist planning.

In 1956, after this long period of intellectual stagnation, Soviet economic thought came to life. The problems of social evaluation, rational planning, and decentralization of economic decision making have all received thoughtful, penetrating analyses since then. No definitive answers to these problems have emerged from the Soviet debates, but the fact that official dogma has not precluded a broad and thorough intellectual campaign to come to grips with these issues is cause for optimism. The Soviet Union has certainly not achieved anything resembling the socialist system envisioned by the great thinkers in the socialist tradition. But with industrialization successfully behind them, and having initiated some beginnings of political and intellectual freedom, they may well be starting on the path to such a socialist system. Only time will tell.

SOCIALIST DEVELOPMENT IN CHINA

Since World War II socialism has been established in several countries. In some it has developed along lines quite different from the Soviet Union's version. China is the largest country in which socialists have triumphed. The Chinese experience differs from that of the Soviet Union in many ways. For these reasons, we shall briefly examine some of the main features of Chinese economic development since 1949.

In 1911, the fall of the Manchu dynasty marked the beginning of a period of rapid social change in China. Between 1911 and 1949, the Chinese economy had been ravaged by revolution, civil war, foreign invasion and exploitation, and flood and famine. When the Communists took over in 1949, they inherited an extremely poor and backward economy.

The industrial sector was very small and mostly foreign owned. In the major urban centers most industry and commerce had come almost to a standstill. Dams, canals, and irrigation systems were in a dilapidated condition. The fighting had destroyed most of the railroad lines. Inflation had nearly ruined the money system. And worst of all, the population that had survived the preceding disasters was abysmally poor, half-starved, and exhausted.

The Chinese economy was basically feudal, with about 80 percent of the population employed in agriculture. The coastal cities had become enclaves of foreign capitalist industry, but in 1949 there was less industry in China than existed in Russia in 1914 or in India when it became independent in 1947.

The firt step taken by the new government was to begin a massive land reform. In 1949, landlords and rich peasants, who constituted less than 10 percent of the population, owned 70 percent of the land.[6] By 1952, the land reform had been completed, and over 300 million poor peasants had benefited.

Other policies undertaken between 1949 and 1952 were designed to restore the economy to its prewar level and to create the necessary economic, political, and social prerequisites for a successful planned economy. Accomplishments during this period were impressive. The government suppressed the banditry that had been rife during the period of social turmoil, restored the dilapidated railroad system, and repaired and extended the irrigation systems. An extensive system of public health, preventive medicine, and sanitation was initiated. Perhaps most significant of all, it undertook to provide a relatively equal distribution of the available food and clothing.

By 1952 the government believed conditions justified launching its first Five-Year Plan, to cover the years 1953–1957. The slogan was "Learn from the Soviet Union." Ministries, each responsible for an industry, were established in Peking. Planning was centralized, with the ministries fixing prices and output targets. A high priority was given to the major capital goods industries.

In education, public health, and industry, most of the plan's targets were achieved. By 1958, the educational system had graduated 431,000 students, including 130,000 engineers, more than twice the number produced in the previous 20 years. The public health program virtually eliminated such diseases as cholera, typhoid, and plague, which previously had regularly decimated the Chinese population.

Considerable increases in the output of heavy industry were also achieved: "Crude steel output increased from 1.5 million metric tons to 5.35 million; coal from 66.5 to 130.7 million; petroleum from 0.44 to 1.46 million; cement from 2.9 to 6.9 million; sulphuric acid from 190 thousand metric tons to 632 thousand; and electric power from 7.3 billion kilowatt hours to 19.3 billion."[7]

There were also failures during the first Five-Year Plan. The size and complexity of the Chinese economy made it extremely difficult to plan everything from the center. Inevitably there were inefficiencies, wastes, dislocations. Light industry was growing very slowly. And there were problems in the agricultural sector remark-

[6]E. L. Wheelwright and Bruce McFarlane, *The Chinese Road to Socialism* (New York: Monthly Review Press, 1970), p. 32. Most of the statistics in this section are from this source.
[7]Ibid., p. 36.

ably similar to those the Soviet Union had encountered in the 1920s. As a consequence, in 1956–1957 the Chinese stepped up the process of agricultural collectivization. By the end of 1957, almost all peasant households were in collectives.

The second Five-Year Plan was never undertaken, for in 1958 the Chinese launched their *Great Leap Forward*, an all-out effort to transform radically the most basic social and economic institutions. This transformation involved a complete rejection of the planning model of the Soviet Union and ultimately an almost complete break with the Soviet Union.

The first and most basic change was the establishment of *people's communes*. China's 752,000 collective farms were reorganized into 26,500 communes. The collectives had included an average of 158 households; in the new communes, the average was 5,000 households. The new organizations were designed to permit effective mobilization of the massive rural labor force to facilitate the construction of many labor intensive capital projects and to increase the production in small-scale industries. These functions were, of course, in addition to the households' more basic role as producers of agricultural products.

The communes undertook such important projects as construction of new irrigation systems and water conservation systems and afforestation programs. They also organized small-scale production in several industries, including cloth weaving, machinery repair, simple tool making, and the manufacture of many other industrial products. (The "backyard" smelting of pig iron that was widely ridiculed in the Western press never did have the importance attributed to it in the West.)

The communes established schools for technical training, research institutes, and spare-time facilities for general education. They also served to ration and distribute food and other consumer goods, and maintained communal kitchens, laundries, and children's nurseries. In general, they were integrated social units performing many social, political, and cultural functions for the people.

In late 1957 and early 1958, there was a widespread attempt to decentralize industrial decision making. The central authorities continued to control the capital goods industries, but consumer goods industries were put under the control of provincial authorities.

The years 1959–1961 were years of crisis. Innumerable problems were encountered in the communes, where radical social reorganization was occurring simultaneously with the introduction of new systems of production and education. The primary cause of the crisis, however, was disastrous harvests. Many Western observers believed China was on the brink of social collapse.

Gradually, however, as Western scholars gathered more information, they realized that along with the failures the Chinese had achieved many successes. The Great Leap Forward

> familiarized millions of backward peasants with industrial techniques at great immediate cost, but at an equally great potential benefit. It liberated China from excessive reliance on the Soviet developmental model which, whatever its strengths, was not suitable to a populous Asian land. . . . It achieved a strategically and economically significant dispersion of industry and an increase in the number of home-made scientists and technicians. . . . By 1962 China's meager army of scientific and technical personnel had almost doubled; important inroads had been made on illiteracy; and the number of types of steel, rolled steel, and non-ferrous metals had increased by 200 percent, and those of machine tools by 150 percent. . . . Contrary to the oft-repeated assertions in the West, the commune system of socio-economic organization was not jettisoned, merely made more rational.[8]

During the 1960s, several changes were made in Chinese economic priorities. First, increased emphasis was given agricultural production and light industries in the national investment program. A larger share of the output of heavy industry was devoted to agricultural machinery, chemical fertilizers, insecticides, fuel, electric power, irrigation equipment, and building materials. Second, much greater stress was placed on improving the quality of all goods produced. Third, there was a general reorganization of the communes aimed at increasing their effectiveness. Between 1958 and the late 1960s, the average number of households per commune fell from 5000 to about 1600.

ACCOMPLISHMENTS
OF CHINESE SOCIALISM

Since the Great Leap Forward the Chinese have not made general production statistics available to the West. Thus we lack quantitative evidence with which to evaluate their economic performance since 1958. Judgments about China's progress must be made from firsthand observations of the general conditions under which the people are living. Many contemporary economists have visited China. When an economist visits China and wants to evaluate its performance, he

> studies the official statistics and publications put out by the government and other institutions. He talks to the country's

[8]Jan S. Prybyla, "Red China in Motion: A Non-Marxist View," in Harry G. Shaffer, ed., *The Communist World* (New York: Appleton, 1967), p. 176.

economists. He moves around as much as he can, visiting various units of production over as wide a field as possible. In his travels, . . . he utilizes his previous experiences and observes the condition of the people—whether they appear well fed and healthy, whether there appears to be substantial unemployment (real or disguised), the absence or presence of beggars, standards of cleanliness and hygiene, the quality and range of consumer goods in the shops, other products exhibited in trade fairs and elsewhere, the standard of public housing, the clothing of the people, the leisure habits of the people, and so on.[9]

Before making such judgments, the economist should keep in mind the conditions prevailing in China after World War II. Over the previous several decades, approximately 100 million people had perished in floods, famines, war, and revolutions. The overwhelming majority of those remaining were starving, poverty-stricken, demoralized people. Intestinal and lung diseases were endemic; the country was regularly devastated by epidemics of various communicable diseases.

Economically, China was much more backward than Russia had been before the Revolution. Russia's petroleum production in 1913, for example, was over 27 times as great as China's was in 1943. Steel production in prerevolutionary Russia was $3\frac{1}{2}$ times that of China. On the eve of collectivization, the Soviets had 210,900 tractors; in 1949, the Chinese had 400. Russia's 1913 railroad mileage was approximately 45,600; China had 13,600 in 1949, and most of its railroads went inland only far enough for foreign capitalist powers to bring its raw materials to the seaports to be shipped abroad.

In agriculture, chemical fertilizers had virtually never been used before 1949. Reckless deforestation and soil erosion had made a large percentage of cultivable farmland subject to periodic devastating floods. Agricultural techniques were abysmally backward. It is only against this background that we can evaluate the Chinese economic performance since 1949.

Agricultural accomplishments are perhaps most important because of the massive, starving population that existed in 1949. The Chinese reorganized their agriculture. They increased the degree of mechanization, produced and used substantially more chemical fertilizers, and greatly expanded the supplies of eggs, vegetables, fruits, poultry, fish, and meat. Today, China feeds her entire population and exports more food than she imports. One American economist has gone so far as to state that "it would not be farfetched to claim that there has been less malnutrition due to maldistribution of food in China

[9]Wheelwright and McFarlane, op. cit., p. 13.

over the past twenty years than there has been in the United States."[10]

In education, there have also been important achievements. Virtually all urban children and most rural children attend school. Illiteracy, which before the Revolution was almost universal, has been nearly eliminated. A wide variety of schools and technical training centers exists at all levels throughout China.

The gains in the medical and public health fields are very impressive. A Canadian doctor recently reported on his visits to Chinese medical colleges, hospitals, and research institutes. He reported that they had high medical standards, used high-quality equipment, and dispensed excellent medical care, which was almost all comparable to Canadian standards.[11] A member of the U.S. Public Health Service has written that "the prevention and control of many infectious and parasitic diseases which have ravaged [China] for generations [was a] most startling accomplishment." He also asserted that "the improvement of general environmental sanitation and the practice of personal hygiene, both in the cities and in the rural areas, were also phenomenal."[12]

In the area of industrial production, China is definitely still a backward nation. Nevertheless, its achievements have been much more impressive than those of other comparably situated less developed countries, and this despite the extremely low starting point, which precluded successful industrialization within a period comparable to that of the Soviet Union.

Considering all of the facts, we can conclude:

> The truth is that China over the past two decades has made very remarkable economic advances (though not steadily) on all fronts. The basic overriding economic fact about China is that for twenty years she has fed, clothed, and housed everyone, has kept them healthy, and has educated most. Millions have not starved; sidewalks and streets have not been covered with multitudes of sleeping, begging, hungry, and illiterate human beings; millions are not disease ridden. To find such deplorable conditions, one does not look to China these days, but, rather, to India, Pakistan, and almost anywhere else in the underdeveloped world. These facts are so basic, so fundamentally important, that they completely dominate China's economic picture, even if one grants all

[10]John W Gurley, "Maoist Economic Development: The New Man in the New China," *The Review of Radical Political Economics*, Fall 1970, pp. 34–35.

[11]G. Leslie Wilcox, "Observations on Medical Practices," *Bulletin of the Atomic Scientists*, June 1966.

[12]Quoted in Gurley, op. cit., p. 35.

of the erratic and irrational policies alleged by her numerous critics.[13]

CHINESE ECONOMIC PHILOSOPHY

Any country undergoing industrialization must devote massive amounts of resources to the building of industrial capacity. This means, of necessity, that the average worker must remain relatively poor for a long period. While the low standard of average consumption must remain for some time, the incentives for labor during industrialization can be achieved in either of two ways.

The first method is the one used by the Soviet Union. There, although the average worker's wage remained very low, the few skilled technicians, engineers, and managers were offered high material incentives. Thus egotistic drive for more material benefits was manipulated to achieve industrialization, just as it had been during capitalist industrialization.

The second method, used by the Chinese, attempts to develop other types of incentives. Materialistic incentives are discouraged. Ideological propaganda emphasizes the importance of overcoming selfish, egotistic behavior. The well-being of everyone and the development of socialism and other social, nonindividualistic motives are stressed.

Many Western observers have noted that the income differential in China between factory worker and factory manager is quite small. Furthermore, the factory manager is expected to take his turn at tedious or menial labor such as sweeping the factory floor. As a consequence, workers and managers have much closer and more amiable personal ties in China than they do in most other countries.[14]

Education and training are less specialized. Each person is trained to do a number of jobs and may rotate from manual to mental labor, from urban to rural employment, and from rank-and-file positions to leadership positions. The Chinese emphasize the notion that narrow specialization prevents an individual from achieving his or her mental, emotional, and creative potential.

Some economists have criticized this policy. They assert that it is inefficient and retards the training of the large number of highly skilled technicians desperately needed for industrialization to be successful.

---

[13]Ibid., p. 34.
[14]See, for example, Barry M. Richman, *Industrial Society in Communist China* (New York: Random House, 1969), chap. 9.

The Chinese reject this criticism on two grounds. First, they argue that they consider the making of well-rounded, intelligent, and creative human beings to be the final goal of industrialization. Rigid specialization, they assert, treats the individual as a *means* and not as an *end* because it stunts his or her development in the interest of greater productive output. Second, they believe that even though rigid specialization may bring short-run advantages in production, in the long run it is disadvantageous. Over the longer period a broadly educated, creative, and happy population, whose motives are social rather than individualistic, will be much more productive. Further, they assert that this is the only concept of human development that is consistent with traditional ideals of socialism.[15]

The Soviet and Chinese models of socialist industrialization are certainly strikingly different. At present, rigorous attempts to compare and evaluate the effectiveness of the two models would be premature. The two countries have so many differences in their histories, cultures, and general economic circumstances that one cannot generalize from the experience of the one to evaluate the other. Nevertheless, they do present contrasting approaches for any less developed country that might wish simultaneously to industrialize and to build a socialist society.

SUMMARY

The first revolution calling itself socialist occurred in 1917, in Russia. Against incredible odds the Russian Communists ended the tsarist autocracy; won a civil war in which 14 foreign countries intervened against them; socialized industry; collectivized agriculture; carried through a successful change from a rural, illiterate, and less developed economy to a predominately urban, highly educated, and advanced economy; and defeated the onslaught of Hitler's fascist armies. Income is distributed more equally than in the United States, and the Soviet rate of production growth exceeds the U.S. rate. Unfortunately, the Soviet Union paid for all of this not only in decades of hard work and postponed consumption, not only in blood and millions of lives lost, but also in political dictatorship that formerly executed its enemies and often represses intellectual life even today.

In 1949, the Chinese Revolution ousted the old, corrupt regime of Chiang Kai-shek after decades of fighting against Chiang's forces and resisting Japanese imperialism. In less than a quarter of a cen-

---

[15]For a good discussion of Chinese economic philosophy, see Gurley, op. cit., pp. 29–38; Wheelwright and McFarlane, op. cit., pp. 197–240; and Edgar Snow, "Mao's Attributes," *The Listener*, May 29, 1969.

tury, they have had remarkable success in raising living standards and hopes in what was once the most backward of all large countries. Their industrialization drive apparently has appealed even more than the Soviets' to social consciousness and less to immediate individual money incomes. It is still too early to undertake a detailed evaluation of their performance (although some other less developed countries are already very much influenced by the Chinese model of development). Thus in the next two chapters we turn to the Soviet experience and examine it in detail.

problems
of
socialist
planning

We assume for the time being that the centralized, dictatorial Soviet model represents a kind of socialism. Although many socialists would argue that the Soviet Union is not really socialist, the Soviet case is considered here simply because it holds the record of the longest experience with some kind of planning under some kind of socialism.

THE SOVIET ECONOMIC MODEL

In the capitalist United States, most land and factories are privately owned. In the socialist Soviet Union, most land and factories are publicly owned, with the government claiming to represent the public. Public ownership, of course, tends to mean public direction and therefore usually means planning. The principal type of household income in the Soviet Union is wage income for labor. In the United States, income consists not only of wages but also of profits, rent, dividends, and interest. The latter incomes are derived basically from private property; thus most U.S. planning is necessarily limited in scope to the confines of single enterprises in which decisions reflect the search for private profit.

In the Soviet Union, the only exceptions to public ownership are a small percentage of cooperative industrial enterprises composed mainly of handicraft workers. There are also many collective farms that are supposed to be cooperatives but are subject to considerable central control (but each farmer also has a small private plot of land).

In the publicly owned enterprises, the Soviet government, or some agency of the government, appoints a manager. He is solely responsible for the performance of the factory, and his bonus is based on how well it performs. His performance and his conduct are checked by numerous agencies, and he may be promoted, transferred, or fired at any time. In turn, he hires and fires all the other workers at the enterprise.

The government grants the enterprise its plant and equipment and initial working capital, although it is now beginning to charge interest on capital. After the initial grant of capital, however, the enterprise is made financially independent. It must meet all costs of wages and materials out of revenue from sales and must also replace or repair depreciated and broken capital out of revenues from sales. And it is normally expected to show a profit above all of its costs.

The Soviet economy is centrally planned. The most important economic orders originate from the USSR Council of Ministers, but additional orders to the enterprise may come from regional or local governmental bodies. Further orders may originate in or be transmitted through the agency directly supervising the enterprise, whether that agency is associated with a regional governing body or with the ministry directing some industrial area. Finally, all of these orders from governmental or supervisory bodies are supposed to be in accord with the plan, which emanates from the Central Planning Commission or its subordinate agencies. The enterprise manager is solely responsible for the performance of the factory, then, only in the sense that he must execute all of the orders he has received within the constraint of the resources allocated to him.

The Central Planning Commission first collects information up the ladder, from enterprise through agencies, in order to evaluate the last year's performance and the present conditions and possibilities. Then the Commission is told by the Council of Ministers what goals it must strive to meet. On these bases it draws up a general plan for the whole economy, although production and allocation details are provided for only, say, 2000 commodities. The draft plan is then shown to all agencies on down the ladder to the enterprise. After all these units have added their detailed modifications and suggestions, the Central Planning Commission draws up the final draft.

The plan is supposed to provide sufficient investment for the desired rate of growth, guarantee balance among all the industrial needs and outputs, and choose the best assortment of goods. At any rate the Central Planning Commission hands the plan over to appropriate government bodies to enact into law. It is then passed on with detailed commands, expanded at each intermediate level, until the enterprise receives a formidable document that is supposed to tell it exactly what to produce for a year (or some other period), how to produce it, what prices to charge, and what funds it may use. Again, the manager is judged on how well he follows these commands, though he has always had some decision-making power over details. The economic reforms of 1965 augmented the manager's decision-making power (discussed in Chapter 37).

PLANNING FOR GROWTH

In the case of a centrally planned economy such as the Soviet Union, it may be assumed that *aggregate* effective demand always rises as rapidly as aggregate supply, although *particular* goods may be unsalable for various reasons. Thus there are no retardations or depressions caused by lack of demand. If the problems of demand are thus eliminated, then growth will depend simply on how fast output can be expanded. The supply problem may be resolved into two questions: (1) How much of each input (labor, capital, natural resources, and technology) can be procured under existing circumstances for use in production? (2) How much output can be obtained from these inputs in the production process?

These questions can be most usefully analyzed in terms of the growth formula explored in Chapter 31. It may be repeated here:

$$\text{Rate of growth of output} = \frac{\text{increase in output}}{\text{investment}} \times \frac{\text{saving}}{\text{output}}$$

If saving equals investment, as it does in the Soviet Union, then this formula is true by definition. The ratio of saving to output then indicates how much new capital is invested per year, and the ratio of increased output to investment indicates the amount of product produced by the new capital invested. Of course that productivity is affected by changes in the labor force and in natural resources and technological improvements.

Consider the following application of the growth formula. If the ratio of saving to output is 9 percent and the ratio of increased output to investment is 1:3, then we find:

$$\text{Rate of growth} = \frac{1}{3} \times .09 = .03, \text{ or 3 percent per year}$$

This has been approximately the performance of the U.S. economy since the Civil War.[1]

[1]For empirical data on the ratios and the average growth rate, see Simon S. Kuznets, *National Product Since 1869* (New York: National Bureau of Economic Research, 1946).

For the years 1950–1970 conservative U.S. estimates place Soviet GNP growth at 6 percent per year; official Soviet figures indicate 9 percent per year.[2] (It is worth noting that China, in spite of political upheavals, also achieved a 6 percent growth rate each year from 1949 to 1966.[3]) Even the conservative American estimate is still high enough to call for an explanation in terms of the growth formula. If it is assumed for the moment that the Soviet ratio of increased output to investment is the same as the U.S. ratio, then in this simple analysis the higher rate of growth can be explained by a higher ratio of saving and investment from current output. Thus if the Soviet ratio of increased output to investment is also 1:3, then a 6 percent growth rate can be explained only by an 18 percent ratio of saving to output. According to the formula,

$$\text{Soviet growth rate} = \frac{1}{3} \times .18 = .06, \text{ or 6 percent per year}$$

One reason for the high Soviet growth rate is that there is always sufficient aggregate demand in the Soviet Union for full employment of labor and full use of capacity. Therefore all Soviet saving is used for investment because the planners can always find a use for new capital. In fact, Soviet planners usually complain of a *scarcity* of capital because they attempt to invest more than the entire available amount of savings. In the United States, however, when businessmen cannot find a profitable investment for all of their savings, some planned saving does not become investment in new capital. American economists often complain of *too much* planned saving, while planned investment in additional capital is less than it could be, sometimes causing depressions.

Another reason for the high rate of Soviet growth is the enormous amount of resources invested in education and scientific research. By this means the Soviets' output per unit of capital has been greatly increased. First, education has given them a highly trained work force capable of very productive labor. Second, education and science have given them a rapidly rising level of technology.

It is obvious from the formula, however, that the Soviet people have to pay a price for their high rate of investment and growth of output. If the Soviets save 18 percent and the United States saves only 9 percent of national output, and if both begin with the same $100 of output, then in the first year U.S. consumption would be $91 while Soviet consumption would be only $82. It is impossible to

[2]The data used in this paragraph are discussed in detail in Howard J. Sherman, *The Soviet Economy* (Boston: Little, Brown, 1969), chap. 5.

[3]See the testimony by John Gurley in U.S. Congress, Joint Economic Committee, *Mainland China in the World Economy* (Washington, D.C.: GPO, 1967), p. 188.

have both higher consumption and higher investment out of the same output (assuming we began with full employment); the Soviets have sacrificed some present consumption for more investment. Furthermore, in reality total Soviet output is still far below the U.S. level, and thus the Soviet consumption level is even lower. In purely human terms, moreover, we must stress that when the Soviets began their rapid industrial expansion, their consumption was at a miserably low level. Therefore each percent of national product taken from consumption in order to make investments meant a very great amount of present human misery accepted as the cost of future growth.

However, the simple growth formula also indicates that if the Soviet Union continues to grow twice as fast as the United States, after some years both their total output *and* their consumption will be larger than those of the United States. That is true, however, only if they continue to build new capital at the same rate and maintain the same increase of output per unit of new investment (through more education and more scientific research). It is no wonder that a major *political* issue in the Soviet Union has been and continues to be how much of national output should be devoted to present consumption. Conversely, how much should be taken away from present consumption and put into investment in order to increase future consumption?

AGGREGATE BALANCE
VERSUS INFLATION

The question of aggregate balance in the Soviet economy is mostly a reflection of the growth problem already discussed. Basically the resources supplied for investment must just equal the amount required or demanded for investment, while the amount supplied to consumers must just equal the amount they will demand at present incomes and prices. The capitalist economy of the United States has frequently been plagued by lack of adequate demand for the products of private enterprise. In the planned economy of the USSR, there has *always* been sufficient aggregate demand since the planning period began in 1928, and there has never been general or aggregate unemployment. In the USSR, however, the problem has usually been that the government has demanded much more for investment than could be supplied and has failed to provide enough consumer goods to satisfy household demand.

Because aggregate demand has always more than equaled the amount of available resources and manpower, aggregate unemployment has been nonexistent since 1928. Of course the Soviet Union does have a considerable amount of frictional and structural unemployment. *Frictional* unemployment may be defined as ordinary labor turnover. *Structural* unemployment occurs when the structure of industry and technology changes, so that millions of workers must change jobs from one place to another, from one industry to another, or from one skill to another. These changes require large amounts of retraining and moving expenses. Many observers recently have reported significant unemployment from this source. The Soviet Union may also have some seasonal unemployment, which occurs because in certain industries, especially agriculture, demand for labor varies during the year. It may not be profitable for a society to transfer these workers to another job for only a few months, although the Chinese now use them to build dams and roads.

As implied earlier, the main problem of aggregate balance in the Soviet economy has not been unemployment created by lack of demand but rather inflation caused by excessive demand for labor and all goods. The main reason for the inflation of the 1930s and 1940s was the excessive increase in government demand for investment goods, military supplies, and free, or nonpriced, welfare services, which created an excess demand for all inputs, including labor. The excess demand for labor pushed up wage rates much faster than productivity, and thus workers' demand for consumer goods rose faster than total production and much faster than the output of consumer goods.

The excessive wage payments (which resulted in inflation) occurred as a result of decisions both at the national level and at the level of the firm. In the initial industrialization and wartime periods, the planners called for much larger increases in investment and military goods than in consumer goods; the discrepancy was usually even greater in the fulfillment of plans. Related to the high level of investment and military spending was the practice of over-full-employment planning mentioned earlier. At the enterprise level, over-full-employment planning meant managers were given output targets that, for most firms, were essentially unachievable with the amount of labor and other inputs legally available to them.

In order to meet their production plans, therefore, Soviet managers found themselves competing strenuously for materials and labor. Prices of material goods going to enterprises were effectively controlled, and most deliveries of goods were ordered by direct central priorities and rationing. Workers, however, did move from job to job according to the incentive of higher wages, and thus this was the path followed by managers competing for labor inputs. In the 1930s and 1940s managers were able to overspend their payrolls with few if any penalties but were under extreme pressure to meet output targets. They would bid notoriously high to obtain the scarce supply of workers, and even hoarded unneeded workers against future needs.

As a final result of this process, the workers attempted to spend their rapidly increasing wages on the much smaller increase in consumer goods. The consequence was too much money chasing too few goods in the consumer goods market, and steadily rising prices until 1947. This is the basic pattern of prewar and wartime inflation: excess demand for labor as a joint result of the high rate of investment and over-full-employment planning, and excess demand for consumer goods as a result of wages rising faster than productivity and faster than the output of consumer goods.

In the face of these extreme inflationary pressures, Soviet policy was always to maintain constant or declining prices by administrative fiat. In practice, the pressures forced them to raise prices for long periods in the 1930s and 1940s. These reluctantly imposed increases did not soak up the full demand, however, and the result was *repressed inflation*, or regulation of prices below the free-market level. Repressed inflation showed up in shortages and long queues for many goods. Because their wages often could not be spent for any goods (because none were available at any price), workers' incentives to labor declined.

Only since 1947 has the problem been brought under some control (although a smaller degree of repressed inflation still exists). Since that time, (1) the State Bank allows enterprises to pay wages above the planned amount *only to the extent* that they increase output above plan, and (2) the degree of over-full-employment planning appears to have been sharply reduced (because the most urgent military demands have lessened).

RELATIONS BETWEEN INDUSTRIES: MICROBALANCES

We have examined the aggregate (or macro) balances between the major parts of the economy, such as consumption and wages or saving and investment. Now the analysis must turn to the individual (micro) balances required between different industries. In this context each *industry* is defined as a collection of enterprises producing a single product for which no close substitute exists.

Soviet planners have been using a fairly simple approach called the *method of balances* to state macro- and microbalances. The following example at least roughly approximates how they would record all the sources from which one product—say, iron—is obtained, and all the uses to which it is put—that is, the total need for iron in the economy.

The balance of sources (or intake) and uses (or outgo) for the iron industry would appear as follows.

Iron industry

1. Imports	1. Exports
2. Reduction in inventory	2. Increase in inventory
+ 3. Production listed by plants or regions	+ 3. Uses by other industries, usually listed by region

e.g., a. Iron from Ukraine
     b. Iron from Latvia
	e.g., a. Iron needed in Ukraine
	     b. Iron needed in Latvia

Total Sources	Total Uses

Of course it is only the totals that must balance. But somehow enough iron must be available to meet each use or need in each area of the country.

This method runs into many problems. It is very difficult to achieve such a balance among all the conflicting needs and available materials in any one industry. Moreover, the balances are all related because each industry relies on others for supplies. For example, more steel is needed to produce more blast furnaces, but more blast furnaces are needed to make more steel. Recently consideration has been given to adopting the input-output method developed in the West (by which a computer can estimate all the balances *if* it is given the correct information).

PRICES AND ECONOMIC PLANNING

One of the most important issues in Soviet planning is the question of how the planners are to decide which outputs society should produce. A related question is which technology is the cheapest for society to use in production.

Under capitalism, the search for profits dictates what is produced. Socialists have been persistent in pointing out that this method of deciding what to produce gives a higher social priority to trinkets, useless gadgets, and other trivia for the wealthy than it does to the necessities of life for the poor. Socialists have always rejected the notion that market prices reflect meaningful social values.

Yet price offers a convenient basis for comparing goods and services that are not directly comparable. If a capitalist determined that he could produce several alternative "bundles" of commodities with, say, the $1 million of resources at his disposal, deciding which bundle to produce would be relatively simple for him. Given the resources at his disposal, he would produce the bundle of commodities that had the highest dollar value. He does not claim to be making a philosophical or moral judgment. He is merely maximizing his profits.

But when socialist planners are faced with the same situation—a fixed group of resources from which several possible combinations of outputs can be attained—theirs is a far more difficult task. They are not attempting to maximize profits. It is the general social welfare that they wish to maximize. In order to choose the combination of commodities that maximizes social welfare, the prices used for calculations must reflect perfectly the goals of a socialist society.

Until the 1950s this was not a terribly important problem for Soviet planners. The USSR was still a backward economy in the 1930s, and therefore rapid industrialization could be achieved simply by copying the product mix and technologies of the most advanced capitalist countries.

During the 1940s, the war and the necessities of reconstruction dictated the product mix to the socialist planners. By the mid-1950s, they had achieved a reconstructed industrial economy with immense productive capacity. Many more possibilities were technologically feasible. Furthermore, although rapid growth was still important, it had lost much of its urgency, while the goal of increasing the general welfare and providing more comforts for consumers had assumed much more importance. Under these circumstances the question of how to evaluate the different possible commodity mixes became a central issue of socialist controversy in the Soviet Union. To understand these issues we must first reexamine some debates in the West.

RATIONAL PLANNING UNDER SOCIALISM

In the 1920s the possibility of rational socialist planning was denied by Ludwig von Mises.[4] Mises argued that the calculation of economic choices requires knowledge of "rational" prices for both inputs and outputs. For example, if a farmer wishes to know whether to produce oranges or apples, he must know their relative prices at the time in order to maximize his revenues. Or if a planner wishes to decide whether railroad locomotives should use coal or oil, he must know the relative prices of coal and oil in order to minimize costs.

In socialism, however, the government owns the coal and oil as well as the locomotives. Therefore according to Mises, because there

[4]See Ludwig von Mises, "Economic Calculation in the Socialist Commonwealth," in F. A. Hayek, ed., *Collectivist Economic Planning* (London: Routledge & Kegan Paul, 1935). A brief history of the whole debate appears in Abram Bergson, "Socialist Economics," in Howard Ellis, ed., *A Survey of Contemporary Economics* (Philadelphia: Blakiston, 1948), vol. I, pp. 412–448.

is no market and no competition between producers, there can be no rational prices. If the coal and oil producers are merely commanded to turn over a certain physical product to the locomotive makers, no one can know which kind of fuel will cost more. In short, Mises argued, if there is no free market in socialism, there are no rational prices; and thus there can be no meaningful calculation or rational planning of allocation of resources.

The answer to Mises was pointed out long ago.[5] It is that economic calculation of optimum allocation does not require prices in an actual market. Only three kinds of information are required: (1) availability of resources, including men and machines as well as raw materials; (2) the preference scale of consumers, whether they are individuals or planners or politicians or some weighted sum of the three; (3) the production function of each output—that is, the combination of resources necessary to produce each output at the present level of technology.

As a concrete example, assume that the Soviet economy produces only two kinds of outputs: apples and oranges. The planners must have information on the given technology of apple and orange production, and they must know the given amount of labor and capital inputs available. Assume next that the economy can produce *only* either (A) 5 apples and 10 oranges or (B) 10 apples and 5 oranges. Which output mixture should be produced to maximize output? That obviously depends on the price of each output relative to the price of the other. The planners will set relative prices according to their knowledge of consumer preferences and social goals. If consumers like apples twice as much as oranges, their price should be twice as high. If the prices (calculated according to preferences) are 2 rubles an apple and 1 ruble an orange, then social value, or output, is maximized by choosing mixture B, 10 apples and 5 oranges. But if the prices (reflecting different preferences) were 1 ruble an apple and 2 rubles an orange, then we would maximize value by choosing mixture A, 5 apples and 10 oranges. (This is simple arithmetic; readers should do it to prove it to themselves.)

Information for Planning

As noted, planners must be informed about resource availability, consumer preferences, and technological possibilities. Both in a private enterprise economy and under socialism, the third kind of information (about alternative production possibilities) is furnished by engineers, although the final choice among technologies is an economic problem relating to the costs of various inputs. In a competi-

---

[5]The clearest statement is in Oskar Lange, *On the Economic Theory of Socialism* (New York: McGraw-Hill, 1964 [written in 1938]).

tive private enterprise economy, however, market prices *automatically* reflect the first and second types of information—that is, the relative scarcity of different resources as well as the relative preference of consumers for different products. Under socialism, the planners have to collect this information themselves. If it can be obtained, then socialist planners will be able to calculate rational prices for all resources and for all products. These prices would be data for planners to use and need never be paid to anybody.

If the planners of socialist industry had access to the same information available to the private enterprise managers, presumably they could then calculate the optimum mix of technology and resource allocation for the maximization of social welfare in much the same way private enterprise managers calculate for the maximization of profit. The problem is that collecting the necessary information and calculating the necessary equations is very difficult, and hence planning is far from perfect. However, the Soviet economy has performed reasonably well, and the deviation from optimal allocation may be less than it is under oligopoly conditions in the capitalist market. The relative inefficiencies of bureaucratic planning and oligopoly price setting cannot be reliably evaluated on the basis of available data.

SUMMARY

Soviet economic planning faces various economic problems, although they are very different from American economic problems. The Soviets have full employment because their planners can always use excess funds for more projects. However, they have had inflation problems because they have tried to produce even beyond their physical capacities and have paid out more wages than there were consumer goods available at current prices.

There is also a constant political fight over producing more consumer goods versus producer goods (for growth) versus military goods versus welfare goods (including education, which also contributes to growth).

Moreover, there is need for balances between individual products; each industry must produce enough to meet the need for its product from every other industry.

Finally, the planners must decide how much of each product to produce and how to produce it. These decisions depend on information about (1) resource availability, (2) consumer and social preferences, and (3) technological possibilities. Getting this information is difficult, but the imperfect planners may still do as well or better than the imperfect markets of capitalism.

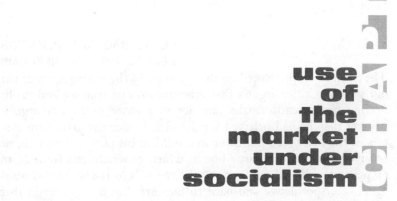

use of the market under socialism

In the modern world socialism has usually meant central planning. In this chapter we shall examine the Soviet debate and reforms, which decreased the degree of centralized power over economic decision making, and the Yugoslav experience with extreme decentralization of economic decision making.

MARXISM AND DECENTRALIZATION

Marx himself wrote very little about the details of socialist planning; he always emphasized that it would be utopian to discuss such details before the advent of an actual socialist economy. But clearly Marx and Engels disapproved of the planlessness of capitalism. In addition, they felt it to be an important cause of the periodic crises of depression or inflation. Nevertheless, this does not indicate that they would necessarily disapprove of the market device under socialism since socialism provides a very different economic environment in which markets can be controlled in accordance with the general welfare of the public.

RECENT SOVIET EXPERIENCE

Soviet planning reforms may have been generated partly by the increasing complexity of the economy. The argument is that rational planning is more difficult and more necessary in relatively advanced than in less developed countries. Technical innovation, which is now one of the most important Soviet goals, depends mainly on continuous local initiative at the production point. By contrast, throughout the 1920s and 1930s the main problem was putting to work in industry the resources that were unemployed or less profitably employed in agriculture. For this purpose central control was very efficacious.

SOVIET MANAGERIAL BEHAVIOR
BEFORE THE 1965 REFORMS

The Soviet debate pivoted on the behavior of the manager under the old system. Critics argued that attention to cost cutting and profit making could hardly make him act in a more greedy, bourgeois manner than he had behaved for decades. Under the prereform system, if the manager fulfilled or overfulfilled his plan each month, he received an additional large bonus, which generally ran from 25 to 50 percent of his salary. Some of the rewards to the successful manager were speculative and hard to measure, but it was certain that the unsuccessful manager would lose bonuses and ultimately lose his job or be demoted to a less important operation.

Because the manager was under great pressure to produce, he resorted to many evasions. His performance was judged by several criteria, including wage and raw material costs per unit and other indicators of productivity and efficiency. But the principal index of success, the one he strove above all to achieve, was simply the value of the gross output produced. If he did not achieve the planned value of output, he received no bonus at all. If, however, he exactly met the planned target, he might receive as much as a full 40 percent bonus, although the average bonus was somewhat less. For each 1 percent overfulfillment of the plan, managers in high-priority industries received an additional 4–6 percent bonus.

The Soviet manager brushed aside bureaucratic regulations and controls when they conflicted with the achievement of output goals. To a great extent he evaded specific regulations only in order to meet his plan. This was not always to the national benefit. In some instances, the manager circumvented red tape in order to obtain materials that should have been his anyway. On other occasions, however, he may have illegally obtained materials that could have been better used by a higher-priority enterprise. Unfortunately some of the manager's devices (e.g., lowering quality in order to produce greater output) yielded a bonus for an *apparent* plan fulfillment. Such behavior constituted, in fact, an antisocial act not dissimilar to the well-known evasions of the corporate income tax or antitrust laws by managers of American corporations.

Practices that reformers called attention to include the following:[1]

False reports Obviously if his production for the month had fallen short of 100 percent of the planned target, and thus the manager had lost his bonus, he might have padded his figures with waste or unfinished goods or "shifted" enough production from a very high month to a low one. Some managers, but not many, actually resorted to outright falsification (the system forced them to do so if they were to survive). Of course falsification was dangerous because the manager had to submit a very large volume of related reports, which were examined for internal consistency by bank auditors or his superiors.

More important, there were many different channels of control over the manager, and these channels were sufficiently independent to make collusion by all agents at best very difficult. First, there was the superior agency that controlled the enterprise. Second, there was the Communist party, which has cells in each enterprise, and these had certain rights to inspect and suggest improvements on enterprise projects. Third there were the trade unions, one of whose functions was the stimulation of production. Fourth, there was the State Bank, in which every enterprise kept accounts. Fifth, there also were agents of the Ministry of State Control whose sole function was to check on the legality of enterprise actions. Finally, there was the Central Statistical Agency. In spite of all of these agents of control, bribery, direct and subtle, reached everywhere, and controllers at the local level tended to form a coalition with managers.

Easier plans The manager himself played an important role in formulating the plan. He naturally bargained for a lower output target and a higher amount of required supplies. In this way output targets were more easily overfilled.

Poorer quality If a plan could not be met in the necessary quantities by producing what was supposed to be produced, it could often be fulfilled by producing goods of poorer quality. Some Soviet consumer goods have been of notoriously poor quality.

Fewer styles If was much easier to produce a large amount of one homogeneous good than it was to produce small quantities of many different goods. The manager therefore had an incentive to produce all of one type of good rather than a variety, although the latter might lead to more consumer satisfaction. Because the price was fixed, the manager did not depend on demand. However, man-

[1]See, for example, Harry G. Schaffer, "Ills and Remedies," *Problems of Communism*, May-June 1963, pp. 27–32; also David Granick, *The Red Executive* (Garden City, N.Y.: Doubleday, 1961).

agers sometimes introduced a new style just to be assigned a higher price.

Easiest mixture   The type or style on which production was concentrated may have been chosen not on the basis of usefulness to the economy but because it was the cheapest method of achieving the output goal.

Extra supplies   It is a well-known fact that managers kept on their payroll men whose only function was to expedite the flow of supplies or to find new sources of supply outside of the planned sources. These men were known as *pushers*, although they had some other title on the official payroll. They often enjoyed pleasant lives on expense accounts, wining and dining officials from other firms and various higher organizations who may have been able to furnish scarce supplies (by barter or bribery). They were the counterpart of the American *expediters* of World War II, who hung around Washington trying to get scarce materials for their firms.

Hidden reserves   A wise Soviet manager piled up inventories of any goods he could get his hands on, regardless of whether he happened to need them at the moment. When his output target was raised, he could use these extra reserves if he was unable to procure more supplies legally. Thus a large amount of resources may have been wasted, frozen in an unproductive storage stage of the productive process.

Extra labor   The manager had a plan for labor and for the total amount of wages he could spend. Overspending on wages, however, was usually very lightly punished, if at all. Of course meeting, and especially exceeding, the output target cleansed him of all crimes.

High-priced raw materials   The manager was penalized very little for high costs and was given a great reward for overfulfilling his output target; thus he had no reason not to use high-priced raw materials. Moreover, he was judged not by the value added by the enterprise but by the gross value of the product, including the value of the raw materials that were merely bought from other firms. Therefore the higher the price of the raw materials he bought the higher the value of his gross output and the greater his own reward. Naturally Soviet managers had considerable incentive to buy the most expensive raw materials.

Resistance to innovations   The manager frequently did not react with enthusiasm to innovations that *may* have increased his productive capacity at lower cost. First, innovations were risky because they might actually lower output for some months while the transition was being made to new machinery. Managers seldom took the long-run view because they were often switched to other jobs on fairly short notice. Frequent reassignment may have prevented or reduced corruption and collusion (or "familyness"), but it also motivated managers to focus their attention on immediate production gains, so that they were unwilling to gamble on higher bonuses from greatly increased production at some future date.

Second, the manager knew that if the innovation succeeded in greatly increasing his capacity to produce, his production targets would be increased, and thus he himself might gain nothing. If the plan were overfulfilled by a large margin, targets were apt to be raised in the same proportion. Therefore a manager was likely to try for a steady 103 percent or 105 percent but not more.

The tendencies we have just described did exist (and still do to a lesser extent), but they should certainly not be taken to mean that Soviet managers were completely inefficient. The Soviet economy has produced higher peacetime growth than the American economy, despite these inefficiencies. This dysfunctional behavior does imply that the growth achieved was at greater cost and sacrifice than necessary, or that growth could have been faster with the same amount of effort. The fact that some degree of inefficiency did exist in the old system of central planning was the driving force behind the decentralization reforms of the 1960s and the continued fight for further modifications.

THE COURSE OF THE DEBATE

In the atmosphere of increased freedom for scientific inquiry after 1956, there arose a faction of economists whose approach was pragmatic. They analyzed organizational matters and very concrete policy issues; through experimentation they hoped to develop solutions for limited problems. During the 1950s criticism of the malfunctions of the enterprise incentive system flowed largely from their evidence and conclusions.

Kharkov Professor Evsei G. Liberman was one of these critics. In fact, he was not the most important critic but was chosen by the political leaders to spark the public debate. Liberman published three papers in Soviet journals during the 1950s. He argued that specific problems created by existing success indicators could be overcome by appropriate changes in the operational constraints on enterprises. The reforms he advocated in 1959 were essentially those that touched off the 1962 controversy. However, until 1962 both the man and his recommendations were ignored by other writers as well as by the general public.

The debate was given urgency when the Soviet political leadership became alarmed over the retardation in growth rates apparent in the early 1960s. In addition to temporary problems (such as increased military spending), these difficulties and the need for reform may have been due to the growing complexity and interdependence of Soviet allocations, which made it increasingly difficult to devise priority rankings and balance the plan.

ESSENTIALS OF THE LIBERMAN PLAN

In September 1962 the Communist party initiated a public discussion by allowing Liberman to publish his plan in *Pravda*. His *Kharkov incentive system* calls for structural changes in the planning process, but only at the level of the firm. All investments, prices, and outputs are to continue to be centrally planned. The relationship of the planning apparatus to the individual enterprise, however, is to be fundamentally changed.

To encourage greater flexibility and initiative, the large number of indicator targets now passed down to the firm is to be streamlined to "key indexes" only. Liberman recommends assigning enterprises targets that pertain exclusively to their final output mix: quantity and assortment of production, product destinations, and delivery dates. The *input* mix is to be determined by each individual firm: The planners will then presumably sum up all the needs of the enterprises and provide them through the centrally planned system of material allocation. (This would be quite difficult.)

How well an enterprise fulfills society's demand for maximum productivity is to be assessed solely on the basis of an evaluation of its efficiency. *Profitability*, which is defined as profits expressed as a percentage of total capital, is to serve as this efficiency evaluator and is to be estimated in yearly plans submitted by all firms. Once the stated ouput goals are attained, the rate of profitability achieved becomes the sole determinant of the amount of bonus funds awarded to the firm and its employees. Liberman depicts the central planners as "relieved from petty tutelage over enterprises" and from "costly efforts to influence production through administrative measures rather than economic ones."[2]

Bonus payments are to be computed by comparing the profitability rate of a particular firm with a profitability norm established for the branch of industry within which each firm is to be included. This is an attempt to set a "single standard of profitability of enterprises in roughly the same natural and technical conditions."[3] Different incentive payment scales will then be set up for the different branches of industry. The bonus premiums earned by the firm under this system will be utilized, as the manager directs, to (1) pay salary bonuses to management and workers, (2) provide

[2]Evsei G. Liberman, "Plan, Profits, and Bonuses," in M. E. Sharpe, ed., *The Liberman Discussion* (New York: International Arts and Sciences Press, 1965), p. 79.
[3]Ibid.

new housing, nurseries, kindergartens, and recreation facilities for workers' families, and (3) finance small, decentralized investments.

To motivate directors to attempt plans as ambitious as their productive potential allows, Liberman advances three proposals: First, incentive premiums per ruble of capital invested are to rise as the rate of profit increases. Second, the firm is to benefit more from fulfilling its own profitability plan than from overfulfilling it. Third, the norms of profitability are to be established for an extended period (from two to five years or more). This will prevent the harmful practice of raising norms whenever a firm surpasses its planned targets. In this way the firm's directors can count on reaping benefits from successful innovations or particularly effective cost-saving programs. The concern for profitability is also supposed to stimulate the manager to search for cost reductions and to produce the output mix demanded by his consumers.

SOVIET CONTROVERSY, 1962–1963

Both moderate and active Soviet supporters of the Liberman system agree that a rational price system is a necessary precondition for a profit-based index to serve as an effective evaluator of enterprise efficiency. Although Liberman himself has been somewhat indefinite about the changes in price methodology that would be necessary to achieve this rationality, others (e.g., V. S. Nemchinov) have taken a strong stand for many years. Because profits derive from selling prices and cost prices, profitability will be a measure of real, and not merely paper, efficiency only if prices reflect the relative values of all inputs into production. Consequently, as a Soviet commentator asserts, a substantial price deviation "above or below the socially necessary outlays, results, regardless of the operation of the enterprise, either in an unjustifiably low profitability, and even loss, or in excessive profitability."[4]

One group of Soviet writers argued further that the existing material supply system was too complex and inflexible to give enterprises the freedom of input determination envisioned in Liberman's incentive scheme. Therefore they advocated replacing administrative allocations with a system of state trade in which enterprises would negotiate independent agreements with suppliers and customers. Nemchinov boldly argued that all planning of intermediate goods should cease; the state should decide only what final products it needs.[5]

The majority of responses to *Pravda*'s 1962 request for discussion,

[4]L. Gatovskii, "The Role of Profit in a Socialist Economy," translated in *The Soviet Review*, Summer 1963, p. 20.
[5]See V. Nemchinov, "Plan, Assignment and Material Incentive," in Sharpe, op. cit., pp. 107–113.

however, were characterized by either total hostility to Liberman's scheme or considerable criticism. For example, A. Zverev, former minister of finance, denounced the theory he sees lurking behind Libermanism: that profit is created not only by the worker's labor but also by fixed and current capital: "It is hardly necessary to prove the erroneousness of such a theory."[6] (Notice that he may be confusing the productivity of capital with the productivity of capitalists. None of the reformers says that *capitalists* are productive, nor does any of them advocate paying profits to individuals.) Zverev also rejected the premise that the central planners are less informed as to the capabilities of enterprises than the enterprise itself. They "are obligated to know, and actually do know, the production capacities of enterprises."[7] In addition, the former minister challenged the profitability norms to be established for branches of industry, asserting that they would not be objective for all firms in a grouping and predicting that constantly changing technical conditions among firms would cause persistent pressure on any norm-setting government agency to revise the norm. The only way to keep norms fair, he concluded, would be to revise them continually.

A full measure of hostility was focused on the increase in decentralized investment likely to occur with the adoption of a scheme like Liberman's. Convinced that existing defects in "capital construction" are due to insufficient centralization, several writers emphatically decried the proposal to leave an increased number of investment decisions with the enterprises. They argued that enterprises are "ignorant of the various national economic interrelations," so that the effect would be to increase "parochialism" and to multiply "disproportions in the national economy."[8] (Actually Liberman never advocated decentralization of major investment decisions.)

Professor Liberman's reply to his critics in 1962 made some interesting points.[9] First, he attempted to clear away the confused notion held by some that profitability would be the single index to regulate enterprise behavior. The production goals society demands of enterprises, including the quantity and assortment of output, are still to be centrally planned and individually assigned to firms. Only after meeting the output targets does profitability take on prime importance for the firm. Second, he countered the charge that successful enterprises will be able to rest on past efficiency achieve-

---

[6]A. Zverev, "Against Oversimplification in Solving Complex Problems," *Problems of Economics*, April 1963, p. 18.

[7]Ibid., p. 16.

[8]Quotations in this paragraph are from K. Plotnikov, "E. G. Liberman: Right and Wrong," translated in Sharpe, op. cit., pp. 161–165.

[9]E. G. Liberman, "Reply to Critics of the Profit Proposal," *Current Digest of the Soviet Press*, December 1962, pp. 18–20.

ments, asserting that "even a small increase in incentive payments is of some interest" and that "every manufacturing enterprise must constantly introduce new production . . . or its incentive scale will drop."[10]

By May 1963, however, the controversy had died down considerably. The government gave no further indication of its readiness to alter the basics of its system of minutely detailed planning and supervision of enterprises. Yet during the lull in public debate, which lingered through mid-1964, problems with unsold consumer goods became critical. It was apparently the unwanted inventory increases that precipitated the first Soviet experiments with profit incentives and direct ties to consumers.

RESUMPTION OF DEBATE: 1964–1965

In 1964 public discussion was again requested by the editors of *Pravda*. The inference is that desires for economic reform from within the party had significantly grown in the interim. The party was probably influenced by the intensification of the Soviet economy's problems between 1962 and 1964, including the rapidly mounting inventories of consumer goods, the grain crop failures in 1963, and the declining growth rate. The Soviet party was surely also influenced by the virtual stagnation of the Czech economy in 1963, the inception in 1964 of profit sharing and a charge on capital in Hungary, and the continued success of the decentralized Yugoslav system.

In 1964 another lead article by Liberman in *Pravda* reiterated his position and, in addition, advocated a charge on capital. Within six months the newspaper received 600 articles and letters in response. Most indicated a substantial shift from the tone of the 1962 controversy. A *Pravda* columnist concluded that the overwhelming majority of writers felt it necessary to "intensify sharply the role of economic levers in the management of the national economy to expand the rights of enterprises, to enhance the importance of profit . . . and to put price formation in order."[11] Expressions of total hostility were practically nonexistent. And an expanded and vocal group of economists, research workers, and enterprise managers became increasingly insistent in their demands for the adoption of widespread change.

The degree of enterprise autonomy urged by some of the writers now went considerably beyond the Liberman plan and its 1962 extensions. Arguing that output plans should be based on orders

[10]Ibid., p. 18.
[11]"Survey of Readers' Letters," *Pravda*, February 17, 1965.

from customers, they asserted, first, that enterprises "should be given the right to amend the output plan with the consent of the customer," and second, that when an enterprise is producing a product "with higher consumer properties than are stipulated by the standards, it should be given the right to fix the price with the agreement of the customer."[12] One Soviet author even proposed that central price setting be replaced by competition ruled by consumer demand.[13]

The goals of most hopeful reformers, however, did not at first include changes that would decentralize price setting. Their main new demand was for the introduction of direct links between enterprises in order to supplant the unwieldly system of central supply allocations. They were also loud in urging a price calculus with capital charges. Nevertheless, complete central control over national parameters (including prices) was still regarded as integral to the preservation of economic balances and a high rate of accumulation. Only after the reforms actually began in 1966 and 1967 was considerable sentiment voiced for price decentralization as well as output decentralization.

OFFICIAL REFORMS

Although "economic experiments" were given varied trials during 1964 and 1965, it was not until September 1967 that the government responded with a major organizational reform in industry, which moved somewhat in the direction of the Liberman proposals. Adopted as law by the Supreme Soviet on October 2, the stipulations of the Kosygin Reform were conservative and tentative, yet they did begin the process of reform. The section pertaining to the individual enterprise contains four significant new policies. First and most important, managers' bonuses are paid for fulfillment of planned targets for sales, profit or profitability, and physical output. The scale of bonuses was designed to provide relatively higher rewards for fulfillment of targets. Moreover, to evaluate the amount of sales, the *gross value of output* indicator was replaced by *output sold*, which implies the necessity to produce what the consumers desire. Numerous detailed target directives were eliminated, including the norms for labor productivity, number of workers and employees, and average wages.

Second, the enterprise can now retain and utilize a large portion of profits (and some portion of depreciation allowances) for bo-

---

[12]V. Belkin and I. Berman, "Independence of the Enterprise and Economic Stimuli," translated in Sharpe, op. cit., pp. 225–230.
[13]O. Volkov, in *Pravda*, August 23, 1964.

nuses, welfare purposes, and decentralized investment. This turned out to be a very significant measure giving financial muscle to the decentralization reforms. Third, half of decentralized investment is financed by repayable and interest-bearing loans from banks, and interest charges are levied (in the form of a tax) on all fixed and working capital put at the enterprise's disposal. Fourth, contracts between enterprises are more strictly enforced, prohibiting superiors from changing enterprise plans at will during the plan period.

Some of the reform measures do approach the spirit, if not the letter, of Liberman's scheme. Attention to what has been left out of the Kosygin system, however, gives us a more pessimistic view of the possibility that the reforms will implement the kind of changes Liberman and his sympathizers have been proposing. For example, it has been pointed out numerous times that any attempt at greater reliance on profitability criteria would be useless (or even harmful) without a rational price system. Yet the wholesale price reform has been very slow in coming, and the more drastic changes requested by Soviet reformers have not been made.

Moreover, the new economic system continues to maintain the method of direct material allocation (there are recent reports of some attempts to replace or modify it through the introduction of large wholesale-warehouse-like establishments in which enterprises can buy anything they need). As long as the system of direct material allocation is continued, the reforms certainly will not result in the Liberman objective of enterprise freedom to vary inputs. Notice that the reformed system also keeps the central limits on total pay-rolls and allows managers to choose the labor mix only within those limits. At the same time the more decentralized investments have resulted in a significant decrease in central control over the determination of future output.

It must be admitted that even these limited reforms have run into bureaucratic obstruction and sabotage. Thus there have been numerous reports of continued extralegal interference by government and party organs in the day-to-day operations of enterprises, including those on the new system. The undoubted difficulties of the new system will be resolved eventually either by retrogression (renewed centralization) or by further reform (toward greater use of the market in socialism). Which direction is taken will depend on many factors, including external ones such as a peaceful world atmosphere.

THE YUGOSLAV MODEL

The Yugoslav experience revealed to the whole world that a socialist economy could be largely decentralized and directed mainly by the market. Although at first it was denounced with the usual Stalinist unanimity, later, when the anti-Stalinist tide began to rise, the Yugoslav economy became a model to investigate.

The Cominform (or Communist Information Bureau) was established in 1947 by Stalin primarily as a means of keeping eastern Europe, and perhaps especially Yugoslavia, on a tight leash. In 1948, however, Yugoslavia broke with the USSR and advocated complete independence and equality for all socialist nations. The Yugoslavs complained that the Russians had attempted to dominate their army, to exploit their economy through joint companies, to use secret agents to investigate and blackmail important Yugoslavs, and to threaten the cutting off of all trade should Yugoslavia take any independent action. In reply the Cominform excommunicated Yugoslavia, charging that it had slandered the USSR and was no longer Marxist because it had stopped pushing collectivization.

The Yugoslavs eventually answered that the USSR had deviated further and further from socialist democracy toward bureaucratic overcentralization. By 1950, as a concrete reaction, the Yugoslavs had begun to decentralize their economy and create their own socialist democracy, focused on *workers' councils* in each factory. During this period the Yugoslavs advanced the economic theory that central or administrative planning may at first greatly help the progress of a less developed or war-torn socialist economy. As the economy becomes more built up, complex, and interrelated, however, such extreme central direction "turns into its opposite" and becomes a barrier to further progress. Some variant of this theory has become the basis for reforms in much of eastern Europe and even the Soviet Union.

FRAMEWORK OF THE
YUGOSLAV ECONOMIC SYSTEM

After 1950 farming in Yugoslavia reverted to private ownership (as it did in Poland after 1957). There are few Yugoslav collectives today, although the goal of collectivization supposedly remains. In fact, the government is very, very gradually buying up individual pieces of land as farmers retire. There is also a private business sector, mostly in the areas of trade and handicrafts. Private businesses and farms may hire up to 5 people, but this limit apparently has been exceeded in practice. Farmers may acquire up 10 hectares of land. The private sector thus plays a very small role in industry but constitutes almost the whole of the farming sector. Private enterprise also plays an increasing role in the catering and service sector.

In the socialist sector of industry each factory is run as a producer's cooperative under the control of its own workers' council. The workers' councils are a feature unique in Yugoslav socialism. Many other eastern European countries are slowly directing their economies toward fully independent activity by each enterprise. Yet at present none of them intends to institute workers' councils as a basic feature, preferring control by government-appointed managers. (When revolutionary tides ran strong, workers' councils were temporarily introduced in Poland [in 1956–1957] and Czechoslovakia [in 1968–1969].) Today only the Yugoslavs consider workers' councils the most vital part of their economic structure. They not only praise their allegedly democratic aspects but also claim that they motivate workers and managers to the highest efficiency. Some Yugoslavs even assert that the workers' councils are responsible for their high rate of growth, which skeptics attribute primarily to a high rate of investment.

How does the system of workers' councils operate? The workers elect a council. The manager is then appointed by the local government, but the workers' council has veto power over the appointment of the manager. The council can also fire the manager; set wages, within limits established by the central government; set prices, also within limits defined by the central agencies; set production targets and determine technology; and dispose of its profits after taxes through additions to wages, collective welfare projects, or reinvestment. Taxes collected by the national government are used to finance major investment projects as well as defense and welfare.

Because all firms compete in the market, the prices set will be rational from the viewpoint of neoclassical economics, provided that there is pure and perfect competition. Nevertheless, because a large percentage of investment is still under central control, capital cannot freely flow to areas of higher profits. This constitutes a barrier to entry of other firms and may allow monopoly or oligopoly to arise in any area in which the central government sets an optimum firm size that is very high in relation to the total market. Because Yugoslavia is a relatively small country and the total market for many commodities is limited, there are many industries in which optimum firm size demands only one or a few producers. As the result of such monopolies, (1) price relationships are distorted away from the socially "rational" price, (2) resources are therefore allocated wrongly from the social viewpoint, and (3) consumers are exploited in the sense of paying higher prices to these particular firms.

Expansion and new investment by a particular firm also have some peculiar aspects under this system. If an entirely new firm is organized, it has its own council to look after the benefits of its own workers. New firms are often, but not always, set up by old ones.

However, a new workers' council does not return any profits to the firm that set it up, although it is obligated to pay interest to the government on the capital it has been given. Some of the "sponsored" new enterprises are treated legally as mere subsidiaries of the old firms and the additional profits are divided among the workers of both the old and new firms. In either case the way a council evaluates a new investment project outside its own plant is far more complicated than the usual profit calculus of a capitalistic competitive firm. One would expect some tendency to limit projects to those that might be considered a legitimate part of the old firm.

In addition to these microeconomic aspects of investment, there is something new in this system with respect to the question of aggregate investment. What is to keep a particular firm's workers from deciding that all of their profits should go into current wages or welfare projects rather than reinvestment and expansion of the productive base? Legally the only constraint is that the firm must first pay its taxes to the central government. The central government does take a very large tax bite, and much of this revenue has been used for investment, which has contributed significantly to Yugoslavia's impressive rate of economic growth. Yugoslavs also claim that the workers are generally very willing to make many large reinvestments, supposedly being content to wait for the large future returns.

The Communist party group within each enterprise also strongly encourages collective welfare projects and reinvestment for expansion of the productive base. And the manager of the enterprise exerts a somewhat independent pressure, in most cases advocating expansion of the enterprise's capital. Actually it appears that the balance of power over the distribution of income between workers and managers and higher authorities varies from plant to plant as well as from year to year. At present the ratio of investment to national income is very high. Therefore a large percentage of all investment, especially that going into new enterprises, must be and is still done by the central government, but an increasing percentage is coming under the control of existing firms and local governments.

It should be noted that the revenue of the enterprise must pay (1) interest on loans from the banking system, (2) depreciation allowances, (3) interest to the central government on the initial capital investment, (4) the turnover tax on sales, (5) miscellaneous taxes and fees, and (6) the income tax on profits. After the firm has paid these expenses, it is free to divide the rest of the revenue between wages and new investment. Yet the workers still must pay an additional social insurance tax on their wages. It is also required that at least 24 percent of investment funds go to a housing fund and to communal investment projects such as recreation centers. One further restriction lies in the fact that the government enforces a minimum wage for each worker.

For some time the total of all taxes, including profit tax, turnover tax, and interest on initial capital, amounted to about one-third of GNP. In the 1960s about 50 percent of government revenues were spent on defense, 35 percent on welfare, and 15 percent on investment. But allocations by enterprises pushed gross investment up to 35 percent of GNP.

In other areas, too, decisions are not made by the enterprise-level workers' councils. Central planning is responsible for (1) all of the most important investment projects, (2) most research and development, and (3) the education of skilled and professional workers.

SOME PROBLEMS OF THE YUGOSLAV SYSTEM

Prices of products in Yugoslavia are set by the enterprises (to the extent allowed by government price control), and the enterprises have every reason for increasing prices at every opportunity. If output demanded does not fall proportionately, then higher prices give the workers' council an opportunity to pay higher wages. Furthermore, as already noted, a small country such as Yugoslavia inevitably has many monopoly producers because a single large-scale, optimum-size enterprise takes such a huge slice of an industry. This problem is mitigated in part by foreign trade because foreign competition helps keep the monopolies in line. The result of the strong wage position and monopoly structure has been a chronic tendency toward price inflation. One interesting consequence of the monopoly pricing is that socialist Yugoslavia has passed an antimonopoly law against combinations in restraint of trade or conspiracies to raise prices.

In addition, the natural reaction of a central government with a planning tradition was the imposition of a large number of price controls. It was noted earlier that by 1967 a large percentage of Yugoslavia's industrial sales were of price-controlled goods. (This was supposed to be a temporary situation, but is still in effect.) Firms either may set prices only within certain limits, or they must get agency approval for any price change. Bureaucracy thus returns to the price-setting stage via the back door, although the enterprises are still the formal sources of all prices.

Another Yugoslav problem has been the continuing importance of regional or national rivalries. This is especially significant in the investment process, in which the allocation is achieved partly by local and regional agencies. Some of the allocation is by central planners, but they themselves may be afflicted by regional biases. Moreover, it is not just a matter of regional rivalries; the regions are in vastly different stages of economic development. To achieve equality in the level of development, it still is necessary to invest, say, in Macedonia, despite the fact that the project could do much better in a more advanced region. This is a profound problem; in the short run at least, it causes a great loss from investment allocation that is inefficient in terms of what might be done were there no extraeconomic regional considerations.

Another problem arises from the attempt to give real power to workers' councils over the specific plants and enterprises. This tends to result in the splitting up of industries into units small enough for democratic participation. But the political objective may conflict with the economic goal of achieving enterprises large enough to utilize all possible economies of scale. Thus the railways of Yugoslavia have been divided into a rather loose association of more than 160 autonomous enterprises, far too many competing firms in an industry that requires integration. Similarly, Yugoslavia has five factories producing entire radios; considerable economies of scale might be obtained by having each factory specialize in a single radio component. In recent years there has been a strong trend in some industries toward merger of enterprises, in spite of the obstacles presented by entrenched workers' councils.

Another problem that socialism was supposed to have avoided but that is found in Yugoslavia today is a certain degree of job insecurity and unemployment. It is theoretically possible that a system of market socialism such as Yugoslavia's might be subject to a certain degree of aggregate unemployment. In the past this has generally been overcome by a sufficient amount of central investment and by exportation of about 400,000 workers, mostly to West Germany. Nevertheless, there is a continuing problem of frictional unemployment, to the degree that inefficient enterprises are allowed to go bankrupt although there is some noneconomic pressure against this. Moreover, there actually was a significant amount of aggregate unemployment in 1966 and 1967.

In addition to the regional biases mentioned earlier, investment allocation under the Yugoslav system is subject to certain distortions due to the limited outlook of individual enterprises operating on purely profit criteria. Because workers are attached to the firm only for a limited time (at most during their lifetime), the workers' councils tend to neglect many long-run considerations in favor of short-run rapid returns. Furthermore, some individual Yugoslav firms, like those under a private enterprise system, tend to overlook the possible social benefits and damages of their investments. For example, each firm does not consider fully the effects on the community of the smog they create.

A quite different problem is posed by the private nature of Yugoslav farming. Because it is not only private but also of generally low productivity, with low yields per worker, this sector tends to conflict with the socialized and rapidly modernizing industries. The official Yugoslav remedy is that farming itself will eventually be socialized, but the lack of significant movement in this direction may leave one skeptical about the political feasibility of the move at any time.

Finally, consider the left-wing Chinese criticism that the Yugoslav system will eventually revert to capitalism. This is based on the notion that workers and managers in particular plants are coming to have a vested economic interest in those plants. It is hard to see, though, how the workers of a given plant in the Yugoslav system can ever use their possession of the plant either to exploit other workers or to pass on their position as an inheritance to their children.

Related to the allegation just described is the charge that the Yugoslav economic psychology is reverting to a bourgeois obsession with profit-making activity. Both Yugoslav workers and managers concentrate on their own individual moneymaking with no care for social needs, and some social welfare projects have actually been reduced to promote "private initiative." While this backward psychological movement certainly is the case to some extent, it is not easy to see that the central-planning alternative produces less of a moneymaking psychology on the part of workers and managers. Moving in a different direction, the Chinese have retained central planning but have drastically reduced the income differentials between unskilled workers, skilled workers, and managers. Thus while the Yugoslavs are relying more and more on individual material incentives, the Chinese claim to be relying more on collective moral incentives.

SUMMARY

For several years in the 1960s, a debate raged in the Soviet Union over how far to decentralize the economy. In 1965, the government passed limited reforms that increased the freedom of action of the plant manager in several areas and made his bonus dependent more on maximizing profits than on following a detailed output plan. The central plan is still very important, and the profits still go to the public rather than to any individual.

Since 1950, Yugoslavia has pursued an extreme form of decentralization and use of the market, leading many observers to question whether it has retained any planning or any socialism. All major decisions in the enterprise are made by a workers' council directly elected by the workers in each factory. It appoints the manager (jointly with the local government) and decides how much income is to be reinvested, how much is to be distributed, and who shall get the income distributed. Thus ownership is no longer really public in Yugoslavia; rather, the ownership resides with all the workers in each enterprise as a collective or cooperative venture. A basic criticism leveled by some radicals has been that this wide use of the market and money incentives instills a more bourgeois psychology and leads back toward capitalism.

political
and
social
problems
under
socialism

So far only the core of purely economic problems under socialism has been discussed. Socialist countries, it has been demonstrated, can plan in a rational manner for the whole economy; they do achieve the necessary balance for full employment (although with some inflation problems); and by using a high rate of saving and investment, they have usually achieved very high rates of growth. Further, there are attempts to overcome some of the problems of overcentralized planning, partly through the application of better economic theory and advanced computer analysis and partly through some decentralization of decision making.

Now we must examine the impact of socialism on the more general problems of equitable income distribution, free social services, racism, sexism, pollution, dictatorship, imperialism, and alienation. Obviously a book could be devoted to each of these problems, so in this brief chapter we shall do no more than pose some problems and note some trends in the socialist countries.

EXPLOITATION OR
EQUITABLE INCOME DISTRIBUTION

The distribution of income in the Soviet Union is very similar to the distribution of wage income in the United States The difference is that there is no upper end to the distribution; there is no private profit income, no rent income, no interest income (except on savings lent to the government). To the extent that only wage income is given to Soviet citizens, we may say that there is no exploitation in Marx's sense of the term.

However, some Soviet income that is supposedly wages paid for labor may be exploitive income in disguise. The incomes of the top government officials, top Communist party officials, and top military men are known to be very high but are state secrets. Officially they are paid labor income; but because they set their own wages, these "wages" may be considerably above an income based on labor alone. To the extent that this is so, it is fair to question just how socialist is the Soviet Union. It may be added that most observers believe the income distribution in China (and Cuba) to be much more egalitarian, as was Soviet income distribution immediately after the 1917 Revolution.

FREE SOCIAL SERVICES

In any event it is a long way to the complete equality, or payment according to "need," that is promised for communism. Still, the highly differential wages paid in the Soviet Union are made considerably more equal by the very large sector of free goods and services available to everyone. Of course all goods and services are produced by human effort and therefore are not free in that sense. But the Soviet government chooses to give many goods and services to its citizens without payment.

The Soviets are particularly proud of their very extensive, excellent, and free medical services. They are also proud of their completely free educational system, from elementary school to graduate school. Good students are also given scholarships large enough to live on without outside work. Their retirement system is comprehensive, as is the right to a paid vacation each year. Paid maternity leaves with job security are also mandatory under the law. The area of free goods and services provided by the public is clearly far larger than in the United States, although just how large is controversial. (The Soviets claim that it amounts to one-third of the real wage.) Presumably, under full communism all goods and services will be free, but the present Soviet leadership is certainly not rushing in that direction (and the leaders with high incomes have a vested interest in the present system).

RACISM

The Soviet government has always propagandized against racism, and there is little or no perceptible prejudice against black people in the Soviet Union (but there are very few blacks there). It does appear that some racial prejudice has been used as a political weapon to get popular support in the verbal struggle between the Russians and the Chinese (and it has apparently been used on both sides). There also used to be much propaganda against anti-Semitism, but Stalin used anti-Semitism as a weapon against his political opponents, and Hitler brought propaganda against the Jews with him when he invaded Russia. As a result of these two sources of prejudice, and because the Jew continues to be a convenient target for prejudice, some Soviet writers still make anti-Semitic statements. (Many racist statements are made under the guise of anti-Zionism, a perfectly legitimate political position that is grossly misused in this case.)

One should not overestimate Soviet use of anti-Semitism. Many Soviet authors are allowed to attack it, if they do not criticize top leadership. Moreover, Soviet Jews have much *higher than proportional* numbers of students and faculty in higher education, as well as scientists, actors, concert artists, and journalists. This by no means results from discrimination in their favor, but it does indicate lack of discrimination in certain educational and economic areas; their high proportions result simply from an urbanized, education-oriented tradition. Only in political positions are Jews almost completely unrepresented.

SEXISM

In combatting sexism the Soviet system has shown its most striking successes. Women are close to equality in number of college students and have a rapidly rising number of Ph.D.'s (now over one-third of the total). They constitute about 20 percent of Russia's associate professors. More than 50 percent of all doctors and lawyers are women, and in the sciences and all other professions the percentages are very high (even including one-third of all engineers). Women account for more than 50 percent of the total Soviet labor force.

On the negative side, it must be admitted that the attitudes of Soviet men have changed very little since pre-Revolutionary days. Or more precisely, the social situation of Russian women was so low that, even with fantastic upgrading, it still appears poor by the standards of the U.S. women's liberation movement. Men and women do take it for granted that the average Soviet woman has a job appropriate to her abilities and *at equal pay*. They also assume that she is entitled to a lengthy maternity leave while being paid and retaining her job. Moreover, most children are given good care each day in child care centers, a service that is well developed in the Soviet Union and is free to all. But men still assume that when a woman returns from a hard day's work she is exclusively responsible for the children in the evening. She is also expected to cook and clean the house while the man, who worked the same number of hours in the day, relaxes and does nothing. This situation has not changed at all in the countryside; it is beginning to change very slowly among educated urban men and women.

POLLUTION

The Soviet Union has much less pollution than the United States, but that is partly a consequence of less economic development—particularly because there are vastly fewer automobiles. Yet the reduction of pollution is also due to the fact that private profit has been replaced by social control. All new facilities, including whole cities, are carefully approved by a sanitation inspector who is pledged to strict protection of the environment. There also is a new set of very strict antipollution laws.

Nevertheless, many cases of environmental destruction have been reported, in loud and agonized voices, by Soviet newspapers and journals. The reasons for the pollution, in spite of social planning and laws, can be traced to the continued private interests of Soviet managers and some bureaucrats. The manager's bonus depends on how much he produces and how low his costs are, but he can produce more at lower costs by paying no attention to pollution. As a countermeasure, fines are beginning to be applied to polluting managers. Yet some managers are protected by higher bureaucrats because their performance too is judged on the basis of how much their district produces and at how low a monetary cost. Under Stalin *production* was the sole goal *at any cost*—monetary, human, or environmental.

And that is natural. People at very low income levels need to increase their food, clothing, and shelter for survival; worry over polluting the environment is a luxury they cannot afford. With economic development and affluence, pollution becomes a major problem, which can and must be solved.

DICTATORSHIP

One reason for the Soviet disregard of human feelings and environmental destruction during the period of rapid industrialization was the lack of democratic control over the leadership. Stalin ruled as a sole and arbitrary dictator. Even at present, decision making is only partially shared with the Central Committee, which consists of a few hundred individuals. A considerable amount of freedom of discussion and criticism does exist now, but it is still very much limited to safe subjects and the criticism of local leaders. Thus there was vast public discussion of educational reforms and new marriage and divorce laws, but no dissent at all was allowed on the invasion of Czechoslovakia, and intellectuals are still carted off to jail for criticizing basic policies of the top leadership.

The Soviet trend to dictatorship over the working class (rather than democratic representation of it) began during the emergency situations of civil war and foreign intervention. The new Soviet government not only was menaced by a violent uprising of the old reactionary forces (tsarist military men, landlords, and so forth) but also was invaded by 14 foreign countries, including the United States. All this in a country with very little democratic tradition, grinding poverty, and 70 percent or 80 percent illiteracy. Still, there was considerable revival of free speech and debate in the 1920s. This was stifled, and Stalin became absolute dictator only later when the all-out industrialization program was launched.

Rapid industrialization implies, as we have seen in previous chapters, a vast concentration of the country's resources in investment in new factories and machinery. These resources for investment could come only (because there was no foreign help) from the effort and sweat of a population provided with very few consumer goods. Because over 70 percent of the population were peasants in agriculture, this meant squeezing out every bit of agricultural product from them above their minimum survival needs (and sometimes, in the early years, even that was taken). The food was given to the industrial workers or exported to buy foreign machinery. Thus most of the population was hostile to the government and would not have backed this drastic program in any democratic vote. Hence it was the attempt to overcome economic backwardness rapidly by heroic means at the expense of the present generation that led inevitably to the terrorist Stalinist dictatorship. In the recent period, with greater affluence, a reduced industrial pace, and the spread of general education, it is possible to see a long-run trend toward political liberalization. (But the trend often gives way to very regressive steps.)

IMPERIALISM

We saw in an earlier chapter that imperialism has tended to flourish under capitalism because it has brought vast gains to the owners of a few large corporations, even though it has meant taxes and inflation and deaths and wounds in wars for most of the population of the imperialist countries. The Soviet Union has no private owners of large corporations, nor can anyone make private profit from an overseas investment or from a military contract. In fact, Soviet planners recognize military spending for what it is, a drain on their ability to produce more consumer and producer goods for the society.

Still, it is a fact that the Soviet Union has taken aggressive actions against Czechoslovakia and Hungary and has subjected them to involuntary military occupation. It is a fact that the Soviet Union and China have clashed on their borders. What are the ultimate causes of these actions if they are not related to private profits? Partly, at least, the causes would seem to be related to the continuing undemocratic character of the Soviet government, and to the fact that top leaders make high salaries and have vested interests in maintaining their positions. It is often easier to keep political power at home by putting people's minds on foreign adventures and always reminding them of the possibilities of foreign intervention. It also means further extension of the Soviet leaders' personal political control over eastern Europe.

The most succinct analysis of Soviet foreign policy has been provided by Andreas Papandreou, a man whose country (Greece) was taken away from him by a military coup known to be backed by the CIA.[1] Professor Papandreou says: "While the expansionist-capitalist dynamic is absent in the Soviet Union, the bureaucratic-militarist dynamic is very present indeed. . . . Thus, while the Soviet Union lacks an imperialist dynamic that springs from its economic organization, it does not lack an expansionist dynamic which reflects the needs of its establishment to consolidate its world position. . . ."[2]

ALIENATION

Legally speaking, the Soviet worker is one of the owners of all the factories in his land. Nevertheless, in his own factory he must still take orders from the foreman, arrive on time, and often do tedious routine work for many hours. Thus although one kind of alienation has been eliminated or reduced by socialism, other kinds still persist because of the needs of any modern industry.

The alienation in the factory is reinforced by the lack of democratic control over national political and economic policies. The Soviet worker is ordered about by the foreman, by the manager above him, by the higher economic agencies, by the police and secret police, by several layers of bureaucracy, and ultimately by the top political leaders, who are self-perpetuating. Thus he still has the feel-

[1]Professor Papandreou was chairman of the Department of Economics at University of California, Berkeley, before he returned to join the cabinet in the last Greek democratic government (of which his father was premier).

[2]Andreas Papandreou, *Man's Freedom* (New York: Columbia University Press, 1970), p. 49.

ing of facing a huge faceless machine. Undoubtedly, greater democratic participation in national decision making would reduce some of this alienated feeling.

Perhaps some greater feeling of control over his life would also be contributed by a wide area of workers' control in the factory. In Yugoslavia, where workers' councils do have full legal control over the manager and the enterprise, some of this type of alienation may have been eliminated. Still, we noted that the Yugoslavs achieved this control at the expense of other kinds of alienation. Specifically, elimination of centralized bureaucracy means substitution of the marketplace as the arena of economic decision making. It thus means even more reliance on purely material motivations, on local gain (sometimes by monopoly profit) at the expense of the rest of society, and on highly differentiated individual incomes.

Both the Soviet Union and Yugoslavia (and to a lesser extent China) retain highly unequal income distributions. The Soviet income distribution is, however, many times less unequal than the American, mainly because the Soviets have no private income from ownership of capital. And the Soviets do have a much wider area of free public goods and services. Nevertheless, they are far from the communist principle of "payment according to need." In a society with this range of income distribution, even though it has socialist ownership of production, there are workers with relatively low incomes who feel left out of the growing affluence. And there are top leaders with very large individual incomes (only vaguely associated with their labor contribution) who have a vested interest in preserving their economic and political privileges. Hopefully, if and when the socialist countries achieve 70 percent or 80 percent of their distribution in free goods and services, workers will feel less alienated, the political structure will give up its coercive powers, and the whole attitude of people toward work and power will change. But for the present that is only speculation.

SUMMARY

From the viewpoint of most American radicals, the Soviet Union has been much more successful in solving economic problems (such as full employment, growth, and income distribution) than social and political problems (such as the elimination of alienation and dictatorship). The other countries calling themselves socialist are still too new to make any definite evaluation, except to point out that they have evolved a remarkable variety of social, political, and economic models, many of which are strikingly different from the Soviet model. All of these countries are still very, very far from the utopian communist ideal of people working for the social good without wages or prices—and with no coercive government. Moreover, since the U.S. economy has already finished the rough road of industrialization, a radical change here can begin with both socialism and democracy. These goals, plus peace and an end to discrimination, are the ideals for which radicals must struggle.

suggested
further
readings

Two journals contain numerous very useful and very interesting articles on every subject mentioned in this book. One is the *Review of Radical Political Economics* (Union for Radical Political Economics, Office of Organizational Services, Michigan Union, Ann Arbor, Michigan 48104). The other is *Monthly Review* (62 West 14th Street, New York, New York 10011).

For Part One on history, the best overall work is Maurice Dobb, *Studies in the Development of Capitalism* (International Publishers). A moving biography and explanation of Marx's ideas is Franz Mehring, *Karl Marx* (Ann Arbor Paperbacks).

For Part Two, an excellent study of the economics of discrimination is Raymond Franklin and Solomon Resnik, *The Political Economy of Racism* (Holt, Rinehart & Winston). A comprehensive book on sex discrimination is Barbara Deckard, *The Women's Movement: Political, Socioeconomic, and Psychological Issues* (Harper & Row). The political influence of economic power is described by the Ralph Nader group in *Who Runs Congress?* (Bantam).

For Part Three, a powerful little book on pollution and ecological problems is Mathew Edel, *Economics and the Environment* (Prentice-Hall). On imperialism, the best single thing is Harry Magdoff, *The Age of Imperialism* (Monthly Review Press). A fascinating case study, written as an autobiography, is Cheddi Jagan, *The West on Trial* (International Publishers).

For Part Four, the classic study of the Chinese Communists is by the journalist Edgar Snow, *Red Star Over China* (Grove). A more up-to-date and very exciting book is Jack Belden, *China Shakes the World* (Monthly Review Press). On the Soviet Union, the best analyses are found in the works of Isaac Deutscher. He gives a comprehensive political history in his biography *Stalin* (Oxford University Press). He is a superb writer and is at his best in his beautiful political biography *Trotsky* (Vintage Books, three volumes). All the books suggested here are in paperback editions.